The Sunday Game

Ohio History and Culture

The Sunday Game

At the Dawn of Professional Football

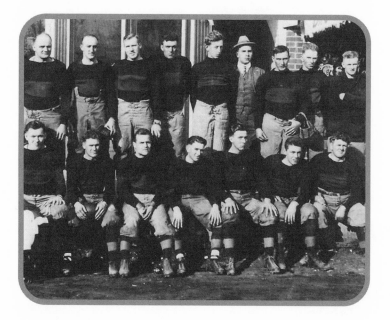

by Keith McClellan

 The University of Akron Press

All inquiries and permissions requests should be addressed to the
publisher, The University of Akron Press, Akron, OH 44325–1703.

Manufactured in the United States of America

First Edition 1998
03 02 01 00 99 98   5 4 3 2 1

Library of Congress Cataloging–in–Publication Data
McClellan, Keith
    The Sunday game : at the dawn of professional football / by Keith
McClellan.
        p. cm.—(Ohio history and culture)
    Includes bibliographical references (p.) and index.
    ISBN 1–884836–35–6 (cloth).—ISBN 1–884836–36–4 (pbk.)
    1. Football—United States—History. I. Title. II. Series.
GV954.M37 1998
796.332'0973—dc21   98–24175
                                                                    CIP

The paper used in this publication meets the minimum requirements
of American National Standard for Information Sciences—Permanence
of Paper for Printed Library Materials, ANSI Z39.48-1984.∞

Contents

List of Illustrations   vii
Acknowledgments   ix

1   The Dawn of Professional Football   3
2   Setting the Stage   16
3   Assumed Names and Anti-Pro Sentiments   29
4   The Art of Scheduling   34
5   The Fort Wayne Friars, 1915   38
6   The Panhandles: Big As Mountains, Strong As Lions   49
7   Native American Players with Altoona   64
8   Evanston North Ends and the Kicking Swede   69
9   The Toledo Maroons and the Adrian College Boys   82
10   The Youngstown Patricians   98
11   Dayton: St. Mary's College and General Motors   117
12   The Detroit Heralds: Like a Ford in Heavy Traffic   132
13   The Cincinnati Celts: River City Champions   162
14   The Greatest Rivalry of Its Time   172
15   A Streetcar Conductor Wins the Day   190
16   Cleveland, Canton, and Massillon: Center of the Hurricane, 1916   202
17   The Akron Pros   232
18   Massillon and Canton: The Rivalry Continues, 1917   240
19   Davenport: When the Players Were in Charge   254
20   The Rock Island Independents   366
21   The Minneapolis Marines: Champions of Minnesota   275
22   Pro Football in Wisconsin   283
23   Wabash: The Little Town that Could   295
24   Racism Rears Its Ugly Head   318
25   Fort Wayne Friars: Indiana Champions, 1916   324
26   Fort Wayne Fizzles, 1917   338
27   Boosterism and the Hammond Clabbys, 1916   346

28   Hammond: New Indiana Champions   354

29   Football Prepared Young Men for the Future   365

30   Sunday Heroes   377

31   Promotion and Financing of Iron-Man Football: 1915–17   382

Appendix A. Rosters and Schedules   397
Appendix B. Professional Players Who Doubled as Coaches   461
Appendix C. All-Professional Teams, 1917   463
Appendix D. Walter Camp All-Americans in Pro Football, 1915–17   464
Notes   465
Index   491

List of Illustrations

1.1. Knute Rockne   13
5.1. Ivan Armon Zaring   43
6.1. The Nesser brothers   50
6.2. Columbus Panhandles (1913)   51
8.1., 8.2., 8.3. Evanston North Ends and the Wabash Athletic
   Association (1913)   71
8.4. Evanston North Ends and the Wabash Athletic
   Association (1914)   72
8.5. Eugene Schobinger   73
9.1. Frank "Tubby" Roush   95
10.1. Horace "Hoke" Palmer   104
10.2. Melvin Lesley McCreary   108
10.3. Franklin "Bart" Macomber   111
11.1., 11.2. Dayton Gym-Cadets and the Wabash Athletic
   Association (1914)   118
11.3. Frank S. White   126
12.1. John A. Roesink   133
12.2. Tom Moriarity   135
12.3. Leon C. Exelby   136
12.4. William Blake Miller   142
12.5. Lewis S. Castle   149
12.6. Rudolph W. Propst   157
12.7. Clarence "Steamer" Horning   158
14.1. George Edward "Carp" Julian   176
14.2. Alfred Earle "Greasy" Neale   179
14.3. James F. "Jim" Thorpe   186
14.4. Robert P. "Butts" Butler   188
15.1. Gideon Charles Smith   198
16.1. Paul R. "Shorty" Des Jardien   203
16.2. Harry Whitaker   209
16.3. James Martin "Butchy" Barron   218
16.4. Howard "Cub" Buck   223
18.1. DeOrmand "Tuss" McLaughry   247

21.1. Bob Marshall   276

21.2. Russell J. Tollefson   279

22.1. Scott "Duke" MacEachron   284

23.1. Mark G. "Mickey" Erehart   296

23.2. Homecoming parade for the Wabash
Athletic Association   298

23.3. Pine Village Athletic Club (1915)   299

23.4. Wabash Athletic Association (1916)   305

23.5. Bill Williams   307

23.6. Pine Village Athletic Club (1916)   309

24.1. Clarence "Smoke" Fraim   321

25.1. Charles "Gus" Dorais   325

25.2. Ralph H. "Bull" Young   329

25.3. Edgar C. "Big Ed" Davis   331

25.4. Notre Dame alumni playing for the Fort Wayne
Friars (1916)   333

27.1. Harold S. "Hod" Ofstie   352

29.1. WWI interrupted the formalization of a professional
football league   375

Acknowledgments

Many people helped me with this book. Foremost was my wife Marian, whose encouragement, research assistance, ideas, and computer work were indispensable over the five-year journey this book required. She has been a true partner and a source of loving support in sickness and in health. Yvonne Johnson typed the first draft of rosters and schedules, a laborious, unrewarding task. Robert Hilsabeck, a mentor, historian, teacher, and friend, read and commented on two rough drafts of this book. His assistance and comments are appreciated. Elton Glaser is a sympathetic and skilled editor who had confidence in the manuscript in its early stages of development and provided encouragement at critical times. I am particularly thankful for his guidance.

A number of public librarians and historical society archivists were very helpful. Of particular note are Mark Burnette, archivist at the Evanston (IL) Historical Society, and Jack Miller of the Wabash County (IN) Historical Society. I am grateful to both for going beyond normal duty to provide assistance. A trunk full of Wabash Athletic Association records dating from the turn of the century was a rare find, and a search of Evanston City Directories unearthed long lost information.

The librarians at public libraries in Akron, Altoona, Canton (Stark County District Library), Chicago, Cleveland, Clinton, Columbus, Crawfordsville, Davenport, Dayton, Decatur, Des Moines, Detroit (including the Burton Historical Collection), Evanston, Fort Wayne, Green Bay, Hammond, Indianapolis, Joliet, Massillon, Milwaukee, Moline, Newcastle, Pittsburgh, Racine, Rock Island, Rockford, Toledo, Wabash, and Youngstown were invaluable. The Library of Congress, the Michigan Historical Society, the Ohio Historical Society, the Indiana Bureau of History, the Iowa Historical Society, the Minnesota Historical Society, the Youngstown Historical Society, the Pro Football Hall of Fame Library, and university libraries at the University of Michigan, University of Notre Dame, University of Detroit-Mercy, Adrian College, Washington and Jefferson College, Georgetown University, Michigan State University, University of Minnesota, Ohio State University, Bucknell University, Susquehanna University, The University of Akron, Cincinnati University, University of Illinois, Purdue University, University of Pittsburgh, and Ohio University were indispensable.

Charles Lamb and Norma Blackman, archivists at the University of Notre Dame; Philip Bantin, director of archives at Indiana University, along with Jim Grace and Brad Cook of that staff; Case Western Reserve University, The University of Akron, the Summit County Historical Society; Vicki Sussman at Denison University; John Riggs, archives researcher at DePauw University; Bertha Ihnot, archives assistant for manuscripts at Ohio State University; Baldwin Wallace College Archives; Ron Frankum and Chad Wheaton of Syracuse University Archives; Earl M. Rogers, university archivist, the University of Iowa; Knox College Archives; Mr. Medlicott, Franklin College reference librarian; George W. Bain, head of Archives and Special Collections, Ohio University; Penn State University Archives; Brown University Archives; and the Alumni Association at Colgate University—all were generous with their time and knowledge, as were Alice Diehl, Lebanon Valley College Library; William R. Massa Jr., public service archivist, Yale University; Lynn Beideck-Porn, University Archives and Special Collections, University of Nebraska; Kathy Byers, administrative assistant to the director, O'Keefe Library, St. Ambrose University; Wanda Finney, University of Illinois Archives; James Bevin, Purdue University Special Collection; Anne Kintner, college archivist, Grinnell College; R. Jeanne Cobb, archivist, Bethany College; Paul Milliman, research assistant, Ohio Wesleyan University; Ron Becker, Rutgers University Archives; Suzy Taraba, Department of Special Collection, University of Chicago; Sandra Nyeman, Marietta College Archives; Jamie Peele, Kenyan College Archives; Gail Piacheck, University of Pennsylvania Archives; Phillip J. Zorich, special collections librarian, Indiana University of Pennsylvania; Susann Posey, associate librarian, Mercersburg Academy; Roland M. Baumann, Oberlin College Archives; Elizabeth A. Nielsen, Oregon State University Archives; Don Link and Nanci A. Young, Princeton University Archives; Diane Jacob, Virginia Military Institute Archives; and H. Dewey DeWitt, Westminster College Archives.

I appreciate the correspondence from Mrs. Dwain (Doris) Cottingham of Otterbein, Indiana, regarding the Pine Village Athletic Club. I also appreciate the correspondence with Vincent Sacksteder of Dayton, Ohio; Carl M. Becker of the Department of History, Wright State University; David W. Kraeuter and Susan M. Isola of Washington and Jefferson College; Lauren K. Landis, Genealogy Division, Stark County District Library, Canton, Ohio; Harold S. Parsons of the Warren County,

Illinois, Genealogical Society; Verl L. Lekwa of Columbus Junction (Iowa), who reported on Ernest McRoberts; and Lutheran pastor Ralph Wallen, Storm Lake, Iowa, who made it possible to obtain church records on the family of Rueben Johnson.

Bob Carroll, president of the Professional Football Researchers Association, and Bob Gill, assistant editor of *Coffin Corner*, were generous with their accumulated knowledge and prior research, both of which were useful and insightful.

Finally, I would like to thank my uncle, Wesley Marquette, who played single platoon football before World War II and taught me, by example, how to play high school football with commitment and courage. I dedicate this book to him and to all of us who played single platoon football for the love of the game.

Keith McClellan
Oak Park, MI
September 1997

The Sunday Game

1. The Dawn of Professional Football

On a gray, overcast Sunday in Canton, Ohio, in late November 1915, local football fans witnessed the dawn of professional football. Professional football is the direct offspring of independent football, so titled by sportswriters of the era because it was played by adults independent of college affiliation. Independent football emerged in the steel and coal towns of Pennsylvania and Ohio shortly before the beginning of the twentieth century and quickly spread across the Midwest from Altoona, Pennsylvania, to Davenport, Iowa, and even beyond, and from Louisville in the south to Minneapolis and Duluth in the north. Usually played on Sunday afternoons, independent football was particularly popular in the medium-sized factory cities of the Midwest that were not blessed with a college team. It never penetrated the South, in part because the Baptists, Southern Methodists, and Christian Evangelicals were strongly opposed to breaking the Sabbath. Massachusetts, Pennsylvania, and parts of New York also passed blue laws that prohibited commerce on Sundays and, consequently, hindered the development of the Sunday football game.[1]

In the early years of the twentieth century, professional football experienced the same stages of development as professional baseball did in the 1870s, when the National Baseball League was taking root. Initially, independent football teams recruited players locally, then teams began hiring a few outstanding individuals from outside the community to win critical games. Later, while most members of the team were paid only if the team made money, teams also hired key players for the season and paid them an agreed-upon amount per game, making these teams semiprofessional. Finally, when all of the players received an agreed-upon amount of money per game instead of splitting the pot at the end of each season, the teams completed the transition to professional status. The progression was not always straightforward or without complications.

According to sports scholar Marc S. Maltby, "it is difficult to pinpoint the exact moment of professional football's origin, particularly when definitions of professionalism are, by no means, precise or static. By the standards of the late nineteenth century, professional players were not at all uncommon. 'Ringers' or 'tramp' athletes were prevalent on many college campuses and were thought by press, public and universities to pose a serious problem."[2] However, it is important to distinguish between individuals who were paid to play football and teams designed to be money-making enterprises and comprised solely of paid players. In 1902, there was an abortive attempt to organize a professional football league in Pennsylvania. Led by David Berry, editor of the *Latrobe Clipper,* and Connie Mack, owner of the Philadelphia Athletics baseball team, the league went broke before the end of the season, possibly because the teams had to play on Saturday, putting them in direct competition with college football, which was much more popular.

In the Midwest, strong community rivalries fueled the change from independent to semiprofessional football. Following the example of baseball, independent football teams schemed for an advantage in important games. As early as 1895, some independent teams recruited an outstanding former college football star or two to play for them in an important game against a team from a rival city. Most players on town teams lived in the town and played just for team spirit and the love of the game. But the ringers, unmotivated by town spirit, expected to be well paid for their efforts.

The evolution of independent football into the modern professional game was a slow process that encountered a number of setbacks. The cost of pay-to-play football frequently escalated beyond the means of the small cities that pioneered the independent sport. Key players moved on or retired; managers, owners, and sponsors tired of the risks associated with the sport or experienced business failures; and, on occasion, local fans lost interest. Innovations such as having a whole team of paid players failed initially, but later they became an integral part of the business.

In the early years, few were concerned about the future of the sport. In 1903, a group of civic leaders decided that Massillon, Ohio, should have a football team. At this time, a local sporting goods store in Massillon was having a clearance sale on black-and-orange-striped jerseys. The team sponsors bought up the jerseys and called the team the Massillon Tigers.

Because the Massillon group knew that a game with Canton would be a good draw, they contacted an attorney in Canton, some twelve miles away, and talked to him about starting a rival team. In this way, the Canton Bulldogs were formed to play the Massillon Tigers, and the greatest rivalry in the country began. The two Ohio teams started a rush to sign up top players anywhere they could find them. Between 1903 and 1906, the rivalry became intense, and both teams attracted paid players from Michigan, Ohio, Pennsylvania, and beyond. At the close of the 1906 season, however, financial difficulties and a scandal around charges of point fixing by players and tampering by gamblers ended professional, independent football in those two cities for a number of years. At the same time, however, strong independent football teams were developing in Akron, Columbus, Elyria, Toledo, Dayton, and Cincinnati, Ohio; Detroit and Ann Arbor, Michigan; Fort Wayne, Wabash, and Pine Village, Indiana; Evanston and Rock Island, Illinois; Racine, Wisconsin; and Minneapolis, Minnesota.

The tradition of paying former college players to play for independent teams continued in these towns and elsewhere. For example, Shelby, Ohio, located near Mansfield, had a reputation for finding the best athletes available in the upper Midwest to represent their community. Shelby was determined to win the state championship of Ohio. On one occasion, Shelby hired Ty Cobb to play on their baseball team in a game to determine the state baseball championship. On another occasion, they hired Guy Schulz, the brother of Adolph "Germany" Schulz, the great All-American center from the University of Michigan. Considered by many to be the best center to play in the first fifty years of American college football, Germany Schulz, at six feet four and 245 pounds, was one of the fastest men on the field and could dominate a game. In 1907, Adolph Schulz almost alone held a strong University of Pennsylvania team at bay for more than forty-five minutes, according to the great sports reporter Grantland Rice.[3] Some argued that his brother Guy, who did not attend college, was as good as Adolph, and newspaper reports sometimes confused the two brothers.

With this kind of history, it is not surprising that, by 1908, the Shelby Blues took the lead in hiring former college players to upgrade their strong, independent team. The Blues hired former Massillon Tigers star, George "Peggy" Parratt, as player-manager. He promptly engaged half a dozen of the best former college stars from various parts of Ohio, and the Blues became the state independent football champions. Because Shelby relied primarily on hired talent rather than local men, the Blues became one of the outstanding semiprofessional football teams in America.

Independent state football championships during this period were entirely unofficial. An informal consensus of sportswriters, team managers, and fan opinion determined the "state champion." The decision was based on all games played, but some games were more important than others. The strength of a team's opponents was the most important factor in the ranking and, if a team played an opponent twice, the second game was given more weight than the first. The system was not as well organized as the modern high school and college rankings, but it usually worked to the satisfaction of those who cared.

Akron, Ohio, offers an excellent case study of the transition from independent football to professional football. The roots of professional football are as deep in Akron as they are in Canton, Massillon, and Shelby, Ohio. As early as 1902, the Akron East End Athletic Club fielded a team that challenged the Massillon Tigers and the Shelby Athletic Club for the Ohio independent football championship. Coached by Bill Laub, the Akron club defeated independent teams from Detroit, Youngstown, and Canton. They also defeated college teams from Mt. Union College and Ohio Northern University. Akron's only loss in 1903 was to the Massillon Tigers.[4]

In 1907, the Akron Indians replaced the Akron Athletic Club. They played their games at the Sherman Street Field and moved to the Nolan Park field a year later. The team was made up almost exclusively of hometown players. The Indians featured Charles A. "Doc" Baker, one of the first African-American professional football players. Baker played halfback for the Akron Indians from 1907 through 1909, and again in 1911.[5] In 1908 and 1909, the Indians were undefeated and claimed the independent football championship of Ohio.[6]

From 1907 through 1911, the Indians shared hometown football fan loyalty with the Akron Tigers. The Tigers were never quite in the same class as the Indians, although they only lost 5–0 in one of the two games played by these teams in 1910. The real competition for the state title in 1910 was between Akron and the Shelby Blues. Named the Blues because the team wore blue jerseys, they were coached by John Miller, their halfback, but quarterback Peggy Parratt was thought to be the man in charge. Parratt and Guy "Germany" Schulz were the stars for the Blues. For some of the critical games, they hired one of the Nesser brothers.

As semiprofessional teams hired more professional players, these teams began demanding guarantees for away games. In 1911, the Shelby Blues demanded and received a $135 guarantee for their out-of-town Sunday games.[7] This was one of the highest guarantees in independent football during these years. Pay to players averaged five dollars per game, with stars receiving as much as twenty-five dollars per game. By contrast, the average worker made five to ten dollars a week.

George Waterson "Peggy" Parratt did more than anyone else in America to foster the transition from independent to professional football. Though largely unrecognized for his contributions, he was one of the football geniuses of the pre-World War I era. While Canton is generally acknowledged as the birthplace of professional football, in reality, the Canton Bulldogs simply completed the job started by Parratt in Shelby and Akron.

Born in May 1882 to the William Parratts, Peggy played football at West High School in Cleveland and entered Case School of Applied Science on September 16, 1902, where he became a campus hero. Playing for Case between 1903 and 1906, he was All-Ohio at end for two years and All-Ohio at quarterback in 1905, his senior year. He was captain and coach of the first baseball team at Case, in 1906, and organized and played on the school's first basketball team. In the fall of 1905, Parratt played semiprofessional football on Sundays for the Shelby Athletic Club while simultaneously playing college football at Case in Cleveland on Saturdays. When this was discovered sometime in 1906, he was declared ineligible to play amateur athletics.[8] In the spring of 1906, he graduated from Case with a mechanical engineering degree.[9]

After declining the head coaching position at Marietta College, in 1906, Parratt became the starting quarterback for the Massillon Tigers, and, on October 25, 1906, he threw the first complete forward pass in semiprofessional football. [10] The Massillon Tigers broke up at the end of the 1906 football season because of financial problems and did not reorganize until 1915, so Peggy played for the Franklin Athletic Club of Cleveland in 1907, organized and coached the Cleveland Broadway Athletic Club, and spent most of his spare time that year making money by officiating.[11]

In 1908, Parratt returned to Shelby where he helped organize, coach, and play for the Shelby Athletic Club. In 1909, the Shelby team claimed a share of the state independent football championship along with Akron. In 1910 and 1911, Parratt helped recruit well-known former Ohio college players for the Blues, who won the state championship both years. The use of a large number of paid players established Shelby as one of the leading semiprofessional teams in the country.

In 1912, at twenty-seven years of age, George "Peggy" Parratt was part of a group that acquired control of the Akron Indians. He became its coach and, as the team's manager, helped to reinstate it as one of the nation's best independent football teams. The process of outgunning Shelby, however, was not easy, as this report in the *Cleveland Leader* on November 4, 1912, indicates:

Professional football is a queer game, with many queer results. . . . Remember Peggy Parratt, that sensational Peggy of a few years back, who brought fame and glory to Case School by his wonderful work at end, by his wonderful speed, and by his still more wonderful pluck?

"Peggy" of late years has been closely identified with professional football in this state.

The power of the [Akron] Indians has been so recognized that the team has frequently had difficulty getting games.

The difficulty had been as great in 1912 as in any other year.

The Indians wanted a game with Shelby. Shelby, home of strong teams of the past, was reckoned as a fine drawing card. Akron likes professional football and turns out well to see the games.

Shelby was scheduled. Shelby's 1912 team was but a shadow of the great teams of the past. The Indians needed a good game, a strong opponent. They realized that their faithful rooters were entitled to a good game.

Parratt thought Shelby could not give good competition. He anxiously inquired about the players on the team. He thought the Indians would win so easily that the Akron fans would be disappointed. That wouldn't do.

Peggy grew charitable. He volunteered to help Shelby. He volunteered to get some good players for Shelby. The Shelby manager appreciated Parratt's help. perhaps cracking his sides at the same time in anticipation of the surprise which would be sprung on Peggy.

The day of the big game arrived. It was last Sunday. Five thousand of the faithful fought for choice positions to watch the contest, and incidentally to watch their favorites annihilate their bitter rivals.

"Peggy" was ostensibly prepared to meet any style of game that Shelby could produce. He himself has imported acknowledged stars for the game to be used in case of emergency. Among the stars were "Hull" Hinaman, former Case guard, and now well known coach of Ohio University. Another was Dwight Wertz, speedy Reserve quarterback of a couple of years ago and now connected with Herman Schleman's great Elyria professional team. Another was Homer Davidson, hero of pro games for a dozen years past and one of the greatest punters and drop kickers that Ohio, if not the world, has ever produced.

Yes "Peggy" was prepared. His convictions were strong. "Peggy" likes to have a little side bet occasionally. He bet a large wad on the game. The exact amount has not been divulged. It was over a couple of hundred at least. The final score was Shelby 14, Akron 7.

"Peggy" was stung.

Thereby hangs the gruesome part of the tale.

Shelby was loaded, and loaded to the guards. Note some of the ex-college stars. There was Gardner, wonderful end of the Carlisle Indians team of a couple of years ago; Goebel, All-American guard of the Yale team. Carson, great tackle of the Penn State team, at quarterback whose name if divulged would be recognized by everyone who ever read a line concerning football as a great national star at his position; Littick of Ohio Wesleyan, and also an All-Ohio fullback; also Jones another alumnus of Ohio Wesleyan, and a few others whose correct names were not revealed.

Parratt is still dazed.

In 1913, Parratt did succeed in winning the independent championship of Ohio for Akron, and, in doing so, he forced rival communities to hire their own former college stars in order to stay competitive with the Akron Indians.

One of the first communities to respond to this challenge was Canton, Ohio, less than twenty miles south of Akron. After six years without a strong independent football team, Canton revived its team in 1912. On November 3, 1912, the *Cleveland Leader* reported: "Akron made use of several college stars in Pendleton of Oberlin, Wells, All-American end from Michigan, Parratt of Case, and Mathews, Kenyon coach. Canton depended on home talent and failed."

Jack Cusack, partner and manager of the Canton Pros from 1912 to 1918, wrote:

Our Canton team of 1912, with the exception of Erb of Allegheny College and Wright of Western Reserve, was made up of strapping local talent able to hold their own against the best competition because they were fast and heavy and kept in fine physical condition. . . . We played nine games during that season, winning six and losing three. We lost two games to Akron and one to Elyria, but since both teams were made up principally of college graduates, we felt that we had made a credible showing. But that was not enough for the fans—they wanted a winner.[12]

An avid football town, Canton would not tolerate losing to rival communities like Akron and Massillon. They demanded that their local independent football team hire an even stronger core of former college all-stars to wrest the state championship away from Akron. In 1913, Canton added several college men to its roster and hired coach Harry Hazlett of Canton's McKinley High School. When Akron still beat them, they upgraded their team again. This time the Akron Indians responded and won the state championship in 1914.

Between 1912 and 1915, Parratt continued the process of creating a team composed of college all-stars he had begun at Shelby. Parratt's Akron Indians won two state independent football championships and beat the best teams from Detroit and Chicago. At this time, most teams limited their schedules to competitors within their state, but the better semiprofessional teams were expanding their schedules to include powerful teams in other states.

In 1914, Parratt hired the best independent football team ever assembled to that point. It was a team of professionals, only two of whom were from Akron, but all of whom represented Akron on the gridiron. This team so dominated Ohio independent football that it forced other teams to seek out and hire college all-stars from around the nation to achieve parity with the Akron Indians.

The 1914 Akron Indians were a colorful array of stars. One of the most popular was Ralph "Fats" Waldsmith, a hometown star and team leader. Ralph played center and was one of the finest single platoon centers ever in professional football. He was on an undefeated football team at Central High School in Akron in 1910, where he first proved himself. In 1911, he attended Akron's Buchtel College and lettered in varsity football for three years. He was captain of the Buchtel team in 1913 and made the mythical All-Ohio team put together by the state's newspapers.[13] Ralph started professional football for the Akron Indians in 1914.

Edmund Leroy Kagy played right halfback for the 1914 Akron Indians. Born on April 21, 1889, in Findlay, Ohio, Edmund was one of seven children. He washed dishes at a local restaurant in the winter months and worked for the Buckeye Pipe Line Company in the summer to pay for his high school education and help out at home. His hard work for the pipeline company built muscles that made him a high school football star. From the beginning of his football career, Ed Kagy had a working man's orientation.

After considering an eastern college, Ed Kagy and his best friend, Dwight Wertz, enrolled at Cleveland's Western Reserve University. While in college, Kagy worked for the Standard Oil Company filling oil cans. He also waited tables at his fraternity house and clerked at the university bookstore. In addition, he worked for the American Express Company and was a gang boss for the New York Central unit laying concrete culverts along the railroad's main line.

In 1909, Kagy became right halfback and end on the Western Reserve varsity team. He captained the 1911 team. He also played varsity baseball three years and varsity basketball one year. One summer, he tried semipro baseball for the civil engineers at Crystal Falls, Michigan, in the Michigan Iron Country League. Following graduation from Western Reserve, Kagy taught physics at South High School in Cleveland, where he coached all sports. In 1913, he became head baseball and basketball coach at Western Reserve and assisted with the football team.

In 1912, Kagy and his friend Dwight Wertz began playing independent football for the Elyria Pros. They accepted a better offer to play with the Akron Indians in 1914.[14] In addition to Kagy and Wertz, Peggy Parratt recruited Milton Claudius "Muffin" Portmann to play tackle for the 1914 Akron Indians. Portmann was born in Jackson, Minnesota, on October 20, 1888, and played football at Jackson High School. In the fall of 1908, he enrolled at Western Reserve University in Cleveland for a bachelor's degree in law. At Reserve, he became an outstanding tackle on the varsity team. Along with his younger brother, he made up the line known as the "Beef Trust." According to his college yearbook,

In 1909, Milton Portmann was elected captain of the varsity football team. One of his professors said of him, "If the opposing team has as strong and nervy men as our captain, we have just cause to fear it."[15]

Portmann was an All-Ohio tackle while at Western Reserve. He also was on the track and basketball teams. In 1912, he played independent football for the Shelby Blues, and he joined the Akron Indians in 1913.

Joe Collins was a Cleveland boy who attended Notre Dame University and played fullback for them in 1910. The following year, Collins played with Parratt in Shelby, switching to the Akron Indians in 1912.[16] It was Joe Collins who suggested that Peggy Parratt recruit some other Notre Dame players for his 1914 Akron team.

On November 1, 1914, Howard "Cap" Edwards joined the Akron Indians and completed the season with them. Edwards, who grew up in South Bend, Indiana, was captain of the unbeaten 1909 Notre Dame team and got the nickname "Cap." The next year, Edwards became Notre Dame's assistant football coach and played independent football for several teams in and near South Bend. Edwards, an outstanding tackle, became an important addition to the Akron Indians team.[17] Later in November, Parratt added Keith "Deacon" Jones and Knute Rockne to his Akron team. Deacon Jones played left tackle at Notre Dame from 1912 through 1914. He also played hockey there.[18]

Knute Rockne played the last two games for Akron in 1914. Rockne is, of course, a legend in American football. Rockne was born on March 4, 1888, in Voss, Norway. His father, a renowned carriage maker and machinist, moved to Chicago, in 1892, to enter his carriages in the World's Columbian Exposition, which he won. Shortly afterward, he sent for his wife and children. They settled in the Logan Square area of Chicago, where Knute attended North West Division High School. He only played high school football one year as a fullback, but he enjoyed success on the track team as a half-miler and pole vaulter. He did not finish high school and, between 1905 and 1910, worked nights as a clerk at the Chicago Post Office. He read voraciously and was an active member of the Illinois Athletic Club.

Rockne's sister urged him to go to the University of Illinois, but he was talked into going to Notre Dame because the tuition was lower and more jobs were available to help him work his way through college. After passing the special examination required of those who lacked a prep school diploma, he entered Notre Dame in the fall of 1910. His roommate, Charles "Gus" Dorais from Chippewa Falls, Wisconsin, urged Rockne to play football, and Joe Collins recommended him to the coach.

At first, the Notre Dame coach, Shorty Longman, was unimpressed with Rockne. When he saw that Rockne excelled on the track team, however, Longman gave him a chance to play on the football team. In 1911, Rockne became varsity end for then tiny Notre Dame University. At 165 pounds, Rockne was slight and short (5'8"), but wiry and tough. He was also several years older than most of his college teammates.

In the summer of 1913, Rockne and Dorais went to work at Cedar Point Amusement Park, where they practiced the forward pass. Whereas previously the only tactical move employed by pass receivers was to try to outrun the defender, Rockne introduced acting, deception, sidestepping, and change of pace as ways to get open for a pass reception. That fall under coach Jesse Harper, they used the pass to beat Army and Texas, making Notre Dame a national football powerhouse. In 1913, the *Chicago Interocean* made Rockne its first team left end for the All-Western eleven, and the *Chicago Evening Post* put him on their second team.

Rockne was a football hero, a track star, editor of the school yearbook, a flutist with the orchestra, and an actor in the drama group, in addition to waiting on tables and performing janitorial duties to earn money for school. He also boxed in South Bend clubs. He majored in chemistry and graduated, in 1914, magna cum laude with a B.S. degree in pharmacy. In the fall of 1914, he became head track coach and assistant football coach at Notre Dame for $1,000 per year.[19]

In Akron, the future of independent football seemed secure. On the last weekend of the 1914 season, Peggy Parratt attended Joe Collins's wedding on Saturday, and the next day his team won the State of Ohio independent football championship by beating the Canton Bulldogs. Peggy had built a dynasty he hoped would dominate Ohio independent football for years to come. His dream, however, was soon shattered.

In late September 1915, the Massillon Tigers were reborn with the financial backing of community leaders, and Joe Collins was hired as coach to resurrect the team's former glory. Collins started his team-

Knute Rockne, end, played professional football for the Akron Indians in 1914; the Massillon Tigers in 1915–17; and the Fort Wayne Friars in 1916–17. *(The Archives of the University of Notre Dame.)*

building program by hiring six starters away from the Akron Indians' championship team. This represented half of Akron's starting lineup, and the loss essentially destroyed Parratt's team. Not to be outdone, Canton hired away the rest of Akron's starters.

With these players, Canton and Massillon became rivals for the world championship of professional football. This rivalry began the football wars for top players and meant that salaries would climb. Other cities began to emulate what Peggy Parratt had done in Akron, and a number of truly professional teams began to emerge.

When Parratt found out that almost all of his starting lineup had been lured away by higher pay, he was forced to cancel the Akron Indians' opening game with the Detroit Mack Park Maroons.[20] On October 31, Parratt finally fielded a patched-up team against the Maroons and also played games in Toledo and Dayton in early November, but for practical purposes the Akron Indians ceased to exist when their team was cannibalized by Massillon and Canton at the beginning of the 1915 season. On October 19, Parratt agreed to coach the Shelby Blues.[21] However, his tenure with Shelby was short-lived. Unable to compete with the new professional teams, Shelby stopped playing major league football before November. Parratt turned his attention to becoming a lawyer, graduating from the John Marshall Law School of Baldwin-Wallace College in 1917 with an LL.B.[22]

In 1915, this drive to be competitive caused several changes in independent football that transformed it from semiprofessional to professional status. Heretofore, many independent teams either passed the hat or charged a modest admission to pay for expenses. If there was money left over at the end of the season, it was divided among the regular players. The cost of a ringer was charged to expenses. However, when more than half the players were paid professionals, the payment method had to change. Players were now paid by the game, and, because of the uncertainty of schedules and gate receipts, player contracts tended to be game to game. Big games that drew big crowds meant lots of stars. Less important games that drew smaller crowds meant fewer stars. Thus, top-flight players were frequently itinerants, uncertain where they would play from one week to the next.

Likewise, teams that drew large crowds tended to become stronger, while teams that could not compete effectively lost stars and good bookings. In order to attract crowds, teams looked to local rivalries and tried to create new rivalries with strong teams from outside their region. Interstate games became more common and more compelling by 1913 and were well established among the best teams by 1915.

Newspaper coverage also became crucial to team survival. Independent football was snubbed by the press and never received the coverage given to baseball or college football. As teams of all-stars emerged, local community support was a critical factor in their survival. Communities that gave good newspaper coverage to their independent teams had a distinct advantage in the uncertain world of big-time independent football in 1915.

Team management was another critical variable in the transition from independent to professional football. With no leagues, no stadiums, no team rosters, and no set schedules, everything was negotiable. Team managers had to put teams together, find places to play, schedule games, make travel arrangements, extract guarantees, agree on officials, advertise games, sell tickets, and account for and distribute gate receipts. This meant that effective team management was vital to survival.

Baseball parks doubled as football stadiums for independent teams, so the independent football season could not begin until the baseball season was over. Typically, this meant that the independent football season started in October and ended on or near Thanksgiving.

Because most teams could not afford to sign guarantees for more than a game or two at a time, schedules were determined week to week. If the weather was good, the crowds were good, and the team won, the schedule got progressively harder as the season advanced. On the other hand, if the weather was bad, the crowds were poor, or the team lost, the manager scheduled less competitive teams that demanded smaller guarantees. In any case, games with strong rivals were usually scheduled for mid-November when players were in better condition and enough money was accumulated to hire the best ringers.

The 1915–17 seasons represent the dawn of professional football in America. During those three seasons, more than twenty independent football teams changed dramatically. They paid salaries to players and offered guarantees to visiting teams. They introduced former college players into their starting lineups on a regular basis. They played interstate games with strong teams in other states, and they began to discuss the need for leagues, schedules, and longer player contracts. Most importantly, the best independent football teams took on an all-star character that was reflected in the number of All-Conference and All-American college players recruited to play on their teams. These conditions marked a transition from independent, semiprofessional football to professional football. This book is about that transition.

2. Setting the Stage

The first successful pro football teams started in a variety of ways. Some prospered because railroad companies helped sponsor their teams. The Columbus Panhandles, the Altoona Indians, the Pitcairn Quakers, and the Pine Village Athletic Club are examples of this type of commercial origin. Others, like the Evanston North Ends and the Toledo Maroons, started out as boys teams and grew into professional status as the players got older and their teams became better managed and coached. Catholic parishes started teams in Youngstown and Dayton, while former college players organized teams in Detroit and Cincinnati, so that they could continue to play the game they loved. An army reserve group in Racine was simply too good for nearby teams. Since few teams in Wisconsin would play them, they were forced to schedule games regionally. But, for most other teams, community boosterism was the primary motivator for the growth of professional football. Medium-sized cities such as Akron, Canton, Massillon, Wabash, Davenport, Rock Island, Fort Wayne, and Hammond saw a winning football team as a source of local pride. Not all of the teams chronicled here became National Football League members, but all contributed to the creation of the league in one way or another. None of the 1921 NFL teams was formed in a city that had not already made the transition from independent to professional football by 1918.

Between 1900 and 1914, strong semiprofessional football developed in midwestern cities that were involved in rivalries with nearby communities. Intense community pride promoted fierce battles with the opposing city's team. For example, Detroit had a natural rivalry with Chicago; as railroad towns, Altoona and Pitcairn were very competitive, as were Wabash and Fort Wayne, Rock Island and Davenport, and Canton and Massillon. In nearly every case, independent football became semiprofessional and, ultimately, professional, because of the intense competition.

Rivalries encouraged the hiring of former high school and college stars or "ringers" to make certain that the home team did not get humiliated by the rival team. Over time, more and more former college players were hired, until teams like the Akron Indians were composed almost entirely of former college stars. But it was not until late November, 1915, that independent football produced a truly professional team. The announcement, on November 12, that Jim Thorpe had signed a contract to play football for the Canton Bulldogs was the culmination of a long process of transition from independent to professional football. Thorpe was probably the only athlete of his generation who could excite enough interest to complete the transition at that time. Without Thorpe, the process undoubtedly would have taken longer.

When Jim Thorpe played for Canton, the size of the crowd doubled and more than justified his $250 per game salary. Once it was demonstrated that former college football stars could attract crowds large enough to support a professional team, other independent, semipro teams followed the lead of Canton and Massillon.

It is hard to explain the electricity that Jim Thorpe created on the football field, but perhaps this report will offer some insight. Coach Clarence Childs had just introduced his new assistant football coach, James Thorpe, to the students at Indiana University:

> A throng of schoolboys more in their glory than when a circus comes to town, greeted Thorpe. The quiet, amiable Thorpe thrilled the audience with his trademark drop-kick exhibition. It was nothing for him to dodge a dozen tackles, or punt 75 yards with an easy nonchalance that seemed almost uncanny.[1]

Despite his importance, Jim Thorpe was not the only reason for the emergence of professional football in this era. It was the love of factory and mill workers for independent football that created the market for this distinctly American fall sport. Without the market they represented, the pro game could not have survived, much less flourished. The 1915 season demonstrated that blue-collar workers in factory towns were willing to pay from fifty cents to a dollar on a Sunday to see good professional teams play. The challenge for team managers was to attract top players who would make a winning football eleven, to schedule strong teams to play them, and to finance it all. This challenge was taken up by several new communities in 1916. Cleveland, Hammond, and Davenport launched strong independent teams, while Youngstown, Dayton, and Fort Wayne upgraded their independent teams significantly.

In 1916, the factories and farms of North America were prosperous. America was serving as the arsenal and breadbasket for Europe, while those great nations were engaged in a deadly war of attrition, no longer able to produce either the tools of war or the goods for life. American factories were working near capacity, and wages for factory workers were good. Long daily hours and relatively high wages, by the standards of the day, made blue-collar workers a good audience for Sunday football.

Most factory workers worked at least a half-day on Saturday, making Sunday their only free day for enjoying recreation and sport. Professional football, unlike the Saturday game of college football, was attractive to blue-collar workers because it was accessible. It was played on their day off in the cities where they worked. Ticket prices were generally lower than for college games, and workers could relate better to professional players than to many of the upper-middle class and well-to-do college players. Men who played for the pros were often rough-and-tumble guys who continued to play football because they loved the sport, with all its violence and raw edges. The working guy relished it when unschooled players like the Nesser brothers, who were boiler-makers, or Norman Speck, an iron worker, showed up the college boys.

Professional football gave the blue-collar worker a way to be proud of his community and, at the same time, gave him an opportunity to let off steam and vicariously hit back at the frustrations of a hard working life. A blue-collar base of support was not always an advantage, however, as workers did not have much money to spend on entertainment, even when times were good and employment was high, because wages were low by modern standards. In 1917, when the average worker earned a dollar or two a day, it cost a day's wages to see a Sunday football game, if travel and admission costs were considered. Often, going to a game required a real sacrifice. If the weather was bad or the game held little interest, attendance would fall off significantly.

With such a tenuous market, it required genuine risk-taking entrepreneurs and community boosterism for professional football to succeed. Community pride fueled independent football for more than a decade before Thorpe made his appearance in Canton, and it is still an integral part of professional football's popularity in America. Creating a professional football team was a shaky business at which few succeeded. The entrepreneur with the heart of a pirate and the mentality of a con artist was frequently drawn to the management of independent football. The emergence of professional football occurred both because of and in spite of these gambling, buccaneer businessmen. Entrepreneurs did not create the audience for professional football; they only attempted to capitalize on it.

Another factor that made the sport a risky financial venture was the negative attitude of sportswriters and college alumni toward pro football. To them, the sport was as disreputable as hanging out in a pool hall. Before World War I, sportswriters generally ignored professional football. Typically, its coverage lagged behind boxing and ranked somewhere near track, hockey, rowing, and bowling. After the baseball season, the sports pages were dominated by college football. Even local high school games often got a fourth of a page, while the pro game was typically limited to one or two column inches and relegated to the bottom of the page. There was a direct link between fan support for professional football and local sports page coverage. In communities like Massillon, Canton, Detroit, Fort Wayne, Dayton, Toledo, Wabash, and Hammond, professional football coverage was good to excellent. Sportswriters in these communities provided profiles of professional stars, gave lineups for games, reported out of town professional football scores, and sometimes even provided play-by-play descriptions of important games.

In the rest of the country, reports on professional football were sparse, at best, and usually did not exist. In 1915, in Washington, D.C. there were less than two column inches of coverage in the *Washington Post* and the *Washington Star* combined for the entire year. In 1916, the *Post* increased its coverage slightly to include occasional very short reports on the Columbus Panhandles, Detroit Heralds, Toledo Maroons, and Pine Village Athletic Club.[2] In that same year, the Minneapolis papers began reporting on Pine Village Athletic Club, Fort Wayne Friars, Massillon Tigers, Detroit Heralds, and Canton Bulldogs.[3]

As in college football at this time, there was often an incestuous relationship between sportswriters and professional football coverage. In college ranks, football coaches often hired sportswriters to referee their games, thereby ensuring newspaper coverage.[4] In Massillon, Canton, Fort Wayne, Hammond, and Davenport, sportswriters had close affiliation with the local professional team. In Davenport, sportswriter Victor L. Littig was the team's first coach.[5] In Massillon, Fred Becker, the local sportswriter, was secretary of the Massillon Tigers organization.[6] It seems likely that some professional football teams failed because they received inadequate coverage in the local sports pages. This no doubt had an adverse effect on the financial fortunes of the Evanston North Ends, the Cincinnati Celts, and the Columbus Panhandles.

The Panhandles received excellent newspaper coverage outside of Columbus, in large measure because their manager Joe Carr, a former newspaper writer, prepared colorful news releases about the Nesser

brothers that could be distributed by the host team to local sports reporters. The Panhandles rarely received more than token coverage in
Columbus during this period, because the fans were focused on Ohio
State University games and were not much interested in games played
by railroad workers. As a consequence, the Panhandles never achieved
much of a hometown following.

Cincinnati newspapers gave the Celts poor coverage, and their home
games never achieved the fan support found elsewhere. One could ar-
gue that local newspapers gave poor coverage because there was little
fan interest, but fan interest generally improved when newspaper coverage increased in cities like Toledo and Dayton.

The opinions of famous sportswriters Walter Camp and Casper
Whitney set the tone of the period. As advocates of "manly virtues,"
"fair play," and the gentleman's sports ethic, these writers were outspo-
ken in their opposition to the mercenary aspects of professional football. As they saw it, athletes were selling their loyalty, instead of playing for the pure joy of sport and their devotion to an institution of
higher learning. The high purpose of football was being perverted into
a lowly job tied to "filthy lucre" and linked to gambling and other sor-
did interests. To these writers, sport was meant to develop the virtues
of strength, courage, loyalty, and order. The amateur athlete was
revered for exemplifying these qualities. Professional football, on the
other hand, tarnished the integrity of the athlete.[7]

By 1915–16, All-Big Nine Conference football players like Jack
Townley began challenging the popular prejudice against professional
football. The *Minneapolis Journal* reported:

There has been some criticism of the Gopher players for turning professional so
soon after [the next day] representing [the University of] Minnesota at Chicago
[against the University of Chicago]. Professional football is not in the best standing here, but in this regard Jack Townley said today "the professional football
played by the Massillon team would surprise the rooters here if they saw it. On
the squad of which we were members last Sunday there were 20 players, all college men, from Ohio State, Notre Dame, Penn State, and many eastern schools.
There were 12 All-American players on the two teams [Massillon and Canton].
They play as good and as clean as college football in the conference, though not
as fast because the men are not in as good condition as the college player."[8]

However, if you were a working stiff—a mill worker, railroad worker, or factory worker—you saw it differently. You were not worried
about developing manly virtues; you had them by the nature of your
work. At a pro football game, you could stand up and root for your
town on your day off, and you did not have to be a college alumnus to
feel ownership of your pro team. Scorned and ridiculed by the college

crowd, loved only by factory workers and a few fanatics, professional football was taking root in America's midwestern factory towns.

There were some risks, however: some workers forgot discretion when gambling was involved and diverted money from necessities of life to wager on their team. Gambling has been linked to sport since ancient times, and nothing increased spectator concern about the outcome of a game more than a small wager. It is nearly impossible to read the newspaper accounts of Sunday football in this period without finding references to wagering on the game. Sportswriters often spoke about the odds given by bettors or made statements such as the one that appeared in the *Pittsburgh Gazette-Times:* "Large sums of money changed hands, as the betting was brisk."[9] Similar references can be found in nearly every in-depth report about professional football games held between 1915 and 1917 in cities such as Canton, Chicago, Cleveland, Davenport, Detroit, Fort Wayne, Hammond, or Youngstown.

The close association between gambling and pro football has continued well into the modern era. In 1946, for example, Arthur "Mickey" McBride was one of the principal investors in the Cleveland Browns. The basis for McBride's fortune was his skill in establishing and operating the gambling "wire" for the crime syndicate's horse racing betting parlors, which incidentally also covered bets on pro football games.[10] The subsequent owner of the Browns also had ties to syndicate gamblers.[11]

An uneasy alliance started in 1915 between the principal owners of pro football teams—the buccaneer businessmen who often either enjoyed gambling or traveled in circles that included serious and persistent gamblers—and the minority investors who saw professional football as a civic enterprise that benefited the home community. Player salaries and stadium expenses increased operating costs for pro teams and made them dependent on higher levels of community support, either through fan attendance or commercial underwriting. The marginal business of football frightened normal businessmen and attracted risk-taking promoters. Still, the teams needed civic support to attract fans, to have access to stadiums, and to get public transportation to accommodate their games. To survive, the football club needed to have the community behind it. It also needed good press from the local newspaper and its advertisers. Newspapers were usually owned and supported by conservative, civic-minded businessmen who in turn profited from the increased traffic and community spirit brought to the town by a successful professional football team.

During the 1915–16 football wars, alliances between the community and risk-taking owners became more essential because of rising costs. This marriage of divergent interests is still apparent in professional football. Pro teams continue to depend on civic support to build and maintain football stadiums, promote team merchandise, sponsor television and radio coverage, and attract crowds to their games. Yet, increasingly, owners have been breaking an implied contract by behaving as if their team's financial success has nothing to do with community support. The success or failure of a professional football franchise has historically been intertwined with a community.

In the second decade of the twentieth century, the supporters of successful professional football teams agreed on the need to have a winning team for the benefit of their town. This drive to win required that the town hire more stars, rather than depend on local talent. As teams hired more and more highly paid players, they incurred greater expenses. In 1910, the Shelby Blues spent about $150 per game. The average player was paid between $5 and $10 a game, and a star might receive as much as $25. By 1914, the Akron Indians had a payroll of $350 for a late season game, and, by 1915, Canton and Massillon were spending $800 or more on players' wages for late season games. By 1916, more than a dozen teams averaged $1000 in salaries for late season games.

Obviously, the transition to professional football carried a significant price tag. In some cases, corporate sponsorship helped ease the burden. In Akron, Canton, and Massillon, for instance, breweries helped the hometown team with cash flow and shortfall, and in Altoona, Pitcairn, and Columbus, the Pennsylvania Railroad provided free transportation to players and purchased playing jerseys. Even so, the best professional teams in 1916 found it necessary to draw between twenty-five hundred and three thousand paying fans per game to break even, because of guarantees to the visiting team, salaries to their players, and officials' fees. Only about half of the top twenty-five professional football teams achieved this standard. Pro football was a marginal business and continued to be so for nearly two decades.

Before World War I, public support for Sunday football was always tenuous. Poor performance by the home team, weak opponents, or bad weather might make any Sunday the last one for the home team. In many communities, there was organized religious opposition to Sunday football, particularly where Calvinist and Evangelical churches were strong. These church groups opposed Sunday football because it distracted from God's day. By contrast, Catholic and Lutheran churches, with few exceptions, had no religious objections to attending a football game on a Sunday afternoon. In towns like Massillon and Fort Wayne, where there were large Catholic populations, Notre Dame players were particularly sought. Catholic players encouraged support among blue-collar workers, many of whom were Catholic. In Youngstown and Dayton, the pro football teams were originally organized by Catholic priests for their own church communities and later developed into professional teams.

Prior to the National Football League, there was no official method for ranking the relative strength of teams. Sportswriters gave rankings within the state, and, for most teams, their highest aspiration was to be the state champion. Since the writers rarely compared teams on a national basis, arguments about which teams were the best in the region raged in many cigar stores and barbershops. Interestingly enough, however, although Pine Village claimed to be the champion of the Midwest, only Massillon and Canton claimed the national championship—a claim with which most pro football fans agreed.

Table 1 shows an unofficial ranking of the top twenty professional teams in 1915, 1916, and 1917 can be made, based on the contemporary observations of sportswriters and team managers, the level of difficulty of team schedules, and won-lost records.

Other teams existed at that time but simply were never among the nation's top twenty independent, semipro, or professional teams of the era. Teams in Buffalo, Rochester, Lancaster, and Brooklyn, New York were not ignored, nor were teams from Elyria, Ohio; South Bend and Muncie, Indiana; Wheeling, West Virginia; or Spring Valley, Taylorville, Aurora, Rockford, Maywood, and Decatur, Illinois; Des Moines, Iowa; or Duluth, Minnesota. They just did not have the caliber of player or the challenging schedules of the teams listed.

Twenty professional teams are chronicled in this book, with special emphasis on the critical period 1915–17, when the foundation for the National Football League was laid. America's full-fledged entry into the First World War ended major league professional football until the Kaiser was defeated. Once the war was over, it took the 1919 season to get teams back to prewar levels. The creation of the American Professional Football Association in 1920, which became the National Football League a year later, was the natural result of events described in this book.

It is dangerous to make comparisons between these players and the modern professional football player. The playing conditions, rules, and equipment were vastly different. From 1906 to 1910, for example, the

Table 1   Unofficial Ranking of Professional Football Teams

1915
1. Massillon Tigers
2. Canton Bulldogs
3. Evanston North Ends
4. Detroit Heralds
5. Pine Village Athletic Club
6. Wabash Athletic Association
7. Fort Wayne Friars
8. Columbus Panhandles
9. Dayton Gym-Cadets
10. Toledo Maroons
11. Cincinnati Celts
12. Detroit Maroons
13. Minneapolis Marines
14. Youngstown Patricians
15. Moline Red Men
16. Rock Island Independents
17. Racine Regulars
18. Altoona Indians
19. Pitcairn Quakers
20. Akron Indians

1916
1. Canton Bulldogs
2. Massillon Tigers
3. Cleveland Indians
4 Fort Wayne Friars
5. Dayton Triangles
6. Youngstown Patricians
7 Pine Village Athletic Club
8. Wabash Athletic Association
9. Minneapolis Marines
10. Columbus Panhandles

11. Detroit Heralds
12. Toledo Maroons
13. Davenport Athletic Club
14. Rock Island Independents
15. Evanston North Ends
16. Hammond Clabbys
17. Cincinnati Celts
18. Chicago Cornell-Hamburgs
19. Akron Burkhardts
20. Washington Vigilants

1917
1. Canton Bulldogs
2. Detroit Heralds
3. Massillon Tigers
4. Akron Pros
5. Hammond Clabbys
6. Minneapolis Marines
7. Dayton Triangles
8. Rock Island Independents
9. Davenport Athletic Club
10. Pine Village Athletic Club
11. McKeesport Olympics
12. Fort Wayne Friars
13. Youngstown Patricians
14. Chicago Cornell-Hamburgs
15. Wabash Athletic Association
16. Pitcairn Quakers
17. Columbus Panhandles
18. Toledo Maroons
19. Cincinnati Celts
20. Buffalo All-Stars

field of play was 110 yards long, the goal posts were on the goal lines, and the end zone added another ten yards at each end of the playing field. There were no quarters in the game, once a player left the game he was barred from returning, and the quarterback could not run the ball across the line of scrimmage within five yards of the hike or throw a forward pass within five yards of the line of scrimmage; the length of a forward pass was limited to twenty yards. The offense had only three downs to move the ball ten yards for a first down. A touchdown was worth five points, and an onside kick was required to cover twenty yards. The game was composed of two thirty-five-minute halves, with a ten-minute rest between halves.

By 1912, the length of the field had been reduced from 330 feet to 300 feet, with a ten-yard forward pass zone behind each goal line. The offense was given four downs to get a first down. The place of kickoff was changed from the center of the field to the forty yard line of the side doing the kicking. Seven men were required on the line offensive of scrimmage when the ball was put in play. The value of a touchdown was increased to six points, and restrictions on the quarterback's right to run and pass, as well as on the length of a forward pass, were removed. However, if a pass thrown across the end zone was incomplete, the defense got the ball on their own twenty yard line.[12] The game was divided into four quarters, with a fifteen-minute break at halftime, and a player who left the game was allowed to return in any subsequent period. Nevertheless, player substitution was still very limited, so it was common for the same eleven players to play the entire game.

Throughout this era, the ball was played wherever it was downed, and, unlike today, the clock did not stop when a player went out of bounds. If a player went out of bounds, the ball was put into play within three feet of the sideline and the clock kept going. Consequently, there was no advantage for a ball carrier to go out of bounds and some disadvantage, since on the next down the ball was put in play next to the sideline. This left no doubt where the next play was going, and a team usually had to waste a down just getting the ball toward the center of the field to gain options.

The "play the ball where it lies" rule also encouraged third-down punts to change field position. If the safety went back to protect against the punt on third down, a team had more room to pass or run. On the other hand, if the safety did not move back to protect against a kick, a quick kick could establish better field position. All in all, with the quick kick and the punt-out, there was considerably more emphasis on kicking. Nearly every team had more than one kicker, who also was required to run, pass, and play defense.

The extra point after touchdown was a difficult ordeal. When a team scored a touchdown, a member of that team would be required to "punt-out" the football so that a player on his team could attempt a fair catch. The punt-out starts with the players on the punter's team standing in the field of play not less than five yards from the goal line and their opponents standing on the goal line. The defensive team may not come within five yards of the punter after the referee blows the whistle and play starts. The ball must be punted-out from within five yards of where the man making the touchdown had crossed the goal line, and the extra point was kicked from wherever the free catch was made.[13] The current method of "try-for-point after touchdown" was not introduced until 1922.

Plays were "called out" while the players were in position to play. The "huddle" system of giving signals was not introduced until 1921. Prior to 1916, the team that made the touchdown retained possession of the ball, and the team that had been scored on was required to kick off to them.

The football equipment and the football itself were much different in that era. The ball was fatter and larger than it is now. The football uniform was the union suit with vest attached. The union suit was padded with splints and papier-mâché. It collected moisture from perspiration or rain and offered little protection from hard tackles or blocks. Often, wool sweaters or jerseys with leather elbow pads and shoulder patches were the primary football gear. Sometimes shoulder pads were used, but they were small and thin. Football shoes were high-topped leather shoes modified with permanent rectangular leather cleats sewed to the soles. A leather aviator helmet with felt lining and chin strap was often, but not always, worn. Some players still used the old head harness with adjustable suspension cushions, forehead bands, and a padded chin piece, but they were little protection against a head-on collision and were so hot and heavy that many players played without a helmet. Some players wore rubber mouthpieces and hip pads; many did not. A few backs had special mud cleats for rainy days; most did not. A few wore nose guards to protect or aid them.[14]

In 1915, the game was much as it had been in 1910, with the exception that the football field was now 100 yards long, the game had been divided into four quarters, and the rules governing the forward pass were somewhat more liberal. The center could no longer fake a hike and run with the ball, as had been possible until 1915, and there were modest improvements in football pants, which were now made of canvas, had some pads sewn in, and had a high waist with a kidney-protecting pad across the back. Fiber pads were sewn into the thighs. Some players now wore chin pads, often homemade, to protect against the common practice of kicking your opponent in the chin.[15]

The only pieces of equipment furnished by professional team owners were the jerseys and a football. Players were expected to bring their own football shoes, pads, helmet, mouthpiece, and football pants. New

Spalding equipment in 1915 would cost a player about $25.00. Padded football pants were $5.00, hip pads were $2.75, shoulder pads were $5.00, a head harness was $3.00, football shoes were $6.00 to $9.00, and a rubber mouthpiece was twenty-five cents.[16]

There were other differences besides players being responsible for their own football equipment. Players had little practice time, as this comment in the *Massillon Independent* on October 9, 1915, suggests: "Packing football duds, members of the Tiger horde will wend their way to this city today, most of them arriving this evening [Saturday], while the balance will reach the scene of their future football battles Sunday morning." Once the player arrived in town, he must meet his fellow players and learn the formations and signals before game time. As Howard "Cap" Edwards, captain of the 1915 Canton Bulldogs, put it:

The trouble with getting together an all-star team in most cases is that most of the fellows think themselves too good to take instructions from a coach or captain. Each wants to play his own style of game and shine individually. Team play under these conditions is clear out of the question. . . . Another thing, those stars nine times out of ten go into the game entirely for money and spend most of their time while playing is in progress figuring up their accounts—salary, meals, car fare, and the like—rather than planning some play which may help him win a game.[17]

Not only did equipment, rules, training, practice, and support services differ, but playing conditions were also different. In 1915, all games were played outdoors on fields that were designed for baseball and were not maintained after the baseball season. Frequently there were holes and wet spots on the field, and sometimes there were icy slicks or boggy places. Sometimes the ground was uneven, and often the grass was high or there was no grass at all where the baseball infield was located.

Most players played the full sixty minutes of a game. There were few timeouts, and all players played offense as well as defense. Versatility was required, and quickness was more beneficial than size in most cases. Blocking and tackling techniques back then were significantly different. Many of the techniques used today were illegal in 1915 and vice versa. For example, you could not use your hands for blocking. Chop blocking was allowed; so was throwing your body in front of someone.

On average, there were many fewer plays in a game because the clock rarely stopped during a period, except for a timeout. It did not stop when a player moved out of bounds, or when the officials moved the chains. Also, there was no time limit on when a play had to be started.

These differences should not suggest that the players of 1915 were not good athletes. On the contrary, most were outstanding players with proven prowess in more than one sport. Nearly all could have been professionals in any era. They might have trained differently or specialized more in modern times, but they still would have been great athletes. The durability of pre-World War I professional football players is demonstrated by the large number of them who later played in the National Football League.

3. Assumed Names and Anti-Pro Sentiments

Before embarking on a detailed history of the twenty teams that pioneered in professional football, it is important to explain how antiprofessional attitudes in sports and opposition to playing football on Sundays caused the widespread use of assumed names by professional football players. It is also useful to describe how the early management of semiprofessional football dealt with scheduling when there were no leagues or guidelines.

In 1916, the *Toledo Blade* reported that the Maroons "will be playing the masked marvels next on [one of Ohio's] big professional teams." The Massillon team got this nickname because of the number of players using assumed names. The *Blade* went on to say:

> Canton and Massillon, as everyone knows, have been football rivals for years. Each season the rival managements scour the country for the best players. It is not always possible to get enough luminaries who have finished college, so players still on big college elevens are contracted with, and played under assumed names—or "covered up."
>
> Just as soon as one team puts a man on the field the rival team gets busy and tries to uncover him. . . . One of the pleasant indoor autumn pastimes engaged in by football partisans of Canton and Massillon is a little game called "uncovering the covered."[1]

The *Toledo Blade* reflects both the fascination and the misinformation surrounding the use of assumed names by professional football players. The assumption was that all of the players who used assumed names were college players who were cheating college rules by earning extra money playing Sunday football. This assumption was incorrect. Nine out of ten times, players used assumed names because of their business ties or their family objections to Sunday football, not because they were in college.

Nearly all of the college players who played pro football did so only after they were barred from college sports for playing minor league baseball or because they had completed their college football eligibility and wanted to continue playing the game. Accepting money for playing summer baseball was the most common reason for ending a college athlete's amateur standing. This practice became a national issue in 1913, when Jim Thorpe was stripped of his Olympic gold metals for playing summer baseball in Rocky Mount, North Carolina, in 1909, and was continued in 1915, when Lorin Solon, captain of the 1914 University of Minnesota football team, and Malcolm E. Galvin, first-team fullback for the University of Wisconsin, were declared ineligible because they allegedly accepted money for playing baseball the previous summer.[2]

The Solon and Galvin incidents generated a significant uproar and efforts to abolish the prohibition against playing professional baseball in the summer. Student petitions were passed at the University of Wisconsin to abolish the "baseball clause."[3] The Indiana University Athletic Committee voted to end the prohibition,[4] and many at the University of Minnesota agreed,[5] arguing that the University of Chicago benefited from such a rule because alumni in large cities could find well-paid summer jobs for athletes, whereas those in smaller communities could not provide such aid except through summer baseball. The rule, however, was not changed, and, in 1916, Christopher Schlachter and three Cornell University players were declared ineligible for playing summer baseball.[6] In 1917, John Leo "Paddy" Driscoll, the Northwestern University team captain, also lost his amateur standing for playing professional baseball.

Some players lost eligibility because they were caught playing more than four years of college football. Among this group were Malcolm "Red" Fleming and William Neill.[7] Others, like Pete Calac, John Kellison, and Alfred E. "Greasy" Neale succeeded in playing more than four years of college football.[8]

Most frequently, college seniors played pro football after the close of their college football season. This group included Frank Whitaker of Indiana University, Bart Macomber of the University of Illinois, and Frank Rydzewski of Notre Dame; Earl Abell, Frederick Sefton, and Charles Edward Stewart from Colgate; Gideon Charles Smith from the Michigan Aggies (Michigan State); Carl Weiler from Case; and Bert Baston, Jack Townley, and Gilbert Sinclair from the University of Minnesota. Only rarely were players competing under assumed names because they were still actively playing college football. When this occurred, the players usually got caught and were barred from further college play, as was the case with William Blake Miller and Jerry Da Prato of the Michigan Aggies in 1915 or George Trafton of Notre Dame in 1919. These cases were far more unusual than was believed by the college opponents of professional football, although at least two players—Homer Stonebraker and Leo McCausland—played semiprofessional football during their college years but did not use assumed names and were not penalized.

The two most common reasons for using an assumed name were employer or parental opposition to Sunday football. David Reese and George Roudebush reported that their parents opposed Sunday football for religious reasons, and they often used assumed names to hide their activities from their mothers.[9] As late as 1923, Ralph and Arnold Horween played for the Chicago Cardinals, under the assumed name McMahon, to keep their mother from finding out that they were playing professional football.[10] Sometimes, however, men played under an assumed name because the high school or college where they coached discouraged or even prohibited their employees from playing professional football. Russell "Busty" Ashbaugh, Frank Dunn, A. A. Wesbecher, Howard Parker Talman, Maurice "Windy" Briggs, Joel P. Mattern, Clarence "Doc" Spears, Bob Boville, Richard C. King, Howard "Cub" Buck, John Kellison, Sam S. Willaman, Gus Welch, and Alfred E. "Greasy" Neale were in this category. Greasy Neale also wanted to hide his professional football activities from his summer employer, the Cincinnati Reds, who prohibited football for their players.

The upper-class and upper-middle-class prejudice against professional football was very pronounced before World War I. Between 1891 and 1899, Casper Whitney wrote a column entitled "Amateur Sport" in *Harper's Weekly* that frequently railed at the intrusion of professionalism into amateur athletics, a theme that he continued for the monthly magazine, *Outing*, until 1910. Whitney argued that it is the task of American colleges to educate gentlemen, and he declared, "We had rather see football forbidden by the university faculties than pained by the exhibition of our college boys, sons of gentlemen, resorting to the intrigues of unprincipled professionals."[11] Walter Camp, the acknowledged expert on American football, agreed. He believed that "amateurs ought not to work at their sport," because "amateurs are expected to be gentlemen" and "football should be fun."[12] Professional sports were associated with gambling and selling loyalties for personal gain. Such work was more suited to "crude blacksmiths, miners and backwoodsmen" than to gentlemen.[13]

In 1905–6, there was a strong movement to outlaw American football. It was considered dangerous, tainted by corrupt practices, and incompatible with amateur athletics (since it was primarily a spectator sport prone to obvious excess). W. J. Brier, president of the State Normal School of River Falls, Wisconsin, who hoped that the regents at the University of Wisconsin would prohibit football, wrote:

Professionalism has so saturated the game that it has become a stench in the nostrils of the more sober and conservative people. The coaches have dictated terms and rules, in their own interests, and there has been a strong following of the sporting element which has over-ridden the thoughtful and those who think there is still room for some profitable work and study in the universities and colleges. To my mind football has lowered the morals and ideals of our higher institutions as much as would recognizing prize fighting and horse racing.[14]

Historian Frederick Jackson Turner, the author of the frontier theory of American democracy, was the leader of antifootball elements at the University of Wisconsin. At a faculty meeting on January 8–9, 1906, the Turner group tried to pass a resolution suspending football at the university for two years. Failing this, they sought to place strict rules on football, requiring one year of college residence before participating in athletics, excluding graduate students from playing football, and forbidding the employment of professional coaches.[15]

Only a noisy rally by students and the involvement of alumni saved football at the University of Wisconsin from those who felt that it should be destroyed "root and branch" if it could not be kept pure and clean from professional influences. Students created that great ceremonial day of the athletic season, homecoming, which was designed to heighten the intensity of alumni feelings, contributions, and sentimental attachments to the university, as an antidote to antifootball sentiments.[16]

Similar beliefs were most strongly held in the Ivy League schools, but were also held by Amos Alonzo Stagg at the University of Chicago, Fielding Yost at the University of Michigan, and faculty representatives of the Western Conference Universities.[17] Thus, it was not surprising that blue-collar universities, with their favorable attitudes toward professional football, and coaches like Glenn "Pop" Warner and Knute Rockne, were considered outcasts and rogues by the "blue bloods" during this era.[18]

Concern about the sanctity of amateur athletics led the Amateur Athletic Union (AAU) to revise its constitution and bylaws in November 1916. The AAU reasserted its definition of an amateur as "one who engages in sport solely for the pleasure and physical, mental or social benefit he derives therefrom and to whom sport is nothing more than an avocation."[19] Without question, professional football was raising troubling problems for the advocates of the "gentleman's view of sports."

Nor should it be surprising that, when the faculty representatives of the Western Conference met in December 1916, they strongly disapproved of professional football. Moreover, they passed a resolution stating that "football players on 'big nine' conference elevens who compete in professional games after the close of the collegiate season will be expelled from school and will lose their letters." They also declared that "employees of athletic departments in any of the 'big nine' universities shall be prohibited from taking part in any professional contest. Violation of the rule will result in dismissal."[20] Many high school teaching and coaching contracts had similar provisions. Hence, those affected by the restrictions felt the need to coach for a Catholic school, where such prohibitions did not exist, or to play under an assumed name.

4. The Art of Scheduling

In early November 1916, the *New York World* ran a bit of cynical big-city wisdom that said, "an amateur pure and simple is generally the latter." However, the art of scheduling professional football games in 1916 was anything but "pure and simple." Take, for example, the negotiations between the Wabash Athletic Association and the Fort Wayne Friars.

The negotiations for their annual game started in September 1916 when Billy Jones, the manager of the Wabash team, telephoned Leo Beltman, the general manager of the Friars, for a commitment to play Wabash in Wabash. He offered a $500 guarantee, plus an additional $100 if Fort Wayne defeated the Wabash Athletic Association. He guaranteed "unbiased officials and fair treatment." Leo Beltman refused the deal, insisting that Wabash play the game in Fort Wayne for the same terms. Billy Jones refused, pointing out that Wabash had played the Friars in Fort Wayne in 1915 and that the Friars owed them several games in Wabash. Beltman countered that "there will be no game between the Friars and the Wabash A.A. unless the Wabash Athletic Association agrees to come to Fort Wayne." Angered by the discourteous way the Friar management had treated him, Billy Jones called a team meeting and put the Fort Wayne proposition to the players for a vote. The Wabash players flatly refused to go to Fort Wayne for a game unless the Friars would reciprocate.[1] Armed with strong player support, Billy Jones wrote an open letter to the Fort Wayne Friars stating the Wabash position. He sent copies of the letter to the *Fort Wayne Journal-Gazette* and the *Wabash Plain Dealer*. In the letter, Jones advised fans that the Wabash Athletic Association was holding open the dates of November 19 and 26 for a home-and-home series with the Fort Wayne Friars.

On October 26, the issues between Fort Wayne and Wabash still had not been settled, when Claire Rhodes, the manager of the Pine Village Athletic Club, contacted Carl J. Suedhoff, president of the Friars, and proposed a game on November 26 in Indianapolis between Pine Village and Fort Wayne and offering a flat guarantee of $1000 for the Friars appearance.[2] On the following day, the Friars telephoned Billy Jones and told him that, unless Wabash came to terms within twenty-four hours, they would sign a deal with Pine Village, even if it left them with an open date. Wabash agreed to send a delegation to Fort Wayne to iron out a deal. The following Tuesday, the Friars general manager offered the delegation of Wabash players, led by William "Red" Milliner and George Yarnelle, a home-and-home contract with a game in Fort Wayne on Sunday November 19 and one in Wabash a week later. Each visiting team was guaranteed $750.[3] On November 1, more than a month after negotiations had started, the deal was closed.

Meanwhile, Hammond offered to play Pine Village in Hammond on November 26 and proposed an $800 guarantee, plus expenses. Claire Rhodes turned the offer down. Only later did Frank O'Rourke, the Hammond Clabbys' representative, learn that the reason he was turned down was that Rhodes had a lease on a football stadium in Indianapolis and could not afford to play elsewhere.[4] At no time did Rhodes have the courtesy to tell O'Rourke why he would not accept his offer. On November 20, Rhodes traveled to Pittsburgh and on that evening signed a contract with P. H. Muteller, manager of the Pitcairn Quakers, to play in Indianapolis the following Sunday.[5]

Sometimes there were complex reasons for making a particular deal. In 1916, the Hammond Clabbys were attempting to upgrade their schedule to be considered among the top twenty independents. To achieve this goal, they wanted to attract one of the better teams to Hammond. The Clabbys, however, had not been very successful in drawing a large hometown following. They had perhaps six hundred very faithful followers, but this was not a large enough base to attract a top-twenty team to Hammond.

The Hammond management believed that, if they could get a better class of team for a home game, fan support would develop.[6] Aware of the fact that Davenport was also attempting to upgrade their schedule and could bring five hundred or so fans with them, the Clabbys offered the Iowa team an attractive contract to play in Hammond.

Although Davenport already had an out-of-town excursion to Taylorville planned for November 19, the Clabbys' guarantee was better, so Davenport agreed to bring their fans to Hammond. The Clabbys immediately raised their ticket price to $1 to recapture $500 of the $800 guarantee given the Davenport Athletic Club.[7]

The question of whom to schedule had several facets. It was important to have a winning record to keep fan support, but it was also important to play worthy opponents. Early in the season, fans were usually happy to pay admission to see the home team beat the Carlisle Indians. There were two teams composed largely of graduates of Carlisle Institute, and both found ample bookings in October. The Carlisle Indians teams were not expected to win. Fans were attracted to these games for the same reason they went to Buffalo Bill's Wild West Show. Both Detroit's Carlisle Indians (also known as the Detroit Braves) and the Altoona Indians put much-needed money in the pockets of Carlisle alumni. Playing one of these teams was a way of working your team into shape, while still drawing enough fans to cover expenses.

Another strategy for early in the season was to schedule semiprofessional teams, which might include Elyria, Wheeling, North Cincinnati, Lebanon, Buffalo, the New York All-Stars, or a variety of industrial teams, such as the Imperial Electrics, the Blepp Knits, or New Kensington Aluminum. When these teams played one of the top independents, they invariably lost. Once the top independents had played themselves into shape, the Pittsburgh-area professional teams were generally good teams to schedule to prepare for a strong rival or to recover from an unexpected loss. The McKeesport Olympics and the Pitcairn Quakers were both fairly good teams that usually gave the top twenty independents a strong game without beating them. In 1917, however, Pitcairn beat Youngstown and Fort Wayne, and McKeesport tied Pine Village.

In the absence of leagues, the object of most scheduling efforts was to play strong rivals in November and to angle for a championship of some sort. Typically, a team tried to be champion of its city, state, or region. If all these plans succeeded, the team might well try for the national championship.

There were hazards to scheduling. Guarantees were potentially risky commitments for home teams. Unfavorable weather could hold down an expected crowd or even cause the cancellation of a game.[8] It was also possible to overschedule a team. On November 21, 1916, the *Davenport Daily Times* observed,

Last Sunday's game plainly indicated that the schedule of eight games had left the men stale or on the verge of staleness and many of them are suffering from injuries sustained at Hammond or in previous games that refuse to yield to treatment. That the men are worn out and ready to call it a season is certain. On the train coming home from Hammond they were listless and completely worn out, although they have played much harder football in previous contests. The long grid of training and the constant nerve strain has finally worn the men down until they are no longer capable of the hard, fast football which has marked their work heretofore.

Jack Cusack's Canton Bulldogs were able to gain a comparative advantage over Massillon, in 1915 and 1916, by passing up a Thanksgiving Day game; in doing so, Cusack rested his players and avoided injuries before playing for the world's championship the following Sunday.

When two teams were located in the same marketing area, it was important to coordinate games, or both teams could lose money. On occasion, it was possible to schedule conflicting games in the same marketing area and get away with it, as was the case when Davenport and Rock Island scheduled big games on the same day. As the *Davenport Daily Times*, November 25, 1916, put it:

With every indication of perfect football weather for Sunday, officials of the Davenport Athletic Club are preparing to care for one of the largest crowds of the season [when they play the Minneapolis Marines], in spite of the counter attraction in Rock Island where the Independents and the Maywood Athletic Club are booked to get together for the Illinois state championship. However, it is doubtful if either of the contests hurts the other to any great extent, and both the Davenport and Rock Island teams are expected to play to huge crowds.

A more common response could be found in Massillon:

The management of the Tigers had hoped to have the team play here next Sunday and had attempted to schedule Pitcairn, but owing to the Canton-Columbus Panhandle game in Canton Sunday, the big battle in Ohio grid circles—decided to take on the Detroit Heralds, who had made a flattering offer to the local management to have the Tigers show in the Michigan city.[9]

All in all, scheduling was a challenging assignment at this stage in professional football.

5. The Fort Wayne Friars, 1915

No story is more typical of the rise of professional football in the American heartland than that of the Fort Wayne Friars. Fort Wayne, Indiana, located in the northeastern part of the state at the confluence of the St. Joseph and St. Marys Rivers, was a major railroad town in 1915. This metropolis of 83,250 people was served by five railroads, four of which had repair shops in Fort Wayne.[1] Railroads were the principal employers in the city. The New York Central Railroad or Nickel Plate Line, The Indiana Railroad system (better known as the Monon Line), The New York, Chicago and St. Louis Line, the Pennsylvania, and the Wabash Line employed more than twenty thousand residents.[2] There were, of course, brewers, grocers, and a variety of manufacturing companies that made knit goods, copper wire, oil pumps and tanks, and agricultural implements. But railroads were the lifeblood of the city.

Like other railroad towns such as Columbus, Ohio, and Altoona and Pitcairn, Pennsylvania, Fort Wayne took to independent football early in the twentieth century and, by 1915, was one of its principal practitioners. As in all railroad centers east of the Mississippi, there was an ample number of Irish and German Catholics who loved Sunday football. Early in the century, the business leaders in the community formed the Friars Club, whose principal role in the fall of the year was to sponsor the town's independent football team. Spearheaded by the cigar stores, breweries, men's haberdasheries, and railroads, the Friars Club sponsored bowling and basketball in the winter, amateur baseball in the summer, and Sunday football in the fall.

For several years, the Friars fielded a solid team of local athletes, who frequently lost to Evanston, Illinois, and interstate rivals like Muncie, Wabash, and even South Bend. Determined to remedy these embarrassments, the Friars decided to hire a few outsiders to bolster their team. In 1914, they hired Louis Island, the star quarterback from Haskell Institute in Lawrence, Kansas. Island, a member of the Oneida tribe, had been a back-up to Frank Mt. Pleasant, in 1907, while at Carlisle Institute.[3] In 1913, Island had played for the Jackson, Michigan

All-Stars, and had performed well against the Friars, so, in early October 1914, the Friars signed Louis Island to a contract.[4] In 1915, they added Kent "Skeet" Lambert of Wabash College and Alvin "Heine" Berger from Notre Dame.

Kent Lambert was a great athlete who came from a family of athletes. One of five children, he was born in Crawfordsville, Indiana, in 1891. He followed his older brother Ward into athletics. They both played on the Crawfordsville High School team under Ralph Jones, who doubled as coach of the Wabash College football squad until 1908 when Jesse Harper took over as the Wabash coach. Jones later made football history when he introduced the "T" formation, first at the University of Chicago and later to the Chicago Bears.

Lambert was an all-around athlete. In high school, he played football, basketball, and baseball and was captain of the baseball team his senior year. He was also class treasurer his sophomore and junior years. After graduation, he joined his brother Ward (nicknamed "Piggy") at Wabash College in Crawfordsville. Kent immediately became a triple threat at quarterback. As he was described, decades later, in *Montgomery: Our County Magazine:* "Lambert was the sort of quarterback that every coach must dream about. . . . his running and kicking made many points. . . . His ingenuity in taking advantage of annual changes in the rules in unexpected ways made him more than famous locally."[5]

Under Kent's field leadership, the 1910 Wabash football team went undefeated. They were unscored on in their first four games, defeating teams like Purdue, Georgetown, and St. Louis. After graduating in 1913, Kent, now known widely as "Skeet," signed a contract to play quarterback for the Fort Wayne Friars. Later he played for the Canton Bulldogs, the Detroit Heralds, and the Massillon Tigers, before accepting an officer's commission in 1917 as a captain in the U.S. Army.[6]

Independent football was very popular in Fort Wayne when the 1915 squad held its first practice just seven days before the first game. Coach Samuel Byroades added three new players: La Pado at left end, Walt Kennedy at left halfback, and Alvin "Heine" Berger at fullback. Alvin "Heine" Berger was a well-known backfield star for Notre Dame.[7] Three more practice sessions were held by coach Byroades before the season opener with South Bend at League Park. By October 1, the coach declared that "the players are in good condition physically" and that they generally were familiar with the new plays and signals.[8]

On October 25, 1914, the South Bend Silver Edges humiliated the Fort Wayne Friars 23–12 in an upset that cost the fans hundreds of dollars in betting losses. Knute Rockne, then an assistant coach at Notre Dame, had a second job as coach of the two South Bend independent football teams owned by the Mussel Brewing Company. He was paid a fee of $300 for the season, plus $50 in expenses. He was also allowed to hire Stanley Cofall, Notre Dame sophomore halfback, as an assistant coach for $100, plus $50 in expenses.

When the Silver Edges were scheduled to play the Friars in Fort Wayne, a great deal of money was bet on the game. Rockne engineered a humiliating upset by introducing the Notre Dame shift and several trick plays. Borrowing liberally from Yale's system of multiple laterals to trailing backs behind the line of scrimmage, designed to drain off defenders and open up the field of play, the Silver Edges devastated Fort Wayne's defense. Rockne also played end in this game under an assumed name and passed off as Silver Edges five top Notre Dame freshmen, including Jimmy Phelan, who became Notre Dame's first-string quarterback from 1915 through 1917.[9] Complaints by Fort Wayne fans resulted in a Notre Dame investigation, but this action did not deter other college players from playing semipro games and betting on the results.[10]

Fort Wayne was poised for revenge when they opened the 1915 season at home against the Merchants Athletic Club of South Bend on October 3. The Friars started La Pado and Louis Island at ends, Miller and D. C. Smith at tackles, Walter Krull and Wilkens at guards, Daniel R. Ball at center, and Skeet Lambert, Walt Kennedy, Laird, and Heine Berger in the backfield. Before the afternoon was over, the Friars played seventeen players and scored seven touchdowns against South Bend.[11] Skeet Lambert was the star in the one-sided, 58–0 win.

Still dissatisfied with the team's performance, Coach Byroades had his players back on the practice field Tuesday night to correct weaknesses that had surfaced the previous Sunday.[12]

The Friars' second opponent was the Newcastle Maxwell-Briscoes, and the Friars used the same lineup as the previous Sunday. However, Christian C. Chambers, a local hero, was now available as a reserve fullback.[13] The Newcastle team was outclassed at every stage of the game. Skeet Lambert and Heine Berger dominated play for the Friars. Lambert gave Fort Wayne fans their first exhibition of dropkicking for the season and made two field goals. He also passed and ran for several touchdowns in the first half. At halftime, he was replaced by Island at quarterback. The Friars played nineteen players in the 79–0 slaughter.[14]

On October 17, the Friars played the Muncie Congervilles, led by Frank "Coonie" Checkaye at quarterback and Hole at fullback. As in the two previous starts, Fort Wayne dominated play, hammering Muncie 109 to 8. Walt Kennedy made five touchdowns for Fort Wayne; Lambert made four; La Pado made three; Chambers two; and Strieder and Island one each. Lambert threw five touchdown passes and had a hand in nearly half of the Friars' points.[15]

On October 24, Fort Wayne played the Chicago Blues, a new team organized by Joe Pliska, the former Notre Dame halfback. Though the Blues starred Notre Dame's Tom Shaughnessy, they lacked depth and teamwork. For the fourth straight game Fort Wayne used the same starting lineup, and, behind the leadership of Skeet Lambert and Heine Berger, they tromped Chicago 43–0.

On the last Sunday in October, the Friars played the independent football champions of Wisconsin in the Indiana team's fifth consecutive home game. The Racine Regulars, managed by Otto Jandl, fielded several standout linemen, including Walter Eck from Lawrence College at right tackle, Phillip Thoennes at left tackle, and Scott "Duke" McEachron at left guard. Right halfback Bobby Foster, who had played at Marquette University, was their primary running threat.

The first quarter of the game was even. Racine scored early, and, for the first time all season, the Friars were on the short end of the score. However, Walt Kennedy soon countered with a series of off-tackle plays that fueled a sixty-five-yard drive. A run by Kennedy tied the score, and the extra point was good, putting Fort Wayne ahead 7–6 at the close of the first quarter. Heine Berger and Skeet Lambert dominated the second quarter, and Fort Wayne took control of the line of scrimmage. At halftime, Fort Wayne led 20–6.

In the second half, Chris Chambers, the Friars' reliable fullback, scored two of his three touchdowns to give the Fort Wayne eleven a 41–6 win. Kent Lambert pulled an outstanding play in the last quarter when he sent his backs into the line, then sneaked around end for a touchdown. The Friars attracted nearly three thousand fans, their largest crowd to date.[16]

The difficult part of the Friars' season was about to begin. Like most other independent teams of the era, Fort Wayne scheduled easier teams in October while they played themselves into midseason form and developed fan support. In November, they tried to establish themselves as champions of some sort by playing teams strong enough to establish them as city, state, or regional champions.

The Friars' first game in November was against the famed Evanston North Ends. Evanston was having another good season. Although they lost a disputed game to the Wabash Athletic Association on October 24, they rebounded to defeat the Detroit Heralds a week later. Led by the kicking genius Reuben Johnson and supported by Guilford Falcon, Robert Specht, and Henry Kilby in the backfield and their "million-dollar line," the Evanston North Ends were formidable opponents.

After struggling for years with ordinary teams, the Friars had images of being one of the best teams in independent football. The Evanston North Ends were the initial test of Fort Wayne's resolve. In 1914, Evanston defeated the Friars 29 to 7, with an amazing display of trick plays that were the equal of the better college teams.[17]

Samuel Byroades, the Friar coach, was unable to make the game because he was taking a special government examination in St. Louis.[18] In his absence, Skeet Lambert filled the coach's shoes. The fortunes of the Friars were dashed in the first quarter when Lambert was badly injured while making a tackle. He separated his left shoulder and was out the remainder of the game. Without Lambert, the Friars' ability to adjust to the North Ends' shifts and alterations was severely hampered. Louis Island filled in at quarterback, and the Evanston North Ends exploited Fort Wayne's weaknesses almost at will.

In the first quarter, the North Ends scored a touchdown on a five-yard pass from Reuben Johnson to Art Pascolini, and Johnson added the point after goal. In the second period, Robert Specht, in the words of the *Fort Wayne Journal-Gazette*, "squirmed off-tackle for a 15 yard run and a second touchdown for Evanston." The extra point was unsuccessful, so the score was 13 to 0 at halftime. In the fourth period, Rube Johnson place-kicked a field goal to make the final score 16–0. In the last half, the Friars played good football, but their rally was too little, too late. The absence of Skeet Lambert significantly changed the course of the game.[19]

It was urgent that the Friars acquire a quarterback for the upcoming game with their arch rival, the Wabash Athletic Association. On the day after the Evanston loss, Friar management representative Roy Lopshire hired Frank "Coonie" Checkaye to replace Lambert at quarterback, until he recovered from his injury. They also made arrangements for the services of Ivan Armon Zaring to bolster their line. Zaring, from

Ivan Armon Zaring, tackle, Fort Wayne Friars 1915–17, grew up in Salem, Indiana, and graduated from Indiana University, which he lettered in football and wrestling 1912–14. *(Indiana University Archives.)*

Salem, Indiana, starred at Indiana University in football and wrestling in 1912–14, and was noted for his strength.[20]

Maneuvering for an advantage in the Wabash-Fort Wayne game was a season-long process that intensified two weeks before the game. The contestants added the names of well-known ringers to their eligible player lists, debated referees and field judges, and generally sparred on every aspect of the forthcoming game from fan seating to locker room arrangements.[21] Wabash claimed that Edgar Davis and Matt Winters, who were on the Pine Village roster, would play for them, as would Harry Routh from Purdue and Everett "Newt" Tibbs. In turn, Fort Wayne claimed to have hired Charles "Gus" Dorais, the Notre Dame great, as quarterback, and Michigan All-American Germany Schulz as tackle.[22] In the meantime, rain inhibited outdoor practice and forced Coonie Checkaye to lead the Friars in blackboard drills and indoor signal calling. On Saturday, November 13, the Friars finally conducted an outdoor workout in which Checkaye called signals and formations for his new teammates.[23] Even at this late date, however, a disagreement over officials threatened to cancel the contest, which was just a week away.

On November 14, Fort Wayne played a good, independent Ann Arbor, Michigan, team. Frank Checkaye had his first opportunity to lead the Friars. Lined up against the Friars was an array of former University of Michigan gridiron stars as well as a graduate or two from other colleges. The Ann Arbor Independents featured former Wolverine Ernest J. Allmendinger, an All-Western Conference tackle. The Independents also had Michigan football greats, Andrew "Dope" Smith at center, Frank M. McHale at right guard, Eberwein at left halfback, John Lyons at right half, and Benton at fullback. Thomas McCall, a Harvard end, was coaching at Michigan and played right end, while University of Michigan freshman star Jack Dunn was the starting quarterback.

The game between Ann Arbor and Fort Wayne was not nearly as exciting as promised. After taking a 3–0 lead at halftime, Ann Arbor played poorly, and the Friars won the game 32 to 3. Checkaye's mix of plays in the second half included fake punts, forward passes, and a running game that exploited Ann Arbor's weaknesses. His efforts were significantly enhanced by the Friars' ability to control the line of scrimmage.[24]

With the Wabash game only a week away, Charles E. Pask, an advertising agent who had been on the freshman football team at Purdue University, in 1906, and quarterback for the Friars through the 1914 season,[25] organized a group he called the "Howling Hundred." Using Schirmeyer's and Pohlmeyer's cigar stores as recruiting centers, he persuaded more than 100 Friar fans to pay an extra twenty-five cents for reserved northside bleacher seats. The group rehearsed cheers, hired a band, and otherwise shouted their support for the home team. Many of the Howling Hundred wore white monk's customs that look dangerously like Ku Klux Klan robes.[26] Fan interest in the Wabash-Fort Wayne game required Friars' management to build more bleachers for the game.[27]

By midweek, the Friars recruited former Notre Dame captain Howard "Cap" Edwards, who had been playing professional football for the Canton Bulldogs. Left tackle Cap Edwards would measurably strengthen the weak side of the Friar line.[28] The Friars also added former Notre Dame players Al Feeney at center and Joe Pliska at halfback. Wabash added only Harry Routh from Purdue University at left tackle.[29]

The gates opened at 12:30, with the Wabash-Fort Wayne game starting at 2:00. The admission price was fifty cents for all adults, "ladies and gents alike." Seats in the reserved section cost an additional twenty-five cents.[30]

Howard "Cap" Edwards, Al Feeney, Joe Pliska, and Reilly (who had been with the Chicago Blues) had little opportunity to practice with the Friars before the game practice. On Friday, it rained for the one pregame practice.[31] After working out with the team, Howard Edwards told local reporters that he liked the Friar spirit:

You seldom see that spirit in independent football. . . . Your fellows certainly get a lot of pep into their work and it comes pretty close to being the same spirit that one encounters on a college gridiron.

On November 22, 1915, the *Fort Wayne Journal-Gazette* declared:

In one of the greatest football struggles ever staged in these parts the Fort Wayne Friars yesterday afternoon played the Wabash A. A.'s to a six to six draw at the Calhorn street lot. "Dutch" Berger put the home warriors in the score column shortly after the game opened when he ran thirty yards through the Wabash eleven for a touchdown while the irresistible Mr. [Jesse] Reno tallied for his side in the second quarter, going over the Friar line after receiving a short forward pass with the scrimmage about eight yards from the Fort Wayne goal.

Dutch Berger was the first Fort Wayne Friar ever to make a touchdown against Wabash, and they had been playing each other since the turn of the century. A record turnout of forty-five hundred fans saw the game in which Mark "Mickey" Erehart and Dutch Bergman were spectacular for Wabash, and Harry Routh "played a whale of a game in the line."[32]

In the week before the game, Dan Ball and Charles Pask drew up plans for a steel shoulder support they believed would protect Skeet Lambert's separated shoulder well enough to permit him to play. They had it built and hauled Lambert to Pask's home where they kept him on a pancake diet in the hope that the pancakes would help heal his injury.[33] With the aid of the brace, Lambert was able to enter the game late in the second quarter to attempt a scoring drive. Starting on their own twenty yard line "and traveling at breakneck speed [the Friars] worked the ball well into Wabash territory only to have the play end just after Lambert had cut in with a second run of fifteen yards or better." The clock ran out on the first half.[34]

Wabash attempted to place Homer T. Showalter in the game at the opening of the second half, but he was not on the approved players' roster and was still playing on the Wabash College team.[35] During the course of the afternoon, Fort Wayne missed three drop kicks for field goal. On one of these occasions, Harry Routh blocked a field goal attempt by Lambert.

Howard "Cap" Edwards and Joe Pliska were the stars of the Fort Wayne effort. "Edwards kept up the pepper in the Fort Wayne line," according to Frank Checkaye, who regarded Edwards as "one of the best players I have ever seen play."[36] To many Friar fans, the tie with Wabash was at least a moral victory.

The final game of the Friars' 1915 season was scheduled for Thanksgiving Day against the Columbus Panhandles. Led by the six Nesser brothers, the Columbus Panhandles were a big draw in a railroad town like Fort Wayne. Nearly all of the Panhandle players worked for the Panhandle Division of the Pennsylvania Railroad, and their reputation was well known in Fort Wayne. The Columbus Panhandles played a schedule that included the Canton Bulldogs, the Massillon Tigers, the Toledo Maroons, and the Detroit Mack Park Maroons. Coming into Fort Wayne, the Panhandles had lost only two games—one to Canton and the other to Toledo. They had defeated Massillon, Detroit, and Dayton, among others.

Lambert again planned to use the steel shoulder harness that permitted him to play the previous Sunday. The Friars kept Cap Edwards, Al Feeney, Reilly, and Joe Pliska on the roster and added the Carlisle Indian Don Peters, who had been playing for the Canton Bulldogs.[37]

The Panhandles brought only four of the Nesser brothers to Fort

Wayne, leaving Phil and John at home to play a game in Columbus against the Columbus Muldoons. The Fort Wayne-Columbus game was hard fought from start to finish. Al Feeney suffered a broken nose. The game was hard-hitting, rock'em-sock'em football with neither team gaining much advantage.

It was fortunate for the Friars that Lambert played, because his drop kick in the fourth quarter produced the Friars' only score and gave Fort Wayne a 3–0 victory over Columbus. Of course, Lambert did not win the game by himself. It was a team effort, with Reilly, Ivan Zaring, La Pado, Joe Pliska, Walt Kennedy, and Cap Edwards each playing an important role in the victory. "What the Friars lacked in weight and the like they made up for many times over by sheer pluck and determination."[38]

After the game, the Panhandles and their manager, Joe Carr, were the guests of the Friars for Thanksgiving dinner. Carr told reporters that "the Friar management had given them the best treatment they had ever received. The Nesser brothers sang several songs to the group and Schneider, the Columbus guard, told a number of stories. The turkey dinner with trimmings was enjoyed by all."[39]

The successful 1915 season encouraged Friar management. They declared that, "independent football [in Fort Wayne] will pay as long as stars can be secured and nothing but hard games with the best in the country are scheduled."[40] Attendance at the Evanston, Wabash, and Panhandle games exceeded three thousand paying fans, and the Friars drew twelve thousand paying customers and grossed more than $7,000 in November.

The Friars were already planning to recruit an all-star team for 1916 that would play the best teams in the country over the course of the entire season. The *Journal-Gazette* observed:

College and University stars have come to see the big field open in independent circles. Several years back the average college star had enough of football by the time he had completed his college career and as a rule only laughed at offers made him to play independent football. A fellow who can star in independent football is now regarded as a big hero as when he was winning games for his alma mater and there can be no denying the fact that the glory attached to athletic accomplishment means a lot, especially when salaries like those offered by the big teams are to be had.[41]

The Friar management pledged to bid for more stars, continue to build strong team play with more depth, and access a playing field early in the season when baseball parks were in use.[42]

On the day after Thanksgiving, Kent Lambert and Howard "Cap" Edwards left for Canton, Ohio, to be in the starting lineup for the Canton Bulldogs against the Massillon Tigers for the world professional football championship. Both were instrumental in Canton's victory over Massillon.

6. The Panhandles: Big As Mountains, Strong As Lions

The Columbus Panhandles and the Nesser brothers were virtually synonymous, and there are few stories about the pioneer days of professional football in Columbus that do not involve this fascinating family.

The Nesser brothers were German Catholics. Theodore Nesser was a powerful, athletic man who fathered twelve children, seven of whom were destined to play professional football. When he was thirty, he and his wife Catherine moved to Ohio from Germany with their six children. According to census records, their oldest son John was born in Germany in April of 1875. Two other sons, Peter and Phillipe, were also born in Germany—Peter in October 1877 and Phillipe in December 1880.

In the early 1880s, the Nessers moved to Denison, Ohio, where Theodore Jr. was born on April 5, 1883. Ted was followed by Fred W. in September 1888, Frank in June 1889, Rosa in May 1891, Alfred L. in June 1893, and Raymond in May 1898.[1]

In about 1890, Ted Nesser Sr. moved his family to Columbus, Ohio, where he took a job in the repair shops of the Pennsylvania Railroad's Panhandle Division. The Pennsy, as the railroad was nicknamed, had a reputation for hiring the family members of existing employees, and, true to form, by 1901 there were five Nessers working for the Panhandle Division.[2]

Ted Jr. went to work for the Pennsy, in 1900, when he was seventeen and became a boilermaker at eighteen.[3] In 1901, when Bill Butler organized a football team among the Panhandle shop employees, Ted and his brother John played on that team. By 1904, Ted coached the Panhandles, and brothers Frank and Phil, along with boilermaker Sebastian "Babe" Green, played on the team.[4] Occasionally, Ted Nesser also played a few games with the Shelby Athletic Association. At that time, Joe Carr,[5] who later became president of the National Football League, was the Panhandles' manager.

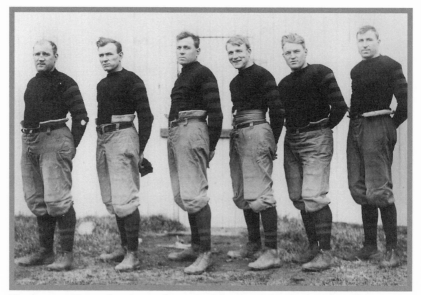

The famous Nesser brothers who starred for the Columbus Panhandles. From left to right: Ted, halfback and tackle; John, quarterback; Phil, tackle; Al, end and guard; Frank, fullback; Fred, end and halfback. *(Pro Football Hall of Fame.)*

Since Columbus did not field a major independent football team in 1905 or 1906, John and Ted Nesser played for the Massillon Tigers and the Shelby Blues.[6] In 1907, the Panhandles reappeared under the management of Joe Carr. Five Nesser brothers played on the team, including Ted who was the coach. The Nesser brothers maintained their loyalty to the Panhandles for nearly two decades. Nowhere is commitment to team better illustrated than in the story told by Joe Carr about Ted Nesser. According to Carr, Ted Nesser broke his arm early in a game in 1908, and two bones of his left arm protruded through the skin. Urged to see a doctor, he stayed with his team until the end of the game. "I ain't going to desert the boys," he exclaimed. "They like to know I'm here."[7] By then, the Nesser brothers excelled at a variety of sports. Fred was a promising boxer, Phil was an outstanding track star, and Frank was on his way to becoming a professional baseball player.

In 1909, brother Alfred played some games with the Panhandles,[8] and his brother-in-law, John Schneider, also a boilermaker at the Panhandle yard, was on the team.[9] Thus, between 1909 and 1916, there were generally six Nesser brothers and one brother-in-law on the Panhandles independent football team. Even brother Raymond, who did not like football, joined the team for a season in 1916.

Between 1909 and 1917, the Columbus team was one of the best independent football teams in America. In 1909, they went 7–1–1 against some of the best competition in Pennsylvania and Ohio.[10] Over that six-year period, the Panhandles never had a losing season.

"Probably no other team in the country is as well organized as the Columbus eleven," wrote the *Massillon Independent* on November 10, 1916. "All the players work in the Panhandle railroad shops in Columbus and every noon they spend at least 50 minutes of their noon hour in practice. They work 10 hours a day in a boiler factory, and at lunch time hustle through their meal and get out for practice." They spent five and a half days a week keeping the iron horses rolling. With the exception of Frank, who played first base in the minor leagues starting in 1911, the rest of the family worked for the Pennsy Railroad and played football on Sundays for the love of the game.[11] Knute Rockne, who played against the Nessers between 1914 and 1917, once declared, "Getting hit by a Nesser brother is like falling off a moving train."[12] It was reported that, even when past the age of forty, Frank Nesser stopped the great Bronco Nagursky three times inside the three yard line.[13]

The Panhandles played most of their games on the road. Because they had free passes on the railroad, they could save the expense of renting a field and the trouble of selling tickets by playing out of town. The few home games were played at Recreation Park and, later, at Neil Park.

In 1913, the Columbus Panhandles, in the dark jerseys, traveled to Wabash, Indiana, where they defeated the Wabash Athletic Association, 13–0. John Nesser is playing quarterback without a helmet, as are Frank Nesser at right guard and Fred Nesser at left end. Ted Nesser is the fullback. *(Wabash County Historical Society.)*

In 1915, Louis Edward "Pick" Pickerel, the star quarterback for the Ohio State University Buckeyes, joined the Panhandles. Born in Jackson, Ohio, in 1894, Pickerel was only five feet ten inches tall and weighed 155 pounds.[14] In addition to Pickerel, the Panhandles started Oscar and Roscoe Kuehner, Emmett Ruhl, and, on occasion, Charles Dunn or Lee Snoots, along with the Nesser brothers and John Schneider.

In 1915, the Panhandles won nine games, lost three, and tied one. Led by John, who was already forty years old, and Ted Nesser, age thirty-two, with support from their four brothers, the Panhandles battered their way through the toughest football defenses and flattened the orneriest offensive lines they played against. They frequently left broken bones in their wake. After playing warm-up games in Columbus and Marion, Ohio, the Panhandles played the Canton Bulldogs, the Toledo Maroons, and the Massillon Tigers on consecutive Sundays.

In Canton, on October 17, 1915, the Panhandles and the Bulldogs battled evenly for three quarters, and the game might easily have ended in a scoreless tie. But Bill Gardner stripped the ball from Louis Pickerel, and Howard "Cap" Edwards recovered it within five yards of the Columbus goal line. Two line plunges by Don Peters, the Canton fullback, produced the winning points. Don Hamilton punted out to Eddie Van Alman, and the goal was kicked. The Bulldogs had capitalized on the fumble to beat the Nesser brothers 7–0.

This victory, however, was a costly one for Canton. On the opening kickoff of the game, Peters kicked to Ted Nesser, who returned the ball six yards to the thirty-five yard line. Ted Nesser was traveling like a bullet when Hal "Hank" Dagenhart, the Canton left guard, tackled him head-on. Nesser went down, but Dagenhart "was carried off the field suffering from injuries about the head and spinal column and was taken to Mercy Hospital. He was conscious but doctors said it would be several days before the extent of his injuries were known." Dagenhart's football career ended that day.[15]

Later in the first period, M. J. Truesby broke his collarbone trying to tackle Frank Nesser. He was replaced by Eddie Van Alman, who had not practiced with the team. Despite his lack of preparation, Van Alman played brilliantly. Bill Gardner injured his knee when he stripped the ball from Louis Pickerel.

The following Sunday, the Maroons ambushed the Panhandles at Armory Park in Toledo. The Maroon players were inspired by the home crowd because the grandstands were so near the playing field that interaction between players and spectators was normal.[16] The Maroons had a good team in 1915. Their backfield featured Billy Marshall and Paul "Dutch" Reule from Adrian College, Jimmy Baxter from Kenyon College, and Ray Eichenlaub, the giant fullback from Notre Dame. The Panhandles were kept off balance all afternoon, and Toledo walloped them 20 to 0.

Determined to turn their season around, the Panhandles traveled to Massillon to play the Tigers on October 31. The Tigers were intent on becoming the independent football champions of Ohio and invested heavily in an all-star team. Having defeated the Detroit Maroons the previous Sunday, Massillon knew that only the Nesser brothers stood directly in the path of their objectives. *The Detroit Free Press* described the attributes of the Nessers well:

These brothers averaged over 200 pounds and are among the cleverest exponents of football extant. John, the eldest, plays at quarterback or right half. He has held the championship of the Pennsylvania railroad employees as all-around athlete for years. Ted, who plays fullback, is the smallest in stature, but weighs over 200 pounds and has the speed of a lighter man. He is credited with bringing a sudden halt to Willie Heston's career [the great University of Michigan All-American] on the gridiron [when he tackled Heston so hard he could not continue in the 1906 Massillon-Canton game]. He also coaches the team. Frank, the largest of the brothers is a tackle and does the punting, being rated one of the best kickers in the middle west. He will give an exhibition of long-distance kicking before the game. Fred is the tallest of the Nessers and plays left end of the aerial attack. He stands 6 feet 6 inches and handles the football with the ease most baseball players do the horse hide. Alfred is the youngest and plays at guard, being rated a great defensive man. Philip plays a tackle and is the real giant of the section. He is a finished athlete and a regular participant in all the athletic meets in this section. He holds the Ohio and Pennsylvania championships for putting the shot, high jump and is a great offensive player on the gridiron.[17]

The Nessers, the two Kuehner brothers, Louis Pickerel, Hiram Brigham, and Emmett Ruhl started for Columbus. Ruhl was a clever halfback, some said, "one of the greatest men ever seen in action while carrying the ball through a broken field." Possessing the ability to dodge and squirm away from would-be tacklers, Ruhl could gain many yards through the opposition's defenses before being brought to the ground.[18] He was particularly difficult to tackle when the Nessers were running interference:

Big as mountains and strong as lions the railroaders from the capitol are among the most feared teams in the state. Led in their efforts by the six Nesser brothers, football players of renown, the Columbus aggregation balks at nothing. They fight from start to finish. Possessing a clever backfield and a heavy line, the Panhandles present a battle front hard to pierce.[19]

On Halloween Day, the Massillon Tigers and the Columbus Panhandles clashed on Driving Park field in Massillon before a crowd of three thousand people. By mutual consent, they played twelve-minute quarters. The first Panhandle touchdown came in the second quarter on a forward pass from Louis Pickerel to Frank Nesser. The next score came in the fourth quarter when Pickerel made a field goal from the fifteen yard line. A few minutes later, a forward pass from Pickerel to Roscoe Kuehner resulted in the final touchdown.[20] Thus, after forty-eight minutes of "thrilling warfare," the Columbus Panhandles had completely crushed the Massillon Tigers 16 to 0. The outcome was a complete surprise to the Massillon fans, who believed their team was the greatest ever assembled. Ted and Frank Nesser had been demons that afternoon. They battered their way through the Tiger defensive line time and time again.[21]

When Massillon played Detroit, their line had controlled the field of play, but the Panhandles manhandled the Massillon front seven all afternoon. Because Massillon was unable to run the ball, they spent the greater part of their time on defense. Charles "Sam" Finnegan and Knute Rockne performed well on defense for Massillon, but Ted and Frank Nesser easily ripped through the balance of the Tiger team. Time after time, they made substantial gains as they battered their way down the field unconcerned with deception or the forward pass.

The first Sunday in November found the Panhandles in western Ohio playing the unbeaten Dayton Gym-Cadets. Comprised largely of former St. Mary's College players trained by the Brothers of the Society of Mary, the Gym-Cadets featured an outstanding core of young players. Norbert Sacksteder, Alphonse H. Mahrt, George "Babe" Zimmerman, George "Hobby" Kinderdine, and Larry Dellinger were destined to have long professional football careers.

Norb Sacksteder scored a touchdown in the first play from scrimmage on a sensational sixty-yard run in which he dodged half the Panhandle team. Although Dayton led Columbus for three quarters, they were no match for the Panhandles when it mattered in the fourth quarter. The first Panhandle score came in the third quarter on a forty-five-yard pass from Louis Pickerel to Lee Snoots, narrowing the Dayton lead to one point. In the fourth quarter, Pickerel spearheaded the Panhandle attack with a thirty-yard pass and several line plunges which culminated in a touchdown by Ted Nesser. While Frank Nesser failed the kick for point, subsequent touchdown passes from Pickerel to Roscoe Keuhner and Fred Nesser resulted in a 24–7 Panhandle victory.[22]

The Panhandles took the train to Detroit the next weekend to play the Mack Park Maroons. Almost the entire Detroit team were former college players. Frank McHale, Arthur "Red" Cornwell, Michael H. Boyle, Thomas Bogle, and Hadden from the University of Michigan; Murray, F.R. Davis, and Faunt "Dutch" Lenardson from Michigan Agricultural College (Michigan State University); Tom McCall from Harvard, Ed Kerwin from Georgetown, and Gus Toumey and Tacks Harding from the University of Detroit were in the starting lineup. With the exception of a last-second loss to Massillon, the Mack Park boys were undefeated.

The game was a titanic defensive battle in which neither team scored offensively. The turning point of the game occurred in the final moments of the first half when Red Cornwell hiked the ball over the head of the quarterback, and the Panhandles fell on the ball in the end zone for a touchdown, showing the "college boys" a thing or two.[23]

On Saturday afternoon, November 20, Joe Carr and a squad of eighteen players took the Pennsylvania Railroad from Columbus to Youngstown. They arrived in Ohio's Steel City at midnight and were met at the Pennsylvania station by Joe Omier, the Patrician manager. He escorted them to their quarters in the Ohio Hotel. While his players went to bed, Carr went to the *Youngstown Vindicator* newspaper office, where he gave them an interview and provided a team picture. Sometime after 1 A.M., Carr made a bed check of his players and went to sleep.[24]

The next morning, the Panhandles ate a heavy breakfast, reviewed their signals, discussed a game plan, suited up, and warmed up. Each man was responsible for his own football gear. Gray clouds and a stiff breeze welcomed the teams when they came on the field to warm up for the 2:30 game. The air had passed from chilly to downright cold by game time. Five thousand fans were obliged to keep moving whenever possible to keep warm.[25]

The undefeated Youngstown Patricians, led by player-coach Ray Thomas from West Virginia University, fielded an all-star team. Their starters included Getz from Ohio State University at left halfback and All-American DeOrmond "Tuss" McLaughry from Lansing, who had played fullback for the Michigan Aggies and Westminster College. The team also included three outstanding defensive players. Elgie Tobin, the Penn State University guard who would lead Akron to a world professional football championship in 1920, and left end George Vedderneck, a former Carlisle Indian star, were rocks on defense. Russell G. "Busty" Ashbaugh, the hometown boy who had been a gridiron star at Brown University, played brilliantly, twice preventing touchdowns by the Panhandles.[26]

Treacherous winds hampered the Panhandle aerial attack, and the tough play of Ashbaugh, Vedderneck, Thomas, and Tobin neutralized the Nesser brothers' ground game. In the first half, play centered in Youngstown territory. Though the Panhandle line had a weight advantage over the Patricians, Youngstown held whenever a touchdown seemed certain. Once again, the presence of the Nesser brothers guaranteed injuries. Benson and Cavanaugh were carried from the field in the first half, but Loos and Duval were strong replacements. When the final gun was sounded, the game ended in a scoreless tie.[27]

Four days later on Thanksgiving Day, two Nesser brothers stayed home and led a group of Panhandles to a 19–0 victory over the Columbus Muldoons, while four of the brothers traveled to Fort Wayne with the balance of the team to play the Friars. Both Fort Wayne and Columbus were railroad towns, but Fort Wayne had no university, so their entire community supported the Friars. Fort Wayne football fans were delighted with a chance to see the famous Nesser brothers. On November 24, 1915, the *Fort Wayne Journal-Gazette* reported:

The Columbus outfit is headed by the six Nesser brothers, big huskies who are easily the equal of the best football players ever turned out by the biggest universities in the country. The club has been strengthened this season by the addition of several new stars and are capable of a rare brand of football.

The game was "one of the most grueling gridiron contests ever staged in independent football circles." Alfred and Ted Nesser played well, but Frank was the big problem for the Friars. His smashes from the fullback position and his kicking caused Fort Wayne considerable trouble. Then it was Fred Nesser, the tall one, who nearly beat the Friars with a triple pass just before the end of the third quarter. The play gained thirty-five yards, and Fred was stopped only eight yards short of the goal line. A Columbus touchdown seemed certain, but the Fort Wayne line held and Skeet Lambert punted the ball out of danger. In the closing minutes of the game, Lambert recovered a fumble, and a long run by Reilly set up a drop kick for field goal from the fifteen yard line. Fort Wayne beat Columbus 3 to 0.[28]

After the game, Friars players told newspaper reporters that "Fullback Frank Nesser is the hardest man to stop they had ever played against. It is next to impossible to stop him with a clean tackle and about the surest way to get him down was to drop in front of him." At least half a dozen opposing players broke bones attempting to tackle Frank or Ted Nesser in 1915. In this game, Al Feeney broke his nose trying to stop Frank.[29]

On the Sunday following Thanksgiving, the Panhandles played a home game against the Columbus Barracks. In that game, Hiram Brigham, the Panhandle center, was kicked in the head when he was down and had to be carried unconscious to the hospital, where he was not expected to pull through.[30] Though he survived, his future play was affected by the experience. In those days, many people played without headgear, but even if they wore headgear, the thin felt provided scant protection. Injuries were serious and often fatal.

The Panhandles won their final game against the Ohio All-Stars and finished the season as one of the eight best teams in American professional football circles. After the 1915 season, however, they began a slow decline as a football powerhouse. While the Panhandles played for another decade, they would never again be as strong as they were in 1915. They never developed much hometown support because Columbus football fans preferred watching Ohio State University on Saturdays to watching pro football on Sunday. Consequently, during the entire pre-World War I era, the Panhandles played on the road.

The availability of free railroad passes cut travel costs to a minimum and made it feasible for them to play the best teams in Ohio, Pennsylvania, Michigan, and Indiana. Playing a schedule dominated by away games, however, had its disadvantages. It placed the Panhandles at the mercy of hometown crowds and officials who usually favored the home team. It also placed pressure on the team because of travel fatigue, difficulty in making connections, and unfamiliar food and water.

The primary problems for the Panhandles, however, were that professional football was becoming more than a part-time job and the Nesser brothers were getting older. Even so, the Nessers were receiving attractive offers from other teams, and they played for other teams to get the money while they still could. In 1916, Ted Nesser was thirty-three years old and had been playing professional football for fifteen years. He was a step or two slower than the year before—his peak playing years in the sport were already in the past.

The Panhandles started their 1916 season on October 8, playing the Marion Questions as a warm-up for the Detroit game the following week. The Detroit Heralds were also an aging team. Like the Panhandles, their principal players had been in the sport for nearly a decade. The Heralds hired Kent "Skeet" Lambert as quarterback in an effort to upgrade their team. In addition, the collapse of the Mack Park Maroons brought Bernard "Bertie" Maher, Danny Mullane, and Art Cornwell back into the Heralds' lineup. But would this be enough? Many of the Heralds' regulars were past their prime, and they had no strong running back to balance their offensive attack.

Six Nesser brothers led the Panhandles onto Detroit's Navin Field. John, aged forty-one, started at quarterback, Frank at right halfback, Ted at fullback, Fred at left end, and Alfred and Phil at right guard and tackle. The Panhandles played a strong first half. "They outrushed, out-kicked, outpassed and out everything" the Heralds, as even the *Detroit Free Press* admitted. Columbus scored nine minutes into the first quar-ter, when they executed a triple pass, including a forty-seven-yard for-ward pass by Frank Nesser to Emmett Ruhl, the right end. Frank had thrown the ball nearly half the length of the football field. The kick for goal failed.[31]

In the second quarter, with just over a minute to play in the half, Frank Nesser made a short kick that was mishandled by the Heralds and was recovered by Lee Snoots on the eighteen yard line. Snoots then picked up the fumbled kick and ran for a touchdown. The *Detroit News* declared: the "Panhandles are the smartest semi-pro ball team Detroit has ever seen. They have any amount of trick plays and strate-gy. It is a nice team to watch, tricky, but always clean."[32]

Ted Nesser gave considerable thought to devising trick plays and other ways of gaining advantage over Panhandle opponents. On Au-gust 27, 1916, he wrote to Walter Camp inquiring about the fair catch, an important part of the game because of the punt-out for extra point. Ted wrote, "I have been playing foot-ball for quite a number of seasons and we always have conference officials. One thing they cannot make plain to me is the opportunity for making fair catch . . . They claim the signal is not necessary. Who is right?"[33]

The Heralds' only touchdown came in the third period on a running play by Lambert. As the *Detroit Free Press* later wrote, "Columbus out-punted Detroit, showed a better defense and proved particularly adept at receiving. . . . It was a good game to look at and a big crowd seemed to enjoy every minute of it." According to the paper, many came out to see the famous Nesser brothers, and they were not disappointed. The crowd enjoyed seeing factory workers outsmart the college boys. The *Free Press* observed, "The Nesser boys are heavy and fast, and when one of the Nesser boys hits you flush there is usually a little work for the water boy and the club doctor."[34]

Following the triumph over Detroit, the Panhandles went to Cleve-land, on October 22, to play Peggy Parratt's team. They started six of the seven Nesser brothers and managed a 9 to 6 victory over the pow-erful Cleveland Indians.[35]

On the last Sunday in October, the Panhandles played the world champion Canton Bulldogs. Jim Thorpe and George "Carp" Julian,

Canton's backfield tandem, each scored rushing touchdowns against the tenacious Nesser crew in the first half. Once Canton gained the upper hand, according to the *Canton Repository*, "the Bulldogs made no great effort to fatten the count in the second half, preferring to play it safe and risk no chances of injury to men who will be needed for hard combats to come."[36] The Bulldogs coasted to a 12 to 0 victory to remain undefeated and unscored on.

Despite the loss to Canton, the Columbus Panhandles were still highly regarded in professional football circles. On November 2, 1916, the *Toledo Blade* observed:

Up to two years ago they were one of the strongest elevens in the country, but then something went wrong and they began losing games—by small margins to be sure—but losing, nevertheless. Everybody figured that the Nesser brothers had shot their bolt; that age was beginning to tell and that the grand old Panhandle machine was about to throw a tire. . . [but] the Columbus, Panhandles are staging the greatest comeback in Ohio professional football.

The Panhandles' next opponent was the Toledo Maroons, who had defeated them the previous year. The *Toledo Blade* credited Ted Nesser, the coach and captain of the Panhandles, with formulating and putting into action the triple pass, the crisscross, and the short kickoff. He was said to have perfected these plays before they were used by college coaches.[37] The Maroons, who had recently hired Johnny Barrett, previously with the Evanston North Ends, were short of money. Because the Panhandles were such a good draw they could demand more for this game. Gentlemen were charged seventy-five cents and ladies fifty cents.

The game with Toledo turned out to be rough—too rough for the spectators who did not want to see that kind of brutality. The Toledo press blamed Phil Nesser, whom they accused of dropping on tackled men with his knees, slugging, and stopping runners by clotheslining them. It seems certain, however, that players on both teams played rough. In 1905, President Roosevelt had interceded to change the rules so congress would not outlaw football completely because of the senseless violence and injuries, but his intervention had only tempered and had not stopped the mayhem.[38]

For the most part, the Panhandles' offense sputtered. Occasionally, Ted Nesser shot through the line for a good gain, but he could not do so consistently, nor could Snoots skirt the ends. By contrast, John Barrett, Charles Nichols, and Jim Baxter all scored touchdowns, and Toledo also made a field goal. The final score was 23 to 0.[39]

Two straight losses demonstrated how much the Panhandles missed the services of Louis Pickerel, who was now an assistant coach at Ohio State University and normally did not travel with the team. They also discovered that their opponents had significantly improved since 1915. By contrast, the Panhandles were growing older, sustaining injuries, and lacking in new talent.

On November 12, they entered Driving Park, the Tigers' den, in Massillon. No one on the Massillon Tigers team took Columbus for a weak opponent. There was ample reason for the Panhandles' loss to Toledo, according to the *Massillon Independent:*

Fred Nesser was out on account of an injured arm and the doctors insisted that he stay out of the game until next Sunday. Emmett Ruh was hardly able to move, and about two hours before the team left Columbus the infant child of Frank Nesser died. The child became ill Saturday morning.[40]

The Nesser brothers needed no introduction since Massillon fans had been watching them play football for twelve or more years. The Nessers were known throughout the country, not only for their football skills, but also for their other athletic endeavors. Raymond, the youngest brother, had joined the team earlier that year as a substitute lineman, and now the seven Nesser boys weighed 1,277 pounds in aggregate. They averaged 211 pounds apiece in 1916, when the average professional lineman weighed about 180. They were a handful for any football eleven.

Frank, the biggest member of the family, who tipped the scales at 238 pounds, played fullback and was the team's punter, forward passer, and line plunger. Fred played end and stood his ground against anyone. Although he was thirty-three years old in 1916, Ted was still 231 pounds of muscle and the star of the team. As a fullback, he could run over All-American linemen with ease. John, Phil, and Alfred played guard or tackle as needed, and John, at age forty-one, also occasionally played quarterback.

While John and Ted had lost a step or two to old age, the Panhandles still played a rough brand of football:

Ted plunged through the Tiger line time after time with as much ease as one would shove a hot knife through butter. He bowled over tacklers, shook them off and carried four or five before he was downed.

Frank's specialty was forward passing and he certainly could heave the leather. It was nothing for him to shoot the ball down the field 50 yards and Columbus made its most sustained gains on this play—Frank on the heaving end and Ruh on the receiving.[41]

Four thousand fans watched the Massillon defense hold the Panhandles scoreless. The next day the *Massillon Independent* told the Tigers' side of the story:

> The Tigers, Massillon's professional gridiron aggregation, in the scramble for pro grid honors of the United States, along with such teams as Canton and Cleveland, demonstrated Sunday that it possesses the punch that means victory. True, the punch did not look effective enough to defeat a team such as Canton has gathered together but any team that can wallop such an aggregation of bulls like the Columbus eleven by a 10 to 0 score certainly carried around a punch that other teams will bear respect for.

Joel Mattern was the leading ground-gainer for the Tigers. Kent "Skeet" Lambert, having already faced the Panhandles earlier in the year while with Detroit, knew what to expect and made appropriate adjustments. He found it easier to run around Columbus's ends than to attempt to run inside the tackles.

In the first quarter, Lambert missed a drop kick from the forty yard line by inches. In the second quarter, he made a field goal by drop kick from the twenty yard line. Finally, in the last thirty seconds of the game, Lambert threw a pass to Red Fleming for the only touchdown of the game. Massillon won 10–0, eliminating the Columbus Panhandles from consideration in the state professional football championship. John Nesser gave Kent Lambert credit for the Massillon win over the Panhandles.[42]

On November 19, 1916, the Panhandles returned to Detroit to play the Heralds. Detroit, in their red-and-white jerseys, no longer had Skeet Lambert at the helm. However, the Heralds' line still included Archie "Dutch" Stewart, Art Cornwell, Norman "Tango" Glockson, Bernard "Bertie" Maher, Richard "Red" Shields, and Nig Lennahan. Although the Heralds' lineup was much the same as it had been earlier, the Detroit newspaper predicted "a much different medium of play. . . . Short passing will be the stunt this time, with the tackles and surrounding territory being the vantage point."[43]

Despite the change in strategy, the Panhandles overpowered Detroit. Three times the Heralds were within scoring distance but were unable to cross the goal line. The Panhandles scored their first touchdown in the second quarter on a pass from John Nesser to Homer Ruhl. In the fourth quarter, Alfred Nesser picked up a Percy Wilson fumble and ran for a touchdown. A few minutes later, Frank Nesser drop-kicked a twenty-five-yard field goal, resulting in a 15 to 0 win for the Panhandles.[44]

The Panhandles were notorious for using trick plays to win games. A week later, when they played Cleveland, E. N. Mayer, a halfback for the Indians, turned the tables on the Panhandles with an outrageous play. As the *Toledo Blade* told the story, "On one of the formations in which Solon smashed outside left tackle for a 15-yard gain, Meyer [sic] fooled the bruisers by tossing a black head guard in the air to a player on the right side of the line. The feint pulled four of the Pans away from Solon." The sports writer went on the say that "brains figured prominently in this pro game."[45]

The Panhandles had at last been tricked by the same kind of deception they so had often used on others, and they lost to Cleveland 7 to 0. In addition, the Columbus Panhandles lost Hiram Brigham, their regular center, who suffered an eye injury and missed the rest of the season.[46]

Thanksgiving found the Panhandles back in Fort Wayne playing the Friars, the 1916 professional football champions of Indiana. In an extraordinary season, the Friars had defeated the Wabash Athletic Association, Pine Village, the Hammond Clabbys, and the Evanston North Ends. On most Sundays, seven of the eleven Friar starters were Notre Dame graduates.

The game was played on a muddy field with uncertain footing, making end runs and passes virtually impossible. Both teams were limited to a ground game devoid of trick plays or excitement of any kind. Deprived of the services of Brigham, Frank Nesser was forced to play center. He had a terrible time hiking the ball, and this further hampered the Panhandles' offense. Fort Wayne nearly scored at one point, but Heine Berger fumbled the ball on the Columbus ten yard line. When Columbus reached scoring position, their drive was stalled by an intercepted pass. The only score of the game came in the second quarter when Friars' center, Al Feeney, kicked a field goal from placement. Keith "Deac" Jones made the final tackle of the Fort Wayne season when he brought down Ted Nesser as the clock ran out with the score Fort Wayne 3, Columbus 0. After the game, the Friars held their second annual football banquet at the Wayne Hotel with the Panhandles as their guests. The Nesser brother entertained the group with a couple of songs.[47]

The Panhandles played two additional games in 1916. On December 3, they played the Youngstown Patricians in Youngstown, and, on December 10, they played the Columbus All-Stars, winning both games to end the season with a 6 and 5 record.

The Panhandles' decline accelerated in 1917. Efforts to rebuild the club were hampered by conscription and the war effort. On May 26, 1917, for example, J. Lee Snoots applied for admission into the Army Officers Reserve Corps and was lost to the Panhandles for the coming season.[48] Moreover, the Panhandles could rarely field more than four of the Nesser brothers. Alfred moved to Akron and was a starter for the Akron Pros, while Frank, who was attempting to support himself as a professional athlete, played only about half the games with the Panhandles and the balance with the Akron Pros or the Detroit Heralds, who paid better. His summer baseball wages were insufficient to support him year round, and it was rumored that Detroit paid him $500 for a two-game package which included the Thanksgiving Day game with the Panhandles and the Canton Bulldog game on November 29.[49] Frank, who was largely responsible for defeating the Heralds twice in 1916, was now playing against his family's team.

Columbus lost to Canton, Massillon, and Youngstown, and the only major professional football team the Panhandles beat in 1917 was the Toledo Maroons. The once proud Panhandles would never return to their 1915 level of competitiveness. The railroad boilermakers from Columbus continued to play with muscle and pride well into the 1920s, but younger men usually won the day.[50] The Nesser brothers legend still haunts the halls of the Professional Football Hall of Fame in Canton, Ohio, near the site of so many early contests of manly strength and skill held between the pipe fitters and the best college stars money could buy at the dawn of professional football.

7. Native American Players with Altoona

A**ltoona was a company town** nestled in the mountains of central Pennsylvania's coal-mining region. Controlled by the Pennsylvania Railroad, it was a refueling and repair center for a steam-powered transportation system that depended on coal for energy. Altoona workers were staunch football fans as early as 1891 when they first fielded an independent team. Originally organized as the Altoona Athletic Association, the Altoona Athletic Club played the best independent football teams in Pennsylvania. Among Altoona's early rivals were the Allegheny Athletic Association, the Greensburg Athletic Association, the Homestead Library and Athletic Club, Latrobe, the Latrobe YMCA, and the Pittsburgh Athletic Club.[1]

At the turn of the century, Carlisle Institute, located twenty miles southwest of Harrisburg, was a Bureau of Indian Affairs sponsored trade school already well known for the athletic prowess of its students. According to coach Glen "Pop" Warner, Carlisle was "a vocational school giving academic work equivalent to ordinary high school . . . but in athletics Carlisle had collegiate rank."[2] With an enrollment of under six hundred boys, Carlisle was soon winning football games against some of the best colleges in the country. In 1905, Frank Mt. Pleasant was the first Carlisle Institute alumnus to play for Altoona, and he has been given credit for persuading others to join the team.

Frank Mt. Pleasant was a member of the Tuscarora tribe, and, by 1906, he was setting records that earned him a place on the United States Olympic team in 1908. He was also the quarterback and field general for the 1905–7 Carlisle football team that established the school as a big-time, university-level football powerhouse.[3] By 1915, most of the players on the Altoona independent football team were former Carlisle Institute players who worked for the railroad, and the team was widely known as the Ex-Carlisles.[4]

At the start of the 1915 season, the team was managed by Mort Henderson and coached by former Carlisle Institute fullback Gus

Wheelock. The starting lineup featured nine Carlisle alumni, including Stilwell Saunooke, Joel Wheelock, [5] and Shipp. In the opening game at Yeagertown, Maryland, they received anything but unbiased officiating. According to the *Altoona Mirror*, three Altoona touchdowns were disallowed by Yeagertown officials, and the ex-Carlisles lost the game 0–6.[6] In a rematch the following Saturday, Yeagertown traveled to Altoona, where the outcome was entirely different even though the players were the same. Altoona defeated Yeagertown 25–0.[7]

On Saturday, October 23, Altoona played the Duquesne Cornells in Pitcairn, a suburb east of Pittsburgh near Monroeville. The Pennsylvania Railroad sponsored the game and provided the team free transportation. Altoona won 25–7.[8] The following Saturday, the Pitcairn Quakers came to Altoona under a similar arrangement. Altoona's new manager, Cyril McGough, formerly coach at Lebanon Valley College, brought his star fullback, Carl G. "King Carl" Snavely.[9] McGough also added Winnshick, Hugh Wheelock, Joe Bender, H. Brennan, Woodring, and several other Carlisle luminaries to ensure victory over Pitcairn.[10] Hugh was Joel's older brother and had also played on the 1911 team with Thorpe.

Train number 12 brought two hundred Pitcairn Quaker fans in four special cars to Altoona to see the game.[11] Even with George "Cotton" Vedderneck and Clark, two strong former Altoona players, in their lineup, the Quakers could not overcome the strength of the Altoona line, and attempts at trick plays were ineffective. That afternoon, Altoona played a conservative game, and their control of the line of scrimmage was the primary factor in the win. Snavely kicked the field goal that defeated Pitcairn 3–0.[12]

Altoona traveled to Canton, Ohio, on free railroad passes for their game against the Bulldogs on Sunday, November 7. Altoona signed up Malcolm "Red" Fleming, [13] the noted Washington and Jefferson College star. However, Altoona was no match for Canton, where players like Greasy Neale, Cap Edwards, and Fats Waldsmith were featured. Altoona lost a lopsided game to the Bulldogs, 38–0.[14] The loss illustrated the gap between the level of independent football in New York and Pennsylvania, and that developing in Ohio and other midwestern industrial cities.

Red Fleming stayed in Ohio to play for Massillon, while the rest of the team returned home to play Latrobe the following Saturday. Beginning in 1895, Latrobe and Altoona were fierce rivals.[15] This game would determine the leading contender for the independent football championship of Western Pennsylvania. Altoona defeated Latrobe 13 to 3 and almost had another touchdown, but it was scored just after time ran out. In those days before there were stadium clocks for the fans and players to watch, one of the officials kept the only clock, so he alone knew how much time was left in the game. In the excitement the official forgot to look at his watch and did not realize that the time had run out until after the touchdown was scored.[16]

The next Saturday, Red Fleming returned to Altoona to play for Swiss Vale, and George Vedderneck rejoined the Altoona lineup. Fleming almost single-handedly won the game. He called the plays, did all the kicking, and was the leading tackler for Swiss Vale. The winning score came in the last five minutes of the game, when Fleming threw a forty-five-yard pass for a touchdown and then kicked the extra point.[17]

The following day, Red Fleming returned to Ohio to help the Massillon Tigers defeat the Canton Bulldogs.[18] On Thanksgiving Day, Red helped Massillon defeat Toledo 3–0 in Toledo.[19]

Red returned to Altoona the next day, where he led the Indians in a 10–0 victory over the Pitcairn Quakers. Three thousand fans saw Red Fleming do "everything to help Altoona gain the victory, but carry the water bucket."[20] Altoona also engaged William Elwood "Red" Swoope[21] to play quarterback for them against the Pitcairn Quakers.[22] Following the victory over Pitcairn, Red Fleming took a train to Canton to play for Massillon in the world's championship of professional football on Sunday, November 28, 1915. In nine days, he played in five games, in four different cities, and on three different teams.

Altoona ended the season with a 5–3 record, but because two of their three losses were to out-of-state teams, they had a 5–1 record within western Pennsylvania and declared themselves the 1915 independent football champions of Western Pennsylvania.

In 1916, the Altoona Indians were managed by agents for the Pennsylvania Railroad. The team now had the "Pennsy" railroad logo on their uniforms, used free railroad passes to travel, and extended their schedule to include more teams west of Pittsburgh. The 1916 Altoona Indians carried over twenty players from the previous season, including Red Swoope, and added ten new players over the course of the season. Its best players, Joe Bergie and Stilwell Saunooke, often played for better teams. William Lone Star Dietz assumed the quarterback duties for Altoona when Red Swoope dropped off the team in midseason.[23]

Altoona opened its season at Canton on Sunday, October 1. Jim Thorpe was still playing professional baseball and was not with Canton for the first three weeks of the season. However, Harry Costello, half-back from Georgetown University and new head coach at the University of Detroit, played nearly as well as Thorpe. Early in the game, two Canton drives were halted by fumbles, and Altoona made a couple of first downs, but they also fumbled. Then Harry Costello returned a punt twenty-seven yards and, after a successful pass and run, he scored Canton's first touchdown. Before the afternoon was over, Canton had scored 23 points while Altoona was held scoreless.[24] The following Sunday, Altoona played Peggy Parratt's Cleveland Indians in Cleveland and lost 7–39.[25] Finally, on Saturday, October 14, the Altoona Indians played their home opener before several thousand fans in Altoona at Cricket Park against the Burnham YMCA and won 30–0.[26]

Immediately after the game, the Indians took a train to Massillon, where they played the Tigers the next afternoon. A crowd of three thousand spectators came to Driving Park Field to see the game. The Massillon Tigers, coached by Red Fleming, fielded a strong team, while nine of the eleven Altoona starters had played the day before. Only John Joseph Donnelly, a track star and graduate of Altoona High School, and Carr, at fullback, were fresh for Altoona. Massillon dominated the game, making fifteen first downs to Altoona's one. Six different Massillon players scored touchdowns in their 54–0 romp.[27]

Altoona next defeated Lewiston, Pennsylvania, at Cricket Park, 25–6.[28] Before traveling to Dayton, they added Jackson "Auggie" Blair, a former University of Pittsburgh lineman, and E. A. Snyder, a former Bucknell center, to their roster. The Wheelock brothers, Ollie Vogel, Yarnell, and Pohle carried the load for Altoona on October 29 against the Triangles, but they lost the game 0–33.[29] By the end of the month, Altoona had played six games in four weeks. The pace was too great, and the number of victories too few, to keep up this schedule. On Saturday, November 4, they ended their 1916 season by defeating Lebanon College 7–0 in the last ten minutes of play.[30] Their 1916 record was 3 and 4. By 1917, Altoona had ceased being a professional football stronghold and only fielded a team for a few October games.

The subsidy provided by the railroad permitted teams like Altoona, Columbus, and Pitcairn to survive. Altoona and Pitcairn wore the Pennsy Railroad logo on the front of their football jerseys for good reason. Without railroad underwriting, it seems unlikely that they would have survived as an interregional team. Ohio pro teams liked to schedule Altoona because they demanded a low guarantee, drew large crowds because of the Carlisle influence, and promised an almost certain victory for the home team. Ohio teams were able to work into midseason form without losing money or harming their chances for a state championship.

Altoona generally attracted a crowd of from fifteen hundred to three thousand fans for an out-of-town game, and two thousand to three thousand for a home game. These were respectable crowds in the early days of professional football, but not large enough to build a national contender or to cover all the expenses for an interstate game.

8. Evanston North Ends and the Kicking Swede

In 1906, a group of high school boys began to play Sunday football on an open field in the Chicago suburb of Evanston. They were managed by Erne Hunt, with the assistance of C. L. "Pat" Pattison, and coached by Earl Scholes.[1] Reuben Johnson quickly emerged as the leader of the group that called themselves the Evanston North Ends. Reuben was an outstanding athlete with extraordinary kicking and passing skills. It was not unusual for him to punt fifty yards or more and to drop kick from thirty or forty yards out.[2]

In the fall of 1906, at the age of fifteen, Reuben became the quarterback for the semiprofessional Evanston North Ends football team.[3] He quickly became known as "the Kicking Swede" and was elected captain of the team. For the first three or four years, the North Ends "played on an open field and passed the hat among the spectators after the game to cover expenses."[4] From the beginning, the Evanston North Ends were a winning team. Their games were not covered by the newspapers until 1909, when the North Ends drew a crowd of thirteen hundred to watch them defeat the previously unbeaten Ripmores of Chicago to become the best team in Illinois. That year they were undefeated and were scored on only once. In 1910, they were again the best independent team in Illinois.

In 1911, the team added Guilford Falcon[5] to its backfield. He, too, was a teenager, but he would demonstrate his extraordinary running skill to professional football fans for the next seventeen years. Guil attended Evanston High School and played football there as a fullback, also playing right field on the baseball team. In 1910, at the end of the high school football season when he was just seventeen years old, Guil started playing semiprofessional football for the North Ends. The following year he became a starter for the team.[6]

Henry Norbert Kilby[7] was also an early star for the North Ends. He played football and baseball at Evanston High School and started playing halfback and reserve quarterback for the Evanston North Ends when the team was formed. In 1909, he became their starting center. He played with the North Ends until they disbanded in 1916 and continued to play professional football during the early 1920s. He was also an active baseball player for the Logan Squares and the Chicago Blues.

Murray J. Battaglia[8] was another early North Ends star. Born in 1894 to a peddler, he was one of eight children. The family moved to Evanston, Illinois, when he was ten years old, and the following year he started playing center for the Evanston North Ends, continuing to play with them through the 1915 season. A solid lineman throughout his career, he was the object of a good deal of razzing because he missed the train for the Wabash, Indiana, game in 1913, which resulted in the North Ends' only loss that season. Often outweighed, he was never outplayed.

In 1911–12, many believed the Evanston North Ends were the best team in independent football in America. In 1911, they were not scored on, and the following year only one team scored on them. In 1913 and 1914, they played nearly all of the quality teams west of Ohio, losing only to Wabash in a game that Evanston believed was stolen from them by hometown refereeing. In 1914, the North Ends defeated Wabash and played the Detroit Heralds to a scoreless tie—the only blemish on their otherwise perfect season. They played games against Wabash, Muncie, Fort Wayne, Detroit, Elgin, Beloit, Aurora, and Rock Island—as difficult a schedule as played by any independent team in the country.

The North Ends team was comprised of clerks, policemen, pipe fitters, telephone repairmen, dairy workers, machinists, and a deep sea diver, none of whom attended college. They played nearly all of their games on the road because the caliber of team they played demanded a bigger guarantee than the meager crowds in Evanston would generally support. Playing on the road had several drawbacks. The team had to travel, often through the night or a significant part of it, to get to and from their games. Crowds were rarely supportive of "the boys from Chicago," and the referees were seldom kind to them. On October 22, 1913, the *Evanston Daily News* explained it this way: "Kilby, Johnson and Falcon . . . played all around the Wabash warriors but were unable to check the gains of the latter players when the referee refused to penalize them for rule infractions." Moreover, a touchdown was called back on a questionable claim of holding.

The core of the 1915 North Ends team had played together for seven years, exhibited excellent team work, and employed an advanced

The rivalry between the Evanston North Ends and the Wabash Athletic Association was one of the most intense in iron-man football. In 1913, Wabash, in the light-colored jerseys, defeated the North Ends, 7–0. Note the Wabash offensive formation where only the center is on the line of scrimmage. This formation was outlawed the following year. *(Wabash County Historical Society.)*

brand of football with shifts and trick plays. Some referred to their strong line as the "million dollar line." The North Ends were capable of beating any independent football team in America on any given Sunday. Nevertheless, the team still depended on the kicking and leadership of Reuben Johnson, by now a nine-year veteran of independent football. Walter Eckersall, the great University of Chicago quarterback turned sportswriter for the *Chicago Tribune,* said repeatedly in private and in print that Johnson, captain of the North Ends, was "one of the greatest kickers the game has ever produced, and if he were on some big college eleven would be heralded as another Pat O'Dea."[9]

On October 3, 1915, Eugene Schobinger's Illinois all-stars came to Mason Park in Evanston to play the North Ends before a crowd of twenty-five hundred. A native of nearby Morgan Park, Schobinger had been a standout halfback and Olympic track star at the University of Illinois. Now a mechanical engineer, he organized a team of all-stars and was its principal offensive weapon. He was, as described in the *Evanston News-Index,* a "well known line plunger and carried the ball around the ends to good advantage."[10] The average weight of the Illinois All-Star line was 175 pounds. Its backfield averaged 173 pounds.[11] The All-Stars included Voight, from a Wisconsin college, at quarterback; Kelly, from the Chicago Ripmores, at halfback; Headriz and Balswick, who had played with the Cornell-Hamburgs; and the Koskie brothers, from an Indiana college.

The North Ends easily won the game 34 to 0. John Hanna and Art Pascolini, the two ends for Evanston, were outstanding both offensively and defensively. Rube Johnson ran the team like a clock. He kicked one punt sixty-five yards and several others for over fifty yards. And, in

In 1914, Evanston, in the dark jerseys, retaliated for its loss the previous year by defeating Wabash, 6–0. *(Wabash County Historical Society.)*

Eugene Schobinger, end, fullback, Illinois All-Stars 1915; Evanston North Ends 1916; Fort Wayne Vets 1919. He grew up in Morgan Park, Illinois, and graduated from the University of Illinois. He was a member of the 1912 U. S. Olympic track team. *(University of Illinois Archives.)*

the opinion of the *Evanston News-Index*, Henry Kilby did "stellar work at right half."[12]

The North Ends played the second game of the season at home against the Cabery, Illinois, town team, considered one of the best teams in Illinois. The game was played at De Paul College Field because the original site of the game, Federal Field, was so wet park officials would not allow them to play on it. Only three hundred fans found the relocated game and were willing to sit through the rain to watch the athletes splash around in the mud.

Cabery did not trust the Evanston official to keep time for the game, so they also kept time themselves. At the close of the scoreless first half, the Cabery timekeeper claimed that the period had lasted three minutes too long. The Cabery man was shown that he had not kept account of all the timeouts, and the matter was dropped.

The muddy field made it impossible for Evanston to run their normal offense with its trick plays, and Cabery had a strong team that kept the ball in the middle of the mud. With the game scoreless and down to the last two minutes, Evanston had the ball on the Cabery ten yard line with three downs left. The Cabery man with the watch ran out on the field claiming the game was over, and the Cabery team quit. After a ten-minute wrangle, the referee ordered the teams to play ball, but the Cabery team was already in the clubhouse. The North Ends made the touchdown, and the game was given to them by the referee.[13]

On the following Sunday, the North Ends played in Wabash, Indiana. They would not play another home game until Thanksgiving Day. The Wabash Athletic Association had one of the best independent football teams in America, losing fewer than six games over sixteen years. They played their home games on Carroll Field, which had barbed wire strung around it within six feet of the sidelines to keep fans off the playing area. The dressing rooms had no showers, and the fans showed no mercy to out-of-towners. The Wabash A.A. entered the field at 2:17 P.M. on Sunday, October 24, and were given a great ovation by the six thousand fans present.[14] Evanston entered a few moments later. After a brisk signal practice, both teams were ready to play by 2:30.[15] Wabash kicked off. Two plays later, Wabash sideback Alfred "Dutch" Bergman intercepted a Johnson pass. The ball changed hands several times in the quarter, but neither team threatened to score. Midway through the second quarter, Reuben Johnson was injured and had to be replaced. A few plays later, Wabash drove the ball to the Evanston twenty-five yard line. At this juncture, Wabash halfback George Yarnelle threw a pass to Jesse Reno, who scored the game's only touchdown. At halftime, Johnson reentered the game. Both teams shifted their style of play from off-tackle runs to a passing game. Several Evanston passes were intercepted, and they never seriously threatened to tie the game. Wabash won 7–0.[16]

On Sunday, October 31, the Evanston North Ends invaded Packard Park in Detroit to play the Heralds. The Evanston players had a $1000 side bet with the Heralds that they would win the game.[17] Evanston kicked off at 3 P.M. and, for three quarters, both teams were scoreless. Johnson's kicking game was unbelievably good. He had punts of sixty-five and seventy-five yards, placing him in the category of kickers with Pat O'Dea and exceeding the performances of legends like Thorpe and Brinkley.[18] In the final quarter, Rube Johnson took control of the game. He ran forty yards on an end run, threw several passes to Art Pascolini, and finally sprinted around end ten yards for a touchdown. Evanston beat Detroit 7–0 and won the bet.[19]

According to the *Free Press*, Johnson's "defensive work is the equal of his offensive contribution. He can hit that line and back it up when they come flocking through it." Overall, the North Ends "exhibited team play the equal of the Heralds. . . . The North Ends showed as fine a football team as you will find anywhere in independent ranks and richly deserved their win."[20]

On November 7, the best independent football game scheduled in the nation was the Fort Wayne Friars-Evanston North Ends clash in Fort Wayne. The Friars had been pointing for this game for several weeks in anticipation of gaining revenge for the beating they took in 1914. The *Fort Wayne Journal-Gazette* reported:

Next week the Friars play the famed Evanston North Ends at the Local League Park and this is expected to be the hardest game of the season. . . . The Fort Wayne backfield headed by hustling little "Skeet" Lambert is thought to be the equal of any college backfield in these parts and no one ever doubted but what the fellows [in the line] would be able to do their share.[21]

In the first quarter, Kent "Skeet" Lambert, star quarterback for the Friars, suffered a separated shoulder making a tackle on left end Art Pascolini after a completed pass, and had to leave the game. The North Ends immediately took charge and scored a touchdown on a pass from Johnson to Pascolini that he ran into the end zone from the five yard line. The loss of Lambert left the Friars without adequate offensive leadership or kicking skills, and their offense sputtered and lacked punch. The North Ends responded with another touchdown in the second quarter on "a squirming off-tackle run of fifteen yards by Robert Specht, a Chicago mounted policeman and Sunday half back." This time, they failed the extra point because of the bad angle resulting from the punt-out. The score was 13–0 in favor of the North Ends. In the fourth quarter, Rube Johnson finished the scoring for the day with a long field goal from placement. As the game clock wound down, the Friars managed a rally, but it was too little too late and did not result in points.[22]

In 1914, the North Ends "displayed a lot of college stuff." That year, according to a story in the *Fort Wayne Journal-Gazette,*

except for several new plays on double and triple passes back of the line, the Evanston attack was almost identical with that . . . presented last season. On every play they resorted to their old shift and secured excellent results through it during the first half. Johnson's punting at times was great, and although he tallied but once out of four tries on place kicks, he missed by inches on two occasions. . . . Theirs is a well handled eleven, every man of which apparently knew his part and played it well, especially during the first half. In Pascolini they have a bear of an end whose ability to receive forward passes caused the Friars a lot of worry yesterday.[23]

Everyone felt that, if Lambert had not been injured, it would have been a different game.

Now the Evanston North Ends set out to secure the state independent football championship of Illinois. First, they played the Moline Red Men in Moline. The *Rock Island Argus* declared that "Evanston's backfield was the best seen in action here. . . . Falcon, Kilby, Specht and Johnson tore-off long runs, displaying some of the most brilliant open field running ever witnessed."[24] Moline fans also marveled at the kicking of Reuben Johnson. "Almost every punt went at least sixty-five yards and one near seventy," according to the *Evanston Index*. Field Judge Sprague of Yale said he had never seen anything like it on the college football field, adding that it was a great pity the Rube had never gone to college.[25] Moline's loss to Evanston reduced the amount of money Moline fans were willing to bet on their upcoming game against Rock Island.[26]

On November 21, the North Ends played the Rockford Athletic Club. For the second week in a row, they played a strong Illinois contingent on its home turf. Only fifteen hundred people weathered the cold to watch the game, and neither team played up to form. A number of the North End regulars were out, including John Hanna and Murray Battaglia. A few minutes after the game started, Rube Johnson kicked a field goal from the thirty-five yard line, and later in that period he ran for a touchdown. Rockford scored on a fifty-yard run and a fifty-five yard pass in the second quarter to lead 14–10 at halftime. The North Ends rallied in the second half. Rube Johnson threw two touchdowns in the third quarter—a tackle eligible pass to Max Palm and a surgical strike to Art Pascolini—to win the game 24–14.[27]

The North Ends had hopes of playing the Detroit Heralds at home on Thanksgiving Day, but they were unable to secure an adequate guarantee, so their season ended on Northwestern University grounds in a rematch with the Moline Red Men. This time they defeated Moline 25–0. After the game, members of both teams were guests of Evanston manager Pattison at a banquet.[28]

The 7–1 record of the Evanston North Ends was one of the best in independent football. The semiprofessional football business, however, was changing rapidly. Canton and Massillon were promoting a revolution. By hiring entire teams of well-paid college all-stars recruited from all over the country, the Ohio football clubs were creating truly professional teams of major league caliber. It was clear that teams of hometown boys would no longer be able to win independent football championships.

In 1916, the Evanston North Ends found it necessary to add some top college players to their roster. While these additions improved their talent pool, they also interfered with the teamwork that had characterized Evanston's play in the past. College graduates had their own ideas about how to run plays, and their ideas frequently made it difficult to play in unison without a strong coach and plenty of practice time, neither of which pro teams had in 1916.

Evanston opened its 1916 season against the Milwaukee Maples on De Paul Field in Evanston. The North Ends' starting lineup included Johnny Barrett, who played for Washington and Lee College in 1915, and Penn Carolan, who attended Dartmouth College for a year or two. They both had grown up in Oak Park, Illinois, and were teammates at Oak Park High School, where they both played halfback for the class of 1913. In 1914, John Barrett attended Keewatin Academy in Prairie du Chien, Wisconsin, to prepare for college. While at Keewatin Academy, he played football in a backfield that also featured All-American Joe Guyon from Carlisle Institute.[29] Eugene Schobinger, from the University of Illinois, was now the North Ends' starting fullback, and Tom Shaughnessy, who had played center at Notre Dame, was a starting tackle.[30] Penn Carolan and Gene Schobinger pounded the Milwaukee Maples line time after time. Then John Barrett went over for the score. Barrett made two touchdowns, Carolan made one, and Max Palm recovered a fumble for the final score. Rube Johnson made all four extra points.[31] Evanston did not play another home game until the end of the month.

Coach Moore took his team to Racine, Wisconsin, the following Sunday. Battery C, also known as the Racine Regulars, were the independent football champions of Wisconsin. They had Bob Foster from Marquette University at one halfback and a fine sandlot player, Joe Dory, at the other. Their tackles, Phillip Thoennes and Walter Eck, were as good as any Evanston would face.[32] A crowd of more than twenty-five hundred turned out for the game. Several times in the first quarter Racine threatened to score, but each time they lost the ball. Rube Johnson drop-kicked field goals in the first and second quarters. The North Ends added a touchdown on a pass from Johnson to John Bosdett, an Evanston Technical High School graduate, playing left end for Evanston.[33] "Racine offered such light opposition," according to the *Evanston News-Index*, "that the North End eleven, after scoring 12 points, decided the game was safe, so made many substitutions. Coach Moore has such a wealth of material this year that he wishes to give all a chance to show their worth before telling any of them to turn in their uniforms."[34] It was not until the third game of the season, in Davenport, Iowa, that the North Ends were to learn that other teams were catching up with them quickly and that 1916 would not be an easy season for them despite their talent. On Sunday, October 15, Evanston took the train to Rock Island and crossed over the Arsenal Bridge to play the Davenport Athletic Club. Wyatt Earp's cousin played tackle for Davenport; otherwise, the team looked innocent enough. This was not the case, however. At no time in the game was Davenport outplayed. Costly fumbles by the Evanston backfield and numerous offside penalties hampered the North Ends. With only three minutes to play, Dick Fort, Davenport's fullback, drop-kicked a forty-five-yard field goal and split the uprights. Davenport won the game 3–0.[35]

On the long ride home, Evanston planned for their next game in Wabash, Indiana. On October 15, five thousand fans had watched Wabash and Pine Village play to a scoreless tie in Wabash. Coming off that bruising game, the Wabash Athletic Association was preparing to face "the speedy pigskin warriors from Evanston," as the *Wabash Plain Dealer* called them.[36] On October 22, Wabash and Evanston renewed their rivalry at the Carroll Street Field. For most of the afternoon, it appeared that Evanston would suffer its second straight defeat. At the start of the fourth quarter, Wabash led 18–0. But in the last ten minutes of the game everything changed. "Fantastical end runs, trick plays, and sensational forward passes featured the contest," according to the Wabash newspaper account. Evanston overcame the loss of Rube Johnson, who had suffered broken ribs in the first half, and numerous penalties called against them by what some believed to be a less than impartial referee. At one point, the referee called back a ninety-five-yard touchdown run by North Ends halfback Johnny Barrett because of an alleged but unspecified foul. With a side bet of $700 or $800 of their own money on the game, the North Ends were infuriated by the call, and they responded by using every trick play and deception they knew to score three straight touchdowns in the last ten minutes of the game. Chicago mounted policeman Robert Specht scored two touchdowns, and right end Fitzgerald caught a long pass from Gilbert, the backup quarterback, for the other score.[37] The final score was Evanston 21, Wabash 18.

Evanston ended October with a home game at De Paul Field against South Bend. John Barrett took a job with the Toledo Maroons, but they hardly missed him. Schobinger was moved to right end, Robert Specht and Penn Carolan played halfbacks, and Baggs Miller, a graduate of Lane Technical High School in Chicago, played fullback. In spite of cracked ribs, Reuben Johnson made two touchdowns and kicked six of seven extra points. Eissler, a substitute halfback, made two touchdowns; Penn Carolan made two; and Baggs Miller made one. Henry Kilby and Rube Johnson shared the quarterback position and made most of the Evanston yardage through their passing game. South Bend was held to a field goal. The final score was 51–3 for the North Ends.[38]

November 1916 was destined to be a disappointing month for the proud Evanston North Ends. Long the champions of the west, they were about to experience a mighty fall from the lofty heights they had been inhabiting. On November 5, they traveled to Detroit to play the Heralds in what should have been a routine victory. The Heralds were not having a particularly good year. Many of their players were beyond their peak, and Detroit had not brought in enough fresh talent to revitalize their aging team. Their record stood at two wins and three losses. Moreover, Skeet Lambert, who had been their quarterback in October, jumped the leaky ship to play for the Massillon Tigers. While Rube Johnson was playing with broken ribs, the North Ends team was talented and had just come off amazing wins against Wabash and South Bend. Furthermore, Detroit had never defeated the North Ends, and Dick Shields, the Detroit captain and quarterback, was suffering from serious injuries and illness and was thirty pounds under his normal playing weight.[39]

The first quarter was hard fought and scoreless. The Heralds recaptured the team play, crisp blocking, tackling, and intense interference that had characterized them in former years. They were quick to diagnose plays and, as the *Detroit Free Press* put it, "rarely failed to spill them."[40] Evanston, on the other hand, "tried its famous lateral pass three times, each time for a loss of from four to seven yards." Their play looked tired and showed little that was new. A lack of coaching was evident. In the second quarter, Dick Shields made a field goal from placement, giving Detroit a 3–0 lead. On the first set of downs following the kickoff, Evanston retaliated by scoring a touchdown on a long forward pass from Reuben Johnson to Gene Schobinger.[41] The North Ends failed to convert the point after touchdown.

Just before the half, a pass from Shields to Bob Boville, an All-American end from Washington and Jefferson who was playing his first game for Detroit, moved the ball inside the Evanston fifteen yard line. Earl Dunn, the Heralds' fullback, smashed the ball in close to the goal line, and Dick Shields finished the drive to give the Heralds a 9 to 6 half time lead.[42] The third quarter was again a standoff, and punts of sixty to seventy yards by Reuben Johnson kept Detroit out of scoring range.[43] But Detroit dominated the fourth quarter. In a smartly orchestrated drive, marked by slashing runs through the center of the line by fullback Earl Dunn, end runs, and trick plays, Detroit scored their second touchdown. Later, Nig Lennahan scored a third touchdown.[44] The Heralds came very near scoring a fourth touchdown, but they were halted when Johnson intercepted a Heralds' pass on the Evanston one yard line. As the clock was running out, Johnson drop-kicked a forty-eight-yard field goal, a feat few kickers ever perform, to make the final score 21 to 9.[45]

Evanston's problems did not end when they left Detroit. The following week, they played the Fort Wayne Friars in Indiana. The North Ends had never lost to the Friars, and the *Fort Wayne Journal-Gazette* considered the North Ends "the best managed team in pro-football," calling Rube Johnson "the best kicker" in the game.[46] Squeezed by rising costs, Evanston chose to limit their traveling team to fifteen players in hopes that conditions for a comeback were favorable.[47]

On Friday, November 10, the Friars announced that Dorais would miss Sunday's game because of illness, leaving quarterback duties to Frank "Coonie" Checkaye.[48] Past experience showed that the Friars were less effective with Checkaye at quarterback than when Dorais led the team. Still, Fort Wayne was undefeated and had just whipped a talented Pine Village team.

Five of the eleven Friar starters were from Notre Dame: Cap Edwards, Deac Jones, Al Feeney, and Mal Elward played in the line, and Joe Pliska played halfback. From the opening kickoff, Fort Wayne was in control of the game. They scored a touchdown in the first quarter and added another in the third. Almost the entire game was played at the Evanston end of the field. The Friars won 14–0.[49]

On November 19, the North Ends had a reprieve when they played the Rockford Athletic Club at Kishwaukee field and thrashed them 41–0 on the outstanding play of Johnson, Eissler, and Specht.[50] On November 30, Thanksgiving Day, Evanston finished their season by playing the undefeated Cornell-Hamburgs of Chicago for the championship of Chicago and Illinois. Prior to the game, Rube Johnson announced that he was retiring from football and that this would be in his last game with the North Ends. The Hamburgs eked out a 7–6 victory in a game shortened by darkness before ten thousand fans at Northwestern University's stadium.[51]

After losing as many games in the 1916 season as they had in their entire history, the North Ends disbanded. In 1917, Rube Johnson played for the Cornell-Hamburgs, and the other Evanston stars found starting assignments with Fort Wayne, Wabash, Toledo, Youngstown, and a variety of Chicago teams.

The North Ends had been a semiprofessional football powerhouse from 1910 to 1915. During this period, they had outstanding teamwork and a deceptive offense, with the latest in shifts and trick plays. The kicking and passing of Rube Johnson, together with the running of Guil Falcon, Robert Specht, and Roger Kilby made Evanston a difficult combination for their opponents. But as the competition got stiffer, they needed better coaching and more hometown games to remain in the top ranks of the sport. In 1916, the North Ends added a number of former college stars to their lineup, but instead of strengthening their team, these additions weakened them, because they no longer showed the teamwork and practiced deception that had made them a winner. Additional talent without proper coaching and coordination just added costs without providing offsetting advantages. The lack of hometown support was the greatest handicap of all. The team could not win consistently when it had to play nearly all its games on the road. As a result of playing on the road, the North Ends suffered from travel fatigue, home-team bias in refereeing, and higher than normal expenses. The Evanston North Ends learned the hard way that the professional football teams that would survive were those with strong hometown fan support. Others would have to learn that valuable lesson themselves.

9. The Toledo Maroons and the Adrian College Boys

The **Toledo Athletic Association** was organized in 1902. Among its early players were Maxy "Mother" Kruse, a slashing halfback; Fred Merkle, who later gained infamy when his failure to touch second base led the New York Giants to lose the 1908 pennant; and quarterback Walter Wright, who later became a well-respected Western Conference football official.[1]

From 1902 until 1908, Toledo compiled a 37–1–2 record. Over that period, the team played their home games at Armory Park, an unsodded field that in part inspired the name "Mud Hens" for Toledo's minor league baseball team, which used the same field. The ground was in such bad condition by 1908 that the management at Armory Park refused to allow the Toledo Athletic Association to play there and, with no place to hold their games, they disbanded.[2]

In 1906, the Toledo Maroons football team was organized for teenagers. By 1909, when young Art Gratop, who had been the team's center, became its manager, the Maroons started playing adult teams and realized just enough profit from their games, as sports scholar Bob Carroll said, to "let every man keep his jersey at the end of the season."[3] At that time, the line between semiprofessional and amateur sports was blurry, since reimbursement was not publicly discussed.

In 1911, Adrian College, a small Methodist school in Adrian, Michigan, enrolled Harry M. Seubert, Charles Nichols, and William Marshall to play football for them. Seubert and Nichols had played for Toledo Central High School in 1909,[4] and all three played for the Toledo Maroons in 1910. Adrian College also recruited Paul "Dutch" Reule from Mississippi State College.[5] On October 30, Adrian beat the Toledo Maroons at home 5–0 on their way to winning the Michigan Intercollegiate Athletic Association[6] Championship.[7] In 1913, Errett Sala, captain of the 1909 Toledo Central High School football team, and Bob Siebert attended Adrian College.[8] By the fall of 1914, the key players at Adrian returned to the Maroons to play for pay. The following year, these players, along with Ray Eichenlaub from Notre Dame and Jimmy Baxter from Kenyon College, made up the core of the Toledo Maroons professional football team.

The Maroons opened their 1915 season at Armory Park against an industrial team, the Cleveland Blepp Knits. The Maroons starting line-up was the same as in 1914. Billy Marshall was the team's captain and quarterback, with former Adrian College colleagues Chuck Nichols and Paul "Dutch" Reule at halfbacks, and King Bowles at fullback. Errett "Monk" Sala and Hugh Hackett started at ends, Louis G. Trout[9] and Tompkinson at tackles, John Schimmel and Louis "Dutch" Mauder at guards, and Julia "Jules" Weiss at center. The Maroon back field averaged 175 pounds and, in the eyes of the *Toledo Blade,* "every man is a speed merchant." In Toledo, Billy Marshall was "looked upon as the greatest field general in the state and there is more than one university team that would like to have his equal."[10]

The Blepp Knits Football Club had Montigney at fullback from the University of Pittsburgh, and a line that featured Hafner from the U.S. Naval Academy, Hucera and Hollicker, veterans of the Cleveland Tomahawks, and Armstrong, who had played with the Erin Brauns football team of Cleveland.[11] The first half of the season opener was scoreless, with both teams showing rough edges. There were frequent fumbles, and punts were short. Dutch Reule hurt his knee on the first play of the game and had to be replaced by West. In the second quarter, King Bowles was injured and had to be replaced by Russ McConnell. In the second half, Louis Trout, Errett Sala, Bill "Bee" Weiss, and Walt Semlow[12] each scored a touchdown. Because they were not the stars of the team, they were an unlikely group to have produced Toledo's 27–0 win.[13] The game resulted in four key injuries to Toledo players: Dutch Mauder broke two ribs, King Bowles got "water on the knee," and Dutch Ruele and Russ McConnell injured ankles.[14]

Because of the loss of King Bowles in the Blepp Knits game, Toledo manager Art Gratop attempted to recruit Ray Eichenlaub, who played fullback for Notre Dame in 1914.[15]After turning down several offers, Eichenlaub finally agreed to play for Toledo only after his college classmate Cameo O'Rourke spoke to him on behalf of the Maroons.[16] However, Toledo was scheduled to play Elyria before Eichenlaub could be signed.

Elyria had an excellent quarterback in Jack Ambrose, a teacher-coach at Elyria High School, who had been a star at the University of Maine.[17] The weather in Toledo on October 10, 1915, was ideal for football, and some twenty-two hundred fans paid to see the Sunday game. Toledo scored first on a run by Chuck Nichols, following a thirty-yard pass from Billy Marshall to Hugh Hackett. Later the Maroons made the score 13–0 on a touchdown pass from Marshall to Hackett that covered more than thirty yards. Elyria scored in the final quarter on a spirited drive in which the team captain, left halfback Nichols, had two twenty-yard runs, the final one resulting in a touchdown. The final score was 13–6 in favor of Toledo.[18]

When the Ann Arbor Independents came to Toledo on October 17, Eichenlaub still had not agreed to terms with Toledo, and the Maroons started Dutch Reule at fullback and used Jimmy Baxter and Chuck Nichols at halfbacks.[19] The Ann Arbor team had laid claim to the independent football championship of Michigan in 1914 and started six former University of Michigan football players and Thomas McCall, a former Harvard University end.[20]

The Maroons made a touchdown in the first period on a forward pass from Marshall to Hackett. They scored again on a pass interception in the second period. Jimmy Baxter intercepted another pass in the final quarter, and Marshall took advantage of the turnover with a fifteen-yard pass to Chuck Nichols, who scored, making the final tally 19–0.[21]

On Wednesday, October 20, Art Gratop went to Columbus, where he met with Ray Eichenlaub and finally signed him to a contract to play with the Maroons.[22] Eichenlaub was just out of college, trying to make a living as an architect, and it seems likely that he needed to supplement his income to make ends meet. Eichenlaub played four years as varsity fullback for Notre Dame, where he was All-Western and a Frank Menke choice for All-American in 1913, and was considered "one of America's greatest athletes."[23]

On October 20, Joe Carr, the Columbus manager, predicted that the Panhandles would defeat the Maroons by three touchdowns the following Sunday.[24] They had to eat their words when they were downed by Toledo 20 to 0 at Armory Park four days later.

The Nesser brothers had a bad day on October 24. Errett Sala's hard tackling jarred the Panhandles ball carriers, and when Columbus roughed Sala up in retaliation in the third quarter, he traded punches with boxing champion Fred Nesser. Even though Fred outweighed him by fifty pounds, Sala held his own, but both men were thrown out of the game.[25]

The hard running of Eichenlaub and Dutch Reule moved the ball through the normally stubborn Panhandle defensive line and kept the Maroons' drives alive. Once their running game was established, sensational passes from Marshall to Hackett resulted in three Maroons touchdowns. The first came after an interception that gave Toledo good field position. The second came on a sustained drive that ended in a pass to Nichols. A pass from Marshall to Hackett set up the final touchdown on a run by Trout, making the score Toledo 20, Columbus 0.[26]

The Dayton Gym-Cadets came to play Toledo on October 31, with what was announced to be "the fastest backfield combination in Ohio football."[27] The Gym-Cadets had an outstanding quarterback in Alphonse Mahrt, who was a skilled passer and good field general. He was supported in the backfield by George "Babe" Zimmerman, a veteran fullback of powerful proportions, Pie Decker, a speedy halfback, and Norbert Sacksteder, the best Ohio-born halfback in pre-World War I pro football. The Gym-Cadets' backfield stars were well known to Toledo sports fans, and to readers of the *Toledo News-Bee,* which called "Norb Sacksteder and Al Mahrt heroes of many hard fought basketball games here" for the St. Mary's Cadets.[28]

The Dayton Gym-Cadets only brought fourteen men to Toledo to play against the Maroons.[29] Nevertheless, they quickly took control of the game. Some six minutes after the opening kickoff, Norb Sacksteder grabbed a punt on his twenty yard line and ran through the entire Maroons team for a touchdown. Billy Marshall, who was playing without a helmet, and Ray Eichenlaub had a shot at the elusive Dayton halfback, but could not catch him. Sacksteder's second touchdown came on an end run later in the first half. The Maroons scored their only points in the third quarter on a drive fueled by two successive forward passes, one to Hugh Hackett and the other to Chuck Nichols.[30] After three running plays resulted in a touchdown by Nichols, Jules Weiss kicked the goal. Eichenlaub had trouble with the signals. Obviously, more practice was needed to integrate him into the Maroons offense.[31] The Gym-Cadets scored again in the last quarter when Sala fumbled a punt, which was recovered by Al Mahrt in the end zone.[32] George R. Pulford, sports columnist for the *Blade,* complained that

the Maroons lacked a united effort. There was no speed to the attack and the old punch was gone. The outfit acted as if it wore weighted shoes. Fumbles were frequent and costly. The interference [downfield blocking] was worthless . . . only one side of the [offensive] line was blocking.[33]

The final score was Dayton 20, Toledo 7.

Disgusted with the performance of his players, coach Tom "Doc" Brown decided to put himself in shape to play in the next game. Brown had been All-Southern at tackle while at Vanderbilt, and he had a thing or two to show the team.[34] Toledo's next opponent was Peggy Parratt's

Indians, only nominally from Akron, because they had not played a home game and went by many names that year. The original Indian squad was hired away by Massillon and Canton in early October.[35] Parratt was forced to recruit an entirely new team in mid-October after most good semipro players were already committed to other teams. In spite of these handicaps, he had managed to find a number of fine athletes. The problem was that they were given little time to jell into a team.

Parratt's Indians started Arthur "Bugs" Raymond and Wilson, an assumed name for a former Dartmouth player, at tackles; Roe from Western Reserve at center; Stanfield Wells from Michigan and Howard Beck from Washington and Jefferson at ends; Carl Weiler and Zachman from Case Institute at guards. His backfield included Jonathan Fred Potts and Orrville Littick from Ohio Wesleyan, Sam Willaman from Ohio State University, and Ed Hanley from the University of Pittsburgh.[36]

In the first period, the Maroons had the ball in Indian territory almost constantly. Ray Eichenlaub did an excellent job for the Maroons' ground game. He had apparently learned the Toledo signals and executed them well. It was not until the second quarter, however, that the Maroons made their first score. Jimmy Baxter drop-kicked a field goal from the thirty-two yard line. Later in the second quarter, the Indians nearly tied the game on a drop kick by Orrville Littick that fell short. The second half gave the twenty-six hundred hometown fans something to cheer about. Led by Sam Willaman, Ed Hanley, and J. Fred Potts—who was playing without a helmet—the Indians pushed the ball down the field to Toledo's three yard line. The Toledo line held, and Littick missed another field goal.

The Maroons' drive started in the shadow of their own goal posts. Four- and five-yard line plunges by McConnell, Nichols, Trout, and Eichenlaub brought the ball to the center of the field. A forty-yard pass from Marshall to Jules Weiss moved the ball to the Indians' ten yard line. After two running plays up the middle failed, McConnell circled the Indians' left end for a touchdown. Following the punt-out, Weiss booted the goal.[37]

With coach Tom Brown in the lineup, the Maroon defense improved significantly. Interestingly, the Maroons all wore the same football uniforms, but each Indian brought his own uniform so the Akron team looked like an all-star conglomerate rather than a unified team. Perhaps the uniforms told the story of the Maroons' 10–0 victory. Without teamwork, Parratt's Indians were unable to score.

On November 15, Toledo played the Cincinnati Celts without the services of their captain, Billy Marshall, who had injured his knee rather badly against the Indians. Jules Weiss was moved to quarterback, and Louis Trout was moved to the backfield as a back-up.[38] The Celts featured Tan Snyder, Keene T. "Peggy" Palmer, and Tilly Schuessler at halfbacks, Al Bessmeyer and Chet Knab at ends, and Frank Lane and Otto Bessmeyer in the line.[39]

Prior to the Celts-Maroons game on November 15, the *Toledo News-Bee* held its first annual horseshoe-pitching tournament at Armory Park from nine in the morning until half past twelve, right before the football game. The playing field was obviously torn up by the more than two thousand participants and onlookers who showed up at the ball park. One sportswriter quipped, "After the horseshoe pitchers get through at Armory Park on Sunday, the Maroons should be able to do some fancy running through a *broken field.*"[40]

The Celts-Maroons game was a hard-fought scoreless tie. Each team had a game plan that centered on straight football with "line plunges" and an occasional end run. The Maroons' passing game was hampered by the absence of Billy Marshall. The Celts were using Chet Knab, normally an end, at quarterback.[41] In a game plagued by holding calls on both sides, each team was happy to settle for a tie.[42]

On the following Sunday, the Massillon Tigers came to Toledo to play the Maroons. Massillon was the best team in America, having defeated Jim Thorpe's Canton Bulldogs the previous week. This game gave the Maroons an opportunity to contend for the state and national professional football championships. The *Massillon Independent* described the condition for the game: "A steady rain, lasting nearly all of Saturday night, followed by a cold, sharp wind . . . made the field very heavy and slow. . . . Fast work by either team was impossible."[43]

Massillon brought an array of football talent that included Knute Rockne and Boyd Cherry at end, Franklin Day and Deac Jones at tackle, Muff Portmann and E. M. Cole at guards, Louis Hayes at center, and Red Fleming, Charles Dorais, and Edmund Kagy in the backfield.[44] Massillon had engaged Norb Sacksteder from the Dayton Gym-Cadets to supplement their backfield. Otherwise, they fielded almost the same team they had employed the week before against Canton. Toledo was back at full strength with Reule, Eichenlaub, Nichols, and Marshall in the backfield, and Hackett, Brown, Mauder, Jules Weiss, Schimmel, Trout, and Sala in the front line.[45]

The Tigers had a weight advantage over the Maroons. Unable to move the ball, Toledo played a defensive game and often punted on first down to gain field advantage. Ray Eichenlaub was the only Maroon back capable of running against Massillon, and Toledo depended on Dutch Reule's impressive kicking to stay in the game. He averaged fifty yards a punt, and some punts traveled sixty-five yards.[46] Toledo made only one first down all afternoon.[47] The Massillon Tigers also had trouble moving the ball, but Sacksteder was somewhat more effective than Eichenlaub. Massillon made seventeen first downs yet failed to make a touchdown.

For forty-three minutes, Massillon and Toledo battled for the state championship without either team gaining significant advantage. Every man did his best. The Massillon Tigers were the aggressors and had the ball in Maroon territory the greater part of this time, but Dutch Reule and Chuck Nichols kept the Tigers at bay with their kicking.[48]

Dorais tried to drop-kick a field goal in the first period and missed. He also threw successful passes to Knute Rockne and Red Fleming, but Massillon could not score. It was Sacksteder's running that set up a Dorais drop kick from a difficult angle with only five minutes remaining in the game. Massillon finally took a 3–0 lead as darkness set in on the muddy field.[49] The five minutes remaining after the field goal were played in darkness. Toledo's title hopes were crushed by Dorais's kicking toe: all that was left was pride and the city championship.

Four days later, on Thanksgiving Day, the Toledo Maroons played the Mack Park Maroons at home. Detroit had a solid team, although they had just lost the previous Sunday to their cross-town rivals, the Detroit Heralds, on a mental error. The Mack Park team was loaded with college stars, most of whom attended Michigan colleges. Bernard "Bertie" Maher, a University of Detroit graduate, was captain and right half. Faunt "Dutch" Lenardson from Michigan Agricultural College (Michigan State), Art Cornwell from the University of Michigan, and Ty Krentler from Kalamazoo Normal were among the other college players in the Mack Park starting lineup.[50] Mack Park scored first. In the second quarter, Moriarity intercepted a forward pass and took it to the Toledo three yard line. Parcell then pushed the ball across goal for the touchdown. Toledo evened the score in the third quarter when Ray Eichenlaub burst through left tackle on a forty-yard touchdown run. The game ended in a 6–6 tie.[51]

Three days later, the Maroons played the Toledo Glenwoods for the city championship. The Glenwoods had an outstanding fullback by the name of Clarence "Smoke" Fraim, a Black athlete playing for an otherwise White team. Smoke Fraim had been one of the stars on the 1912 Toledo Central High School team that claimed a share of the national high school championship. Nicknamed the Mastodons of 1912, Central High was undefeated against teams like Detroit Central High School and Chicago's Hyde Park High School and averaged a point for every minute they played that season.[52] On Thanksgiving Day, Fraim scored two touchdowns in their 26 to 6 win against Fremont, Ohio.[53]

The Toledo Maroons made easy work of the Glenwoods. Ray Eichenlaub made two touchdowns, and Walt Semlow, Jimmy Baxter, and Dutch Mauder also scored. In addition, there was a safety against the Glenwoods. When Ray Eichenlaub left the field at the end of the game, the crowd gave him a hand, knowing his contract was completed and it was his last game for the Maroons.[54] Fraim ran well against the Maroons and proved that he could play in that league. He created two or three scoring chances for the Glenwoods, but, without the supporting cast necessary to convert these opportunities, his team lost 56–0.

Toledo played one last home game on December 5 before a thousand fans to close their season. The game against the Cleveland city champion, Favorite Knits, was never in doubt. The Maroons won 34 to 0.[55]

Toledo had an outstanding season in 1915. They lost only two games: one to Dayton, the other to Massillon, the teams with the two best records in independent football in Ohio. Moreover, they played a strong schedule. Of course, they had the advantage of playing all home games, but they also incurred injuries and faced playing conditions that were less than ideal. Without question, the 1915 Toledo Maroon team ranks high in pre-World War I era football circles.

As October 1916 approached, football news began to crowd baseball off the sports pages. On the opening day of Toledo's season, none of the six players who had attended Adrian College in 1911 returned to the Toledo Maroon lineup. William "Billy" Marshall, Chuck Nichols, Hugh Hackett, and Jimmy Baxter were playing baseball for the Rail Light team and were in the middle of a tournament,[56] while Bob Siebert, Harry Seubert, Paul "Dutch" Reule, and Errett "Monk" Sala had quit professional football.[57] Also missing were Ray Eichenlaub, King Bowles, Tompkinson, Russ McConnell, and others. The 1916 Maroon squad was smaller because only four newcomers were hired to replace the twelve missing players. The only new player with college experience was Golly Jarvis, a halfback who had played with Adrian College prior to 1909. The other newcomers were Art McIntyre, from Scott High School (Toledo), at right end,[58] Red Wells, who had played for

Racine in 1915 at fullback, and McMahon at left halfback. Tom Merrill, the football coach at Scott High School,[59] coached the Maroons in 1916.

A sizable crowd greeted the Maroons when they took the field on October 1 against the Elyria Andovers. Jack Ambrose was quarterback for Elyria, but his front line had difficulty protecting him. He was sacked behind his own goal line for a safety. Toledo's new backfield had the benefit of last year's front line and did well. In the *Toledo Blade*'s account of the game, a pass from Billy "Bee" Weiss at quarterback to Art McIntyre "gave the speedy end an opportunity to squirm through a broken field for a twenty-yard touchdown. It was all the scoring Toledo got and all they needed." The final score was Toledo 9, Elyria 0.[60]

On October 8, the Maroons played the Buffalo All-Stars at Armory Park. By and large, professional football in New York state was weaker than watered tea. Buffalo featured Frank Mt. Pleasant, who was well past his prime, as he had been a star with Carlisle Institute in 1903. Mt. Pleasant was aided by Douglas Jeffery from the University of North Carolina and Edward J. Dooley. Buffalo played competitively against the Rochester (NY) Jeffersons, the Lancaster Malleables, the Buffalo Oakdales, and the Brooklyn Lakewoods, but, whenever these teams ventured into Michigan or Ohio, they were almost always defeated by lopsided scores. This, of course, was not the pitch given to the newspapers. Buffalo claimed to have scored 148 points in 1915, "while keeping their own goal uncrossed." The truth of the matter was that the Buffalo All-Stars were defeated by the Detroit Heralds in 1915 by a score of 69–0.[61]

Even without Nichols, Marshall, Hackett, and Baxter, Toledo defeated Buffalo 15–0. Art McIntyre scored the first Toledo touchdown in the opening quarter on a blocked punt by Jules Weiss: the blocked punt allowed Art to pounce on the ball in the end zone. Later that quarter, as reported by the *Toledo Blade,* "Toledo mounted a sustained drive on the ground, and 'Red' Wells took it over the goal line on a straight line plunge." In the final quarter, Wells kicked a field goal to complete the scoring.[62]

Toledo's third game in 1916 was against the Akron Imperial Electrics, a team that started five former players from the Municipal University of Akron, including Don Ross, who was player-coach.[63] The Electrics also had Bullet Mitchell, a former Purdue University player, and Sisler from Case Institute.[64] Toledo won easily, 20–0, over Akron's industrial team. With Billy Marshall, Hugh Hackett, and Chuck Nichols back on the field for Toledo, the Maroons' passing attack "must have looked like a Zeppelin attack to the rubber-town men," in the colorful phrase of the *Toledo Blade*.[65]

After playing three relatively easy teams, Toledo finally faced the Massillon Tigers on October 22. Manager Art Gratop raised admission prices from fifty cents to seventy-five cents to cover the guarantee required by Massillon.[66] The game attracted more than six thousand paying fans, who saw Massillon very nearly lose to Toledo. As the *Massillon Independent* wrote, "For three quarters of the fray Toledo was very much in the race and held the upper hand, the Tigers battling hard to overcome the seven point lead established by the Maroons" on a second quarter pass from Marshall to McIntyre.[67] Massillon scored fifteen points in the last twelve and a half minutes of "unabated fury." As the darkness was closing in, Joel Mattern, Massillon's left halfback, ran for a touchdown, then Red Fleming scored the go-ahead points with a field goal from placement. On the ensuing kickoff, Knute Rockne picked up a live ball that was mishandled by Maroons quarterback Jimmy Baxter and scored the last touchdown.[68] As always, the Maroons line was solid, and Billy Marshall played well without a helmet. Doc Brown, Jules Weiss, and John Schimmel were particularly good on both offense and defense. The *Toledo Blade* was impressed by the contest: "High class football was the order of the day."[69]

In the days following the loss to Massillon, Art Gratop had been approached by Johnny Barrett and Penn Carolan, who were unhappy with their current arrangements with the Evanston North Ends. Seeing an opportunity to improve the Maroons, he signed John Barrett.[70]

The Maroons ended the month of October by playing the Cleveland Telling-Strollers. Johnny Barrett and the Maroons had a field day against the Cleveland industrial team. After a scoreless first quarter, Toledo scored four touchdowns in the second quarter and five more in the second half. McIntyre, Barrett, Hackett, and Marshall each scored two touchdowns, and Nichols made one. Weiss kicked five extra points. The *Toledo Blade* story surged with superlatives:

Johnny Barrett . . . played right half most of the game, and proved himself a remarkable gridder. He ran with rare judgment and tremendous power; in the open he bowled the would-be tacklers over with ridiculous ease, and seemed about the hardest man to stop that has performed at Armory Park this year.[71]

Not everyone was impressed. George Pulford, sports columnist for the *Toledo Blade*, wrote, "Since the acquisition of Johnny Barrett the Maroons have looked better, but before becoming too enthusiastic over the former Oak Park star, wait and see him in action against the powerful Panhandles, when his skill will be needed."[72]

Beset by personal tragedy, the Panhandles were unable to play with their normal intensity. Fred Nesser missed the game because a doctor had ordered him to rest his injured arm. Emmett Ruhl was hardly able to move because of injuries. After having taken ill that morning, Frank Nesser's infant child died just two hours before the team left Columbus.[73] Consequently, Frank did not accompany the team, and only four of the Nesser brothers started for the Panhandles—Phil, Al, John, and Ted. None of the Toledo fans or players were aware of the problems.[74]

The Maroons scored in the first quarter on a run by Nichols, but, under the leadership of the forty-one-year-old Ted Nesser, the Panhandles fought back. Early in the third period, they got possession of the ball on a muffed punt and shot a forward pass from Ted Nesser to Roscoe Kuehner for a touchdown, giving Columbus the lead 7 to 6. Not long afterward, according to the *Toledo Blade:*

Johnny Barrett tore off a 43 yard run from a kick formation, spilling Panhandles like ten pins. Barrett spun like a ten when tackled. He started from his 40 yard line, ran diagonally across the field to the Panhandles 45, then shot to the opposite side, where he was pulled down from behind while dodging a tackler on the enemy's 25.

Later Barrett made a spectacular run in which he covered the field with tacklers for a touchdown.[75]

In the fourth quarter, after Jimmy Baxter scored on a ten-yard run, a distraught Phil Nesser jumped on him and injured him. Late in the game, Hugh Hackett kicked a field goal to make the final score 23–0.[76]

The next Sunday, the Maroons played the Dayton Triangles led by Norb Sacksteder, Babe Zimmerman, Lou Partlow, and quarterback Al Mahrt. The *Toledo Blade* covered the contest: "Mahrt picked his man and shot the ball, like a bullet, into his hands. Pass after pass was successful, netting long gains." Though he was injured on the first play of the game, Barrett kept playing because he was Toledo's only competent kicker. Without a healthy backfield, Toledo often punted on first down and depended on their defensive skills. Dayton's passing, together with Norb Sacksteder's ability to run to the outside, won the game for the Triangles, 12–0.[77] Because of the injuries, Art Gratop was forced to hire Penn Carolan and Jack Fluhrer to boost his backfield for their upcoming game with Pine Village.[78]

The Pine Village Athletic Club was a formidable foe. From 1903 to 1916, this small community of four hundred souls had fielded an undefeated football team. Frequently, Claire Rhodes, the center and manager of the team, hired the best semiprofessional football players in the nation to represent Pine Village. On November 19, the Pine Village starting lineup featured Ernie Soucy and Richard King from Harvard, Ed Davis and Matt Winters from Indiana, Cub Buck from Wisconsin, Charles Helvie and Cliff Milligan from Indiana, and Emmett Keefe from Notre Dame.[79] About two thousand fans witnessed the game. The contract arrangements gave Pine Village half the gate, a much better deal than usually given to visiting teams. The admission price was seventy-five cents for men and fifty cents for ladies, though few women attended what was considered too violent a game. In the battle of a lifetime, the game ended in a scoreless tie.

On November 26, Toledo played the Lancaster (New York) Malleables, a team that had formed in 1904. Lancaster had defeated the Altoona Indians and the Buffalo All-Stars and had played the Detroit Heralds to a scoreless tie in 1915.[80] In a well-played game that received little press coverage, Toledo defeated Lancaster 10 to 0.[81]

On Thanksgiving Day, Toledo played the Racine Regulars, the champions of Wisconsin. The Maroons had Johnny Barrett back in the lineup, along with Penn Carolan, Billy Marshall, and Red Wells. Penn Carolan played a remarkable game for Toledo. His end runs and Billy Marshall's passing were responsible for the Maroons' 19–0 win.[82]

Except for a charity game against the Toledo Police Department held on December 10, Toledo ended their 1916 season against Peggy Parratt's Cleveland Indians, one of the five best teams in professional football that year.[83] Their star-studded team had David Walter Hopkins from the University of Pennsylvania and John Wagner from the University of Pittsburgh at ends, Thomas H. King from Notre Dame and Thomas Gormley from Georgetown at tackles, E. M. Cole and Jim "Butchy" Barron at guards, and Whitey Schultz at center (in place of Paul Des Jardien, who was sick). The Indians' backfield featured Lorin Solon from Minnesota, Derby, said to be from West Virginia University, Honus Graff from Ohio State University, and I. R. Martin from the University of Missouri.[84]

At Armory Park, for three quarters, neither team threatened to score. Most of the game was played in Indians' territory or around the center of the field. Doc Brown was a defensive standout for Toledo and Barrett played "a whale of a game." Only a lucky pass in the gathering darkness made it possible for Lorin Solon to kick the field goal that won the game for Cleveland.[85]

Once again the Maroons had completed a successful season. Their only losses were to Massillon, Dayton, and Cleveland—three of the four best teams in the state. Art Gratop succeeded in attracting decent crowds even when he charged seventy-five cents per game, and he limited his payroll so as not to lose money at a time when the bidding for scarce football talent was driving up players' wages.

In 1917, Jimmy Baxter took over the management of the Toledo Maroons, and Byron Dickson replaced Tom Merrill as coach.[86] America was at war with Germany, and young men were joining the army or working in defense industries. Only six members of the 1916 Toledo Maroons team returned to play in 1917: the Weiss brothers, John Schimmel, Louis "Dutch" Mauder, Noble Jones, and Joe Schuette.[87] Only four had been starters the previous year.

The Maroons football team had to be completely rebuilt. Its backfield combination of Marshall, Nichols, Barrett, and Wells was out of pro football. The new backfield was Billy "Bee" Weiss at quarterback, Jimmy Lalond at left halfback, old-timer Maxy "Mother" Kruse at right halfback, and Frank "Tubby" Roush at fullback. Mother Kruse had played for Toledo in 1903 and, at thirty-five years of age, was past his prime. Frank "Tubby" Roush had been the star left halfback for the Morrison R. Waite High School in Toledo in 1915 and 1916.[88] The 1917 Toledo line had veterans Jules Weiss at center, Noble Jones and John Schimmel at guards, and Louis "Dutch" Mauder at tackle. Paul Sinclair Mason, who had played for Toledo Central High School in 1911 and for Purdue University while in medical school, was at the other tackle position,[89] and Red Nicholson, Dority, and Taylor, all new men, were at ends.[90] Later in the season, John T. Bachman, a graduate of Mercersburg Academy where Frank Sommer, the football coach at Michigan Agricultural College, had coached in 1910–11, was hired to play left end.[91]

Toledo opened its 1917 season on October 7 against the Carlisle Indians of Detroit, a team coached by Ed Morin and composed almost entirely of Native Americans who had attended Carlisle Institute in eastern Pennsylvania. Most of the Carlisle players worked at the big Ford Motor Company plant in Highland Park.[92] Almost two thousand fans showed up at a new, bigger venue, Swayne Field. Because Swayne Field was not as intimate as Armory Park, fans complained that they missed the close relationship between players and spectators.[93] In an effort to offset this problem, the Maroons introduced numbered jerseys to help fans identify players. Toledo scored early and often in their 47–0 win. The local newspaper explained the lopsided score: "The Maroons outrushed, outkicked, and out guarded their opponents and on the defensive the locals were like a wall." Most of those sitting on the Maroons bench got an opportunity to play. Leslie M. Jones, the starting

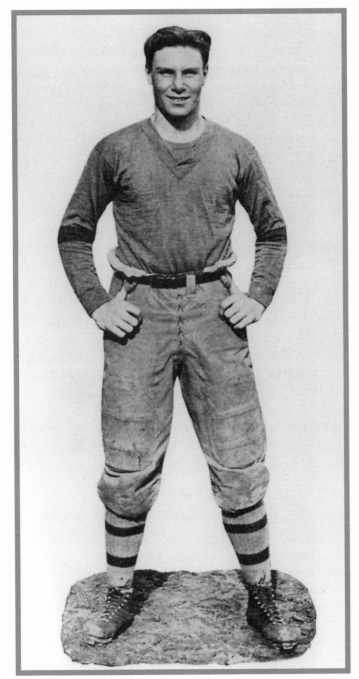

Frank "Tubby" Roush, fullback, Toledo Maroons 1917, was a standout for
Morrison R. Waite High School in Toledo in 1916. *(Toledo-Lucus County Public Library, Library Legacy Foundation.)*

left guard for the Maroons, broke his left leg and was out for the season.[94] The following week, when Toledo played the South Bend All-Stars, another blowout resulted, the Maroons winning 49–0.[95]

On October 21, the Maroons finally played a strong team, the unbeaten Dayton Triangles, who had defeated Toledo in 1915 and 1916. It was the first out-of-town game for Toledo in four years, and over five thousand fans showed up at Dayton's Triangle Park. Al Mahrt, George "Babe" Zimmerman, and Louis Partlow were in the opponent's backfield, and Lee Fenner and Harry Kinderdine played ends.[96] The Maroons received the initial kickoff but were unable to move the ball. Shortly after receiving the Toledo punt, Mahrt threw a pass to Babe Zimmerman, who ran the ball across the goal line for a touchdown, but the Triangles missed the kick for the extra point. In the second quarter, neither team got within scoring distance, but Butch Miller grabbed a Triangle fumble and ran fifty yards before being stopped by John Devereaux. It was the Maroons' best play of the day. In the third quarter, another pass from Mahrt to Zimmerman resulted in a touchdown. Later that period, Babe also kicked a field goal to make the final score 15–0.[97] While the Maroons had played well, it was a long ride home.

The next two Toledo games were also on the road. On October 28, the Maroons played the Detroit Heralds at Navin Field. Entering this game, the Heralds had not been scored on. The Detroit lineup included some of the best players in professional football, including Norbert Sacksteder, Harry Whitaker, Ray Whipple, and Nany Shanks.[98] Toledo started Taylor, Schuette, Mauder, Jules Weiss, Schimmel, Freehart, Dority, Butch Miller, Jimmy Lalond, Red Nicholson, and Frank Roush.

Both teams scored in the first quarter. Soon after the game started, Norb Sacksteder made a series of fifteen-yard runs that resulted in the Herald's first touchdown and point after. Later in the quarter, an exchange of punts gave Toledo field advantage. Detroit chose to punt on first down, but Earl Dunn's kick went straight up in the air and came straight down, giving the Maroons the ball on the Detroit fifteen yard line. Bee Weiss took advantage of the opportunity, and Nicholson ran the ball for a touchdown on the next play. Detroit went ahead again in the second quarter on a pass from Harry Whitaker to Danny Mullane, then stretched the lead to 20 to 7 on another touchdown by Norb Sacksteder in the third quarter. Although Toledo played an impressive fourth quarter, they lost 20–7.[99]

Toledo played another game on the road on November 4 when they met the Fort Wayne Friars at League Park. The Friars' all-star lineup included several Notre Dame greats, a player from Indiana University, and a veteran from the Evanston North Ends. Charles "Gus" Dorais usually played quarterback for Fort Wayne, but was replaced by Jack Ambrose of Elyria for this contest.[100]

From beginning to end, Toledo was overmatched. After a slow start, the Friars scored a touchdown toward the end of the first quarter before three thousand cheering fans. Before the final gun, Robert Specht scored one touchdown, Pliska two, Ambrose two, and Helvie, Berghoff, and Dority one each. An eighty-yard run by Ambrose was the highlight of the game for the Friars, who overpowered the Maroons 45–7.[101] Weiss scored the only Toledo touchdown. A reporter for the *Toledo News-Bee* underreported the Fort Wayne score by more than twenty points in the Toledo newspaper the next day,[102] and was accused by Fort Wayne of a coverup.[103]

The bleeding did not end, however, and the Maroons lost to Dayton, Akron, and Detroit again before the season finally ended on December 1. Only a win against the Toledo Navy Training Center on November 25 offered a reprieve. Toledo ended the season with a 3–7 record, the worst in their history.

The Maroons resumed professional football in 1919 but did not join the American Professional Football Association in 1920. Jim Thorpe and baseball Hall-of-Famer Roger Bresnahan applied for an American Professional Football Association franchise on June 18, 1921, but they did not field a team. The following January, Bill Harley, who had sought the Chicago franchise that was awarded to George Halas, was awarded the Toledo franchise.[104] So the Maroons entered the National Football League in 1922, featuring such prewar stars as Guil Falcon, Tom Holleran, Clarence "Steamer" Horning, and John Kellison. With this talent, they managed a 5–2–2 record, but the next season they had a losing record and dropped out of big-time professional football.[105]

10. The Youngstown Patricians

The **Patricians Club** of Saint Patrick's Catholic Church in Youngstown, Ohio, encouraged by Rev. Father Charles Alfred Martin, organized and financed a football team in 1911.[1] The Pats, as they were nicknamed, were composed of local players who played other local teams for the next three years. The *Youngstown Vindicator* later remarked, "at that time Youngstown fans were not interested in football outside the clashes between local school teams."[2]

In 1914, the Pats, who were from the south side of Youngstown, played the Crescents, from the other side of the city, for the championship of Mahoning County.[3] The Pats won the game on a field goal before a crowd estimated at more than eight thousand, according to the *Youngstown Vindicator*, and set their sights on a regional schedule for the 1915 season.

The 1915 Patricians team was "well supplied with college stars of the first water, as well as natural gridders no less deserving of praise because they have had no 'scientific training.'" All of the Pats' players were Youngstown products and "they play[ed] the strenuous college game in much the same snappy fashion that it [was] played in the foremost American colleges."[4] They were managed by Joe Omier and coached by Ray Thomas, who had grown up in Youngstown and had been a football star at Youngstown's Rayen High School before attending the University of West Virginia, where he was again heralded for his work on the gridiron.[5] Other notable former college players who had grown up in Youngstown and returned home to play for the Patricians included Russell Gilman "Busty" Ashbaugh, who had been an All-American end at Brown University in 1911 and 1912, and Elgie Tobin, who had attended Penn State University.[6] The Patricians also recruited Rayen High School football coach Philip P. Edwards, who had graduated from Oberlin College,[7] Fred Stiver from Case Institute, and Leo Eberhardt from Buchtel College (The University of Akron).

By 1915, the Patricians were a winning team and continued to draw large crowds. The Pats played their first four games against relatively weak town teams from locations within sixty miles of Youngstown. All of the games were played in Youngstown and drew crowds of five thousand or more fans, although the income was modest because the admission price was only twenty-five cents, which often went unpaid.[8] The Patricians' home opener was on October 10 against Alliance, Ohio. The game was held at Willis Park and was a total mismatch, with Youngstown winning 72–0.[9]

On October 17, the Patricians played Barberton, Ohio. Eight thousand fans came to watch "the grand autumn sport" played in a manner pleasing to the hometown folks in ideal weather. Barberton never threatened to score. Fans were impressed by the quickness of the Youngstown offensive play. As the *Vindicator* noted, "There was little of the tiresome delay and repetition of signal calling so frequently met with in the semi-pro game." Busty Ashbaugh scored two touchdowns, as did George "Whitey" Yeckel. Philip Edwards, Wilber S. Davidson, and Ray Thomas each scored a touchdown as well. Elgie Tobin scored a field goal and seven extra points after touchdown. Youngstown "played like a well seasoned college machine" in their 52 to 0 victory over Barberton.[10]

October 24 found "derby day" weather conditions for the Youngstown Patricians as they greeted the B.F. Goodrich football team from Akron. The Akron team featured two University of Wisconsin stars, a former University of West Virginia football starter, and a Buchtel College man.[11] The Pat's sandlot star fullback Ralph Funkhouser scored two touchdowns. One was a sensational seventy-two yard return after intercepting a forward pass. On the return, he dodged three Akron players, "using the stiff-arm with charming accuracy." The final score was 21 to 0. An estimated five thousand fans saw the game played at Wright Field.[12] Sunday football was finally becoming a fixture on the athletic schedule of Ohio's Steel City, and fans were anxious to see a higher caliber of opponent for the November portion of the season.

The final Sunday in October found the Salem, Ohio, town team at Wright Field. Salem was the last of the nearby towns to play Youngstown in 1915, and the Pats made short work of the Columbiana County gridders, 20 to 0. Bill Lavin, who had attended Youngstown's Rayen High School, scored a touchdown in the first quarter. Ed Gillespie recovered a potentially costly fumble in the third period, and George Yeckel and Busty Ashbaugh added touchdowns in the final quarter.[13]

In the last half of the season, the Youngstown Patricians became one of a handful of independent teams that was emerging as a truly professional team of national status. The transition started on November 7 with a game against the McKeesport Olympics. Like Youngstown, Mc-

Keesport, Pennsylvania, would soon be making the transition from regional intrastate games to an interstate schedule that required players who could not always be recruited from the local stocks available. In the meantime, the McKeesport team's manager bragged that not one of his players had ever seen the inside of a high school or college. They were all steelworkers who toiled hard six days a week and devoted the seventh to the even more strenuous duty of semiprofessional football.[14] McKeesport lacked a powerful running back and was forced to pass the ball in order to move it. They also lost opportunities because they fumbled several hikes from center. Ray Thomas scored the first touchdown for the Patricians, and Ashbaugh kicked two field goals in the first quarter, adding a touchdown in the second period. At halftime, the score was 20 to 3, the McKeesport score coming on a forty-yard field goal by Hardesty in the second quarter. It was the first time that the Pats had been scored against in the 1915 season. The Pats' fullback, Getz from Akron, scored an additional touchdown in the fourth quarter. The final score was 27 to 3.[15]

On November 14, the Pats played a team from suburban Pittsburgh, the Pitcairn Quakers. Pitcairn had evenly contested Red Fleming's Altoona Indians early in the season, losing 0 to 3. The Quakers featured George "Cotton" Vedderneck and the Adams brothers, among others. They had played and defeated Irwin, Pennsylvania, on Saturday, then traveled to Youngstown Sunday morning to play the Pats.

The Quakers scored in the first quarter on a run around left end, putting the Pats behind for the first time all season. However, the punt-out for goal try was blocked, and Philip Edwards recovered the ball for Youngstown, preventing Pitcairn from trying an extra point after touchdown. At the end of the opening quarter, Pitcairn led 6–0. Ray Thomas and Busty Ashbaugh rallied the home team in the second quarter. Ashbaugh caught a seventeen-yard pass to set up a three-yard tally by Thomas. Ashbaugh kicked the extra point, and at halftime the Pats led 7–6. In the second half, the rigors of playing back-to-back games over the weekend began to take its toll on Pitcairn. During the second half of the game, Wilber Davidson broke his leg but continued play for some time before being replaced by Yeckel.[16] In the third period, as the Quakers' endurance began to give way, Ashbaugh kicked a thirty-five-yard field goal, and, in the final frame, the South High School coach made a touchdown and extra point to give Youngstown a 17 to 6 win.[17]

After beating two of the best semipro teams in Pennsylvania, the Patricians prepared to battle the Nesser brothers' Columbus Panhandles.

The Panhandles were having a winning season. They had already defeated the Massillon Tigers, the Detroit Mack Park Maroons, and the
Dayton Gym-Cadets, among other teams, and had given the Canton
Bulldogs and the Toledo Maroons all they could handle. The Panhandles were a mixture of young knights and old warriors. They presented
the most severe test of the Pats' strength and ability. The core players
on the Panhandles had played together for fourteen years and were
ranked among the top ten independent teams in America. If the Pats
could beat the Panhandles, they could play against the best in 1916.
Youngstown hired George "Cotton" Vedderneck, who had played with
distinction against them the previous Sunday, to play left end against
Columbus.[18]

Gray clouds, a stiff breeze, thirty-degree temperatures, and minia-
ture swamps that were hazardous to footing greeted both the Pats and
the Panhandles at Wright Field on Sunday afternoon, November 21, at
2:30 P.M. The Panhandles used trick formations to advantage in the
first quarter, but the Pats soon figured out the tricks and the Panhandles were finally held on downs. The struggle was even all afternoon,
as players matched muscle and wit without gaining significant advantage. The Panhandles outweighed the Pats, but the muddy field neutralized this advantage. George Vedderneck, the long-time pro and former Carlisle Institute star, helped stabilize the Pats line against the
Nesser brothers. In the third quarter, Vedderneck stepped up and carried his Pats teammates with him. He was in the middle of nearly every
play. "Clean and decisive, he frequently brought his man to the earth
without ceremony," the *Youngstown Telegram* said of Vedderneck, and
when Ted Nesser blocked Ashbaugh's field goal attempt and gained
control of the ball, Vedderneck came to the rescue, tackling Nesser before he could advance the ball. When the final gun sounded, the game
ended in a scoreless tie.[19]

On the last Sunday in November, the Washington D.C. Vigilants
were given a $1,000 guarantee to come to Youngstown to play the Pa-
tricians.[20] The Vigilants styled themselves the "Champions of America,"
having won ninety games while losing only three over a seven-year
period.[21] The Vigilants, however, played a relatively weak schedule and
did not even begin practice until the end of October.[22] They generally
played few teams stronger than the West Park Athletic Association of
Baltimore.[23] In a game marked by more grit than glitz, five thousand
fans watched the Youngstown Patricians slip past the Vigilants 13 to 7
and end their season undefeated.[24]

The Patricians were ready to challenge the best teams in Ohio in

1916, but, like most good professional football teams of the era, the Pats wanted to play themselves into shape before facing Massillon and Canton. Youngstown started the season against Lisbon, Ohio. However, because of a more difficult schedule and the need for more former college players, the Pats increased ticket prices from 25 cents to 50 cents. Forty percent of the admission price went to Paul Powers, who held the lease for Wright Field, which in turn was owned by the streetcar company. The Pats guaranteed Lisbon $400 to play them on opening day. When perfect weather brought out five thousand fans, the Pats grossed $800 after paying the visiting team and paying for the stadium. They would need to continue to build their treasury to cover the larger guarantees demanded by the better teams they hoped to play in November. As in 1915, Busty Ashbaugh, Elgie Tobin, and Ray Thomas were the hometown heroes, but Tuss McLaughry and Hoke Palmer also distinguished themselves in the Pats' 21–0 victory over Lisbon.[25]

The Pats followed their home opener with four straight wins. They defeated the Ex-Carlisle Indians on October 8, the Jamestown (New York) Alcos on October 15, the Martins Ferry Athletic Association (Wheeling, West Virginia) on October 22, and the Pitcairn Quakers on October 29, 1916. During the month of October, the Pats scored 103 points and were unscored on. Clyde E. Bastian, University of Michigan varsity football and track letter holder, popular student leader, and well-regarded literary student graduate from Williamsport, Pennsylvania, played fullback "like a whirlwind" for the Patricians against the Martins Ferry Athletic Association until injured late in the first quarter.[26] Tom Gormley, formerly with Georgetown University, made his first appearance with the Patricians at left tackle in their game with Pitcairn.[27]

Youngstown fans were eager to play Massillon, Canton, Columbus, and Cleveland and urged the Patricians to upgrade their competition quickly.[28] In anticipation of a stronger schedule, the Pats had been hiring more former college players than in the previous year. In addition to Tom Gormley, they signed Jim "Butchy" Barron of Georgetown University, Charles H. Roberts from Yale, R. M. Smith from Penn State, J. "Auggie" Blair from the University of Pittsburgh, Lester Thomas Miller from Marietta College, Horace "Hoke" Palmer and Douglas McWilliams Hawkins from Ohio University, and Stilwell Saunooke from Carlisle Institute to supplement college graduates Ashbaugh, Tobin, Yeckel, Stiver, and Thomas from the Pats' 1915 squad.[29] By the end of October 1916, Youngstown had finally signed agreements to play Massillon twice and Canton, Cleveland, and Columbus at least once in November. They also arranged to give the Vigilants a rematch near the close of the season.[30]

The first Sunday in November found Massillon paired with Youngstown at Wright Field. A special train carried Massillon fans to the game,[31] where more than five thousand Youngstown fans were cheering against the black and gold invaders. Massillon was unable to hire Charles Dorais and Knute Rockne for this game, as both had previous commitments. But Massillon did have Kent "Skeet" Lambert at quarterback, Carl "Dutch" Thiele and Fred Heyman at ends, J. Franklin Day and Bob "Nasty" Nash at tackles, Louis J. Hayes at center, and Joel Mattern, Malcolm "Red" Fleming, and Ed Kagy in the backfield. Youngstown, in gray jerseys, started Ray Thomas at quarterback, Busty Ashbaugh and Charles H. Roberts at end, R. M. Smith and Tom Gormley at tackles, Fred Stiver and George Yeckel at guards, Lester Thomas Miller at center, and Stilwell Saunooke, Horace Palmer, and Getz in the backfield. The Pats had luminaries like George Vedderneck from Carlisle Institute, Elgie Tobin from Penn State, and Dickle, reported to be from Ohio University, on the bench.[32]

From the opening kickoff, "the Patricians and Tigers . . . locked horns." Both teams were scoreless in the first half, but, unbeknown to the crowd, Ray Thomas broke a bone in his left wrist. Nevertheless, he started the second half. Soon after the start of the third quarter, Thomas fumbled the ball on the Patricians' thirty-five yard line. Massillon recovered the ball, and, shortly after that, Skeet Lambert dropkicked a field goal from the forty yard line.[33] According to the *Massillon Independent*, "His kick sailed squarely between the uprights and he hoisted the leather from a difficult angle."[34] It was the only score of the afternoon. The Pats had done their best to tie a knot in the Massillon Tigers' tail, but they could not cross the Tigers' goal line. After this game, some of the out-of-town recruits deserted Youngstown for higher pay in Cleveland. While it was reported that upwards of eight thousand men saw the game, only 3,049 paid admission. Massillon received $1,525 or 50 percent of the gross; $457.35 went to pay the park lease; $700 was paid Patrician players; and the balance went to the Patrician Athletic Club and the coach.[35]

Despite personnel changes, the Pats recovered their winning ways the following week against the McKeesport Olympics, defeating them 20–3 in a rough, hard fought outing. After relinquishing a three point lead to McKeesport on a short kick caused by a missed blocking assignment, Youngstown rallied with a touchdown by Getz in the second period and scores by Ashbaugh, who was playing quarterback in place of

Horace "Hoke" Palmer, fullback and captain of the 1914 Ohio University football team, played right halfback for the Youngstown Patricians in 1916. *(Ohio University Archives.)*

Ray Thomas, and Getz in the final period.[36] The game acted as a reprieve, allowing the Pats a breather before facing Canton, Massillon, and Columbus.

On November 19, the Pats played the Canton Bulldogs, the best professional team of the pre-World War I era. Jim Thorpe was at his peak, and he had an outstanding supporting cast. The Pats recruited Hughitt from the University of Michigan to take Ray Thomas's place at quarterback, but he would not be available until November 26 after the close of the University of Michigan season. Earnest F. "Tommy" Hughitt played quarterback and halfback for the University of Michigan between 1911 and 1916 before turning professional.[37] In the meantime, Busty Ashbaugh, who normally played end, continued to handle the quarterback chores. A great athlete, he was considered the best candidate for the position from those available.

Canton was also short-handed for the game. On Saturday, Ernie Soucy and Howard Buck were in Minneapolis with the University of Wisconsin, as assistant coaches, and were unable to make connections to reach Youngstown for the game. Instead, they played for Pine Village against the Toledo Maroons rather than for Canton that Sunday.[38] More importantly, Jim Thorpe had a case of stomach flu and was nursing an injured ankle. Moreover, George "Carp" Julian was sick with what turned out to be tuberculosis. Canton started Milton Ghee at quarterback. Ghee had been coached at Oak Park (IL) High School by Bob Zuppke, where his teammates included Franklin "Bart" Macomber and Pete Russell.[39] In 1916, Ghee was coaching at Dartmouth and, in late September, had agreed to play for Canton, but because of his coaching duties this was the first game for which he was available. Harry Costello from Georgetown replaced Thorpe in the starting lineup at halfback. M. E. "Red" Wilkinson played the other halfback position and, despite his illness, Carp Julian started at fullback.[40] Canton's personnel problems became more complicated when Harry Costello injured his foot in the first quarter. Thorpe, whose doctor had advised him not to play, took Costello's place. At halftime, Thorpe could not carry on and was replaced by Carp Julian, who finished the game in spite of sickness.[41] Youngstown fans were unhappy at the absence of the great Native American athlete, and hundreds chanted "Has Jim Thorpe a yellow streak?" The very thought that Thorpe was afraid or even fainthearted was "a libel on such a fair name," declared the *Youngstown Telegram*.[42] In fact, Thorpe had played sick and injured, at significant risk to his health and career, and still the fickle fans were not satisfied.

Neither team scored until the last three minutes of the fifty-two-minute game, when a pass from Milton Ghee to Red Wilkinson resulted in a touchdown.[43] Wilkinson failed on the try for goal, giving the Bulldogs a 6 to 0 victory. This loss eliminated Youngstown from the race for the world's professional football championship. As a consequence, Cleveland refused to play their scheduled game with Youngstown on Thanksgiving Day, figuring that there was little to gain by such a contest.[44] Instead, Cleveland booked a game in Detroit, and Youngstown scheduled the Washington D.C. Vigilants for November 26, and an away game at Massillon for Thanksgiving Day.

Seeking satisfaction for their 13 to 7 loss in 1915, the Vigilants pointed for their rematch with the Pats for an entire year. Washington won the toss and chose the ball. Shortly after the start of the game, the Vigilants' left halfback, Cranston, kicked a twenty-three-yard field goal and Washington took a 3–0 lead, which held up until the fourth period when Cranston scored a touchdown for the Vigilants.[45] At that point, they chose to kick out for position, but failed and lost their chance to kick goal, making the score 9–0. With only eight minutes left to play, Tommy Hughitt, in his first game for Youngstown, finally rallied the Pats and led them on a drive that resulted in his drop-kicking a forty-five-yard field goal. After a strong defensive stand and with time running out, Hughitt hurled a fifteen-yard pass to Busty Ashbaugh, who raced another forty-five yards through half the Vigilant team to tie the score. Ashbaugh then kicked the extra point to win the game 10–9.[46]

Braced by the comeback victory over the Vigilants, Youngstown traveled to Massillon on Thanksgiving in hopes of getting revenge for their 3 to 0 loss to Massillon twenty-five days earlier. The Pats started nearly the same team that had defeated Washington. Massillon, on the other hand, hired Russ Goodwin to play quarterback for the Tigers. Goodwin and Red Fleming played together at Washington and Jefferson College and were familiar with one another and the offense that Red had brought to Massillon from his college experience. Fred Heyman, Goodwin's favorite receiver at college, was also on the Massillon roster, so Goodwin had two familiar passing targets. Passes from Goodwin to Heyman broke the game wide open. Massillon completed twelve of fourteen passes and coasted to a 27–0 win.[47]

Youngstown closed the season with a 0–13 loss to the Columbus Panhandles in Youngstown. Ashbaugh replaced Tommy Hughitt at the pivotal position, and most of the other out-of-town stars were dropped from the roster in anticipation of a small turnout. The Nesser brothers were in top form, and Columbus defeated the Patricians with little difficulty.[48] The venture into major league football had been a disappointment to the fans. After a promising build-up in October, the Pats lost all four games against their Ohio rivals in November. Obviously they would have to recruit better players if they hoped to keep up with Canton, Massillon, Columbus, and Cleveland. Melvin Lester McCreary, captain of the 1916 Ohio University football team, was recruited to start at center for Youngstown. The Pats had tried six different centers in the previous six games without satisfaction.

In late September 1917, Ohio football fans were already beginning to look beyond the World Series to speculate about the upcoming professional football season. On September 24, the sports writer at the *Toledo Blade* wrote:

> In addition to Massillon and Canton, Youngstown will be in the field for the "big football" championship this fall.
>
> The first named pair have battled for the state title for so long that they are not accustomed to real opposition, but the announcement of the men signed to play with the Patricians makes the team look dangerous.
>
> To begin with Stan Cofall, the former Notre Dame back will coach the team and will probably play one of the backfield positions at times.
>
> Men already under agreement for play with the team are Peck of Pittsburgh, Schlachter of Syracuse, Beckman, Fitzgerald and Ward of Notre Dame, Thornhill of Pittsburgh, Macomber of Illinois, Johnny Barrett of Washington and Lee, Gilroy of Georgetown and Rayan of Cleveland.
>
> Cofall has been given permission to "go as far as he likes" in putting together a championship team. The Patricians plan to give both Canton and Massillon a battle for the national professional championship and expense isn't considered when a star is wanted.

Stanley B. Cofall was born in Cleveland, Ohio, in 1894. He played football at Cleveland's East Tech High School in 1910 and then moved to East High where he became an All-Scholastic star in football and hockey. He also played on the Cleveland Athletic Club hockey team while in high school. During a series of hockey games between Notre Dame and the Cleveland Athletic Club, he became acquainted with Deac Jones, captain of the Irish team. As a result of that friendship, Cofall enrolled at Notre Dame, in 1913, where he became a close friend and frequent dinner companion of Knute Rockne, captain of the Irish varsity football team. In 1914, as a sophomore, Cofall became Notre Dame's regular left halfback and helped Rockne coach two South Bend independent teams owned by the Mussel Brewing Company. In 1916, he was on several All-American teams. At the suggestion of Rockne, Cofall was hired as player-coach of the Youngstown Patricians in 1917.[49]

Melvin Lesley McCreary, center and captain of the 1916 Ohio University football team, played center for the Youngstown Patricians late in the 1916 season. *(Ohio University Archives.)*

The Pats opened their season against the Wheeling, West Virginia Martins Ferry Athletic Association on October 7 with a new team manager—Joe Mullane, who was a clerk at the I & S Company—only four players from the 1916 season, and an admission charge of $1 per ticket.[50] They added David Reese to their lineup at left end. Reese was originally from Massillon and had starred at Denison College before playing professionally for the Cincinnati Celts and coaching at Cincinnati University.[51] Cofall and John Barrett led the Pats to a 36–0 win.

Bart Macomber played quarterback in the season opener, but, unsure about his passing skills, Mullane was negotiating by mail with Tommy Hughitt to sign a contact for the season to play the pivotal position. When Hughitt laid out his terms, Mullane telegrammed his acceptance. For some unexplained reason, the wire did not reach Hughitt, who, thinking Youngstown was not willing to meet his terms, agreed to play the first two games of the season with the Detroit Heralds, while he negotiated with Massillon. Anxious to know why the former University of Michigan star quarterback had not accepted his offer, Mullane called Hughitt by long distance telephone at his home in Buffalo, "despite the high cost," and completed the contact to begin October 21. Claude Thornhill, the All-American tackle from the University of Pittsburgh, signed a contract to play with the Pats but soon broke it to take the job of coaching the McKeesport Olympics. He then had the audacity to try to schedule a game between McKeesport and Youngstown. Mullane turned him down flatly, and, when it was rumored that the Pitt star was negotiating with Massillon to play for them, Mullane threatened to enjoin him if he attempted to play football in Ohio.[52]

On October 16, the Pats played the Pitcairn Quakers. Macomber again started at quarterback and was supported by the same lineup as the week before, except for Reese, who was replaced by Barry from Georgetown.[53] The Pats built up a 10–0 lead early in the game and apparently relaxed. In the fourth quarter, the Quakers turned the tables, scoring sixteen points in the last five minutes to defeat Youngstown 16–10.[54] Patricians fumbles and poor pass defense proved to be their undoing.[55]

On the following week, with Tommy Hughitt at the helm at last, Youngstown played a second-rate Dayton team, the Dayton Shamrock Wolverines, who were called the Cadets by Youngstown.[56] The old Dayton Gym-Cadets team had merged into the Dayton Triangles who were playing host to the Toledo Maroons. The visiting team left Dayton at 10:45 P.M. on Saturday, but before long, four coach cars jumped the track, occasioning a long delay. Their train encountered another wreck at Crestline and did not reach Youngstown until 3:30 Sunday afternoon, an hour after the scheduled starting time.[57] Totally worn out, the Dayton road team offered little competition for the Pats, who steamrolled over the interlopers 44 to 0.[58] The new Pats lineup included Stanley Cofall at left halfback, Hughitt (Michigan) at quarterback, Bill Kelleher (Notre Dame) and George Vedderneck (Carlisle) at ends, Tom Gormley (Georgetown) and Bill Ward (Penn) at tackles, George Yeckel (Western Reserve) and Jim "Butchy" Barron (Georgetown) at guards, Freeman Fitzgerald (Notre Dame) at center, and Ed Hanley (Pittsburgh) and Johnny Barrett (Washington and Lee) in the backfield. It was a star-studded lineup with virtually no local players in it.[59]

On October 22, the Youngstown Patricians signed Bart Macomber, former University of Illinois quarterback, to a season-long contract for $125 per game.[60] Franklin Bartlett Macomber was five feet seven and 165 pounds. Macomber, coached in high school and college by Bob Zuppke, was a triple-threat on offense and a sound defensive player. In 1916, he was one of the best fifteen players in college football. Off the football field, he was mild-mannered and enjoyed taking leading parts in student operas and dramatic theater. On the field, he was tough and fearless. In 1916, Bart was selected to be on Walter Camp's first team All-American squad, but, at the last hour, Camp dropped Macomber in favor of Elmer Oliphant and left Bart off his All-American list altogether.[61]

On October 28, the Patricians faced the Columbus Panhandles. Though they were a weak imitation of past Panhandle teams, Columbus still played with pride and was capable of winning. With Hughitt at quarterback and Macomber at right halfback, the Pats manhandled them 30 to 0. Stanley Cofall seemed faster than a runaway truck down a mountain road. He made all the touchdowns, and Macomber added to the total by booting three goals and kicking a forty-seven-yard field goal from placement. Johnny Barrett and Tommy Hughitt were the defensive stars for the Pats.[62]

The first Sunday in November was a big day in Youngstown. The largest crowd ever to attend a football game at Wright Field showed up to watch the Patricians face off against the world champion Canton Bulldogs. The *Youngstown Vindicator* captured the cockiness of the home team: "When asked about the Patricians chances of defeating the Canton this year, John Barrett told a reporter, 'Jim Thorpe is all right, but he's only one. If the Patricians can't beat that Canton bunch we ought

Franklin "Bart" Macomber, quarterback and right halfback, Pine Village Athletic Club 1916; Youngstown Patricians 1917; Fort Wayne Vets 1919; from Oak Park, Illinois, he graduated from the University of Illinois in 1917. *(University of Illinois Archives.)*

to hide our face, for we have one of the greatest backfield any professional grid team ever had.'" Barrett expressed "all the respect in the world for Thorpe's ability," but refused to be awed by his presence in the game.[63] The teams were evenly matched. The feature match-up of the day was head-to-head competition between the two centers, Bob Peck of Youngstown (who was playing under an assumed name) and Ralph "Fats" Waldsmith of Canton.

Robert D. Peck was born on May 38, 1891, in Lock Haven, Pennsylvania. After playing halfback at Lock Haven High School and Pawling School in New York State, Peck enrolled at the University of Pittsburgh, where he was converted to center by head coach Pop Warner. Peck played on the 1914–16 football teams, which lost only one game in three years. He was captain of the 1916 National Champion Pitt Panthers and was on the Walter Camp All-American team in 1915 and 1916. As the roving center on defense, he played much like a modern linebacker. At 185 pounds, Peck was extremely aggressive. He attracted attention by taping his wrists, ankles, and helmet so others could recognize him in a pileup. He was a ferocious tackler with great defensive range, and on offense frequently made more than one block during a single play. The newspapers called Peck "one of the greatest centers that ever played," and Knute Rockne listed him as the best center for the first quarter of this century. Peck was "in every play. . . . He sprinted down the field with the ends and floored punt catchers with startling frequency." Coach Warner declared, "never have I known a man who could inspire his mates as Bob Peck."[64]

Ralph "Fats" Waldsmith was also one of the finest single platoon centers ever to play professional football. Ralph grew up in Akron, Ohio, where he played center on an undefeated Central High School team in 1910. In 1911, he attended Buchtel College in Akron and played varsity football for three years. In 1913, he was elected captain and was honored as All-Ohio first team at center. The next year, Ralph started his professional football career with the state champion Akron Indians team. In 1915, Waldsmith joined the Canton Bulldogs and was considered by Jim Thorpe to be the best center he had ever played behind.[65]

In their first face-to-face meeting, both Peck and Waldsmith were out to win and to prove that they were better than the other. It was an eye for an eye and a tooth for a tooth between them. Peck played a rough game throughout in an effort to knock the courage out of Waldsmith, but the Bulldog center never flinched. Both men were outstanding. Peck showed physical strength and a quick ability to diagnose the opposing team's attack, while Waldsmith played steady, strong, and without error. Peck sat out the third quarter to rest up, but Waldsmith played the entire game. It was the consensus of opinion that Fats Waldsmith was the better player on this particular afternoon.[66]

The Canton-Youngstown game was an even match-up. Canton stars Pete Calac, Alfred E. "Greasy" Neale, and John Kellison lived and played college football in West Virginia, in violation of intercollegiate football regulations. They also played Sunday football for the Canton Bulldogs under assumed names. Fearful of being recognized and exposed because Youngstown was close to West Virginia, they decided not to play this game. To further complicate matters for Canton, in the first half Milton Ghee cracked a rib and Frank Dunn was carried off with a sprained ankle, and both had to be replaced.

Although the Canton Bulldogs gained 168 yards with their rushing attack and passed for an additional eighty-two yards, they could not cross Youngstown's goal for a touchdown. The Youngstown defense was outstanding whenever Canton threatened to score. Howard "Cub" Buck's drop kick from the fifteen yard line in the first period produced the only points in the game. Three times, Bart Macomber tried to tie the score with a field goal but failed each attempt. Canton won 3–0.[67]

Youngstown had opportunities to beat Canton but did not capitalize on them. The Pats had proved that they could play with the best pros in America, and, on November 11, they faced the Massillon Tigers at Wright Field. Prior to the game, there was a dispute between officials of the two teams. Youngstown complained that Claude Thornhill should not be allowed to play for Massillon because he had a prior contract with the Pats. Massillon countered that Jim Barron had been taken from them by Youngstown.[68] Team managers all over the country were beginning to worry about the lack of talent. The Panhandles lost five of their players who were conscripted into the armed services.[69] Massillon signed Dexter Very, former Penn State University end, to a contract only to have him drafted into government service.[70] In Fort Wayne, soldiers agreed to play for the Friars, only to have their weekend passes canceled by their superiors.[71] Though Massillon managed to add Jack Scott to their roster to play Youngstown, he missed the game because of poor train connections.

In past years, most Massillon fans traveled to Youngstown by train to watch the game. As a measure of progress, it should be noted that the Massillon newspaper gave automobile routing instructions to fans for the first time. The instructions gave some sense of the difficulty of motor travel in 1917. It took a determined fan to drive his car to the game in those days. The paper reported on November 9 that "the preferred path from Massillon to Youngstown" was as follows:

Massillon to Canton. Canton to Alliance, then to Sebring. From Sebring head for Beloit, where the road ends. Turn left for about 25 feet, turn to the right and drive east to an old coal mine. At this point head north and continue until the first road to the right. A mile on this road will reach the macadamized road. Left on the Macadam straight to Berlin center. Turn right and travel five miles east to Ellsworth. Turn left and another five miles drive north brings Jackson to hand. Turn to the right on the bricks and drive straight east to Youngstown.[72]

Five thousand fans paid to watch the two great teams play. Games varied in playing times depending on agreements between the teams; this one was scheduled for forty-eight minutes because of a late start and the prospects of early darkness. Massillon received the opening kickoff, made a first down, but could not continue to move the ball and was forced to punt. On the Pats' first offensive play, John Barrett gained thirty yards around left end, taking the ball to the Massillon thirty-eight yard line. From there, Cofall threw a thirty-yard pass to Martin, who scored. In the second quarter, "Tuss" McLaughry scored a touchdown for Massillon, but Eugene Elseworth "Shorty" Miller missed the extra point because of the difficult angle involved. At half-time, the score was Youngstown 7, Massillon 6. Neither team gained further advantage until the last three minutes when, as the *Massillon Independent* reported, "unobserved by a Tiger warrior, Quarterback Hughitt walked leisurely to the extreme left of the Patricians line and waited until Cofall heaved a pass into his open arms, carrying the ball to the Massillon's five yard line where two bucks by Barrett and Cofall brought a second touchdown."[73] The 14–6 upset put Youngstown back into the race for the world professional football championship.

The next game was a rematch with the World Champion Bulldogs. Nearly one thousand Bulldog fans accompanied their team to Youngstown.[74] Once again, Kellison and Calac did not play for Canton, perhaps because so many Youngstown fans were from nearby West Virginia. Greasy Neale, however, did play fullback for the Bulldogs under an assumed name, because he planned to resign as coach at West Virginia Wesleyan following the basketball season and had less concern about being recognized. He suggested to Pittsburgh reporters that John Kellison, his assistant coach, also might resign.[75] Calac, Neale, and Kellison used up their college eligibility but continued to play football for two and three years. Neale and Kellison coached and played for West Virginia Wesleyan, and, for a time, nobody at the college cared. However, there were beginning to be rumors in Pittsburgh and elsewhere about them playing beyond their eligibility. More importantly, there were rumors that they were playing pro football on the Sabbath, and, at a Southern Methodist school, this was not acceptable to the board of trustees. There was the further complication that Neale was playing professional baseball, and the owners were not happy about the possibility of him getting injured in a football game.

Once again the match-up between Fats Waldsmith and Bob Peck was a focus of attention. This time, Peck played under the assumed name Cripp, because of his job as football coach for the Culver Military Academy in Indiana. Fats Waldsmith more than held his own and was declared by Canton newspapers to be the best center in pro football.[76] Canton defeated the Pats without the services of Jim Thorpe, who sidelined himself to allow an injured leg to heal so he would be in top shape for the Massillon game.[77] Samuel Willaman, playing under the assumed name Williams, replaced Thorpe at halfback. In the 1920s, Willaman would be head coach at Iowa State University and Ohio State before his untimely death. As it turned out, Alfred Earle "Greasy" Neale was instrumental in the Canton win. As he told the story forty-seven years later,

Jim Thorpe was coaching the team, but wasn't playing that day. We came up to Youngstown's 22-yard line on a third down with one to go. In our huddle, our quarterback, Milt Ghee, an All-American from Dartmouth, said 'Greasy, what will we do?' I said to pass. . . . [One of the other players] said, 'no let's buck the line for the one yard and the first down.' I told him . . . 'We'll get that yard on the next down if the pass fails'. . . . Well, sir, Ghee throws me a pass into the flat, and I get away with only Tommy Hughitt of Michigan, then safety man, between me and the goal line. At the five-yard line Hughitt leaves his feet for the tackle, and I leave my feet at the same time. Hughitt goes under me. I land on my shoulder in the old baseball roll and come up and I walk the game from Youngstown 13 and nothing.[78]

The Youngstown Patricians were scheduled to play the Akron Pros to end the season, at Wright Field in the Steel City. Hundreds of Akron rubber workers were planning to motor to Youngstown to see the game. A paved highway between Akron and Youngstown made the trip possible, and Mac MacGinnis, one of the owners of the Akron team, chartered three large motor buses and a flock of jitneys to make the trip.[79]

The weatherman forecast cold weather for the game and, when Frank Nesser arrived in Akron from Columbus Saturday morning on the Pennsylvania Railroad, he was quoted as saying, "This is ideal weather for Akron and you can bet your last nickel that we will win over Youngstown. I feel fit to play the game of my life."[80] It began to snow in Youngstown Saturday afternoon, and by 3 P.M. there was nearly a foot of snow on the ground. Faced with these conditions, the Pats canceled the game. Suey Welch, the Akron manager, told friends that "Fear of defeat prompted Youngstown to cancel with Akron. Frank Nesser is at his best in cold weather and Stanley Cofall and his Patricians knew it. They did not want to risk having another blot placed upon their record."[81] It is more likely that fear of losing money due to a poor turnout, rather than fear of losing the game, motivated Youngstown team owners to call off the game.

The Patricians brought their football season to a close Saturday night, November 24, with a banquet at their club rooms where they celebrated the sixth anniversary of the organization of the club. The featured speaker was Fr. Charles A. Martin, founder of the club. Patrick Barrett was the toastmaster, and Mr. Dwyer was the current president of the club.[82]

In the meantime, Stanley Cofall, Bob Peck, and Freeman Fitzgerald signed to play with Massillon against Canton on December 3.[83] Thus, a season that had started with such high hopes ended with an unseasonable snowstorm and a modest 4 and 3 record.

In 1919, the Youngstown Patricians staged a brief comeback under the leadership of coach-manager Ray Thomas. The Pats hired Harry Gaskeen of Syracuse, Tommy Hughitt, Bill Kelleher, Tuss McLaughry, George Vedderneck, and George Yeckel. But after a 27–0 pounding by the Massillon Tigers on October 5, 1919, the Pats concluded their professional football history in Youngstown.[84]

11. Dayton: St. Mary's College and General Motors

The **Gym-Cadets** were organized in 1913 by the Athletic Association of St. Mary's College in Dayton. St. Mary's College was founded in 1849 by the Brothers of the Society of Mary, an order established in 1817 by Brother William Joseph Chaminade. The school later became the University of Dayton. Since the school's varsity team was called the Cadets, they named the independent team the Gym-Cadets, because it was composed of young adults who used the St. Mary's gym. In their first year of independent football, the Gym-Cadets capitalized on the forward passing wizardry of Alphonse H. Mahrt, who had recently graduated from St. Mary's, winning all seven games they played. Both of the Cadets' touchdowns in their 14–9 win over the Dayton Oakwoods for the city championship came on forward passes from Mahrt, and on Thanksgiving Day the Gym-Cadets won the rematch 26–21, overcoming an eight-point deficit going into the final quarter. In between these two Oakwoods games, they traveled to Redlands Field in Cincinnati, where they defeated the Cincinnati Celts to win the championship of Southern Ohio. All of St. Mary's touchdowns came on forward passes from Mahrt. Indeed, three of every four Dayton plays were forward passes. The school newspaper remarked, "To forward pass in your own territory is considered poor judgment, but not when you can get away with it."[1] In 1914, the Gym-Cadets had a good season but lost to the Wabash A. A. 19 to 14 in Wabash, Indiana.

Norbert and Hugh Sacksteder, Alphonse H. Mahrt, George "Babe" Zimmerman, Ernie Dugan, John Devereaux, Larry Dellinger, William Zile, Carl Storck, and Pie Decker were on the original Cadets squad. All had played for St. Mary's, and some were still playing for the college varsity team as well as the Gym-Cadets team when it was organized.[2] The three St. Mary's College alumni who gave the most character to the Gym-Cadets were Norbert Sacksteder, John Devereaux, and Alphonse H. Mahrt.

Norbert Sacksteder attended St. Mary's College from 1910 until the

In 1914, the Dayton [St. Mary's] Gym-Cadets journeyed to Wabash, Indiana, where they lost a hard-fought game, 19–14. Notice the barbed wire fence within six feet of the out-of-bounds line and how close to the out-of-bounds line play is initiated. *(Wabash County Historical Society.)*

spring of 1914. His brother Hugh J. also attended St. Mary's High School and College from 1907 to 1912. While in college, Norbert played basketball, baseball, and track as well as football. Norbert and Hugh played on the original 1913 Gym-Cadets team. Concurrently, he also played on the St. Mary's College varsity team. Norbert quickly became a star on both Saturdays and Sundays.[3]

John Devereaux started his football career in high school in Lexington, Kentucky, where his team won the state championship in 1911 and played an exhibition game against Kentucky State University. In the fall of 1912, Devereaux enrolled at St. Mary's College, where he immediately became a starter. As a sophomore, he was elected captain of the varsity football team and was a starter on their basketball team. He also played Sunday football for the Dayton Gym-Cadets that year. In the fall of 1914, Devereaux transferred to Christian Brothers' College in St. Louis and played football for them. In 1916, he was the catcher for Evansville in the Central Baseball League.[4]

Alphonse H. Mahrt grew up in Dayton, graduated from Emanuel School, and played football at St. Mary's High School and College from 1907 to 1915.[5] At one time, there were three different Alphonse Mahrts playing football at St. Mary's Institute—Alphonse M., Alphonse H., and Alphonse G. Mahrt. A. H. Mahrt, who was preparing to become a priest, attended the high school division until the fall of 1910, when he entered the college division. By December, he was the starting right forward on the St. Mary's Cadets varsity basketball team. In the fall of 1911, he was the starting quarterback for the varsity football team and was also a starter on the basketball team. At that time, the St. Mary's football program was gaining prominence. In 1911, they played Otterbein, Antioch, Earlham, Heidelberg, Kenyon, St. Patricks, Wilmington, and St. Xavier colleges and even had an offer to play Notre Dame (which was turned down as "conditions are not yet favorable enough for such a meet"). St. Mary's College won four games, lost three, and tied one that year. The college newspaper declared, "Already St. Mary's is in demand throughout the state for a place in the schedule of the leading colleges in 1912."[6]

In 1912, Alphonse H. was awarded college monograms in football, basketball, and baseball. St. Mary's won all but two of their football games that year, and Mahrt was now a star. In the first game of the season, he scored a touchdown within three minutes of the start of the opening kickoff. In the second game, his forward passing was so good that only once did he misjudge a throw. Against Otterbein, he was the "individual star of the game," according to the college newspaper: "He used splendid judgment in directing his play and kept his men on a fighting edge throughout."[7] A. H. Mahrt graduated magna cum laude with a B. A. on June 15, 1913 and went to work as an office clerk at Dayton Breweries for $9 a week.[8] A. H. Mahrt's best years of football were yet to come. In the fall of 1913, he became an advisory coach for St. Mary's College and played quarterback for the newly created Gym-Cadets.

In 1913 the *Cincinnati Enquirer* wrote,

Mahrt is a small cuss probably weighing no more than 138 pounds, but he has the nerve and gets away with many a great play that some less strong hearted warrior would not attempt. He evaded one Celt charge after another, and then when satisfied that the time was ripe, deliberately stepped in the midst of a bunch of huskies and tossed. The rest was easy.[9]

Sacksteder, Devereaux, and Mahrt each played professional football for a number of years. Norb Sacksteder went on to play until 1926 for such teams as the Massillon Tigers, the Detroit Heralds, the Detroit Tigers, the Canton Bulldogs, and the Dayton Triangles. Devereaux also played for Dayton and Detroit, and Mahrt starred with the Triangles through the 1923 season.

In 1915, the Dayton Gym-Cadets had many of the same players who had been with the team from its origins. Only Babe Zimmerman and Hugh Sacksteder reported giving up the game.[10] Like other semipro teams, the Gym-Cadets started their season after the first of October and played themselves into shape by scheduling weak teams at the beginning of the season and more competitive teams later. Though Dayton had a good team, they lacked the fan support necessary to be a statewide football powerhouse. They could schedule the few good teams that were willing to accept modest guarantees, but were unable to play top teams like Canton, Massillon, or Detroit, so they stood little chance of challenging for the state title.

Their first game, on October 10, at Westwood Field in Dayton against the Valley Athletic Club of Cincinnati, was never in doubt.[11] Norb Sacksteder made three touchdowns and negotiated several long end runs in the 50 to 0 rout.[12] One week later, North Cincinnati was also an easy win in the Cadets' first out-of-town game. Again, Norb Sacksteder scored two touchdowns in the 33 to 7 victory.[13]

Cadets manager Gessler completed the round robin of the Cincinnati teams by scheduling the Celts to play in Dayton on October 24. The Celts claimed to be the southern Ohio champions and held the Cadets to a scoreless tie. The Cadets had no trouble keeping the ball in Cincinnati territory, but the Celts stiffened when the Cadets got within scoring range.[14]

The Gym-Cadets traveled to Toledo on the first day in October. Both the Toledo Maroons and the Cadets were undefeated, and Toledo had just beaten the Columbus Panhandles in convincing fashion. With Ray Eichenlaub and Dutch Reule in the backfield, the Maroons were expected to have plenty of offense. The more relevant issue was whether or not the Gym-Cadet offensive line could get back on track. The answer came early in the first quarter when Norb Sacksteder received a punt on his one yard line and ran the entire length of the field for the first touchdown. Shortly after that, he scored a second touchdown on a pass from Mahrt, and before halftime Mahrt turned a Toledo fumble into a third touchdown. In the third period, the Maroons passed for a touchdown, but after that score the Cadet defense tightened up and Dayton won 20 to 7.[15] However, in the process of winning the game, Al Mahrt was injured.[16]

Dayton fans acknowledged that this was "the best team in Cadet history" and began to evaluate their chances for a state championship.[17] Their dream, however, was short-lived. On November 7, the Columbus Panhandles, led by five Nesser brothers, redefined the Cadets' season. On the first play from scrimmage, just forty seconds into the game, Norb Sacksteder ran sixty yards for a touchdown and Walters kicked the goal. It was to be the only scoring from the Cadets that afternoon. The Panhandles' defense keyed on Sacksteder and smothered the Cadets' running game, and, without Mahrt, Dayton had no passing game.[18]

The Panhandles dominated the game in the second half. A forty-five-yard pass from Pickerel to Fred Nesser resulted in the first Columbus touchdown. After the kickoff, Dayton intercepted a pass and punted out of danger, but the reprieve was temporary. In the fourth quarter, Pickerel completed a thirty-yard pass and, after three line plunges by Ted Nesser, the Panhandles went ahead 12 to 7, then scored two more touchdowns. The final score was Columbus 24, Dayton 7.[19] The loss to the Panhandles allowed Canton and Massillon to ignore the Gym-Cadets, and, without a game of that stature, Dayton had no prospect of a state championship.[20]

Unable to schedule a contender for the state title, Dayton had to be satisfied with a game against Peggy Parratt's Akron Indians. Parratt was having a bad year because his best players had been lured away to Massillon and Canton, and he negotiated this game on the strength of his past reputation. Although the Cadets won 39–0, no one took notice because Akron no longer resembled its 1914 state championship team.[21] After the Panhandles game, fan support waned. Dayton had not yet proven itself to be a strong Sunday football town, and, without paying customers or business subsidies, the Cadets were doomed to the backwaters of Ohio independent football.

The Gym-Cadets finished their 1915 season by playing local teams that gave them only token opposition. Norbert Sacksteder was lured away on November 22 to play for the Massillon Tigers. He finished the season with them,[22] although he did play with the Cadets on Thanksgiving Day against the West Carrollton Paper Company, an industrial team that drilled nightly under electric lights.[23] While playing West Carrollton, the Gym-Cadets discovered Lou Partlow, the best of a pair of brothers playing for the paper company, and recruited him to replace Sacksteder for their final game of the season against the Dayton Wolverines, which the Cadets won 20–0, ending the season with a 7–1–1 record.[24]

In the summer of 1916, F. B. McNab, an attorney with Dayton Engineering Laboratories, and Michael W. Redelle, manager of General Motors recreational activities in the city, approached their employers at General Motors about hiring Nelson Talbott to assist Redelle in directing sports programs. Talbott was born in the Gem City and recently graduated from Yale, where he was captain of the football team and a Walter Camp All-American at tackle. McNab hoped to save professional football in Dayton by using the resources of General Motors.

In the meantime, industrial leaders Colonel Edward A. Deeds of Dayton Metal Products and Charles F. Kettering of Dayton Engineering Laboratories purchased a sizable plot of land at the confluence of the Great Miami and Stillwater Rivers. The property was to be used as a recreation park for their companies, giving Redelle a focus for the employee recreational activities he coordinated. It was named Triangle Park because of its shape, and because it served three General Motors plants—Dayton Engineering Laboratories (later known as Delco), Dayton-Wright Aeroplane Manufacturing, and Dayton Metal Products. The property was not properly developed until 1917.[25]

McNab used the Triangle Park development to reorganize the Gym-Cadets.[26] It was clear to the St. Mary's Athletic Association that new leadership was needed to expand support beyond the Catholic Church if professional football was to survive and grow in Dayton. Triangle Park was a logical sponsor for this necessary transition.

When it came time to start practice for the 1916 season, nearly everyone on the 1915 Gym-Cadets team transferred their allegiance to the Dayton Triangles coached by Nelson Talbott and assisted by Carl "Dutch" Thiele.[27] Team backers wanted to ensure that Al Mahrt, star quarterback of the Gym-Cadets, would became part of the new team. When they offered him a better-paying position as accounts payable clerk for Dayton Metal Products, Mahrt gave up his $9 per week job with Dayton Breweries. Ambitious for further advancement at his new company, Mahrt studied accounting at the YMCA in the evenings.[28]

Dissident members of the Dayton Gym-Cadets management tried to field a team in Fort Wayne on September 30, 1916, but ended up using players from the Dayton Munitions industrial team. The Dayton Munitions boys were no match for the Fort Wayne Friars, who manhandled them 101 to 0.[29]

The Triangles opened their 1916 season in much the same manner as the Gym-Cadets had in 1915. They played a weaker than normal Cincinnati Northern team, whose key players were still engaged in minor league baseball. Once again, "the individual work of [Norb] Sacksteder stood out most prominently. . . ." and the Triangles won the game 72 to 0.[30]

On October 7, the Triangles faced Wellston, a team led by "Walters, who formerly played with the Gym-Cadets, and Joe Galigher, who starred as quarterback with the Christian Brothers team in St. Louis." They were ineffective against Norb Sacksteder, who scored three touchdowns in a 67–0 romp.[31]

As mid-October approached, Coach Talbott's drilling showed results, and the Triangles worked "in a more machinelike manner." The *Dayton Daily News* observed,

This is the first season that any local grid team has had the benefit of any real coaching, but under the tutelage of the former Yale captain they should develop into one of the best aggregations in the state. The return of Al Mahrt to his old time form and the addition of Zimmerman gives the team the much needed punch.[32]

Talbott and Redelle scheduled another easy game for Dayton on October 15. On a rainy day before a sparse crowd, the Triangles methodically dissected Elyria. Only a slippery ball and a muddy field held the score down in the Triangles' 20 to 0 win.[33]

Coach Talbott now believed his team "sound enough" to play some of the better pro teams in the region. Despite more wet weather that hampered outdoor practice, the Triangles felt ready to travel to Detroit on the 11:30 sleeper Saturday night to face the Heralds.[34] For the first time, the Triangles, who were still referred to as the Gym-Cadets by Detroit newspapers, were playing big league football before a sizable crowd. There were more than seven thousand fans at Navin Field, the summer home of the Detroit Tigers. The Heralds featured Kent "Skeet" Lambert from Wabash College, the Shields brothers from Michigan Wesleyan, Norman Glockson, an old pro, and Earl Dunn from Syracuse. They also started Bill "Chief" Newashe from Carlisle Institute, Nig Lennahan and Harry Schlee from the University of Detroit, and Percy Wilson from St. Louis University.[35]

The Triangles started Lee Fenner, Larry Dellinger, Arthur "Red" Murray, Lou Reese, Glen Tidd, Harry Cutler, Craig, Al Mahrt, Lou Partlow, Norb Sacksteder, and George "Babe" Zimmerman. Five of them had attended St. Mary's College, and all were hometown Dayton boys.[36] Dayton won the toss and chose to receive. Archie "Dutch" Stewart kicked off for Detroit, and Norb Sacksteder received the ball on his own ten yard line. With the wedge blocking of his teammates, he split the oncoming Heralds up the center of the field and ran ninety yards for a touchdown, "twisting, dodging and squirming his way to the goal line." Seconds later, Lou Reese added the extra point and, fifteen seconds into the game, Dayton led 7–0.[37]

Detroit tied the score in the second quarter when runs by Wilson and Lambert set up a forward pass from Skeet Lambert to Red Shields that resulted in a touchdown. Shields kicked goal to tie the game. The Triangles countered with a passing game of their own. Al Mahrt threw passes to Sacksteder and Lou Partlow that resulted in a Partlow touchdown in the second quarter. Again Lou Reese kicked goal. After going ahead, the Triangles played outstanding defense. At one point Detroit had four chances to score from the four yard line, but failed on all four attempts. Glen Tidd, Larry Dellinger, and Lou Reese were outstanding on defense.[38] The *Detroit Free Press* considered the 14–7 Dayton victory to be the best game held at Navin Field that season.[39] The upstart Triangles had entered the den of the Detroit Tigers baseball team and proved that the Triangles were no minor league football team. The Detroit newspapers were particularly impressed by Norbert Sacksteder and Al Mahrt. The *Free Press* called Sacksteder "the most sensational back that has ever been here. . . ." The *Free Press* called Al Mahrt "a wonderful quarter" and said,

[He] has even Lambert beaten for throwing the forward pass. They come out like a rifle shot and had the Dayton ends and backs been a little keener on the 'catch' there is no telling what might have happened to the Herald cause. He gets the ball to his man faster and with more accuracy than anybody who has ever raced around on the Detroit football greens.[40]

Fresh from their successful invasion of Detroit, the Triangles prepared to play the Altoona Indians on the following Sunday. Altoona was sometimes referred to as the "Panhandles of Pennsylvania," because, like Columbus, they traveled on free railroad passes supplied by the Pennsylvania Railroad System.[41]

The victory over Detroit fueled speculation about playing Canton, Massillon, or Cleveland. Hometown fan support for the Dayton Triangles and their predecessors the Dayton Gym-Cadets had never been very strong. It was hoped that attendance at the next two games—one against Altoona, the other against the Pitcairn Quakers—would be sufficient to host a major team like Detroit, Cleveland, Massillon, or Canton. If not, the Triangles would have to consider playing more games on the road.[42]

Altoona fielded fair to good independent football teams for more than a decade. The majority of their players were from Carlisle Institute, but some were from Susquehanna College, Penn State, or Bucknell. The Altoona Indians were not rated in the top echelon of pro teams in the nation, although they might have been ranked just outside the top twenty. They were willing to accept a relatively low guarantee because they had minimal travel costs and a payroll of less than $500. Without much effort, the Triangles defeated Altoona 33 to 0.[43] Unfortunately, only fifteen hundred fans paid admission to the game.

The first game in November attracted two thousand fans to see the Triangles play the Pitcairn Quakers, led by quarterback Frank S. White, who had been captain of the Indiana Normal College football team in Indiana, Pennsylvania, in 1914.[44] The Quakers lost close games to Canton, Cleveland, and Youngstown during the month of October. Like the other contenders for the state championship, the Triangles defeated the Quakers by the narrowest of margins, 7 to 3. Norb Sacksteder scored the only touchdown in the first quarter on a pass from Al Mahrt.[45]

The home games against the two Keystone State teams demonstrated once again that fan support for Sunday football in Dayton lagged significantly behind Cleveland, Canton, Massillon, Youngstown, and Detroit. On November 13, 1916, the *Dayton Daily News* reported it unlikely that the Triangles would be given an opportunity to play Canton and, therefore, would not be seriously considered for the state title.

The Triangles traveled to Toledo on November 12 to play the Maroons, who supported a 6–1 record, having lost only to the Massillon

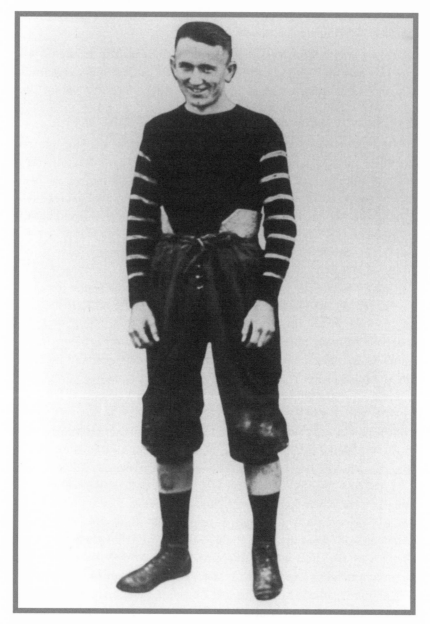

Frank S. White, captain of the 1914 Indiana Normal School football team of
Indiana, Pennsylvania, was quarterback for the Pitcairn Quakers in 1916–17
and played one game at halfback for the Massillon Tigers in 1916. *(Indiana, University of Pennsylvania Archives.)*

Tigers, 15–7. Moreover, they were just coming off a 23 to 7 win over the Columbus Panhandles and were believed to be a contender for the state title. The game was hard fought throughout. Toledo shut down the Triangles' running game by keying on Norb Sacksteder. Dayton responded by playing an open game with a strong emphasis on the forward pass. Toledo's star halfback John Barrett played the game injured, and Toledo frequently resorted to the quick kick to stay out of danger. Dayton scored three times: Lou Partlow scored a touchdown for the Triangles in the second quarter, and, in the final quarter, Al Mahrt used the forward pass to set up two field goals. In the last minute of play, substitute fullback McCorkle broke his leg and was lost for the season.[46]

On November 19, the Celts journeyed to Dayton to play their chief rival at Westwood Field. The only score of the game came in the second quarter when passes from Mahrt to Partlow and Sacksteder set up a ten-yard run by Partlow. Dayton prevailed 6 to 0.[47]

In a return match the following week in Cincinnati, the Triangles finally bowed. Their unbeaten season was lost in the third quarter when a field goal by Celts' halfback Keene Palmer locked up the 10–7 win for Cincinnati. The fierce contest was dominated by Celts' stars George Roudebush, the famous Denison College star, who scored a touchdown, and Albert "Whitey" Bessmeyer, a University of Cincinnati graduate who was outstanding on defense. The Dayton score came on a defensive play when an attempted Celts pass was fumbled and was picked up by lineman Earl Stoecklein, who ran forty yards for the touchdown.[48]

Following the second Celts game, Norb Sacksteder signed a contract to play for the Detroit Heralds. While with Dayton in 1916, Norb scored 86 of 243 points, or thirty-five percent of the points tallied by the Triangles. He scored one or more touchdowns in each of the first six games of the season. Only when teams began to key their defenses against Sacksteder did Lou Partlow become the primary scorer. Over those same nine games, Partlow accounted for 60 points, or twenty-five percent of Dayton's points. Without question, Sacksteder's running set up the Dayton passing game. During the first nine games of the season, the Triangles had thirty-three scoring drives. Forward passes played an important role in fifteen of these scoring drives, and Norb Sacksteder was one of the primary targets in Al Mahrt's passing game.

The final game of the 1916 Triangles' football season was played on Thanksgiving Day at Westwood Field. Carl "Scummy" Storck, who had been attending George Williams YMCA College in Chicago, returned home for the holiday and was signed to take Norb Sacksteder's place in the Dayton lineup.[49]

Scummy Storck was born in Dayton, Ohio, in 1893, and attended Stivers High School where he played football and basketball. As a high school fullback, he was extremely fast and was hard to tackle because he ran with his knees high. He graduated from Stivers in the spring of 1913 and, later that year, enrolled at George Williams College in Chicago. Scummy occasionally played for the Dayton Gym-Cadets while in college, particularly at Thanksgiving time or when he was home for the long weekend.[50] Despite his willingness to play, however, Scummy never made it into the final game of the 1916 Triangle season against the Pitcairn Quakers. Instead, Pie Decker and Babe Zimmerman did the honors. Lou Partlow, who scored two touchdowns, and Lee Fenner, who was outstanding on defense, were the stars in the 20 to 9 Dayton victory.[51]

Scummy Storck was poised to play an important part in the Dayton Triangles' future, however. When he completed his degree at George Williams YMCA College in the spring of 1917, Scummy returned to Dayton, where Mike Redelle hired him to be assistant manager of the Triangle Park recreation program. Redelle enlisted in the U.S. Army in 1918, and Storck took his place as director until the war was over. In that role, he helped manage the Dayton Triangles and, when the American Professional Football Association was formed in 1920, Scummy and Mike Redelle purchased the franchise for Dayton. In 1922, when the National Football League was created out of the APFA, Storck was elected to be secretary-treasurer for the NFL. He became president of the NFL in 1939, when Joe Carr died.

The entrance of the United States into World War I was already having an impact on professional football when the Dayton Triangles opened their 1917 season. Nelson Talbott had been one of the first to join the army and was now coaching and playing at Camp Sherman. A patriotic motif was used to launch Dayton's professional football season in a game against the 42nd Aviation Squad from Wright Field in Dayton. In hopes of enticing baseball fans to the home opener, the Triangles featured a play-by-play account of the World Series by megaphone before the game and at halftime. The megaphone service was also resumed during any lull in the football game so that the fans attending the game would not miss the World Series results. An airplane flew by to drop a football on the field to start the game.[52]

The starting lineup for Dayton had a couple of new faces in it.

George "Hobby" Kinderdine started the game at center. Hobby played high school football in Miamisburg, Ohio, and had a long career with the Triangles. He and his brother Harry B. "Shine" Kinderdine, whose nickname was acquired in grade school when he was a shoe shine boy,[53] had played for the Dayton Gym-Cadets in 1915. George Kinderdine's pro football career would not end until 1929.[54] Carl "Scummy" Storck started at fullback, Dick Abrell[55] from Purdue University started at right halfback, and John Devereaux was the starting right end.

The *Dayton Daily News* reported that "The Triangle football squad literally 'flew' away from the boys of the 42nd Aviation squad. . . ." Lou Partlow was the most prominent player for the Triangles, scoring three touchdowns. Scummy Storck scored two touchdowns, and passes from Al Mahrt to Devereaux and Collins also resulted in touchdowns.[56]

After two easy games, the Triangles were scheduled to play the Toledo Maroons. George "Babe" Zimmerman decided to end his retirement from football to help his former teammates put together a winning season. A crowd of more than two thousand (the *Toledo Blade* said five thousand) fans welcomed the Maroons at Triangle Park. The Maroons received the initial kickoff, but were unable to move the ball against the stonewall defense of the Triangles. After an exchange of punts, Al Mahrt threw a pass to Babe Zimmerman, who carried the ball over for a touchdown. The Triangles missed the extra point. Neither team threatened to score in the second quarter, but in the third quarter another pass from Mahrt to Zimmerman gained forty yards, and the same combination on the next play gave the Triangles their second touchdown. Later in the quarter, Zimmerman kicked a field goal to make the final score 15 to 0.[57]

On the last Sunday in October, the Triangles were scheduled to play the Cleveland Tomahawks, a semipro industrial team. The game was canceled because of a heavy rainstorm on Saturday, in order to save the field and avoid financial losses from a poor turnout.[58] Though the Tomahawks required a low guarantee, at an admission price of fifty cents one thousand fans were required to break even.

The McKeesport Olympics, led by William Clay and Stanley and Frank Graf, rode the train in from Pittsburgh for a game on the first Sunday in November. The McKeesport team held Dayton in check for the first half before three thousand fans. Early in the first quarter, the Triangles scored on a pass from Mahrt to Devereaux. Devereaux kicked the extra point, and Dayton led 7–0. With Zimmerman on hand, Storck had only limited playing time. In the second quarter, Mahrt was sidelined with a knee injury. His absence from the lineup put a damper on the Triangle offense. However, when Mahrt went back into action in the third quarter, his passing broke the game wide open. Partlow and Devereaux were his favorite receivers, and both scored touchdowns in the third period. Partlow added another touchdown in the final quarter for a 27–0 win.[59]

On November 11, the Triangles met the toughest team on their schedule, the Cincinnati Celts. The Celts had lost to the Detroit Heralds and the Fort Wayne Friars, but tied the fabled Pine Village Athletic Club in Lafayette, Indiana, and beat the Pitcairn Quakers 7 to 6 the previous Sunday. The Celts and the Triangles were natural foes, because of their geographic proximity. The Celts figured to have a powerful line, so the Triangles' game plan centered on Mahrt's passing skills. The Celts, who traditionally wore bright green jerseys, came to Dayton with red jerseys.[60]

Dayton won the toss and received the ball. Shortly after the initial kickoff, Babe Zimmerman fumbled, and the Celts took over with good field position. A defensive battle ensued. After several exchanges of the ball, Partlow drove the Triangles into scoring position, but Devereaux missed an attempt for field goal. The two teams played even until the third quarter, when the Celts opened up their game with a series of passes. As the Celts threatened, they threw one pass too many. Mahrt intercepted it, and the Triangles mounted a counterdrive. After Partlow failed to gain ground on an end run, Mahrt broke loose for a twenty-five-yard run, but the drive stalled. At one point, the Triangles succeeded in kicking a field goal, but it was called back because of a holding penalty. After four quarters of grueling football, the game ended in a scoreless tie.[61]

On November 18, the Triangles played in Toledo. They were short-handed because of injuries to Devereaux and Shine Kinderdine. In the course of the game, Cutler was sidelined with a broken nose, and Abrell was injured and could not play the second half. Nevertheless, the Dayton team was brilliant throughout. Lee Fenner caught three touchdown passes, and Hobby Kinderdine scored a defensive touchdown.[62]

The Triangles traveled to Cincinnati on November 25 for a rematch with the Celts. Cincinnati took the lead in the first quarter when Mahrt fumbled an attempted punt and Celt lineman Williams picked up the ball and took it in for a touchdown. In the second period, the Triangles tied the Celts on a touchdown from the two yard line by Lou Partlow and an extra point by Zimmerman. Neither team could score for the balance of the game.[63]

As a result of their second tie, the Celts and Triangles agreed to play one final game in Dayton on December 1. The third match-up between the two teams was never close. Three thousand fans watched the Triangles score on a pass from Mahrt to Partlow in the first period. In the fourth quarter, Zimmerman tallied again on a short run. The Celts never threatened to score against the Triangles.

Dayton ended its season undefeated. The Triangles scored 188 points, their opponents only 13 points. Under ordinary circumstances, the Triangles deserved an opportunity to play for the state professional football championship, but weak fan support kept them from playing a stronger schedule since they could not afford a large enough guarantee to make a game with Canton, Massillon, or Detroit feasible. Hence, the undefeated record was suspect because the Triangles had few real tests of their ability. Although they deserved a good ranking among the best pro teams, they ranked no higher than fifth in the nation on the basis of their schedule.

The Dayton Triangles were a charter member of the American Professional Football Association and the National Football League. Their franchise was sold to the Brooklyn Dodgers on May 12, 1930.[64]

12. The Detroit Heralds:
Like a Ford in Heavy Traffic

Virtually all evidence of the once proud Detroit Heralds has been obliterated in trash dumps and fires. Only old newspapers give testimony that the team ever existed. The Heralds were organized, in 1905, by William H. Marshall and several fellow Detroit College players, when, because of a fiscal crunch, the college was unable to field a team.[1] After World War I, the University of Detroit had a nationally ranked football program that, starting in 1925, was under the stewardship of Athletic Director Charles "Gus" Dorais. However, for the first decade of the twentieth century, the Detroit College varsity—nicknamed "the Tigers"—played high school, freshmen, YMCA, and small college teams and could not even field a team in 1905 and 1908.[2] So the idea that a group of players from that school could start a professional football team seems farfetched. Nevertheless, the Heralds adopted the red and white team colors of Detroit College and began playing at Belle Isle, where games had to be stopped every few plays to push the crowd back. The team was supported by passing the hat. In 1909, William Marshall and Bernard "Bertie" Maher graduated from Detroit College, after playing a successful basketball season as starters for the Detroit College Tigers.[3] In 1910, the Heralds were still referred to in the newspapers as an amateur team, when they won the city independent football championship.[4] The following year, Bertie Maher called signals for the Heralds, and they won both the city and state independent football championships.[5]

On November 5, 1911, the Heralds became a semiprofessional football team when they began playing at the newly built Mack Park baseball field on the far east side of Detroit. Mack Park was built by John A. Roesink on land owned by the Webb Realty Company. Opened May 22, 1910, it was fenced in, had wooden grandstands that seated five thousand for football, and was designed so that admission could be charged, games and players publicized, and baseball and football teams

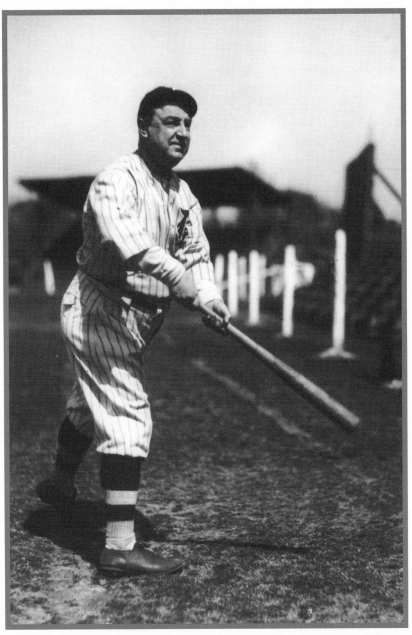

John A. Roesink, leaseholder of Mack Park in Detroit, organizer of the Mack Park Maroons, and business agent for the Detroit Heralds from 1916–1922. In 1926, when this picture was taken at Mack Park, Roesink owned the Detroit Stars of the Negro National Baseball League. *(The Archives of Labor and Urban Affairs, Wayne State University.)*

could be managed as businesses.[6] In later years, the Detroit Stars of the Negro National Baseball League would play their home games at Mack Park.[7]

William H. Marshall, no relation to Billy Marshall in Toledo, became business manager-coach for the Heralds when the team moved to Mack Park. Marshall was a mediocre halfback at Detroit College (soon to be the University of Detroit) and for the Detroit Heralds. He was a good "line plunger," but he did not possess the natural speed or broken field running ability of a first-class back. However, he was trusted by his fellow players, was a good coach, and became a decent business manager.[8] In 1913, the Heralds became the first independent football team in America to wear numbers on their jerseys.[9] Prior to 1914, the Heralds played few teams from outside the Michigan-Windsor area, with games against Ann Arbor, Bay City, the Cleveland Tomahawks, the Detroit Argonauts, the Detroit Myrtles, and the Detroit Morrells being the most challenging.

There were innumerable problems in running an independent football team in the first two decades of the twentieth century. The careers of promising players were cut short by parental objections, sometimes because of fear of injury,[10] other times because they did not want their sons playing football on Sunday.[11] Games had to be scheduled; fields rented; players recruited, drilled, and coached. Marshall solved those problems on a regular basis, but his business sense did not always go unchallenged.

In 1901, John Aaron Roesink, a promising young baseball player, was transferred from Grand Rapids, Michigan, to Detroit, where he was engaged as the display and advertising manager for a clothing store.[12] On August 10, 1903, he married the store's bookkeeper and the following year returned to Grand Rapids to work at Grand Rapids Dry Goods Company.[13] He returned to Detroit in 1909, formed a semiprofessional baseball team, and began making plans to become a sports promoter. The following year, Roesink built the Mack Park baseball field at Mack Avenue and Fairview on Detroit's east side, and, in November 1911, he invited the Detroit Heralds to make it their home field. This invitation was instrumental in the creation of Detroit's first venture into professional football. When, in 1913, the Federal League attempted to lease or buy Mack Park to place a rival major league baseball team in Detroit, Roesink refused the deal and ingratiated himself with Frank J. Navin, the owner of the Detroit Tigers.[14] In 1914, Roesink decided to form the Mack Park Maroons and forced the Detroit Heralds to seek out Packard

Tom Moriarity, tackle for Detroit Mack Park Maroons in 1915 and Camp Custer in 1917, graduated from Georgetown University and was an assistant coach at the University of Detroit in 1915. *(Georgetown University Special Collections.)*

Leon C. Exelby, end, Detroit Mack Park Maroons 1915, was All-Western in 1910 for Michigan Agricultural College and considered by many as the most consistent two-way end in the school's history. *(Michigan State University Archives and Historical Collections.)*

Park, a mile west at Mack and Seminole, as their home field.[15] In prior years, after the close of the baseball season, Packard Park had featured soccer rather than football.[16]

At the same time as the Detroit Heralds were emerging as Detroit's new, semiprofessional football powerhouse, Bernard "Bertie" Maher, a former Detroit College football hero, was establishing himself as their star player.[17] In 1915, Roesink apparently decided that the Detroit Heralds were drawing too many fans away from Mack Park to Packard Field and cutting into his potential gate, so he offered to make Bertie the player-coach of his Mack Park Maroons, with a view to drawing Sunday football fans back to his venue. Bertie Maher was delighted with the opportunity to coach his own team and persuaded a couple of his teammates to switch teams with him.[18] In its second year of operation, the Mack Park Maroons would be the equal of any independent team in Michigan,[19] particularly when Bertie Maher and Cyril Moran were joined by new recruits Tom Moriarity from Georgetown, who was coaching at the University of Detroit; Faunt "Dutch" Lenardson, All-Western in 1913 from Michigan Agricultural College; and several University of Michigan players.[20]

Even after the defection of Maher, the Heralds had Richard and Guy Shields (with the team since 1911), Archie "Dutch" Stewart, Harry Schlee, and Percy Latham from their 1914 starting lineup. Despite the schism, the Heralds still had a good team. Late in September 1915, the Heralds once again took up residence at Packard Park and began the serious business of preparing for the season ahead. After practicing on September 26, 27, and October 2, the Heralds opened their season at their home park against an industrial team from Cleveland, the Erin Brauns.[21] The Heralds started Richard Shields and Joseph Malcomson—who had been a track star at Detroit University School—at ends, Guy Shields and Harry Schlee at tackles, Bill "Chief" Newashe and Webster Pierce at guards, Archie "Dutch" Stewart at center, and Percy Latham, Percy Wilson, Gerald Kelly, and Earl Dunn in the backfield[22] (although, on the Monday after the game, the two Detroit newspapers did not fully agree on who had played for the Heralds).

Meanwhile, the Detroit Mack Park Maroons, with Leon C. Exelby, the 1910 second team All-Western star from Michigan Agriculture College, at end, played host to the Toledo Glenwoods and eked out a 7–0 win.[23] The season opener also went well for the Heralds. Joseph Malcomson, the 1909 national Amateur Athletic Union 220-yard low-hurdles champion for the Seattle Athletic Club,[24] and Gerald Kelly led the Heralds to a 34–0 win over Erin Braun. The Heralds amassed 27 points in the first two quarters and used the rest of the game trying out new plays and practicing teamwork.

On October 10, the Akron Indians were scheduled to play the Mack Park Maroons, and the Cincinnati Celts were scheduled to play the Heralds. However, on Thursday, Peggy Parratt called to report that his best players had been lured away by Massillon and Canton "with exorbitant salaries," making it necessary for Akron to cancel the game. On Saturday, the Celts also canceled because their quarterback was sick, and no one else could call signals.[25] The Maroons quickly replaced Akron with the Buffalo Oakdales, but the Heralds were forced to sit idle.

On the Saturday before the game, the Mack Park Maroons finally signed the three University of Michigan alumni who had made a commitment to play for them—Frank McHale, Tom Bogle, and John Lyons.[26] The three Michigan stars were immediately placed in the Maroons' starting lineup for the game against Buffalo. After a scoreless first half, the Maroons scored two touchdowns but could not master the punt-out for the goal after. Mack Park defeated Buffalo 12–0.[27]

The Heralds practiced on Tuesday after work, and prepared to play the Cincinnati Celts the following Sunday. The Maroons prepared for the Blepp Knits, an industrial team from Cleveland.[28]

The Heralds and the Celts played a torrid game. The Heralds' first touchdown came early in the encounter on a pass from Percy Wilson to Dick Shields, but the extra point was missed. Detroit continued to dominate the first half, but in the third quarter the tables turned. The Celts gained three times as much territory as the Heralds and were able to stop three drives inside their own ten yard line. Finally, Thomas Gaither, the strong Celts halfback, tied the score. At one point, it seemed almost certain that the Celts would go ahead, but Chief Newashe recovered a Celts fumble near the goal line to avert a second Cincinnati score. With less than three minutes left in the game, the three thousand fans saw the hometown team surge ahead on a thirty-five-yard pass from quarterback Latham to captain Dick Shields, the red-headed end for Detroit.[29] The final score was 12–6 in favor of Detroit.

On their Sunday morning sports page, the *Detroit News Tribune* expressed its displeasure with Bertie Maher for leaving the Heralds, with a headline that said, "Professional Base Ball Cannot Touch Semi-Pro Football for Jumping Acts: Managers Never Know Just When Their Teams Will Hop To Another Park For Better Pay."[30] Although there was no accompanying story, the meaning was clear to all its readers. Despite the criticism, a determined Maroons team scored on a line plunge by Tacks Harding, the Detroit fullback, after a scoreless first quarter. A defensive struggle ensued. On three occasions, the Maroons drove within scoring position against the Cleveland Blepp Knits, only to have Tom Bogle miss field goals. Jimmy Mount, playing his first game for the Maroons, ripped off tackle to set up a touchdown by Bertie Maher in the final frame. The Maroons defeated Cleveland 13–0.[31]

The first games of the season had been designed to help the Detroit teams get into shape and practice teamwork. All of the better teams followed the same strategy. The games scheduled for October 24 would finally test the mettle of the Heralds and the Mack Park Maroons: they were about to play host to the best teams in Ohio, the Canton Bulldogs and the Massillon Tigers.

The Mack Park Maroons matched up well with the Massillon Tigers. Both were new to big time independent football. Massillon had not fielded a major independent team since 1907, and the Mack Park Maroons had never before been considered a major team. Both squads were now dominated by former college players, and the balance of the players were seasoned independent football pros. Massillon featured Knute Rockne, Keith "Deac" Jones, and Joe Collins from Notre Dame; Jim Flynn, Edmund Kagy, Cass, and Dwight Wertz from Western Reserve; and E. M. Cole from the University of Michigan. Arrayed against them for Detroit were the products of Michigan colleges in Tacks Harding, Danny Mullane, and Bertie Maher from the University of Detroit; Hadden, Art Cornwell, and Thomas Bogle from the University of Michigan; Ty Krentler from Kalamazoo Normal College; Faunt Lenardson from Michigan Agricultural College; and Jimmy Monat from the Detroit Athletic Club.[32]

The Massillon Tigers and the Mack Park Maroons played fine football for the large crowd that paid fifty cents each to see the game. The first quarter was an even battle, although Homer Davidson tried a field goal for the Tigers. As the game wore on, however, the Massillon line outplayed the Maroons line. On the first play of the second quarter, after a Detroit offside call, Edmund Kagy scored a touchdown for Massillon. The extra point failed, leaving the score 6–0. Toward the end of the third quarter, the Maroons took the ball on their own thirty yard line. A long pass from Bertie Maher was caught by Ty Krentler, who outran the defense for the tying touchdown. When Bogle made the extra point, Detroit took a 7–6 lead. In the fourth quarter, Massillon, undertook a drive that stalled inside the twenty yard line. Davidson again missed a twenty-two-yard kick from a poor angle. Later in the quarter, Kagy drove the ball to the twelve yard line, and Davidson kicked a field goal. Bogle had one last chance to beat Massillon on a forty-yard field goal, but it missed by inches.[33] Mack Park lost to Massillon 9–7 in one of the best-played games of the season.

Meanwhile, at Packard Park the Canton Bulldogs fielded a solid team that had Howard Axtell and Bill Gardner at ends, Howard Edwards and Dutch Powell at tackles, Whitey Schultz and Bill Dagenhart at guards, and Ralph "Fats" Waldsmith at center. In the backfield, the Bulldogs started Don Hamilton at quarterback, Ed Iddings and George "Carp" Julian at halfbacks, and Don Peters at fullback. Lined up against them were Dick Shields, Guy Shields, Mitchell, Archie Stewart, Bill "Chief" Newashe, Harry Schlee, and Norman "Tango" Glockson in the line, and Latham, Kelly, Wilson, and Dunn in the backfield for the Heralds.

Canton jumped out to a three-point lead on a thirty eight yard field goal by Don Hamilton from the right side of the field. In the second quarter, the Heralds responded by scoring a touchdown on a pass from Wilson to Dick Shields for a 6–3 lead. Canton's right side proved to be weak, and the Heralds exploited that weakness both offensively and defensively. Chief Newashe, Harry Schlee, and Tango Glockson had a wonderful day. In the third quarter, Shields kicked a third field goal. The final score was 9–3.[34] The *Detroit Times* called the Heralds-Bulldogs game "the most spectacular independent game in the history of local football."[35]

The Heralds would not have much time to savor their victory over Canton. Their next game was against the Evanston North Ends, arguably the best team in independent football in 1913, 1914, and the first half of the 1915 season. In 1913, Evanston beat Detroit. In November of 1914, the North Ends and Heralds played again. To offset the possibility of a small purse resulting from low attendance, the teams bet $1000 on the results, and, when the game ended in a scoreless tie, both teams lost money.[36] Now, in hopes of recouping their losses from the previous year, Ruben Johnson and his blue-collar team bet several hundred dollars of their own money that they would beat the Heralds. Coach Bill Marshall and his team immediately took a big slice of the 1915 bet themselves.[37]

The North Ends had no college players on their team, but they did have some of the most talented independent football players in America. Rube Johnson was an outstanding athlete with extraordinary kicking and passing skills. It was not unusual for him to punt fifty or more yards and to drop-kick from thirty or forty yards out. In addition, Guilford "Hawk" Falcon could run as well as any fullback in football. Robert Specht was as good as any college-trained halfback, and Henry Kilby was a solid all-around player.

At 3:00 P.M. on Halloween Day, the North Ends took the field at Packard Park. The battle between these two great teams surged back and forth for three quarters. In the first half, the teams played evenly. Evanston was more interested in maintaining control of the ball than in scoring. Their strategy was to wear down the Heralds. At one point, Archie Stewart blocked a Reuben Johnson punt, but the North Ends defender dropped on the ball to avoid a Heralds' touchdown. Johnson's punts usually carried sixty-five or seventy yards and provided good field position to the North Ends. Reuben Johnson made the difference in the game: in the fourth quarter, he took charge. He ran forty yards on a fine sweeping run from a fake kick formation. Then two forward passes from Johnson to Pascolini yielded thirty-five yards. Finally the Evanston leader sprinted around end for the final ten yards and the only score of the game. Evanston left Detroit that evening with nearly $1500 of Motor City money.[38]

Across town, the Mack Park Maroons were playing a disappointingly poor opponent. The Peggy Parratt eleven paraded this week as the Shelby Blues and the week after as the Akron Indians. The Ohio team brought decent players, but they had never practiced together, much less played together. The 21–0 victory for the Maroons was no surprise. Maher made two touchdowns, and Ty Krentler scored the third.[39]

The Heralds faced another good team on November 7. The Lancaster (NY) Malleables, who called themselves the champions of New York, played the Heralds to a scoreless tie.[40] On Saturday, Neno "Jerry" Da Prato, All-American halfback and the leading scorer in college football, had been the principal ball carrier for the Michigan Aggies against Marquette University.[41] The following day, he came down from East Lansing to play for Detroit, but he retired at the end of the first half. Da Prato did not have enough energy left to play his normal game.[42]

The Detroit Mack Park Maroons also played the Ann Arbor Independents to a scoreless tie on November 7 at home. The Maroons had been defeated by Ann Arbor in 1914 and hoped to do better this year. Comprised principally of former University of Michigan players, the Independents proved to be a good match. Eberwein and Dutch Reule were the leading ground gainers for Ann Arbor. Ty Krentler made a thirty-three-yard run for Detroit, and a pass from Maher to Krentler resulted in a twenty-one-yard gain, but neither breakout resulted in a serious scoring opportunity.[43]

The Maroons' next opponent was the Columbus Panhandles with the six Nesser brothers. Perhaps the best known independent football players of the era, according to newspaper reports, "these brothers average over 200 pounds and are among the cleverest exponents of . . . [and] the biggest draw in football." The Maroons strengthened their backfield by hiring Parcell and Gus Toumey, both former University of Detroit backs.[44] To their credit, the Maroons held the Panhandles scoreless for three of the four quarters of their game at Mack Park on November 14. Ted, Frank, and Fred Nesser played with power and strength few had witnessed before, yet the Maroons held their own. The only lapse of the game came in the final seconds of the second quarter when the Maroons tried to punt out of their own end zone. The

William Blake Miller, end and halfback, Detroit Heralds 1915–16, 1919–20; Camp Custer 1917; Detroit Panthers 1921. He won nine letters and All-American honors at Michigan Agricultural College before being barred from college athletics for playing pro football. He was an assistant coach at MAC in 1919 and, later, a golf pro for the Lansing Country Club. *(Michigan State University Archives and Historical Collections.)*

hike from center hit the ground before reaching Tom Bogle, the punter. Bogle tried to pick up the ball, but it bounded away from him, and Oscar Kuehner of the Panhandles fell on the pigskin for a touchdown.[45]

Toumey had to be replaced early in the contest after making a jarring tackle on J. Lee Snoots, the Panhandle left halfback. Snoots got up; Toumey did not. Cornwell and Maher were also injured trying to tackle the Nesser brothers and had to leave the game. Most of the game was played on the ground. The Maroons completed only three passes for a total of fifty-eight yards. The Panhandles completed only one pass, for a one-yard gain.[46] The Maroons threatened to tie the game on three occasions when they made it inside the Panhandles' fifteen yard line. On each occasion the Panhandles held, winning the game 7–0.

At Packard Park, the Heralds faced the Buffalo All-Stars. Two Michigan Agricultural College all-conference stars, who were still in college, played for the Heralds: Neno "Jerry" Da Prato and William Blake Miller entered Michigan Agricultural College in 1911 and played together on the freshman team.[47] In mid-November 1915, when their college football careers were over, these college roommates decided to play for the Heralds. Both were all-around athletes, and Miller had earned nine varsity letters.[48] They played on the M.A.C. basketball team, and Blake Miller was also on the baseball team, but their first love was football. As a result of playing in this game, both were declared ineligible for future college athletics.[49] Blake Miller,[50] a native of Tonawanda, New York, went on to become assistant coach at Michigan Agricultural College in 1919.

The Heralds routed the Buffalo All-Stars 69–0. Everyone on the Heralds team enjoyed success. Dick Shields, Earl Dunn, Percy Wilson, Jerry Da Prato, Larry Nedeau, Ed Schlee, and G. Herbert "Hubby" Weekes each scored a touchdown, William Blake Miller scored three, and Jerry Da Prato made nine extra points. As the *Detroit Free Press* reported, the Heralds also had plenty of time to experiment with "fan formations, intricate shifts, and spoiled plays out of which came forward passes, kicks, end runs, split plays and everything conceivable. It was a good exhibition of diversified attack" that had Buffalo mystified all afternoon.[51]

The most important game of the 1915 season in Detroit came on November 21 at Packard Park, when the Mack Park Maroons and the Detroit Heralds met to determine the best team in the city and the state. It was the culmination of the season for the Detroit fans. Going into the game, the analysts figured that the Maroons "had the better line," but the Heralds "offset this in backfield and on the flanks."[52] Nearly eight thousand people paid fifty cents each to see the game. The winning team was to get 70 percent of the gate. The Maroons scored early in the first quarter on a run by Bertie Maher. About eight minutes into the game, Jerry Da Prato punted the ball for the Heralds, and it came down beyond the Maroons' goal line. Parcell, who was playing safety, received the ball. Unaware of where he was on the field, he attempted to run the ball out of the end zone, even though three Heralds' players were closing in on him. As he crossed the goal line, he was hit and driven back for a safety, which gave the Heralds two points. This mistake turned out to be the deciding factor in the game. In the second quarter, Da Prato threw a pass to Dick Shields. When the Heralds successfully kicked goal, that settled the final score at 9–7. The importance of Parcell's "boner" was not lost on Detroit newspapermen. All three dailies compared Parcell's misplay to Fred Merkle's failure to touch second base that cost the New York Giants the National League Pennant, or to Snodgrass's muff in the 1912 World Series. They reminded their readers that Parcell's "idiot play" cost the loser heavily in real money and a chance for the city title.[53] Happy to have survived the Maroons game with a 5–1–1 record, the Heralds ended their season in the black as a result of the $2800 earned on November 21.

The Maroons' accounting ledger, on the other hand, was still in the red, so they suited up on Thanksgiving Day to play the Toledo Maroons in Armory Park in Toledo. Detroit scored first in the second quarter when Moriarity intercepted a forward pass, taking it to the Toledo three yard line, and, on the next play, Purcell powered off tackle for a touchdown. Toledo tied the score in the third quarter when Ray Eichenlaub, the former Notre Dame fullback, burst through left tackle on a forty-yard touchdown run. The game ended in a 6–6 tie.[54] It was the last professional game for Purcell.

The 1915 season was a costly one for both the Heralds and the Mack Park Maroons. The competition for players, fans, and opponents had left both teams in a precarious financial situation, so John Roesink and William H. Marshall joined forces in 1916 in an effort to elevate professional football to the status of major league baseball. Roesink became the Heralds' business manager and arranged to have them play their games at Navin Field. William Marshall remained team president and coach. The Mack Park Maroons continued to play semiprofessional football, but they did not answer the call as an interstate professional team for the 1916 season.[55]

In 1916, the Ford Motor Company entered into an arrangement with Carlisle Institute to conduct an apprenticeship program for Native Americans. Among the students apprenticed to Ford were Pete Calac and some forty other Carlisle Indians who had played football under Pop Warner at the well-known Pennsylvania school. These ex-Carlisle football men started a professional football team in Detroit. Though they had no home field, they did manage to schedule games with the Detroit Heralds, Flint, and Fort Wayne.

Bill Marshall's Detroit Heralds opened their season against the Detroit ex-Carlisles on September 30 at Navin Field, the summertime home of the Detroit Tigers. The ex-Carlisles lineup included Lookaround, Woffert, Potter, Black Bird, Morrin, Briler, and Two Guns. All-American Pete Calac would join the team later in the season.[56] The Heralds' lineup included a number of former Mack Park Maroons such as Art Cornwell, Ty Krentler, and Bertie Maher, who were now playing side by side with Dick Shields, Archie Stewart, Larry Nedeau, Percy Latham, and Norman "Tango" Glockson. The Heralds played poorly. Their tackling in the first half was miserable, and their offense sputtered. Only the ineffective play of the Ex-Carlisles allowed Dick Shields and Earl Dunn to score the touchdowns that gave the Heralds a 12–0 victory.[57]

On October 1, the Heralds announced that Kent "Skeet" Lambert would be the new quarterback. Unfortunately, he had no time to work out with the team and establish signals before his first starting assignment against the Cincinnati Celts on October 8. Lambert was an all-around athlete, who also played alongside Jim Thorpe for the Canton Bulldogs when they defeated the Massillon Tigers for the world's professional football championship.[58] He was a skilled passer who invented intentional grounding to avoid a sack.[59] His complete knowledge of the game made him an outstanding field general at a time when quarterbacks, not coaches, determined play selection and game plan adjustments.

On October 8, Navin Park was hot as a baking oven. It was a day better fit for swimming than for football. Prior to the Celts game, the Heralds added Frank Gardner, who had been a teammate of Jim Thorpe at Canton and an All-American end at Carlisle.[60] For three quarters, neither the Heralds nor the Celts could score. In the first quarter, Tilly Schuessler, captain of the Celts, intercepted four Heralds passes. On one occasion, he returned the ball to the doorstep of the Heralds' goal only to have the Celts quarterback fumble, allowing Lambert to save a touchdown by recovering it. In the second quarter, the Heralds started substituting generously to offset the effects of the heat. The Celts threatened again in that quarter, and again fumbled the ball, which was recovered by Dick Shields. Later, Schuessler intercepted another pass and raced for the Heralds' goal line, but was stopped short. A forward pass thrown by Thomas Gaither towards Chet Knab was intercepted at the last second by Lambert, and Dick Shields then punted out of danger.

At the start of the second half, Latham replaced Lambert to give him a rest. Two plays later, Latham intercepted a Celts pass, but, after a Heralds punt, the Celts made another drive toward the Heralds' goal. They reached Detroit's thirteen yard line before their drive stalled.[61] Lambert came back into the game in the fourth quarter. Shortly after that, according to a *Detroit News* reporter, "Lambert stepped back and hurled a beautiful forward pass to Dick Shields, who caught it with the Cincinnati defense behind him and raced over for the first touchdown." It was a thirty-four-yard gain but a forty-six-yard pass. Following the extra point, Cincinnati received the kickoff and, after three plays, was forced to punt. On the following plays, the Heralds rushed the ball into scoring territory, and Lambert drop-kicked a field goal for an additional three points. Tired out and short of substitutes, Cincinnati was pushed back almost at will. Detroit made a final touchdown on a pass from Lambert to Percy Wilson.[62] The Heralds defeated the Celts 17–0.

The six Nesser brothers returned to Detroit on October 15 to play the Heralds. The Columbus Panhandles were well prepared for the game. The *Detroit Free Press* report of the game did not spare the home team, who were outplayed in every aspect of the game during the first half.[63] However, the Motor City's blue-collar crowd loved it. They rooted for the pipe fitters who taught the college boys how the game should be played. At halftime, the Panhandles led 13–0. The first touchdown came on a triple pass that fooled the Heralds. Ted Nesser tossed a lateral to Frank Nesser, who threw the ball forty-eight yards to Emmett Ruhl, who leisurely ran over for the touchdown. The other touchdown came on an obscure onside kick trick. The Heralds' lone touchdown came on a running play by Lambert, "who started for the Detroit eleven and played a brilliant game most of the afternoon."[64] The Detroit line was not as strong as the Panhandle front seven, and Detroit lacked a good line plunger who could move the ball against heavy line play. Some of the key Herald players were beyond their prime or did not have the skills of some of the younger people coming into professional football. The final score was 13–7 in favor of Columbus.

On October 22, the Dayton Triangles, comprised largely of the Dayton Gym-Cadets of 1915, came to Detroit for the first time. Coached by Nelson S. Talbott, the Yale All-American, they starred Alphonse Mahrt, Norbert Sacksteder, George "Babe" Zimmerman, and Lou Partlow. The game was just fifteen seconds old when Sacksteder returned the opening kickoff ninety yards for a touchdown. With the help of splendid downfield blocking, Sacksteder ran through the entire Heralds team. In the words of the *Detroit Free Press*, "The startling suddenness of this feat stunned the Herald supporters and players alike."[65] For a time, the game settled down to a tough defensive battle. The only other scoring opportunity in the first quarter came on the concluding play when Dayton attempted a field goal from the Heralds' thirty yard line. In the second quarter, the Heralds went ahead on a long forward pass from Skeet Lambert to Dick "Red" Shields. Dayton responded quickly, however, with a pass from Al Mahrt to Lou Partlow and a short run for the touchdown. The halftime score of Dayton 14, Detroit 7 stood up. On one occasion, Dayton threatened to score on the "New Haven lateral" that involved a triple pass from Mahrt to Sacksteder to Partlow, all behind the line of scrimmage and in direct alignment. This play moved the ball from midfield to the Heralds' ten yard line. But the Heralds held. After that, neither team threatened to score.

The *Free Press* wrote that "Mahrt is a wonderful quarterback and has even Lambert beaten for throwing the forward pass," but gave Lambert credit for being a better field general. Percy Wilson and Dick Shields played well for Detroit, but Norb Sacksteder won the game for Dayton with his touchdown on the opening kickoff.[66]

The Heralds faced their third straight tough opponent on October 29, when the Massillon Tigers came to Detroit. The visitors boasted a team with several All-American and All-Conference players, including Knute Rockne and Fred Heyman at ends; Joel Mattern and J. Franklin Day at tackles; Carl "Dutch" Thiele and Ed Harley at guards; and Maurice "Windy" Briggs at center. The Massillon backfield featured Freeman Fitzgerald at quarterback, Edmund Kagy and Malcolm "Red" Fleming at halfbacks, and Joe Bergie at fullback. However, several Tigers were starting at unfamiliar positions. Briggs, who usually played end, was playing center. Fullback Harley was playing guard; halfback Mattern was playing tackle; and Freeman Fitzgerald, normally a tackle, played quarterback. To compensate, Massillon shifted its players around during the course of the game so that no one had to play out of position for the entire game.[67]

Detroit hired William Sykes Tucker to start at halfback. Tucker grew up in Mobile, Alabama, and led a short but heroic life. After attending Harvard for a year, he transferred to the University of Pennsylvania, where he became an outstanding football and wrestling star. While a lieutenant serving in France, he was awarded the Croix de Guerre for gallantry, but died in St. Louis on January 14, 1920, of appendicitis.[68] Despite the addition of Tucker, Detroit did not play an opportunistic game. Their blocking was erratic, and their tackling was poor. They attempted to brush-block skilled players like Rockne and Thiele, when firm blocks were needed. Their offense was out of sync, and they played without heart. The Heralds were lucky to lose by only 6–0. Two forward passes from Fitzgerald to Rockne were responsible for the Massillon touchdown.[69] When Massillon left town, they took Skeet Lambert with them. It was advantageous for him to play for a team with more money and better prospects, while it was also helpful for the Heralds to build for the future, as they had little chance for a championship of any sort in 1916.

On November 5, the Heralds played the Evanston North Ends, who came to town with several injured players, including Rube Johnson, playing with cracked ribs. Since Detroit had never defeated Evanston, a difficult game was projected. Dick Shields took Lambert's place at quarterback, Washington and Jefferson College All-American Bob "Rube" Boville—a graduate of Central High School in Detroit—was recruited to play end, and Bill Schultz was used at left halfback.[70] Dick Shields, who had been suffering from injuries and illness, was thirty pounds underweight but played normally for the first time since the Cincinnati game.[71] Though he had not played quarterback for four years, his skills were sharp, and he played particularly well on defense. The *Detroit News Tribune* praised Shields highly: "He handled the long twisting spirals of Captain Johnson faultlessly, ran back these kicks in a highly artistic manner and, what counted most, restored the "Wallop" to the Heralds' offense."[72] Under his leadership the entire Heralds team blocked and tackled better. Norman Glockson was reported to be the most improved.

The Heralds were the first to score when Dick Shields kicked a goal from placement in the second quarter. Evanston responded with a long pass from Reuben Johnson to Gene Schobinger that resulted in a touchdown, making the score 6 to 3 in favor of the North Ends. However, before halftime, Dick Shields passed to Bob "Rube" Boville to set up a one-yard run by Shields that put Detroit ahead 9 to 3.[73] Boville, who

While at Syracuse University, Lewis S. Castle played left halfback. In 1916, he moved to Detroit where he became a trader on the Detroit Stock Exchange and played pro football for the Youngstown Patricians and the Detroit Heralds. After World War I, he played basketball for the Detroit Athletic Club. *(Syracuse University Archives.)*

returned to Northwestern High School to coach football in 1920, played particularly well until he was badly injured in the third quarter and had to be taken to the hospital.[74] Alma College star Andrew "Ox" Edgerton entered the fray for Detroit for the first time in this period. Edgerton, a science teacher at Cass City High School, had been a football, basketball, and track star in college. In the fourth quarter, Dunn and Lennahan scored touchdowns for Detroit to put the game out of Evanston's reach. Reuben Johnson, regarded as the best kicker in the west, kept that reputation when he drop-kicked a field goal from the forty-eight yard line in the fourth quarter. Detroit won the game 21 to 9. [75]

Four new players wore the Heralds' red and white colors when the Pitcairn Quakers lined up against Detroit on November 12. Bernard "Bertie" Maher, who had been with the Heralds early in the season, was in uniform at end. Lewis S. Castle, a Syracuse University halfback from 1910 to 1914,[76] was on hand, as were Collins, a tackle, and D. Miller, an end. The new players gave spark to the Detroit attack. According to the *Detroit News Tribune*, "Maher at one time saved the Heralds a desperate scrape when Shields punted weakly to midfield. 'Birdie' avoided a blocker, dove and nailed the receiver in his tracks."[77]

Dick Shields was responsible for both Detroit touchdowns. He started as the Heralds' quarterback for the second straight week. The first Detroit points came on a safety, when Quaker captain Rupp attempted to run from a kick formation and was tackled behind the goal line by Detroit halfback Bill Schultz. Later in the second quarter, Shields drove the ball over the goal line when the Pittsburgh eleven expected another back to carry the ball. The last touchdown came shortly after the beginning of the second half. Castle ran seven yards, then Percy Wilson threw a twenty-seven-yard pass to Mullane. Wilson ran off tackle for a long gain, and finally Dick Shields ran the ball in from the five yard line. At times, the Detroit fans were nasty. They jeered the decisions of the referee, instantly questioned every ruling, and, generally, made it difficult for the game to continue.[78] The final score was Detroit 15, the Pitcairn Quakers 0.

The Columbus Panhandles returned to Detroit on November 19. This game provided an accurate measure of the progress the Heralds had made in rebuilding. For three quarters, they played even with the Panhandles. Three times, the Heralds were within striking distance but were unable to score. According to newspaper accounts, the game was marred by wrangles, timeouts for injuries, and the use of questionable tactics. The Panhandles' superiority began to show in the fourth quarter. Homer Ruhl and Frank Nesser made touchdowns for Columbus, and Frank kicked a twenty-five-yard field goal. The first touchdown came on a forward pass and the second on a Detroit fumble near their own goal line. The 15–0 win by the Panhandles proved that Detroit had a lot of rebuilding left to undertake.[79]

Detroit played the Akron Burkhardts on the last Sunday in November. The Burkhardts had started the season against Peggy Parratt's Cleveland Indians but generally played a second-rate schedule against such teams as the Massillon Blues, the Youngstown Struthers, the Akron Imperial Electrics, Elyria, and Barberton. The Burkhardts, who had few stars and were outweighed by ten pounds a man, should have been easy pickings for the Heralds. With the exception of the first two minutes of the second half, the Heralds played a lackluster game. While the men from Ohio were light and fast, and played well defensively, they were not as talented as the Heralds, who seemed uncertain and indifferent. A fumble by Castle on Detroit's one yard line gave Akron its scoring opportunity. Joe "Dolly" Gray made the touchdown. The Heralds, however, scored twice in the third quarter, and Detroit narrowly won the game 13 to 7.[80]

The Heralds closed out their 1916 season by playing the Cleveland Indians, one of the five best teams in professional football. Cleveland had several All-Americans in its starting lineup, including Paul "Shorty" Des Jardien from the University of Chicago, Bob "Butts" Butler from the University of Wisconsin, Murray Shelton from Cornell University, and Lorin Solon from the University of Minnesota. Detroit loaded up for the game. They hired Norb Sacksteder away from Dayton and brought in All-Western tackle Herbert Straight, a Holland, Michigan, native from Michigan Agricultural College (Michigan State). Both would continue to play for Detroit in 1917.

Cleveland kicked two field goals in the first quarter, and Campbell "Honus" Graff added two touchdowns, one a few minutes into the second quarter, the other in the fourth quarter. Paul Des Jardien's punting gave Cleveland good field position throughout the first half. Detroit improved in the second half. The *Free Press* reported, "Norb Sacksteder, Dunn, Wilson and Lennahan matched anything Cleveland served up. Stewart and Collins were bears on the line for the Heralds." But Sacksteder's lone touchdown was not enough. Cleveland won the game 20–6 before 8,000 disappointed Motor City fans.[81]

The 1916 season was a transitional year for the Heralds. Aging hometown players were being supplemented by out-of-town stars. The process, however, was too slow and uneven to give the Heralds a winning season, which left Detroit fans angry and disappointed. The teamwork of prior years was lost, without the benefit of the skills of a host of star players. Detroit ended the season with a 5–5 record.

The declaration of war against Germany and conscription began to reduce the pool of professional football players by the fall of 1917. In September, over five thousand draftees came to Camp Custer in Battle Creek for preliminary military instructions.[82] Among these were former Heralds players Jerry Da Prato, Blake Miller, Frank Gardner, and Tom Bogle. Former Detroit Mack Park Maroon player Ed Kerwin and Canton Bulldog player Harry Costello were also at Camp Custer.

Detroit opened its 1917 season, on October 7, against the Hammond Clabbys, named for Jimmy Clabby, the former world's welterweight boxing champion, who first sponsored the team. Seven of eleven Detroit starters had not been with the team for their home opener in 1916, although Edgerton, Straight, and Sacksteder had joined the Heralds in November of the previous year. The Hammond Clabbys were an up-and-coming team. They had players like All-Western Conference tackle Frank Blocker from Purdue University, Ted Blocker from Indiana University, and George Volkman from the University of Wisconsin. Their backfield stars were Wallie Hess, who had played for Indiana University, Harold "Irish" Sheridan, who had played for Pine Village, and A. R. Longenecker, from the University of California doing graduate work at Purdue.

Arrangements were made to have telegraphed results of the World Series available during the Hammond-Detroit game.[83] Four thousand fans paid to watch the game at Navin Field. Tommy Hughitt, the former University of Michigan star, was in negotiations with Youngstown and Massillon for his services, but in the absence of a signed agreement with either of them agreed to play a game or two with the Heralds.[84] In the second quarter, with Tommy Hughitt at the helm and Norb Sacksteder at halfback, the Heralds took control of the game. Passes from Hughitt to Sacksteder and from Sacksteder to Hughitt, together with a forty-three-yard run by Sacksteder, put Detroit ahead 12 to 0. Sacksteder added another touchdown on a punt return in the third quarter to make the final score 19–0. Newcomers Carl "Dutch" Thiele from Denison College and Ray Whipple from Notre Dame played well for Detroit at the ends. They caught several passes and looked good on defense.[85]

On October 14, the Heralds played the Cincinnati Celts at Navin Field, using the same starting lineup as in their home opener. Detroit

The Detroit Heralds: Like a Ford in Heavy Traffic   153

scored in the opening period on a pass from Tommy Hughitt to Carl "Dutch" Thiele. Norb Sacksteder scored on an eighty-yard run in the fourth period. The Detroit front seven played well throughout.[86] Hughitt finally came to terms with Youngstown and played the balance of the season in eastern Ohio.[87]

The Buffalo All-Stars followed Cincinnati to Navin Field and offered scant opposition. On Sunday, October 21, the Heralds humiliated the All-Stars 67 to 0. Detroit started Weekes at quarterback. Danny Mullane returned as left end, Windbile played left tackle, Harry Schlee played left guard, Archie Stewart started at center, Guy Shield replaced Herb Straight at right guard, Nany Shanks played right tackle, Ray Whipple started at right end, and the backfield had Bertie Maher in place of Dunn. In short, six of the eleven Detroit starters were older players standing in for newer players. No explanation for the change is available, but management might have been saving money in a game against a weaker team.

Detroit made four touchdowns in the first quarter, and two each in the second, third, and fourth quarters. Norb Sacksteder tallied four touchdowns, Nig Lennahan scored three, Bertie Maher two, and Mullane one. Buffalo stars Doug Jeffery and Gene Dooley exhibited some great individual performances, but their team did not play well as a unit. Buffalo did complete eleven passes in the second half, but each drive was stopped on downs or an interception before they could score.[88]

When Detroit played the Toledo Maroons at Navin Park on October 28, Whipple, Usher, and Dunn were back in the starting lineup, and Harry Whitaker from Indiana University was the new quarterback. Whitaker, from South Bend, was captain of the 1915 Indiana University team and a letterman in baseball and basketball as well as football.[89] He played the last game of the season for the Canton Bulldogs in 1915 and a couple of games for Canton in 1916. These players, together with Danny Mullane, Nany Shanks, Herb Straight, Archie Stewart, Windbile, Bertie Maher, Norb Sacksteder, and Earl Dunn, made up an outstanding team.

The game was even during the first quarter. An outstanding Toledo punt pinned Detroit near its own goal line, and Earl Dunn managed only a two-yard punt. Nicholson, the Toledo halfback, took advantage of the break to score the first touchdown. However, Sacksteder responded with an eighty-yard run to tie the score. In the second period, Sacksteder scored again. Finally, Danny Mullane caught a Harry

Whitaker pass in the third quarter for the Heralds' last score. They defeated the Toledo Maroons 20–7.[90] One of the casualties of the game was Ray Whipple, who broke his nose and badly bruised his eye.[91]

The Wabash Athletic Association came to Detroit for the first time on November 4. Wabash had been playing independent football for twenty years and had lost only six games in that time. The Indiana team had several outstanding pros on their 1917 squad, including Jesse Reno, Max Palm, Homer T. Showalter, Alfred "Dutch" Bergman, and Guilford Falcon. Palm and Falcon had played for the Evanston North Ends, Dutch Bergman for Notre Dame, and Homer T. Showalter for Wabash College. However, the Wabash quarterback and captain, Red Milliner, was over thirty-five years old.

The first half of the game was relatively evenly played. Then a mental mistake by Snyder and Falcon of Wabash gave Detroit an easy touchdown. Just after the teams switched ends, Wabash had the ball "fourth down and six to go," when the Wabash center, Snyder, mistook the goalpost for Falcon and hiked the ball over Falcon's head into the end zone. Instead of dropping onto the ball for a safety, a stunned Falcon just stood there while a Detroit player recovered the ball for a touchdown.[92] Before the afternoon was over, the difference between a safety and a touchdown made no difference in the outcome. Detroit made four additional touchdowns, including one by Sacksteder, who, as the *Detroit Free Press* enthusiastically reported,

put on his specialty of stopping and starting like a Ford in heavy traffic, scooted past everybody and hit the open. Then he only had to pass Checkaye, the halfback safety man of the Hoosier layout. This he did by running right up to him and then throws her "into reverse", and then into "high."[93]

The final score was Detroit 34, Wabash 0.

Through the first five games of the 1917 season, the Heralds scored 154 points, their opponents 7. Now the Heralds played one of the most important games of the season against the Camp Custer team, which included as fine a combination of football players as found anywhere in the pros. Eight of the eleven starters for Camp Custer had played pro football before entering the army. Several were all-stars, including Frank Gardner, Ed Kerwin, Harry Costello, Blake Miller, Tom Moriarity, and Jerry Da Prato. The Heralds started Bertie Maher and Ray Whipple at ends, Nany Shanks and Usher at tackles, Windbile and Herbert Straight at guards, Archie Stewart at center, and Whitaker, Lennahan, Sacksteder, and Dunn in the backfield.[94]

All of the scoring in the game took place in the first half. Camp

Custer's points came as a result of former University of Detroit football coach Harry Costello's kicking, two by field goal, the other on a touchdown pass from Costello to Thompson that was set up by field position gained by his punting. The army team keyed on Norb Sacksteder and completely stopped his running attack. Neither Sacksteder nor his teammates made a first down until the final quarter of the game, when they earned two. The Camp Custer front seven repeatedly broke through the line, throwing the Heralds' runner for a loss. The game nearly got out of control on several occasions. Tom Moriarity was thrown out of the game for slugging, and Blake Miller had to be hospitalized because of injuries.[95] Uneven officiating worked to the advantage of Camp Custer, giving them a questionable touchdown in their 13–0 victory.[96]

The Racine Regulars traveled to Navin Field to play the Heralds on November 18. Though Racine had its share of former college players, including Bob Foster from Marquette University and Walter Eck from Lawrence University, it was mainly a team of blue-collar workers. Detroit fans were unfamiliar with the Racine team whose "net strength [was] a matter of conjecture."[97] On game day, the *Detroit Free Press* explained,

A cool searching wind swept over the field and the rather small crowd of onlookers were forced to hop around a bit to keep their radiators from freezing up on them. Along in the second half the breeze shifted right through the thin "bennies" and the cast off sweaters of the battling athletes were at a premium on the sidelines.[98]

When Norb Sacksteder ran thirty yards or more twice for touchdowns in the first quarter, it looked as if it would be a lopsided game. Racine showed some spirit, however, and mounted a comeback drive. The Wisconsin team got to the Heralds' eleven yard line before an intercepted pass killed their drive. Later in the quarter, Racine drove to the Detroit twenty-four yard line. Again, their drive stalled. Sacksteder retired from the game early in the second period after he injured his leg, but he returned in the last quarter when Racine began making things too warm for the Heralds.[99] Neither side showed much of an offense until the final quarter. In that period, Sacksteder's sixty-yard run was called back. In response, he threw a forward pass to Danny Mullane that resulted in another Detroit touchdown. The final score was Detroit 19, Racine 0.[100]

Detroit raised its ticket prices to $1.00 and $1.50 for its last two home games of the 1917 season. The Heralds played the Columbus

Panhandles on November 25, and, on Thanksgiving Day, they played Jim Thorpe's Canton Bulldogs. In 1916, Columbus had defeated the Heralds twice, and now Detroit was out to even the score. Everyone in Detroit considered the forthcoming games as the toughest of the year.[101] Determined not to lose both games, William Marshall, the team president, and John Roesink, the business manager, hired Frank Nesser to play for Detroit against his brothers in the Panhandle game and against Thorpe in the Thanksgiving Day game.[102] The Heralds also hired Clarence "Steamer" Horning,[103] the Walter Camp All-American tackle from Colgate, to strengthen their line.[104]

Detroit's first touchdown against Columbus came in the first minute of the game when Harry Whitaker threw a pass to Norb Sacksteder, who ran thirty-five yards for a touchdown. Later in the quarter, Frank Nesser drop-kicked a field goal to give the Heralds a 9–0 lead. The new Heralds' tackles Frank Nesser and Steamer Horning closed down the Columbus inside running attack, and at halftime the 9–0 score stood.

In the fourth quarter, the Heralds got the ball in Panhandle territory on a fumble. A pass from Whitaker to Frank Nesser resulted in another touchdown. Finally, Ray Whipple caught a Whitaker pass for the last touchdown of the day. Detroit got its revenge 23–0.[105]

Four days later, Detroit played Jim Thorpe's Canton Bulldogs, one of the greatest teams in the history of single platoon football. Bill Marshall realized that the lineup he had been playing all season would not defeat Canton. He increased ticket prices so he could hire new talent. He hired Elmer E. Carroll, a former Washington and Jefferson star, Carl Thiele of the Cincinnati Celts, and Rudolph Propst, and kept Clarence Horning. Rudolph Propst,[106] captain of the 1912 Syracuse University team and a Walter Camp All-American, was hired to play right tackle.

On Thanksgiving Day, Navin Field was a sea of mud. Jim Thorpe did not start the game and declared that he would not play unless he was absolutely needed. Thorpe had a badly battered shoulder, a bad knee, a few broken ribs, and a collection of bruises and scratches.[107] The Heralds outplayed Canton in the first half, but neither team scored. Most of the play was on the Ohio side of the field, but, inside the twenty yard line, Canton held. Archie Stewart tried a field goal for Detroit, but the mud-covered ball skidded away.

Thorpe, deciding he was needed, started the second half. He and Pete Calac then dominated play, ripping off runs of from five to thirty yards at a crack. Thorpe went off tackle and around end. He scattered Detroit players whenever he plunged into the line. Thorpe ran many of his

Rudolph W. Propst, captain of the Syracuse University football team in 1912, was a Walter Camp All-American. After serving as an assistant coach at Syracuse in 1914–15, he played a couple of games for the Detroit Heralds in 1917, before making the army his lifelong career. *(Syracuse University Archives.)*

Clarence "Steamer" Horning, tackle, was a Walter Camp All-American at Colgate University in 1916 and played for the Detroit Heralds in 1917, 1919–20; Detroit Panthers, 1921; Rochester Jeffersons, 1921; and Toledo Maroons, 1922–23. He later coached at the University of Detroit and Highland Park High School. *(Archives of Labor and Urban Affairs, Wayne State University.)*

plays from a punt formation so that he could hit the line at full speed. Then, when everyone was focused on Thorpe, the ball was hiked to Milton Ghee who threw a pass to Greasy Neale for a touchdown. Thorpe kicked the extra point, and, thereafter, Canton played it safe. Thorpe and Calac still moved the ball, but they took no chances. Their priority was to protect their lead.

The crowd saw enough of Thorpe to realize why he has been called the best football player in history. The *Detroit News* praised his athletic prowess: "Big, powerful, wonderfully fast, Thorpe gets by on brute strength, speed and his instinctive strategy. It is next to impossible for one man to stop him." Greasy Neale was also recognized as "the best man on the forward pass game Detroit has seen."[108] Clarence Horning, Ray Whipple, and Norb Sacksteder stood out for Detroit. Sacksteder made several runs of twenty-five yards or more, but did not have sufficient blocking when Detroit got inside the Canton twenty yard line.[109] Canton won the game 7–0.

On December 2, the Detroit Heralds ended their season in Toledo, Ohio, against the Maroons. Six Heralds players narrowly escaped serious injury en route to their train in Detroit, when the taxi they were riding in collided with a touring car. Horning, Sacksteder, Shields, Dunn, coach Marshall, and manager Roesink were thrown from the taxi. Dick Shields bruised his knees so badly he could not play the game. Luckily, he was not needed. The Heralds romped over Toledo, 23–0. Dunn, Sacksteder, and Whitaker made touchdowns, and Dunn kicked a field goal. Burliegh Edmund Cruikshank, a native of West Somerville, Massachusetts, and All-American from Washington and Jefferson College, played guard for Detroit.[110] The Maroons never had a chance to score.[111]

The Heralds closed the 1917 season with an 8–2 record. They played a tough schedule and scored 218 points, while their opponents scored only twenty-seven points. Norbert Sacksteder was the offensive star for Detroit. He accounted for 108 of the 218 points scored, or nearly half of Detroit's offensive output. Over the course of the year, Detroit fielded some of the best new linemen to enter pro football. Herbert Straight, Ray Whipple, Nany Shanks, and Rudolph Propst all played well and had promising pro careers ahead.

The city of Detroit proved early on that it was a staunch supporter of professional football. Detroit teams attracted large crowds, and fans were willing to pay the unheard-of price of $1.50 to see Jim Thorpe or the Nesser brothers play. Moreover, the Heralds played one of the most difficult schedules in independent football. At one time or another, they played nearly every first-rate team that suited up for the fall sport. The Heralds played a harder schedule than either Massillon or Canton because they played Chicago and Indiana teams as well as those from Ohio, Pennsylvania, and New York.

The Heralds also demonstrated that great talent would flow from places like Dayton to Detroit when the smaller towns did not reward their athletes well enough. Norbert Sacksteder was an outstanding talent with deep roots in Dayton, but he found a greater measure of success in Detroit, where he was offered higher pay and better fan support. Others would follow this pattern.

The Heralds were always a good football team, but their rebuilding program of 1916–17 made them one of the best professional football teams in America. In 1919, the Heralds recruited Harry Costello to quarterback the team and College Football Hall of Fame tackle, Walker

Carpenter from Georgia Tech, but lost games to Canton and Massillon. The following year, Norb Sacksteder returned to Dayton to play for the Triangles, and Harry Costello also moved out of Detroit. In 1920, the Heralds were a charter member of the American Professional Football Association but fell on hard times. They played most of their games on the road, because the University of Detroit had emerged as a college football powerhouse and began playing its home games at Navin Field. The Heralds were relegated to playing home games back at Mack Park. Heavy rains caused the cancellation of games with the Akron Pros and the Detroit Armadas in early November,[112] and the aging team could only manage one win and three ties.

The following year, in an effort to capitalize on the growing popularity of the Detroit Tigers baseball team, William H. Marshall changed the name of the Heralds and became president of the Detroit Tigers of the American Professional Football Association. Walter "Tillie" Voss, the six foot four, 215-pound, All-American tackle who had recently graduated from the University of Detroit, became the team's vice-president, and Clarence "Steamer" Horning became its captain, secretary, and treasurer.[113] John Roesink apparently had a significant stake in the ownership of the Heralds.[114] The Detroit Tigers football team encountered difficulty early in the 1921 season. They lost their first two games on the road to Rock Island and Dayton. They then came home to Navin Field to play the Akron Pros, who featured Fritz Pollard, Paul Robeson, Al Nesser, and Elgie Tobin. Akron, the 1920 American Professional Football Association league champions, required a $3,000 guarantee, and the Detroit Tigers reported $2,200 in expenses per week, including payroll. Altogether, the single home game cost was estimated to be $7,200 when stadium cost, ticket sellers, officials, and promotional costs were included.[115] At least six thousand paid admissions were needed to break even, according to William Marshall.[116] The winless Tigers did not break even. The following week, the Tigers lost a home game to Rock Island and nearly went broke. After losing road games to Buffalo and Chicago, Marshall's Tigers decided that they could not host return games with those teams, as required by league rules. On a bitter cold Armistice Day, they played Bay City on their field before two thousand fans and finally won a game, 33–7.[117] After tying a road game with Dayton, the Tigers, using long-time Heralds players Norb Sacksteder, Earl Dunn, Jerry Da Prato, Ray Whipple, Guy Shields, and Clarence Horning, attempted to close out their 1921 season against the Mack Park Maroons with a victory, as the Heralds had done in 1920.[118]

However, on November 27, 1921, the Tigers canceled the game because of a soggy playing field, although some felt that the real reason was their inability to muster eleven players for the game.[119]

The Maroons, coached by Danny Mullane and starring Jimmy Kelly, Red Cullen, Larry Nadeau, and Ty Krentler—all former Heralds' stars—finally played the Detroit Tigers, absent DePrato, Voss, Whipple, and Horning, at Navin Field on December 5, the day after the University of Detroit played Alfred "Greasy" Neale's Washington and Jefferson College team before a crowd of twenty-two thousand fans. Less than four thousand paid to see the Maroons defeat the Tigers 7–0.[120] This humiliating defeat ended the Detroit Tigers' football franchise. Detroit did not field a major league professional football team again until 1925, when the Cleveland Panthers franchise was moved to Detroit.[121] In 1925–26 and 1928, the Detroit Panthers were in the National Football League before disappearing forever.[122] Finally, on June 30, 1934, the Portsmouth (Ohio) Spartans franchise was purchased and moved to Detroit by George A. Richards and a group of twenty-six or so other investors. Richards had been manager of the Firestone Tire and Rubber Company in Akron before purchasing the WJR radio station in Detroit. The radio magnate renamed his team the Detroit Lions, and Detroit has been a strong NFL franchise since 1934.

Walter C. "Tillie" Voss, the Detroit-born, University of Detroit Titan great who had attempted to usher the Detroit Tigers into the National Football League, played professional football for eleven teams over nine seasons and professional basketball for six teams over five seasons, was a WPA project worker, and ended his career as a plant guard for the Ford Motor Company.[123] John Aaron Roesink went on to own the Detroit Stars in the Negro National Baseball League and to introduce night baseball to Detroit in 1930, before the Detroit Stars went broke in 1931 during the great depression.[124] He also ran for the Detroit City Council in 1941, but, when he died on July 19, 1954, John Roesink was unheralded and forgotten by nearly everyone. He did not receive an obituary in the *Detroit Free Press*, left no children, and was survived only by two sisters. Not even a picture of the Mack Park Field survived his death.[125]

13. The Cincinnati Celts: River City Champions

The Cincinnati Celts, organized before 1910, had a strong rivalry with the North Cincinnati Colts that continued until 1916. The Celts were considered the independent football champions of southern Ohio as a result of playing well against the high-ranked Columbus Panhandles in 1912 and the Dayton Gym-Cadets in 1913. The early Celts teams drew a number of their players from the alumni of the University of Cincinnati. Like the Columbus Panhandles, they had to play on the road frequently to cover expenses. The out-of-town games were rarely reported in the local papers, so information about them is sparse. In 1912, they had games against Toledo and Detroit. In 1913, the Celts played Wabash, Dayton, Columbus, and Muncie, among other teams.

The Celts starting lineup for their 1915 season opener had Albert "Whitey" Bessmeyer and Chet "Shine" Knab at ends, Otto Bessmeyer and Gaylor at tackles, Frank Lane and Meister at guards, Magley at center, Davis at quarter, Tilly Schuessler at left half, Tom Gaither at right half, and David Reese at fullback. Three of the starters had attended the University of Cincinnati: Albert Henry Bessmeyer was a cooperative engineering student from 1908 to 1911; Tilly Schuessler attended from 1907 until 1910; and Davis was at the university in 1908. Also in the starting lineup were Gaylor from Kenyon College and David Reese from Denison University.[1]

The Celts were scheduled to open their 1915 season on October 10 in Detroit against the Heralds but rescheduled the day before the game because Davis, their star quarterback, was ill, and no one else could call the signals.[2] The season opener was played the following Sunday at Packard Park before three thousand fans. The Heralds, who had already played one game, made fewer first quarter mistakes than the Celts. The first Detroit score came shortly after the game started, on a long pass from Percy Wilson to Dick Shields. Shields missed the extra point. The six-point lead held up in the first half, but the Celts were noticeably better by the second quarter. In the third quarter, Cincinnati tied the score on a "grunt-and-dust drive" that culminated in a touchdown by Tom Gaither. The Celts very nearly scored a second touchdown later, but Chief Newashe stripped the ball from Davis and recovered the fumble. The score remained even until the last forty-five seconds of the game, when a pass from Dick Shields to Percy Latham resulted in a 12–6 win for Detroit. In spite of the loss, the Bessmeyer brothers, David Reese, and team captain Tilly Schuessler played well.[3]

The following week in Dayton, the Celts played the Gym-Cadets to a scoreless tie. The Celts fielded nearly the same team, except Meister replaced Gaylor at left tackle and Love took Meister's spot at left guard. In the backfield, Janzen replaced Davis, and Weheringer replaced Reese.[4] Reese played most of the season for the North Cincinnati Athletic Club with his old college teammate George Roudebush.

The Celts played the next two Sundays in Cincinnati against local independent teams that offered little competition but required less expense. Old-timer Paul Roy Stewart, who had attended the Virginia Military Institute for one year and had played football there in 1901, made it into the Celts' lineup at left end.[5] On November 14, they traveled to Toledo to play the Maroons, one of the best teams in the state, whose strong fan support made them difficult to beat at home. Toledo, led by Ray Eichenlaub from Notre Dame, was having a good season and sported a 5–1 record.

The Celts attack was led by the Bessmeyer brothers and Tilly Schuessler, who were outstanding on defense. The game was fought primarily on the ground, and the last quarter was played at dusk, making it difficult for players and spectators to follow the movement of the ball. The evenly fought game ended in a scoreless tie.[6]

The season ended in Cincinnati, on November 21, with a game against the Muncie Congerville Athletic Club. The Muncie team had been directed by skilled quarterback Frank "Coonie" Checkaye. However, when Fort Wayne quarterback Kent "Skeet" Lambert was injured on November 7, Coonie was hired by the Friars.[7] Consequently, Muncie offered little opposition to the Celts, who won 48 to 0.[8]

The Celts had not had one of their better seasons in 1915. Their cross-town rivals, the North Cincinnati Athletic Club, siphoned much of the available local talent away from the Celts, while other communities concentrated talent in a single professional team. Obviously, the Cincinnati market was too small to support two pro football teams.

The Celts started the 1916 season in Detroit at Navin Field against the Heralds, on October 8, with essentially the same team that had closed the 1915 season. They had Albert Bessmeyer and Chet "Shine" Knab at ends, Ellis B. Gregg Jr. and Otto Bessmeyer at tackles, Meister and Frank Lane at guards, Magley at center and Rowlette, Schuessler, Weheringer and Tom Gaither in the backfield.[9] The game was played, in the *Detroit News Tribune's* description, on

a hot July day that was a little delayed in shipment . . . and good football was out of the question. However, the boys tried hard out there in the blistering sun, and it is really remarkable that an exhibition worth looking at was staked. And it was a game crammed with tense and interesting situations.

Arthur "Red" Cornwell, the great University of Michigan center, had come back to the Heralds after the collapse of the Mack Park Maroons, and Bertie Maher, the veteran halfback from the University of Detroit, came with him. Ox Edgerton from Alma College and Bill Schultz were newcomers in the Detroit lineup. Only Dick Shields, Dutch Stewart, Harry Schlee, Percy Wilson, and Earl Dunn were starters from the 1915 Heralds team.[10]

The teams were locked in a scoreless tie for three quarters. The Heralds substituted freely throughout the game, but the Celts were hampered by their financial decision to bring only eighteen men to Detroit. In the second half, the heat began to take its toll on the Cincinnati starters. Shortly into the final quarter, Lambert unleashed a pretty-looking, long forward pass to Dick Shields from midfield. Because of where Lambert was standing, the ball flew forty-six yards in the air. Dick Shields caught the pigskin on the sixteen yard line and raced over the goal for the Heralds' first touchdown.[11] Shields made the extra point to give Detroit a seven-point lead. After the ensuing kickoff, the Celts' offense sputtered, and they were forced to punt. The Heralds again engaged their ground game and rushed the ball into scoring position. Lambert drop-kicked a field goal for another three points.[12]

With the Celts tired and out of substitutes, the Heralds were now clearly in command of the game: the Cincinnati eleven could be pushed back at will. Nevertheless, the Celts did manage one last drive. Tilly Schuessler broke free for a long, spirited run, and only a spectacular desperation tackle by safety Skeet Lambert saved a touchdown. The tackle sent Schuessler into the air and out of bounds.

Playing at a disadvantage next to the out-of-bounds line, the Celts attempted an obvious end run to the wide side of the field that resulted in a fumble. Dick Shields booted the ball out of danger. When Detroit got the ball again, two long passes from Lambert to Percy Wilson and then to Nig Lennahan resulted in a score by Wilson. The Heralds scored all of their points in their 17–0 win in the last ten minutes of the game.[13]

The Celts returned home on Sunday, October 15, to play Lebanon, coasting to a 61 to 0 win. A week later, they played the Friars in Fort Wayne. The Celts came supplied with new numbered uniforms. For the first time in Indiana, professional players could be identified by number from a scorecard given out before the game.[14]

The Friars team featured seven former Notre Dame players including Howard "Cap" Edwards, Keith "Deac" Jones, Joe Pliska, Alvin "Heine" Berger, Allen "Mal" Elward, Al Feeney, and Hugh "Pepper" O'Donnell, who later became president of Notre Dame. Dorais, also from Notre Dame, was absent because of an injured leg and was replaced by Frank "Coonie" Checkaye.[15]

The Celts added George Roudebush[16] to their backfield and David Reese at center. After graduating from Denison in the spring of 1915, George Roudebush enrolled in law school at the University of Cincinnati and earned spending money by playing professional football for the North Cincinnati Athletic Club. In 1916, he also coached football at Xavier University. He would continue to play pro football for a decade.

The Celts' game strategy called for open formation runs by Weheringer and Roudebush, with passes from Roudebush to Schuessler, Albert Bessmeyer, and Chet "Shine" Knab. On defense, they relied on the Bessmeyer brothers, David Reese, Roudebush, and Tilly Schuessler for roughneck tackling and aggressive obstruction of interference. Schuessler, the Cincinnati captain, was a particular standout on defense. He defended well against the pass, intercepting three. Roudebush and Albert Bessmeyer delivered as planned, but Pepper O'Donnell and Al Feeney also played well defensively for Fort Wayne. At one point in the third quarter, the Celts threatened to score, but Pepper O'Donnell intercepted a pass to kill the drive. The Friars had two chances to score field goals in the second half, but both drop kicks missed. The game ended in a 6 to 6 tie.[17] Joe Pliska scored the Friars' touchdown, and a pass from Roudebush to Albert Bessmeyer gave the Celts their points.[18]

The following Sunday, the Celts played the fabled Pine Village Athletic Club in Lafayette, Indiana. Pine Village claimed they had won 112 games without a loss over the prior thirteen years. To be sure, they had been tied two or three times, but they had never lost a game.[19]

The game between Cincinnati and Pine Village, according to the *Lafayette Journal*, was "an excellent exhibition of the popular fall sport and the game was hard fought every inch of the way. The Celts scored a touchdown in the second quarter on a 'peculiar' . . . kick" that caromed off a Pine Village player and was picked up by a Celts player for a touchdown. The Celts drop-kicked for three points in the third period. In the fourth quarter, Eli Fenters skirted left end on a fifty-five-yard run for the Pine Village Athletic Club to score their only touchdown. The final score was Cincinnati 9, Pine Village 7. More than two thousand spectators left the game dazed. No one expected the Pine Village winning streak to end in this way.[20]

Roudebush was the star of the game. He threw several long passes to Albert Bessmeyer and Shine Knab which kept the pressure on Pine Village and resulted in the field goal that won the game.[21] Reese was outstanding on defense; Weheringer kicked the field goal; and Roudebush scored the Cincinnati touchdown. The addition of Roudebush and Reese made the Celts one of the top ten teams in American independent football circles.

On November 5, the Celts played an easy game when they again trounced Lebanon, Ohio, 67 to 7. The Celts cleared their bench, allowing twenty-two players to get into the fray at Redlands Field in Cincinnati.[22]

A week later, the Celts played the Cleveland Indians, but not their first team. During the course of the season, Peggy Parratt, the manager of the Cleveland Indians football team, found it necessary to upgrade his team in order to be competitive with Canton and Massillon. So, he created a second team, comprised of players who had started for him at the beginning of the season and were under contract to him, but who were not good enough to beat teams like Canton, Massillon, and Detroit. Peggy scheduled his second team to play games in Columbus and Cincinnati so that he could cover the expenses his contracts with these players entailed.

It is not clear how Frank Marty, the manager of the Celts, came to schedule the Cleveland Indians second team. Nonetheless, on November 12, 1916, the Celts played a one-sided game against the Indians castoffs. Campbell Graff was advertised as one of their starters but was reported to be in the hospital. However, Boyd Cherry, E. M. Cole, Whitey Schultz, Thomas H. King, Roy "Tommy" Burrell, and Howard Lester Beck did play for Cleveland. Several of these players had been with Massillon or Canton for the 1915 season and had been stars on winning teams. The Celts loaned the Indians Keene T. Palmer to replace Graff. Several of the Cleveland second team played well, but they lacked teamwork and coordination. By halftime, the Celts regulars had built up a nineteen-point lead and coasted to a 25 to 0 win.[23]

The next game was held at Westwood Park in Dayton on November 19. The Celts starters were the same as they had been since October 22.

The first period was nip and tuck, with neither side making much head-
way and the ball changing hands several times. The quarter ended with
the ball near midfield. In the second period, Al Mahrt, the Triangles'
quarterback, opened up the attack by going to the air. A forward pass
from Mahrt to Partlow picked up twenty yards, and then Partlow
plowed the ball across the goal line for the touchdown. But the Celts
were not disheartened. Roudebush completed a pass to Shine Knab for
a thirty-yard gain. However, Norb Sacksteder intercepted a subsequent
pass and stopped the drive.[24] The Celts and the Triangles struggled on.
Cincinnati challenged again, and an interception by Lee Fenner of Dayton killed this drive, too. Wonderful plays by Celt David Reese, who recovered a Triangle fumble, and Lou Partlow, who sparked the Triangle
ground game, resulted in a close game. The final score was 6–0 in favor
of Dayton.[25]

The same teams met the following week at Redlands Field in Cincinnati, but with a different outcome. The Celts scored a touchdown in the
first quarter when George Roudebush skirted the Dayton left end for a
twenty-yard touchdown run. Schuessler kicked the goal. The Triangles
tied the score in the second period on a lucky break: right tackle Cutler
partly blocked a Roudebush forward pass on the fifty yard line, and the
ball bounced right into the hands of Dayton right guard Stoecklein,
who ran for a touchdown without much trouble. Williams kicked the
Dayton goal. In the third quarter, the Celts targeted the area defended
by Lou Partlow. Pat Reece caught several passes because Partlow was a
poor pass defender. Keene T. Palmer kicked a field goal that gave the
Celts a 10–7 lead. The last quarter was played in darkness. The Triangles worked the ball to the Celts' twenty yard line. At this point, the
Celts broke up the Triangles passing game and held them on downs.
Schuessler then made a forty-yard dash through tackle, and the danger
was over.[26] The Celts lead held up, and Cincinnati won the game 10–7.

A return engagement was arranged between the Pine Village Athletic Club and the Cincinnati Celts in Indianapolis on Thanksgiving, November 30. Pine Village fielded an outstanding team that included several All-Western and All-American players. The starting lineup had
Harold Sigvold Ofstie, the All-Western Conference end from Wisconsin,
and Arthur Krause from Indiana University at ends: Matt Winters, All-
Western Conference from Indiana University, and Indiana University
assistant coach Edgar "Big Ed" Davis at tackle; Wisconsin All-American
Howard "Cub" Buck and Notre Dame All-American Emmett Keefe at
guards; Cliff Milligan from Indiana University at center; and Illinois All-
American halfback Bart Macomber, Clair Scott from Indiana Universi-

ty, Eli Fenters,[27] and Harvard All-American Richard S. C. King in the backfield.

The Celts scored first when they recovered a Pine Village fumble on the Pine Village thirty-eight yard line. Keene Palmer drop-kicked the field goal shortly afterward. Bart Macomber matched the feat for Pine Village later in the first quarter. The first half ended in a 3 to 3 tie. Time after time, Celt passes were broken up, and, without a passing game, they could not work their running game. Gordon Thomas replaced Clair Scott at right half and had a field day. Thomas, Richard King, and Charlie Helvie each scored touchdowns for Pine Village in the second half. Eli Fenters made two of three extra point attempts. Pine Village gained revenge for their loss to the Celts earlier in the season. The final score was 23 to 3 in favor of Pine Village.[28]

Three days later, the Celts played the Hammond Clabbys in Hammond. The Clabbys had experienced only three losses—one to Fort Wayne, another to Davenport, and a third to Elyria. The game might have ended in a scoreless tie except for a spectacular drop kick by the Clabbys' Johnny Finn of Purdue. The Celts rallied: Palmer made sixty yards in three plays and was on the point of scoring when time ran out.[29]

The 1916 Celts were ten points shy of a truly successful season. An extra point against Fort Wayne, a touchdown against Dayton, and a field goal against Hammond would have made the Celts a contender for the championship. The difference between success and failure was a matter of inches and a field goal or two.

The American entrance into the great war in Europe stripped the Celts of their best players. When George Roudebush, William Goebel, and Herbert Goosman entered the army, the Celts recruited Carl "Dutch" Thiele, a Denison University graduate, to play left end. Thiele became one of the era's best players. Born in Dayton, Ohio, in 1890, he was an outstanding athlete at Dayton's Stivers High School. He enrolled at Denison University in 1911 and graduated in 1915. While at Denison, he earned sixteen varsity letters, four each in football, basketball, baseball, and track. Dutch Thiele played for the Massillon Tigers professional football team, in 1916, at left tackle and left end for $35 per game. In 1917, he played for the Cincinnati Celts, the Dayton Triangles (against Camp Sherman),[30] and the Detroit Heralds. Sometimes Thiele played under the assumed name "Williams" to hide his Sunday play from his devoutly religious mother. During World War I, he was a fighter pilot and, in 1919, after the war, returned to Dayton to work at Dayton-Wright Airplane and continue playing football for the Dayton Triangles. He played pro football and pro basketball until 1924. During those years, the Triangles paid him $85 a game.[31]

The Celts also added Frank "Swede" Sorenson[32] to play fullback. Enrolling in engineering at Ohio State University in the fall of 1913, he became a starter on the varsity football team in 1915 and was team captain in 1916. He was five foot nine inches tall and weighed 170 pounds. Ohio State's good showing in 1915 "was in no small measure due to the splendid work of 'Swede' Sorenson at fullback," according to the 1916 yearbook, *The Makio:*

His work at fullback all season was marvelous, demonstrating scientific football at all times. "Swede" showed up best for short sure gains of six or seven yards, especially on split bucks, while his defensive play was admirable. He received mention from Walter Camp.

The Celts opened their 1917 season, on October 14, in Detroit against the Heralds. Detroit played their first game against the Hammond Clabbys a week earlier and whipped them 19–0. The Celts had lost to the Clabbys in the last game of the 1916 season, so this was not an easy way for Cincinnati to start the new season. Former Celts end, Carl Thiele, was now playing for the Heralds, as was Norb Sacksteder, the former Dayton Triangles star. David Walter "Hoppy" Hopkins[33] was added to the Celts' starting lineup at left end.

In the second period, the Heralds took a 7–0 lead on a touchdown pass from Tommy Hughitt, the University of Michigan star, to Carl Thiele. His score stood until Norb Sacksteder chewed up thirty yards in four plays with his elusive running and followed up with a fifty-yard run to double the score against Cincinnati. While Frank Sorenson and Chet "Shine" Knab played well for Cincinnati, Detroit outplayed the Celts every quarter.[34]

One week later, the Celts traveled to Fort Wayne. Because they lost players to the military, Fort Wayne was not as strong as it had been in 1916. The Friars announced that, after the Cincinnati game, ticket prices would be raised to seventy-five cents "to avert a financial catastrophe."[35] "In the neighborhood of twenty-two hundred football enthusiasts crowded into the stands" for the Cincinnati game. In the past the Celts had worn green jerseys, but this year, according to the *Fort Wayne Journal-Gazette,*

they made a natty appearance in their red jerseys, and were given a hand when they trotted onto the field. . . . The Celts started out like whirlwinds and for the first [quarter] played the Friars to a standstill. . . . Practically all of the thrills in the game were concentrated in the second quarter. . . . A forward pass perfectly executed from Pliska to Huntington, landed the ball squarely into the waiting pursuers, Huntington raced across the goal for the first score of the game. Dorais, a moment later made a perfect kick over the goal posts and the score stood 7 to 0 in favor of the Friars. [Later that quarter] Sorenson [the Cincinnati fullback] booted the ball squarely into the back of his own player. It bounced behind the goal posts, was caught by a Celt who fumbled it and quick as a flash [Walter] Berghoff dropped in the sphere, converting what ordinarily would have been a touchback into the second touchdown of the game. Pliska place-kicked to Dorais, who added one more point to the Friar total.

The third quarter was a wonderful defensive battle. In the final quarter, Chet "Shine" Knab of the Celts scored a touchdown, but Cincinnati could not convert the extra point. When the Friars got the ball back, Joe Pliska added another touchdown, making the final score 21 to 6.[36]

The Cincinnati Celts closed out the month of October in Lafayette, Indiana, against the Pine Village Athletic Club. The Celts planned an aerial attack to offset Pine Village's strong defensive line. Their aerial barrage, however, was stymied by Pine Village's sidebacks Richard King, W. V. Van Aken, and Paul "Chesty" Sheeks, who intercepted several Cincinnati passes. The Celts' defensive play, bolstered by the outstanding efforts of Carl Thiele and Chet "Shine" Knab, kept the game a scoreless tie.[37] The month ended without a win or a home game for the Celts.

Cincinnati finally had their home opener, on November 4, against the Pitcairn Quakers. The Celts were greeted in the Queen City with indifference. A small crowd attended their game, and they were lucky to eke out a 7–6 win.[38]

The Celts beefed up their line with Pat O'Brian for their game against the Dayton Triangles, but otherwise they relied on old pros Frank Lane, David Reese, Sam Foertmeyer, and Otto Bessmeyer. At ends, they fielded Williams and Ed Krueck. Shine Knab played right halfback, with Thompson at left half, Freye at quarter, and Frank Sorenson at fullback. The game was held at Triangle Park in Dayton, on November 11, 1917. The Triangles were not powerful enough to pierce the Celts' excellent defenses on the ground, and neither team managed a sustained aerial attack. Dayton had two scoring opportunities, but a fumbled pass and a missed field goal ended those chances. The Celts also had scoring opportunities but did not have the backfield punch when they needed it. The Celts players with German ancestry—Foertmeyer, Bessmeyer, Krueck, and Knab—played well, as did Thompson. The *Dayton Daily News* reported, "Dayton right tackle Cutler and Sam Foertmeyer squared off in an impromptu fight, but cooler heads prevailed and, after a handshake, the football contest resumed." Throughout the game, there was considerable holding and occasional tripping. The game ended in a scoreless tie.[39]

The Celts played an exhibition game against the Camp Sherman army team, on November 17, then returned to Redlands Field in the Queen City to play the Dayton Triangles on Sunday, November 25. The Triangles caught the 9:05 Big Four special train from Dayton to Cincinnati Sunday morning.[40]

The Celts added some men who had played with them in 1916 in an effort to gain advantage over their long-time Dayton rivals. Costello started at left tackle and Meister at left guard. Frank Lane was moved to center because David Reese was playing quarterback. Tom Gaither was back at the fullback slot and Tully was at left half, while Chet Knab played right half.[41]

The Celts scored first in the opening quarter on an opportunity created when Mahrt fumbled a bounding punt. Williams picked up the ball and, with a clear field ahead of him, scored the touchdown. Bessmeyer kicked goal, making the score 7–0. In the second quarter, Knab shanked a punt, giving the Triangles the ball on the Celt twenty yard line. Mahrt picked up ten yards on an end run, and Partlow punched the ball across for the touchdown. Zimmerman's extra point tied the game. For the rest of the game, neither team was able to move the ball, and the contest ended in a 7–7 tie.[42]

On December 1, the Celts and the Triangles played for a third time to determine the championship of southern Ohio. This game was played at Triangle Park before three thousand fans, the largest crowd to attend a pro game in Dayton prior to the end of World War I. The two new backfield men, Harlan and Hall, were unable to provide either an offensive or defensive spark to the Celts. The Celts were outplayed throughout the game, although the score was only 6–0 entering the final quarter. The Triangles stuck to their passing game and ultimately won 13 to 0.[43]

It was a disappointing season for the Celts, who ended with a 1–3–3 record. The Celts were determined to make Cincinnati a football town, but, in 1917, the prospects did not look good. The Celts made a brief appearance as part of the American Professional Football Association league, in 1921, when they posted a 1–3 record. Their lone victory came at the expense of the Muncie Flyers. Ironically, this win was wiped out of the NFL record book because Muncie dropped out of the league before completing the season. In 1922, the Cincinnati Celts NFL franchise was canceled when they failed to post the necessary league fees. On July 8, 1933, the Cincinnati Reds were granted an NFL franchise, which in turn was sold to St. Louis in 1934.[44] Cincinnati did not return to the NFL until 1968.

14. The Greatest Rivalry
of Its Time

Canton and Massillon are located less than twelve miles apart in
Ohio, and for years there was intense rivalry between them. They
competed for new industries, for new residents, and in all forms of athletic endeavor. The creation of semiprofessional football teams in these
communities sustained and escalated existing antagonisms.

When the Canton Athletic Club was formed in November 1903, it
played only two games, losing to archrivals Massillon and Akron. The
damage to town pride made it impossible to field a major semiprofessional team the following year, but, in November of 1904, the Canton Athletic Club announced that it planned to reorganize itself for
the 1905 season as a "professional organization" with a "professional
coach."[1] The club hired Bill Laub, Akron's captain and coach, to lead
the team. However, in November of 1905, Laub was injured in a game
with Latrobe and was replaced by Charles E. "Blondy" Wallace,[2] who
had been captain of Connie Mack's famous 1902 Philadelphia football
team.

During 1905 and 1906, the Canton Bulldogs won eighteen games
and lost only three. Two of those losses, however, were to Massillon,
which did not endear the team to the hometown fans. As a result of financial difficulties and rumors of point fixing in the 1906 season, the
Canton Bulldogs disbanded. Another semipro team was not reorgan-
ized until 1912, when Ed Piero and Dr. Lothamer formed the Canton
Professionals. They avoided using the Bulldog name because it was associated with the scandal. Jack Cusack, then only twenty-one years
old, became the secretary-treasurer of the team. H. H. Halter was the
team manager, but could not schedule a game with Akron, as Peggy
Parratt refused to meet with him because of past conflicts over arrangements. Since such a game was necessary to the financial success of the
team, Cusack gained control of the situation when he negotiated a contract for a game. He also secured a five-year lease on Canton's League
Park, ruthlessly squeezing out Halter as the team's manager.[3]

Canton's 1912 team started Norman "Dutch" Speck, Smoke Smalley, Harry Turner, Monk Oberlin, and several other notable local players. They lost only three games, two to Akron and one to Elyria. Since both teams were made up largely of college all-stars, Cusack felt his team had a good season, but Canton fans, who hated losing to Akron, put pressure on him to improve his team.

The need to upgrade the Canton Professionals forced Cusack to change the way he paid players. In 1912, the team split profits evenly among the players at the close of the season. This arrangement kept capital expenses low but limited access to out-of-town players. To hire former college players, most of whom lived out of town, Cusack was required to pay them on a game-by-game basis. To do this, someone had to take financial responsibility. So in 1913 Monk Oberlin and Jack Cusack became the co-owners of the team and changed the name of the Professionals back to the Canton Bulldogs. They immediately put all the players on salary. Jack Cusack later wrote:

This new arrangement left us free to start building a team that could compete with Akron and Elyria, and we added several college men, including Ray McGregor of Mt. Union, also Henry and Bill Dagenhard, together with Eddie and Norm Van Alman.[4]

But again Canton was unable to beat Akron.

The first few games of the season often lost money, while later games with Shelby and Elyria generally drew fifteen hundred fans, and games with Akron drew twenty-five hundred. With admission at fifty cents, and no reserved seats to add to the income, there was usually a cash flow problem in October. In 1914, J. J. Foley, president of the Home Brewing Company, cosigned a $10,000 line of credit at First National Bank, which helped the Bulldogs relieve the cash flow problems caused by high salaries and low attendance early in the season.

In mid-November 1914, Canton's center, Harry Turner, a well-liked hometown player, died of a broken back and severed spinal cord incurred in Canton's first triumphant win over Peggy Parratt's Akron Indians. In the return game two weeks later, the Bulldogs charged seventy-five cents admission and set aside twenty-five cents from each admission for Harry Turner's widow.[5] This event proved that fans would pay more money for a good game and a good cause.

Still dissatisfied with their losses to Akron and Elyria, Canton was determined to upgrade their team once again in 1915. Prior to the opening of the season, they hired three new backfield men and three new linemen, and it was clear that more changes were in the offing.

They rehired the Dagenhart brothers, Vince Zettler, Norman "Dutch" Speck, and Eddie Van Alman, and renewed the contracts of Don Hamilton, a former Notre Dame quarterback now coaching at Wittenburg College in Springfield, Ohio, and Don Peters, a fullback from Carlisle now coaching at Northern Ohio College. When five starters from the 1914 State Champion Akron Indians became available, Cusack jumped at the opportunity to hire them. On opening day, the Bulldog lineup had Howard Axtel and Vince Zettler at ends, Dutch Powell and Don Drumm at tackles, Whitey Schultz and Art Schlott at guards, Ralph "Fats" Waldsmith at center, and Don Hamilton, M. J. Truesby, George "Carp" Julian, and Don Peters in the backfield.[6]

Harold Thompson "Dutch" Powell was born in Columbus, Ohio, in 1891. He played football at Central High School in Columbus before going to Ohio State University, in 1908, where he was All-Ohio tackle for three years. According to his college yearbook:

Possessed of a fine physique and agile as a cat, he successfully performed the tasks of running with the ball, taking forward passes and doing anything any man on the team could do, besides playing his position at tackle equally well. Quick to diagnose plays, he invariably drove himself through and over the opposing line and there were no ends powerful enough to box him.[7]

Powell graduated in 1912 with a B.A. in law, having earned three letters in football and one in basketball.[8] In 1912, he played professional football for the Shelby Blues and the Akron Indians, and he continued to play for Akron in 1913–14.

Norman J. "Dutch" Speck was born in 1886 in Canton, Ohio. After playing sandlot football, in 1904 he began playing semiprofessional football for the Canton Shamrocks. Speck's professional football career lasted twenty-five years, a feat which landed him an appearance in the Ripley's Believe It Or Not series. He played for the Canton Bulldogs off and on from 1914 through 1926. In 1920, he joined the Hammond Pros; in 1921, he played with the Evansville Crimson Giants; and, in 1924, with the Akron Pros. Speck was a close friend of Jim Thorpe; in the 1920s, his daughter married Pete Calac, the famous Native American fullback who played for Carlisle Institute and later for the Canton Bulldogs.[9]

The Bulldogs opened the 1915 season against a hapless Duquesne Athletic Club of Wheeling, West Virginia, and scored seventy-five points, while holding Wheeling scoreless. The Bulldogs made twenty-seven first downs and yielded none to their opponents. The Canton Repository reported:

Interest centered in Julian, the famous Michigan Aggie star whose college days ended last June, after a brilliant career covering several years on the grid. He looked the part of an All-American backfield man, exceedingly hard to stop because of his zigzag, twisting manner when running with the ball. His 195 pounds of bone and muscle is well fortified with speed. . . . Julian is a bear at carrying the ball. . . . Another new-comer in the Canton backfield . . . was Truesby, the little half from Painsville whose career was limited to one year with Oberlin Academics. He is fast, nervy and can find the holes in a broken field.[10]

George "Carp" Julian gained large chunks of ground and scored two touchdowns. Don Peters scored on an eighty-seven-yard punt return and made two additional touchdowns.[11] A disappointingly small crowd of only six hundred showed up for the game, so, after paying their players, the officials, and the visiting team their $150 guarantee, the Bulldogs were in the hole.

After the opening game, the Bulldogs hired Bill Gardner, the great Carlisle Institute All-American end. On October 15, the *Repository* reported:

Since leaving Carlisle, Gardner has spent most of his time during the grid season coaching. This fall he has been in North Dakota, but agreed to come back to Ohio when given a good offer to enter the ranks of the Canton Professionals.

On October 17, Canton added Bill Gardner to the roster for their game against the Columbus Panhandles at home. Henry "Hank" Dagenhart started at left guard but did not last long. On the opening kickoff, he tackled Ted Nesser, who was "traveling like a bullet." Nesser went down, but Dagenhart suffered head and spinal column injuries and had to be carried from the field to Mercy Hospital. These injuries ended his playing career. Later in the game, M. J. Truesby, the Canton left halfback, broke his collarbone and had to be replaced by Eddie Van Alman. Finally, Bill Gardner injured his knee and was replaced by Vince Zettler. Football was a dangerous game, but it was particularly dangerous to play the Nesser brothers.

Only a lucky break allowed the Bulldogs to win. The scoreless game took a favorable turn for Canton late in the fourth quarter when the Panhandles fumbled a punt near their goal line. Canton took advantage of the turnover, with Don Peters driving the ball over the goal line for the game's only touchdown. After the punt-out, Don Hamilton kicked the extra point.[12]

The following week, Canton faced an even tougher opponent, the Detroit Heralds. Over the ten years of their existence, the Heralds had a reputation for playing sound football and had defeated most of the country's finest independent football teams.[13] Its core group, together

George Edward "Carp" Julian, fullback, Canton Bulldogs 1915–16, graduated from Michigan Agricultural College and was an outstanding pro player before being hospitalized with tuberculosis. After recovering from TB, he worked for the State of Michigan Department of Agriculture and was President of the Michigan State University Alumni Association, 1938–40. *(Michigan State University Archives and Historical Collections.)*

for more than five years, called a good mix of running and passing plays. Percy Latham was the Heralds' quarterback, and his favorite receivers were Richard "Red" Shields and Gerald Kelly. Earl Dunn and Percy Wilson were their principal running backs. The real strength of the Heralds, however, was its line. Guy Shields, Bill "Chief" Newashe, Dutch Stewart, Harry Schlee, and Norman "Tango" Glockson were solid linemen who were rarely pushed around.

Harold "Eddie" Iddings from the University of Chicago was brought in to replace Truesby, and Norman "Dutch" Speck replaced Hank Dagenhart. Both were improvements. Canton scored in the first quarter on a thirty-eight-yard field goal by Don Hamilton. In the second quarter, however, the Heralds moved down the field using the forward pass to circumvent the Canton defense. A pass from halfback Percy Wilson connected with Red Shields, the Heralds' captain, who ran for a touchdown. After a punt-out, the point after goal was missed, leaving the score 6–3.

In the third quarter, Harry Schlee recovered a fumble for Detroit, and Red Shields kicked a field goal to extend the Detroit lead 9–3. A desperate flurry of passes in the final quarter failed to put any more points on the scoreboard for Canton. The next day the *Canton Repository* reported:

> Although the greatest team that has represented Canton in professional or other football since the days of the famous Bulldogs of 1905–6, Jack Cusack's "pro" combination of 1915 is not invincible. This was shown at Detroit Sunday afternoon, when the red and white machine was sent to its first defeat . . . The Heralds presented a defense that was even too much for the Canton backfield . . . The Detroiters displayed defensive ability even greater than that of the Panhandles a week ago. . . .
>
> The Heralds put on the field a college combination just as formidable as those which are boasted by Canton and Massillon here in Ohio, even though this has been the hot-bed of "pro" football for years. Most of the Detroit men hail from Michigan, the Michigan Aggies and other western colleges. One, Newashe at right guard, is from Carlisle.[14]

As the midpoint of the season approached, no Ohio team was undefeated, and Canton, Massillon, and Toledo had identical records. Columbus sported two losses, one to Canton and a second to Toledo. Akron, Cincinnati, and Dayton were also-rans. The state championship was clearly up for grabs. Before facing the other contenders for the title, Canton played the ever interesting but mediocre Altoona Indians. Altoona boasted some fine athletes, but they rarely beat any team west of Pennsylvania. November 7 was no exception: the Canton Bulldogs won

38–0. Alfred "Greasy" Neale, who was to become a key player in the Bulldogs' championship drive, made his first appearance for Canton under the assumed name Fisher.

Alfred Earle "Greasy" Neale was born in Parkersburg, West Virginia, on November 5, 1891. A childhood friend nicknamed "Dirty" gave him the nickname "Greasy." Neale, an average student at Parkersburg High School, went to college at West Virginia Wesleyan primarily to play football, basketball, and baseball. In the 1912–13 basketball season, he scored 139 field goals, an amazing record for the time. He graduated in the spring of 1915 and became coach of his college football team that fall, while continuing to play on the team. In November, Greasy Neale started three games for the Canton Bulldogs, two of them against the Massillon Tigers. He played under an assumed name to avoid confrontation with members of the West Virginia Wesleyan Board of Trustees for playing Sunday football, and to avoid questions about his college eligibility.[15]

Later, Neale brought John Kellison to Canton to play for the Bulldogs. Also a graduate of West Virginia Wesleyan, Kellison was Neale's assistant coach there and, like Neale, continued to play college football after using up his college eligibility. In those years, the rules were often loosely enforced. In November 1915, Kellison played two games at tackle for the Canton Bulldogs against the Massillon Tigers. He continued to play for the Bulldogs, often under an assumed name, until 1920. In 1922, he played for the Toledo Maroons and worked as an assistant college coach for many years.[16]

Jack Cusack made wholesale changes in his starting lineup in November. He hired John "Hube" Wagner from the University of Pittsburgh and Greasy Neale and John Kellison from West Virginia Wesleyan, and he persuaded Bill Gardner to help recruit his friend and former teammate, Jim Thorpe, to play for the Bulldogs. Thorpe, considered by nearly everyone to be the world's greatest athlete, was a professional baseball player with the New York Giants and, after the baseball season, had been lured by 1912 Olympic teammate Clarence Childs, head football coach at Indiana University, to take a temporary assignment as a backfield coach for his team at a salary of $2,078.69 for the season.[17] Cusack sent Gardner to Bloomington, Indiana, to meet with Thorpe and to offer him $250 a game to play for the Bulldogs.[18] After discussing the offer with Childs, Thorpe agreed to the terms offered. The addition of Jim Thorpe to the Canton roster changed the course of independent football in America.

The event that triggered the entry of Jim Thorpe into independent

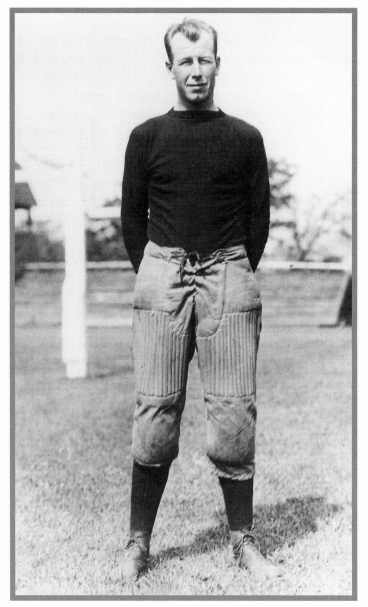

Alfred Earle "Greasy" Neale, end, Canton Bulldogs 1915–17, was born in Parkersburg, West Virginia, and attended West Virginia Wesleyan University from 1912–14, where he played football, basketball, and baseball. He played major league baseball for the Cincinnati Reds and coached at West Virginia Wesleyan, Marietta College, Washington and Jefferson College, and Yale. He also coached the Ironton Lions and the Philadelphia Eagles. He invented man-to-man pass defense and the five-man defensive line. He hit .357 in the 1919 World Series, took Washington and Jefferson to the Rose Bowl, and coached the Eagles to two NFL Championships. Neale was inducted into the Pro Football Hall of Fame in 1969. *(Washington and Jefferson College Archives.)*

football was the rebirth of the Massillon Tigers. Between 1903 and 1906, Massillon, Ohio, with a population of 26,400, had fielded one of the best semiprofessional football teams in America. The Massillon Tigers were organized on September 3, 1903, when thirty-five local civic leaders and businessmen gathered at the Hotel Sailer in Massillon to initiate an independent football team that would represent the entire community.[19] Massillon had fielded amateur teams since the early 1890s, but they had not fared well against Canton teams, a situation that caused much concern in Massillon, where local pride made all events involving Canton extremely competitive. The get-together in the Hotel Sailer, in 1903, was designed to repair local pride and replenish a few pocketbooks that had been made lighter by the large sums of money lost on betting on Massillon against the cursed Canton teams.[20]

Massillon made Jack Goodrich, a local halfback, the team manager and named Edward J. Stewart from the *Massillon Evening Independent*, a former college player for Western Reserve University and Mt. Union College, as the team's coach.[21] Needless to say, football coverage in the *Independent* was outstanding, whereas in many towns it was sketchy at best. As Jack Goodrich began the process of organizing a strong semiprofessional football team for the town, a local sporting goods store was having a clearance sale on black-and-orange jerseys. Clerk of Courts J. J. Wise was put in charge of buying supplies and bought the lot for Massillon's new independent football team. The black-and-orange jerseys gave rise to the team's nickname "Tigers."[22]

From 1903 through 1906, Massillon claimed to be the independent football champions of Ohio, losing only two games in four years, one to Wooster College and the other, in 1906, to the Canton Bulldogs. During those four years, Massillon recruited players from Pittsburgh, Akron, Canton, and elsewhere, rather than relying on local players. More than half the Massillon starters were on salary.[23]

In 1906, Massillon claimed the professional world's football championship.[24] But a good deal of dissatisfaction arose over the conduct of the Massillon team in the game with Canton. The *Massillon Independent* accused Blondy Wallace, coach and captain of the Bulldogs, of attempting to fix the game. Few doubt that Wallace, a veteran of the 1902 football wars in Pennsylvania, knew all the tricks of the business. Several Massillon players were implicated, although no wrongdoing was proven. However, the professional teams in both cities were deeply in debt and disbanded soon after the game. Strong independent football was not revived in Canton until 1912, when the Canton Professionals were formed. The Canton team resumed the use of the name Canton Bull-dogs in 1913. The Massillon Chamber of Commerce discussed the possibility of reviving the Massillon Tigers independent football team in 1914 but could not find appropriate leadership.[25]

When it became clear that J. J. Foley, president of the Home Brewing Company in Canton, was going to underwrite the Canton Bulldogs in 1914, Bill Schuster, manager of the Massillon Brewery of the Stark-Tuscarawas Breweries Company, decided to get behind the Massillon Tigers project and persuaded John "Jack" Whalen Jr., Jack Donahue, and sportswriter Fred Becker[26] of the *Massillon Independent* newspaper to help form the Massillon club.

Whalen, whose financial resources were key to the project, agreed to support the proposed team on one condition: "We want good clean players with clean records, someone who I'm not ashamed to introduce to my wife Rose and our beautiful daughter."[27]

On October 2, 1915, Bill Schuster and John "Jack" Whalen Jr. officially announced the formation of the Massillon Tigers Football Association.[28] The project had been in the works for more than a year, but firm commitments were apparently less than two weeks old.[29] John Whalen Jr.'s commitment of financial support was key to the formation of Massillon's professional football club. As general superintendent of the Massillon Coal Mining Company, Whalen had the financial resources and the community standing necessary to put a first class team on the field.[30]

As the *Massillon Independent* put it, on October 5, 1915:

Clothed in the orange and black worn by the Tigers of old, whose fame traveled far and wide . . . [the new Massillon lineup] banded together by Joe Collins, playing manager and coach, will be here next Sunday to start the campaign to replace Massillon on the map as a football town and bring another championship to the old Tiger town. That's the honest intention. Nothing but a championship will satisfy the fans of Massillon because in days gone by they have had the best in the world as regards football and they want it yet.

Team management hired Joe Collins[31] to coach and help recruit players.[32] Joe Collins of Cleveland was a star end at Notre Dame from 1908 to 1910, where he suggested that coach "Shorty" Longman give freshman Knute Rockne a chance to try out for the team. Collins played fullback and was captain on the 1914 Akron Indians independent football team that won the mythical state of Ohio professional championship.

His first move as Massillon coach was to hire six first-team players away from the Akron Indians. Collins was charged with building a strong team, and he wanted proven quality at its core. Parratt fumed that the wages Collins offered his men were exorbitant, but that year he did not have the financial backing to match them.[33] Among the Akron Indian stars Collins lured away from his good friend were: Knute Rockne, Keith "Deac" Jones, Milton "Muff" Portmann, Homer Davidson, Dwight Wertz, and Carl "Bull" Olsson. Collins also had a tentative commitment from Howard "Cap" Edwards, one of his old Notre Dame teammates who had played with the championship Akron Indians, but Edwards received a better offer from Canton that nixed the deal. Canton also hired Howard Axtel, Harold "Dutch" Powell, and Ralph "Fats" Waldsmith away from Akron.[34]

When Peggy Parratt found out that almost all of his starting lineup had been lured away by higher pay, he was forced to cancel Akron's opening game with the Detroit Mack Park Maroons.[35] Parratt finally fielded a patched-up team, on October 31, against the Mack Park Maroons and also played games in Toledo and Dayton in early November, but for practical purposes the Akron Indians ceased to exist when their team was cannibalized by Massillon and Canton at the beginning of the 1915 season. On October 19, Parratt agreed to coach the Shelby Blues.[36]

In addition to the players lured away from the Indians, Massillon hired Clarence Erb from the Canton Bulldogs, Joe Esch from the Elyria Pros, E. M. Cole, who had left the University of Michigan after the 1912 season, Charles "Sam" Finnegan, recently of Notre Dame, and Howard J. Bowie, just out of Western Reserve University. Massillon Blues starter, Harold A. Boerner[37] played left tackle in the home opener. After the first game, Wertz, Erb, and Bowie were replaced by Boyd Cherry of Ohio State, Jim Flynn of Western Reserve, and Morris of Ohio State, and Boerner returned to the Massillon Blues.[38] As Fred Becker, secretary of the team, wrote in the local newspaper,

> With five former Notre Dame players in the line up, the Tigers will undoubtedly resort to the style of play taught at that school, and as Notre Dame has always been proficient on the gridiron game, excellent football is expected.[39]

Massillon had planned to open its season on October 10 with a game against the Shelby Blues, but Shelby was in the midst of a baseball tournament and did not have time to think about fielding a football team.[40]

The opening of the Massillon Tigers season against the Cleveland industrial team, the Blepp Knits, was a big occasion. The Massillon high school band was on hand to celebrate the event. Before the teams went to Driving Park, there was a grand parade. The rival teams gathered at the Hotel Sailer in their uniforms and marched up Main Street behind the band before being loaded into automobiles and taken to the football field.[41]

Two thousand spectators packed the park to watch the Massillon Tigers win the home opener against the Cleveland Blepp Knits, 43–3. Although one-sided, the game exposed a weakness, and a few days after the game the *Independent* commented, "Massillon's line is not as strong as it will be. . . . Massillon will have to secure additional talent to bolster up the weak spots. This is now being done. . . ."[42]

Massillon did not have access to a home field and was unable to schedule a home game for October 17.[43] Instead, they took twenty men to Detroit for their second game, confident that they "had the greatest collection of gridiron stars ever brought together."[44] "A special car load of fans" left from Massillon bound for Detroit at noon Sunday morning. An advanced guard left Saturday afternoon on the Pennsylvania Railroad for Detroit, where the Massillon Tigers would square off against the undefeated Mack Park Maroons.[45] The Maroons kept their perfect record intact by defeating the Toledo Maroons 7–0 on October 3, and the Buffalo Oakdales 12–0 two weeks later.

More than three thousand fans paid to watch the Maroons play the Tigers. Massillon fielded a strong team led by Knute Rockne, Sam Finnegan, Carl "Bull" Olsson, and Edmund Kagy. The game was closely fought. Massillon scored a touchdown in the second quarter after a solid drive, when Kagy drove through tackle for the score, but Massillon failed the goal after the punt-out.

In the third quarter, the Detroit Maroons scored a touchdown on a beautiful pass from Bertie Maher to Ty Krentler. Goal was kicked, and Detroit led 7–6.[46] That score stood until the final minutes of the game, when Massillon's Homer Davidson drop-kicked a field goal from the eighteen yard line. Davidson, a graduate of Central High School in Cleveland, was a veteran semipro player who could hold his own with the college all-stars.[47] Detroit did get an opportunity to win the game on the final play, but Thomas Bogle, a University of Michigan product, missed a forty-yard goal from placement by inches.[48]

On October 31, 1915, Massillon returned home to play one of the best teams in Ohio, the Columbus Panhandles. Massillon added Ed Hanley and David Reese to the Tiger squad for the game.[49] The Panhandles started six Nesser brothers, with Frank and Ted Nesser as the team leaders. Frank weighed in at 225 pounds and was a tower of strength at right tackle. Fullback Ted Nesser had been a star for ten years and played for the 1906 Massillon Tiger team, yet no one felt that age had slowed him down significantly.[50] The Panhandles were coming off a 20–0 defeat at the hands of the Toledo Maroons, and Toledo was already claiming to be the team to be beaten for the state independent football championship.[51]

By mutual consent, Columbus and Massillon agreed to play twelve-minute quarters. A crowd of three thousand surrounded the field at Driving Park at kickoff time. From the opening kick onward, Ted and Frank Nesser dominated the game. Although Knute Rockne and Charles "Sam" Finnegan played an outstanding game for Massillon, Columbus battered their way through the Tiger defense to a 16–0 victory. Massillon lacked unified team play, while Columbus worked together like a well-oiled machine. Though Massillon fans believed that individually their players were better than those of the Panhandles, Columbus created mismatches and used their ground game to control the ball.

Columbus capitalized on their weight advantage and ripped and tore their way through the Massillon line. On nearly every offensive play, it took nearly the entire Tiger team to tackle Ted or John Nesser. On offense, Massillon was unable to move the ball against the stubborn Columbus defense.[52] Clearly the Massillon Tigers would have to strengthen their team if they hoped to contend for the state championship in November.

In an effort to regroup, add new players, and create better teamwork, the Massillon Tigers scheduled a game against Wheeling, West Virginia, at Martins Ferry, Ohio, on November 7. Massillon players were asked to assemble in Wheeling on Saturday night and Sunday morning for the game to be played at Central League baseball park in Martins Ferry, across the river from Wheeling. The field was used because the Ohio side was better suited to building a football field, and because blue laws prohibited football in West Virginia on the Sabbath.[53]

The game against the Duquesne Athletic Club of Wheeling was viewed as a practice game to tune up for the Canton match the following week. Knute Rockne was again the team leader at Martins Ferry. Superior on defense, he broke up play after play and nailed the ball carrier regularly in the one-sided 47–0 victory over Wheeling.[54] At Martins Ferry, Massillon's teamwork improved markedly.

The two upcoming games with the Canton Bulldogs were the high-

light of the Massillon season. The games had not been officially scheduled until October 20, when the directors of the Massillon team chased
down Jack Cusack, the Bulldog manager, and forced a decision out of
him. According to Fred Becker in the *Massillon Independent* on October
21, 1915, Jack Cusack was scheduled to meet with John Whalen Jr.,
Bill Schuster, and Joe Collins at the Hotel Conrad in Canton to agree on
the dates for a home-and-home series between the rival cities. However, when Cusack did not show up as agreed, the Massillon delegation
piled into an automobile and decided to find Jack Cusack if it took all
night. Sometime after midnight they found his house, got him out of
bed, and negotiated and signed an agreement to play in Massillon on
November 14 and in Canton on either Thanksgiving or the Sunday following Thanksgiving.

On November 12, Jack Cusack made an announcement that would
ensure the full-fledged professionalization of American independent
football. On Sunday, November 14, the *Canton Repository* announced,
"Jim Thorpe, the most famous of all Indian athletes, will play half-back
for the Canton Bulldogs!" Cusack declared that he "had entered into
agreement with Thorpe some time ago but was keeping the great Carlisle star covered. Somehow the fact leaked out and crept into one of
the Cleveland papers, although," he said, "it did not come from me.
Massillon was not supposed to be put 'wise' to Thorpe's presence until
Sunday."[55]

Cusack had just completed the transformation of big-time independent football to professional football. By offering Thorpe the unheard-of
sum of $250 per game, he caught the attention of professional athletes
everywhere. Thorpe was capable of extraordinary feats on the football
field. One eyewitness reported seeing Thorpe kick a football 100 yards
in 1915. According to his story, Thorpe had just arrived in Bloomington, Indiana, to coach kicking for Indiana University, and was asked by
one of the players, "What was the longest kick you ever got off, coach?"
Thorpe replied, "I'll try to show you." He told the center to hike him
the ball. Catching the ball on the goal line, he took a couple of strides,
gave the pigskin a terrific smash with his foot, and the ball sailed seventy-five yards in the air, then rolled to the other goal line.[56] The presence
of Jim Thorpe on the field in football-crazy northeast Ohio doubled the
attendance at the game and escalated the demand for former college
all-stars to the point where no team could hope to become a state, regional, or national championship contender without a significant number of paid former college stars on its team.

James F. "Jim" Thorpe teaching Clair Scott how to punt. Jim Thorpe was the greatest athlete in the world during the first half of the twentieth century. His presence made pro football possible in 1915. Clair Scott, president of the Indiana University class of 1916, played left end for the Pine Village Athletic Club in 1916. *(Indiana University Archives.)*

The November 14 game between Canton and Massillon was billed by the *Canton Repository* as "the greatest professional football conflict in ten years."[57] Massillon arranged to bring Charles "Gus" Dorais in from Iowa to revive the Dorais-to-Rockne aerial attack made famous in 1912 when Notre Dame used the forward pass to beat Army. They also hired Boyd Cherry and Maurice "Windy" Briggs, the All-Ohio ends from Ohio State University, and J. Franklin Day, Louis J. Hayes, and Malcolm "Red" Fleming, who were playing illegally at Muhlenberg College in Allentown, Pennsylvania. All five of these newcomers to the Massillon Tigers played under assumed names. Canton also had a couple of players playing under assumed names: Alfred E. "Greasy" Neale and John Kellison were playing as Fisher and Davis.

The price of admission to the Canton-Massillon game on November 14 was increased to seventy-five cents, with reserved seats an additional twenty-five cents. Despite the high price of tickets, six thousand fans paid to see the game at Massillon's Driving Park. Only the game between Wabash and Evanston held on October 24 and the games between Youngstown and Barberton and Youngstown and McKeesport had equaled that size crowd. Since the other teams charged between twenty-five and fifty cents for admission, this was the largest gate in the history of independent football.

Ed Conners, University of Maine graduate and coach at Cleveland's Lincoln High School, officiated the game. Jim Thorpe arrived in Canton on Saturday from Bloomington, Indiana. Many of the other players did not arrive until late Sunday morning. Don Hamilton, for example, coached a Wittenburg College game held in Cincinnati on Saturday and could not leave until he got his college team back to Springfield.

On game day, the *Massillon Independent* reported, "Nowhere in this country today are there two football teams possessing such a galaxy of stars as do the Tigers and Bulldogs." Because it rained all day Saturday and the Driving Park football field was poorly drained, the field was muddy and slippery. The skies were gray and gloomy, but the fans were at a fever pitch.

Thorpe was unfamiliar with the Canton offense, so he did not start the game and, because of playing conditions, was not particularly effective. Nevertheless, he gained seventy yards on ten attempts, including one run of forty-two yards. Not bad for a man unfamiliar with the Canton offense and his teammates.

The real hero of the day, however, was Charles "Gus" Dorais. He ran the Massillon offense with skill, completing seven of nineteen passes for 119 yards. His pass to Edmund Kagy in the second quarter set up the game's only touchdown. More importantly, he made three splendid field goals on drop kicks of thirty-three, forty-two, and forty-four yards in four attempts.

Canton had opportunities to win the game that were foiled by the slippery field. In the second quarter, Jim Thorpe caught a nine-yard pass and ran forty-two yards before he slipped and went out of bounds on the Massillon eight yard line. Four plays later, the Bulldogs had a touchdown called back when a Massillon player tipped a forward pass which was subsequently caught by Canton guard Don Drumm, who scored. Under the rules of 1915, the Canton touchdown was not allowed and the ball was turned over to Massillon, ending the scoring threat. On another occasion, Thorpe skirted Massillon's left end and had a clear field in front of him but slipped and fell when he tried to make a cut to take advantage of the opening. The greatest part of the last quarter of the game was played in darkness. "The unknown halfback from the East," Greasy Neale, and George "Carp" Julian both played well for Canton. The biggest disappointment for Canton was the

Robert P. "Butts" Butler, tackle, Akron Indians 1914; Canton Bulldogs 1915; Cleveland Indians 1916. He was a Walter Camp All-American at the University of Wisconsin in 1912 and 1913, and a member of the University of Wisconsin coaching staff in 1914–16. *(University of Wisconsin Archives.)*

play of its line. The younger, faster Massillon front seven dominated play in the trenches.[58]

After a lapse of nine years, Massillon still held sway over Canton. As the *Canton Repository* put it, "the same old Massillon jinx still holds its mystic power over Canton."[59] Massillon's 16–0 win made them the odds-on favorite for the championship of professional football in 1915. Cusack's mission was to break the Massillon jinx and bring the championship to Canton. Beating Massillon was more important than money at this point, so he was prepared to spend whatever was necessary to get the job done. Game-day analysis of the Massillon win indicated that Dorais had clearly outplayed Don Hamilton at the quarterback slot. When Cusack expressed displeasure at how Hamilton had called the game, Hamilton quit on the spot, leaving Canton without a quarterback. It was also evident that Canton would have to strengthen its line if it hoped to win the rematch.[60]

The Canton manager decided to single-mindedly focus his attention on beating Massillon. He chose not to play a game on either the following Sunday or on Thanksgiving. Instead, he began rebuilding his team for the November 28 rematch with Massillon. For the most part, Cusack relied on existing networks to recruit new talent, but he also reviewed the ranks of college seniors, whose college season would end by Thanksgiving, for possible players.

Looking over the list of All-American nominees, Cusack picked Earl Abell,[61] a senior and a Walter Camp All-American at Colgate.[62] In turn, Abell recommended that Cusack hire his classmates at Colgate, Frederick Sefton and Charles Edward Stewart.

Cusack also had his eye on Wisconsin University assistant coach, Robert Parker "Butts" Butler, who had been an All-American tackle in 1914 and had played for him under an assumed name against Akron at the end of the 1914 season.[63]

On the advice of George "Carp" Julian, Cusack hired Gideon Charles Smith, Carp's former teammate at Michigan Agricultural College and All-Western tackle in 1913–15.[64] Likewise, Dutch Powell recommended former Ohio State University lineman Arthur "Bugs" Raymond.

Because Canton chose not to schedule a game on Thanksgiving, many of its best players played for other teams and scouted talent for Canton. Jim Thorpe started for the Pine Village Athletic Club against the Purdue University All-Stars, and Howard "Cap" Edwards played for the Fort Wayne Friars against the Columbus Panhandles on Thanksgiving, where he met Kent "Skeet" Lambert. Impressed with Lambert's skills as a field leader and triple threat, Edwards recommended that Cusack hire him to replace Hamilton at quarterback. Jim Thorpe also brought Big Ed Davis, coach of the Pine Village team, and Indiana University All-Conference quarterback Harry Whitaker of South Bend to Canton to play for the Bulldogs on November 28.[65]

Massillon played Toledo on Thanksgiving Day. The Tigers added Norbert Sacksteder from the Dayton Gym-Cadets to their team as a running back. On a muddy field, Massillon squeezed out a 3–0 victory over Toledo on a fourth quarter field goal by Gus Dorais.[66] Perhaps the Massillon players were looking ahead to the upcoming contest with Canton.

15. A Streetcar Conductor
Wins the Day

The final football game of the 1915 season between the Canton Bulldogs and the Massillon Tigers was billed as the world's professional football championship. Held in the League Baseball Park in Canton, it promised to be one of the most exciting games played in the United States that year. Both teams had scoured the nation for the best available players, and both the Massillon Tigers and the Canton Bulldogs were prepared to field all-star teams of a caliber never before seen in independent football. Nearly every player was a headliner, and some were considered among the best ever to play single platoon football.

Leading the list was the great Native American Jim Thorpe, considered by many sportswriters to be the best football player of the century and nearly everyone's "eternal All-American."[1] According to those who played with him, Thorpe "could go sixty minutes at top clip. He was the best, without question the best all-around football player and the best all-around athlete of his era." Hall-of-Famer Joe Guyon recalled, "When he tackled you, goddang, he'd almost kill you. Give him the ball and he'd delight in running through a whole team."[2] Jim Thorpe's presence on the field doubled the size of the crowd for the pending game.

In addition to Thorpe, there were thirty-six superb athletes suited up for the game. All played offense and defense, and the teams were evenly matched. Many in the Massillon lineup played under assumed names in an attempt to protect their amateur status or to hide their activities from their day employers. Boyd Cherry called himself White. J. Franklin Day played under the assumed names Southern and Campbell. Louis J. Hayes played under the names Lee and McGuire. Ed Hanley used the name Hogan. Malcolm Fleming played as Maurie, and Maurice Briggs played as Burne. Canton's Alfred "Greasy" Neale used the name Fisher. Only the best-informed fans knew who was really playing.

It is useful to reenact large portions of the Canton-Massillon game on a play-by-play basis to contrast the football game of 1915 with the modern game. At that time, pro teams played by the same rules as college teams. The game was scheduled to start at 2 P.M. on November 28, just outside the Canton city limits. It was an overcast, gray Sunday afternoon, and the field was soft from the soaking rain that had drenched the area all day Friday and up until noon on Saturday. The gray skies, however, did not deter the crowd. League Park was filled to capacity, and standing room was even sold in the end zones. Altogether more than sixty-five hundred fans paid one dollar each to attend the game, and half of them paid an extra twenty-five cents for a grandstand seat. In addition, upwards of fifteen hundred fans climbed the fence or crept past the gate unnoticed. The game was officiated by referee Ed Conners, a Cleveland teacher, umpire Cosgrove of Cornell University, and head linesman Jones of Ohio State University. All were experienced football officials who had officiated both college and independent games in the past.

Before the game started, ground rules were discussed. Jack Cusack, the Canton manager, later reported that both teams had agreed to the ground rules, one of which was that, owing to the crowd in the end zones, any player crossing the goal into the crowd must be in possession of the ball when he emerged from the crowd. Charles Dorais, team captain for Massillon, could recall no such agreement.

Massillon brought eighteen players, and Canton suited nineteen players. The starting lineups were as follows:

Canton		**Massillon**
Bill Gardner, Carlisle Institute	LE	Knute Rockne, Notre Dame Univ.
Earl Abell, Colgate Univ.	LT	Keith "Deacon" Jones, Notre Dame Univ.
Howard Edwards, Notre Dame Univ.	LG	E. M. Cole, Univ. of Michigan
Ralph Waldsmith, Buchtel College	C	Louis J. Hayes, Muhlenberg College
Edgar Davis, Indiana Univ.	RG	Milton Portmann, W. Reserve Univ.
Robert Butler, Univ. of Wisconsin	RT	J. Franklin Day, Muhlenberg College
John Wagner, Univ. of Pittsburgh	RE	Ed Kagy, W. Reserve Univ.
Kent Lambert, Wabash College	QB	Charles Dorais, Notre Dame Univ.
Jim Thorpe, Carlisle Institute	LH	Bill Kelleher, Notre Dame Univ.
Alfred Neale, W.V. Wesleyan College	RH	Malcolm Fleming, Wash. and Jeff. College
Geo. "Carp" Julian, Mich. Ag. College	FB	Ed Hanley, Univ. of Pittsburgh

The Canton Bulldogs had several Walter Camp All-Americans in its starting lineup: "At tackle we have Abell, captain of the Colgate team, another heavy man and one of the best linemen that has played that position in several years. He was practically the only man in the Colgate line who could really stem the tide of the Syracuse avalanche."[3] Butler was All-American at Wisconsin the previous year and was now coaching linemen at his alma mater.[4] Gardner had been All-American while at Carlisle, when Jim Thorpe was just starting to play big-time college football. Edgar Davis was All Big Nine (now Big Ten) at Indiana. George "Carp" Julian and Howard "Cap" Edwards were All-Western. Julian was second team All-Western on both the *Chicago Evening Post* and *Chicago Interocean* squads in 1913 and on their first team in 1914.

Some less heralded players were also outstanding. Ralph "Fats" Waldsmith was one of the best centers to play single platoon football. Waldsmith had played undergraduate football at Buchtel College (now The University of Akron). He was in the tradition of great centers at Buchtel where Harry Clark, under coach Heisman, invented the hike to the quarterback in 1893 that replaced rolling the ball to the quarterback.[5] Jim Thorpe considered Waldsmith the best center with whom he had ever played. Norman "Dutch" Speck,[6] already close friends with Jim Thorpe, was on the bench. In addition, there was Gideon Charles Smith,[7] the great African-American tackle, on the Canton bench. Smith had almost single-handedly defeated the University of Michigan earlier in the fall, when he led the Michigan Aggies to a win over Coach Yost's Wolverines. He was on the second team All-Western squad named by the *Chicago Evening Post* in 1913. Deprived of All-American honors because of his race, G. Charles Smith would become the first Black professional football player to play in a world championship.

Massillon had almost as many stars. Knute Rockne and Charles "Gus" Dorais had revolutionized football in 1912 when they used the forward pass to defeat what was thought to be an unbeatable army team. Both were All-Western in 1913. Keith "Deac" Jones was captain of the 1913 Notre Dame team, while Boyd Cherry was All-Ohio and All-Big Nine as an end for Ohio State in 1912 and 1913. Milton "Muff" Portmann, along with Knute Rockne, had played for the championship the year before while with the Akron Indians and had been on the winning team. Red Fleming from Bellwood, Pennsylvania, had been All-Pennsylvania while at Washington and Jefferson. Massillon had two fine players on the bench, ready to fill in as needed: Norb Sacksteder, a St. Mary's College All-Star with the Dayton Gym-Cadets, and Ohio State all-purpose player Maurice "Windy" Briggs.

As was usual in such long-standing community rivalries, the *Canton Daily News* noted, "There was a large amount of money [bet] up on the game and the fans, crowded into a stadium much too small for the crowd, were at fever pitch when the game started."[8] Because the ball park was outside the city limits of Canton, city police were not available to control the crowd, and the sheriff's deputies would not work on the job for the amount of money offered.[9] As a result, there were no policemen to keep order. At Wabash, Indiana, they had strung barbed wire around the field to keep the fans from interfering with play, but this was not done at Canton.

The game got started later than scheduled to allow additional fans into the "standing room only" section of the ball park, which included the end zones of the playing field. The temperature at game time was forty-nine degrees, almost perfect football weather.[10]

The team captains, Charles Dorais for Massillon and Howard Edwards for Canton, both Notre Dame graduates, met with the officials at midfield for the toss of the coin to determine goals and possession of the ball.[11] Canton won the toss and chose to defend the west goal with Massillon kicking off. Red Fleming kicked the ball from placement from the forty yard line at a point equidistant from the sidelines, in accordance with the rules. Hube Wagner received the kick and ran the ball back to the thirty-eight yard line where he was tackled by Deac Jones, who stood five feet eleven inches tall and weighed nearly two hundred pounds. On the first play from scrimmage, Canton lined up in a wing formation, and Greasy Neale attempted a sweep to the right. Kagy, the old pro who had played for the Ohio professional championship teams in Elyria and Akron, stopped Neale for a one-yard loss. Kagy was a strong defender who had toned his muscles on a railroad work gang. On second down, the teams lined up and the signals were shouted, as the huddle would not come into use until 1921, when the University of Illinois pioneered the strategy. On this play, Jim Thorpe took the ball on direct snap from center Fats Waldsmith and headed around Knute Rockne's end with Skeet Lambert, Greasy Neale, and Carp Julian running interference. Lambert, who was playing with an injured shoulder, boxed Rockne out of the play, and Thorpe gained six yards. On the next play, Massillon was penalized five yards for being offside, and Canton was given four more downs.

Thorpe put his fingers in his mouth to moisten them, then took a hand-off from Lambert on first down and bucked into the line for three yards. On second down, Julian ran at Muff Portmann for six more yards. However, on two additional attempts up the middle, first Julian and then Thorpe failed to get a first down. Massillon took over the ball near midfield on downs. The crowd roared its approval.

Massillon lined up in the Notre Dame box. Dorais was about three yards back of center with Bill Kelleher two yards further back and to his left, Red Fleming at the same distance back on his left, and Ed Hanley three yards directly behind Dorais. On Massillon's first play from scrimmage, Dorais received the ball from center and handed it off to Hanley, who attempted to run through Butts Butler at right tackle. He was stopped without gain. Butler, the University of Wisconsin All-American, was like a rock on the defensive right side. On second down, Massillon faked a hand-off to Hanley and gave the ball to Fleming who ran at Earl Abell, the Canton left tackle. Massillon believed that Abell might be the weak link in the Canton line. Fleming gained less than a yard. On third down, Kelleher also ran at Abell without success, so on fourth down Dorais punted the ball.

Jim Thorpe received the punt on his own twenty-four yard line with Massillon players closing in on him. He returned the ball just four yards before being downed. Canton lined up in a normal set, similar to Massillon's offensive set. All four backfield men went down in a three-point stance. Lambert yelled out three sets of numbers, and the four backfield men rose up in unison and moved into a single wing formation right and reset. Lambert yelled out another set of numbers. The ball was hiked to Lambert who handed it to Greasy Neale who ran over right tackle for two yards. On the next play, Abell pulled from left tackle, ran parallel with the line of scrimmage, and was handed the ball for a play off right tackle while the backs faked left. The trick play carried for only two yards. On third down, in a surprise move, Canton shifted into a short punt formation, and Jim Thorpe proceeded to punt the ball sixty yards. Dorais ran back in an attempt to return the punt but lost it in the sun that had momentarily returned, and he fumbled the ball on the Massillon seventeen yard line where Canton's Hube Wagner pounced on it.

Canton prepared to take advantage of the turnover by taking the ball directly to Massillon. Two line bucks by Greasy Neale and one by Jim Thorpe netted only five yards. On fourth down, Thorpe drop-kicked a goal from the twenty yard line, giving Canton a 3–0 lead.

In 1915, the team that was scored on was obliged to kick off to the team that had scored; thus, Massillon again kicked off to Canton. Jim Thorpe received the ball and returned it to the thirty-three yard line. After Kagy stopped Greasy Neale on an attempted end run, and side-back Fleming blitzed the Canton quarterback for a loss of four yards, Thorpe swung around Rockne's end for two yards and on fourth down punted to the Massillon twenty yard line. Dorais returned the ball to the thirty-five yard line. Up to this time, the Canton Bulldogs had gained only twenty-five yards, or less than two yards per try. Massillon had earned only four plays from scrimmage and had gained only three yards. A tough defensive battle was shaping up.

On the first play, Hanley had the ball stripped from him, and Hube Wagner recovered his second fumble of the afternoon. Then the Canton Bulldogs' offense went back into action. Lambert handed the ball to Greasy Neale, who produced two yards over center. Carp Julian followed up with a six-yard gain, but Canton was penalized fifteen yards for holding. Lambert threw a pass that was nearly intercepted by Dorais, and on third down Thorpe galloped around right end for fifteen yards before being tackled by Knute Rockne. Thorpe attempted a drop kick, but it was blocked. Massillon recovered the ball on their own forty-five yard line, giving them good field position.

On first down, Massillon again tried the Canton line but failed to gain ground. The play, however, set up a fake into the line on second down, which allowed Dorais to bootleg the ball around left end for eight yards. On third down, Hanley plunged up the middle for only one yard, so Dorais was forced to punt. Unfortunately, he shanked the ball, and it went out of bounds on Canton's thirty-four yard line. Up to this point, the game had been all Canton's.

With the ball placed just three feet in from the north sideline, the entire line was to the right of the center. Canton tried Carp Julian up the middle on first and second downs, but with the sideline limiting the area of play he made only four yards altogether. So Jim Thorpe tried a long pass to Hube Wagner, which fell incomplete on the Massillon twenty yard line. Thorpe punted, and the ball went out of bounds on the Massillon twenty-five yard line.

Now the Tigers were pinned against the north sideline and were forced to line up their entire front six to the left of the center. As the first quarter drew to a close, Fleming tore off a six-yard gain for Massillon around left end. Butler then stopped Dorais for no gain, and the quarter ended when Canton was penalized five yards for being offside. The score was Canton 3, Massillon 0. Canton had gained fifty-two yards rushing, while Massillon had been held to eighteen yards. Neither team had completed a pass, but Massillon had two turnovers, one of which had resulted in a field goal for Canton.

The second quarter was again evenly fought. The Canton line stopped the Massillon running game cold at the beginning of the quarter. Massillon and Canton traded punts twice before Massillon's Ed Kagy wrenched his ankle and was replaced by Boyd Cherry. When Canton was held on downs at its fifteen yard line, Thorpe punted to

Dorais, who was tackled by Abell and Wagner on the Massillon thirty yard line.

At this point, the Massillon offense began to click. Red Fleming reeled off five yards, and Norbert Sacksteder was brought into the game at left halfback in place of Kelleher. Sacksteder proceeded to twist and slide off four more yards for Massillon over Earl Abell's spot at defensive left tackle. After being stopped on third down, Ed Hanley made a first down on a fake punt formation.

Braced by the success of their running game, Dorais now began to pass the ball. He threw an arching, "fluffy" pass that was deflected by Carp Julian but was nevertheless caught on the rebound by Red Fleming, who made another first down. Dorais then threw a twenty-five-yard pass to Knute Rockne, who caught the ball over his shoulder with two men defending—one attempted to intercept the ball, and the other tackled Rockne as soon as he caught the ball. However, on the next play, Thorpe intercepted a Dorais pass and returned the ball to midfield, thereby halting the Massillon drive.

Canton's offense bogged down again, and the ball was turned over to Massillon, whose offense was still on track. Sacksteder made nine yards over Abell, and Hanley followed with five yards over the gap at center. Massillon drove the ball to the twenty yard line, where Dorais tried a drop kick in hopes of tying the game, but the kick was blocked. Canton recovered the ball in the middle of the field. George "Carp" Julian pounded the ball up the middle on a hand-off from Lambert for eight yards, and then went through the center of Massillon's line for thirty-two yards before safety Dorais saved a touchdown by spilling Julian. Carp Julian's run would be Canton's longest gain of the game.

The hometown crowd got so excited, it surged onto the field, and play had to be stopped to clear the field before the game could continue. When play resumed, Thorpe twice tried to pass, but each attempt failed. Canton's end, Bill Gardner, felt he had been tripped by Red Fleming as he attempted to run his pass pattern, but the referee had not seen the infraction. Gardner and Fleming exchanged unpleasantries, but the game continued. Thorpe then tried an end run but was thrown for a two-yard loss by Knute Rockne. The half ended with the score still 3 to 0 in favor of Canton. In the first half, Canton had rushed for 110 yards. Massillon had rushed for fifty-eight yards and had made an additional thirty-seven yards passing. The big difference was the three turnovers committed by Massillon and the field goal by Thorpe.

The teams went into their unheated dressing rooms. Canton held onto a narrow lead, but it was clear to Massillon that they had found a way to make their offense move and, if they could eliminate turnovers, they could win this game. They talked about ways to take advantage of Canton's weaknesses in the second half. Deac Jones was convinced that he and Rockne could drive a wedge between Abell and Gardner that would open the left side of the line.

In the meantime, Cusack, the manager of the Canton Bulldogs, was beginning to worry about Abell. The big tackle had traveled a long way with poor connections to reach Canton from Hamilton, New York, in time for the game, and he had flu symptoms. Cusack was not sure Abell would last another half and asked Jim Thorpe during the recess about whether or not to replace Abell with Gideon Charlie Smith, the African-American tackle from Michigan Agricultural College. Thorpe was reluctant to take an All-American out of the lineup, but he deferred to Cusack who replaced Earl Abell with G. Charles Smith to start the second half.

The move was propitious. According to the *Canton Daily News,*

No one player received more attention after he got into the game than Smith. Smith only weighed 178 pounds, but he played like a raging bull. The first ten times Massillon had the ball, Smith either broke interference or got around and made the tackle. . . . Smith was the biggest star on Canton's defense.

When Jim Thorpe kicked off to start the second half, Smith tackled Ed Hanley who had returned the ball to the Massillon ten yard line. On the following play, Smith stopped Sacksteder for a loss, then he stopped fullback Hanley without a gain. On third down, Dorais punted the ball on a quick kick, and Lambert, the Bulldog safety, downed the ball on Massillon's forty yard line.

Massillon's defense held like a stone wall, giving up only three yards in three plays. Thorpe tried a drop kick from the forty-eight yard line, but the ball fell short. Because it went over the goal line, the ball was brought out to the twenty yard line, where Massillon took over.

Each team punted twice before Sacksteder was stripped of the ball by Smith. Canton guard Norman "Dutch" Speck recovered the fumble. He was a hometown Canton boy who had never attended college and frequently earned his living as an ironworker. Speck had replaced Edwards in the previous defensive series to help save the captain of the Canton team for the fourth quarter when his experience was bound to be needed.

The hometown crowd, of course, went wild when one of their own boys gathered in the college star's fumble. Three line plunges netted five yards for Canton, and on fourth down Thorpe dropped back to the

Gideon Charles Smith, tackle, Canton Bulldogs 1915, was All-Western at
Michigan Agricultural College and became assistant director of physical education at Hampton Institute. While he played only one half a game of pro football, it was one of the best performances in iron-man pro football. Smith was
the first Black to play in a pro football championship game. *(Michigan State University Archives and Historical Collections.)*

thirty-seven yard line for a place kick. Lambert held the ball, despite the fact that neither had trained together for the maneuver. The kick was good. Canton led 6–0.

Massillon kicked off again. Greasy Neale received the kickoff near the end zone and returned the ball to the fifteen before being dropped by a host of Massillon Tigers. The Canton offense was unable to move the ball, so Thorpe punted to Dorais, who returned Thorpe's towering punt to the Massillon thirty yard line. On the next play, Thorpe threw Sacksteder for a three-yard loss, but Massillon got the yards back on an offside call on the second down. Gideon "Charlie" Smith then leveled Windy Briggs, who had replaced Sacksteder, for a loss of five yards. A tackle eligible pass to Deac Jones yielded eight yards more, but Massillon was forced to punt for the fourth time in the quarter.

Lambert received the punt and was immediately tackled by Muff Portmann on the Canton twenty-six yard line. After licking his hands, a distinguishing habit, Thorpe then ran around the right end for twenty yards, his longest gain of the day. On the next play, however, defensive sideback Red Fleming intercepted a Canton forward pass on his own four yard line.

The third quarter ended there, with the score still 6–0, Canton. Canton also held a decided advantage in overall offense. They had gained 142 total yards to Massillon's ninety-three yards. Two months of football had now boiled down to fifteen minutes that would decide who would be the champions of professional football for 1915. Rockne reminded his Massillon teammates that he was not a loser and did not expect them to be either. When the fourth quarter got underway, it was with renewed determination on the part of the Massillon Tigers, who could win this game with a touchdown and a point after—no easy trick in this era of the punt-out for extra point after touchdown.

Dorais started the fourth quarter by throwing a pass to Knute Rockne, who deceived the defender with his acting, sidestepping, and change of pace. The pass covered thirty-three yards, and Rockne ran for an additional twelve yards. The little Norwegian was playing big as usual. The ball was now resting on the Canton eighteen yard line, and the game had an entirely different complexion. Gus Dorais made three yards around left end on first down, but Windy Briggs gained only two yards on second down, and Ed Hanley was held without gain. On fourth down, Dorais tried a pass to Rockne. It was incomplete in the end zone, and, under 1915 rules, on an incomplete pass in the end zone the ball went over to the opposing team on the twenty yard line.

The Bulldog offense still sputtered. During this series of downs, Bill

Gardner and Red Fleming got into a shouting match. Gardner called Fleming a dirty cheat, and Fleming replied, "You're the biggest baby on the whole Canton team. You're yellow." A fistfight was imminent until referee Conners stepped between them. Gardner again complained about Fleming's illegal tactics. On fourth down, Thorpe once again was forced to punt. The ball ended up near midfield, and the Massillon Tigers went to work again. Dorais threw a forward pass to Windy Briggs who netted twelve yards on the play. Hanley plunged into the line for a single yard, then on a play action pass, Dorais threw to Boyd Cherry, the 170-pound end from Ohio State University. He gained twenty yards on the play.

Another short pass to Cherry yielded only two yards. Now it was second down on the Canton seventeen yard line, and the crowd in the end zone pushed past the goal line to get a better look at the game. Dorais went over to the referee and asked that the goal line be moved out ten yards and that the ball be moved back ten yards to make the end zone more accessible. Cosgrove, the umpire, told him to get on with the game.

On the next play, Dorais threw a pass to Windy Briggs, who caught the ball on his outstretched fingertips as he dove for the end zone, but in doing so he disappeared into the crowd. A few minutes later, Charlie Smith, the Canton tackle, emerged from the crowd with the ball. Briggs insisted that a policeman had kicked the ball from his arms after he crossed the goal line and that he should be awarded the touchdown that would tie the game. Canton argued that there were no policemen on the premises, and hence Briggs's story was a fantasy. A long argument ensued. The crowd streamed onto the field, threatening to lynch the officials if they made the wrong decision, and any decision would be considered the wrong decision by nearly half the people in attendance.

Finally, after twenty minutes or more of debate, the last of the day's light was gone. Reluctantly, it was agreed that the game would be called on account of darkness, even though there were still eight minutes on the game clock. The officials would submit their decision in writing to the clerk of the Cortland Hotel with their verdict to be read at 12:30 A.M., to give the referees an opportunity to catch the train out of town unmolested.

Based on the ground rules agreed on at the outset of the game, the touchdown was disallowed, and Canton was declared the winner of the game. Massillon offered a $10,000 winner-take-all bet on another game, but Jack Cusack, manager of the Canton Bulldogs, replied that, "I'm through for the year. . . . I could cover the $10,000 with good Canton coin but it might spoil the sport for next year."[12]

Years later, Jack Cusack ran across a streetcar conductor who claimed to have won the game for Canton. He told Cusack that he had $30, his entire two weeks wages, bet on Canton, and when Windy Briggs crossed the goal line, he was so mad he kicked the ball out of Briggs's hands, and the ball popped over to Charlie Smith, who fell on it for a touchback. Because of the brass buttons on his conductor's coat, Windy Briggs mistook him for a policeman, opening himself to ridicule because no policemen were working the game that day.[13] So ended the first great professional football play-off game.

16. Cleveland, Canton, and Massillon: Center of the Hurricane, 1916

Peggy Parratt's Cleveland Indians opened the 1916 football season with a team that could have won the 1915 world's championship but proved to be insufficient for the new season. Professional football was improving week by week. Older players, unfamiliar with new styles of play, were having a difficult time keeping pace with the changes.

Parratt secured strong backing for his newly organized Cleveland Indians and was determined to get even with Massillon and Canton for breaking up his 1914 championship Akron team. He started building his 1916 team by hiring back many of the stars Massillon and Canton had stolen from him in 1915, and a few others as well. He hired Milton "Muff" Portmann, Boyd Cherry, Ed Hanley, Carl "Bull" Olsson, Cass, Homer Davidson, E. M. Cole, and Dwight Wertz away from Massillon. He hired Bob Butler, John "Hube" Wagner, and Harold "Dutch" Powell away from the Canton Bulldogs. He also offered quarterback Harold Pogue, from the University of Illinois, $50 per game for a twelve-game season, but Pogue turned down the offer because it would have required him to move from Decatur to Cleveland.[1] Before the season was over, Parratt would pirate players from three or four other teams and recruit a number of former college stars directly into his organization.

Parratt's Cleveland Indians opened their season on September 24 against Elyria. Nearly all of the opening-day players had been with Massillon or Canton in 1915. The starting lineup featured Roy "Tommy" Burrell and Boyd Cherry[2] at ends, Milton Portmann and Bob Butler at tackles, E. M. Cole and Carl "Bull" Olsson at guards, C. "Whitey" Schultz at center, and Homer Davidson, Campbell Graff,[3] Arthur "Dub" Schieber,[4] and Ed Hanley in the backfield. All were seasoned professionals, although some may have been past their years of peak performance. The Cleveland Indians narrowly won the game 6–3.[5]

On October 1, 1916, Cleveland added Walter Camp first team All-American center Paul "Shorty" Des Jardien from the University of Chi-

Paul R. "Shorty" Des Jardien, center, Cleveland Indians 1916; Hammond Pros 1919; Chicago Cardinals and Chicago Tigers (player-coach) 1920; Rock Island Independents 1921. He was an All-American at the University of Chicago and had a brief career in major league baseball before playing for Peggy Parratt's team in 1916. *(College Football Hall of Fame.)*

cago. The nickname "Shorty" was a joke, because he was six feet five inches in height, so he had excellent vision as a linebacker on defense.[6] Des Jardien played professional baseball for the Cleveland Indians during the summer of 1916, but he was cut from the major league team a few days before joining Parratt's team.[7] For Cleveland's game against the Akron Burkhardts, Parratt added Guy L. "Chalky" Williamson, a notable quarterback from the University of Pittsburgh. In spite of opening the season against weak teams that would not rank among the top twenty in independent football, the Cleveland Indians were having difficulty winning. A lack of teamwork plagued Cleveland, who struggled to beat Akron 3–0.

By October 8, Cleveland began to play better. They added Thomas H. King from Notre Dame at left tackle, Stanfield Wells from the University of Michigan at end, and Howard Lester Beck from Washington and Jefferson at end.[8] An unknown player with the name "Goldberg" showed up among the substitutes as a guard.

Cleveland, like all of the other teams in northeast Ohio, made quick work of the Altoona Indians, 39 to 7.[9] They also disposed of the Pitcairn Quakers in a more competitive contest on October 15. The *Cleveland Plain Dealer* bragged, "Indians Win Brilliant Contest from Pitcairns."[10]

Even at this early date, Cleveland and Pittsburgh had no love for one another when it came to football. Chalky Williamson delighted in sending a message back to Pittsburgh that Cleveland was developing a football team to contest Canton and Massillon for the world's championship. Ed Hanley and Chalky Williamson, both from Pittsburgh, each scored a touchdown in Cleveland's 14–6 win over the Quakers. Carlisle Institute luminary, Joe Bergie, together with Frank White and Sutter, from Indiana Normal School in Pennsylvania, led the Pitcairn attack. Sutter had a touchdown called back, for holding, that would have made the game much closer. Even Peggy Parratt got into the act by throwing a thirty-five-yard pass to Ed Hanley. [11]

By October 12, 1916, the *Toledo Blade* reported that "the baseball war has passed into history, but it's different in the professional football world." The article went on to say:

The Federal League example is being followed by football promoters, and if reports are true a football war has broken out, to the joy of the players and the ultimate sorrow of the managers of professional elevens.

At present Cleveland, Massillon and Ft. Wayne are embroiled in the controversy, each claiming that one of the other teams has stolen players using money as the bait, while on the other hand each manager emphatically denied having tampered with players supposed to be members of other teams.

Massillon claims that Peggy Parratt stole Chalky Williamson and induced the Pitt quarter to report to the Cleveland Indians.

Parratt on the other hand declares that he had lined up Rockne and Fitzgerald of Notre Dame; "Red" Fleming, of W. & J.; Joe Mattern, ex-Minnesota star and now assistant coach at University school. All these men played Sunday with Massillon.

Peggy declares his negotiations with Mattern and Rockne had gone so far that he gave these players the Cleveland plays and signal code.

And then comes the howl from Ft. Wayne, which declares that Rockne and Fitzgerald do not belong to either Cleveland or Massillon, having originally agreed to play with Ft. Wayne.

Canton, while not yet in, is ready to fight, claiming that several Canton stars have been approached with offers of more money to play other elevens. Incidentally, Cleveland, Massillon, and Ft. Wayne are making the same howl as Canton.

But the Canton management has taken the real sensible move by trying to get the other managers to agree not to tamper with another team's players.

Tampering will soon demoralize players, as they will be jumping to the team which offers the most money, wrecking team play and upsetting plans.

Canton also points out that unless this "stealing" of players ceases professional football will again be in a bad way, and instead of having several teams in the fight there will not be enough first-class elevens left in the country to enable the professional managers to fill out schedules.

Canton proposes that each team shall keep the players now playing and shall sign an agreement not to approach a member of any other bonafide professional eleven without the consent of the management under which the said player is then playing.

On October 22, Parratt got a wake-up call when the Nesser brothers came to Cleveland to begin the round robin that would determine the independent football championship of Ohio. Six thousand fans paid to see the famous Nesser brothers play the upstart Cleveland team. For three quarters, the teams played evenly. In the first quarter, Cleveland gained more yards than the Panhandles, but they were stopped on the Panhandle ten yard line without scoring.

In the second period, the Panhandles took charge of the game when Lee Snoots intercepted a Cleveland forward pass on his own forty-five yard line. Frank and Ted Nesser then powered their way to the Cleveland thirty-five yard line "like runaway railroad cars," knocking down two or three prospective tacklers before scoring the only Columbus touchdown of the game.[12]

Cleveland fought back to tie the game on a series of passes from Homer Davidson to Beck and a run by Ed Hanley. Beck scored the tying touchdown. Late in the fourth quarter, Emmett Ruhl drop-kicked the field goal that won the game for the Panhandles.[13]

Peggy Parratt was deeply disappointed with the outcome of the Pan-handles game. The last weekend in October, he split his team. Half the team played a rematch with the Akron Burkhardts in Cleveland, and the other half played the Mendel Pirates in Columbus.[14] Parratt was stuck with players who turned out not to be good enough to challenge Canton and Massillon, and he needed to hire others to upgrade his team.

Parratt signed up eleven new players to meet his dual commitment. He added linemen Harold "Dutch" Powell, Frey, Getz, Brooks, Fay, and Zeeman. He also added backfield stars Pickerel, Yocum, Willaman, Wertz, and Smith. F. A. Yocum was a football hero for the class of 1915 at Oberlin College.[15]

Louis Edward "Pick" Pickerel was born in Jackson, Ohio, in 1894, and studied law at Ohio State from 1911 to 1916, where he played quarterback and left halfback. He was five feet eleven inches tall and weighed 155 pounds. In 1915, he played quarterback for the Columbus Panhandles. He also played a game for the Cleveland Indians in 1916, when he was assistant coach at Ohio State.[16]

Future pro star Samuel S. "Willie" Willaman was born in Salem, Ohio, in 1891. He enrolled in the engineering school at Ohio State in the fall of 1910, where he played halfback and end. He made All-Ohio, in 1913, at halfback. His accurate passes to Boyd Cherry, in 1914, were well publicized. After graduating in the fall of 1915, Willaman coached at the high school in Alliance, Ohio. He played for Peggy Parratt's Akron Indians, and, in 1916, he played for Parratt's Cleveland Indians, while coaching football at East Tech High School in Cleveland. In 1917, he played with the Canton Bulldogs, sometimes using the assumed name "Williams" to avoid trouble with his high school administration. In 1922, he become a successful head football coach at Iowa State College. He became assistant football coach at Ohio State in 1926. After the 1933 season, he resigned to become head coach at Western Reserve in Cleveland. He died unexpectedly following an emergency operation on August 18, 1935. He was buried in Salem, Ohio.[17]

With the help of these great stars, the Indians managed to win both games on October 31, but neither by impressive scores. Parratt attributed his problems to lack of teamwork. Cleveland defeated the Mendel Pirates 13–0 with a team composed of Boyd Cherry, Thomas King, Dutch Powell, Whitey Schultz, E. M. Cole, Bull Olsson, Roy Burrell, Homer Davidson, Sam Willaman, Dwight Wertz, Louis Pickerel, and Honus Graff. A team of this stature should have won by a larger margin.[18]

Meanwhile, in Cleveland, Guy L. "Chalky" Williamson, Ed Hanley, Muff Portmann, Bob Butler, Stan Wells, Dub Schieber, Paul Des Jardien, Smith, Frey, Brooks, and Zeeman barely got by the Akron Burkhardts 13–0 in what the *Plain Dealer* called a "poor contest."[19] The Burkhardts, with players like John Larsen and Leo McCausland at tackles and Joe Gray at halfback, proved stronger than Parratt had anticipated and the Indians came off looking weak to hometown supporters. There were already indications that, even with the new talent, Parratt's team would not be strong enough to win against Canton and Massillon. These were the very teams Cleveland would face over the next three weeks.

When the Canton Bulldogs opened their 1916 season, they were committed to championship football. Jack Cusack, the Bulldogs owner-manager, had a core of stalwarts from his 1915 team and played the free-agent player market like a chess master. He tied up players like Milton Ghee, who was coaching at Dartmouth, even though Ghee was unlikely to be available to play until after the close of the Dartmouth College football season in mid-November.[20] He used players like Park Crisp, Harry Whitaker, Art Schlott, and George Roudebush to start the season, knowing full well that they would not be good enough to face Massillon, Cleveland, and Youngstown late in the season. He used his resources skillfully, even under adverse circumstances, to quickly find competent replacements when unexpected problems arose. The Canton lineup changed weekly in 1916 depending on the availability of first-rate players.

Tom F. Gormley, a lawyer who had starred for Georgetown University in 1914 and 1915, had a verbal commitment to play the opening game for Canton, but he got a better offer from Youngstown. Later, he did play a game or two for Canton and then took a job with Cleveland. As unreliable as he was, one would expect that teams would avoid using him, but he was so good that he continued to play well into the 1920s. Because of his talent, his cavalier attitude toward commitments was overlooked.

Ernie Soucy and Howard Buck missed games because their coaching positions sometimes made it impossible for them to make railroad connections to Canton in time for the Sunday game, so on occasion they played for nearby Pine Village instead. Yet, despite these problems, Jack Cusack always fielded a strong lineup and managed to win even with the injuries and sickness that affected stars like Jim Thorpe and George "Carp" Julian (see Table 2).

Table 2: Canton Roster Changes, 1916

Date	Action	Pos	Players
October 1		E	M. J. Truesby, Charles E. Stewart
		T	Ed Russell, Art Schlott, Bell
		G	Park Crisp, Norman Speck
		C	Ralph Waldsmith
		QB	Harry Whitaker
		H	George Lowe, Harry Costello, George Roudebush
		F	George "Carp" Julian
October 8	ADD	E	Fredrick Sefton, W. Davis Ward
		T	Tom Gormley, Bill Gardner
	DROP		Bell, Truesby
October 15	ADD	H	Jim Thorpe
		E	Ernie Soucy
	MOVE	G	Bill Gardner
October 22	DROP	H	George Roudebush (to Cincinnati Celts)
October 29	ADD	H	Richard C. King
		C	William Garlow
	DROP	H	George Lowe (to Cleveland)
November 5	ADD	T	Howard Buck (from Pine Village)
		H	M. E. "Red" Wilkinson
	DROP	T	Tom Gormley (to Cleveland)
		H	Richard King
November 19	ADD	QB	Milton Ghee
		T	John Kellison (Playing as Ketchem)
	MISSED GAME	E	Ernie Soucy
		LT	Howard Buck
November 26	ADD	FB	Frank Dunn
		RG	Doc Spears
	DROP	FB	George Julian (illness)
December 3	ADD	FB	Pete Calac
		T	Howard Edwards (from Ft. Wayne)
		QB	Bart Macomber (from Pine Village)
		HB	Gus Welch
	DROP	QB	Harry Whitaker

Of all the new players recruited by Cusack, his most important acquisitions were Harry Costello and Ed "Unk" Russell. Costello had been an all-around player at Georgetown University, whose good judgment on the field quickly highlighted his running, passing, and kicking skills.[21] Pop Warner said that Costello, "for his [size] was one of the greatest players that ever lived."[22] As head football coach for the University of Detroit, Costello played under an assumed name to avoid

Harry Whitaker, quarterback, Canton Bulldogs 1915–17 and Detroit Heralds 1917, was the signal-caller for Indiana University 1913–15. *(Indiana University Archives.)*

problems with his new employer. Ed Russell was an excellent tackle. He replaced the captain of the 1915 Bulldogs, Cap Edwards, without weakening the team.

Cusack courted fan support by holding the general admission price to fifty cents during the month of October.[23] Whatever he lost in gate receipts early in the season, he expected to make up in November when the big games were scheduled with archrivals Cleveland and Massillon.

Meanwhile, Massillon was facing problems of its own. The Tigers were counting on Dorais to be their quarterback, perhaps not at the start of the season, but certainly when the chips were down and the championship was on the line.[24] Since Dorais had also promised to play for the Fort Wayne Friars, this was a problem for the Tigers.

Massillon was not satisfied with the team that ended the 1915 season. In late September, Massillon hired Malcolm D. "Red" Fleming as its new head coach to keep him from playing for Cleveland. Upon getting this assignment, Fleming took a trip east to recruit new players. En route, he stopped in Pittsburgh and discussed his plans with the *Pittsburgh Press*. Fleming claimed to have signed Charley Barrett, Cornell's great kicking star, to a Massillon contract, but Barrett never played for Massillon. He also talked to Russ Goodwin, the Washington and Jefferson quarterback, who was now coaching; A. A. "Buzz" Wesbecher, the great center at Washington and Jefferson, who was now athletic director at Bethany College; and Frank Dunn, the Dickinson College All-American fullback.[25]

Canton opened its season at home on October 1, 1916, against the Altoona Indians. Harry J. Costello dominated the Bulldogs offense. "Silk Hat Harry," the pride of Georgetown University, was called "a bigger man than Taft" by his classmates because of how well he played football, even though at 180 pounds he had nowhere near the girth of the 345-pound President.[26] His pass to former Colgate University end, Charles Edward Stewart, gave Canton its first six points of the season. His kick for extra point was good for a 7–0 lead. Later, his running and passing set up a second touchdown by Harry Whitaker.[27] The final score was 23–0 in favor of Canton. The failure of starters Fred Sefton and Tom Gormley to show up for the season opener did not deter the Bulldogs.

One week later, Gormley finally appeared in the Canton lineup, along with college dropout William Ward from Georgetown University playing under the assumed name Moriarity, perhaps because he was a

Sherlock Holmes fan but, more likely, to pass for former teammate Tom Moriarity, who had played for the Detroit Maroons in 1915. In the first half of the Canton-Pitcairn game, Canton was held to four first downs while the Quakers made one. In the second half, the Bulldog defense stopped a Pitcairn drive on their own two yard line. They won on a touchdown by George "Carp" Julian and an extra point by Harry Costello. Costello missed four earlier field goals, each by less than a foot. However, he distinguished himself on defense, as did Dutch Speck, William Ward, and Carp Julian. Canton was lucky to win the game 7–0.[28]

At the close of the major league baseball season in mid-October, Jim Thorpe returned to the Canton lineup. George Roudebush, from Denison University, was used to back up Jim Thorpe in the Buffalo All-Stars game, because Cusack felt that Thorpe needed time to regain his football legs. Ernie Soucy, a new end from Harvard, playing under the assumed name of Drake, was added to the team. The starting Bulldog lineup remained the same, with the exception of Thorpe and Soucy. The Bulldogs scored eleven touchdowns, three each by Thorpe, Costello, and Soucy and two by Carp Julian. Buffalo was no match for Canton and lost 77–0. Thorpe played only half the game. Before being relieved by George Roudebush, Thorpe threw a thirty-nine-yard pass to Stewart.[29]

On October 22, the *Canton Repository* reported that the home team "Mauled, trampled, trounced and humiliated the New York All-Stars 67–0." Harry Costello and Jim Thorpe each made two touchdowns, and Carp Julian made four. Thorpe made five of seven extra points, and Costello made two of his three extra points.[30] Canton looked unbeatable throughout the month of October.

At the same time, the Massillon Tigers were also putting together an undefeated October. Nearly 10 percent of the city's population showed up for the October 8 home opener and watched Massillon romp over Elyria 31–0. Massillon's starting lineup found Knute Rockne and Ed Harley at ends, Carl "Dutch" Thiele from Denison University and J. Franklin Day at tackles, Carl Rambaud from the Massillon sandlots[31] and Freeman Fitzgerald from Notre Dame at guards, and Louis J. Hayes at center. The Massillon backfield started Ed Kagy at quarterback, Malcolm "Red" Fleming at right half back, Bill Kelleher at fullback, and Joel Mattern at left half.[32]

Joel P. Mattern attended the University of Minnesota, in 1913, and Lehigh College the following year. In 1916, while he was coaching and teaching at University High School, he played football under the assumed name DeMars to avoid problems with the school board. In 1919, he played for the Cleveland Indians, and for the Detroit Heralds and Cleveland Panthers in 1920. Later, he became head football coach at Dunwoody Institute and played for the Minneapolis Marines. He was known as a great open field runner.[33]

Freeman C. Fitzgerald was born, in 1892, in Parkersville, Oregon, and enrolled at Notre Dame in the fall of 1912. He was a strong, two-hundred-pound lineman and immediately became a first team guard on the varsity team. He played for two years at guard and two years at center, winning All-American honors at both positions. Fitzgerald, who was captain in 1915, was Notre Dame's last four-year varsity football monogram winner. He also won a letter in basketball. After graduating as a mechanical engineer in the spring of 1916, Fitzgerald coached the freshmen at Notre Dame. In the fall, he played right guard for the Massillon Tigers. He also played a game or two for the Fort Wayne Friars that year. In 1917, he played the first half of the season with the Youngstown Patricians and the balance with the Tigers. After the 1917 football season, he joined the army and earned the rank of lieutenant in aviation. In 1920–21, Fitzgerald played professional football with the Rock Island Independents of the NFL and was the head football coach at Creighton College. In 1922–29, he was line coach at Marquette University. Subsequently, he became the Milwaukee manager of the Ceco Steel Company and was president of the Notre Dame Club of Milwaukee. He died on May 6, 1942, at the age of fifty, after a long illness.[34]

On October 11, 1916, Massillon added 1915 All-American guard Christopher Schlachter. Playing under the assumed name Schmidt, Schlachter had a conflict with his coach at Syracuse and dropped out of college to play pro football.[35]

On October 15, Massillon defeated the Altoona Indians 54–0.[36] The first real test for the Tigers came on October 22 against the Toledo Maroons. Massillon played Windy Briggs at quarterback and Joe Bergie at fullback, but otherwise their lineup stayed the same. The game attracted six thousand spectators to Armory Park in Toledo. Toledo took a 7–0 lead in the second quarter, which held until the last twelve minutes of the game. At the end of this bitterly contested struggle, as darkness settled over the field, the Massillon Tigers rallied by scoring fifteen points on touchdowns by Knute Rockne and Joe Mattern and a field goal by Red Fleming.[37]

Finally, Massillon played the Detroit Heralds at Navin Field, the major league baseball stadium in Detroit, on October 29. Big Robert "Nasty" Nash, at six feet two inches and 210 pounds, joined the Massillon Tigers for their game in Detroit. A second team Walter Camp All-American in 1914, Nash was a significant addition to the lineup.[38] In a poorly played game, Massillon barely beat the Heralds, 6–0. As the *Detroit Free Press* reported,

[Massillon's] team work was not there, nor did it evidence itself on the Herald side for that matter. But the Tigers brought a couple of fine ends to town in Rockne of Notre Dame and "Dutch" Thiele of Denison. Still, neither of these men would have been so deadly effective if the Herald backs blocked like first grade backs should. With one or two exceptions, the Herald backs never once left their feet to block on an end skirting or tackle dive. They attempted to brush men like Rockne and Thiele aside with their shoulders and their laughable and feeble efforts in this direction got them nowhere in particular.[39]

Despite the fact that the Massillon lineup contained two All-Americans and at least six others who had won country-wide recognition, the Heralds played them pretty even.[40] The Heralds quarterback Kent "Skeet" Lambert played well, but his receivers had bad cases of butterfingers, and Massillon barely escaped with a 6–0 win. Nevertheless, the Tigers passed one more milestone in the race for the professional football championship of the United States.[41] After the game, Massillon spoke with Lambert and enticed him to become the new Massillon quarterback.

Like Massillon, Canton remained undefeated and unscored on in their 12–0 win over the Columbus Panhandles. Thorpe and Julian each scored rushing touchdowns against the tenacious Nesser crew in the first half. Once they had gained the upper hand, the *Canton Repository* said, "the Bulldogs made no great effort to fatten the count in the second half, preferring to play it safe and risk no chances of injury to men who will be needed for hard combats to come."[42]

The first Sunday in November found Massillon paired with the Patricians in Youngstown. A special train carried Massillon fans to Wright Field,[43] where more than five thousand Youngstown fans cheered against them. Massillon was unable to hire Charles Dorais and Knute Rockne for this game, both having previous commitments, but they took a strong team to the Steel City.[44]

Massillon		**Youngstown**
Carl Thiele, Denison Univ.	LE	Russell Ashbaugh, Brown Univ.
Freeman Fitzgerald, Notre Dame Univ.	LG	Fred Stiver, Case Institute

(Continued)

Massillon		Youngstown
Robert Nash, Rutgers Univ.	LT	R. M. Smith, Penn State Univ.
J. Louis Hayes, Muhlenberg College	C	Lester Miller, Marietta College
Christopher Schlachter, Syracuse Univ.	RG	George Yeckel, Western Reserve Univ.
J. Franklin Day, Muhlenberg College	RT	Tom Gormley, Georgetown Univ.
Fred Heyman, Wash. and Jeff. College	RE	Charles H. Roberts, Yale Univ.
Kent Lambert, Wabash College	QB	Ray Thomas, West Virginia Univ.
Joel Mattern, Univ. of Minnesota	LH	Stilwell Saunooke, Carlisle Institute
Malcolm Fleming, Wash. and Jeff. College	RH	Horace Palmer, Ohio Univ.
Ed Kagy, Western Reserve Univ.	FB	Getz, Akron Central High School

The Patricians and Tigers battled fiercely for a scoreless first half, according to the *Massillon Independent*, but, soon after the start of the third quarter, Kent "Skeet" Lambert drop-kicked a field goal from the forty-yard line. "His kick sailed squarely between the uprights and he hoisted the leather from a difficult angle."[45] It was the only score of the afternoon. The Pats had done their best to tie a knot in the Massillon Tigers' tail, but they could not cross the Tigers' goal line.

On November 12, the Tigers played the Columbus Panhandles, who featured 1,477 pounds of Nesser brothers. The Panhandles were a well-organized aggregate of railroad workers that could give any football team in America a lesson in teamwork and old-fashioned "three yards and a cloud of dust" football. The Panhandles had daily workouts in which they practiced signals and punting and had scrimmages. While most of the Columbus players were over twenty-five years of age, they put everything into each play because they truly loved the game.[46]

Ted Nesser dominated Panhandles play, cutting through the Massillon line like a "hot knife through butter," in the cliché of the *Massillon Independent*, and Frank demonstrated that he knew how to heave the pigskin as far as anyone in the game.[47] The Massillon offense depended on Joel Mattern, who often "submarined himself through the Columbus line." Skeet Lambert drop-kicked a field goal to give Massillon its lead, then, in the last thirty seconds of the game, threw a pass to Red Fleming that put the game on ice.

A Massillon newspaper reported, "Eleven snarling, snapping, fighting Tigers . . . plunged, drop kicked and forward passed themselves to a 10 to 0 victory over the heavy Columbus Panhandle football team on the Driving Park gridiron east of the city, before a crowd of spectators estimated at 4000."[48] While Massillon did not yet have enough punch to defeat Canton, the black-and-orange eleven were good enough to whip Columbus. However, Massillon might have scored three additional touchdowns had they been able to capitalize on all of their scoring opportunities.

Willmon "Fats" Keiser from Bucknell College in Lewisburg, Pennsylvania, played his first game for Massillon. Willmon Keiser was from Mt. Carmel High School in Pennsylvania and was captain of Bucknell's football team from 1913 to 1915, where he was the starting left end and fullback for three years. He could also play right halfback with skill. He graduated and became an electrical engineer.[49] "His laugh is the best imitation of a hen's cackle," his college yearbook declared.[50] But, once on the football field, few laughed at Fats. According to the *Massillon Independent,* "Keiser at fullback could rip through the Columbus line just about as well as Ted [Nesser] could plow through the Massillon line."[51]

On November 5, in Canton, an important game was underway. The day before the game, the *Canton Repository* reported,

Realizing that he was going up against the most powerful professional football machine ever welded together, Peggy Parratt, field marshall of the Cleveland Indians has gone east and west in his search for new stars to hurl against the Canton Bulldogs. . . . He had unearthed four new men for his line and claims to have two others, both All-American rating, on the way. All of which indicates a rather rugged struggle. Peggy is well backed financially and is in the game to the limit with orders to spare nothing in the effort to give Cleveland a winner.[52]

The lineups of both teams read like a 1916 *Who's Who* of American football:[53]

Cleveland		Canton
John Wagner, Univ. of Pittsburgh	LE	Ernie Soucy, Harvard Univ.
Milton Portmann, Western Reserv. Univ.	LT	William Ward, Georgetown Univ.
William Neill, Univ. of Penn.	LG	Norman "Dutch" Speck, Canton sandlot
Paul Des Jardien, Univ. of Chicago	C	Ralph "Fats" Waldsmith, Buchtel College
C. "Whitey" Schultz, Sandlot	RG	Bill Garlow, Carlisle Institute
Bob Butler, Univ. of Wisconsin	RT	Ed Russell, Univ. of Penn.
Roy "Tommy" Burrell, Canton sandlot	RE	Charles Stewart, Colgate Univ.
Homer Davidson, Clev. Central H.S.	QB	Harry Costello, Georgetown Univ.
Arthur Schieber, Ohio State Univ.	LH	Jim Thorpe, Carlisle Institute
Dwight Wertz, Western Reserv. Univ.	RH	M. E. "Red" Wilkinson, Syracuse Univ.
Ed Hanley, Univ. of Pittsburgh	FB	George "Carp" Julian, Mich. Ag. College

From the opening kickoff, the game was never in doubt. Cleveland's team was still in the process of development, and they lacked teamwork. Cleveland failed to make a first down.[54] Jim Thorpe played one of the best games of his life. The *Cleveland Plain Dealer* declared, "Thorpe proves too much for Parratt's gridders." The newspaper went on to say,

Jim Thorpe jammed through the line. Jim Thorpe whirled around the ends. Jim Thorpe punted. Jim Thorpe hurled forward passes, and Jim Thorpe did just a little more than almost any other human being could do.

Thorpe numbered among his feats a spectacular dash of more than seventy yards. He sidestepped through a broken field for thirty yards and a touchdown. Frequently he gained from five to fifteen yards. Almost invariably he tossed off a few tackles before being stopped.[55]

Thorpe carried the ball more than half the time and scored three touchdowns. The *Canton Repository* wrote,

"Carp" Julian, Jim's running mate at fullback, likewise made the Cleveland delegation often feel sick at heart, and so did quarterback Conley [Harry Costello], and so did—but why go on, just scan the line-up. Canton advertised a team of stars, and eleven men starred for Canton."[56]

The *Cleveland Plain Dealer* echoed the praise,

Canton's set of forwards [linemen] would lose no luster compared to the great collegiate lines. Practically every one of the forwards as a famed character in his collegiate days, and apparently they have lost none of their skills and little of their dash.

From the outset the Indians played a defensive game almost entirely. There were times when the line held brilliantly. Inside of Cleveland's five-yard line Canton had a terrible time gaining. Twice the Indians held for downs inside their one yard line.[57]

Before the game, George "Peggy" Parratt questioned the value of having so many illustrious names as Canton had, saying, "Names don't win games." Canton's answer was, "If your name is Jim Thorpe, it does."[58] More than seven thousand fans watched the Cleveland-Canton contest at $1 each. It was the second largest gate in independent football history, and the best of the season was yet to come.

On November 6, the *Canton Repository* sports page headline read, "Count the Cleveland Indians . . . out of the race for the professional championship of the world this season," but it was still premature for that epitaph. Canton still had to play Cleveland in Cleveland the following week. Peggy Parratt was convinced that his team was not as bad as it had looked on November 5. He decided to play himself at quarterback and strengthen his backfield with Derby of the University of Virginia at left halfback. In violation of a gentleman's agreement not to tamper with players signed by other teams, Peggy Parratt hired Tom Gormley and Jim "Butchy" Barron away from Youngstown.[59] He also added Lobert from Villanova at right end and George "Bull" Lowe at left halfback playing under the assumed name Hunter. Jim "Butchy" Barron played under the assumed name Roberts and Tom Gormley played as Gordon, presumably to misdirect Youngstown Patrician management.[60]

Canton fielded essentially the same team, except that Harry Whitaker started at quarterback in place of Harry Costello, who was injured the week before.[61] The game was played in Cleveland's American League baseball park, and the *Plain Dealer* reported that a crowd of ten thousand attended the game.[62] Jack Cusack, Canton's general manager, later complained that he was paid for only four thousand fans. Since more than one general manager complained that Peggy Parratt liked to "divide the money half-horse and half-rabbit, his preference being the horse end,"[63] we may never be able to get an accurate report on the size of the crowd and the gate. It is certain that, as the *Cleveland Plain Dealer* reported, "several thousand Cleveland residents and some hundreds from other points in northern Ohio, including a large cluster from Canton and Akron" collected at Cleveland's League Park

to feast their eyes on the greatest athlete of all time—Jim Thorpe—and, incidentally, to see the Cleveland and Canton professional football elevens wage battle.

Several of the [Cleveland] players, for business reasons, have been forced to play under assumed names. The seven are players of recent college experience. Practically every one of them gained fame on big college teams.[64]

For the second week in a row, professional football fans in northeast Ohio saw Jim Thorpe at his best. This time, Cleveland was better prepared, and the game was a thriller. Fans saw "two elevens of magnificent strength and skill with all the energy and spirit of big college elevens struggling for a championship."[65] According to the *Plain Dealer* report,

Without Thorpe the results might have been different. Of course, that was to have been expected. He furnished the punch in the crisis. Twice when Canton hovered in the shadow of Cleveland's goal, Thorpe's backfield running mates were stopped. And twice Thorpe went to the rescue, with an exhibition of playing which scarcely could be excelled. . . . The play was remarkable even in the first period, with the rival clans fighting viciously for inches and the Cleveland delegation watching Thorpe with catlike ferocity and holding him well in check.

Canton scored within forty seconds of the call of time at the close of the second period, with Thorpe carrying the ball across from the ten-yard line, after a stirring attack had advanced the ball about sixty yards. It was then that Jim

James Martin "Butchy" Barron, guard, Canton Bulldogs 1916–17, 1919; Cleveland Indians 1916; Youngstown Patricians 1916–17. He was a star at Georgetown University before turning pro. *(Georgetown University Special Collections.)*

showed the stuff which has made mild mannered and conservative critics rave. A comparatively ordinary man before that, he suddenly became a giant, tearing loose from two or three tacklers before he finally ended his run behind the goal line.

In the next period, Cleveland tied the score, because of a good piece of individual work by left tackle Gordon, who isn't Gordon at all, but who really is a great big Irishman with a more Irish name than Gordon and with the nerve of a bulldog and strength of a bull. Gordon [Tom Gormley] blocked a punt and then gave chase to the free ball. George "Bull" Lowe fell on the ball for a touchdown and Gordon kicked goal to tie the game.[66] This would be the only score against Canton in 1916.[67]

In the final quarter, Jim Thorpe again "swung around the Cleveland end and hurled aside several would be tacklers to cross the line for a touchdown."[68] In the process of making the winning touchdown, Thorpe twisted his ankle and had to leave the game.

Jim Thorpe, a colorful character in American sports history, was the greatest athlete of the century. One measure of his status among contemporaries is a statement made by the great Harvard halfback Eddie Mahan, who was coaching at the University of California in 1916. According to Mahan, "I have often smiled in silence when football enthusiasts grew warm debating who was the greatest player of them all. That possibly is the one point in the realm of football that coaches never discuss. They know. Name, Jim Thorpe, Indian. The big chief stands alone in a class by himself, and will for a long time, I expect."[69] Stories about Thorpe's football exploits were legend and appeared frequently in the newspaper.[70]

James Frances "Jim" Thorpe was born May 28, 1888, in the Oklahoma Indian Territory near present-day Prague, Oklahoma. He was given the Sac and Fox tribal name "Bright Path." His mother was one-quarter French and claimed descent from Black Hawk, chief of the Chippewas. His father, Hiram Thorpe, was a farmer and trader of mixed Sac and Fox descent. An indifferent student, Thorpe attended the Sac and Fox Reservation School and was sent to Haskell Institute for Indians in Lawrence, Kansas, where he excelled at outdoor sports. He was shipped to Carlisle Institute in Pennsylvania when he was sixteen years old. A glorified trade school, Carlisle was known for its military discipline and work programs. Because he detested farm work and loved athletics, Thorpe played all sports. He particularly excelled at football, track, and baseball. He first started on Glenn "Pop" Warner's highly talented football team, in 1908, and scored two long touchdowns against the University of Pennsylvania on his way to being named to Walter Camp's second team All-American squad. In the spring of 1909, Jim left school and played baseball for Rocky Mount, North Carolina, in the East Carolina league, hiring out for manual labor to support himself. At that time, college athletes often played professional baseball in the summer under an assumed name. Thorpe, who did not understand the ramifications, used his own name.[71]

At Warner's urging, Thorpe returned to Carlisle for the 1911 football season. During that season, Jim Thorpe was named All-American when he led Carlisle to eleven wins and only one loss. The following summer, he won both the pentathlon and the decathlon and was declared "the world's greatest athlete" by King Gustav of Sweden. In 1950, a poll of the nation's sports writers concurred: they voted Thorpe the best athlete of the first half of the twentieth century.[72] When Thorpe returned to Carlisle that fall, he set a new college football scoring record and was again named All-American. Soon after reports surfaced that Thorpe had played professional baseball in 1909–10, he was declared ineligible to compete in college athletics and the Olympic Committee demanded that he return his Olympic medals.

Discouraged, Thorpe left Carlisle and joined the New York Giants baseball team. His major league baseball career was only average, as he had difficulty hitting a curve ball. However, his hitting weaknesses were exaggerated. He played major league baseball from 1913 through 1919, and batted .252. He played in the 1917 World Series and finished his major league baseball career with the Boston Braves in 1919. In 1920, he hit .358 and drove in 112 runs with the Akron team of the International League.

During the 1916 and 1917 professional football seasons, Thorpe played and coached football in and near Canton. In 1916, he coached backs on a part-time basis for the Municipal University of Akron. He also helped coach two high school football teams in towns near Canton. In 1917, he coached kicking one week for Glenn "Pop" Warner at the University of Pittsburgh.[73]

Thorpe had a voracious appetite. Prior to a football game, he would blow into the dining room of the hotel about 10 A.M. and would immediately be surrounded by waiters, because he was known to be a generous tipper. According to the *Youngstown Vindicator*, "He would always begin by saying he wasn't very hungry" and would proceed to order "grapefruit, cereal, half a dozen fried eggs with ham, a sirloin steak with onions, two orders of fried potatoes, country sausage, wheat cakes, rolls and a pat of butter."[74]

The November battle for the 1916 world's championship of professional football was focused almost exclusively on the Big Four teams in northeast Ohio. Jim Thorpe's Canton Bulldogs were the clear favorite. They were undefeated and unscored on, and they had a cast of all-stars second to none in the history of independent football.

Massillon was a worthy rival for Canton. The Tigers had played better than Canton in 1915, and there was a tradition of the Tigers beating the Bulldogs when their teams were evenly matched. While Massillon victories had been narrower than the impressive Canton wins, it could be argued that Massillon played a harder schedule in October.

On November 19, 1916, Canton played the Patricians in Youngstown. Youngstown quarterback Ray Thomas was missing because he broke his hand in the Massillon game. The Pats recruited Ernest "Tommy" Hughitt from the University of Michigan to take his place, but Tommy would not be available until November 26. In the meantime, Russell "Busty" Ashbaugh, a hometown boy who graduated from Brown University, was handling the position. Ashbaugh was twice a third team All-American end (in 1911 and 1912) while at Brown.

Canton was short-handed for the game. Ernie Soucy and Howard Buck, assistant coaches for the University of Wisconsin, were in Minneapolis for the Wisconsin-Minnesota game and unable to make connections in time to play for Canton. More importantly, Jim Thorpe was nursing a bad ankle and a case of stomach flu, and George "Carp" Julian was sick. Canton started Harry Whitaker at quarterback, but he was relieved by Milton Ghee. Ghee, who had played under coach Bob Zuppke at Oak Park High School near Chicago, was coaching at Dartmouth and in late September had agreed to play for Canton, but this was the first game he was able to make. Harry Costello replaced Thorpe at halfback. M. E. "Red" Wilkinson played halfback, and Julian played fullback, even though he was ill. John Kellison, playing as Ketcham, was starting his first game for Canton in 1916, in place of Howard Buck.

Canton's problems became more complicated when Harry Costello injured his foot in the first quarter. Thorpe, whose doctor had advised him not to play, took Costello's place. At halftime Samuel Willaman replaced Thorpe. Canton won the game 13 to 0.[75]

The home-and-home series between unbeaten Massillon and unbeaten Canton for the professional football championship of the world was held November 26 in Massillon and December 3 in Canton. Both games drew more than ten thousand fans, and some say fifteen thousand attended the game in Massillon. Charles "Gus" Dorais was added to the team to play Canton, but he did not prove to be as effective as he had been in 1915.

The starting lineup for the first game was:

Canton		Massillon
Ernie Soucy, Harvard Univ.	LE	Knute Rockne, Notre Dame Univ.
Howard Buck, Univ. of Wisconsin	LT	Robert Nash, Rutgers Univ.
Ed Russell, Univ. of Penn.	LG	Chris Schlachter, Syracuse Univ.
William Garlow, Carlisle Institute	C	A. A. Wesbecher, Wash. and Jeff. College
Clarence Spears, Dartmouth College	RG	Freeman Fitzgerald, Notre Dame Univ.
John Kellison, W.Va. Wesleyan College	RT	Jack Townley, Univ. of Minnesota
Charles Stewart, Colgate Univ.	RE	Fred Heyman, Wash. and Jeff. College
Harry Whitaker, Indiana Univ.	QB	Charles Dorais, Notre Dame Univ.
Milton Ghee, Dartmouth College	LH	Joel Mattern, Univ. of Minnesota
M. E. Wilkinson, Syracuse Univ.	RH	Malcolm Fleming, Wash. and Jeff. College
Jim Thorpe, Carlisle Institute	FB	Howard Talman, Rutgers Univ.

It was a gala day at Driving Park in Massillon. Thousands of Canton fans were bedecked with red and white. They had a forty-piece band backing them up on the east side of the gridiron. Massillon fans were dressed in orange and black, and they too had a band. Unfortunately, there was a strong south wind, the field was soft, and the footing was unsure. Jim Thorpe was still not fully recovered from a twisted ankle, an injury to his hip, and stomach trouble, but he was prepared to play regardless of injuries.[76] Carp Julian, on the other hand, a victim of "blood poisoning," had already undergone surgery and was confined to the hospital in Akron for another week.[77] Julian's defensive play particularly was missed because "he had backed up the line flawlessly all season." Jack Cusack, the Canton general manager, used Harry Whitaker of Indiana University to handle the quarterback position, shifted Ghee to left half, and moved Jim Thorpe to fullback. It was not a perfect solution, but it was serviceable. All-American Frank Dunn was available as a back-up fullback or halfback, and William Garlow, a member of the Tuscarora tribe from New York, was installed at center. Garlow had played with Thorpe at Carlisle in 1908–9. In 1910, he dropped out of school to play baseball in Ontario. Later, he attended West Virginia Wesleyan, where he played football with Greasy Neale and John Kellison.[78] College Hall-of-Famer Clarence "Doc" Spears, who attended

Howard "Cub" Buck, guard, tackle, center, Canton Bulldogs 1916–17, 1919–20; Pine Village 1916; Green Bay Packers 1921–25. He was a Walter Camp All-American at the University of Wisconsin in 1915, on Wisconsin's coaching staff in 1916–17, and a member of the Green Bay Packers Hall of Fame. *(University of Wisconsin Archives.)*

Knox College for one year before becoming an All-American at Dartmouth, was the starting right guard for Canton.

According to eyewitnesses, from the opening kickoff to the final gun, "the wind interfered continually with the quality of the football, making punts and passes extremely uncertain." "A slippery field made conditions under foot just as hindersome, robbing both Bulldogs and Tigers of their speed." A fumble by Frederick Sefton gave Massillon an opportunity to start a drive on the Canton thirty yard line. A fifteen-yard penalty, an eleven-yard dash, and several short drives brought the ball to the Canton eight yard line, but, when the drive stalled, Charles Dorais was unable to make the field goal. The wind "twisted and turned the ball from the goal posts."[79] On another occasion, Dorais also missed a field goal, and, when Skeet Lambert came on in relief of Dorais, the wind conditions and the stubborn Canton defense never gave him an opportunity to score.

For his part, Jim Thorpe did not look like a world-beater. Still, he carried the ball eight times and gained twenty-eight yards for an average of three-and-a-half yards per carry.[80] On one occasion in the fourth quarter, Jim Thorpe broke free for a fourteen-yard run, but Canton never threatened to score.[81] As the Massillon paper put it, "It wasn't a question of Canton scoring. The big issue was could Massillon score?" Canton was lucky to make a first down. Even the *Canton Repository* admitted, "Bulldogs escape defeat but are outplayed by the Tigers." The *Massillon Independent* wrote,

In a contest replete with many brilliant tackles, end runs, line plunges and everything that goes to make up a corking good football game, the Massillon Tigers and the Canton Bulldogs Sunday afternoon battled to a scoreless draw . . . in the first big struggle for the Professional Football Championship of the United States.[82]

On Thanksgiving the following Thursday, Massillon played Youngstown at Massillon's Driving Park. Fresh off a thrilling victory over the Washington D.C. Vigilants, which was won in the closing minutes by Tommy Hughitt's sixty-yard pass, Youngstown hoped to get revenge for their 3–0 loss to Massillon earlier in November.

Massillon added Russ Goodwin at quarterback for his first professional game. Red Fleming, a former teammate of Goodwin's, signed him up at the beginning of the season, but coaching duties at Washington and Lee prevented him from playing earlier. Goodwin was one of the best college quarterbacks of his era. He attended Washington and Jefferson College in Washington, Pennsylvania, from 1911 until 1915. He lettered in football all four years and in his senior year led his team to a 10 and 1 record against the best teams in the nation. Generally underrated, he consistently passed and ran with great skill. Goodwin would become mayor of Wheeling, West Virginia, and, as a college referee, worked a number of Rose and Cotton Bowl games. In 1990, he was posthumously inducted into the Wheeling, West Virginia, Hall of Fame.[83]

The Thanksgiving Day game against Youngstown turned out to be a one-sided affair. With Massillon High School graduate Fred Heyman, who was also Goodwin's college teammate, at end, Goodwin felt right at home. Passes from Goodwin to Heyman broke the game with Youngstown wide open. Massillon won 27–0. After the game, the Massillon Tigers held a big turkey dinner at McDonaldsville's restaurant (McDonaldsville is a village a few miles northeast of Massillon) for the men who financed the team and as many of the players as could come.[84] The financial backers present were J. H. "Johnny" Lodwick, William A. Schuster, Jack Whalen, Edwin B. Lord, J. P. Fischer, W. S. "Red" Bloomberg, Paul V. Sibila, Vincent Henricks, Jack Dowling, Bert Laylin, Frank A. Vogt, Jack Smucht, Louis P. Maugher, F. H. Fetworthy, S. S. Miller, and Fred J. Becker.[85] This dinner guest list gives the only known record of the financial backers for the Massillon Tigers in 1916. By separating the football players from the other guests, it is possible to see who probably financed the Tigers.

Fearing injuries and failing to get an adequate guarantee, the Canton Bulldogs canceled their game with the Detroit Heralds and allowed the Cleveland Indians to play in Detroit.

The world professional football championship game for 1916 was held in Canton on December 3. The Bulldogs were hoping for a hard, dry field to help them accent their speed.[86] Massillon arranged to have three members of the University of Minnesota, the Big Nine football champions, come to Canton the day after they beat the University of Chicago to bolster the Massillon line.[87] College seniors Bert Baston, Jack Townley, and Gilbert Sinclair, having just completed their college football eligibility, were willing to pick up much-needed money by playing pro football. Baston had been named to the *Boston Post*'s first team All-American squad the day before.[88] As it turned out, however, Big Nine administrators were very unhappy that Massillon hired college players before their graduation.[89] For their part, Canton brought Howard "Cap" Edwards back from Fort Wayne where he had been playing all season, enticed Pete Calac to play fullback, and imported All-America Frank Dunn, the great Dickinson College star, to play right halfback. Milton Ghee was moved back to quarterback, and Ralph "Fats" Waldsmith was reinstated as the starting center. Massillon started the same team as the week before, except that they put Goodwin at quarterback.

The Bulldogs were in top shape. They had practiced during the week, and Thorpe's ankle had mended.[90] The playing field was muddy, but Canton was prepared. The Bulldogs scored once in the first quarter when Massillon fumbled the ball deep in their own territory and Fats Waldsmith scooped up the fumble and ran fifteen yards for a touchdown. Canton failed the point after touchdown but Canton led 6–0. In the second quarter, Jim Thorpe broke through the Massillon defenses for a fifty-one-yard run, but he was stopped short of the goal line. Pete Calac plowed through for the second touchdown. Again, Canton missed the point after touchdown after the punt-out. At halftime, the score was 12–0. After a scoreless third quarter, Canton put the game on ice with two touchdowns in the fourth quarter. A long pass from Milton Ghee to Ernie Soucy resulted in one touchdown, but Thorpe missed the goal after Calac made the punt-out. After a Massillon drive stalled, a "stirring sprint by fullback Calac," followed by Thorpe ramming the ball through the Massillon line, yielded the final touchdown. Doc Spears missed the kick for extra point by inches after Thorpe's punt-out.[91]

The *Cleveland Plain Dealer* summarized the game as well as any one:

Massillon was outplayed and outclassed. Jim Thorpe and company gave an artistic exhibition of all that is great in the rough sport, through laboring under trying conditions. A muddy field proved a woeful handicap, robbing the contest of many of the anticipated features. . . . Jim Thorpe was a veritable demon and Pete Calac was extraordinary. . . . This was a regular victory. It had no semblance of a fluke. It left no room for alibis.[92]

Jack Cusack considered his 1916 Canton Bulldogs to be the best team he had ever put on the field. They were undefeated and scored on only once the entire season. On December 4, 1916, the *Canton Daily News* described the sad farewell to a happy football season:

Canton's professional football team, champion of its class in these United States, disbanded Sunday night at the hotel Courtland. Handshakes were many, and hopes were expressed that friendly exchanges would ensue in 1917.

Every member of the Bulldog team, imported for the season, will go to other cities, except "Indian" Garlow who plans to make Canton his home. Garlow did good work at center in some of the big game.

Captain Thorpe, with his wife and young son, Tuesday departs for home in Oklahoma City. Thorpe is anxious for an outdoor life, devoid of care and worry attendant on an important football series. He intends to hunt birds until the first of the year, and in 1917 will resume baseball duty. The New York Giants hold an option on the Indian who finished the 1916 campaign with the Milwaukee club of the American Association.

Much of the credit for the successful 1916 Canton Bulldog season must go to Jack Cusack. Still under thirty years of age, Cusack was an excellent judge of football talent and had an honest, unassuming way of handling players. In an era when many people treated American Indians as if they were an inferior race, Cusack treated Thorpe, Calac, Garlow, and Welch as equals. He valued their opinions, gave them responsibility, paid them appropriately to their talent, and, when asked to do so, managed their money with honesty and integrity. As a result, Cusack got the best out of his players. They rarely left his team for another, at a time when loyalty by either players or owners was rare. In 1916, and again in 1917, the Canton Bulldogs had one of the most stable teams in independent football. Cusack provided good stable management during this highly volatile, risky period when professional football was still just taking root.

Massillon ended the 1916 season with a record of seven wins, one loss, and two ties. They were tied by Cleveland and Canton, and lost the final game of the season to Canton. This was an enviable record for any team but Massillon. Their failure to defeat Cleveland and Canton cost Red Fleming his coaching position.

When it was clear that the team Cleveland fielded in Canton on November 5 would not defeat the Bulldogs, Peggy Parratt recruited five new players to face Canton on November 12. However, because he had a number of players under contract for that week, Parratt scheduled a game for his second team with the Cincinnati Celts in Cincinnati and used seven extra Celt players to complete his second team. Dwight Wertz, Bull Olsson, Whitey Schultz, and Dutch Powell led Cleveland's second team and lost to Cincinnati by a score of 25–0.[93] From Peggy Parratt's point of view, he was able to honor his contracts with old friends and defray his costs. The humiliating loss, however, made additional second team games unlikely.

After the one-man show by Jim Thorpe against the Cleveland Indians on November 12, Peggy Parratt prepared to face the hated Massillon Tigers, who had cannibalized his 1914 dream team. There was bad blood between Peggy Parratt and the management of the Massillon Tigers. The conditions for the game had to be negotiated by Parratt's financial backers.[94]

The game was important to Parratt, and he expected a good-sized crowd. The *Cleveland Plain Dealer* observed on the day of the game that

there'll be no Jim Thorpe to act as drawing card when the Massillon Tigers clash with the Cleveland Indians at League Park today, but a team with such players as Dorais (whose individual work surpassed that of the great and only Thorpe a year ago), Mattern, Talman, Fleming, Rockne, Nash, etc. scarcely needs a Thorpe to gain recognition as great football eleven.

For his part, Peggy Parratt "wanted to beat Massillon in the worst way." He was not satisfied with the strength of his team and signed up Lorin Solon, the ex-University of Minnesota captain who was playing for an independent team in Duluth. Dissatisfied with the Indian's quarterback play, he had reportedly released Chalky Williamson but changed his mind because he was unable to find a strong replacement.[95] On game day, Cleveland started Lorin Solon at fullback, Chalky Williamson at quarterback, and Martin from Georgetown at end; otherwise the Indians had nearly the same lineup that played Canton. Massillon started Lambert at quarterback, Thiele and Heyman at ends—Rockne played in relief of Heyman—Nash and Day at tackles, Fitzgerald and Schlachter at guards, and Hayes at center. Mattern, Fleming, and Kagy rounded out the backfield. Dorais was playing for Fort Wayne on November 19. About five thousand fans attended the game.

The teams were too evenly matched to make an exciting game. In general strength, the Indians had an advantage. In the first two periods, Mattern "wiggled" his way for substantial gains, but at halftime Cleveland made some adjustments, and after that Massillon's efforts were confined almost exclusively to defense. As the *Cleveland Plain Dealer* pointed out, "There was no time when a score for Massillon seemed imminent." Massillon was never close enough even for a try for field goal. Cleveland missed two field goals and "on one occasion Cleveland missed a chance for a touchdown when end Wagner muffed a beautiful long pass [from Parratt] after getting the ball in his arms."[96] While both teams were outstanding on defense, Cleveland center-linebacker Paul Des Jardien was brilliant, and Chalky Williamson and Tom Gormley also stood out as defensive stars for Cleveland. Cleveland's offensive stars were Lorin Solon at fullback and E. N. Mayer at halfback. Mayer, who was reported to be from Washington and Lee University,[97] was instead from the University of Virginia.

The scoreless tie was a moral victory for Cleveland, considered to be the underdog. On the Monday after the game, Fred Becker, sportswriter for the *Massillon Independent* and secretary of the Tigers football team, wrote,

Parratt, the sixth city mogul [Cleveland was the 6th largest city in the USA] placed a wonderful team upon the field, one that is too wonderful for Parratt to hold together. Combinations like that which upheld the Cleveland colors Sunday cost a mint of money, more than it is believed Parratt can afford to pay after sizing up the attitude of Cleveland fans toward him and professional football. But there is no getting away from it, Parratt had a team that with some practice would be world beater and it was only Massillon's stiff defense, that held like bands of steel and glistened with brilliant tackling, that kept the Clevelanders safe and away from a possible chance to score a touchdown.[98]

The game was so evenly matched that it did not provide the flash fans enjoyed.

Cleveland was scheduled to play the Youngstown Patricians the following week, but Peggy Parratt canceled the game, believing he had nothing to gain by playing a team that had just lost to Canton. Instead, he scheduled the Columbus Panhandles for a rematch in Cleveland.[99] Using almost the same team he had used the week before, Peggy Parratt wanted revenge for the Indians' early-season loss to the Panhandles. The one change Cleveland made was at quarterback. They replaced Guy "Chalky" Williamson with a "famous" college quarterback playing under the assumed name James, who has not been identified.

The Cleveland Indians were not the financial success that had been anticipated, and team backers hoped that this final home game of the season would help balance the books.[100] In truth, Peggy Parratt had signed too many players during the course of the season for the Indians, as a first-year team, to show a profit.

The game between Cleveland and the Columbus Panhandles was a thriller from start to finish. Cleveland played their best game of the season. Their new quarterback James proved to be the person Parratt had been looking for all season. He handled his job with skill. It may have helped that the entire team was now familiar with the signals. The rest of the Cleveland backfield also played like a finely tuned piano. Lorin Solon sparkled at fullback, while Mayer and Graff complemented both offensive and defensive play. At one point, Mayer tricked the Panhandles by using his helmet to fake a pass, and the defense chased the wrong man while Solon made six yards by running around the opposite end.[101]

The only points of the game were made by Cleveland in the third quarter, when a coordinated attack of passing and running moved the ball steadily toward the Panhandles' goal line. Graff made eight yards, a forward pass advanced the ball thirty-five yards, then Solon smashed for fifteen yards and followed up with a two-yard gain. Two successive plays by Mayer made sixteen yards. With the ball on the Panhandles' five yard line, Solon hurled himself over the Panhandles' line for a touchdown. Following the punt-out, he also kicked goal for a 7–0 win. The famous Nesser brothers were able to dive to the Cleveland ten yard line, but were unable to score.[102]

When the Canton Bulldogs refused to sign a contract to play the Detroit Heralds on Thanksgiving Day because Cusack could not get what he considered a satisfactory guarantee, Peggy Parratt stepped in and signed the contract. Consequently, Cleveland played Detroit on Thanksgiving in Navin Park. Parratt also scheduled the Toledo Maroons on the following Sunday to make the trip west cost-effective.[103]

The first half of the Thanksgiving game in Detroit was all Cleveland. The Indians outplayed the Heralds and showed more spirit. Shorty Des Jardien's punting kept the Heralds on the defensive.[104] Lorin Solon kicked two field goals from placement in the first quarter, and Campbell Graff, the former Ohio State fullback, made a touchdown in the second quarter to give Cleveland a 13–0 halftime lead. Detroit finally came alive in the second half. As the *Toledo Blade* described it: "Three times they were inside the Cleveland 20-yard stripe but couldn't put over the wallop that was needed."[105] Thanks to Des Jardien's punting, Cleveland got out of trouble after each failed Detroit drive in the second half, and they generally mired the Heralds in poor field position all day. James, the All-American quarterback playing under an assumed name, was a flawless field general. Norb Sacksteder played well for Detroit. His slick running was Detroit's only bright spot. He "tore some long gains," and in the fourth quarter "sprinted through the entire Indian team for a touchdown after he clutched a 20-yard toss."[106] However, Cleveland countered with another touchdown by Campbell Graff, and the final score was 20 to 6.

Cleveland had played its best game of the season before eight thousand Detroit fans, and Lorin Solon had lived up to his nickname "The Crusher."[107] Overall, Detroit fans saw "one of the best demonstrations of line-plunging ever displayed in that city" in pre-World War I football.[108]

Encouraged by their performance on Thanksgiving, the Cleveland Indians managed an afternoon workout at Armory Park in Toledo on December 1.[109] Paul Des Jardien became sick and returned home to Chicago on doctor's advice.[110] Nevertheless, defensive standouts Tom Gormley, Butchy Barron, and Fred Walker—a new end on the team from the University of Chicago, who played his first professional game in Detroit on Thanksgiving Day—had an excellent workout and were looking forward to the Toledo game on November 3.

Toledo proved to be a better match for Cleveland than expected. Without the punting skills of Des Jardien, the Maroons managed better field position than Detroit had. Neither team scored until the last ten seconds of the game when Lorin Solon set up for a place kick and scored a field goal as time was running out.[111] Gilbert Sinclair traveled from Minneapolis to play left guard for Cleveland, after playing against the Minneapolis Marines on Thanksgiving Day, although the *Minneapolis Journal* reported that he was playing for Massillon.[112] Sinclair was an interesting success story. After being on the second team at West High in Minneapolis in 1911, he went to the University of Minnesota and was named to the second team All-Conference team for the Big Nine in 1915 and 1916.[113]

Cleveland ended their 1916 season with eight wins, three losses, and a tie. Of course, their second team had an additional loss to the Celts.[114] More importantly, Peggy Parratt's Cleveland Indians had lost money, and his backers refused to field a team in 1917.[115]

17. The Akron Pros

In 1916, the semiprofessional Akron Burkhardts played on the edges of professional football. The team was named for Akron brewers Gus and Bill Burkhardt who sponsored the team. Depending largely on homegrown talent, they were more at the level of the better industrial teams than of the powerful professional teams. They played the Cleveland Indians twice and the Detroit Heralds once, losing all three games though they played well. The Burkhardts tied the Massillon Blues and defeated Elyria, the Barberton Pros, and the Imperial Electrics of Akron. The Burkhardts had the makings of a solid professional team with players like Howard Welch from Case Institute, Joe "Dolly" Gray from the University of Chicago, John Larsen from Notre Dame and Princeton, Frederick Stanley Sefton from Colgate and currently the coach of the Municipal University of Akron (formerly Buchtel College), Leo McCausland from Akron High School, who would later play football for the University of Detroit, Tom Holleran from Akron South High School, and sandlot stars Chick Ulrich, Carl Carderelli, Cliff "Chief" James, and Chick Conway.[1] Indeed, the *Minneapolis Journal* called Dolly Gray "the best ground gainer for the University of Chicago eleven in 1914."[2]

Over the summer of 1917, Stephen "Suey" Welch and Vernon "Mac" McGinnis acquired control of the Akron Burkhardts and changed the name of the team to the Akron Pros. They recruited Alfred Nesser, Carl "Bull" Olsson, Roy "Tommy" Burrell, and a former Purdue University player named Bullet Mitchell, who had played with the Akron Imperial Electrics in 1916. These additions made the Akron Pros competitive with most other professional teams in Ohio. They adopted blue and gold as their team colors and leased Grossvater Park for their home games.

Of all the new recruits, the biggest star was Alfred Nesser,[3] already well known in professional football circles. He was the youngest of the seven famous Nesser brothers who played for the Columbus Panhandles between 1904 and 1922. Born in 1892, in Columbus, to a Roman

Catholic family, Alfred joined his five brothers on the Panhandles in 1909. They all worked in the yards and shops of the Pennsylvania Railroad's Panhandle Division and practiced football every day during lunch breaks. They never attended college. Alfred's playing weight was 190 to 200 pounds, and he often played without headgear or shoulder pads for extra speed. In 1913, Alfred moved to Akron, Ohio, but continued to play with the Panhandles until 1915, when he also played some games with the Massillon Tigers. In 1916, he was back with the Panhandles, but the next year he switched to the Akron Pros and started for them from 1919 to 1924. In 1925, he played with the Cleveland Bulldogs and a team in Toronto. When the Bulldogs were sold and became the Cleveland Panthers, in 1926, he remained with them. For the next two years, he played with the New York Giants, who won the NFL Championship in 1927. He ended his professional football career, in 1931, with the Cleveland Indians, after playing for teams in Alliance, Ohio, and Grand Rapids, Michigan. Like his brothers Ted and Phil, he played football until well after his fortieth birthday. Ted's last professional game was in 1922 at the age of forty-six, and Phil played until he was forty-two years old. In later years, Alfred was known as "the Iron Man of Football."

Alfred Nesser and Park "Tumble" Crisp were the anchors of the Akron front seven. Crisp was a hometown favorite at left tackle. As a member of the Pi Kappa Epsilon fraternity, with a history as a star first baseman and right guard in basketball, and with a brother (Michael) who was also an Akron sports hero, Tumble Crisp had a large local following. He had been a starter in football at Buchtel College, from 1912 through 1915, and had played for the undefeated Canton Bulldogs in 1916.[4]

The Akron Pros opened their 1917 football season on October 7 against the Salem, Ohio, semipros at home. Akron's starting lineup had Howard Welch and Red Forrest at ends, Park "Tumble" Crisp and Joe "Dolly" Gray at tackles, Alfred Nesser and Carl "Bull" Olsson at guards, Carl "Squash" Carderelli at center, and a backfield consisting of Tommy Holleran at quarterback, Roy "Tommy" Burrell and I. R. Martin (playing under the assumed name Johnson) at halfback, and Bullet Mitchell at fullback.[5] Akron won the game 34 to 0.

On October 14, they played the Columbus Panhandles at home. Akron, outweighed, was kept on the defensive most of the game. The Panhandles had three chances for a field goal, but Frank Nesser missed all three times. Park "Tumble" Crisp, on the other hand, booted a field goal that provided the winning margin. Alfred Nesser played a strong game against his five brothers. The final score was Akron 3, Columbus 0.[6]

On October 14, the Massillon Tigers cut Fleming from their team. At the beginning of the 1917 season, Fleming had come back to Ohio with the Pitcairn Quakers to play the Canton Bulldogs. He signed a one-game contract with the Massillon Tigers for the following Sunday, but, because of his failure to defeat Canton in 1916 when he was the Massillon coach, he was not welcomed by the fans.[7] Some also felt that Fleming was a step or two slower than he had been in 1916. He was then hired by the Akron Pros.

Buoyed by their victory over the fabled Panhandles, the Akron Pros entertained the Cleveland Tomahawks on October 21. This was Red Fleming's first game for Akron, and he made an immediate impact both offensively and defensively with his aggressive play. Akron walloped the Tomahawks 40–0.[8]

Akron's next opponent was Massillon. This game was likely to draw a big crowd, as there was a natural, long-standing rivalry between the two towns. Tickets were sold at all of Akron's rubber factories and downtown cigar stores.[9] The game was held at 2:30 P.M. on October 28, at Grossvater Park in South Akron. Massillon reported that its starting lineup would include Knute Rockne and Jim Dettling at ends, Claudia (generally represented as "Claude") Earl Thornhill and Charles Copley at tackles, Fritz Rehor and Carl "Bat" Rambard at guards, Buzz Wesbecher at center, and Eugene Elseworth "Shorty" Miller, I. R. Martin (playing under the assumed name Jones), DeOrmond "Tuss" McLaughry, and Blackburn in the backfield. As it turned out, Rockne was not scheduled to play, and Robert "Nasty" Nash played left end for Massillon.[10]

The leading light in the Massillon lineup was Tuss McLaughry. DeOrmond "Tuss" McLaughry grew up in East Lansing, Michigan, and entered the freshman class at Michigan Agricultural College (now Michigan State) in 1911.[11] Judging him an outstanding college football prospect, Westminster College in New Wilmington, Pennsylvania, just east of Youngstown, Ohio, offered McLaughry a scholarship to play for them. He transferred after his sophomore year because he was tired of living at home and wanted to be on his own. In 1914, he married, while still a college senior[12] and went on to become one of the best coaches in America and a member of the College Football Hall of Fame.

I. R. Martin, born in Youngstown, Ohio, was an all around athlete at the University of Missouri before taking the athletic director's job with Goodyear Tire and Rubber Company in Akron. In 1916, Martin played minor league baseball for St. Paul, Minnesota, and Sunday football for the Fort Wayne Friars under the assumed name Johnson. He opened the 1917 season with the Akron Pros under that name but jumped to Massillon.[13] Massillon also featured Eugene "Shorty" Miller from Penn State University at quarterback. A triple threat, Shorty Miller had made a seventy-eight yard run against Pitcairn the previous week.[14]

The Akron Pros signed up Frank Nesser for their game with Massillon. A number of other lineup changes evolved since the season opener. In addition to Crisp, the Pros started Howard Welch and Carl "Bull" Olsson on the left side of the line. The right side of the front seven featured Alfred Nesser, Joe "Dolly" Gray, and Roy "Tommy" Burrell. Carl Carderelli played center, and Tom Holleran, Red Fleming, Frank Nesser, and Rube Bechtol filled out the backfield. Bechtol had played college football at Wooster College and was coaching at South High School in Akron.[15] Twenty-three-year-old Clinton C. Prather, a 1916 graduate from Indiana University and starting end for the Hoosiers in 1914 and 1915, was scheduled to start for Akron, but he never made it into the game.[16]

Permanent stands with a seating capacity of twenty-eight hundred were built at Grossvater Park in Akron to augment the three thousand circus seats being placed at the western end of the field. In addition, a redwood fence was built around the field to keep spectators off the gridiron. Arrangements were made to have a section of the main grandstand, which had a full view of the field, reserved for newspaper men.[17]

Special cars on the Northern Ohio Transit Company trolley line were arranged for October 28 to make it easy for Massillon fans to travel the twenty miles to Akron for the game.[18] Massillon and Akron had not met in professional football since 1906. As two of the first towns in Ohio to get into big-time independent football, both cities had fans excited about the game. Stephen "Suey" Welch and Vernon "Mac" McGinnis were anxious for the game to revive their dwindling bank accounts. The process of starting up the Akron Pros had been expensive, and they needed a good gate to permit the team to be competitive in November.[19]

The game itself was hard fought. Massillon's passing was likened to a Zeppelin attack by the *Akron Beacon Journal*.[20] Massillon scored touchdowns in the second and third quarters on passes from Shorty Miller to

Nasty Nash, the Massillon player-coach. Massillon made nine first downs and completed five passes in nine attempts over the course of the game, while Akron managed only two first downs. Akron tried fifteen passes; seven were incomplete, and six were intercepted. Red Fleming was not a factor in the game, and Frank Nesser did little but throw intercepted passes.[21]

More than thirty-five hundred fans paid to see the game. A "boneheaded" play by Carl Carderelli gave Massillon its first chance to score. Carderelli grabbed a Nesser pass as an ineligible receiver, and, under the rules of 1917, this automatically turned the ball over to Massillon on the Akron thirty yard line.[22] In the second quarter, however, Akron had a chance to score when Frank Nesser threw a beautiful pass to Bechtol, who took the ball to the Massillon one yard line. Three runs and a fourth-down pass failed to score any points for Akron. Massillon defeated the Akron Pros 14 to 0.[23]

Akron Pros' management was disappointed with the performance of Red Fleming. They announced that "he had been overrated, and it is more than likely that the sorrel-topped gridder will sit on the bench next Sunday or may be given his release. Fleming did not play the game that was expected of him against Massillon and he was responsible for the visitor's pair of touchdowns."[24] Many Akron supporters agreed. They felt that if Fleming was not good enough for Massillon, he was not good enough for them. Red, however, was kept and moved to a position as back-up lineman.[25]

On the following Sunday, Akron played the Buffalo All-Stars, who were sponsored by the Irish-American Athletic Club. Coached by Abbott, formerly an Allegheny College coach, and featuring Douglas Jeffery, Barney Lepper, Wesley Talchief, and Bob Gill (a baseball star for Buffalo in the International League), Buffalo promised to be a good match for Akron.[26]

Bechtol was unable to play because he tore a ligament in his right leg in the game against Massillon. Bullet Mitchell replaced him in the starting lineup, and Dolly Gray shared halfback duties with Red Fleming, who was given one last chance to prove himself as a back. Frank Nesser stayed on at fullback, and a player called Colgate was scheduled to start at left end.[27] "Colgate" was really Frederick Stanley Sefton, All-American from Colgate, who was now coaching at the Municipal University of Akron.[28] Frank Nesser ended up playing left tackle in place of Crisp, who played for Youngstown that afternoon. Howard Welch and Clinton C. Prather started at ends, although Sefton substituted at right end.[29] Conway started in place of Carderelli at center, and Cartwright, from Indianapolis, played fullback. Holleran and Mitchell scored touchdowns for Akron, winning the disputed game 12 to 7. Eugene Dooley, the manager and quarterback for Buffalo, claimed that "The real score to be published should be 13 to 12 in favor of Buffalo." According to Dooley, "In the second quarter the ball was fumbled by one of Akron's men and picked up by Lepper and carried for a touchdown. As the official saw our man running down the field for a goal, he blew the whistle and declared it a dead ball. That was the second time a fumble was picked up by our side. The first one being so plain and apparent that when this same official wanted to declare the other touchdown a dead ball even the Akron team wouldn't stand for such raw work."[30]

On November 11, bitter rivals Akron and Canton met for the first time since 1914. The Bulldogs were unable to start Milton Ghee at quarterback because he was home in Chicago nursing tonsillitis,[31] so Jim Thorpe played quarterback.[32] On October 28, Thorpe had thrown a pass fifty yards in the air, so it was not expected that Canton would miss Ghee very much.[33] Frank Dunn was able to return to the Canton lineup and would start the game at fullback.[34]

There were high hopes in Akron that they could reclaim the world's championship from Canton, and the papers made much of this opportunity, but everyone knew that Canton was favored to win. While the Canton Bulldogs were not as strong as they had been in 1916, they were still undefeated and had been running up high scores against weak teams. But the week before, Canton was lucky to defeat the Youngstown Patricians 3–0.

Akron started Fred Sefton and Tommy Burrell at ends, Park Crisp and Frank Nesser at tackles, Carl "Bull" Olsson and Alfred Nesser at guards, Carl Carderelli at center, and Tom Holleran, Bullet Mitchell, Gardner, and Cartwright in the backfield. Conway, Fat Howard, Red Fleming and Joe "Dolly" Gray substituted for Akron.[35] Two Akron boys—Ralph Waldsmith and Ollie Dreisbach—were starters for Canton. The Bulldogs also had Alfred "Greasy" Neale and Charles E. Stewart at ends, Howard "Cap" Edwards and Howard "Cub" Buck at tackles, Unk Russell at guard, and Thorpe, Schwab, Jackson, and Dunn in the backfield. Canton substituted Norman Speck at guard.[36]

Canton, in its red and white colors, was held scoreless in the first quarter. Early in the game, the Bulldogs fumbled on their own eight yard line, but the Akron Pros could not take advantage of the break. After three rushing plays failed to move the ball more than a few feet,

Park Crisp's attempted field goal was blocked by Jackson.[37] Akron executed their only successful forward pass in the third quarter. The toss from Frank Nesser to Howard Welch, who ran for thirty yards to the Canton fifteen yard line, set up a second scoring opportunity, but once again Akron failed to take advantage of it. In contrast, six thousand fans saw Canton make their opportunities count. In the second quarter, a thirty-yard pass from Thorpe to Greasy Neale put the ball on the Akron fifteen yard line. Jim Thorpe ran the ball in from there, and Unk Russell kicked the extra point. Again in the fourth quarter, Greasy Neale made a spectacular catch and carried the ball to the ten yard line. Thorpe scored on the second try to make the score 13–0. Russell added another point after the punt out. The final score was 14–0 in favor of Canton.[38]

On November 18, Massillon brought their team back to the Summit County seat. Three weeks earlier, Massillon had easily disposed of the Akron Pros, and there was no reason to believe they would not do it again. As a consequence, Tiger fans were looking beyond Akron to their two games with Canton.

On November 15, the *Massillon Independent* announced that Charles E. Brickley, the former Harvard All-American, would be taking charge of the Massillon Tigers on November 17, in time to play Akron as a warm-up for the Canton series. Many sportswriters believed that Brickley was the equal of Jim Thorpe as an all-around football player. With Brickley in charge, the Massillon Tigers had a chance to take the world's professional football championship away from Canton.[39]

Brickley flashed into prominence in 1912 and 1913 as the result of his "wonderful kicking ability." Brickley often engaged in halftime exhibitions where he drop-kicked for fifty-five yards. In November of 1912, he had booted the ball from placement over the goal posts from forty-seven yards in a game against Princeton. He had drop-kicked the ball for field goals of twenty-three, twenty, and fifteen yards in that same game. In 1913, he had single-handedly beaten Yale with five field goals—only one of which was more than thirty yards. Of course, being from Harvard, he was the darling of the east coast football crowd.

There were rumors that Akron had signed up Fred "Fritz" Pollard, from Brown University, for their game with Massillon. Akron management had been pursuing Pollard all fall, but he was not signed until 1919. Except for Brickley, both the Massillon and Akron lineups for the game were essentially the same as they had been three weeks earlier.

In the third quarter, Eugene "Shorty" Miller fumbled the ball, and Al

Nesser scored by kicking a field goal from placement after three unsuccessful running plays. During the entire game, Akron relied almost exclusively on their running attack to move the ball. They only tried three passes all afternoon, one of which was intercepted by Shorty Miller. Frank Nesser did manage to give Brickley a kicking lesson, punting for fifty and sixty yards.[40]

Massillon, having passed up opportunities for field goals early in the game, had one chance to score in the second half and that was a forty-five-yard field goal that Brickley missed by more than five yards. Unfamiliar with the professional game, Brickley underestimated his opponents, and his bad judgment resulted in the second loss of the season for Massillon, 0–3.[41] His misjudgment gained attention throughout the Midwest.[42] After the game on November 18, Akron released Red Fleming.[43]

The Pros were scheduled to play the Youngstown Patricians, but a snow storm that dumped more than a foot of snow on Youngstown made it impossible to play Akron's only out-of-town game. Akron lost hundreds of dollars on the cancellation, since it had to pay players who had traveled to Akron or Youngstown for the game.[44] Akron's final game was scheduled at Grossvater Park on Thanksgiving against the Toledo Maroons.[45]

The Toledo Maroons, who were having the worst season in their history, hired Toledo fireman Jim Flynn at left guard.[46] Flynn, a well-known boxer, tried his hand at professional football without much luck as he was matched up against Frank Nesser. Toledo scored early on an intercepted pass, but, after the initial touchdown, Akron scored three times in the first half and added another touchdown in the fourth quarter. Welch, Holleran, and Gardner accounted for Akron's four touchdowns. Park Crisp made three extra points. Akron ended their 1917 season by outplaying the Toledo Maroons 27 to 7.[47]

The Pros had an impressive 6–2 record and promised to play professional football again after the war. Akron was among the first members of the American Professional Football Association, which later became the NFL. Sponsored by Frank Neid, a cigar store owner, and Art Ranney, the Akron Pros won the league championship in 1920, when they were undefeated. The Pros thrived until 1926, when, in the throes of hard times, they resumed their ancestral name, the Akron Indians. On July 16, 1927, the Akron Indians, still unable to draw enough paying fans, suspended operations. A year later, they forfeited their NFL franchise.[48]

18. Massillon and Canton:
The Rivalry Continues, 1917

The world champion Canton Bulldogs opened their season on October 7, 1917, in Canton, against the Pitcairn Quakers, without many of their 1916 starters. Jim Thorpe was playing professional baseball, Pete Calac was in college, George Julian had tuberculosis while Ernie Soucy and Harry Costello were in the army. Canton listed the following starters against Pitcairn:

Ends—Fredrick Sefton, Colgate Univ.; Charles E. Stewart, Colgate Univ.

Tackles—Howard Edwards, Univ. of Notre Dame; Ollie Driesbach, Municipal Univ. of Akron

Guards—Norman Speck, Canton sandlot; Jim Barron, Georgetown Univ.

Center—Ralph Waldsmith, Buchtel College

Quarterback—Milton Ghee, Dartmouth College

Halfbacks—John McNamara, Georgetown Univ.; John Schwab, Wash. and Jeff. College

Fullback—Frank Dunn, Dickinson College

The Bulldogs were in great need of practice and showed little uniform teamwork. Individual Canton players performed like all-stars, but they did not play as a team. The game started off well for Canton. According to eyewitnesses, "after taking the kick-off Schwabe and Dunn tore off 20 yards on two plays." But on the next play, the Pitcairn Quakers recovered a fumble in excellent field position. A pass for thirty yards and another for ten yards put the ball on the Canton two yard line. Crawford carried the ball over the goal line on a line plunge. Schiller kicked the point after, and Pitcairn led 7–0. After that, Pitcairn did not threaten Canton again until the second half, when they reached the twenty yard line twice, only to be held on downs. In the third and fourth quarters, Schwab and then Dunn scored touchdowns for Canton to make the final score 12–7. It was not an impressive start for the world champions.[1]

On October 14, 1917, Canton played the Altoona (Pennsylvania) Indians, and Massillon opened their season at home against the Buffalo All-Stars. Canton added John Kellison at right tackle and moved Ollie Dreisbach to right guard.[2] Norman Speck was used as a substitute. Pete Calac returned to the Canton lineup as fullback, and Frank Dunn took Schwab's place at right half.[3] The Altoona game was little more than practice for the Bulldogs' stars. Within three minutes of the opening kickoff, Canton scored on a pass from Ghee to Sefton. A few minutes later, McNamara scored Canton's second touchdown on a sixty-yard run. Then Sefton intercepted an Altoona pass and created a second opportunity for McNamara to score. By the end of the game, Canton had run up an 80–0 win.[4]

A few miles to the west, Massillon was belatedly opening its season with this starting lineup:

Ends—Knute Rockne, Univ. of Notre Dame.; C. Meyers, Canal Fulton High School

Tackles—Robert Nash, Rutgers Univ.; Charles Copley, Muhlenberg College

Guards—Fred "Fritz" Rehor, Univ. of Michigan; Carl Rambaud, Massillon sandlot

Center—Stuart Scruggs, Lehigh Univ.

Quarterback—Eugene "Shorty" Miller, Penn State Univ.

Halfbacks—Blackburn, Massillon High School; Malcolm "Red" Fleming, Wash. and Jeff. College

Fullback—DeOrmond "Tuss" McLaughry, Westminster College

Robert "Nasty" Nash played tackle and end for Rutgers University from 1912 to 1915. In 1916–17, he played left tackle and left end for the Massillon Tigers. He was player-coach for Massillon in 1919. The following year, he played for the Akron Pros and the Buffalo All-Americans and continued to play for Buffalo until 1925, when he joined the New York Giants, where he ended his career.[5] Newcomer Fred "Fritz" Rehor, who had attended the University of Michigan, started at guard. He stood six feet tall and weighed 225 pounds, a very big lineman by the standards of the day. Tuss McLaughry operated a three-hundred-acre farm and enjoyed Sunday football as a reprieve from livestock and harvesting, while the starting center was Stuart Briscoe Scruggs, originally from Dallas, Texas, and a 1917 civil engineering graduate from Lehigh University. Scruggs had been the starting center on the Lehigh football team for three years and was a letter winner in lacrosse and wrestling, as well as football.[6] Finally, Massillon used two local players in their starting lineup, C. Meyers from Canal Fulton and Blackburn, a Massillon High School graduate, who had been playing professional baseball in Buffalo.

The Massillon Tigers management had made a number of improvements on a new home field at the Massillon Baseball Athletic Club field on Clay Street where they would open the season. They built a picket fence around the entire playing field, and along the field's west side they put up two hundred feet of bleachers fourteen tiers high, large enough to accommodate over twenty-five hundred people. A big banner had been placed across West Main Street at Clay giving directions to the park.[7] The admission price was seventy-five cents, children under twelve were admitted for twenty-five cents, and auto parking was free.

The *Massillon Independent* reported,

A crowd of at least 1200 spectators saw the orange and black warriors in their initial attempt. Bob Nash, ex-Rutgers star and generalissimo of the 1917 Tigers, played on the field a likely looking crowd of gridders, which strengthened by the addition of other stars as the big battles with Canton, Akron and Youngstown approach, should make good in retrieving the honors lost in 1916.

It took the 1917 Tigers just one minute and 10 seconds to annex their first seven points. Buffalo received but fumbled, Fleming covering on the visitor's 31 yard line. Five plays later Blackburn drove a wedge through the visitors for a touchdown. Fleming kicked goal.[8]

Russ Sherman, the Buffalo fullback, scored their touchdown in the second quarter, and Eugene "Shorty" Miller secured the game in the fourth quarter with Massillon's final touchdown. The Tigers made fourteen first downs and punted six times. They had two completed forward passes, while missing on seven. Three Buffalo passes were intercepted. Before the afternoon was over, Buffalo left town on the short end of a 14–6 score.

After the game, Red Fleming was released.[9] The Massillon management wanted nothing to remind their fans that they had failed to defeat Canton in 1916. A few days later, Jim Dettling, formerly of the University of South Carolina and more recently from Muhlenburg College, was added to the team to play right end.[10]

The following week, Massillon played the Pitcairn Quakers. Fresh from their victory over Youngstown, the Quakers were led by Joe Bergie, the former All-American center from Carlisle, and quarterback Frank White, captain of the 1914 Indiana Normal School football team. The Quakers did not prove to be as difficult an opponent as anticipated. Using I. R. Martin in the halfback slot vacated by Red Fleming, Claude "Tiny" Thornhill, the All-American from the University of Pittsburgh, in place of Scruggs but at tackle, and Dettling at right end in place of Meyers, the Massillon Tigers scored six points in the first quarter and twenty-one points in the second half to coast to a 27 to 0 win.[11] Massillon did not use a substitute in the game. The muscle and brawn provided by Tiny Thornhill was, in large measure, responsible for shutting down the Pitcairn Quaker offense.

Claudia Earl "Tiny" Thornhill was born in Richmond, Virginia, on April 14, 1893, and attended high school in Beaver Valley, Pennsylvania. At the urging of John "Hube" Warner, he enrolled in the School of Mines at the University of Pittsburgh and played football for coach Glenn "Pop" Warner. In 1916, some newspapers named Thornhill All-American at left tackle. In 1917, Thornhill agreed to play for the Youngstown Patricians but broke the agreement to coach and play for the McKeesport Olympics. After two games, he was hired away by the Massillon Tigers, despite strong objections from Youngstown. Thornhill played with the Cleveland Indians professional football team in 1919. The following year, he started for the Buffalo All-Americans, and in 1926 he played with the Cleveland Panthers. Throughout this time, Thornhill coached, ending up at Stanford University from 1933 through 1939. While at Stanford, he took three consecutive teams to the Rose Bowl, losing to Columbia 7–0 in 1934 and to Alabama 21–13 in 1935, but then defeating Southern Methodist University 7–0 in 1936. Thornhill died June 29, 1956.[12]

Meanwhile in Canton, Jim Thorpe, fresh from the World Series, played in only one quarter in his debut with the 1917 Canton Bulldogs, who piled up 54 points against the hapless Columbus Panhandles. The Columbus game also marked the return of Greasy Neale, John Kellison, and Pete Calac to the Bulldogs' lineup. As usual, the West Virginia contingent were all playing under assumed names. Greasy Neale made three touchdowns against Columbus, Frank Dunn made three, and Thorpe and Charles Stewart each made one.[13] Although the Panhandles were a mere shadow of the team they had been in earlier years, they were also hampered by a lack of sleep. Though they were expected to arrive in Canton about midnight, a train wreck kept them from reaching their destination until morning and deprived them of much-needed rest.[14]

Pete Calac, the Carlisle Indian star fullback, had lived in Detroit in 1916, where he worked at Ford Motor Company on a special program arranged through Carlisle to apprentice their graduates.[15] While in Detroit, he played a game or two of professional football for the "Carlisles of Detroit" and played the final game of the 1916 season for the Canton Bulldogs. In the fall of 1917, at the urging of John Kellison and Greasy Neale, who had played with him on the Canton Bulldogs team and who coached the Wesleyan College football squad, Calac enrolled at West Virginia Wesleyan College. Thus, Calac, who was technically ineligible to play college football, was the team leader for West Virginia Wesleyan on Saturdays and a star, under an assumed name, for the Canton Bulldogs on Sunday.[16] Perhaps these weekly trips from West Virginia to Canton were motivated, in part, by Calac's growing friendship with Norman Speck, whose daughter he would marry after World War I.[17]

On October 28, Massillon played at Akron and won 14–0 before thirty-five hundred fans in Grossvater Park. Canton ended an easy October schedule by rolling over the Forty-seventh Infantry team from Syracuse, New York, 41–0. The Syracuse army boys did not even make a first down. Unfortunately for the infantry team, their best players had been shipped south to another camp on the Friday before the game. According to the *Canton Repository*, October 29, 1917:

On account of the war most of the soldier stars were missing when the Syracusans blew into Canton. Uncle Sam had interfered with the program by ordering the 47th to one of the southern camps late Friday night. Hence Farnham, the great guard from Brown, Alex Eilson, the All-American halfback from Yale, and a dozen or so other college lights could not come to Canton. Orders from the War Department must be obeyed, football or no football.

Jim Thorpe did not start the game but did enter the fray later. Kellison, Greasy Neale, and Frank Dunn were the pacesetters in this game. Greasy Neale scored two touchdowns, and Frank Dunn one touchdown, with Milton Ghee, Charles Stewart, and Fred Sefton scoring the others.

On November 4, Canton played the Youngstown Patricians in Youngstown and had its hands full. Although the Canton Bulldogs gained 250 yards, they could not make a touchdown. Milton Ghee and Frank Dunn were both injured in the first half of the game and had to be replaced. Still, Fats Waldsmith, the Bulldog's center, played an outstanding game against Bob Peck, the Pat's All-American center. As the *Canton Repository* described it:

Peck played a rough game all through in an effort to knock the courage out of Waldsmith but the Bulldog center never flinched. It was an eye for an eye and a tooth for a tooth all afternoon except for a time in the third period when Peck was on the bench.[18]

While Canton fans expressed great respect for Peck as a football player because he was "full of fight and aggressiveness, with the physical strength and ability to diagnose the enemy's attack," it was the consensus that Fats Waldsmith was the better player.[19] The only score of the game came on Howard Buck's fifteen-yard drop kick in the first period. The Pats had three chances to tie the score with a field goal, but Bart Macomber failed each attempt.[20] Canton sneaked out of town with a 3–0 win.

Meanwhile, Massillon opened its November schedule at home against the Columbus Panhandles. Weakened by the loss of two of the Nesser brothers to the Akron Pros and the loss of three other stars to the war effort, Joe Carr was worried about playing Massillon, particularly after losing to Canton 54–0.[21]

Massillon ripped through the line and tore around the ends of the Columbus Panhandles for a 28–0 win over Joe Carr's team. I. R. Martin, Earl Blackburn, Shorty Miller, and Bob Nash scored touchdowns for Massillon, and, as usual, Nash, Wesbecher, and Thornhill were outstanding on defense. The orange and black from Massillon made their first touchdown four minutes into the game, scoring fourteen points in the third quarter and seven more in the fourth quarter.[22]

Going into the second Sunday in November 1917, both Canton and Massillon were undefeated. They each had just two games to play before facing each other. Of the past sixteen games, Canton had won fifteen and tied one. Massillon had won sixteen, lost two, and tied three over the same period of time.

Massillon played Youngstown on November 11. The Youngstown Patricians featured All-American Bob Peck along with Tommy Hughitt, Stanley Cofall, Bill Kelleher, Bart Macomber, and Jim Barron. The Pats were a powerful team. The prior week, they had nearly upset Canton, and there was bad blood between the managers of the Massillon and Youngstown teams. Youngstown complained that Massillon had stolen Thornhill from them by offering him more money.[23] Thornhill, angered by threats of an injunction to enforce his contract with Youngstown, declared that "he would rather play with Massillon for nothing than to receive pay and play with Youngstown."[24]

The game was held at Wright Field in Youngstown before six thousand spectators. Massillon moved the ball well against Youngstown but could not score. Massillon made seventeen first downs and gained 296 yards, while Youngstown made only 107 yards. The Patricians scored their first touchdown shortly after the game started. Massillon received the opening kickoff but was held on downs and punted. John Barrett, formerly with the Evanston North Ends and the Toledo Maroons, gained thirty yards around left end. Then Stanley Cofall threw a thirty-eight-yard pass to left end Martin, giving Youngstown a 7–0 lead. In the second half, Tuss McLaughry plowed through the Youngstown line for a touchdown, but Massillon missed the punt-out, losing the extra point. A turnover by John Beck in the third quarter cost the Tigers a scoring opportunity that could have put them ahead. In the last three minutes of the game, Youngstown scored again when Cofall intercepted a Massillon pass on the Tiger twenty-five yard line. Tommy Hughitt then pulled the "sleeper" play on Massillon, and Cofall threw a pass to him that took Youngstown to the Massillon two yard line. Two line bucks later, Cofall made the second Youngstown score, giving the Pats a 14 to 6 victory.[25]

On that same afternoon, Canton defeated Akron 14–0. This game gave Canton a lead in the race for the state championship.

Canton and Massillon traded opponents on the following Sunday: Canton played in Youngstown and Massillon in Akron. Massillon brought in Charles E. Brickley,[26] the Harvard kicking star, to lead their team against Akron and Canton. The new Massillon pilot misjudged the strength of Akron and lost to them 3–0. Canton, on the other hand, waged a bitter battle against Cofall's gang. The Pats' game plan called for an aerial attack to overcome the Bulldogs' strong defense. The Bulldogs got the jump on the Patricians when Alfred "Greasy" Neale made a spectacular catch of a pass by Milton Ghee and forced himself over and past several Youngstown players for a touchdown. Gus Welch and Samuel Willaman were outstanding as Bulldog halfbacks. Welch made an eighty-yard dash later in the first quarter for Canton's second touchdown. Once Canton led by thirteen points, they played a defensive game and won the contest 13–0.[27] Youngstown fans were disappointed not to see Jim Thorpe in action, but he and Frank Dunn rested up for the Massillon game the following week.

Preparing for the Massillon-Canton series was a season-long process for both teams, but on Thursday, November 22, Massillon brought Charles Brickley back to town to take charge of team practice planned for Saturday. Although Massillon had lost their game to Akron the previous Sunday, Brickley had impressed the crowd before the game and between halves with his demonstration of kicking, by lofting some balls over the goal from fifty-five yards away.[28] Massillon also reported that they had hired Everett Tuttle, who had attended Oregon Agricultural College, to play guard, although it is not clear that he was actually brought to Massillon for the game.[29]

The forthcoming contest was billed as the Brickley vs. Thorpe

DeOrmand "Tuss" McLaughry, fullback, Youngstown Patricians 1916 and Massillon Tigers 1917, was an outstanding player at Michigan Agricultural College and Westminster College before becoming one of the country's most successful and enduring football coaches. *(Westminster College Archives.)*

game.[30] Massillon fans argued that Harvard's great football star would prove the superiority of eastern college football by outmaneuvering the Indian luminary. It was admitted in Massillon that Jim Thorpe was a crafty leader and the world's greatest athlete, but, it was argued, Brickley would outsmart him. It was generally believed that Massillon was in good hands now that the Harvard star was in absolute control.

Most of the November 25th Sunday game at Meyer's Park near Canton was played in a driving snowstorm and, in the last quarter, it was so dark that the players were barely discernible from the sidelines. Although the team started by Massillon was well drilled, it was no match for the Canton Bulldogs who started the following players:

Samuel Willaman, Ohio State Univ.	LE
Neil Matthews, Univ. of Penn.	LT
Ed "Unk" Russell, Univ. of Penn.	LG
Ralph "Fats" Waldsmith, Buchtel College	C
Clarence "Doc" Spears, Dartmouth College	RT
Alfred "Greasy" Neale, W. Va. Wesleyan College	RE
Milton Ghee, Dartmouth College	QB
Gus Welch, Dickinson College	LH
Frank Dunn, Dickinson College	RH
Jim Thorpe, Carlisle Institute	FB

Pete Calac, Ollie Driesbach, Fred Sefton, William Ward, and John McNamara came off the bench for Canton.

Brickley had a secret plan for beating Canton. He would start a team composed of players from the Allentown Army Ambulance Corps and some worthy local players. Then, after the first quarter, he would bring in Massillon's first team. By making Canton play two groups of fresh athletes, he expected to catch Canton by surprise, wear them down, and defeat them with fresh players. It was a plan worthy of a Harvard graduate. The question on all the fans' minds was, "Who would win? Ex-Harvard star or Indian Jim?" There were plenty of fans willing to bet on the outcome.[31]

Canton won the toss and chose to receive. True to his plan, Charles Brickley started his shock troops, a "mysterious eleven" unidentified to the audience. Who they were mattered little to Thorpe and his team. Like a steamroller, Thorpe led his team seventy-five yards in four minutes and scored the touchdown himself. Frank Dunn kicked goal. Instead of wearing Canton down, Brickley had succeeded in spotting the Bulldogs a one-touchdown lead. In the second period, Brickley attempted and missed a thirty-six-yard field goal. He missed two other tries for field goal—a drop kick of forty-nine yards and a goal from placement of thirty-eight yards. Massillon used twenty-seven of the thirty-two men they suited in their attempt to wear Canton down. This strategy was a bad idea. Thorpe's crew toyed with all of them. In the final period, Frank Dunn scored the second touchdown, and Canton won the game 14 to 0.[32]

The Massillon-Canton game did not end without incident. Fritz Rehor, a former University of Michigan 255-pound guard, either said something or did something to Canton's Unk Russell, and Russell's fists did his talking. They found their mark twice before the referee broke up the fight and banished Russell to the bench for the outbreak in the fourth quarter.[33]

A Canton reporter observed, "So decisively were the Tigers outplayed that they could make only one first down during the battle, which truly was a battle."[34] "Even though the Tigers were laying for him, Jim Thorpe managed to lead his comrades in average gain [per carry]. Before he injured his right shoulder and arm in the second period, he carried the ball nine times for fifty-three yards or about six yards per carry."[35]

Brickley, the ex-Harvard hero, carried the ball seven times for a net of only four yards. He also was thrown for a loss on three occasions.[36] A reporter for the *Toledo Blade* later remarked, "Brickley was just too slow. . . . [He] failed to deliver what was expected of him."[37] On successive Sundays, Frank Nesser and Jim Thorpe had proved that they were better players than the college boy, and this had not gone unnoticed by the mill workers who attended Massillon's games. On Monday, November 26, Massillon released Brickley, to the delight of the average mill worker, who knew in his heart that football players from the big eastern schools tended to be overrated by Walter Camp and his Ivy League crowd. Brickley had again underestimated the Canton team, and he proved to be a better exhibition kicker than a game kicker. Clearly, several professional players outperformed him in 1917, including Reuben Johnson and Frank Nesser, who had never gone to college. It also was clear that Brickley was not the equal of Jim Thorpe.

On the advice of Knute Rockne, Massillon hired Stanley Cofall to rebuild the Massillon Tigers before the next Massillon-Canton game less than one week away. Rockne had a commitment to play in Fort Wayne on Thanksgiving Day, but he agreed to travel to Massillon the day after to help the Tigers prepare for the final game of the season, one last chance to redeem some self-respect for Tiger fans.[38]

As Massillon tried to pick up the pieces, Canton prepared to play the Detroit Heralds on Thanksgiving Day. The Heralds had offered Canton a $2000 guarantee. It was just too good a deal to pass up.[39] Right before their game with the Columbus Panhandles, the Detroit Heralds signed Clarence "Steamer" Horning to a contract to play right tackle for them.[40] Horning had been a Walter Camp All-American at Colgate and was outstanding on both offense and defense. On November 30, after his first game with the Heralds, the *Detroit News* commented, "Horning's exhibition was the best given by a linesman on Navin field." The Heralds had also recruited Harry Whitaker to play quarterback and Carl Thiele to play end. When combined with Whipple, Sacksteder, Bertie Maher, Dick Shields, and Danny Mullane, Detroit had a good team. Because of the hefty guarantee being paid to Canton, the Heralds charged $1.50 admission to the Thanksgiving Day game.[41] The high ticket price did not deter Detroit fans: more than eight thousand came to watch Jim Thorpe in action.[42] They were not disappointed. The first half ended in a scoreless tie. In the third quarter, Jim Thorpe sparked a seventy-yard drive, ten to twenty yards at a time, on a muddy field. A short pass from Milton Ghee to Greasy Neale resulted in the touchdown, and Thorpe added the extra point. Pete Calac also played a good game for Canton. The sixty-minute game ended 7–0 in favor of Canton.[43]

Stanley B. Cofall[44] was hired by the Massillon Tigers to work with Knute Rockne as coach for the final game of the season between Massillon and Canton. At Notre Dame in 1913, Cofall became a close friend and frequent dinner companion of Knute Rockne, captain of the Irish varsity football team at the time. In 1914, as a sophomore, Cofall became Notre Dame's regular left halfback, and, in 1916, he was listed on several All-American teams. After graduation, he played professional football, in 1917, with the Youngstown Patricians. In 1918, he was accepted in the tank corps as a first lieutenant and was assigned to Camp Gettysburg under the command of Dwight D. Eisenhower. They had played football against one another when Eisenhower played for Army. Cofall served as a battalion drill instructor until 1919. That same year, Cofall revived the Cleveland Indians professional football team, but the team did not last long. He continued to play professional football until the mid-1920s. He coached at a Roman Catholic high school in Philadelphia for three years and played for professional teams in Philadelphia and Pottsville, Pennsylvania. He then moved to Baltimore, where he coached three years for Loyola College before ending his coaching career, in 1928, at Wake Forest College in North Carolina.

Stanley Cofall and Knute Rockne managed to totally rehabilitate the Massillon team for their most important game, the last game of the season in Ohio, held at Meyers Lake Park near Canton. In the five days following the dismissal of Brickley, Stanley Cofall had recruited many of the best players from the Youngstown Patricians team to play against Canton, and added Irving W. Rogers, a college dropout who had been a brilliant freshman quarterback at Princeton in 1913.[45] In other words, the second and third best pro teams in America were being merged in hopes of beating undefeated Canton. In the last two years, Canton had not lost a game and had only been scored on three times. But the combined Massillon-Youngstown team, playing as the Massillon Tigers, was formidable. It featured;

Bob Nash, Rutgers Univ.	LE
Charles Copley, Muhlenberg College	LT
Fred Rehor, Univ. of Mich.	LG
Bob Peck, Univ. of Pittsburgh	C
Freeman Fitzgerald, Univ. of Notre Dame	RG
Claude Thornhill, Univ. of Pittsburgh	RT
Knute Rockne, Univ. of Notre Dame	RE
Eugene "Shorty" Miller, Penn State Univ.	QB
Stanley Cofall, Univ. of Notre Dame	LH
Irving Rogers, Princeton Univ.	RH
DeOrmond McLaughry, Westminster College	FB

Rockne drilled his team Friday evening and twice on Saturday. Not all were present Friday night, but they all made it for the Saturday practice session except Peck.[46]

The game was a defensive battle from start to finish. Canton made ten first downs and Massillon only two. However, a blocked kick in the first quarter resulted in a thirty-four-yard field goal by Cofall. In the second quarter, a poor punt by Canton and a fifteen-yard penalty gave Cofall another opportunity for a field goal, which he made. Those were the only scores in the game.[47]

The Canton papers remarked about Massillon's dirty play. Thorpe, in particular, was upset by Cofall's behavior. The *Canton Repository* reported,

Several times he piled up after the play was dead, for which a penalty can be inflicted and probably would be in a college game. . . . On one occasion he rammed into Thorpe after the Indian had been stopped. It was a plain case of roughness and Thorpe resented the tactic. He started after Cofall but never reached him, because several of the Bulldogs restrained Big Jim. A mix between these two huskies ought to be interesting. There would be no stalling and no bell at the end of three minutes. . . . Strangely enough, Russell didn't get mixed up with Cofall. The Notre Dame halfback didn't seem to aim at Russell's position.[48]

The *Massillon Independent* credited "some very capable coaching by Knute Rockne, former Tiger star and assistant coach at Notre Dame" for the victory.[49] After the game, the Massillon band went to the Cortland Hotel, the home base for the Canton Bulldogs, and commenced playing in the lobby. Hotel management turned off the lights in order to get rid of them.[50] While Canton retained the title of professional football champions of the world because of their superior record, they were no longer undefeated, and Knute Rockne clearly had a future as a coach.

Massillon fielded a team in 1919, but never joined the American Professional Football Association, although there was an effort to leave the door open for their entrance into the league. Canton, on the other hand, played an instrumental role in the formation of the APFA and the NFL. After the 1917 season, Jack Cusack went to Oklahoma to work in the oil business. In the spring of 1919, he turned his lease on Canton's League Park over to his friend Ralph Hay, the local Hupmobile automobile dealer.[51] Ralph Hay was instrumental in calling the meetings that led to the formation of the American Professional Football Association, that became the National Football League in 1922.

In 1919, the Canton Bulldogs were coached by Jim Thorpe, and nearly half their players were holdovers from 1917. Dutch Speck, Cub Buck, Butchy Barron, Bull Lowe, Pete Calac, Al Feeney, John Kellison, I. R. Martin, Clarence Spears, and Fred Rehor were among the Bulldog players that year, and Canton claimed the world championship of professional football.[52] In 1920, Thorpe again coached the Bulldogs with nearly the same cast of players as the previous year, but the results were less satisfactory. However, Canton halfback Joe Guyon, who was selected for the Professional Football Hall of Fame in 1966, managed a ninety-five-yard punt, the longest in professional football history.[53]

The following year, Jim Thorpe and many of his teammates moved to Cleveland Indians, while the Bulldogs rebuilt under a new coach. Cleveland won only two games and suffered serious financial problems both at the hands of rival teams, who frequently did not give an honest accounting of gate receipts, and from the lack of hometown fan support.[54] Canton fared only slightly better. In 1922, however, the Bulldogs hired Guy Chamberlin as player-coach, and he brought glory back to Canton. The Bulldogs, behind such stars as Wilber "Fats" Henry, Link Lyman, Norb Sacksteder, Ralph Waldsmith, and Dutch Speck, went undefeated and won the NFL Championship. With the addition of All-

American Ben Jones, from tiny Grove City College in Pennsylvania, Canton went undefeated again in 1923, but struggled financially. Sam Deutsch, owner of the Cleveland franchise, purchased the Canton Bulldogs in August 1924 and combined the best players from the two teams into the Cleveland Bulldogs, while keeping the Canton franchise inactive.[55] Still under the leadership of coach Guy Chamberlin, the Cleveland Bulldogs won the NFL Championship for the third consecutive year in 1924. In 1925, the Canton Professional Football Company was formed to purchase the Canton franchise from Sam Deutsch. They paid $3,000 for the franchise, twice the cost paid for it by Deutsch a year earlier.[56] Harry Robb and Wilber Henry were placed in charge of a Bulldogs team that featured Pete Calac, Ben Jones,[57] Link Lyman, Norb Sacksteder, and Dutch Speck.[58] The revived Canton Bulldogs only managed a 4–4 season, and at the end of the season Ben Jones was traded to the Frankfort Yellowjackets, who went on to win the NFL Championship in 1926, while the Canton Bulldogs slipped to a 1–9–1 record. The Canton Bulldogs were disbanded at the end of the 1926 season, and their NFL franchise was canceled.[59]

19. Davenport: When the Players Were in Charge

In early September 1916, a coalition of merchants and professional men in Davenport, Iowa, led by Dr. C. V. McCormack, John Malloy, Reed Lane, Gene Halligan and Victor L. Littig, a sportswriter for the *Davenport Daily Times,* formed the Davenport Football Athletic Club.[1] There had been an independent football team in Davenport in 1912, 1913, and 1914, but it had failed for lack of adequate financial backing and for its inability to beat Rock Island, its archrival.

Football was a popular sport in the Davenport, Rock Island, and Moline or Tri-cities area during the second decade of the twentieth century. Both Rock Island and Moline supported strong semiprofessional teams for more than ten years, despite a riot after a 1911 high school game between the fans of the two cities that threatened to sever all athletic relations between them.[2]

The Rock Island Independents and the Moline Red Men were two of the strongest independent football teams in Illinois. Just across the Mississippi River in Davenport, civic leaders, led by the *Davenport Democrat and Leader* sports department, decided it was time to contend for a share of football honors in the Tri-cities by creating a major league team of their own.

The Davenport Athletic Club began football a full two weeks before any other professional team in the country.[3] Victor Littig[4] was the team's coach.

In his column in the *Davenport Daily Times,* Littig said that he "believes only in straight, simple, and strategic football," and asserted that "he will coach no other kind." He further

insists upon good tackling, quick starting, fast running, powerful charging, sufficient interference, sudden openings and thrusts through the line, forward passes far down field, and short bullet-like, forward passes over the line, almost instantaneous kicking, the kick formation threatening a kick, pass or run at all times, prompt lining up, deliberation and judgment in giving signals, followed by very speedy execution, no running back with the ball, no fumbling, no grand-stand playing of any sort, no unnecessary roughness or underhanded work, and he insists upon the entire team playing all the time, covering up every muffed or fumbled ball, and being on the look out for opportunities at all times, regardless of all else.[5]

He opposed "shift formations and trick plays,"[6] and did not like back-field men who played with "the hands on the knees in a semi-erect po-sition as it has never been prescribed for speedy work."[7]

Initially, the newly formed Davenport Athletic Club team drew its players from recent graduates of Davenport High School and the Mo-line independent football team. Richard M. Fort, who had been captain of the 1915 Davenport High School team and was considered to be an all-around athlete and "a natural football player of ability as a runner, tackle, punter and drop kicker, and a typical emergency man," was re-cruited to be the team's fullback.[8] Tom Kennedy, who had also been a fine athlete at Davenport High School, between 1912 and 1915, was recruited as the team's right guard. Other Davenport High graduates included Herbert Ross Tomson at right halfback; Ray "Waddle" Kuehl, who had recently played halfback for the Moline Red Men, at right halfback; and Frank T. Killian, who played quarterback for the class of 1912.[9]

The captain of the Davenport team was Red Wolters, who was an es-tablished independent football veteran with the Moline Red Men. Duffy "Bum" Stuehmer, Raymond "Slim" Crowley from the St. Am-brose College team of 1913,[10] Ward Shaw, Edgar Rumberg from Mon-mouth High School,[11] Hauser from the Moline Red Men, Albert Her-man Miller from the University of Nebraska,[12] and the Wellendorf brothers—Art and Carl—completed the initial squad. Poe, who had at-tended an Indiana college, was a back-up quarterback. On September 23, Ray Mitten, a Davenport High School graduate, was recruited to play left tackle. Mitten was one of Davenport's best all-around athletes. He ran, hurdled, boxed, swam, and rode the bicycle, as well as playing football and baseball. At 185 pounds, he was seen as an important ad-dition to the team.

Fred W. Earp at 210 pounds was recruited to play right tackle. A cousin of the famous Wyatt Earp, Fred had grown up in Monmouth, Illinois, the son of a poultry dealer, and was reported to have attended and played football at Knox College in Galesburg, Illinois, just a few blocks from the birthplace of Carl Sandburg, the famous poet, although there was no record that he completed any classes at Knox.

Fred Earp was already twenty-six years old when he became the star lineman for the Moline Red Men. He joined the Davenport Athletic Club in 1916.[13]

The Davenport Athletic Club practiced at the East Davenport playground in preparation for its first game with Oelwein, Iowa, held at 3 P.M. on Sunday, October 1, 1916 in Davenport. Some 848 football fans paid fifty cents admission at Davenport's Three-I Park to watch Davenport win 27–0.[14]

Despite the easy win, conflicts were beginning to surface between Coach Littig and the team. In this era, the players, not the coaches, determined on-field strategy. Plays could not be signaled in from the sideline. Once the game started, the players were on their own. Consequently, differences between the players' philosophies and the coach's philosophy began to surface. Coach Littig was unhappy with play selection.

The next game with the Moline Red Men promised to be a difficult game. On October 8, the Davenport Athletic Club traveled across the river to play Moline before fifteen hundred fans. Seven truckloads of Davenport fans followed their team across the river to the Moline field on this warm Sunday afternoon. A pass from Ray Kuehl to Murphy, a new recruit at right end, led to Davenport's only score, and Davenport beat Moline 7–6. The most exciting play of the game was a punt return by Fred Earp, who, in the words of the *Davenport Daily Times*, "like an electric current following the line of least resistance . . . drew the spectators to their feet when he clipped off a pretty run of about 30 yards. He also played a cracking good game on defensive, seldom if ever did his opponent get through."[15]

The third game was with the Evanston North Ends. Several members of the Davenport team who had played for Moline were familiar with Evanston, having lost to them twice in 1915. They knew what to expect and felt that Coach Littig's strategy was ill suited to defeat the reigning Illinois state independent football champions. Captain Red Wolters, Dilk Holm, Hauser, Bum Stuehmer, Fred Earp, Ray Kuehl, and E. Carl Wellendorf felt strongly that both offensive and defensive shifts and "trick" plays were needed to even the odds against the better independent teams, such as Evanston. These views were strongly opposed by Coach Littig. There was also concern regarding the way Coach Littig pontificated about how football should be played, particularly when he had no recent football experience himself. In his anxiety to control the team and to produce a winner, the coach "sometimes said pretty sharp things in hopes of getting results." Some veteran players took offense, particularly when their work kept them from practice or caused them to be late only to have the coach publicly humiliate them in his newspaper column by implication, if not by name.[16]

The close score against the Moline Red Men was taken as a warning by the veteran football players, and, for his part, Coach Littig complained, "I have never coached a team before that tried to tell me how to coach them. The team used the style of football I desired in the Oelwein game, but disobeyed my instructions last Sunday in Moline. Without being given the authority to enforce my methods, I no longer care to be responsible for the showing of the team."[17]

Captain Wolters responded, "Coach Littig could not get along with the boys. The coach was to blame in part and the boys were to blame in part."[18] Because of the near miss at Moline, Wolters petitioned the coach and general management of the Davenport Athletic Club to allow them to play a more advanced style of football. The addition of Freeburg, Magerkurth, and Nig Wright, all former Moline Indian players, in preparation for the game with Evanston, increased the pressure to add shifts and "trick plays."[19] On October 11, Coach Littig complained in his column in the *Davenport Daily Times* that "numerous setbacks . . . have impeded the progress and the development of the team has slowed up considerably." He complained about the team's "on the field defensive strategy." In particular, he complained that "shifting with the shift is simply playing with it, and making more possible the ruse of the attack when the ball is sent in the opposite direction." He also criticized the team's offensive play selection.

The resulting internal friction led to a directors' meeting to which the entire team was invited. At the meeting, the coach's teaching methods were found unacceptable by nearly the entire team and, when reconciliation seemed impossible, Coach Littig resigned.

"I sincerely hope," said Coach Littig, "that my action will be the means of restoring good feeling in the club. My idea was to give the men a thorough course of football principles, keeping them to the simple style until they had mastered it. Then to give them the shift formation and the trick plays that they want. Certain members, however, demanded these plays at once and I could not consent to teach the kind of football that I do not believe in." On that same night, it was announced that Ray Mitten was moving to the Dakotas and would not be available for the balance of the season.[20]

The team was turned over to the care of team captain Red Wolters until a new coach could be hired. In the meantime, Davenport was scheduled to play the Evanston North Ends. The North Ends had been perennial independent football champions of Illinois since 1911, and were one of the best teams in the country. They played a fast, shifting offensive game with lots of trick plays. The core of their team had been playing together for nearly a decade. The star of the team was Reuben E. Johnson, who could kick, pass, and run with the best college stars in America, although he had never attended college. Moreover, the Kirby brothers, the Falcon brothers, Lane Tech High School graduates Robert Specht and Baggs Miller, Northwest Academy graduates Frederick "Blad" Meyers, Fitzgerald, Roy Whitlock, and Lindal, together with college players John Barrett, Penn Carolan, Tom Shaughnessy, Art Pascolini, and Gene Schobinger, constituted an awesome aggregate for a start-up team that was without a coach.

The North Ends had scheduled themselves tightly, not expecting much trouble from the upstart team from "the backwoods of Iowa." The North Ends arrived in Rock Island about noon on Sunday and were brought by automobile to Three-I Park in Davenport. The game started promptly at 2:30, since Evanston had to catch a return train to Chicago at 4:30. Because of the cramped schedule, the teams agreed on twelve-minute quarters. Much to Evanston's surprise, "at no time in the game was Davenport outplayed."

According to the *Daily Times*, "Several costly fumbles were committed by the Evanston backfield, and their line was penalized numerous times for offside play." With only three minutes to play, the game was still scoreless. Then, with the ball on the thirty-eight yard line, Dick Fort, Davenport's fullback, drop-kicked the ball from the forty-five yard line and split the uprights to give Davenport a 3–0 lead. "Evanston played desperate football in the few remaining minutes of the game, but was unable to penetrate the Davenport defense and the game ended with the ball in Davenport's possession on their own thirty yard line."[21] It was only the third time in four years that the North Ends had been defeated.

In addition to Dick Fort, the offensive star of the game, Fred Earp and Red Wolters were the defensive standouts for Davenport.[22] The fast pace taught by Coach Littig, together with good "on the field" decisions, contributed to the win.

The search for a successor to Coach Littig began immediately after the win over Evanston. One of the first applicants for the job was Penn Carolan, the former Dartmouth College fullback who was now playing with the Evanston North Ends. In addition, the directors of the Davenport Athletic Club considered George Jones, the coach at St. Ambrose College and a former Holy Cross College football star, and Carl Anderson, the Rock Island High School coach.[23] George W. Jones grew up in Worcester, Massachusetts, and attended Worcester Academy, before distinguishing himself as an all-around athlete at Holy Cross College as a member of the class of 1911. While at Holy Cross, Jones lettered in football, baseball, track, and basketball. He went on to teach and coach for three years at St. John's in Danvers, Massachusetts, before coaching at Worcester Polytechnic Institute in 1915. He was brought to Davenport, in the fall of 1916, to head the athletic department at St. Ambrose College.[24]

On October 16, the directors announced that they had hired Dr. C. F. Wright as trainer for their team. They ruled out Penn Carolan as coach. While his terms were reasonable, his insistence on bringing Johnny Barrett to Davenport with him doomed his application because the directors "failed to see where Barrett could help the backfield they now boast."[25] Finally, on October 18, 1916, the directors appointed Carl Anderson, coach of Rock Island High School, as the club's new coach. A Grinnell College graduate, Coach Anderson immediately added a number of plays to the team's signal book.[26]

Meanwhile, Walter H. Flannigan finally secured a lease on the Rock Island Three-I ball park, which allowed the Rock Island Independents to schedule home games for the first time in the 1916 season.[27]

On October 22, Davenport loped to a 51–0 win over the Peru Socials.[28] Every player on the Davenport team played in the game, an unusual event in the days before free substitution, since a player could only re-enter the game once, and that at the beginning of a quarter.[29]

In the week following the game with the Socials, the *Davenport Democrat and Leader* reported that the Davenport Athletic Club made "special efforts to stop the Osborne shift plays of the [Rock Island] Independents as taught them by 'Nips' Murphy, their quarterback and former star of Clinton [Iowa] high school when Osborne, the originator of the plays, was coaching that team."[30]

On the Saturday before their game with the Rock Island Independents, Herbert Ross Tomson went home ill with an attack of the grippe. He was replaced by Freeberg, "an old time independent football player" who began playing with the Moline East Ends in 1908, when they won the state championship, and then joined the Moline Illini until they won the state championship in 1911.[31]

When the game got underway, there was considerable interest in what a Rock Island group christened the "Suffragette Float."[32] According to newspaper reports, "Besides those who chose to decorate the grand stands there were many automobiles and truck loads of yelling fans. One truck which attracted considerable attention carried a number of 'sparkling damsels' from this side of the river."[33] Meanwhile, "On a field that would have been almost ideal for an aquatic meet instead of a grid battle, the Davenport Athletic Club downed the Rock Island Independents . . . by a score of 6 to 0, before a crowd of nearly 4000 [only 3100 of whom paid for a ticket]."[34]

Davenport field generals "Freeberg and Kuehl kept the Islanders guessing whenever they had the ball." Fakes and tricks kept the Independents off guard all afternoon. In the third quarter, Bum Stuehmer scored the only touchdown, a short-yardage play that culminated a forty-yard drive.[35]

The November schedule started with a rematch between Davenport and the Moline Red Men, held in Davenport. On Tuesday before the game, Kemmerling, Moline's manager, reported that they had added the "Masked Marvel" for their game. In turn, Davenport added Mark Donavan to its backfield.[36] Later in the week, it was determined that, due to illness, Fred Earp and Ray Crowley would be unable to play Sunday for Davenport.[37] They were replaced by George W. Jones, a former Holy Cross College halfback. Davenport also added Charles Schuler, who was living in Des Moines and had played quarterback for Cornell University.[38] Finally, it was reported that Fred Earp would play on Sunday after all.[39] The "Masked Marvel" of Moline turned out to be Churchill, a former University of Minnesota tackle. Jones and Schuler started for Davenport, and Earp, who was sick, played in only one quarter.

Davenport stepped out to a 7 to 6 lead in the first half but fell behind in the third quarter. Nearly four thousand Tri-cities residents were watching the game when Adams kicked a field goal for Moline, making the score Moline 9, Davenport 7. With only six minutes to play, Moline still led by two points, and neither Davenport's running game nor its short passing game was working. At that juncture, Charles Schuler took charge of the game. With the ball on the Davenport twenty-five yard line, he threw a long, wide pass to fullback Dick Fort for a twenty-yard gain, and followed it up with a second long pass to Freeberg for another twenty-yard gain.

The ball was now on the Moline thirty-five yard line. Schuler attempted a run but failed to gain any yardage, so he threw another long pass to Kuehl, who was wide open near the goal line. However, the pass was short, and it was now third down. Most of the fans expected a short pass or a run to set up a field goal attempt. To nearly everyone's surprise, Schuler chose a "Dick Merriwell finish" instead. He called another long pass pattern and "hurled the oval" nearly fifty yards diagonally across the field to Kuehl, who caught the ball in stride just ahead of the defender, crossed the goal line, and ran around to put the ball down back of the goal posts for an easy punt-out for extra point. The story in the *Davenport Democrat and Leader* caught the delirium of the Athletic Club supporters: "Horns tooted, hats were thrown in the air, fans yelled themselves hoarse in their frenzy and mauled one another in their delight."[40]

Dick Fort kicked an easy chance to make the score 14 to 9. With only three and a half minutes to play and almost no way to stop the clock under the rules of 1916, Moline was forced to take desperate chances if it hoped to regain the lead. A few moments later, however, "a mighty punt by Fort" put the ball within a foot of the Moline goal line, where Harold "Peg" Graham, the Moline halfback who had played for St. Ambrose College the year before, fielded the punt. Thinking that he was behind the goal line, he stepped back after he caught the punt and touched the ball down for what he believed was a touchback. Instead, he was called for a safety, because Freeburg tackled Graham immediately, making the final score 16–9.[41]

The following week, the undefeated Davenport Athletic Club played Rock Island again. In the intervening two weeks, Rock Island placed long-time pros Ted Davenport and Art Salzmann in their starting line-up. Art Salzmann had been a high school football star for Rock Island, in 1911, and had five years of semipro experience. Player-coach Ted Davenport, also a well-established pro player, worked himself into shape and was now starting at halfback. Jones, who had played his first professional game for Davenport the week before, was working with Coach Anderson to develop a new style of offense for the team.[42]

On Sunday, November 12, the cross-river rivals played to a scoreless tie before 2,970 fans. The day was bitterly cold, and the piercing wind added to the unfavorable weather conditions. While Davenport played most of the game in Rock Island territory, the Tri-cities champions could not score. Rock Island never penetrated the Davenport territory farther than the thirty-six yard line. Rock Island did use all sorts of shifts and even tried a triple pass, but to no avail. The defensive unit led by Earp and Red Wolters of Davenport was too strong to be scored on.[43]

Sometime after midnight on November 18, 1916, a special train with approximately one hundred Davenport fans, newspaper reporters, two Davenport Athletic Club officials, the coach, the trainer, and about twenty professional football players left from Rock Island, Illinois, bound for Hammond, Indiana. Originally, Davenport had been scheduled to play at Taylorville, Illinois, on November 19, but, on November 4, Hammond had made a better offer, guaranteeing the Iowans $700 to play in Hammond. The deal was quickly accepted, and now they were facing their most important game since beating the Evanston North Ends.

The train was noisy. Between 2 A.M. and 5 A.M., Davenport fans rehearsed yells, while Dick Fort and Waddle Kuehl kept up a noisy chatter. Only Bum Stuehmer was able to sleep, having promised to bruise up anyone who pestered him.[44] When the train reached Hammond, the DAC players were already tired, although keyed up. A band and a big delegation of Clabby Athletic Association members met them at the train.

The team was taken to rooms at the Association of Commerce, where a dressing room and rubbing table were furnished. The Davenport fans were transported to Jimmy Clabby's buffet. Clabby, the former welterweight boxing champion of the world and now a middleweight contender, was in Australia where he was preparing to fight, but his cafeteria was a favorite place with the Davenporters.[45]

The game drew only fifteen hundred fans at $1 admission each, but they were lively, and a considerable amount of money was bet on the game.[46] Davenport kicked off to the Clabbys. The Clabbys were unable to move the ball and punted to the Davenport ten yard line. For the greater part of the game, the ball stayed in Davenport territory. Telling smashes by Hammond backs "ripped the Davenport line to pieces with a regularity that boded no good for the Iowans." Hammond exhibited the better teamwork, and the Davenport players "gave every indication of being slightly stale."[47]

Midway through the first quarter, Johnny Finn, the former Purdue University star who played quarterback for Hammond, kicked a field goal from the thirty yard line, giving the Clabbys the lead. Shortly afterward, a pass from Galvin to Clinks Meyers, followed by two line bucks, gave Hammond a 10–0 lead. In the second quarter, George Jones intercepted a Hammond pass some six minutes into the period, and, on the very next play, Ray Kuehl started around right end, cut back against the grain off tackle, and ran forty-seven yards for a touchdown. Murphy kicked goal, and at halftime the score stood Hammond 10, Davenport 7.

George Jones, Davenport's quarterback, sat out the third quarter. Nevertheless, Davenport pulled ahead in the game when Hammond fumbled the ball on the Davenport eight yard line, and Dilk Holmes picked up the ball and ran ninety-one yards before being tackled two feet short of a touchdown. Two plays later, Ray Kuehl pushed across the goal line for a touchdown. Murphy, the right end, kicked goal, and the score was Davenport 14, Hammond 10.

The most exciting part of the game occurred during the last two minutes. At that juncture, the Clabbys had the ball third down on the Davenport three yard line. On two consecutive off-tackle plays, the Davenport line, led by Fred Earp, Red Wolters, and Hauser, held Hammond. The two heartstopping smashes left the ball less than a yard short of a touchdown.

With the clock running down, George Jones used his football brain to secure the game for Davenport. He called for Hauser, the center, to pass the ball directly to him, and he fell to the ground in the end zone for a safety, making the score Davenport 14, Hammond 12. Time ran out as Davenport prepared to kick off to Hammond from their own twenty yard line.[48]

The Hammond game extracted a heavy toll from the Iowa professionals. Every man on the team suffered bad bruises or other injuries, and they returned home totally exhausted. Red Wolters had his left leg laid open from the knee to the ankle, Dick Fort suffered from a badly wrenched arm, and Ray Kuehl had numerous bruises around the face and a stiff neck.[49] The injuries sustained in this game, together with earlier injuries and illnesses that refused to yield to treatment, left the Davenport team worn out and ready to call it a season. "On the train coming home from Hammond they were listless and completely worn out although they have played much harder football in previous contests." According to the sportswriter Donald Hutchinson of the *Davenport Daily Times*, "the long grind of training and the constant nerve strain has finally worn the men down until they are no longer capable of the hard fast football which has marked their work heretofore."[50]

The team was unable to practice until Friday because of injuries.[51] On Sunday, November 26, they lost a close game to the Spring Valley (IL) Moose, 9–7. Earlier in the season, Davenport would have made easy work of Spring Valley, but Dick Fort fumbled because he was playing injured, and Albert Woodyatt, the Moline Indian's quarterback who had been hired to play for Spring Valley, took advantage of Davenport's weaknesses.

In the second half, George Jones settled Davenport down and they played well, but it was too little, too late. According to the *Democrat and*

Leader, "Overconfidence, poor generalship, costly fumbles, and a questionable decision by the referee which robbed Davenport of a touchdown" were the cause of the Athletic Club's first loss of the season. Two weeks later, the Rock Island Independents beat Spring Valley 13–0.[52]

The last game of the Davenport Athletic Club's 1916 season was held at Three-I League Stadium, on December 3, against the Minneapolis Marines. The Marines were organized in 1905 and had never before played outside of Minnesota. The original Marines team was pretty much intact. All-American Bob Marshall, "the great University of Minnesota Negro end," had been added to the team in 1909, and Eber Simpson was added sometime after 1911; otherwise, the team had been playing together for eleven years. They kept a permanent club room in Minneapolis and had put together an enviable record. During the 1916 season, they were undefeated, although tied by the Minnesota All-Stars, and had only been scored on once, by Duluth in a 54 to 3 blowout.[53]

The Davenport Athletic Club reinforced its lineup for the game. They added Archie Raymond Kirk from the University of Iowa to play tackle and Koppas to play guard. Kirk was the *Chicago Evening Post* All-Western second team tackle in 1914.[54] They also added Meersman and Stowe from the Moline Indians. The game was scheduled for 2:30 Sunday afternoon. The Marines had been guaranteed $700 and could earn 60 percent of the gate—estimated to be worth an additional $200—if they won. The Marines brought seventeen players with them, plus coach Russell J. Tollefson and manager John Dunne.

The Minneapolis team used the old-time Minnesota shift and featured "wonderful interference." They received the kickoff and, over the next four minutes, marched steadily down the field for a touchdown. This was followed by a Davenport fumble and a second Minnesota score, despite outstanding defensive play for Earp and Wolters. Rube Ursella, however, missed the second point after touchdown, and the score stood 13 to 0. In the second quarter, the Marines scored a third touchdown and led at halftime 19 to 0. In the second half, the tide shifted. Davenport played the Marines even in the third quarter and, in the fourth quarter, twice drove the ball to within five yards of the Minneapolis goal line before finally scoring a touchdown in the last minute of play. Davenport lost the game 19–6.[55]

Despite the loss of their final two games in the 1916 season, the Davenport Athletic Club demonstrated that they were one of the fifteen best professional teams in America that year. The Minneapolis Marines management observed that Davenport had the makings of a championship team,[56] and Johnny Walker, a *Davenport Daily Times* sportswriter, declared that the DAC team was unequaled in the history of the Tri-cities and all of Iowa.[57]

Officials for the Davenport Athletic Club were already dickering with a number of men of All-American and All-Western Conference stature for next year's team, and scheduling offers were coming in from the Fort Wayne Friars, Evanston North Ends, Cornell-Hamburgs, Pine Village, the Wabash A.A. and the Toledo Maroons.[58] Without question, the 1916 Davenport Athletic Club football team had made a strong statement with their on-field play at a time when the players and not the coach determined game strategy.

20. The Rock Island Independents

The Rock Island Independents were organized in 1912 around the talents of Arthur W. Salzmann[1] and Frank "Fat" Smith, the stars of the 1911 Rock Island High School team that defeated Moline High School and caused a riot between the fans of the two schools. In their first semiprofessional game, held on October 13, 1912, the Rock Island Independents beat the Moline Illini 6 to 0, a significant feat because the Moline Illini, along with the Evanston North Ends, had claimed the 1911 Illinois state independent football championship.

The Independents went on to an undefeated, unscored-on season in 1912.[2] In 1913, the Independents were also undefeated, and their winning streak continued until the last two games of the 1914 season, when they lost consecutive games to the Moline Red Men and the Evanston North Ends by scores of 9–0 and 6–0.

In 1915, the Rock Island Independents had such a wealth of backfield candidates that they turned down an opportunity to sign Ray Kuehl, the Davenport halfback who had set new records for the Moline Red Men in 1914.[3] Instead, they concentrated on developing backfield men Edward "Nips" Murphy, Edward Swanson, Ted Davenport, Ernest McGinnis, Victor Bredimus,[4] and Tom Kennedy. The 1915 Independents averaged 173 pounds and brought considerable experience to the field. With the exception of Zeb, who now played left end for the Moline Red Men, the 1914 team had returned. Walter H. Flannigan, a former player for the 1912 team, was now manager of the Rock Island Independents, a position he had been elevated to, in 1914, after serving two years as assistant manager.[5] There was talk of the Independents playing "the fastest independent machine in the country," including the Detroit Heralds,[6] but instead Flannigan settled for games with relatively weak regional teams in 1915.

Rock Island was an avid football town with strong fan support. There was, in the enthusiastic prose of the *Rock Island Argus*, a "dyed-in-the-wool 18-karat band of fans from Schneider Brother's Smoker" and the Bijou Cigar Store who called themselves "the Royal Rooters." The main purpose of the "Royal Rooters" was to yell "knock 'em in," "slam 'em down," and "drag 'em out" at Independents football games, and, like many other Rock Island fans, they tended to bet heavily on their team's games, particularly when they played the Moline Red Men.[7]

On November 16, 1915, the local newspaper reported that "one man in Rock Island . . . placed $500 in pool rooms and cigar stores . . . on the Independents at even money. Others have offered $100, and many $50 and there are scores betting smaller sums,"[8] and Herman Hansen, a Rock Island contractor, "offered every player on the Independent football team a new sweater coat if they win from the [Moline] Injuns Sunday."[9]

Hansen did not have to buy the sweaters. Despite the weak schedule, Rock Island was held to a scoreless tie by Moline on October 17, 1915, and was soundly defeated by the Red Men on November 21, 1915. The Moline Red Men, led by Ray Kuehl, Red Wolters, Honey Meersman, and Fred W. Earp, went on to challenge the Evanston North Ends for the Illinois state championship. On Thanksgiving Day, the North Ends beat the Moline Red Men 25–0.[10]

While Moline was playing Evanston for the state championship, the Rock Island Independents were planning to reorganize their team with new players under new management. The local newspaper sensed the team's weariness: "Many of the veterans feel that they have played enough football and have announced their intentions of quitting the gridiron sport. Among these are Captain Art Salzmann, Roy Salzmann, Ted Davenport, Loyal Robb, 'Eatem' Smith and Cook."[11] Thus, a team that had lost but three games in four years had cause for concern because it had failed to defeat its archrival for two consecutive years.

During the off-season, Flannigan and the core players from the 1915 season reconsidered their threat to reorganize and/or quit independent football, and began practicing for the next season on September 24, 1916. Whereas the admission price had been twenty-five cents in 1915, it had now doubled.[12] Ted Davenport was the new coach for the Independents. A rival team was also organized in Rock Island by Jack Roche, and they had signed a lease for Three-I Park, leaving the Independents no place to play.[13] Consequently, Flannigan scheduled two road games to open the season, one in Rockford, the other in Moline. After the preliminary contest between the Union (Colored) Giants and the 706 Club, the Independents launched their season at Kishwaukee Park in Rockford at 3 P.M. against the Rockford Athletic Club. Their hopes were smashed 0–25.[14]

Flannigan's competitor, Jack Roche, promised a Rock Island team that included Woodyatt, Wright, Boyle, Nelson, Johnson, Neilson, Gillman, Hufford, and Freeburg from the 1914 Moline Red Men; Harold "Peg" Graham, who had played for St. Ambrose College the year before; Plummer of Auburn; Bailey of the Moline Olympics; McEniry of Notre Dame; and several recent local high school stars.[15] Roche scheduled a game with the Aurora Greyhounds to be held October 22, 1916. It proved more difficult than anticipated for Roche to form his new Rock Island team, and on October 20, 1916, he transferred his lease for Three-I Park and his game with Aurora to Walter Flannigan.[16]

In the meantime, because of poor team development, the Independents were also in trouble.[17] On October 8, 1916, the Rock Island Independents had played without Art and Ray Salzmann, Loyal Robb, and Keith Dooley. After the loss to Rockford, it was also determined that the team was weak "at one tackle position and at the ends."[18] On October 12, Roy Salzmann returned at tackle and Keith Dooley at end. Jake Lazerous, a graduate of East Des Moines High School, was added at the other end[19] and Ted Guyer, a 1912 All-American tackle from Cornell University, was hired.[20]

Their game in Moline, on October 15, was an even contest. Early in the first quarter, with the ball on the Rock Island fifteen yard line, the Moline quarterback, Al Woodyatt, showed good judgment when he signaled for a place kick. Adams kicked a twenty-yard field goal that turned out to be the game's only score. During the balance of the game, Edward Murphy, the Rock Island field general, used the Osborne shift to dominate the game. The twenty-one-year old Murphy, known to his friends as "Nips," was the Clinton (Iowa) High School quarterback from 1911 through 1914. During his junior and senior years at Clinton High, Duke Slater was his left tackle. Noted as an offensive whirlwind, Murphy was an outstanding open field runner.[21]

The Osborne shift was developed in 1913 by coach Clint Osborne, a native of Rockford, Illinois, who was coaching at Clinton High School. The following year, the use of the shift, which was similar to the Minnesota or Shevilin shifts, made it possible for Eddie "Nips" Murphy to become an All-State quarterback and lead Clinton to the state high school football championship.[22] In 1915, Murphy attended Notre Dame and played for their freshman squad for several weeks before dropping out of college. Now, as the Rock Island quarterback, he introduced the Osborne shift into professional football, with good results. When the Rock Island Independents shifted on offense, the Moline Red Men frequently failed to shift on defense, with devastating effect. The strong side of the Rock Island backfield would attack the less numerous side of the Moline line with consistent success. Only strong goal line defenses kept the Independents from scoring, and quick kicks were used by Moline to keep Rock Island out of scoring position. Over the course of the game, the Independents outgained Moline nearly twenty to one but were unable to score. Nevertheless, Rock Island served notice that if teams failed to make adjustments to their shifts, they would have problems with Rock Island. Once the Independents started taking advantage of their scoring chances, they were destined to have a successful season.[23]

The collapse of Jack Roche's team, on October 20, 1916, ended the professional football war in Rock Island, leaving Walter Flannigan's Independents in control. The players who had signed with Roche sought placements elsewhere. Albert Woodyatt returned to the Moline Red Men full time, Magerkurth and Nig Wright accepted contracts with Davenport, while Brandt joined the Rock Island Independents.

Money, or rather the lack of it, undermined Jack Roche's attempt to create a team. Davenport and Moline were paying up to $25 a game for players. The price was too high for Roche, who led a chorus of criticism, supported by some newspaper interests, against "commercializing" the grid game.[24] They complained that

a Moline player who goes to Davenport to perform, or any other star who leaves his home city to play for another town, cannot be expected to retain that fighting spirit that he would show for his home club. In former years teams were organized and the players would split the earnings at the end of the season. In those days the main object of the players was to uphold the reputation of their team and city. This so-called commercializing of the game will eventually kill the independent sport if it is kept up.[25]

When Rock Island played their home opener, their famous shift play "had the visitors [Aurora Greyhounds] in the air most of the time and they were unable to solve it." The Independents scored three touchdowns and coasted to a 21–0 victory.[26] However, Ted Davenport injured his ankle in the game, keeping him out of the lineup for the next month.[27]

On October 29, 1916, Rock Island played their cross-river rivals, the Davenport Athletic Club, on a muddy Three-I Park field in Rock Island. The entire center of the field was a sea of mud several inches deep from the morning rain. End runs and open field work were of little practical value under these conditions. Most plays were straight-ahead runs without fancy cuts or unnecessary hand-offs. The entire first half saw the ball seesawing back and forth without much advantage for either team. Finally, in the third quarter when they were on their own forty yard line, Rock Island attempted to gain a first down on a fourth-down short yardage situation only to have Quinn slip and fall, turning the ball over to Davenport on downs. Davenport took advantage of the situation and put together a forty-yard drive, scoring the game's only touchdown. Rock Island lost 6–0. Vic Bredimus nearly scored a tying touchdown in the fourth quarter when he picked up a wobbly drop kick and ran forty yards to the Davenport thirty yard line with only one man to beat for a touchdown, but he ran out of bounds, and the Davenport defense held.[28]

After standing idle on November 5, the Independents played Davenport to a scoreless tie, on November 12, before four thousand shivering fans at Davenport's Blue Sox baseball field. Davenport marched twice to within the shadow of Rock Island's goal, only to have the Independents hold like a brick wall. Although the Independents did not get near the Davenport goal, they played well, particularly on defense. Each team made only one substitution during the entire game.[29]

On November 19, Rock Island played Moline at Island City Park at 3 P.M. Admission was fifty cents for men, twenty-five cents for women. Three thousand fans attended the game, nearly all of them men. The Rock Island Independent starting lineup averaged 178 pounds, while the Moline Red Men averaged 174 pounds per man.[30] The Independents had not defeated the Plow City team since November 15, 1914, and they were focused on redeeming community pride. It was a perfect day for football, "the temperature being about right for players and spectators alike." Captain Edward "Nips" Murphy won the toss for the Independents and defended the south goal. Moline kicked off to Rock Island, and, after returning the ball to the twenty yard line, the Islanders unleashed a string of dazzling trick plays, forward triple passes, and shifts that caught Moline by surprise. The final score was 21 to 3, leaving no doubt which team was better. Every man on the Rock Island team played well, and Nips Murphy and Walter Brindley[31] played particularly well.[32]

Rock Island closed the 1916 season with wins over three Illinois teams: Maywood, Rockford, and the Spring Valley Moose. During the 1916 season, Flannigan had strengthened his team and its fan base in the Tri-cities area. While still not the best team in the region, the Independents were contenders for that role. They averaged nearly three thousand fans per game, and they doubled their admission charge over

1915. But it was unlikely that Rock Island, Moline, and Davenport could all maintain a national standing in professional football circles. The 1917 season would determine which team succeeded in consolidating their efforts in that direction.

The 1917 season in Rock Island and Davenport opened on September 23. The Rock Island Independents played Sterling, Illinois, and gave the entire squad a chance to participate in their 33–0 win.[33] Across the Mississippi River, Davenport made short work of Oelwein in their tune-up game, 50–0. A week later, both teams repeated their winning performances by scoring thirty or more points: Rock Island beat Alton 33 to 3, and Davenport beat Moline 31–0. Davenport's new coach was Malcolm Galvin, who had played with the Hammond Clabbys in 1916, and had been quarterback and tailback for the University of Wisconsin in 1914 and 1915, before being required to leave college sports after being caught playing pro baseball.[34] Galvin was also hired to coach at St. Ambrose College and became the head coach there when George W. Jones[35] joined the U. S. Army's 102nd Field Artillery.

On October 7, the Rock Island Independents played the first of three games with the Davenport Athletic Club. It was a bitter struggle that resulted in a 3–0 win for Rock Island.[36] The following week, Rock Island romped over the Peoria Socials, while Davenport lost to the Hammond Clabbys 3 to 9 in Davenport.

John Leo "Paddy" Driscoll made his professional football debut in this game and ran sixty-five yards for a touchdown to give the Clabbys the winning points. Bernard "Swede" Halstrom from the University of Illinois also made his first appearance for the Clabbys and "looked awfully good." Frank Blocker, the former Purdue University star, played offensive center and was the defensive star of the game.[37] Davenport's loss served notice that staying competitive in the national ranks of professional football would require the Tri-cities teams to hire more college all-stars to keep abreast of their competitors.

This message was delivered even more strongly on October 21, 1917, when the Minneapolis Marines beat the Davenport Athletic Club 40 to 0. As the best independent football teams increasingly became truly professional teams, Davenport was clearly not staying competitive with them. The following Sunday, Davenport did manage to defeat the Camp Dodge team 9 to 6, when they blocked two drop kicks by McCormick, the Camp Dodge fullback, set up a successful twenty-yard drop kick by Albert Woodyatt, and saw Ray Kuehl pick up a "doughboy's" fumble and run sixty yards for a touchdown.[38]

Because of their weaker schedule, the Rock Island Independents did not yet have to face this problem, but the facts were apparent to anyone in the Tri-cities area who read the local sports pages. The Independents played the Racine, Wisconsin, Football Association on October 28 and defeated them 12 to 0, but, on November 4, they lost to the Minneapolis Marines 7 to 3. A crowd of 6,425 fans watched the monumental struggle. Two fumbles by Rock Island in the third quarter cost them the game. After a seventy-yard kickoff return, the Independents drove the ball to the Minneapolis three yard line before fumbling. Later in the quarter, the Independents had the ball in scoring position again, only to fumble a second time.[39] In the meantime, on November 4, the Davenport Athletic Club traveled to central Illinois to defeat the Peoria Socials, 27 to 6.

On November 11, 1917, Rock Island and Davenport met at Rock Island's Douglas Field before 4,748 fans. Davenport presented a much faster, better-coached team than five week earlier and "at times bewildered the Islanders." Coach Malcolm Galvin, the five-foot eleven-inch, 180-pound backfield star, recruited former University of Wisconsin teammate William Walter "Polly" Koch, a 1913 graduate of Davenport High School, to strengthen the right side of his line.[40] Koch played the balance of the season for Davenport. Mark Donavan kicked two field goals for Davenport and Honey Meersman made a touchdown to give Davenport twelve points. The Rock Island Independents could only muster one field goal in four attempts by Walter Brindley. Brindley also scored a touchdown and point after for Rock Island, but failed with a drop kick from the twenty yard line with less than a minute to play.[41] It was the second loss in a row for the Independents and caused Flannigan, the manager of the Independents, to reassess his roster and blueprint for a successful season.[42] Flannigan's concerns were reinforced on November 18, when the Minneapolis Marines crushed Rock Island 33 to 14.[43]

Meanwhile, the Davenport Athletic Club team was getting stronger. On November 18, Davenport faced the Cornell-Hamburgs, led by Reuben Johnson, former Evanston North Ends star, and defeated them 14 to 6. A week later, Davenport walloped the St. Paul Bilbow Athletics, from Minnesota, 30 to 2.

On December 2, 1917, the last day of the pro football season, Rock Island played Davenport for the area championship. These two teams had split their regular season series, and both teams had good records. Rock Island had six wins and three losses, while Davenport had seven wins and three losses. Both teams had lost to each other and to the

Minneapolis Marines. Davenport had also lost to the Hammond Clabbys, who were playing for the professional championship of Indiana
against the Fort Wayne Friars that same afternoon.[44]

The game between Davenport and Rock Island promised to be a
close one, with Davenport given a slight advantage because of the
strong finish to their season, until Walter Flannigan recruited five players from the Minneapolis Marines to represent his team. Walter Buland, Rube Ursella, Fred Chicken, Edward Novak, and Harry Gunderson were the core players for the Minneapolis Marines, and their presence on the Rock Island team tipped the scales heavily in Rock Island's
favor. The Davenport newspapers accused Flannigan of "selling out the
public for the sake of a few 'tin can' gamblers who laid a little money
on the game."[45] Davenport recruited Bob Marshall from the Minneapolis Marines and McCormick, the South Dakota star from the
Camp Dodge team, but these additions were not enough to counter the
Rock Island ringers.

With the regular Rock Island players playing a subservient role to
the Minneapolis Marine ringers, Davenport was unable to stop the line
bucks and sweeping end runs of the Minneapolis Marine backfield
men. From the opening whistle to the final gun, the Minneapolis im-
ports dominated the game held at Douglas Park in Rock Island. Unlike
other games between Davenport and Rock Island, fans were less invested in the contest.

The Davenport papers claimed that only four thousand fans attended the game, whereas eight thousand would have been present if Rock
Island had not imported the core of the Minneapolis Marine team. For
many Davenport fans and the leaders of the Davenport Athletic Club, it
was clear that the practice of eliminating local players in favor of the
best available talent without regard for their roots made it impractical
to maintain more than one professional team of national stature in the
Tri-cities area. The leaders of the Davenport Athletic Club had no stomach for what they considered "unfair arrangements" and consequently
refused to compete with Flannigan by matching his tactics. The impor-
tation of the five Marine players spelled the end of big-time professional football in Davenport. While the Davenport Athletic Club fielded a
team in 1919 and 1920, they never pretended to be competitive with
Hammond, Rock Island, and the other teams that entered the American Professional Football Association on September 17, 1920. Rock Island played a prominent role in the National Football League until July
1926, when they suspended operations in the NFL and joined the re-

cently formed American Football League.[46] In 1927, unable to garner the financial support that teams in Chicago, New York, and other big population centers could command in the competition for talent, and unable to garner the fan support obtained in Green Bay (a much smaller metropolitan center than Davenport/Rock Island/Moline), perhaps because of cross-river rivalries, the Tri-cities ceased being represented by a franchise in the ranks of big-time professional football.

21. The Minneapolis Marines: Champions of Minnesota

The Minneapolis Marines were already an established independent football team when Bob Marshall joined them in 1908.[1] Marshall was a superb athlete. From 1897 through 1902, he played football and baseball for Minneapolis Central High School and, in 1904, became the first African-American to earn a starting position on the University of Minnesota varsity football team. Marshall and team captain Ed Rogers combined to make one of the strongest set of ends to play single platoon college football. Rogers played for Carlisle Institute before attending the University of Minnesota law school, and, in 1904, he played for Carlisle as an alumnus to defeat Haskell Institute at the World's Fair in a game advertised to determine the best American Indian football team.[2] The high point of Marshall's gridiron career at the university took place in 1906 when he kicked two field goals to defeat the University of Chicago 4–2. One of his field goals hit the cross bar and bounced over.[3] Marshall was named to several All-American teams that year.[4]

By 1911, the Minneapolis Marines also featured Reuben Ursella, Fred Chicken, Edward Sundby, Walt Buland, Mike Palmer, Dewey Lyle, and Sheepy Redeen, as well as Bob Marshall. The Marines played a schedule that included the best independent teams in Minneapolis-St. Paul and in Duluth, including Adams, Bakula, and Kents.[5]

Managed by Frank Hammer of Minneapolis,[6] the Marines were already the best independent team in the state. By 1913, the Marines were the independent football champions of Minnesota and played an All-Star team on Thanksgiving to close out their season.

In 1914, the Marines, coached by Oscar "Ossie" Solem, a University of Minnesota football star who became an assistant football coach at Grinnell College in 1916, completed their regular season undefeated, beating teams like the St. Paul Kents, the St. Paul Banholzers, and the Minneapolis Beavers.[7] John McGovern, the 1909 University of Minnesota captain and All-American quarterback, organized an all-star team

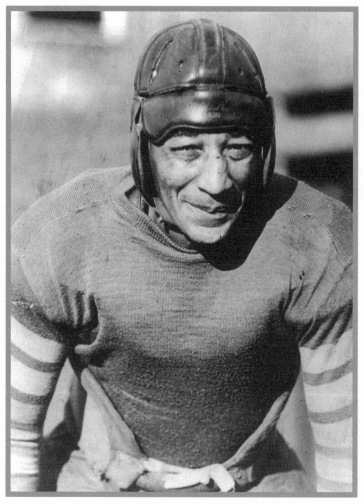

Bob Marshall, end, ranks as one of the most resilient professional football players in history. He played football for twenty-seven years—five years for Minneapolis Central High School, four years for the University of Minnesota, and eighteen years as a professional with the Minneapolis Marines. He was a Walter Camp All-American and later played for the Davenport Athletic Club and the Rock Island Independents. *(College Football Hall of Fame.)*

of former collegiate players to compete against the Minneapolis Marines for the independent football championship of the state. The game was billed as a Thanksgiving benefit for "Belgian War Sufferers."[8] The Marines starting lineup during the 1914 season included Jimmy Rush at fullback, Frank Dries at right halfback, Costello at left halfback, Reuben Ursella at quarterback, Bob Marshall at left end, Dewey Lyle at left tackle, Mike Palmer at left guard, Selvig at center, Art Gaustad at right guard, Walt Buland at right tackle, and Sheepy Redeen at right end. John Dunne, Wegfors, Ed Sundby, and Charles Jonason came off the bench to keep the Marines strong on the field. The Marines squad was a mixture of college and sandlot stars. Buland, Ursella, Palmer, Gunderson, and Gaustad were sandlot stars, while Fred Chicken played for the University of Kansas and Dewey Lyle for the University of Minnesota. The 1914 College All-Stars in red jerseys included University of Minnesota stars Ralph Capron (RH), Morrell (C), Boleslaus Rosenthal (FB), Robinson (RT), and John McGovern. The all-star team also included Bud Dougherty (LH) from St. Thomas College, and John Nichols (RE) and Dan Smith (FB) from Cornell University. About seven thousand rooters witnessed the game.

The Marines experienced bad luck from the outset. On the first play their fullback, Jimmy Rush, broke his collarbone, and, a few plays later, Frank Dries was injured and had to leave the game. The All-Stars scored first, making four straight first downs in a sixty-yard drive that resulted in a two-yard touchdown by McGovern and a 7–0 lead. A pass from Ursella to Bob Marshall tied the score, but a Marines fumble on their own six yard line allowed the All-Stars to take a 14–7 lead. The Marines scored another touchdown but missed the point after. The Marines had one last chance to win the game on a twenty-yard field goal, but Ursella missed an easy drop kick to allow the All-Stars to defeat them 14–13.[9]

In 1915, the Marines again completed an undefeated regular season and played John McGovern's All-Stars for the independent football championship of Minnesota. This year the All-Stars added Lorin Solon, the 1914 Gopher captain; John Markoe from West Point; George Bromley from St. Thomas; and Joe Thompson from Yale. They also attempted to recruit Knute Rockne but failed.[10] Moreover, they played a warm-up game that ended in a scoreless tie before five thousand fans in Duluth on November 14 against an independent team headed by Lorin Solon.[11]

The Thanksgiving game drew sixty-five hundred fans. The Marines tried a forty-yard field goal in the first quarter that missed by less than a yard. It was their only scoring opportunity of the day. Later that quarter, Lorin Solon carried the ball over the goal line on a short-yardage play. This touchdown and extra point resulted in the Marines' second straight loss to the All-Stars, 7–0.[12]

The 1916 season was the turning point for the Marines. They added Eber F. Simpson Jr. to their team. Simpson, a quarterback and halfback, was captain of the University of Wisconsin freshman team in 1914, and went on to star for the Badgers in 1915, along with teammates Cub Buck, Malcolm Galvin, Paul Meyers, and William "Polly" Koch, before leaving college later that year.[13] Simpson was an outstanding kicker, an adequate passer, and a reliable ball carrier. For the first time, the Marines scheduled regional games outside of Minnesota, and they finally succeeded in tying the All-Stars to regain a share of the state championship. Except for the loss of Jimmy Rush, Frank Dries, and linemen Hoffmar and Wegfors, and the addition of Costello and Labe Safro, who was also a welterweight boxer, the Marines lineup was pretty consistent after 1911.[14] In 1916, Russell J. Tollefson, a former University of Minnesota lineman, took over the coaching duties, and John Dunne replaced Frank Hammer as the team manager. The Marines opened their season against West Duluth with a 54–3 win. Ursella was the outstanding player for Minneapolis both offensively and defensively.[15] In succeeding weeks, they defeated the Merrimacs, Laurels, and Banholzers of St. Paul and the East Ends of Minneapolis.[16] Ursella, Chicken, and Marshall did not play against the Merrimacs. On October 22, they played for West Duluth where they could make more money. However, just two minutes into the game, Ursella dislocated his elbow.[17]

Only the East Ends, coached by Johnny McGovern, offered real competition to the Marines. Their lineup included Axel Turnquist, the 1915 University of Minnesota star tackle; Brown, a former Lehigh halfback, currently attending engineering school at the University of Minnesota; Steve Hopkins, the great African-American fullback for the Banholzer team; O'Hara, formerly of Notre Dame; and Morton from Indiana University.[18] Two thousand fans came to Nicollet Park to see the 7–0 victory by the Marines. Safro scored the only touchdown of the game, and Simpson kicked the point after. Bob Marshall and Simpson were the stars of the game for the Marines.[19]

The St. Paul Laurels also loaded up with ringers, including Lorin Solon, in an attempt to defeat the Marines, but all of their extra former college stars did not help them. They lost 34–0.[20]

Russell J. Tollefson, tackle and coach for the Minneapolis Marines in 1916, graduated from the University of Minnesota and coached at Grinnell College in 1917. *(Grinnell College Archives.)*

Three thousand fans came to watch St. Paul champions, the Banholzers, play the Marines at Nicollet Park, but touchdowns by Chicken, Marshall, Dunne, Sundby, and Safro resulted in a lopsided 39–0 win for the Marines. Steve Hopkins was one of the few bright spots for the Banholzers.[21]

The Marines and the East Ends engaged in a rematch on the last Sunday in November. Rube Ursella, who had been out of football for a month because of injuries, was back in uniform leading the Marines. McGovern's East Ends added Curt Timm, formerly with the Banholzers, and Harold Hansen, a West High School graduate, to strengthen their team.[22] However, the East End eleven was outplayed from beginning to end. While Ursella's timing was off, he played only half of the game, and though the Marines fumbled twice in the second half when they were within scoring distance, they defeated the East Ends 17–0 for the city championship.[23]

The annual game between the Marines and the College All-Stars held on Thanksgiving was the real test of the Marines' season. The All-Stars fielded the best team ever in 1916. They drew heavily from the 1916 University of Minnesota squad. Jack Hanson at center, Archie Carlson at halfback, Bert Baston at end, Gil Sinclair at guard, and Jack Townley at tackle were all recruited for the All-Star team. Johnny Mc-Govern, Axel Turnquist, Dunnigan, Earl Pickering, and George Capron —all former Gopher stars—were also in the starting lineup, along with Frank Ward, former captain of the St. Thomas College team, Joe Thompson from Yale, and Bud Dougherty of St. Thomas. Reserved seats for the 2:30 game were $1, and grandstand seats were fifty cents, according to Mike Cantillon, the game's promoter. The betting odds were 10 to 7 in favor of the All-Stars, and wagers on the game were reported to be brisk, with a number of bets in the $100 to $200 range.[24]

The Thanksgiving game was evenly fought. During the first three quarters, the College All-Stars maintained a slight advantage, but Ursella's kicking kept the College team's ground game from leading to points. In the final quarter, the Marines finished strongly before the seventy-three hundred paid admissions cheering in the stands and the additional seven hundred or so believed to have managed free admission by one means or another. Ursella had three drop kicks blocked by McGovern, who almost single-handedly kept the Marines from winning the game, although Bert Baston was also a defensive star for the Collegians and Jack Townley played well on offense. Good teamwork by the Marines offset any advantage the All-Stars might have had in youth or talent.[25] The game ended in a scoreless tie. The gate receipts came to $5,194, of which $1,558.20 went to the Marines, $1,817.90 to the All-Stars, and $1,817.90 to the promoters. The promoters paid all expenses from their share.[26]

The following Sunday, the Minneapolis Marines closed out their season against an overworked Davenport Athletic Club team in Davenport, Iowa, winning 19 to 7.[27]

The undefeated 1916 season marked the emergence of the Marines as a recognized power in professional football circles. The outstanding coaching job done by Russell J. "Tolle" Tollefson earned him the head coaching assignment the next fall at Grinnell College,[28] and in mid-October of 1917, Labe Safro joined the army and was assigned to Camp Dodge in Des Moines, Iowa.[29] In 1917, the Minneapolis Marines, managed by John Dunne, found few Minnesota teams willing to challenge them, and only the Rock Island Independents gave them a close game. The Marines opened their 1917 season, on October 7, against the West Side Tigers of St. Paul[30] and played their second game, on October 14, against the Seatons of St. Paul. Before the end of October Costello, Gunderson, Buland, and manager John Dunne, like Labe Safro, joined the armed services "to fight the Hun," but were not inducted until the close of the football season.[31] The Marines played only four home games. Over the course of the season, Minneapolis scored more than 232 points: their opponents scored 24 points. The Marines played road games in Davenport, Duluth, and Rock Island. They also defeated the Camp Dodge 313th Engineer team coached by Axel Turnquist, 28–0.[32]

The Camp Dodge Engineers drew thirty-five hundred fans to Nicollet Park at admission prices of fifty and seventy-five cents. The vast majority of these fans rooted for the "Sammies" from the Des Moines cantonment.[33] Former Minneapolis Marines halfback Labe Safro was the starting right half for Camp Dodge. The soldiers' team showcased fullback Obe Wenig, a former Morningside College star end, who was credited with making more tackles than any other player in the game.[34] From 1920 through 1923, Wenig played in the NFL for the Rock Island Independents.[35]

Bob Marshall was still one of the featured stars of the Minneapolis team. According to a *Minneapolis Journal* article,

Marshall had a continuous line of chatter on defense that sometimes sounded like this, "Whoa, there, boy: 'most got away from ole Bob that time, hey, boy? My lan', most scared me to death."

Marshall wears an ingenious armour under his jersey, consisting chiefly of a stiff wrapping around his ribs. He says the modern forward passing game is harder on ends than the old style game and brought the need of added armour. This was made clear to him the first year passes were popular, when his ribs were black and blue from being tackled when receiving a pass. Marshall is well along in his 30s. He is a good baseball player.[36]

After the Marines beat the Camp Dodge team on November 25, Ursella, Chicken, Gunderson, Buland, and Novak played for the Rock Island Independents against the Davenport Athletic Club and Bob Marshall played for Davenport.[37] This game drove the Davenport Athletic Club from the pro ranks and opened the way for Rock Island to represent the Tri-cities market in the National Football League in the early 1920s. From 1919 to 1921, Walt Buland, Fred Chicken, Ed Novak, Dewey Lyle, Reuben Ursella, and Bob Marshall played for the Rock Island Independents.[38] Rube Ursella coached those teams. In August 1921, the Minneapolis Marines were granted a franchise in the American Professional Football Association and again appeared on the national professional football stage with old team members Art Gaustad, Charles Jonasen, Harry Gunderson, Mike Palmer, Sheepy Redeen, and Eber Simpson still in uniform. Their standing in the league, however, was stricken from the record because they did not play a complete schedule. In 1922, the Minneapolis Marines welcomed Fred Chicken and Bob Marshall back on the team and struggled to a 1–3 record in the National Football League. The Marines fielded NFL teams in 1923 and 1924, before dropping out of professional football in 1925.[39] In 1924, Rube Ursella and Dewey Lyle played with Jim Thorpe on the Rock Island Independent squad, while Bob Marshall, Ed Novak, Fred Chicken, and Eber Simpson played a winless season for the Minneapolis Marines.[40] Bob Marshall completed his twenty-seventh season in football that year, ranking him with the Nesser brothers and Dutch Speck for longevity in the game.

22. Pro Football in Wisconsin

The **Racine Regulars,** also called Battery C and the Racine Football Association, played their home games at Bi-State League Park and W. I. League Park in Racine, in 1915, and claimed to be the independent football champions of Wisconsin. Few could honestly dispute their claim. The Regulars, managed by Otto Jandl, played the best independent teams in Wisconsin, Illinois, Iowa, and Indiana. Occasionally, they also took on teams in Ohio and Michigan. In 1916, they traveled to Toledo, Ohio, to play the Toledo Maroons, and, in 1917, they played the Detroit Heralds at Navin Field in Detroit. Racine was the first professional football team in Wisconsin to play in the big leagues of post-college football. The Regulars were primarily sandlot players who had never gone to college, or who played college football for a year or two before dropping out of school. In 1915, they ranged in weight from 139 pounds to 251 pounds and averaged 160 each. The Racine line averaged 166 pounds, the backfield 157 pounds,[1] three or four pounds below the average weight of most of the top independent teams.

Racine had two outstanding linemen in Scott "Duke" McEachron and Walter Eck, both of whom were particularly good defensive players. McEachron,[2] an all-around athlete, graduated from Grinnell College in 1909, where he had been a solid college football player. McEachron usually played left guard, but he was Racine's best kicker and on occasion played in the backfield.[3] Eck attended Lawrence College and played for the Ernst Athletic Club before joining the Racine Football Association. Bobby Foster, the Racine right half, grew up in Milwaukee and played college football at Marquette University and was considered by some to be "the best all round man who ever played football with the Racine team."[4] Phillip Thoennes, weighing 155 pounds, was the lightest man on the Racine line, but what he lacked in weight he made up for in speed and aggressiveness at left end. Thoennes played college football at Carroll College. Red Wells, a new man from Toledo, Ohio, started the season at fullback.[5]

Scott "Duke" MacEachron, guard, Racine Regulars 1915–17, graduated from Grinnell College (Iowa) in the class of 1909. Athletic fields at Grinnell are names for the MacEachron family. Scott went on to become executive secretary of the Oregon Banker's Association and vice president of the Federal Reserve Bank of San Francisco. *(Grinnell College Archives.)*

By 1915, Racine already had a reputation for being one of the best independent football teams in Wisconsin, and it was difficult for them to schedule Wisconsin teams. At the beginning of the 1915 season, the Milwaukee Maple Leafs canceled their October 3 game with Racine because they felt overmatched. Otto Jandl, Racine's manager, hurried to Milwaukee to find a replacement game. He contacted the Schmidt Colts, an industrial team supported by the Schmidt brewing company, but was turned down. He also attempted to schedule the U.S. Navy Great Lakes Training School for the following Sunday and obtained a tentative agreement, only to have the game canceled the following Tuesday. He also contacted Kenosha, Oshkosh, and Appleton without a taker.[6] Jandl finally settled on a game with the Milwaukee Arlingtons and requested a $50 forfeiture to insure that the game was played.

Racine finally opened their season on Sunday, October 10, at Bi-State League Park. A big automobile parade was planned, and Mayor T. W. Thiesen was given the honor of kicking the first ball. A preliminary game between the Eagle Athletics and the Mascarillas, two local teams, was played at 1:30, with the big game starting at 2:45. The Arlingtons, the Milwaukee football league champions in 1911, 1913, and 1914, had been the only team to defeat Racine in 1914.[7] The Racine Regulars charged twenty-five cents admission. Ladies were admitted free.[8] Over fifteen hundred fans gathered at Bi-State to watch the fray, but it was later reported that only eight hundred of them paid admission.[9] Racine made two touchdowns in the first quarter using their running game and kicked goal in both instances. Wells added two more touchdowns and both extra points in the second quarter. The halftime score was 23–0. Scott "Duke" McEachron, the star tackle for the Regulars, also made a touchdown, but, in the second half, he broke his leg and had to be moved to St. Mary's Hospital by ambulance. With the game already safely in hand, Racine put in its second team to give them experience. The final score was 33 to 0.[10]

Some of the Racine players were discouraged by the feeble opposition presented by the Milwaukee Arlingtons and called for a harder schedule.[11] Otto Jandl was forced to look outside Wisconsin to find worthy opponents. The first out-of-state team to visit Racine in 1915 was the Illinois All-Stars. The contract between the Illinois All-Stars and Racine gave 60 percent of the gate to the winner. Racine added Mossteck to replace Duke McEachron. The Illinois All-Stars included veteran independent players from the Cornell-Hamburgs, the Ripmore Athletic Club, and several colleges,[12] and they turned out to be good competition for the Racine Regulars. Eugene Schobinger, from Morgan Park, Illinois, a former University of Illinois star halfback and Big Nine pole vault record holder, was the featured player for the Illinois All-Stars. Schobinger graduated, in 1915, as an engineer but continued to play football to supplement his income.[13]

On October 17, it rained to the point that the field was like a pond, but, because the Illinois All-Stars were already in town, the game was played at the appointed time. The two teams splashed and seesawed back and forth in the center of the field. At no point was either team a threat to score. The *Journal-News* reported,

The ball became so heavy that it could not be punted any distance, and so slippery that it could not be handled in the forward pass plays. . . . If a man could have got away there could have been no stopping his flight, but no one could get a start. There was no earth to run on. Everything was afloat.[14]

The line play on both sides was good, and, with no chance for trick plays, little ground was exchanged. The game ended in a scoreless tie.[15]

The Milwaukee Ernsts followed the All-Stars to town the next Sunday. Racine had beaten them 14–6 in 1914, so these long-time rivals had old business to settle.[16] The Ernsts had two well-regarded players, Walter Eck, a tackle, and Robert Foster at right halfback.[17] The contest was played at W. I. League Park in Racine. The Milwaukee team started strong. They kicked off to Racine and held them on downs. A few minutes later, the Ernsts scored a touchdown, and Walter Eck kicked the point after. The Racine Regulars responded by driving the ball sixty-five yards on the ground, completing the drive with a pass from Maxted to Beam. At the end of the quarter, it was 7–6 in favor of Milwaukee. In the second period, the home team scored the go-ahead touchdown. At halftime, Racine led 12 to 7. Racine dominated in the second half but took few chances. Wells scored the final touchdown, and Racine won 19 to 7.[18] After the game, Bob Foster and Walter Eck were recruited to play with Racine for the balance of the season.

Racine traveled to Indiana, on October 31, to play the unbeaten Fort Wayne Friars. Fort Wayne was being directed by Kent "Skeet" Lambert, one of the best quarterbacks in pro football. Lambert was a graduate of Wabash College, where he had mastered the running, kicking, and passing games. He was supported by Joe Pliska and "Heine" Berger from Notre Dame, and stood behind a line that featured veteran independent players Dan Ball, La Pado, Reb Russell, Baird, and Walter Krull. Although not yet the champions of Indiana, the Friars were fast company by the standards of independent football in 1915.

The Racine Regulars left home on the train at 5:35 on Saturday night for Fort Wayne, arriving just after midnight. The Sunday game started shortly after 2 P.M. at League Park. Racine tallied first when halfback Dietrich grabbed a forward pass near the center of the field and sprinted for a touchdown. It was the first time all season the Friars were behind, and it stirred some determination in the home team. In less than five minutes, the Friars evened the score, and, by halftime, they led 20 to 6. Lambert's passing game overwhelmed Racine in the second half. The final score was a humiliating 41–6.[19]

The Wisconsin champs limped back to Racine that night happy that their defeat had not been witnessed by their hometown fans. The only way to regain pride was to play well the following Sunday in their rematch with the Illinois All-Stars. Gene Schobinger's All-Stars caught the 11 A.M. Chicago and Northwestern train from Chicago and arrived in Racine at 12:33. The players on both teams were numbered for the convenience of the fans. The Racine Regulars averaged 170 pounds per lineman and 160 pounds per backfield man. The Illinois All-Stars averaged 176 pounds in the line and 173 in the backfield.[20]

The game was even in the first quarter. The Illinois All-Stars kicked off, and Foster returned fifteen yards. Racine moved the ball to midfield, then lost the ball on downs. The ball changed hands several times, with each side fumbling once before the end of the first period. In the second quarter, the All-Stars finally succeeded in establishing a promising drive when a Schobinger pass was intercepted by Dietrich. The blue-and-white-clad sideback streaked forty yards, leaving a tackler or two in his wake. Downing kicked goal. At halftime, Racine led 7–0. The second half was rather matter-of-fact—hard fought but not sensational. In the third period, Racine increased its lead to 13–0 on a run by Bob Foster. That score stood at game's end.[21]

The Regulars traveled to Comiskey Park, the summer home of the Chicago White Sox, to play the Cornell-Hamburgs on Sunday, November 14. A special football train left Racine Sunday morning at 9:30 and arrived at 10:50 in Evanston, where the team was escorted on the elevated train to Comiskey Park. The Hamburgs claimed to be the Cook County and Middle West champions in 1913 and 1914, but so did the Evanston North Ends. Supported by Chicago back-of-the-yards ward politicians, the Hamburgs drew large crowds for their games.[22] The Chicago eleven had two thousand paying rooters on hand at kickoff time. The star players for the 1915 Cornell-Hamburgs were the Pressler brothers and La Ros. Late in the first quarter, Al Pressler made a long diagonal pass to La Ros, who caught the ball in the right corner and stepped over the goal for a touchdown. Chicago failed to make goal and led 6–0. Great football action followed. Bones Nelson at end and Billie Pressler at halfback played well for the Cornell-Hamburgs, but the score stayed 6–0 at halftime. In the third quarter, Chicago sustained another touchdown drive, gaining four and five yards each down. Another pass to Bones Nelson made the score 13–0. Both teams played hard for the balance of the game, but neither team scored. Al Pressler attempted a drop kick that failed, and a Racine drive stalled on the Chicago twenty yard line in the raw, cold wind of Chicago's south side. The game ended shortly afterward. The final score was Cornell-Hamburgs 13, Racine 0.[23]

The Regulars played and defeated two Wisconsin independent teams before closing the season against the Elgin (IL) Athletic Club in Racine on December 5, 1915. The Racine Regulars were nearly invincible on their home ground. The Regulars got the jump on Elgin with a long pass from Maxted to Downing, who scored the first touchdown of the game. Racine continued to outplay Elgin, and the visitors were forced to resort to the forward pass to get back into the game. The Elgin aerial attack failed. The score remained 6–0 until the fourth quarter, when Racine made three more touchdowns. The stars of the Racine cause were Maxted, the quarterback; Bob Foster, the fullback; Eck and McEachron at tackles; and Murray, an end, who played at Illinois Normal at Macomb, Illinois. The fans found the game interesting and were sorry to see the season end.[24]

In 1916, the Racine Regulars were renamed the Battery C team, presumably because, in a patriotic gesture, the 1915 Regulars had joined the First Wisconsin Artillery Reserve Battery C. They played their home games at W. I. League Park. The Battery C eleven opened their season against St. Charles (IL) in what turned out to be a one-sided game: Racine won 41–0.[25]

On October 8, 1916, Racine played one of the legendary teams of the era, the Evanston North Ends. For the previous six years, the North Ends had been one of the best teams in the Midwest. They had made easy work of the Fort Wayne Friars, the Detroit Heralds, the Wabash Athletic Club, the Moline Red Men, the Cornell-Hamburgs, and the Rock Island Independents, among others. The 1916 North Ends featured Rube Johnson, Guil Falcon, Penn Carolan, John Barrett, and Gene Schobinger, plus their Million Dollar Line. The new Racine squad included Walter Eck and F. O'Connors from Lawrence College, Scott "Duke" McEachron from Grinnell College, Murray from Ripon College and Illinois Normal, John Heiller from the University of Wisconsin, Bob Foster from Marquette University, Phillip Thoennes from Carroll College, and independent football veterans Wallace "Red" Kelly, Cowgill, Maxted, and Joe Dory.[26]

A large crowd of nearly three thousand watched the champions of independent football in Wisconsin battle the heralded North Ends. Several times in the first quarter, Racine's offense moved the ball near the North End goal. On one occasion, Racine linebacker Cowgill intercepted a North Ends pass and returned it forty-five yards. Each time, the North Ends defense tightened and denied Racine points. The North Ends made three points in the first quarter on a field goal by Rube Johnson.[27] In the second quarter, Rube Johnson again drop-kicked a field goal from the twenty yard line. At halftime, the North Ends led 6 to 0. Racine attempted a field goal in the third period, but Scott McEachron's seventy-five-yard kick narrowly failed. The final points of the game came on a pass from Rube Johnson to John Bosdette in the fourth quarter that covered sixty yards and was followed quickly by a short-yardage line plunge that added six points.[28] A *Journal-News* reporter observed, "Racine held its own as far as straight football was concerned, but forward passes and the kicking of Johnson won the game for the North Ends," by a final score of 12–0.[29]

The Battery C eleven traveled to Maywood, Illinois, on Sunday, October 15. The trip was made in a special coach on the Northwestern railroad, and a large crowd of rooters accompanied the team. Racine added Beam from Kenosha, Murray of Marinette, and Jack Dory to their squad. All three had played for the Racine Regulars in 1915. Battery C defeated Maywood 24–6.[30]

The Racine team played another one-sided game at W. I. League Park at Racine against the Schmidt Colts of Milwaukee. Racine earned thirteen points in the first quarter. Joe Dory scored the first touchdown, following up a sensational forty-five-yard run by Bob Foster. Dory also made the second touchdown on a fifteen-yard run. Milwaukee scored in the second quarter on an intercepted pass that was returned forty-five yards. Soon after that, Racine secured a safety, adding two points to their total. Racine also intercepted a pass for another touchdown. At halftime, the score was 21 to 7. Racine added thirteen points in the third quarter and twenty-one in the fourth quarter. By scoring three touchdowns, Joe Dory was the principle star of the game, but Bob Foster and John Heiller made two touchdowns each. A mere six hundred people saw the game.[31]

On October 29, Racine traveled to Moline, Illinois, where they lost 19–0 in a game that was given minimal newspaper coverage. A week later, Racine was in Hammond to play the up-and-coming Clabbys. The Racine-Hammond game was a serious, seesaw struggle. Coach Ted Dumphy's team played well against a Hammond team that featured several Purdue University stars, including Frank Blocker, Johnny Finn, Henry Ruffner, and Talbot. Racine took the lead in the first quarter on a pass from Maxted to Murray but missed the extra point. Hammond rallied and scored its own touchdown and extra point, giving them a 7–6 lead. The Clabbys made another seven points in the third quarter, and Racine answered with seven points of its own. Racine lost the game 14 to 13 because of a missed field goal.[32]

Racine's First Wisconsin Artillery Battery C team played the Cornell-Hamburgs on November 12, 1916, at Schorling's Park on Chicago's south side. About 100 Racine fans accompanied their team to Chicago, where they joined over three thousand south-side fans to witness the game. Several times in the first quarter, the Cornell-Hamburgs carried the ball within a few yards of the Racine goal. On one occasion, the Hamburgs were stopped on downs on the one yard line. Late in the first quarter, William Pressler finally scored for Chicago, and Al Pressler kicked the extra point. In the second quarter, O'Connor moved the ball within twenty yards of the Chicago goal, and Wallace "Red" Kelly kicked a field goal for Racine. It was Racine's only score that afternoon. The teams played even until the Cornell-Hamburgs scored in the last minute of the game against a tired Racine defense. The Cornell-Hamburgs walked away with a 13 to 3 win.[33]

Racine was scheduled to play the South Bend Jolly-Fellows at W. I. League Park. On the Wednesday night before the game, an enthusiastic group of Racine Football Association supporters met at the Commercial Club room and was warned that if the team did not draw two thousand paying fans on Sunday the association would lose money for the season. The managers for the Racine team said that they had been offered $1000 to play the Toledo Maroons but had turned it down because the hometown fans wanted a game.[34] A larger crowd than usual showed up at the W. I. League Park for the South Bend-Racine game, but not as large a crowd as was sought. The locals lost $250 on the game.[35] In a fast-paced game, in which the Racine line dominated the line of scrimmage, Bob Foster scored two touchdowns for the Racine football club and determined the course of play. The final score was 13–0.

Racine ended their 1916 season on Thanksgiving against the Maroons at the Toledo Armory. Penn Carolan and John Barrett, who had played with the North Ends against Racine earlier in the season, made the difference for the Maroons. Carolan's end runs and Barrett's punting controlled the game. Barrett's punting kept Racine out of scoring range, and Carolan's running set up the forward passes that brought a 19–0 Toledo victory in what was one of the hardest fought games of the season for both teams.[36]

The 1916 season completed the transition to big-time professional football begun in 1915. The results, however, were mixed. The Racine club lost five of nine games. All of the teams they played were closely matched with them, and it was reasonable to believe that, with some modest improvements in personnel, Racine could be part of an emerging national professional football association. However, there was a catch. Hometown fan support was not good enough to play in those circles. While other teams in that group regularly attracted two thousand or more paying fans at gate admission prices ranging from fifty cents to $1, Racine had never produced a $2000 gate and was lucky to collect $1000 total for a home game. This was far short of the support needed to sustain a competitive team and attract worthy out-of-state opponents.

In 1917, Ted Schliesman became president of the Racine Football Association, and Fairbanks-Morse and Company of Beloit helped to sponsor the team. They also acquired a new manager, Ed Hegeman. The Racine Football Association, still called Battery C, had its first signal practice of the 1917 season on September 21.[37] There had been talk of opening the season against the South Bend Athletic Association on October 7, but this game could not be worked out.[38]

Many of the Racine Regulars from 1916 were now in military service,[39] and Scott "Duke" McEachron was in Grinnell, Iowa, as an assistant coach at Grinnell College.[40] Despite these losses, Racine appeared to have a stronger team than in 1916. They increased their admission charge to fifty cents a game. Racine played their opening game at home against the Cornell-Hamburgs of Chicago on October 14, 1917, after three weeks of practice. Racine's opening lineup had Ratchford and Ed Hegeman at ends, G. "Babe" Reutz and Walter Eck at tackles, O. Hegeman and Grover C. Lutter at guards, Art Sehl at center, and Fred Newton, Richard Schnell, Bob Foster, and Meyers in the backfield.[41] Only Bob Foster, Walter Eck, O. Hegeman, and Art Sehl were returning starters from 1916.[42] Fred Newton, a former college quarterback at River Falls Normal College in Wisconsin, was the starting field leader for the Regulars. Joe Dory was injured and could not start for Racine.[43] The game with the Cornell-Hamburgs was not close. Rube Johnson, formerly with the Evanston North Ends, scored two touchdowns in Chicago's 27–0 win, and he was in command of the game from start to finish.[44]

Racine played the Hammond Clabbys, on October 21, in Hammond. A crowd of nearly two thousand paid to see the Clabbys' home opener. The substantially improved Hammond Clabbys included a backfield of stars that included John Leo "Paddy" Driscoll from Northwestern, Bernard "Swede" Halstrom from the University of Illinois, and Ted Blocker and A. R. Longenecker from Purdue. Racine got Big Duke McEachron, "prince of tackles," and John Dory—Joe Dory's brother—

back in their lineup. Wallace "Red" Kelly and Joe Schnell, captain of the 1916 Kenosha High School team, were added to alternate at full-back.[45] Racine also hired Norman "Tango" Glockson, an experienced professional football lineman who had played with the Detroit Heralds in 1915 and 1916.[46]

Racine showed surprisingly good teamwork in Hammond, and they got a few good breaks. In the first quarter, Paddy Driscoll received the kickoff and had it stripped from him at midfield by Norman "Tango" Glockson, who recovered the ball for Racine.[47] Racine then drove the ball on several line plunges, until Bob Foster pushed the ball near the goal line, only to have the ball ripped from his hands. Fortunately for Racine, the ball bounced over the goal line, where Walter Eck fell on it for a Racine touchdown. Hammond had nearly everything go wrong for them. Their fullback, Longenecker, sustained a broken shoulder, and their left tackle, George Volkman, fractured a rib. The Clabbys fumbled the ball on several occasions and, in general, just could not get their offense rolling. Hometown fans chided the Clabbys, suggesting that perhaps the Red Cross should knit them some mittens so their cold hands could hang onto the ball.[48] Neither Paddy Driscoll nor Swede Halstrom had much opportunity to show their stuff, because the Clabbys' offensive line was like tissue paper. On a trick play in the last quarter, Joe Schnell went around end for the Racine Regulars' second score, making the score Racine 12, Hammond 0. The punting of Tango Glockson, averaging better than fifty yards per attempt, and the defensive play of Bob Foster, who intercepted a pass, helped keep the Clabbys on their heels, and the 12–0 score stood at game's end.[49]

Buoyed by their win over the Clabbys, the Racine Regulars took the 9:45 Saturday night train to Chicago, where they got a sleeper train on the Rock Island Railroad to play the undefeated Independents. Three thousand fans paid fifty cents each to see the game, and many paid an extra twenty-five cents for grandstand seats. Racine soon discovered that it would not be an easy game. The line play of Frank "Fat" Smith, Louis Kolls, and Ted Guyer was as good as could be found in pro football, and quarterback Edward "Nips" Murphy, who had been a promising Notre Dame freshman a couple of years before, had a shift offense that caused problems for many teams. The Rock Island Independents shut out Racine 12–0.[50]

On November 4, Racine had a rematch with the Cornell-Hamburgs, which they lost 21–0.[51] One week later, they traveled to Fort Wayne to play the Friars. Fort Wayne continued their winning ways by tromping

Racine 28 to 0. With Charles Dorais, famous Notre Dame star, at the quarterback spot, and Robert Specht as the designated running back, the Friars scored two touchdowns in the second quarter and two more in the third quarter to put the game out of Racine's reach. A thirty-five-yard forward pass from Dorais to Mal Elward resulted in the first touchdown, with Al Feeney kicking the point after. Ralph Young caught a pass from Dorais five minutes or so later for the second score. In the second half, Robert Specht, a Chicago cop playing with Fort Wayne, and Charles Dorais each scored a running touchdown.[52] It appeared as if the Friars were well on their way to a second straight Indiana state championship, with their 28–0 win over Racine. Racine's policeman-football player Grover C. "Dovey" Lutter played as well as he had in Rock Island,[53] as did Tango Glockson, who outkicked Dorais.[54] Glockson decided to stay in Fort Wayne after the game to join up with the Friars, since the Racine season was not doing so well, having now suffered four losses in five starts.

The next week, Racine played the greatly improved Detroit Heralds at Navin Field in Detroit. The Heralds had built a strong team. They had two All-Americans, Herbert Straight from Michigan Agricultural College, and Ray Whipple from Notre Dame, at tackle, and a backfield that featured Norb Sacksteder, Hubby Weekes, Bertie Maher, and Earl Dunn. Nany Shanks also bolstered the Detroit line. The Heralds were just coming off a bloody battle against the U.S. Army's Camp Custer that resulted in a 13–0 loss for the pros. There were, of course, more pros on the Camp Custer team than were available to the Heralds. As a matter of fact, the Camp Custer eleven had several former Heralds starters. In any case, the Heralds were smarting from the loss and were out for blood. They found it before three thousand hometown fans.

Bob Foster won the toss and chose the east goal. It was the only thing the Racine Regulars won all afternoon. Shortly after the game started, Norb Sacksteder circled around left end on a fake punt and ran fifty yards for a Detroit touchdown. Later in the quarter, Norb Sacksteder circled around right end and ran another fifty yards for a second touchdown. Foster succeeded in moving the ball on several occasions in the second quarter, but Racine never threatened. Norb Sacksteder made a thirty-five-yard run, but the Racine line held. At halftime, the score was 13 to 0. Detroit made its final score in the fourth period on a forward pass from Weekes to Guy Shields. Racine suffered its fourth straight loss, 19–0.[55] Racine was scheduled to end the season with a game against Beloit, but no such game was reported in the local press.

Although Racine had been a powerful local team, it generally hired people from southeast Wisconsin rather than looking for All-Americans, so it could not compete against top interstate rivals. But later, a Wisconsin town to their north did recruit top talent, and that made all the difference. On November 11, 1917, the Green Bay independent football team played its first professional football game.[56] Sponsored by George Whitney Calhoun, a sportswriter for the *Green Bay Press-Gazette*, this charity game for the Brown County Red Cross drew a large crowd at League Park where the Green Bay All-Stars, led by Earl "Curly" Lambeau, beat the Marinette Badgers 27 to 0.

In 1918, Curly Lambeau went to Notre Dame, where he played one year as a freshman for Knute Rockne, then dropped out of school. In 1919, he and George Calhoun, sports editor for the *Press-Gazette*, organized the Green Bay Packers professional football team. They joined the American Professional Football Association in September 1920, and before long they recruited Howard "Cub" Buck, who had played with the Canton Bulldogs in 1916, 1917 and 1919, and Francis "Jugs" Earp, whose brother had played for the Davenport Athletic Association in 1916 and 1917. With their help, Green Bay became a National Football League legend.[57] While the Racine Regulars never became part of NFL lore like the Green Bay Packers and the Milwaukee Badgers, they were charter members of the NFL. They were all granted NFL franchises on June 24, 1922. Racine played under the name Racine Cardinals, in 1922, and as the Racine Legion, in 1923, their last year in major league professional football.[58] The Green Bay Packers went on to become one of the great professional football franchises in America.

23. Wabash: The Little Town that Could

The **Wabash Athletic Association** fielded a veteran team, in 1915, comprised entirely of local players, most of whom had never even played high school football.[1] Two important newcomers, Alfred "Dutch" Bergman from Notre Dame and Mark G. "Mickey" Erehart from Indiana University, were the only college stars on the Wabash team when they started the season. Bergman was from nearby Peru, Indiana, and Erehart was from Huntington, Indiana, also nearby.[2] They strengthened an already first-rate team. Wabash was carrying on a proud tradition that started late in the 1898 football season when J. B. Hutchins and Ed Colbert organized a football team for the recently incorporated Wabash Athletic Association. They asked the players to chip in enough money to buy a football and expected every man on the squad to furnish his own moleskins or go without. Their first game was played on an old hog lot known as Daugherty Field west of Canal Street in Wabash. Only a handful of fans turned out for the game, which the home team won 44–0.[3]

Energized by the victory, Wabash scheduled a game for Thanksgiving in Huntington, twelve miles to the east. J. B. Hutchins reports,

we went in style, chartered a train on the Wabash Railroad, decked ourselves in pickle dish hats of the vintage of '76 or earlier, and put on a parade that was worth the money. They put on a parade too—they went through us for 28 points—we came home a sorry and wiser bunch. I have often wondered if we couldn't have won that game if we had paid as much attention to practice as we did to parade.[4]

Hutchins went on to say, "Our reverse at Huntington must have put a damper on us, as we did not get started in 1899 until nearly Thanksgiving." On Thanksgiving, they beat Lagro, a small neighboring town, 10–0. This started a proud tradition of winning independent football.

Starting in 1900 and ending with the close of the 1912 football season, the Wabash Athletic Association played an ever-stronger array of independent and college football teams. In the process, they scored 1,801 points to their opponents' 126 points, and won fifty-five games

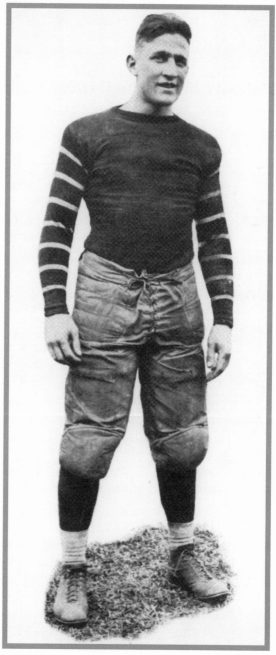

Mark G. "Mickey" Erehart, halfback, Wabash Athletic Association 1915–16, grew up in Huntington, Indiana, attended undergraduate school and medical school at Indiana University and later returned to his hometown, where he was an eye, ear, nose, and throat specialist. He was one of the few former college players on the Wabash team. His brother played for the Muncie Flyers in 1921. *(Indiana University Archives.)*

while losing only four and tying two. At first they played teams like the Marion Owls, Warsaw, Logansport, and South Bend. On occasion, they also played college teams. They beat Earlham College and lost only to DePauw and Butler Universities. By 1904, Wabash was playing strong independent teams like Fort Wayne, Lafayette, and Sheridan, and beating them handily. Wabash played out-of-state competitors by 1909 as well as strong Indiana independent teams. That year, they traveled to Cincinnati and defeated the highly touted Cincinnati Celts. By 1913, they were playing the Evanston North Ends, the Dayton Gym-Cadets, and the Chicago All-Stars, as well as the best teams in Indiana.[5]

Until 1913, the Wabash Athletic Association played under the management of J. B. Hutchins as an amateur team and did not hire ringers to supplement their team. But, when the Wabash Athletic Association gym was closed because of financial problems, the amateur team was turned over to Billy Jones, who made it a semiprofessional team.[6] Up until that time, they used hometown spirit and group bonding to attract local players for their squad. Once a young man joined the team, he often played football with the Wabash A. A. for many years. William Burgess "Red" Milliner, for example, started playing for them in 1900 and was still their starting quarterback in 1917.[7] In other cases, members of the same family played for the association from 1898 through 1904. James Showalter played for Wabash at the turn of the century, and, by 1909, Howard Showalter was playing for the town team. In 1916, his nephew Homer T. Showalter, just out of college, joined the team and played with distinction.[8]

The camaraderie developed by participation on the Athletic Association football team generally lasted a lifetime. The association held annual homecoming dinners, parades, and award ceremonies well into the 1940s. These events were important community social occasions and drew large crowds. Letters and speeches generated for these events testify to the depth of friendship that resulted from being on the Wabash town team. These friendships elevated Red Milliner to fire chief and helped elect Homer T. Showalter mayor in 1929, 1934, and 1942. In all, Homer served as mayor of the City of Wabash for fifteen years.[9]

While the Wabash Athletic Association's football team forged fierce loyalties, it also resulted in ferocious rivalries. The rivalry between Wabash and the Fort Wayne Friars began in 1904, when Wabash beat Fort Wayne 11 to 0. Over the next ten years, Fort Wayne did not score a touchdown against Wabash, much less beat them.

Homecoming parade for the Wabash Athletic Association football team during the early 1920s. Former players are riding on a telephone pole. *(Archives of the Wabash County Historical Society.)*

In 1915, a rivalry also developed between Pine Village and Wabash. Pine Village, a small town of only four hundred souls, started an independent football team in 1903 as a hometown enterprise. Their goal was to beat Morocco, a town on the railroad line to the north. The Pine Village Athletic Club was organized by Claire Rhodes, a former University of Chicago center coached by Amos Alonzo Stagg. Rhodes grew up near Pine Village and returned home to operate his family's diary farm.[10] After whipping Morocco, Pine Village went on to defeat Rensselaer, a town of four thousand, and to award itself the 1903 state independent football championship. By the opening of the 1915 season, the Pine Village Athletic Club had never been beaten and was rarely even scored on; they wore W.I.C. on their football jerseys to indicate that they believed themselves to be the "Western Independent Champions." And who was to say that they were not deserving of that title?

The Pine Village football team had no training program other than the hard work of daily life in a rural setting. Milking and farming occupied most of Claire Rhodes's time, and the same was true of his players. Originally, the team was composed chiefly of young men who had stayed home or come back home to work instead of "treading the path of bright lights," and later of former collegians who had won fame at Indiana, Purdue, DePauw, or one of the other Indiana colleges. In 1915, Pine Village played some of its home games in Lafayette or Indianapolis to accommodate the large crowds that were attracted by games between the best teams in the region. Underwritten in part by

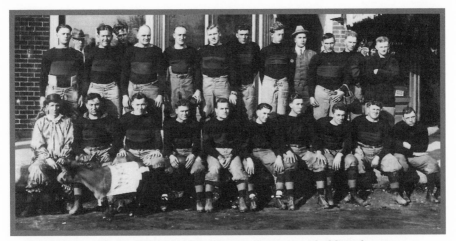

Pine Village Athletic Club 1915. Front row: John Rutter, holding the goat; James Hooker, guard; Matt Winters, tackle; Eli Fenters, quarterback; Charles Helvie, end; McKinley Martindale, halfback; Paul Odle, halfback and end; Claire Rhodes, center and manager; George Cain, fullback. Back row: Oral "Skinny" Brier, end; Ray "Snowy" Fenters, halfback and end; (just the head showing) Charles Metzger, guard; Edgar Davis, tackle; Joe Pliska, halfback; Bill Williams, tackle; John Carr, fullback; Lloyd "Jersey" Crain, halfback; Luther Mann, guard; Charles Sims, guard; Lee "Dusty" Rhodes, halfback; Wilfred "Beekie" Smith, tackle. *(Warren County Historical Society Archives.)*

the Monon Railroad, Pine Village did not hesitate to supplement its basic team with imported former college stars when they were needed to ensure victory on any given Sunday afternoon. Indiana independent football fans eagerly awaited the games between Wabash and Fort Wayne, and between Wabash and Pine Village. These rivalries were likely to draw some of the largest crowds in professional football anywhere in the United States.

The Wabash Athletic Association opened its 1915 football season, on October 3, against the Dayton Oakwoods. The Oakwoods were the 1914 city champions of Dayton, having defeated the Gym-Cadets the previous Thanksgiving. Opening day was a community celebration. The Dayton team arrived in Wabash at eight o'clock Saturday night on the Big Four Train and stayed at the Tremont Hotel. At 2:15 Sunday afternoon, the Urbana band gave a concert in front of the Tremont Hotel, then marched with the two teams around the business district before heading to Carroll Street Park, where the game started at 2:30.

The Wabash team had practiced for two weeks and was in excellent condition. Manager Billy Jones had some difficulty getting Alfred "Dutch" Bergman to the game because his contract with Wabash did not call for him to play until mid-October, but Jones felt they should have him available from the start of the season.[11] Wabash won a close contest, 19 to 14.

On October 10, Wabash played the Illinois All-Stars organized by Eugene Schobinger,[12] former University of Illinois football and track star. The Illinois All-Stars featured several former college players from the University of Wisconsin, Indiana University, and the University of Illinois. They also had several veterans of independent football in Chicago. The All-Stars were fresh off a loss to the Evanston North Ends.

A one-sided game, "full of thrills" for the Wabash fans, took place at Carroll Field. The *Wabash Plain Dealer* reported,

The locals played an almost perfect game and it was easily seen that they had digested all the arts of the great college pastime. The line was invincible while the backs and ends played a brand of ball that bordered on the phenomenal. Bergman, for the locals, drew the fans to their feet with a run the entire length of the field when he received a punt and, shaking off the entire visiting squad, melted one of the neatest markers ever made here.[13]

Alfred Bergman made two touchdowns; Mickey Erehart, Red Milliner, Jesse Reno, and McMurray made one each.[14] Wabash thrashed the All-Stars 41–0.

Wabash's third game was with Jackson, Michigan. Again Alfred Bergman, the marvelous all-around athlete from Notre Dame, made several remarkable runs and led in the scoring. Wabash humbled Jackson 49 to 0.[15] The next Sunday, according to the local newspaper, "The greatest crowd that ever camped on Carroll field went mad" with joy watching their hometown boys against the famed Evanston North Ends. The Wabash starting lineup included George Yarnelle at quarterback, Bergman and Mickey Erehart at halfbacks, and McMurry at fullback. The Wabash front seven had Jesse Reno and Red Milliner at ends, Oscar Bricker and Earnest Scheerer at tackles, Sayveskie and Moses Johnson at guards, and Harold W. "Bud" Caldwell at center.[16] Early in the first quarter, Alfred "Dutch" Bergman intercepted an Evanston pass to halt a drive by the North Ends. Wabash then drove the ball to the Evanston two yard line but did not score. The quality of football on both sides was phenomenal. The North Ends had an aggressive game plan and their defensive work was excellent, particular when Wabash threatened to score. As always Reuben Johnson, Robert Specht, Guil Falcon, John Hanna, and the other Evanston stars played a fast-paced game with plenty of trick plays and shifts. Wabash scored in the second quarter shortly after Evanston captain Reuben Johnson was forced out of the game with rib injuries. George Yarnelle threw a twenty-five-yard pass to Jesse Reno in the spot normally defended by Johnson. Oscar Bricker kicked the extra point, and Wabash led 7–0.[17] Rube Johnson returned to the game in the third quarter and played injured. It mattered little, because the damage had already been done. Wabash defenders intercepted several Evanston passes in the second half when both sides changed from a ground game to a more open passing game. In the last few minutes of play, Evanston tried hard to score but was unable to make the necessary progress. Wabash won 7–0.

In the meantime, Pine Village was also compiling an undefeated season. They had already won games against the Lafayette town team, Sheldon (IL), and the Marion Club of Indianapolis, although Claire Rhodes had broken a bone in his right hand in their game with Lafayette.[18] On October 31, the Pine Village eleven came to Wabash for one of the games that would determine the state independent football championship. Though the crowd did not approach the size or enthusiasm of the hometown crowd for the Evanston game, the low attendance did not reflect the importance of the game.

The visiting Pine Village team had few hired ringers, though they did engage Joe Pliska, a Chicago native, who had been a starter at Notre Dame in 1914. The Fenters brothers, Eli and Ray, and Big Ed Davis, assistant coach at Indiana University, were the usual standouts for Pine Village. Beginning at 2 P.M., the contest was well played and ended in less than two hours. Late in the first quarter, it appeared that Pine Village was going to score when they took the ball to within eight yards of the Wabash goal line. Then, on two line plunges, they got the ball within two feet of the goal—on fourth down, Pine Village scored. In the fourth quarter, Wabash advanced to within a few feet of the Pine Village goal, only to lose the ball on downs. This was Wabash's last opportunity to win. The final score was Pine Village 7, Wabash 0. It was only the third loss for Wabash in thirteen years.[19]

Wabash rebounded, on November 7, with a win over a team from Montreal, Canada. Both teams played straight football, with few passes being thrown. Jesse Reno made two of the three Wabash touchdowns, each scored on one of the rare passes thrown by George Yarnelle. One touchdown came late in the first half on a ten-yard pass, the other in the fourth quarter. The Wabash team in their blue-and-white jerseys played well on defense, allowing only a thirty-five-yard drop kick for the Canadian team in the second quarter. Mark Erehart made the first touchdown for Wabash when he skirted left end and ran twenty yards for the score.[20] The final score was 24–0.

Wabash was scheduled to play the Detroit Athletic Club at Carroll Field on the second Sunday in November, but the game was canceled. No reason was given for the cancellation.[21]

The big game of the Wabash season came on November 21 at League Park in Fort Wayne. Five thousand enthusiastic football fans paid fifty cents each to watch the game between "the state's two foremost gridiron machines." The Friars built additional bleachers for the game and set aside space for bands and special cheering sections.[22] Moreover, Fort Wayne hired additional players for the game. They brought in Howard "Cap" Edwards and Al Feeney, Notre Dame football alumni, to beef up their line.[23] The Wabash Athletic Association hired Harry Routh, a University of Purdue football alumni, to play left tackle in this game.[24]

The Friars' star quarterback, Kent "Skeet" Lambert, was injured two weeks earlier and was not at full strength for the game. Nevertheless, his replacement, Frank "Coonie" Checkaye, was a good quarterback. The balance of the Fort Wayne team was solid. They had Notre Dame stars Joe Pliska and Heine Berger as halfbacks; veteran independent football star Chris Chambers at fullback; and a solid line.[25] The game was an exciting, well-played contest. Both teams scored in the first half. Early in the first quarter, Heine Berger had the honor of registering the first touchdown ever made by Fort Wayne against Wabash when he ran thirty yards through the Wabash eleven for the score.[26] In the second quarter, Jesse Reno caught an eight-yard pass from George Yarnelle to tie the game. Neither team made the extra point.[27]

At the start of the second half, Billy Jones, the manager of the Wabash Athletic Association, attempted to play Homer T. Showalter, even though he was not on the list of players approved in the contract. According to the *Fort Wayne Journal-Gazette*, "Jones knew that as well as any one, yet he attempted to run Showalter, a Wabash College player in at end at the start of the second half, although the latter's name was not on the list."[28] Lambert, who had also graduated from Wabash College, recognized Showalter. Homer was not allowed to play in the game, which, incidentally, preserved the balance of his eligibility at Wabash College, where he was later inducted into the athletic hall of fame.

The game ended in a 6–6 tie. Dutch Bergman played an outstanding game for Wabash. His fifty-yard run set up the Reno touchdown. Both George Yarnelle and the Fort Wayne star, Lambert, kicked well, and Harry Routh blocked a Fort Wayne field goal attempt that would have won the game for the Friars.[29] According to the *Indianapolis Times*,

$3500 was wagered on the Wabash-Fort Wayne game.[30] Wabash ended its 1915 season on Thanksgiving at home against Corby Hall of Notre Dame.[31] Wabash won the game and ended the season with a 6–1–1 record.

Homer T. "Showy" Showalter was the pride of Wabash, Indiana. He was born in a log cabin northwest of Wabash, on November 20, 1892, to Daniel and Elizabeth (Wenzel) Showalter, and was a lifelong resident of Wabash. He played high school football from 1908 through 1910, following a tradition already established by his uncles and cousins, several of whom played football for the Wabash Athletic Association. Homer also played on his high school basketball team.[32] In September 1911, he took the train to Crawfordsville, Indiana, to attend Wabash College, where he joined the football team coached by Jesse Harper. Harper had learned the sport under Amos Stagg at the University of Chicago and was one of the new breed of professional athletic administrators.[33] In 1912, Harper become the football coach and athletic director at Notre Dame.

Wabash College was loaded with outstanding athletes in 1911. Among its players at that time were Kent "Skeet" Lambert, Homer Stonebraker, and Ward Lambert, all of whom gained national attention for their athletic skills. Homer quickly became an outstanding end on the Wabash College football team. In 1911, as a freshman, he became a starter on the varsity team. He was captain of the team in 1913 and president of the class of 1914. He also played college basketball with the great All-American Homer Stonebraker, whom many considered the best basketball player of the pre-1932 era.

Edward Duggan, born May 19, 1891, on a farm in southern Indiana, played halfback for the Wabash Athletic Association in 1916. Eddie Duggan had played for Notre Dame from 1912 to 1914. He coached for a time at Franklin College in Indiana and, in 1921, played for the Rock Island Independents of the National Football League. Duggan moved to Houston, Texas, after playing with the Rock Island Independents and was athletic director at Sam Houston High School until 1948.[34]

Alfred H. "Dutch" Bergman,[35] born in Peru, Indiana, also played for the Wabash A.A. Bergman enrolled at Notre Dame, in September 1910, and became one of the greatest all-around athletes in the school's history, earning eleven monograms in four years: three in football, four in track, two in baseball and two in basketball—the only intercollegiate sports at Notre Dame at the time. In October 1915, he joined the Wabash Athletic Association professional football team and played with them through the 1917 season at left halfback. In fall 1917, he joined the army and was assigned to the officer's training school at Fort Benjamin Harrison. He continued to play football for Wabash on weekends during the 1917 season.

The other Wabash stars included William "Red" Milliner, Jesse Reno, Kenny and George Yarnelle, and John "Doc" Redmond. While Doc Redmond was a college star from the University of Indiana, the others were hometown boys with extraordinary athletic ability. In 1917, Max Palm and Guil Falcon from the Evanston North Ends, Frank "Coonie" Checkaye from Muncie and the Fort Wayne Friars, and Myron "Mike" Yount from Franklin College supplemented the Wabash town players. With this kind of talent, it cannot be denied that the Wabash Athletic Association was one of the nation's best professional football teams in the pre-World War I era.

Football is a sport that requires physical strength and agility, but more importantly it requires desire, drive, grit, and determination, particularly in single platoon football where specialization was not allowed. In modern football, some players only kick or block or tackle. Indeed, specialization has gotten to the point that some players only play on third downs, others only on goal line situations, and still others only run back punts and kickoffs. In 1916, players were required to do it all. They had to kick, pass, run, block, and tackle, as well as call their own plays. Moreover, they often had to play hurt, because, if they were taken out of the game, they could only return once, at the start of a subsequent quarter.

Each performance on the football field requires high energy, adjustments to the play of the opponent, and physical contact. It is a test of manliness and determination. Frequently, the individuals and teams with the most desire and adaptability win the game. This was particularly true of single platoon football, where the skill levels and the game plans of a coach were less critical to success than in modern football. In this environment, the success of the Wabash Athletic Association is truly noteworthy. This relatively small community fielded a football team dominated by local talent who received little compensation. Over the span of ten years, these local boys, few of whom played high school, much less college football, took on all comers and beat the teams of big city boys, wealthy athletic clubs, and college all-stars. They did it with fierce team play and the determination not to lose. For more than ten years, they did not even allow the Fort Wayne Friars to score on them.

The great strength of the Wabash Athletic Association team was its cohesion and team loyalty. To be a member of the Wabash A.A. team

Wabash Athletic Association 1916. Bottom row: John Farr, Homer Showalter, Henry Schneider, John "Doc" Redmond, Oscar Bricker, Frank McHale, Jesse Reno, Alfred "Dutch" Bergman. Top row: Frank Gurtner, William "Red" Milliner, Edward "Eddie" Duggan, George Yarnelle, J. Kenneth Yarnelle, Everett O. "Newt" Tibbs. *(Wabash County Historical Society.)*

was to join a community of lifelong friends.[36] It was the most important thing a young man in Wabash, Indiana, could do in the first two decades of the twentieth century. It was unthinkable to let one's friends down by being responsible for the loss of a football game. If the Wabash A.A. had an advantage over opponents, it was its desire to win. To be sure, there were some exceptional athletes on the Wabash football team, but most of their opponents also had exceptional athletes. Frequently, the difference was the desire to win, also a characteristic of their chief rival in the 1914–16 era, the Evanston North Ends.

The 1916 Wabash A.A. team started the season against the Muncie Congerville Athletic Association in a game played on September 30. According to eyewitnesses, "Mingling heavy line plunging with sensational forward passes and by end gains, the Wabash A.A. football team defeated the Congerville eleven . . . on the Carroll street field."[37] One week later, they were scheduled to play the Toledo Glenwoods but canceled the game because the Glenwoods had a Negro player. To his credit, Red Milliner, team captain, tried to persuade any eleven players on the team to go ahead with the game, but he could not muster the necessary number for a starting lineup. The incident, of course, reflects the prejudices held in central and southern Indiana against African-Americans at that time, and it is noteworthy that at least a portion of the team was willing to play under those conditions.

On October 13, Wabash played the Pine Village Athletic Club in a game that had implications for the state independent football championship. As usual, Pine Village loaded up for the game. Their manager Claire Rhodes and coach Ed Davis always structured their team for the competition, but they rarely came to a game without a strong complement of college stars. At ends, Pine Village started Cliff Milligan at six feet and 170 pounds and Charles Helvie at five foot eight inches, 185 pounds. Both had played at Indiana University. They had twenty-six-year-old Matthew Winters at six feet two inches and two hundred pounds from Poseyville, Indiana, at left tackle, and Big Ed Davis at five feet nine inches, two hundred pounds at right tackle. They, too, were Indiana University stars. Emmett Keefe from Notre Dame and James Hooker, a veteran Pine Village player, were the guards. Claire Rhodes was the center. Claire was five feet ten inches tall and weighed 215 pounds. The Pine Village backfield found Harold "Irish" Sheridan from Purdue University at quarterback; Eli Fenters, the great Pine Village athlete at five feet nine inches and 190 pounds of farmer muscle at left half; Bill Williams at five feet nine inches and 165 pounds from Indiana University at fullback; and Ray Fenters, at five feet nine inches and 170 pounds at right half. This was certainly a strong team, and a thousand fans came along to cheer them on.[38]

Wabash countered with Jesse Reno and Homer T. Showalter at ends. Each of these hometown boys could hold his own against any end of that era. The Wabash starting tackles were Harry Routh from Purdue University and Oscar Bricker. The Wabash guards were Frank McHale from the University of Michigan as well the Detroit Mack Park Maroons, and John "Doc" Redmond from Frankfort, Indiana, and a football and track star at Indiana University. Harry Schneider, a local player, was the center.[39] The backfield had George Yarnelle at quarterback and his brother Ken Yarnelle at left halfback. Eddie Duggan from Notre Dame was the fullback, and William "Red" Milliner, the team captain, played right halfback. Alfred Bergman, the "Flying Dutchman" from Notre Dame, came off the bench to help the team.[40]

On a perfect day for football, some five thousand fans paid fifty cents each to see the game at the Carroll Street Field in Wabash, where the Indiana state championship was at stake. Wabash chose the south goal and kicked off to Pine Village. After several exchanges of the ball,

Bill Williams, fullback, Pine Village Athletic Club 1915–16, stood five feet nine inches tall and weighed 165 pounds; he was a solid runner and sideback. *(Indiana University Archives.)*

Wabash rushed the ball to within fifteen yards of the Pine Village goal, only to lose possession on downs. Pine Village punted out of trouble. It was the only scoring opportunity in the first quarter. The second quarter resembled the first. Both teams were unable to advance the ball very far. Near the end of the half, Kenneth Yarnelle raced thirty-five yards up the field after breaking away from three Village tacklers. It was the longest run of the game, but it brought no scoring opportunity.

Wabash kicked off to Pine Village to start the second half. First downs rarely punctuated the seesaw battle held between the twenty yard lines. Near the close of the game, Pine Village, aided by a penalty, marched to the Wabash one yard line, only to be held on downs. The clean, hard-fought game ended in a scoreless tie. The game was one of the best in Indiana independent football history. The Fenters brothers and Harry "Irish" Sheridan were the outstanding players for Pine Village; Showalter, Routh, and the Yarnelle brothers for Wabash. Redmond and McHale, the new players for Wabash, strengthened the locals' line play.[41]

The following week, Pine Village played Decatur in Pine Village. On October 15, as reported in the *Decatur Review*, the Decatur team had started by automobile for Hammond to play the Independents, but "when they got to the Sangamon River, their machines started sliding from one side of the road to the other, kept turning around and started back toward Decatur because of the previous night's rain. Finally one car went into the ditch so it was decided to call off their trip to Hammond."[42] A benefit dance was held the following Wednesday to raise enough money to keep the Decatur Indians afloat due to the lost revenue from the prior Sunday.[43] On October 22, the Decatur squad took a train to Attica, Indiana, then traveled north ten miles by automobile to Pine Village, only to lose the game 12–7.[44]

On October 21, the Wabash A.A. played their rivals, the Evanston North Ends, who had been given a $1,500 guarantee for the game. They bet Wabash fans another $800 on the outcome.[45] Wabash started the same team that played against Pine Village. Evanston had John Bosdett and John Hanna at ends, Max Palm and St. Germain at tackles, Fredrick "Blad" Meyers and Roy Whitlock at guards, Tom Shaughnessy from Notre Dame at center, and Reuben Johnson at quarterback. The balance of the backfield had Johnny Barrett and Robert Specht at halfbacks, and Penn Carolan at fullback. Nearly five thousand fans paid to see the game that started at 2:30 P.M. Sunday afternoon.

Wabash chose the south goal and kicked off to Evanston. Evanston

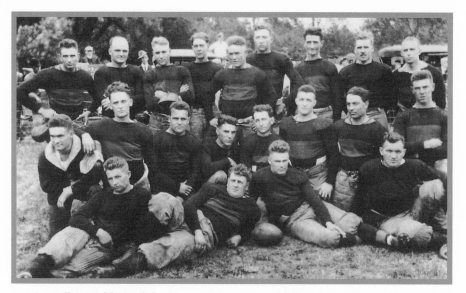

Pine Village Athletic Club 1916. Front row: Harold "Irish" Sheridan, quarterback; Claire Rhode, center; Eli Fenters, quarterback; Matt Winters, tackle. Second row: Roy "Squint" Fenters, halfback; Oral "Skinny" Brier, end; Arthur Krause, end; Lee Brutus; Charles Metzger, guard; David E. "Kinks" Hawthorne, tackle and guard; Jim Hooker, tackle and guard; Bill Fisher. Third row: McKinley Martindale, center; Edgar Davis, tackle; John Sailor; Leslie Hole; Ray "Snowy" Fenters, halfback; Paul Odle, halfback and end; Cliff "Tuck" Milligan, center and right end; Bill Williams, fullback; Emmet Keefe, guard. *(Warren County Historical Society Archives.)*

steadily advanced the ball to the Wabash thirty-five yard line. Reuben Johnson tried a field goal from placement from that point and failed. A few minutes later, Evanston got the ball back to about the same position on the field and again tried a field goal, this time by drop kick, and for a second time the field goal failed. Even though Evanston controlled the ball most of the time, they did not score.

At the start of the second quarter, Dutch Bergman replaced Red Milliner at halfback. On the first play of the quarter, he made a fifteen-yard gain. Steady progress followed for Wabash, until Showy Showalter caught a nine-yard touchdown pass from George Yarnelle to put Wabash ahead 6–0. The point after touchdown failed. After the kickoff, Evanston's offense sputtered, and Wabash again got possession of the ball. A sensational pass from George Yarnelle to Dutch Bergman followed. Bergman then ran fifty yards for the second Wabash score. Again the point after failed.

Evanston received the ball, and Robert Specht made a nifty fifteen-yard run. Heavy line plunging netted Evanston several small gains, before a smashing tackle cracked Rube Johnson's ribs. He had to be carried from the field. Gilbert took his place. A couple of plays later, Jesse Reno, the Wabash star end, sprained his ankle and was removed from the game. Frank Gurtner[46] replaced him, and, shortly afterward, Evanston lost the ball on downs. Just before the end of the first half, Wabash threw a double pass, George Yarnelle to Dutch Bergman to Kenneth Yarnelle. This sensational play resulted in a Wabash touchdown and an 18–0 lead at halftime.

The third quarter was a tug-of-war with neither team gaining much advantage until the end of the quarter, when Wabash had the ball on the Evanston ten yard line. As the fourth quarter started, Evanston regained its pep, which seems to have left them when Rube Johnson was injured. They stopped the Wabash drive and punted out, held Wabash, and forced them to punt. When they got the ball again, Evanston drove steadily for a touchdown. Johnny Barrett kicked the point after, and the score was now 18–7. Before long, Evanston intercepted a pass near the center of the field, and, two plays later, Robert Specht ran forty-five yards for Evanston's second touchdown. Again Barrett made the point after. Wabash was held on downs after they received the kickoff, and, on the ensuing punt, Specht ran the punt back ninety-five yards for a touchdown. The touchdown, however, was called back by a claim that Evanston held on the play.

A long argument followed, but finally the ball was placed on the Evanston twenty yard line and play resumed. Evanston was mad, and they played with superhuman energy, marching down the field four and five yards at a time for a touchdown. For a third time, Barrett kicked the extra point to give Evanston a 21–18 victory. The Evanston players had $700 to $800 of their own money bet on the game and were not going to be denied victory.[47]

The loss to Evanston was devastating, particularly given the financial condition of the Wabash Athletic Association. On October 23, a group of investors in the Wabash A.A. filed suit in the circuit court to place the association in receivership because of financial insolvency.[48] Nevertheless, Wabash prepared for a game with the Decatur Indians the following Sunday and fielded the same team. Decatur had a reputation for being one of the stronger teams in Illinois. Moreover, Decatur had prospects for adding Harold Pogue[49] to their team. Pogue had been a Walter Camp All-American in 1914 at the University of Illinois and a broad jumper on their track team.

After giving the offer serious consideration, however, Pogue decided not to play against Wabash. As he explained it, "First of all, I should have to have more time to practice with the bunch . . . [because] it would be natural for [Wabash] to "lay" for me to put me out of the game. If I knew the players better, I would know what to look for in cases of this kind. When I was in prime condition at Illinois, I had a bad shoulder, my hips and my knees hurt me all the time, and I had a fractured bone in my arm . . . [playing football] is hard work, and I'm glad I'm through."[50]

The game turned out to be a one-sided affair. Wabash scored in the first two minutes and quite often thereafter, with Bergman and Duggan most frequently doing the honors. The final score was 45–16.[51] The Decatur players complained that the only commendable aspect of their treatment in Wabash was that Billy Jones "did not hesitate to come across with the contract price." Early in the game, Charles Dresen, the Decatur quarterback, was socked in the jaw, and the other Decatur players complained that "slugging was so common that it was decided to just play the game. . . . We let them go, for our lives were more valuable, and to lay down and to quit entirely would have canceled the contract. . . . We would have been wise," said an Indian player, "had we taken the advice of the Pine Village players. They told us that the Wabash team had none too good a reputation."[52]

With the same starting lineup, Wabash played Wheeling, West Virginia, on November 5, and defeated them 32–0.[53] Twenty-five hundred people saw the lackluster game. Kenneth Yarnelle, Alfred Bergman, and Homer Showalter each scored a touchdown, and Eddie Duggan scored two.[54]

On November 12, Wabash played an away game with the Pine Village Athletic Club. More than five thousand fans paid fifty cents each to see the game. Three hundred Wabash fans took a special train car to Lafayette. Wabash kicked to Pine Village to start the game. Pine Village started Charles Helvie and Arthur Krause at ends, Matt Winters and Edgar Davis at tackles, Harrison Walker and Emmett Keefe at guards, Cliff Milligan at center, and Eli and Ray Fenters, Clair Scott, and Harvard University All-American Richard King in the backfield. Six of the eleven Pine Village starters had played for Indiana University, one for Notre Dame, and one for Harvard. On the first series of downs, Richard King pounded the ball to the Wabash fifteen yard line before Wabash stiffened and held for three downs. On fourth down, Ray Fenters slashed off tackle and scored the game's only touchdown. Eli Fenters made the point after. Neither team moved the ball far for the balance of the quarter. In the second quarter, Jesse Reno failed to make a catch that could have tied the score. In the third quarter, the ball moved freely between the twenty yard lines, but, once inside, neither team could score. In the final quarter, Wabash had a good drive stopped by a pass interception. Dutch Bergman, who sat out the first quarter, was the outstanding back for Wabash, but Ken Yarnelle also played a noteworthy game. Wabash lost 7–0 because its passing game did not work.[55] Wabash ended the season with a home-and-home series against Fort Wayne and a game against the Louisville Goldbergs. They lost the first game to Fort Wayne, 7–13, but defeated the newly crowned state football champions in the rematch, 3–0. The Goldbergs were easy prey, and Wabash beat them 46–0 to end the season.

Nineteen seventeen was the last year the Wabash Athletic Association had a major league professional football team. In 1915, Wabash had a 6–1–1 record and claimed a share of the Indiana independent football championship. They had a very respectable 5–3–1 record in 1916, but, in 1917, they fell to a 3–5–1 record and were unable to sustain the income necessary to field a first-rate professional football team that could defeat the best in the country.

There are several reasons for the relative decline of Wabash football, the foremost of which was the overall improvement of professional teams. Prior to 1915, nearly all independent teams recruited local talent. Occasionally, regional players supplemented local players, and a few college stars were hired for important games. This was the pattern followed by the Wabash Athletic Association. Fortunately, Wabash County had a fair amount of athletic talent. When combined with local pride, the result was an outstanding independent football tradition that grew with success. However, teams like Massillon, Canton, Pine Village, Hammond, Fort Wayne, Rock Island, and Detroit began recruiting entire teams of college stars, including players from outside their community and region. These teams were now consistently better than hometown teams. They were also more expensive to operate and required larger crowds and higher admission rates to sustain. To succeed, professional teams typically required a larger population base than that of Wabash.

The 1917 season, the twentieth for independent football in Wabash, began on October 7 against the Anderson [Indiana] Remys.[56] The starters were essentially the same as in the 1916 season, except some like captain Red Milliner were older and less able. The blue-and-white jerseys of the Wabash A. A. boasted a starting lineup of Jesse Reno and

Homer T. Showalter at ends. They were among the best six or eight ends in pro football in 1917. Myron Yount, from Whiteland, Indiana, and John "Doc" Redmond were the starting tackles. Both were solid players and had played college football—Yount in 1913 while a freshman at Franklin College, and Redmond at Indiana University. Earnest Scheerer and Henry Schneider started at guards, and Everett "Newt" Tibbs at center. The backfield had Red Milliner at quarterback, Frank "Coonie" Checkaye at left halfback, Frank Gurtner at right halfback, and Frank Allen, a three-time letterman from Indiana University at fullback. Alfred "Dutch" Bergman was in the army, Second Officers' Training Corps, but would play when he was on leave.

The Wabash schedule included four away games, the most for one season in the history of the team, and featured games with the Toledo Naval Training team, Pine Village, Hammond, Detroit, and Fort Wayne. Wabash won the season opener from Anderson 20–6. Milliner, who was starting his fifteenth season for Wabash, and Dutch Bergman, with two touchdowns, were the stars of the game.[57] Fewer than nine hundred fans attended.

On October 13, manager Billy Jones announced that he had signed Max Palm of the Evanston North Ends to a contract to play left tackle. The Carroll Street field was the site of the Wabash Toledo Navel Training Center game on October 14. Frank Checkaye replaced Milliner as starting quarterback. Twelve hundred fans paid to see the game. Again, Alfred "Dutch" Bergman was the star. He scored a spectacular eighty-yard touchdown on a punt return in the fourth quarter, when, as the *Wabash Plain Dealer* emoted, "he dodged through a maze of black and orange players . . . with catlike agility and the speed of a 'bird' found his way through and sprinted down the open field fifty yards for six points." Bergman also intercepted a Toledo pass and made two punt returns for touchdowns.[58] Wabash won 20–0, and Dutch Bergman accounted for eighteen of the twenty points.

On October 22, Wabash added Guilford Falcon, of Evanston, to their team to play the Pine Village Athletic Club at Carroll Field. A crowd of almost four thousand flocked to the game, many of them rooters for Pine Village. Pine Village suited an all-star cast that included Charles Helvie and Harry Banjan at ends. Charles Helvie was a solid pro player whose career included the NFL after World War I. He had been a starter at Indiana University. Harry Banjan had been a starting end at Notre Dame and later would serve for forty-eight years as coach and athletic director at the University of Dayton.[59] Cliff Milligan and Big Ed Davis, both from Indiana University, were the starting tackles. Finally, Emmett Keefe from Notre Dame and Roy Fenters, a fifth-year pro with Pine Village and a legendary sandlot star, were the starting guards.

Homer Stonebraker[60] was the starting center for the Wabash College football team for three years and played for Pine Village on at least two occasions in 1917. His linebacker work was of professional quality. The Pine Village backfield had Paul Sheeks at quarterback, Francis Bacon and Eli Fenters at halfbacks, and Richard King, the Harvard University All-American, at fullback. Paul Sheeks was head coach at Wabash College at that time but had been an All-State right halfback for Mitchell High School in South Dakota before starting at Dakota Wesleyan and the University of South Dakota in Vermillion, South Dakota.[61] Pine Village wore yellow-and-black jerseys. A movie man with his Kodak was on the field, taking moving pictures of the game for the local theater.[62]

The hostilities opened with Wabash kicking off to Pine Village. From the outset, it was a defensive battle. Forward passes failed, and running plays were bottled up. In the second quarter, Newt Tibbs, the Wabash center, hiked the ball to Frank Checkaye, who was to punt. Checkaye fumbled the hike, picked it up, and tried to run with the ball to avoid being sacked. In doing so, he ran into his own end zone and was tackled for a safety. It was the only score of the game.[63] Wabash lost 2–0.

On the last Sunday in October, Wabash traveled to Hammond to play the Clabbys. It was not a happy road trip. The Clabbys gave Wabash its worst defeat since the Huntington Lime City team defeated Wabash 29–0 in 1898. Football fans in Lake County, Indiana, were treated to an outstanding game from the Hammond Clabbys. Both teams had loaded up for the contest. Hammond played Tom Shaughnessy, formerly with the Evanston North Ends and Notre Dame, for the first time. Whitlock from the Evanston North Ends, Wilber Henderson, Frank Blocker of Purdue, and Bernard "Swede" Halstrom of the University of Illinois were an excellent supporting cast for Paddy Driscoll. Wabash started Homer T. Showalter, Myron Yount,[64] Max Palm, Jesse Reno, Doc Redmond, and Guil Falcon.[65]

The two teams played a scoreless first half, but, on the opening kickoff of the second half, Paddy Driscoll received the ball on a short kick and ran sixty yards through the center of the field past the entire Wabash team for a touchdown. Another touchdown was scored by Driscoll a few minutes later on an end run, and he scored a third touchdown in the final period. Driscoll also accounted for two extra points, thus scoring all the Clabbys points. Led by future NFL Hall of

Famer, Paddy Driscoll, Hammond won on straight running football before a crowd of only eight hundred fans.[66]

On November 4, 1917, the Wabash A.A. played in Detroit against the Heralds. Again the game proved to be a mismatch. The Heralds won a lopsided 34–0 game. The Wabash A.A. team finished its road trip in Lafayette, Indiana, on November 11, in a game against the Pine Village Athletic Club. Guil Falcon scored the only touchdown of the game, although Frank Checkaye recovered a fumble that would have led to another score if Frank Allen had not been found offside.[67] Wabash won 7–0. It was the only road game they won all season.

On November 18, Wabash returned home to play a return match with Hammond. The absence of Bergman continued to handicap Wabash. Bergman had not played since the second game of the season, and his speed was sorely missed. The backfield speed of Bernard "Swede" Halstrom, John "Paddy" Driscoll, and Clinks Meyers gave Hammond an edge. The fullback play of Guil Falcon and Ted Blocker offset each other, and the line play was even, except that Homer "Showy" Showalter was missing from the Wabash lineup. He was replaced by Frank Allen. Frank Gurtner was at right halfback for Wabash.[68] Red Milliner, the oldest player on the field, played a solid game for Wabash, and Jesse Reno, Frank Allen, and Guilford Falcon also played well. Falcon's punting was outstanding. For the first three quarters, the game was scoreless. In the early part of the game, Wabash outplayed Hammond, but, in the second half, the tide turned. Finally, Swede Halstrom crossed the goal line with the game's only touchdown. Driscoll kicked the extra point to defeat Wabash 7–0.[69]

Wabash played their annual game with the Fort Wayne Friars on November 25. With the exception of their one-point loss to the Pitcairn Quakers, the Fort Wayne Friars had looked good all season. Wabash was having the worst year in its nineteen-year history. The association had already lost four games and had won only three. The match-up with Fort Wayne appeared to be the prescription for another loss. Fort Wayne was having a good season; Wabash was having a bad one. It was as simple as that—or was it?

Not content with their roster, and mindful of all the times Wabash had defeated them in the past, the Friars decided to strengthen their starting lineup for the game. Frank Rydzewski was scheduled to play his last college game for Notre Dame against Washington and Jefferson College near Pittsburgh on Saturday. Rydzewski was perhaps the best college center in 1917, and the Friars felt that he could improve their team. Consequently, they arranged to have both Knute Rockne and Frank Rydzewski leave the train in Fort Wayne early Sunday morning en route back to South Bend.[70] Despite these last-minute efforts by Fort Wayne to upgrade, Wabash fans were not shy about betting on their team. The Fort Wayne newspaper reported that Wabash fans were betting significant amounts of money on their team to win Sunday's game: "Numerous wagers at even money were posted, among them being one for $100."[71]

Four thousand fans crowded into League Park in Fort Wayne to witness the game between bitter rivals. The home team, in orange-and-black jerseys, kicked off to Wabash. Doc Redmond received the ball and ran it back twenty yards. Late in the first quarter, after five exchanges of the ball, Fort Wayne marched relentlessly up the field four or five yards at a time until Joe Pliska scored a touchdown and Dorais kicked the point after. The Fort Wayne lead held up until the fourth quarter. Both teams made what had appeared to be touchdowns in the third quarter, but in each case they were called back. Reno made a sixty-five-yard run that was called back because of an offside penalty, and on another occasion, Specht ran for a touchdown for the Friars, only to have the play called back because of the illegal use of hands by Robbins, the Fort Wayne guard. In the final quarter, however, Homer T. "Showy" Showalter recovered a fumble resulting from a poor hand-off between Dorais and Specht. Wabash got the ball on the Fort Wayne eighteen yard line. Guil Falcon powered the tying touchdown across the goal line a few plays later. Alfred "Dutch" Bergman kicked the extra point. The game ended 7 to 7.[72]

Rydzewski played an outstanding game for the Friars. "He is full of pep and has a way of communicating it to the balance of the team that works wonders," declared the *Fort Wayne Journal-Gazette* the Monday after the game. Knute Rockne also proved his worth. "Wabash lined up for a trick play in the second quarter, but Rockne had it spotted and broke it before the ball could be advanced a yard."[73] The Yarnelle brothers, who were now in the armed services, were on hand to cheer Wabash on from the sidelines, and Alfred "Dutch" Bergman, on leave from the army, played one of his last football games for Wabash. He later spent more than twenty years in a TB sanitarium, and never again played the professional game he loved so much.

On Thanksgiving Day, Wabash closed out its season in Indianapolis against Pine Village. Pine Village made short work of Wabash. Captain Red Milliner, who for many years had been the dominating spirit of the

Wabash Athletic Association, had to content himself with officiating as head linesman. Red had cracked three ribs in the Fort Wayne game the previous Sunday. Wabash added La Pado, who had played for Detroit, at right halfback and Fredrick "Blad" Meyers from the Evanston North Ends at guard. Dutch Bergman played quarterback for Wabash, but, when his voice gave out in the second half, Guil Falcon piped out the signals for him. Harvard All-American Richard King battered a path through the white-and-blue line for big gains. He was the star of the game for Pine Village. Frederick "Blad" Meyers did not enter the game for Wabash until the second half, when he played defensive linebacker and offensive guard for the home team. While he played well, Wabash was no match for Pine Village and lost 20–6.[74]

Early in the 1917 season, Wabash, Pine Village, and Hammond had signed an agreement creating a professional football league among the three teams. They had hopes of expanding their arrangement to other teams.[75] But the expansion of the league never materialized, and the declining fortunes of the Wabash Athletic Association made the club's future in professional football uncertain, at best, and unlikely given the war in Europe. One of the bright lights of independent football was dimming as professional football, with all-star teams, replaced home-town heroes. Nineteen seventeen was the twilight of independent football in Wabash.

24. Racism Rears Its Ugly Head

One genuinely noble aspect of early pro football was its accessibility by athletes of all ethnic groups. At a time when racial and ethnic parochialism was gripping the nation, pro football was a relatively open institution. World War I had encouraged open hostilities toward Germans, Italians, Catholics, and Jews. Southern control of the administrative branches of national government had also allowed anti-Negro feeling to flourish. In spite of this context, pro football allowed persons of all races and nationalities to play the sport if they had the talent. Jewish athletes, Hymie and Louis Bleich, played for the Lancaster Malleables and the Buffalo All-Stars, Joseph J. Schuette was a stalwart for the Toledo Maroons, David and Abe Cohen were the featured stars of the Aurora Greyhounds, Goldberg played for Cleveland, and Jacob Lazerous played for the Rock Island Independents. Native American athletes played for Altoona, Buffalo, Canton, Detroit, Fort Wayne, Massillon, Pine Village, and Pitcairn. Even a few exceptionally talented African-Americans played for some professional teams. This is not to say that football was immune to local social pressures, as was the case in Wabash in 1916, yet it is amazing that African-Americans such as Gideon Charles Smith and Frederick D. "Fritz" Pollard were actively recruited to play pro football at a time when Blacks were barred from playing professional baseball.

Unlike baseball in this era, college football was not closed to African-American athletes. Thirteen African-American men played intercollegiate football before 1900, including two Walter Camp All-Americans, and an additional twenty-seven played at predominately white colleges through 1914.[1] There were also several African-American players in the professional football ranks. In 1915, Bob Marshall, an All-American from the University of Minnesota, was the starting left end for the Minneapolis Marines, Clarence Fraim was the star fullback for the Toledo Glenwoods, Steve Hopkins was starter for the St. Paul Banholzers, and Gideon Charles Smith, from Michigan Agricultural College, played for the Canton Bulldogs. Moreover, there were several African-Americans playing for major college teams. Frederick D. "Fritz" Pollard, at Brown University, was considered the best halfback in college football in 1916 and was a Walter Camp All-American.[2] Pollard played high school football for Lane Technical High School in Chicago from 1908 to 1912 and later became the first African-American to coach professional football. His sister, Naomi, was the first Black woman to graduate from Northwestern University, and his older brother, Leslie, had played football for Dartmouth College in 1908.[3] In 1914, Lane Tech featured an African-American halfback named Blueitt, who showed signs of football stardom beyond high school;[4] Brown and Morrison were the first team tackle and guard for Tufts University;[5] Paul Robeson—who later became world famous as an operatic bass and classical actor—played halfback at Rutgers and was a Walter Camp All-American end in 1918;[6] and Fred "Duke" Slater, an Iowa University freshman, was soon an All-American tackle.[7] All of these men would play professional football by 1922.[8]

Moreover, African-Americans had been playing as paid football players since 1904, when Charles W. Follis, a high school and college star from Wooster, Ohio, signed a contract to play halfback for the Shelby Blues (Shelby, Ohio)[9] and led them to an 8–1–1 season. In 1907, Charles A. "Doc" Baker was paid to play football for the Akron Indians and continued to play for them in 1908, 1909, and 1911.[10] Bob Marshall began playing football for pay with the Minneapolis Marines in 1908 and continued to play pro football until 1925.[11] Henry McDonald, who was born in Haiti in 1890, grew up in Canadaigua, New York, and graduated from East High School in Rochester, New York, also played professionally for the Rochester Jeffersons, in 1911, and later for the Lancaster Malleables.[12] Steve Hopkins played halfback for the St. Paul Banholzers through 1916.[13]

However, in 1916, the Ku Klux Klan experienced a rebirth in Indiana, and Jim Crow laws were tacitly supported by Woodrow Wilson's administration in Washington, D.C. Newspaper headlines warned white working Americans that "Negros were coming north to work."[14] A popular brand of smoking tobacco called "Nigger Hair" was advertised in newspapers.[15] In Paducah, Kentucky, a mob of white townspeople lynched two black men, one for allegedly attacking a white woman and the other for opposing the lynching. The mob put ropes around the necks of the two black men, threw the ropes over a limb, then tied the ropes to an automobile bumper and drove the car away.[16] Under these conditions, it should be no surprise that racism reared its ugly head in Wabash, Indiana, near the beginning of the 1916 season.

The Toledo (Ohio) Glenwoods were scheduled to play the Wabash Athletic Association in Wabash on October 8, 1916. The Glenwoods used the Glenwood bowling alleys in Toledo as their base of operations,[17] and played a moderately tough schedule against teams such as the Detroit Harvards, Flint, and Ann Arbor. In 1915, the Glenwoods signed a promising African-American fullback named Clarence Fraim, star of the famous Toledo Central High School football eleven, known as the Mastodons of 1912.[18] Because of his leadership and strong play, both on offense and defense, his Glenwood teammates elected him captain in 1916.[19]

The Glenwoods practiced every night the week preceding their October 8 game in Wabash, because they had a tentative booking with the Elgin, Illinois, team that was contingent on a good showing against Wabash.[20] The Glenwoods traveled by train from Toledo to Wabash, leaving Saturday night at 7 P.M. When they arrived in Wabash, there was a crowd of fifteen hundred fans who had paid fifty cents each to see the game. The Glenwoods' guarantee was for only about $250, so it stood to be a profitable booking for the Wabash Athletic Association.

It is interesting that a Toledo team would feature a black player in 1916 because, in 1905, when Shelby played the Toledo Maroons in Toledo, Shelby halfback Charles Follis was jeered by the crowd, until the Toledo Maroon captain Jack Tattersall addressed the crowd by saying, "Don't call Follis a nigger. He is a gentleman and a clean player and please don't call him that!" Tattersall was applauded for his sentiment, and Follis was not molested during the rest of the game.[21]

By contrast, however, when the Wabash team learned that there was a black player on the Toledo team, "they absolutely refused to play against the darky."[22] Racial prejudice was taught at an early age to young people in Indiana and elsewhere around the country. Prevailing attitudes were reflected in the Wabash High School class yell created by their junior class in 1911, which ran, "Nigger, nigger, hot potater. Half past alligator. Ram, ram, bulla-gam. Chi-awa-daw, 1911, Rah! Rah! Rah!"[23]

This is how the Wabash daily newspaper reported the events of October 8, 1916:

At 2:30 o'clock the sidelines were crowded and the bleachers were full. A few minutes later the Toledo players appeared on the field. They were a husky bunch of speedy young fellows and all indications were that they really could play football. Fans, however, noted something unusual in their team—that their captain was a negro—a big fellow by the name of Frame [sic], who, according to the line up was scheduled to hold the position of fullback.

Clarence "Smoke" Fraim, fullback, Toledo Glenwoods 1914–16, graduated
from Toledo Central High School, where he was a football star when this picture was taken in 1912. *(Toledo-Lucus County Public Library, Library Legacy Foundation.)*

It was three o'clock when the W.A.A. eleven made their appearance on the field. The local boys took one glance at their opponents and saw the negro. A short practice followed and then the referee signaled the players to start the game. The Toledo bunch formed in line but the Wabash eleven retained their seats at the west side line of the field. They or a majority of them refused to start the game if the negro captain of the team was permitted to play. A consultation between the managers of the two teams followed and at one time the big darky consented to leave the field. But the members of his team were obstinate and refused to play without him. Likewise the W.A.A. players were steadfast in their determination not to play against the African. Captain Milliner of the W.A.A. used every effort to form a team but from among all the regulars and substitutes he could not find eleven men who were willing to play. The Toledo squad then walked from the field and the referee announced to the fans that because of a disagreement that had not been previously settled, the game had been canceled.

Difference in opinions existed in the crowd of fans toward the action of the local players. While the matter of whether or not the negro should be allowed to participate in the game was being argued cried of 'take him out' and 'leave him play' arose from all parts of the field. Many fans, however, gave their opinion that the W.A.A. men were right in their determination not to play against the negro.

Those who had paid admission to the field were refunded their money as they left the gates or given tickets to next Sunday's game, in which the Pine Village eleven will meet the W.A.A. on the local field.

Captain Frame of the Toledo squad disbanded his team here Sunday night when a disagreement arose over the afternoon's affair. It is said that the Toledo men left in defiance of their captain's orders who wished them to play without him. All future games which had been booked by the Toledo association were canceled last night.

In truth, the Glenwoods did not cancel their remaining games. On October 16, they played the Detroit Harvards.[24]

While this was the only incident of overt racism in professional football in 1916, it was not the only incident in Indiana in 1916. On October 27, 1916, Tufts University went to Bloomington, Indiana, to play the University of Indiana. Among Tufts' squad of twenty-two players were two African-Americans, Brown and Morrison, their starting tackle and guard, respectively. The Hotel English refused to give the black players a room or allow them to eat in their main dining room. Tufts officials threatened to refuse to play the game with Indiana University if the hotel would not make accommodations available to the African-American players. Because thirty-five thousand tickets had been sold, University of Indiana officials effected a compromise by hiring a private dining room for the black players and forcing the hotel to give them a room.[25]

Fortunately, professional football never erected formal barriers against African-American players, although George Halas, George Preston Marshall, and Art Rooney instituted a "gentlemen's agreement," honored by Joe Carr, that excluded African-American players from the league between 1933 and 1946.[26] Team owners like Frank Neid of the Akron Pros, Alva Andrew Young of the Hammond Pros, and Walter H. Flannigan of the Rock Island Independents hired African-American players during the formative years of the NFL. Among the most notable stars of these National Football League teams were African-Americans Bob Marshall, Frederick "Fritz" Pollard, Paul Robeson, Fred "Duke" Slater, Jay Mayo "Inky" Williams, Edward "Sol" Butler, and John Shelburne.[27]

25. Fort Wayne Friars: Indiana Champions, 1916

True to their promise, the Fort Wayne Friars set out to establish a team of all-stars and to upgrade their schedule to professional status. Instead of playing weak independent teams, they scheduled games with Dayton, Hammond, Detroit, Cincinnati, and Pine Village, overall much higher caliber teams than in 1915. Of course, some mistakes were made in the process. Unaware that the Gym-Cadet players had signed with the Dayton Triangles, the Friars scheduled the Gym-Cadets, only to end up with the industrial league Dayton Munitions parading as the Gym-Cadets. Otherwise, the 1916 Friars' schedule was as difficult as that of the Cleveland Indians, the Detroit Heralds, or the Canton Bulldogs.

The first indication that the Friars were determined to build an all-star lineup came in mid-September when quarterback Kent "Skeet" Lambert was allowed to sign up with the Detroit Heralds, and the Friars announced that they "landed Charles Dorais for the season." The *Fort Wayne Journal-Gazette* declared,

Next Sunday's game at League Park marks the close of the baseball season and the Friars will then begin work on the gridiron. The playing field will be extended across the diamond and will make possible the use of the grandstands, which will enable the club to handle much larger crowds than was the case in the past. Bleachers will also be constructed at the north end of the grandstand and along the entire east side of the playing field. This will give the Friars one of the largest and best football fields in the middle west.

The Friar football management made a lucky strike when it landed Charles Dorais. . . . The clever youngster is a product of Notre Dame University and he was made All-American quarterback in 1914, the greatest honor to be attained by a footballer.[1]

Charles E. "Gus" Dorais was born July 2, 1891, in Chippewa Falls, Wisconsin, the son of David Dorais. After graduating from high school, in 1910, he entered the University of Notre Dame, where he roomed with Knute Rockne. Only five feet, seven inches tall, and 140 to 145

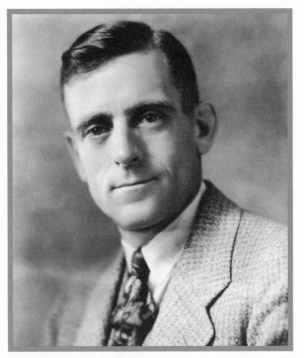

Charles "Gus" Dorais, quarterback, Massillon Tigers 1915–16 and Fort Wayne
Friars 1916–17, traveled by train from Dubuque, Iowa, to play Sunday foot-
ball. After helping to make Notre Dame a national football power as an All-
American, Dorais coached at Columbia College (Dubuque), Notre Dame,
Gonzoga University, and the University of Detroit. *(Portrait by Lee F. Redman, De-
troit; University of Detroit-Mercy Archives.)*

pounds, he endured sarcastic remarks by the Notre Dame coach before
he played quarterback and, in 1912, as team captain, led Notre Dame to
its first undefeated season. The following summer, Rockne and Dorais
worked at Cedar Point Amusement Park in Sandusky, Ohio, and spent
their spare time practicing the forward pass to take advantage of new
rules allowing longer forward passes. So far as can be determined, Dorais was the first one to throw a football by the overhand method, off
his ear with a snap that is akin to the throw of a catcher in baseball. The
result was an arching, "fluffy" pass that was easy to catch. In fall 1913,
Dorais and Rockne stunned the eastern football establishment by completing twelve consecutive passes and defeating unbeaten Army at West
Point. The win marked the rise of Notre Dame as a national football
power and earned Dorais All-American honors. After he graduated, in
1914, with a bachelor of law degree, he became athletic director and

football, basketball, and baseball coach at Columbia College in Dubuque, Iowa, where his football team won nineteen, lost nine, and tied two over four years. He also earned a masters degree. In November 1915, Dorais played three games for the Massillon Tigers, winning two and losing only the final disputed game. Dorais played for both Fort Wayne and Massillon in 1916, choosing the team with the most challenging and important game. He ended up playing five games for Fort Wayne and three for Massillon, which did not endear him to either team.

In 1917, Dorais played nearly all season with the Fort Wayne Friars, traveling there on Saturday evening and returning home by Monday afternoon. The following year, Dorais entered the U.S. Army and was appointed director of sports at Camp MacArthur in Waco, Texas, where he coached an undefeated team. That same year, Knute Rockne became head coach at Notre Dame. In 1919, after the war, Rockne hired Dorais as his assistant. The following year, Dorais became athletic director and head football, basketball, and baseball coach at Gonzaga University in Spokane, where his football team won twenty, lost thirteen, and tied three football games.[2] From 1925 until football was dropped in 1942 because of World War II, Dorais was athletic director and head football coach at the University of Detroit. During his eighteen years there, the Titans became a Midwest football power, winning nineteen consecutive games from 1927 to 1929. His overall record at Detroit was 113 wins, forty-eight losses, and seven ties.[3]

In 1937, he coached the first college All-Stars to a 6–0 win over the NFL champion Green Bay Packers. Dorais became coach of the Detroit Lions in 1943 and transformed them into a winning team over the next two years. In 1948, his contract to coach the Lions was not renewed. His overall pro coaching record was twenty wins, thirty-one losses, and two ties.[4]

On September 18, Keith "Deacon" Jones entered the Friars training camp. Jones played left tackle at Notre Dame, from 1912 through 1914, and, after the college season ended, he played professional football for the Akron Indians. The next year, he was appointed assistant coach at Notre Dame and on Sundays played right tackle for the Massillon Tigers. In 1916, Deacon played for the Fort Wayne Friars. He joined the U.S. Army in 1917 and was assigned to officers' training corps at Fort Taylor in Louisville, Kentucky. After the war, he played a game or two with the Fort Wayne Vets, a professional football team.[5]

Howard "Cap" Edwards joined the Friars squad on September 24,

1916.[6] Joe Pliska also joined the locals that day. Within a week, Frank Checkaye, Alvin "Heine" Berger, Don Peters, and Al Feeney joined the team.[7]

On opening day, October 1, the Friars launched their season against the Dayton Munitions team, billed as the Dayton Gym-Cadets. The industrial team was no match for the improved Friars. The final score was 101 to 0. Dayton made only four first downs in the game, each because of a Friar penalty, and never threatened to score.[8]

The next week, the Friars played the up-and-coming Hammond Clabbys. The Clabbys brought three hundred fans on a Nickel Plate Railroad special. Hammond was earnest about challenging the Friars for the state championship of independent football. The excitement generated by Clabbys fans led the *Fort Wayne Journal-Gazette* to observe "the professional game is changing rapidly . . . and is forcing its way forward until it now comes pretty close to being the equal of the college game. The fans are gradually acquiring the real college spirit as was demonstrated time and again yesterday at League Park."[9]

The game was a hard-fought contest before twenty-six hundred fans. Ironically, Friars halfback Ralph "Bull" Young, who grew up near Hammond, scored the only touchdown of the game. Young's touchdown, together with a field goal by Dorais, made the final score Fort Wayne 9, Hammond 0. Only depth of personnel and greater experience permitted the Friars to win the game.[10]

Several of the Fort Wayne out-of-town stars did not play in the third game. The starting lineup featured Chris Chambers and Baird at ends, Deac Jones and Cap Edwards at tackles, Wilkins and Al Feeney at guards, Dan Ball at center, and Checkaye, Johnson (an assumed name for I. R. Martin), Pliska, and Ralph "Bull" Young in the backfield.[11] Charles Dorais did not play for Fort Wayne. He wired the Friars' management that his leg was still giving him trouble and asked to be excused from the game.[12] In the first half, the ex-Carlisles of Detroit played the Friars to a scoreless tie. In the second half, I. R. Martin and Joe Pliska engineered a rally in which the Friars scored twenty-seven points.[13]

On October 22, the Friars played the Cincinnati Celts. The Celts were led by David Reese, George Roudebush, Tilly Schuessler, and Chet "Shine" Knab. The Celts were defeated by the Detroit Heralds in their opening game, so by most measures the Friars were favored to win the game.

The Celts came to Fort Wayne with numbered uniforms so that the fans could identify the players with a published program or the pregame newspaper lineup. The Friars responded by giving each of their players a letter of the alphabet.[14] The Friars also declared the game "kids day" and permitted all youngsters fifteen years of age and under to enter the game free if they picked up a ticket before game day.[15] The Friars hired Notre Dame lineman J. Hugh "Pepper" O'Donnell to play guard. O'Donnell played center for Notre Dame in 1914 and 1915. After graduating, he entered Congregation a Sancta Seminary at Notre Dame. The Congregation of the Holy Cross is the order that oversees Notre Dame. The Friars announced in 1916 that Pepper O'Donnell had suited up for five games. However, he played in only three games, and it seems likely that he was only hired for those games. He played against the Cincinnati Celts as a guard, against the Elyria Athletics as a center, and against the Wabash Athletic Association as an end. His play for Fort Wayne was generally noteworthy. After the Cincinnati Celt game, the *Fort Wayne Journal-Gazette* reported, "O'Donnell and Feeney certainly balanced the center of the Fort Wayne line. They made numerous tackles in the open and generally brought their man down with a crash." On November 27, the paper reported, "O'Donnell is a center but one would not have thought so yesterday. He took the vacant place on end and put up a wonderful game, his defensive play being just about perfect. Wabash made no gain around . . . O'Donnell." In 1922, Pepper O'Donnell was assigned to work with Knute Rockne on stadium operations and alumni events, and, by 1927, Father O'Donnell was the prefect of discipline for Notre Dame. In 1935, he was appointed vice-president, and, in 1940, he became president of Notre Dame, an office that he held until 1946.[16]

The Friars attracted another big crowd for the Celts game. Players on both teams welcomed the colder weather. The Celts scored six points in the first quarter on a pass from George Roudebush to Tilly Schuessler. Fort Wayne later countered with their own touchdown. The balance of the game was a defensive struggle. Schuessler, the Cincinnati captain, was a particular standout on defense. He intercepted three passes and was one of the leading tacklers. Roudebush and Albert Bessmeyer were also strong defensively for the Celts. The Friars, however, missed three field goals. Pepper O'Donnell saved the day for the Friars when he intercepted a pass in the third quarter as the Celts were threatening to score. The game ended in a 6–6 tie.[17] The Celts had stoked their mental fires, while the Friars failed to play at peak performance. They needed to turn up their game a notch or two if they hoped to contend for the

Ralph H. "Bull" Young, fullback, Fort Wayne Friars 1916–17; Hammond Clabbies 1916; Chicago Tigers 1920. He grew up in Crown Point, Indiana, spent his freshman year in college at the University of Chicago, and his last three years at Washington and Jefferson College, where he was considered by some to be an All-American. In 1916, he coached at DePauw University. Later, he coached at Michigan State University before becoming their Athletic Director until 1954. *(Washington and Jefferson College Archives.)*

state independent football championship of Indiana. They needed to show more drive, desire, and determination, of the type exhibited by Pepper O'Donnell.

On October 29, the Friars faced the Elyria (Ohio) Athletics led by Jack Ambrose, the Elyria High School football coach, who had played quarterback for the University of Maine. The Athletics only brought eighteen players[18] but promised Fort Wayne a gritty game. The Friars won 24–13 to end the first half of their season undefeated.

Pine Village, the Indiana state independent football champions, came to play in Fort Wayne for the first time on November 5. Pine Village was coming off the first loss in the team's history. The Cincinnati Celts defeated them 9–6 in Lafayette, Indiana, on October 29. Not used to losing, Pine Village was certain to be a very tough opponent for the Friars. Coached by their star tackle, Edgar C. "Big Ed" Davis,[19] Pine Village had a strong lineup, with plenty of college experience. Big Ed had graduated from Indiana University in 1914 and was currently an assistant football coach there. At five feet nine inches tall, he weighed two hundred pounds. He played professional football until 1922, when he ended his career with the Columbus Panhandles. Left tackle Matthew Winters, at six feet two inches and two hundred pounds, played as well on the left side as Davis did on the right side of the Pine Village line. Winters was not only a good football player but an outstanding scholar. In 1915, he was awarded a $2000 scholarship at Indiana University as the senior "who had attained greatest proficiency in athletic and scholastic work."[20]

In addition to Davis and Winters, Pine Village started Howard "Cub" Buck and Emmett G. Keefe at guards, Clair Scott at left end, and Arthur C. Krause at right end. The Pine Village backfield featured Harold "Irish" Sheridan, Ray Fenters, Richard King, and Bill Williams at fullback.[21] David Earl "Kinks" Hawthorne came off the bench to relieve Howard Buck.

David Hawthorne was born in West Point, Indiana and grew up on a farm near Wingate. He entered DePauw University in Greencastle in fall 1908, where he played left guard for four years and basketball for three years. Later, when he was asked what he did at DePauw, he responded, "Course pursued—Liberal Athletics, with especial glory in two." He claimed to be "a faithful striver in every form of athletics on campus."[22] Hawthorne[23] graduated from DePauw, in 1912, and attended Indiana University Medical School, where Ed Davis recruited him to play for Pine Village.

Edgar C. "Big Ed" Davis, tackle and coach, Pine Village Athletic Club 1915–17; tackle, Canton Bulldogs 1915; Fort Wayne Friars 1915; guard, Hammond Pros 1920; Dayton Triangles 1920–21; and Columbus Panhandles 1921–22. He was team captain as an undergraduate at Indiana University and, later, as a medial student, assistant coach along with Jim Thorpe. At five feet nine inches and two hundred pounds, "Big Ed" often dominated the line of scrimmage. He later practiced medicine in Muncie, Indiana. *(Indiana University Archives.)*

Clair Scott, the Pine Village left end, was also an achiever at Indiana University, where he was president of his senior class.[24]

Gus Dorais led the Friars against Pine Village. Notre Dame alumni Edwards, Jones, Feeney, and Pliska were a large part of his supporting cast. Dan Ball, I. R. Martin, Joseph D. Trimble (of Rose Poly Tech), and Chris Chambers were also in the Friars' supporting cast, along with Young, Hunter, Smith, and Daley.[25] The Friars controlled the line of scrimmage most of the afternoon. The hard running of Pliska, with downfield blocking by Dorais and Feeney, set up Fort Wayne's two scoring opportunities. Dorais tallied the only touchdown of the afternoon in the third quarter on a short-yardage run. He also kicked the extra point. The *Fort Wayne Journal-Gazette* sportswriter observed, "Every minute of the contest was hard fought by Pine Village." But Chris Chambers blocked a drop kick that kept Pine Village scoreless. For the second week in a row, Pine Village suffered a loss.[26]

According to the Fort Wayne sportswriter, "They don't make better sports than Ed Davis. After the game he complimented the Friar players on their victory and said that his team had never received better treatment than they got here." The *Journal-Gazette* went on to say, "all of the Pine Village players are strong for Davis and that is the reason that they are playing there instead of other places where they might get more money." The balance of the Fort Wayne schedule figured to be as difficult as the Pine Village game. The Evanston North Ends, "probably the largest drawing card in professional football," were the Friars' next opponent.[27]

Dorais reported sick for the game against Evanston,[28] and Frank "Coonie" Checkaye took his place at quarterback. Allen H. "Mal" Elward[29] replaced Trimble at left end. Elward was an outstanding left end at Notre Dame, where he played on the varsity eleven all four years. In 1917, he joined the armed services but played one professional game for the Friars against Racine. Later that year, he played for the Newport Naval Reserve team in Rhode Island against Yale. After World War I, he became head football coach and athletic director at Purdue University.

Evanston only brought fifteen players to Fort Wayne for the game. They had never been beaten by the Friars and expected to continue their dominance over them.[30] Two of Evanston's star backs, Penn Carolan and John Barrett, had deserted the team and were now playing for the Toledo Maroons.[31] Baggs Miller and Eissler were playing in their stead. Gene Schobinger, normally a halfback, started at left end, while Fitzgerald was starting at right end. This was not the strongest eleven used by the North Ends that season.

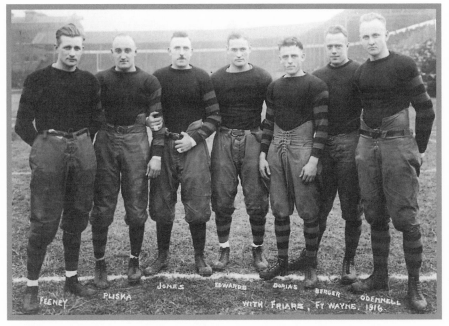

Nine Notre Dame alumni played for the Fort Wayne Friars in 1916. The seven featured in this picture, taken on October 29, 1916, at League Park before the game with Elyria, are: Al Feeney, center; Joe Pliska, halfback; Keith "Deac" Jones, tackle; Howard "Cap" Edwards, tackle; Charles "Gus" Dorais, quarterback; Alvin "Heine" Berger, halfback; and Hugh "Pepper" O'Donnell, guard and center. In 1940, O'Donnell became president of the University of Notre Dame. Al Feeney became major of Indianapolis, and "Gus" Dorais coached the Detroit Lions from 1943–47. *(The University of Notre Dame Archives.)*

The Fort Wayne front seven and the defensive play of Chris Chambers were again the deciding factors in the game. The Friars' line manhandled what was left of Evanston's famed "million dollar line," and Chambers interrupted the North Ends' passing and kicking games. Checkaye scored a touchdown in the first quarter for the Friars, and Pliska finished the scoring in the third quarter, when he tallied a touchdown and Feeney kicked the extra point. Elward, Daley, and Deac Jones were cited for their good defensive play. Rube Johnson made a twenty-five-yard run for Evanston, but Coonie Checkaye forced the play to the sideline, where Johnson was knocked out of bounds to avert a touchdown. Robert Specht also played a strong game for the North Ends, but the rest of the team did not play up to par. The Friars won the game 14–0.[32]

The state championship was on the line when Fort Wayne played Wabash on November 19. Despite Fort Wayne's undefeated season, most observers picked Wabash to win.[33] Although Fort Wayne was the leading contender for the state title, in twelve years of competition they had never defeated Wabash. Indeed, they did not even score against Wabash until 1915. Moreover, Wabash was also anxious to win because a victory would put them back into the thick of the title race. There were all sorts of stories regarding the various ringers that Wabash had allegedly hired for the game. The names Jim Thorpe and Frank Blocker were among them.[34]

More than fifty-two hundred fans paid to see the game. The Friars claimed it was the largest crowd to see a professional football game in the history of northern Indiana. Fort Wayne's "Howling Hundred" fan club met on Saturday evening and again an hour before the game to practice their yells. Nearly four hundred fans traveled to Fort Wayne from Wabash on a special train, and scores made the trip by automobile. Wabash even brought their own band to the game.[35] The round-trip train ticket was $1.30, and admission to the game was fifty cents. Both sides had enough fans to generate plenty of noise while cheering for their favorites.

The match-up between twenty-six-year-old Harry Routh, the left tackle for Wabash, and Howard "Cap" Edwards, the right tackle for Fort Wayne, was one of the keys to victory for each team. Both players weighed in at about two hundred pounds, were about the same age, and had similar levels of experience, and each helped determine the tenacity of their team's line play. The match-ups between Homer T. Showalter and Mal Elward and between Doc Redmond and Wilkins also would be telling. While Showalter and Elward were evenly matched, Wilkins was likely to need help against Doc Redmond. Showalter was a four-year letterman at right end for Wabash College, and Elward was second only to Knute Rockne as a star end at Notre Dame during his tenure there. On the other hand, Doc Redmond, at 210 pounds, had just graduated from Indiana University, while Wilkins was only a sandlot player. Any advantage that Wabash might have at guard was more than offset by the appearance of Gus Dorais at quarterback for Fort Wayne. Still, the Yarnelle brothers, Red Milliner, and Dutch Bergman were great offensive weapons for Wabash. The game promised to be an even contest.

Sunday, November 20 in Fort Wayne was ideal for football. The *Wabash Plain Dealer* reported, "The Friars kicked off to Wabash shortly after two thirty. Kenneth Yarnelle received the ball and returned it twenty yards." The Friars held on downs, and Wabash was forced to

punt. The entire first quarter was a seesaw battle for territory, with neither team winning much ground. In the second period, Fort Wayne got
close enough to try a field goal but failed to score. Finally, after an exchange of punts, Dorais made a big run around right end and scored
Fort Wayne's first touchdown. The Friars missed the extra point, so the
first half ended with Fort Wayne leading 6–0.

Dutch Bergman relieved Red Milliner at halfback in the second half.
Midway into the third quarter, Smith, the Friars' reserve halfback,
fumbled the ball. Kenneth Yarnelle, the Wabash left halfback, picked
up the fumble and ran sixty yards to tie the score. Harry Routh kicked
the point after touchdown, giving Wabash a 7–6 lead. Well into the
fourth quarter, it appeared that Wabash's luck would hold, giving them
the victory. However, after getting the ball on a punt nearly midway
into the period, Dorias threw a long forward pass to Earl Huntington,
the Friars' player-coach. Huntington took the ball to within twelve
yards of the goal line. The *Plain Dealer* reported, "Eight successive line
smashes and Pliska scored the Friars' second and decisive marker." The
point after touchdown made the final score 13–7.[36]

On that same afternoon, the Toledo Maroons tied the Pine Village
Athletic Club in a scoreless game held in Toledo. Given the Maroons'
mediocre record, Pine Village was virtually eliminated from the Indiana state championship. Concurrently, Hammond was losing to Davenport 14 to 12, removing any remote prospect they had of challenging
Fort Wayne for the title.

The return engagement between Wabash and Fort Wayne in
Wabash was played for pride. With victories over Hammond, Pine Village, and Wabash, the Fort Wayne Friars had already wrapped up the
state championship, but the Friars had their sights set on an undefeated
season. The Fort Wayne players did not like traveling to Wabash because the locker room facilities for visitors did not have showers. Moreover, the playing field was ringed in tightly by a barbed wire fence just
five feet or so from the sideline. It could be hazardous to run out of
bounds at Carroll Field. To make matters worse for Fort Wayne,
Charles Dorais decided to finish the season playing for Massillon. Massillon was playing Canton for the world championship of professional
football, and that was far more rewarding than playing Wabash and
Columbus in an effort to achieve an undefeated season. After all, Fort
Wayne had already clinched the state title and stood little to no chance
of challenging Canton or Massillon for the national championship.

One thousand Fort Wayne football enthusiasts braved a cold, rainy day and traveled fifty miles southwest to witness the Friars play Wabash. The Notre Dame contingent in the Friars' starting lineup was increased to include Pepper O'Donnell, who played left end, and Heine Berger, who replaced Pliska, out with an injured leg. Coonie Checkaye took over for Dorais at quarterback. Wabash added ex-Notre Dame full-back Eddie Duggan, former Indiana University guard Doc Redmond, and Purdue University tackle Harry Routh. Otherwise, their team was made up of hometown players, only one of whom had gone to college, though some, like Jesse Reno, were of all-pro caliber. All were experienced and competitive, and they were playing on familiar ground. They had more than four thousand hometown fans in attendance to cheer them on.

By mutual agreement, the quarters were twelve and a half minutes each. For the first forty-five minutes of the game, the teams were score-less. Then, according to the *Wabash Plain Dealer*,

By a splendid big forward pass [George] Yarnelle to [Ken] Yarnelle the ball was brought to within fifteen yards of the Wabash Athletic Association goal and after six minutes of play had taken place in the forth quarter. Three line plays were tried without avail and then the W.A.A. line formed a place kick. [Harry] Routh, left tackle, was the hero. Planting his toe heavily on the pig skin, the ball soared through the air and directly between the goal posts.[37]

Wabash won the game 3–0 before the capacity crowd. Each home team in the Wabash-Fort Wayne series had guaranteed the visiting team $750. At fifty cents a ticket, each home team grossed approximately $2,600 before expenses. After paying the visitors' guarantee, referees' fees, and miscellaneous expenses, each netted $1750, out of which they paid the players and coaches, and underwrote team operating costs.[38]

Fort Wayne finished their season on Thanksgiving. They hired Jack Ambrose to replace Dorais at quarterback. When Ambrose played for Elyria on October 29, he scored two touchdowns against the Friars. They also had to play without Joe Pliska, who was recovering from blood poisoning.[39] Despite the absence of two of their stars, Fort Wayne played a plucky game. The surprise hero of the game was Albert Feeney. Feeney was riding high, having just entered the airplane man-ufacturing business as president of the American Aircraft Company of Anderson, Indiana.[40] The Fort Wayne paper describes the Friars' Thanksgiving victory this way:

Albert Aeroplane Feeney, all the way from America's interurban center, Indi-anapolis talked place-kicking to Coach Byroades and Captain Edwards ever since Sunday, and he got his chance yesterday afternoon, delivering a boot from the fifteen-yard line in the second quarter and thereby winning for the Fort Wayne eleven over the Columbus Panhandles 3 to 0 in the final game of the season.[41]

Nineteen-sixteen was the Friars' best year. When the National Football League was formed, they did not choose to join it. While the Friars had good teams in 1917, in 1920, and for a few years thereafter, they would never match the 8–1–1 record of 1916, when they were the professional football champions of Indiana.

26. Fort Wayne Fizzles, 1917

About half of the 1916 Indiana State independent football championship team returned to the Friars' starting lineup. For most of the professional football world, the 1917 season began on October 7. Patriotic themes abounded. The Fort Wayne Friars played Camp Custer, the team from the newly constructed cantonment near Battle Creek, Michigan. The Camp Custer team was composed of former professional and college stars who practiced every day as part of their of military conditioning. The Fort Wayne backfield still featured Charles "Gus" Dorais at quarterback. According to the *Canton Repository,* October 15, 1917, Gus told Massillon that he could not play for them because he would soon be entering the army. But as it turned out, he was inducted after the football season. Also in the backfield were Joe Pliska and I. R. Martin (playing under the assumed name Johnson), with the old veteran Chris Chambers at fullback. They had Earl D. Huntington[1] at right end and Al Feeney at center. However, several important linemen were missing. Howard "Cap" Edwards returned to Canton to play for the Bulldogs, Freeman Fitzgerald decided to play for the Massillon Tigers, Keith "Deac" Jones was in the army and unable to play for Fort Wayne every Sunday, and Hugh "Pepper" O'Donnell was busy with ecclesiastical pursuits at Notre Dame.

The new recruits for the Friars front seven were not quite on par with the missing guards and tackles. Lee Percy Mehlig, Lockwood, Tom Shaughnessy, and Wanzer could not contain the Camp Custer eleven nor open the holes on offense necessary to defeat a team led by Harry Costello, Neno Jerry Da Prato, William "Blake" Miller, William O'Neill, and William Ward, all of whom were outstanding college and professional football players before entering the U.S. Army. Jerry Da Prato had earned All-American honors while at Michigan Agricultural College.[2] Harry Costello nearly matched Jim Thorpe in play while they were teammates in Canton in 1916, and O'Neill and Ward were tough, solid linesmen. Dorais started at quarterback for Fort Wayne. Tom

Shaughnessy, Moses Bashaw, and Robert Specht took the train from Chicago to play for the Friars. All three had been with the Evanston North Ends in 1916. Fort Wayne also started at guard a former All-State high school player by the name of Lockwood.

Toward the end of the second quarter, fullback Langhoff scored the only touchdown of the game for Camp Custer. In the fourth quarter, Harry Costello drop-kicked a twenty-five-yard field goal to give Camp Custer a 9–0 lead. "The game was one of the prettiest seen here [in Fort Wayne] in several seasons," according to the *Fort Wayne Journal-Gazette*. Camp Custer's winning advantage was practice time, with the resulting advantage in teamwork. Teamwork gave them a 9–0 win before two thousand witnesses.[3]

The Friars dedicated their second game to benefit the American Red Cross, and half of the net proceeds were promised to them. Their opponents were the ever-popular Carlisle Indians from Detroit. The hometown crowd enjoyed seeing the Friars defeat the "Redskins." The Friars were able to arrange a weekend pass for Keith "Deac" Jones to travel from Fort Taylor in Louisville, Kentucky.[4] They also recruited Walter E. Berghoff, son of a local German brewer, to play for them.[5]

The Friars made easy work of the Carlisle Indians of Detroit, who knew enough not to take the game too seriously. Fort Wayne scored eight touchdowns and a field goal to win 56–0. Walter Berghoff and Ralph "Bull" Young each scored twice and Pliska, Ambrose, Dorais, and Specht each scored one. Ambrose also drop-kicked a field goal. Again two thousand Fort Wayne fans paid to see the game. The entire Fort Wayne team saw action in this crowd pleaser.[6] Ralph "Bull" Young added significantly to Fort Wayne's scoring punch. Currently coaching at DePauw University, Young had been a standout at Washington and Jefferson College[7] after spending his freshman year at the University of Chicago. Later he became director of athletics at Michigan State University, where he presided until 1954.[8]

Up to this point, the Friars had only been charging fifty cents for general admission, when teams like Canton, Massillon, Toledo, and Detroit regularly charged from seventy-five cents to $1.50.[9] On October 21, Fort Wayne increased its price to seventy-five cents for the Celts game.[10] In 1916, the Celts had played Fort Wayne to a 6–6 tie, so no one on the Fort Wayne team was underestimating the Celts. Cincinnati made a natty appearance in their new red jerseys, replacing the green jerseys of earlier years. Neither team scored in the first quarter. In the middle of the second quarter, however, the Friars generated plenty of excitement for the hometown fans. Charles "Gus" Dorais threw a series of passes to Pliska, Huntington, and Berghoff that resulted in touchdowns by Berghoff and Huntington, and extra points kicked by Dorais. Fort Wayne had a 14–0 lead at halftime. The Celts did drive the ball to the Friars' ten yard line late in the second quarter before being stopped on downs.

In the third quarter, Joe Pliska, who was playing one of the best games of his career, made an outstanding catch, leaping to meet the ball, and eluded several tacklers in a forty-yard pass-run combination for a touchdown. When Dorais kicked the extra point, Fort Wayne had a commanding 21–0 lead. Throughout the second half, Fort Wayne played wonderful defense. Deacon Jones and Walter Berghoff were the stars of the defensive line play, and Dorais's punting kept Cincinnati out of good field position. In the fourth quarter, a "pretty forward pass" from Sorenson to Carl Thiele put points on the score board for the Celts. The final score was Fort Wayne 21, Cincinnati 6.[11]

The last Sunday in October found Joe Bergie's Pitcairn Quakers in Fort Wayne against the Friars. Stephen Rowan Crawford was the Quakers' backfield star. At five feet nine inches and 172 pounds, Crawford's punts averaged fifty yards. He did his college prep training at Indiana Normal School Academy in Indiana, Pennsylvania, and played college football at Washington and Jefferson. Pittsburgh sandlot player Buldowsky, at 195 pounds and five feet nine inches, was a strong guard for the Quakers.[12] The game was played on a muddy field at Fort Wayne's League Park. From the outset, the Quakers team outplayed Fort Wayne. They controlled the line of scrimmage behind professional football veterans Joe Bergie, Adams, and Buldowsky in the center of the Pitcairn line. Fort Wayne guards Denny Dennison and Lockwood were out of their depth and were pushed around at will by the Pitcairn veterans. The Quakers took the opening kickoff and moved the ball steadily down the field on line plunges that yielded three to five yards per play. Only a fine play by Walter Berghoff that threw 165-pound quarterback Frank White for a substantial loss stopped the drive. When the Friars gained possession of the ball, Dorais booted the home team out of danger on a quick kick.

The first score came in the second period when the Pitcairn fullback Crawford followed perfect interference from Bradley and went around end for fifteen yards, a run that set up a twenty-yard field goal to give the Pittsburgh suburb a 3–0 lead.[13] Later that quarter, the Friars drove to the Pitcairn one foot line before turning the ball over on downs. Quaker fullback Crawford attempted to punt out of trouble, but the kick was blocked. Pitcairn end Warner dropped on the ball for a safety. The score stood Quakers 3, Friars 2 at halftime.[14] In the third quarter, Dorais attempted a long pass to Joe Pliska, who slipped at a critical moment; Plaxico intercepted the pass and returned the ball thirty yards for a Pitcairn touchdown. When Bradley kicked goal, the visitors led 10–2.[15]

Fort Wayne fought back in the fourth quarter with a solid running game from Specht, Young, and Pliska. A fifteen-yard pass from Dorais to Huntington also helped the cause. Finally, Ralph "Bull" Young broke through the line between tackle and end for five yards, then on the next play went around end for a Friars touchdown. Dorais kicked the extra point, making the score 10–9 in favor of the Quakers. The Friars had one last scoring opportunity but could not convert, and lost a game they had been favored to win.[16] Twenty-five hundred fans paid to see the contest.[17]

On the first Sunday in November, the Toledo Maroons came to Fort Wayne to oppose the Friars. It was the first meeting between these two clubs and the third straight out-of-town game for the Maroons this season. Five hundred youngsters under sixteen years of age were the guests of the Friar management as a way of building greater fan support.[18] The game was sold as likely to be the Friars' hardest game of the season. Fort Wayne added Charles Helvie at end to improve their defense and strengthen their passing attack, but it was hardly necessary. The Toledo Maroons were a pale imitation of their 1915 team and put up little fight against the Friars. Fort Wayne scored in every quarter and never fell behind. Specht, Helvie, and Berghoff each scored a touchdown, and Pliska and Ambrose scored two each in the 45 to 7 rout of Toledo. The entire Friars team got an opportunity to play in a game in which they did no wrong.[19]

The Indiana State professional football championship took a curious turn on November 4, 1917. The Hammond Clabbys beat Pine Village Athletic Club 13 to 0 in Indianapolis, while Wabash was crushed in Detroit 35 to 0. Consequently, with only three weeks left in the season, the four leading teams in Indiana had nearly identical records, and no single team was emerging as the favorite for the state championship.

The Racine Regulars followed Toledo into Fort Wayne. Having recently defeated the Hammond Clabbys, the Racine Regulars had one of their best teams. On November 10, I. R. Martin (playing again as Johnson) let Friars management know that he might be available to play a couple of additional games this season for Fort Wayne. After the opening game, Martin signed to play with the Massillon Tigers, but now that Massillon hired Charles Brickley at halfback, Martin was no longer needed and was looking to finish the season with Fort Wayne.[20] He was not needed for the Racine game, though he did play later for Fort Wayne. The Friars hired Mal Elward as a back-up end, but otherwise stayed with their regular lineup. After a scoreless first quarter, the Friars made two touchdowns in the second and two more in the third quarters, while holding Racine without a score. Except for Norman "Tango" Glockson, who played well for Racine, the balance of the team seemed overmatched. The Friars' passing game scored the first touchdown on a pass from Dorais to Elward. Running plays by Ralph "Bull" Young, Robert Specht, and Gus Dorais accounted for the balance of the scoring. Accurate kicking yielded all four extra points by Dorais.[21]

Having lost to Hammond the week before, Pine Village had hopes of defeating their perennial rival, the Wabash Athletic Association. Pine Village had defeated Wabash three straight times, including a 2–0 win earlier in the season. The 1917 season had not been kind to Wabash. They were in danger of having the first losing record in the history of their Athletic Association. Coonie Checkaye almost made amends for the fumble that caused Wabash its loss against Pine Village earlier in the year by recovering a fumble and racing thirty yards for a touchdown, only to have it called back on an offside penalty on Frank Allen, the Wabash defensive end. Fortunately, Guil Falcon was able to move the ball in the second quarter when the Wabash eleven marched eighty yards in a sustained drive topped off by Falcon's plunge that resulted in the game's only score.[22]

At the end of the day on Sunday, November 11, the four major professional teams in Indiana had nearly identical records. Fort Wayne and Hammond were 4 and 2, while Pine Village was 3–1–2, and Wabash was 3 and 3. Hence, with just two weeks left in the regular season, Pine Village, Wabash, Fort Wayne, and Hammond all had a shot at the Indiana independent football championship.

The Friars hired Glockson to finish the season with them, to strengthen their line. On November 18, Fort Wayne played the Columbus Panhandles. This was always a popular game, because Fort Wayne was a railroad town and the Columbus players were nearly all employees of the Panhandle district of the Pennsylvania Railroad Company. But the 1917 Panhandle team was not up to its usual high standards. The normally close game between the two teams was an easy victory for the home team. Fort Wayne won the game 13–0.

Meanwhile, the Hammond Clabbys defeated Wabash to eliminate them from the championship, and Pine Village played a one-sided game against the 328th Machine Gun Battalion to stay in contention for the state title. November 25 was bound to decide the players in the championship, because Fort Wayne played Wabash and Hammond played Pine Village on that date.

Fort Wayne and Wabash were bitter rivals. The Friars had only defeated Wabash once in the previous seventeen years, so the game was likely to be bitterly fought with the possibility of roughness and fights from both sides. The Friars hired Knute Rockne and Notre Dame's star center, Frank Rydzewski, for this critical game. Rydzewski grew up in Chicago and was an All-American center at Notre Dame in 1917. After the close of the 1917 college season, he dropped out of college and started two games with the Fort Wayne Friars before joining the U.S. Army. In 1919, he started for the Hammond All-Stars and, in 1920, he suited up for the Hammond Pros, the Chicago Tigers, and the Cleveland Panthers at tackle as well as center. In 1921–22, he joined the Chicago Cardinals. In 1923, he played for the Chicago Bears and the Hammond Pros. In 1925, he also played for the Milwaukee Badgers, but he continued to represent Hammond until 1928.[23] Notre Dame closed their football season near Pittsburgh on the Saturday before the Wabash game, so Rockne and Rydzewski had to catch a train west to Fort Wayne after their Saturday game and play on Sunday with relatively little rest.

The Friars kicked off to Wabash. John "Doc" Redmond received the ball for Wabash and returned it twenty yards. However, after three running plays failed to make first down yardage, Wabash punted. The two teams traded punts before Fort Wayne began to move the ball. A forty-five-yard pass from Dorais to Pliska gave the Friars good field position, but they were stopped once they got inside the twenty yard line, first by a fumble that lost yardage and then by a blocked punt. However, as soon as the Friars regained possession of the ball, they resumed their march into Wabash territory on runs by Robert Specht and Joe Pliska. Late in the first quarter, Pliska put Fort Wayne ahead 7–0.[24] Red Milliner, a seventeen-year veteran, was playing an impressive game. The old man made fifteen yards around left end. Then Guilford Falcon reeled off ten more yards before fumbling. The Friars recovered the ball. On the ensuing play, Joe Pliska ran for another touchdown, but the Friars were holding on the play and the ball was brought back to the twenty-five yard line as a penalty. At that point, the Wabash line became a stone wall. The Friars tried a passing attack but failed to score.

Late in the second quarter, Jesse Reno ran sixty-five yards for what appeared to be a Wabash touchdown, but it was ruled that he stepped out of bounds. No further threats were made by either side, and the half ended with Fort Wayne ahead by a touchdown.[25]

The game was evenly played during most of the second half. Rydzewski was a "tower of strength to the entire [Fort Wayne] line."[26] Wabash tried a fake drop kick, run play but was unable to fool Fort Wayne. Later, a punt by Wabash was mishandled by Gus Dorais who dropped the ball. Specht tried to recover the loose ball, but Homer T. Showalter fell on the fumble. Then a pass from Milliner to Showalter moved the chains forward for Wabash. After a couple of successful short runs, Guil Falcon tied the score with a touchdown and an extra point by Alfred "Dutch" Bergman.[27] The game ended in a 7–7 tie. Since Pine Village defeated Hammond, Fort Wayne was scheduled to play Hammond on December 2 for the state title. Hammond had a 6–3 record going into the game, and Fort Wayne had a 4–2–1 record. Both teams had lost games by narrow margins and might well have won an extra game with a field goal or a missed opportunity of one kind or another.

The last game of the season was played in Hammond on December 2. The Friars took a special sleeper on the Nickel Plate line and arrived in Hammond at 6:45 Sunday morning. They fielded nearly the same team that played Wabash, except I. R. Martin (still playing as Johnson) replaced Robert Specht at halfback, and Knute Rockne was coaching Massillon against Canton.[28] A good-sized delegation accompanied the Fort Wayne players to Hammond. Wearing black and gold, the Friars were ready for their cross-state rivals. As it turned out, Hammond was also ready for Fort Wayne. They hired Emmett G. Keefe, the famous Notre Dame left guard, to play right guard. Keefe was born in 1893 and played football for Notre Dame from 1913 to 1915. His weight in college was 180 pounds, and he stood five feet eleven inches tall. In 1916 and 1917, he played professional football for the Pine Village Athletic Club. On December 2, he started for the Hammond Clabbys against the Fort Wayne Friars. During the war, Emmett Keefe[29] became a captain at the Great Lakes Naval Station and was in the 1919 Rose Bowl with the victorious Great Lakes team led by Paddy Driscoll. After the war, Keefe played professional football for the Massillon Tigers, the Chicago Tigers, the Green Bay Packers, the Rock Island Independents, and the Milwaukee Badgers.

The Clabbys scored two touchdowns in the first quarter against Fort Wayne and never looked back. They controlled the ball, played outstanding defense, and mixed their plays well between passing and running. Paddy Driscoll was the star for Hammond. He scored three touchdowns against Fort Wayne, aided by the blocking of Lee Percy Mehlig, Emmett Keefe, Frank Blocker, Wilber Henderson, and C. M. McCardy. Great line play opened the way for Paddy Driscoll and led to the Clabbys' 25–0 victory over the Friars.[30]

This was the last season that Fort Wayne was a professional football contender. In 1919, every effort was made to return professional football to prewar standards. The Friars were replaced by the War Vets, who sought to take advantage of the residual of wartime patriotism. Well known stars such as Walter Berghoff, Jack Ambrose, Freeman Fitzgerald, Deac Jones, Bob Peck, Jesse Reno, Gene Schobinger, and Bart Macomber played for the Vets, but the team garnered little support and did not challenge for a regional championship. Fort Wayne was affiliated with the American Professional Football League for part of the 1921 season but quickly faded from the professional football scene.[31] The city did not have the interest in interregional football that they had in basketball,[32] and the active leadership that promoted the Friars before the war did not respond to the challenge of travel schedules, high risk contracts, or full-time sports promotion.

27. Boosterism and the Hammond Clabbys, 1916

Jimmy Clabby, the welterweight boxing champion of the world in 1910–11 and later a middleweight contender, was from Hammond, Indiana. He owned a cafeteria in his hometown and sponsored an independent football team known as the Hammond Clabbys. The Clabbys were managed by Hartley and played a regional schedule that included the Standard Athletic Club of Chicago, the Chicago Monarchs, the Gary Techs, and the First Regiment of Chicago.[1] The 1915 Clabbys started a number of solid football players, including George Blocker, J. Nolan, George Volkman, and Paul D. "Clinks" Meyers.[2] Clinks Meyers and George Volkman were college men who had played for the University of Wisconsin, and George Blocker came from a football family that included All-Western conference center Frank Blocker from Purdue and quarterback Ted Blocker. However, the 1915 Hammond Clabbys were not a major independent team.

In 1916, the Hammond business community was tired of scrub football and wanted a strong independent team for their community, so they hired Edward L. Green to coach the Clabbys. Green, formerly a star halfback with the University of Pennsylvania, had come to Indiana in October 1915 to be an assistant coach at Purdue University.[3] He moved on to become an advertising agent in Chicago and was determined to use his promotional skills to make the Hammond Clabbys one of the strongest independent football teams in America.[4] Recruiting key players from Purdue and the University of Wisconsin, Green began the process of making Hammond a professional football powerhouse. He scheduled games with a better class of teams in Illinois, Indiana, and Iowa, and began promoting football in Hammond. When hometown crowds were insufficient to support a strong schedule, he raised prices and promoted more vigorously.

Hammond opened its 1916 football season on September 24 against Peru, Illinois, and discovered too late that Peru sent their second team to Hammond. The Clabbys beat Peru 76–0, but Hammond merchants and fans were not happy watching their team play against scrubs.[5] On October 1, the Clabbys played the Rockford Badgers at the Hammond baseball park. John R. Finn, the former Purdue University quarterback and baseball star, was the field leader for the Clabbys, while Malcolm Galvin from the University of Wisconsin, Ted Blocker from Indiana University, and Blair supported him in the backfield. The Clabbys line included J. Nolan and Melvin Joshua "Red" Stinchfield at ends, George Volkman and Henry V. Ruffner at tackles, Herbert and Seliger at guards, and Frank A. Blocker at center.[6] Four of the Clabbys starters were varsity starters for Purdue in 1915. Henry Ruffner had already made a career of football. In 1907, he was the starting end for Purdue, and, in 1908, he was their quarterback.[7] The six-foot two-hundred-pound Ruffner dropped out of college and did not return until 1911.[8] He played guard in 1911 and 1912. From 1913 through 1915, he was the Purdue freshman football coach and an assistant varsity coach.[9] M. J. "Red" Stinchfield was also a long-term athlete. Red was an All-State high school football player and an all-around athlete at Purdue. The quiet, steady Stinchfield was on the varsity football, basketball, and track teams.[10] Behind its seven college stars, Hammond won the game 27–2.

The 1916 Fort Wayne Friars were building one of the best teams in their history, and they opened the season with a 101–0 victory over the Dayton Munitions. They had an all-star lineup led by Charles "Gus" Dorais, the great Notre Dame quarterback, and a backfield that included halfbacks Alvin "Heine" Berger and Joe Pliska from Notre Dame, with Ralph "Bull" Young from Washington and Jefferson College at fullback. The Friars started Chris Chambers and Baird at ends, Keith "Deac" Jones and Howard "Cap" Edwards at guards, and Dan Ball at center.[11] The weekly payroll for the Friars was said to be $700.[12]

The Hammond Clabbys were also a serious ball club. "I'm going to bring a football club to your city," declared Forest M. "Heine" Morrow of the Clabby Athletic Association to Friar president Carl J. Suedhoff, "that is out for the state title, and we are coming determined to win. You will not have a patched up and disorganized club against yours," he continued. "You can recommend our team to your rooters as being well organized, coached and in good condition. At present there are four coaches working with the team and we are working out daily."[13] The Clabbys had been working out since August 20 and had already played two games. That amount of work together as a team was almost unheard of in independent football ranks in 1916.

Edward L. Green and the Hammond Commercial Club organized a vestibule train of seven coaches on the Nickel Plate Line out of Hammond Sunday morning, October 8. Every seat was taken for the three-hour ride to Fort Wayne. Some three hundred rooters and many of their ladies were on the special along with the Clabbys football team, coach Floyd Murray, Pop Clabby, Forest M. Morrow, and Max Klein the singer.[14] When the train reached Fort Wayne, the entourage formed a line and marched down the main street of Fort Wayne led by a band. Twenty-six hundred fans paid to see the game. Few intercollegiate games exceeded the spirit exhibited by Fort Wayne and Hammond fans.[15]

The first three quarters of the game were scoreless. The 1915 captain of the Purdue Boilermakers, Frank A. Blocker, was all over the field on defense: he played linebacker with relish. While a member of the secondary line of defense, he did not wait for plays to come to him. He threw his big body into every drive made into the Hammond defensive line.[16] J. Nolan and Clinks Meyers were particularly good at shutting down the Friars' sweeps, and Ted Blocker and Malcolm Galvin, at sidebacks, defended well against Gus Dorais, one of the great passers of the era. It was not until Frank and Ted Blocker and Malcolm Galvin had to leave the game because of the pounding they were taking that Fort Wayne finally scored. Ralph Young,[17] called "Bull" Young because of his powerful play at fullback, scored the only touchdown of the game. While Hammond played a standup game, they lacked the depth and experience to beat Fort Wayne. The final score was Fort Wayne 9, Hammond 0.

On October 15, Hammond returned home to play the Aurora (Illinois) Greyhounds. The Greyhounds were ranked about tenth among Illinois independent football teams. They were a decent team, but not as good as Evanston, the Cornell-Hamburgs, Moline, Rock Island, and the other leaders in Illinois. A crowd of over one thousand fans paid fifty cents each for general admission. Hammond was still nursing injuries from the game with Fort Wayne. Malcolm Galvin, Ted Blocker, and George Volkman were unable to start, and Frank Blocker could not complete the game because of injuries incurred in Fort Wayne.[18] Davie and Abe Cohen were the Aurora stars. Davie Cohen scored the only Greyhound touchdown on a forty-yard run. The Clabbys stars J. Nolan and Clinks Meyers scored five touchdowns, and Red Stinchfield kicked four extra points in the 34–6 Hammond win.[19]

It was growing increasingly clear that the task of building a first-rate professional team was more difficult than expected. Hammond fans were not satisfied with games against the likes of Aurora, Peru, and Rockford. They wanted to see Detroit, Pine Village, Evanston, Fort Wayne, and Wabash, but these teams demanded at least five hundred dollars in guarantees, and Hammond's gate receipts were not large enough to support guarantees of this size.[20] Moreover, no one considered the Clabbys to be on a par with the better teams. The question facing the Clabbys' promoters was how to continue to build the Clabbys and increase local fan support. The initial answer to the problem was to play out of town.

On October 22, the Clabbys scheduled a game in Lafayette, Indiana, against the Sheridan Warriors. The Clabbys took only sixteen players to Lafayette and used them all in the game.[21] Five hundred Hammond fans crowded into nine Monon Line coaches; each fan paid $5.00 for travel, meals, and game tickets. The Hammond Commercial Club hired a band and prepared banners and emblems. The Hammond rooters ate at several Lafayette locations, including the Fowler Hotel, the College Inn, the Oriental Inn, the Elks clubrooms, and the Germania Cafe. While Lafayette was dry on Sunday, the Hammond fans managed to find alcohol disguised as tea.[22] At one o'clock, the Lafayette citizens' band serenaded the Clabby and Sheridan teams at their hotels, then headed a procession to the football stadium. Several photographers and a moving picture operator were taking pictures. Max Klein, the entertainer, gave the crowd of three thousand fans several solos.[23]

Hammond won the coin toss and chose to defend the south goal. After they kicked off, Sheridan was held on downs, and the Hammond offensive effort, led by Johnny Finn at quarterback, opened up a running attack in which Clinks Meyers and Blair advanced the ball steadily. The drive was stopped by a fumble which Sheridan recovered. They failed to move the ball again, and Hammond went back on the offensive. Johnny Finn then threw a pass to Blair, who carried the pigskin twenty-five yards for a touchdown. Toward the end of the first quarter, Malcolm Galvin was injured, and the fullback spot was taken over by Talbot. In the second quarter, Clinks Meyers recovered a Sheridan fumble, but the Hammond drive stalled on the Sheridan twenty-five yard line. Hammond scored its second touchdown when Johnny Finn intercepted a Sheridan pass then threw a fifteen-yard pass to Kohl, who scored the touchdown, making the score 14–0 at halftime.[24] In the second half, Hammond kicked two field goals and won the game 20–0. Emboldened by the win over Sheridan, the *Hammond Times* suggested that a professional "Big Nine" Conference be formed. It was argued that "professional football is by far a greater advertising medium" than baseball and that the commercial clubs of these cities should be happy to sponsor such a league.[25]

Unable to schedule a major independent team with the guarantee available, Hammond brought the Montpelier, Ohio team to Parduhn Field for Sunday, October 29. Montpelier only brought thirteen players to the game and proved to be little competition for the Clabbys, who ran up a fifty-six-point lead before calling it an afternoon. Montpelier only made two first downs and never threatened to score.[26] A slim crowd attended the game, and the gate receipts amounted to only $315. The guarantee to Montpelier was $200, hence expenses exceeded income. As a business proposition, the Clabbys were on the verge of bankruptcy.[27] In order to schedule a worthy opponent at home, they needed at least $500 for a guarantee. The Clabbys had to appeal to the commercial club to bail them out. County Coroner J. A. Graham raised $150 from Crown Point fans in hopes of attracting Ralph "Bull" Young to play for Hammond.[28]

On November 3, the Clabbys agreed to a $700 guarantee to bring the Davenport Athletic Club to Hammond. Davenport planned to bring several hundred fans to the game, each of whom would pay $1 gate admission, so that the risk to Hammond was less than the $500 available to them at that time. Marvin Monnett served as a special envoy in securing the contract. The *Hammond Times* proudly announced, "This was the highest price ever paid to bring a football eleven to Hammond and there is no doubt but that Davenport has the highest class team ever engaged to defend the visitor's goal on the Clabby gridiron."[29]

On November 5, Hammond played the Racine Regulars, also known as Battery C, the independent football champions of Wisconsin. Racine carried twenty men on their roster and promised to give the Clabbys a good football game. The admission price was fifty cents. As promised, the Hammond-Racine game was well played and hard fought. Racine scored first, giving them a 6–0 lead at the end of the first quarter, but, over the next two quarters, Hammond scored twice. Clinks Meyers and Ted Blocker each made a Hammond touchdown. Late in the fourth quarter, Joe Dory, the star halfback for Racine, made a sensational eighty-yard run after he intercepted a misdirected Johnny Finn pass. Although there were three professional prize fighters on the Racine team, the Wisconsin champions did not have enough fight to beat Hammond. The final score was Hammond 14, Racine 12. The crowd was large enough to cover expenses.[30] The next day, Hammond offered Pine Village an $800 guarantee to play the Clabbys in Hammond on Thanksgiving.[31] The offer was declined.

On November 12, Hammond played the Ann Arbor Independents at Parduhn Field. Ann Arbor had shared the football championship of Michigan in 1914, and was very competitive in 1915, but, in 1916, they had dropped from the schedule of every major independent football team in Michigan, Ohio, and Indiana. So the 30–0 win over the Independents impressed almost no one.

On November 19, the Davenport Athletic Club traveled east to play the Clabbys. Hammond increased its admission price to $1 to make good on its guarantee.[32] The game was hotly contested. Hammond backs ripped through the Davenport line consistently, and, on the whole, the team exhibited superior teamwork. Some six or seven minutes into the game, Johnny Finn kicked a field goal from the Davenport thirty yard line, giving the Clabbys a 3–0 lead. Shortly after that, Galvin threw a forward pass to Clinks Meyers that took the ball into scoring position, and two plays later Hammond led 10–0.[33] In the second quarter, Davenport executed an off-tackle run that resulted in a forty-seven-yard touchdown. At halftime, the score was 10–7 in favor of Hammond. In the third quarter, Davenport recovered a Hammond fumble on their own eight yard line and ran it down the field ninety-one yards before being tackled on the one yard line. Two plays later, Ray Kuehl, the Davenport right halfback, scored the go-ahead touchdown. The teams played evenly until the last two minutes of the game, when Hammond drove the ball to the Davenport three yard line. On two consecutive off-tackle plays, Davenport held. The ball was turned over to Davenport on the one foot line. With the clock running down, Davenport took a safety rather than risk turning the ball over and won the game 14 to 12.[34]

The loss to Davenport did not deter the Clabbys' management. They took their team to Elyria, Ohio, the following Sunday and lost to the Elyria Athletics.[35] On Thanksgiving, they played the Detroit Harvards at Parduhn Field. The Detroit Harvards were comparable to the Ann Arbor Independents but gave the uneducated Hammond fan the illusion of playing a strong Detroit team. Hammond won 20–0, and the crowd was just large enough to keep from losing money.

Hammond continued playing football after most independent teams closed their season. On December 3, they beat the Cincinnati Celts in Hammond by a field goal, then lost to Pine Village in Lafayette, on De-

Harold S. "Hod" Ofstie, end, Pine Village 1916, was an All-Western end when he played for the University of Wisconsin. *(University of Wisconsin Archives.)*

cember 10, by the same margin. Pine Village had a host of former college stars. David Earl "Kinks" Hawthorne[36] starred at DePauw University in Greencastle in 1911. Henry "Hank" Rowan[37] from Brookline, Massachusetts, also played for Pine Village. Like Hawthorne, he attended DePauw University, where he was the starting halfback for three years and became captain of the team in 1915. The Pine Village team also included Franklin Bart Macomber, the All-Western quarterback from the University of Illinois; Frank Allen, Ed Davis, and Cliff Milligan from Indiana University; Emmett Keefe from Notre Dame; the Fenters brothers; the Harvard All-American Richard King; and Harold "Hod" Ofstie, the All-Western end from the University of Wisconsin. Macomber was probably paid $75 for the game.[38]

It was a great credit to Hammond that they held this entourage to three points. The Clabbys ended the season with a 9–4 record, and, while they defeated Sheridan, Racine, and Cincinnati and showed considerable promise, most of their victories were against secondary teams. The Clabbys had fallen to the Fort Wayne Friars, the Davenport Athletic Club, the Elyria Athletics, and the Pine Village Athletic Club. More telling, their home game receipts averaged less than $500, with the exception of the Davenport and Cincinnati games.[39] At season's end, they were only able to pay their players $10 per game, except for Frank Blocker who had a season contract, while other teams paid an average of $35 a game for big-time professional football talent, and stars often received $100 or more.[40] This was hardly the foundation for a strong professional football franchise, yet the Hammond Clabbys pushed ahead with plans to promote their team to big-time professional football status.

28. Hammond: New Indiana Champions

The **Hammond Clabbys** were committed to developing a first-rate team in 1917. They were also certain that professional football must form a league to be successful. On September 16, 1917, Ed Leech of the Fort Wayne Friars, Billy Jones of the Wabash Athletic Association, Frank Blocker of the Hammond Clabbys, and Claire Rhodes of the Pine Village Athletic Club met to discuss the formation of a league.[1]

When the other teams insisted on a schedule based on both home and away games, the Friars refused to join the league. In the past, Fort Wayne had played their entire schedule at home and established strong fan support for this arrangement. The other three teams refused to allow an exception for the Friars, so Fort Wayne dropped out of the discussion. A week later, the remaining delegates met in Lafayette, Indiana, to complete the details for the new league. The delegates expected that teams from Rock Island, Davenport, Joliet, Toledo, Cincinnati, and Columbus would join the group later. In the meantime, the managers of the teams in the league pledged to work together to help each other schedule games with the best professional football teams.[2]

The new league members agreed to schedule games on a home-and-home basis with the other teams in the league. Moreover, they agreed on a rule that only eighteen men would suit up on each team for these games, and that managers must submit a list of players to the other team at least five days before the game. The league teams would all start their seasons by playing some outside team.[3]

Paul Parduhn, from Gary, Indiana, acquired control of the Hammond Clabbys and became the team's manager. He also supplied a new home field for the team. Melvin Monnett became his assistant. The new owner terminated several coaches and promoters from the year before, leaving Edward L. Green as the lone surviving coach from 1916. Some of the starting lineup from the previous year had moved on: Malcolm Galvin became head coach in Davenport, Ralph "Bull" Young signed a contract with the Fort Wayne Friars, and Johnny Finn and Talbot were in the army.[4]

The Clabbys' management was working on a schedule that would be one of the most difficult in professional football. "Like Barnum & Bailey's circus, Hammond's town football team will be 'bigger and better' than ever this year," declared the *Hammond Times*. Negotiations were already underway to hire John Leo "Paddy" Driscoll, captain of the Northwestern University Wildcats and a third team Walter Camp All-American selection in 1916.[5]

Hammond opened the season in Detroit against the Heralds, then traveled to Davenport to play the Davenport Athletic Club. On October 21, they played their first home game against Racine, then played Wabash at home before taking on Pine Village in Lafayette. On November 11, they played the Cornell-Hamburgs at home. They played in Wabash on November 18 and closed the season with home games against Pine Village, the Cornell-Hamburgs, and the Fort Wayne Friars. Clearly a schedule of this stature constituted an amazing act of faith given the record and financial difficulties of the 1916 season. The Clabbys were gambling everything on their ability to develop a winning team and their faith in advertising and self-promotion.

Of course, Hammond was not the only team in the Chicago area with an eye on a major league professional football franchise. The Cornell-Hamburgs hired Reuben Johnson from the Evanston North Ends in hopes of moving beyond the championship of the Chicago Independent Football League to at least a regional championship. The Hamburg Athletic Association, sponsor of the Cornell-Hamburgs, was located in a rambling, somewhat anonymous-looking building at 37th Street and Emerald on Chicago's south side. Organized around the turn of the century, it was similar to the Chicago Athletic Club which was controlled by "Big Bill" Thompson and the other stalwart Chicago Republicans, except that the Hamburg Club targeted south side ethnics. Located in the back-of-the-yards area, the Hamburg Athletic Association was the only organization of consequence in that part of the city, and its alumni included an extraordinary number of men who made it big in local government.[6]

In 1914, Tommy Doyle parlayed the presidency of the Hamburg Athletic Association into an aldermanic seat in the Eleventh Ward and became a U.S. congressman in 1918. His protege, Joe McDonough, a Villanova football hero, succeeded Tommy Doyle as club president and, in 1917, as alderman and ward committeeman. In turn, Joe McDonough took young Richard Daley under his wing, and, in 1924, Daley began a fifteen-year reign as president of the Hamburg Athletic Association.

The most visible activity of the Hamburgs, in the period from 1914 to 1917, was its semiprofessional football team, the Cornell-Hamburgs. In 1917, they were coached by "Big Joe" McDonough, and sixteen-year-old Richard J. Daley, the future mayor of Chicago, was the team's water boy. McDonough frequently ate at a tavern at 47th and Wentworth and was known to eat an entire chicken with all the trimmings for lunch. Allied with west side Bohemian Alderman Anton J. Cermak, McDonough would later become treasurer of Cook County and spend most of his time in speakeasies, eating establishments, and racetracks. He finally died, in 1934, of too much booze, too many women, and too much to eat. But in 1917, at the age of twenty-eight, Big Joe was a ferocious leader, devoted to getting his constituents a fair share of Chicago's spoils and winning the professional football championship of the Midwest.[7] His plans, however, hit a snag when the Hamburgs played the East Chicago Gophers, on September 30, at the East Chicago Athletic Field before eight hundred rabid fans. Much to the surprise of the Chicago champions, the Gophers used a clever mixture of forward passes, end runs, and trick plays to defeat the Cornells 20 to 12.[8]

In Detroit, four thousand fans crowded Navin Field, the summer home of the Detroit Tigers, to watch the Heralds kick off their season against the upstart Clabbys. The Clabbys started G. Kohl and J. Nolan at ends, George Volkman and L. Seliger at tackles, Hugo "Hugs" Volkman and Plum at guards, Frank Blocker at center, and Wallie Hess, Harold "Irish" Sheridan, Clinks Meyers and A. R. Longenecker in the backfield. Wallie Hess played under the assumed name Herrin because he coached at Hammond High School and the Board of Education refused to allow him to play Sunday football.[9] The Clabbys' defense played well, although their defensive secondary had a difficult time containing Norb Sacksteder once he broke through the line.

The Detroit Heralds rebuilt what had been an aging team in 1916 into a contender for the national title. Led by Norbert Sacksteder, Tommy Hughitt, All-Western lineman Herbert Straight, Notre Dame great Ray Whipple, and Denison College star end Carl "Dutch" Thiele, the Heralds had few weaknesses.[10] After a scoreless first quarter, Detroit took control of the game when a pass from University of Michigan star quarterback Tommy Hughitt to Norb Sacksteder resulted in six points for the home team. Later in the quarter, Sacksteder scored a second touchdown on a forty-three-yard run. He added a third on a punt return in the second half. The final score was Detroit 19–Hammond 0.[11]

Hammond's offensive problems were solved the following week when the Clabbys signed Paddy Driscoll, one of the finest halfbacks in the Midwest. Born on January 11, 1895, John Leo "Paddy" Driscoll attended Evanston High School, where he became a hometown football hero. In 1914, he enrolled at Northwestern University and played halfback for the Wildcats, where he was an outstanding kicker and open field runner. The next year, he was captain of the team and All-Conference halfback. Paddy ended his college eligibility in the summer of 1917 when he played baseball for the Chicago Cubs as a utility infielder. In thirteen games, he made only three hits and batted .107.

On January 1, 1919, Driscoll played in the Rose Bowl as a member of the U.S. Navy Great Lakes Blue Jackets. After the First World War, he played with the Decatur Stanleys, the Chicago Cardinals, and the Chicago Bears. He also coached for St. Mel's High School in Chicago, Marquette University, and the Chicago Bears. He is a member of the National Football Hall of Fame.[12]

The Clabbys also hired Bernard "Swede" Halstrom, the fine left halfback who had dropped out of the University of Illinois, for their second road game.[13] They left Hammond Saturday night at 8:12 P.M. and, after a transfer in Chicago, took a sleeper to Davenport early Sunday morning. The new Hammond backfield with Driscoll, Halstrom, Irish Sheridan, Clinks Meyers, and A. R. Longenecker was considered good enough to play the best professional teams in America. The Hammond line still needed improvement, particularly at the ends and at one of the guard positions.[14]

The Davenport Athletic Club had also improved their team, but could not keep up with Hammond. Frank Blocker, who played offensive center and defensive tackle for the Clabbys, was the defensive star of the game, and Paddy Driscoll was sensational on offense. Driscoll's sixty-five-yard touchdown run in the first quarter, another long run later, and a field goal demonstrated that Hammond would not be defeated by Davenport two years in a row. The final score was Hammond 9, Davenport 3.[15]

The home opener for the Clabbys turned out to be a disappointment for the fans. At this game, the Clabbys introduced new golden yellow uniforms. The two thousand fans who paid seventy-five cents and $1 for admission had little to cheer about, so there was almost no home field advantage.[16] The Racine Regulars, led by Norman "Tango" Glockson and Walter Eck, upset the Clabbys 12 to 0. In the process, Longenecker separated his shoulder and George Volkman fractured a rib, so both were lost to Hammond for much of the season. Paddy Driscoll and Swede Halstrom had little opportunity to show their skills, because the line was tissue paper thin until Wilber Henderson made his appearance as an end for the Clabbys. The Hammond offense was hampered by frequent fumbles that led some Hammond fans to quip that the Clabbys needed to buy woolen mittens or to use baskets to eliminate their atrocious ball handling.[17]

The Cornell-Hamburgs, meanwhile, were rounding into midseason form and defeated the Rockford Badgers 40 to 0.[18] The southsiders played all of their second team and part of their third team in the one-sided fray. Nicholson scored three of Chicago's six touchdowns.[19]

The following Sunday, when the Clabbys played the Wabash Athletic Association at Parduhn Field, they lost money because they drew only eight hundred fans.[20] Hammond, however, continued to upgrade its line. They hired Thomas J. "Tom" Shaughnessy, the former Notre Dame end, who played for the Evanston North Ends in 1916,[21] and for the first time, they also started Roy Whitlock from the Evanston North Ends at left tackle.[22]

The *Chicago Examiner* sent a reporter who made fun of professional football, calling the game "Prairie Football." In areas where there were no grandstands, fans parked near the field and watched the game from their cars, giving Hammond's League Park the appearance of the Indianapolis Speedway on Declaration Day. The grandstands were enclosed by barbed wire to keep little boys from sneaking in. The reporter also observed that the Clabbys sold Curley Kimball's hot dogs and depended on "old Doc Young," the club sawbones, to keep the players on the field.[23]

In the second period, Hammond intercepted a Wabash pass, and, a few plays later, Driscoll scored a touchdown and kicked the extra point after the punt-out. When Wabash kicked off to start the second half, Driscoll ran the kickoff sixty yards down the center of the field for a touchdown. Later, he executed an end run for the Clabbys' third touchdown and kicked the extra point to win the game 20–0. It was the highest score against Wabash in eighteen years.[24]

The Hammond Clabbys took a special train to Lafayette, Indiana, to play the Pine Village Athletic Club on the first Sunday in November. Owner Paul Parduhn personally put up the $100 guarantee for the train. Fans paid $2.16 for a round-trip fare, the sixteen cents being the war tax. The Hotel Fowler was the designated headquarters for the

Hammond group. Game admission was seventy-five cents.[25] The details of the November 4th games are scarce, but, according to the *Chicago Evening Post*, "La Ross and Brennan aided the Cornell-Hamburgs in beating the Racine team, 21 to 0, at Schorlings' Park" and "Paddy Driscoll kicked two field goals, made a touchdown and made a goal from touchdown in their [Hammond's] 13 to 0 game against Pine Village at Lafayette."[26]

On Sunday, November 11, three thousand fans crowded into Hammond's League Park to watch the Cornell-Hamburgs, the most likely challenger for the metropolitan Chicago Independent Football Championship, face off against the Clabbys. Hammond's record was 3–2 to Chicago's 5–1.[27] The match-up that interested fans the most was between Paddy Driscoll and Rube Johnson, the kicking wonder. Both were from Evanston, Illinois, and each was considered by many to be in the same category as Jim Thorpe—All-Pro caliber. Reuben Johnson made the only points for the Cornell-Hamburgs on an impressive drop kick in a brutal battle. "Harter, [the] Cornell-Hamburg halfback, sustained a broken leg and internal injuries" and when Paddy Driscoll, the Hammond star, was tackled by Brennan, the Chicago left tackle, the *Chicago Evening Post* reported that Driscoll was "knocked out on his feet."[28] Nevertheless, Hammond won the match-up 13–3.

On November 18, seventy Hammond fans and eighteen players took the train for the next game with Wabash. On the train, L. Seliger lost $1.25 in a game of rummy before he realized that they were playing for keeps. That was a whole day's salary in those years. The Hammond lineup had Henderson and Kohl at ends, Whitlock and Ruffner at tackles, Seliger and Green at guards, Frank Blocker at center and Driscoll, Halstrom, Ted Blocker and Clinks Meyers in the backfield. Simmons, Plum, A. R. Longenecker, J. Nolan, and Hugo "Hugs" Volkman played as substitutes.[29] During the course of the game, Hammond used sixteen players, Wabash only thirteen, showing how little substitution took place in a normal game. Wabash kicked off to Hammond. They executed an onside kick, recovered the ball, and advanced it to the Hammond twenty yard line. On second down, however, Wabash fumbled the ball, and Hammond recovered it. After two attempts to run between the tackles, Hammond quick-kicked the ball. For the balance of the quarter, the game was a seesaw battle played near the middle of the field. At one point, Paddy Driscoll tried a drop kick from the forty yard line, but it was blocked. The game remained even until the closing minutes of the first half, when a series of off-tackle runs and a couple of passes brought Hammond into scoring position. However, the Wabash line stiffened near their goal line, and the half ended in a scoreless tie.

There was not much excitement until the fourth quarter. Wabash drove the ball to the Hammond fifteen yard line but failed to score and turned the ball over on downs. Two plays later, Swede Halstrom skirted the Wabash left end and ran more than eighty yards for the only score of the game. Paddy Driscoll kicked the extra point, and the game ended 7–0. The victory gave Hammond a share of the Indiana independent football championship.[30]

As Thanksgiving week approached, Paul Parduhn announced that he planned to bet $500 that the Clabbys would defeat Pine Village on Sunday, November 25, $1000 that they would defeat the Cornell-Hamburgs on Thanksgiving Day, and $2000 that they would defeat Fort Wayne on December 11.[31]

Seventeen hundred fans attended the Pine Village game in Hammond on November 25. Clinks Meyers was unable to start the game because of a knee injury, so Kohl started at right halfback for the Clabbys. Pine Village received the opening kickoff and, after several exchanges of the ball, Harvard All-American Richard King ran thirty yards for a Pine Village touchdown. Eli Fenters kicked the extra point. In the second quarter, Halstrom fumbled on a running play, and J. McCarthy recovered for Pine Village and then ran for a touchdown. When Eli Fenters kicked the extra point, the score was 14–0. It remained that way until halftime.

Coach Green gave Hammond players a stinging halftime talk. No one was spared, and, in the third quarter, Hammond played better. Driscoll, Halstrom, and Blocker each averaged nearly five yards per carry, and Meyers returned to the lineup. Midway through the third quarter, Driscoll ran around end for the final eight yards of an eighty-yard drive to give Hammond six points. In the final quarter, Bacon intercepted a Clabbys pass and ran thirty-five yards to give Pine Village a 21–6 victory.[32]

Paul Parduhn had been unable to bet more than $20 on the game because few from Pine Village were willing to wager on their team. Altogether, less than $100 was bet on the game. Even though he did not lose much money, Parduhn was outraged with the results and discharged Sheridan, Simmons, and Longenecker to make room for new players.[33]

Despite the loss, Hammond was the winner of the Indiana State

League, having won three of four games from Wabash and Pine Village, and would play Fort Wayne for the state championship. But first Hammond was scheduled to play the Cornell-Hamburgs on Thanksgiving for the Chicago area championship. On November 25, the Cornell-Hamburgs had challenged the undefeated Joliet Steel Workers, sponsored by the Wilson Steel Works and coached by Artie Scanlon, who also coached the undefeated Chicago Hyde Park High School football team that had won the city championship the day before.[34] Scanlon's minions in Joliet had won eight straight games and faced the Cornell-Hamburgs in Comiskey Park. In a closely fought contest, the Hamburgs fended off the Steel Workers. In the first quarter, Reuben Johnson managed a forty-five-yard place kick to give Chicago a three-point lead. The Hamburgs padded their lead with a touchdown in the third quarter, after Joliet fumbled on their own thirty yard line and a Chicagoan fell on the ball. Gels, the Chicago halfback, led the drive and scored the winning touchdown while Johnson kicked goal for a thirteen-point lead. Finally Joliet got its offense into gear and made a touchdown, but could not convert the extra point.[35] Shortly after their win over Joliet, manager Bill Finn of the Cornell-Hamburgs announced the signing of Bart Macomber and former Cornell University star Gillies to play for them on Thanksgiving Day against the Hammond Clabbys.[36] As it turned out, Macomber did not play for the Cornell-Hamburgs, although the Youngstown Pats season was over and Macomber was free to play for Chicago.

On Wednesday, Hammond hired Johnny Barrett from the Youngstown Patricians to play for them on Thanksgiving. Barrett had previously played for the Evanston North Ends and the Toledo Maroons after leaving Washington and Lee University.[37] The Clabbys also added All-Western conference tackles Lee Percy Mehlig from the University of Wisconsin and C. M. McCardy from Michigan Agricultural College, who was considered by many to be the best tackle in college football in 1917.

The Hamburgs had a decided kicking advantage because of Reuben Johnson. Most of their team was composed of tough, street-smart men who did not go to college. The Cornell-Hamburgs were 6–3 for the season, having lost only to East Chicago, Hammond, and Davenport. The game started out as an even contest, but, midway through the second quarter, Paddy Driscoll drop-kicked a field goal from the fifteen yard line to give Hammond a 3–0 lead at halftime. At the end of the third quarter, according to the *Hammond Times,*

Ross de Wop of the Cornells whose methods were anything but sweet scented, pulled the rough stuff once too often with P. Driscoll and the mad Irishman remonstrated just after the whistle had blown. Now in the best regulated clubs when such things happen after the bell has struck, the boys shake hands, but these chaps didn't.[38]

Alderman McDonough insisted that Driscoll be thrown out of the game, but the referee and umpire ruled that the roughness had been fifty-fifty.[39] In the third quarter, Johnny Barrett made a thirty-five-yard run and topped off the drive a few plays later with a touchdown. Barrett made a second touchdown in the fourth quarter, and the final score was Hammond 15, Cornell-Hamburgs 0. Hammond used its entire squad of seventeen men and "shifted them about to confuse Ralph Young, who was scouting the game for Fort Wayne."[40]

As a safety precaution, Paul Parduhn added Emmett G. Keefe to the Clabby roster for the state championship game. Keefe played left guard for Notre Dame from 1913 through 1915, and then played for Pine Village. At five feet eleven inches tall and 180 pounds, Emmett Keefe was a solid guard.[41]

Parduhn also added Thomas J. Shaughnessy at fullback, playing under the alias "T. Howard Gangway."[42] The Clabbys started G. Kohl and Wilber Henderson at ends, Lee Mehlig and Henry Ruffner at tackles, L. Seliger and Emmett Keefe at guards, Frank Blocker at center, and Paddy Driscoll, C. M. McCardy, Johnny Barrett, and Tom Shaughnessy in the backfield. Hugo Volkman relieved Kohl, and Halstrom replaced McCardy during the second half. Plum also saw some playing time.

The Fort Wayne Friars had a strong team with Walter Berghoff and Charles Helvie at ends, Deac Jones and Ed Davis at tackles, Lockwood and Bashaw at guards, and Frank Rydzewski at center. The Fort Wayne backfield featured Gus Dorais, Robert Specht, Joe Pliska, and Ralph "Bull" Young.

Almost from the outset, Hammond dominated the game. Two minutes into the contest, Hammond's mysterious fullback (Tom Shaughnessy) scored a touchdown, but Paddy Driscoll failed to kick the point after. Later in the quarter, Driscoll ran around end for a dozen yards and a touchdown, and again the punt-out for extra point was unsuccessful. In the second quarter, Driscoll scored another touchdown, and the score stood Hammond 18, Fort Wayne 0.

Late in the third quarter, the mysterious Hammond fullback scored his second touchdown, and this time Driscoll made the point after. The final score was 25–0.[43] For the first time, the Hammond Clabbys were state champions of Indiana, thanks in large measure to the leadership of John Leo "Paddy" Driscoll and the mystery fullback, Tom Shaughnessy.

Paul Parduhn's payroll was $700 for each of the last three games of the season.[44] Although they tripled their average game attendance over 1916, the Clabbys still lost money. There was talk about playing Detroit to close the season, but, when the weather turned cold, "calmer heads prevailed," and, on December 7, 1917, the management of the Clabbys declared, "We've played the last game until the end of the Kaiser."[45]

Since early October, some small town newspapers had called for an end to football as a gesture to the war effort. On October 10, the *Rensselaer Democrat* (Indiana) had written,

There are entirely too many young men today wasting good time playing baseball, football, golf and what not, who ought to be over in the trenches killing Huns or doing something to help the boys who are there and who are getting ready to go. . . . It is little less than criminal to take a bunch of husky young boys out to spend their time in nothing more profitable than football and kindred sports.

As the war effort progressed, there would be little sympathy for Sunday football. Everywhere, pro players were joining the armed services. Swede Halstrom and Paddy Driscoll enlisted in the radio service of the Great Lakes Naval Training Center.[46] Bob Peck joined an artillery regiment.[47] Milton Ghee, Canton's quarterback, got married and entered aviation training in the U.S. Army.[48] Frank N. Rydzewski, who had recently played pro football for Fort Wayne after being captain at Notre Dame, began service in the army ordnance department in Columbus, Ohio.[49] Frank Mt. Pleasant was given an army commission at the Second Reserve Officers' Trainers Camp.[50] Bill Garlow and Stilwell Sanooke joined the marines and were playing football for the 319th Regiment in Pennsylvania.[51] Soon there would be no healthy players available to play football. For all serious intents, professional football was over until the war ended.

In 1917, the original sponsor of the Hammond Clabbys' semiprofessional football team, former world welterweight boxing champion and Hammond native Jimmy Clabby,[52] had a net worth of at least $100,000. After outgrowing the welterweight division in 1912, he began taking on and defeating middleweight boxers, including Mike Gibbons and Jack Britton. When he retired from the ring, Jimmy settled down back in Hammond and made a number of investments, including one in a stable of racing horses. His money slowly slipped away from him. He was ultimately obliged to take odd jobs to stay afloat. Finally, on October 5, 1931, penniless and unable to pay his room rent, forty-one year old Jimmy Clabby went down to the railroad yards and slid underneath an eastbound boxcar to finish his life as a hobo.[53]

After the First World War, promoter Paul Parduhn established a strong Hammond team that competed for the mythical U. S. professional football championship. The team played its home games in Chicago at Cub Park (now Wrigley Field). As in 1917, Dr. Alvah A. Young was the team physician. A descendant of Brigham Young's brother, "Doc" Young was a big fan of horse racing, boxing, and football. He received his medical degree, in 1905, from Central College of Physicians and Surgeons in Indianapolis, and founded a company called A. A. Young Laboratories, that manufactured his invention of a vitamin-calcium supplement for thoroughbreds called Min-O-Lac. In 1920, Doc Young represented Hammond at the formation of the American Professional Football Association, and was instrumental in forming and shaping the National Football League. He owned the Hammond Pros until 1927, when the franchise suspended operations.[54] Throughout the 1920s, the franchise was plagued by a lack of local support and the absence of an adequate ball park, which required the team to play most of its games on the road and made it difficult to retain talented players.

29. Football Prepared Young Men for the Future

Slightly more than eleven hundred different men played for the twenty-four teams tracked in this study of the best independent football teams of the era. Approximately half of these men attended high school or college, where they played football. However, fewer than two hundred of these men graduated from college. The Canton Bulldogs, the Cleveland Indians, and the Massillon Tigers were the most likely teams to hire college players: the Columbus Panhandles, Evanston North Ends, Rock Island Independents, and Wabash Athletic Association were the least likely to hire college players. This profile suggests that the pioneers in professional football were better educated than the communities in which played, and that the movement toward professionalization drove independent team managers to hire former college players because they were the best-trained football players available.

Football, no doubt, helped in the socialization of both second generation Americans and farm boys making the transition to urban life. It fostered skills and social values that were useful in an urban, manufacturing society with a free enterprise economy. It placed emphasis on teamwork, specialized roles or assignments, planning (with improvisation when necessary), and pursuit of common goals. Football players were taught by the coach to view their interests as secondary to the best interests of the team, mirroring the way the supervisor and his workers functioned in the factory. Football players also were taught that job acceptance is contingent on performance, improvement, and winning. This conditional acceptance, by the coach and fans, taught the athlete to rely on external standards for his sense of identity and self-worth, as was the case in the work world. And, as was true elsewhere in urban society, a successful performer was given prestige that usually developed a general and lasting sense of self-worth. Finally, playing football often required an education, since the game was most often played in high schools and colleges. Consequently, interest in the game almost always promoted education and upward mobility.

By promoting the education of physically active boys, and encouraging conditional acceptance, external control of standards of behavior, a focus on outcome rather than process, acceptance of competition, and upward mobility, football embodied the very characteristics valued by an industrial, technical society in a free market economy.[1] Moreover, in a society that required much more than academic success to thrive, football enhanced intellectual and social development.[2] Certainly, for many, football bridged the gap between social classes.

In the first two decades of the twentieth century, football created opportunities for the sons of working-class families that were unlikely to have been available to them under ordinary circumstances. It may be difficult for many of us to understand the social barriers that existed at that time in many parts of the country between rich and poor, Black and White, Catholic and Protestant, Irish and Germans. Working-class children rarely attended high school and almost never went to college. In 1900, almost one in four children did not attend school at all, and only ten percent of high school aged children attended high school.[3] Both economic and social pressures conspired to limit school attendance. Families had a difficult time making ends meet, and many working-class men did not see the value of education. However, without social contact between people of different religions, nationalities, and racial groups, social mobility was limited. In the areas of the country where professional football flourished, sports—and particularly football—appear to have been an important factor in breaking down many of the social barriers that limited opportunities for boys from working-class families. Football opened doors for fellows like Norman Speck, Reuben Johnson, and Alfred Nesser, who never attended college, giving them employment opportunities and introducing them to social networks that were unlikely to have been available to them if they had not played football. Murry J. Battaglia went from being a peddler's son to foreman for the Bowman Milk Company, at least in part because of the leadership skills he developed on the football field.[4]

Football also made it possible for many to attend college who would not have otherwise attended. Between 1900 and 1917, on average, less than 30 percent of high school graduates graduated from college.[5] For those who attended college, football gave the sons of working-class families a chance to compete on a level ground with their social "betters" and to be considered their equal, at least on the playing field. Evidence of the role of sports in breaking down barriers can be found in the careers of most of the pioneers in professional football.

Football proved to be helpful in establishing personal networks that assisted in the average player's lifetime work, whether that be law, medicine, politics, or labor union leadership. Profiles of the players of the period demonstrate the point. No fewer than a dozen pro players developed successful medical practices, including Edgar Davis, Gordon Thomas, Clarence Spears, David Hawthorne, Paul Mason, and Mark Erehart.[6] Many became important community leaders. Homer T. Showalter and Al Feeney were elected mayors, Homer Stonebraker and Harry "Shine" Kinderdine[7] were elected sheriff, while Grover C. Lutter and Norman Speck were appointed deputy sheriffs. Dwight Wertz became president of a chamber of commerce. George Roudebush, Harold Powell, and J. Fred Potts became prominent lawyers. Orville Littick became a publisher and president of radio and television stations. Burliegh Cruikshank became a well-known minister, Reuben Ludvig Johnson became vice-president of a Federal Reserve Bank, David Reese became a dentist, and Maurice Briggs and Rudolph Propst became stock brokers. Harold Boerner was appointed fire department captain, while William "Red" Milliner was made fire chief. Earnest Scheerer and Frank Gurtner owned and operated grocery stores. Joseph J. Schuette became a jeweler. Walter E. Berghoff, Al Mahrt, Hank Rowan, Earl Abell, and David Hopkins became corporate executives, and J. Hugh "Pepper" O'Donnell became president of the University of Notre Dame.

True, football was not a major factor in altering the social climate for working Americans. Larger trends were remaking the country. The Progressive Movement put pressure on big companies to change their business practices. A number of states enacted laws limiting working hours for women and children, imposed health and safety regulations on factories, and even set minimum wages. In 1916, the Keating-Owen Act established federal child labor laws limiting the tasks and hours children were allowed to work. This legislation freed more children to attend school. The Progressive Movement also promoted physical education as a means of developing the bodies, as well as the minds, of an increasingly urban population. Henry Ford found that it was profitable to pay his workers enough to buy the automobiles he manufactured, and the war in Europe gave American businesses the chance to grow at the expense of English, French, and German competitors. These conditions drove wages up, and as wages improved, so did school attendance, high school graduation rates, and college attendance.[8]

Nevertheless, athletes appeared to be more likely than their peers to be motivated to attend high school and college, and those who played professional football made useful contacts that helped them succeed.

Rising high school and college enrollments, together with the introduction of physical education into the school curriculum, provided new career opportunities for the star athletes of the era. For the first time in American history, the generation of school athletes who came to adulthood after the turn of the twentieth century had the option of making athletics a career. The adoption of physical education as a college major was a slow process that started at Amherst College in 1861[9] and continued at a leisurely pace over the next forty years.[10] High schools began adopting physical education programs in the 1870s, but, like colleges, they were slow to see the value of such programs.[11] In the 1890s, there was a movement to pass state laws requiring the adoption of physical education programs, but it took until 1901 for the first state, Pennsylvania, to pass such legislation. Michigan followed in 1911, and, by 1932, 80 percent of all three-year high schools and 70 percent of all four-year high schools required physical education.[12] As more teenagers attended high school and college and more schools adopted physical education programs, there were expanding opportunities to teach physical education and coach football. These trends were developing at the same time that America was becoming wealthy enough to support professional athletic teams.

The generation born around 1890 was in an ideal position to create new occupations centered around athletics. In the past, except for those in baseball and boxing, young men could not dream of a career in sports beyond college. In the final third of the nineteenth century, athletic clubs emerged as a means of playing and promoting track and field, gymnastics, and other sports, but these clubs offered few, if any, careers in athletics.[13] Now, professional football could prolong an athlete's career and supplement his income to the point where he could afford to apprentice himself as an assistant college coach before becoming a head coach in college or high school. Nearly one hundred future coaches got their start in this way (see Appendix B). Without question, professional football prepared these athletic boys for a career in coaching or other positions that required leadership. They became the best coaches of the 1920s and 1930s and helped usher in what has been called "The Golden Age of Sports."[14] Fifteen pro football players from the 1915–17 era later became National Football League head coaches (see Table 3).

Several men who played professional football prior to World War I gained national recognition as coaches. Knute Rockne, DeOrmond McLaughry (who coached college football for thirty-two years), Carl Snavely, Charles "Gus" Dorais, Claude Thornhill, Ralph Young,[15] and Alfred E. "Greasy" Neale are just a few of those who were able to transform their football experiences into a lifelong career.

One of the concerns frequently raised about sports at the turn of the century was, "Does it prepare one for life?" In the 1915–17 era, football did indeed prepare football players for life. Football turned out to be good training for becoming an officer in the armed services during World War I. In 1916 and 1917, there was no way for young men to avoid the pending U. S. involvement in the great war in Europe. By fall 1916, compulsory military training for college males who were freshmen and sophomores was being imposed in colleges and universities around the United States. "It is quite generally acknowledged," according to university personnel, "that the immediate and greatest need in any case [that might involve military action] is going to be for a body of trained men to serve as officers. Modern warfare has come to be one of the most highly technical and specialized of the professions. Much of the training necessary for an officer can even now be furnished by the university."[16]

In spring 1917, Germany engaged in unrestricted submarine warfare against American ships, and, on April 2, 1917, President Woodrow Wilson asked Congress to declare war on Germany. There was an initial rush of volunteers to join the army, but, in April 1917, Americans only vaguely realized that war with Germany would involve American men fighting in France.[17]

President Wilson personally did not like conscription, preferring instead the spirit of volunteering. Consequently, Congress did not pass the Draft Act until mid-May 1917. Draft registration began June 4, 1917, and conscription did not begin until after July 20, 1917. Between July 20 and December 15, 1917, 516,000 young men were sent to boot camp to prepare for action in the Great War in Europe. Sixteen semipermanent camps were built in the North, and sixteen tent camps were to be built in the South to train the new draftees. Each camp had a capacity to train from forty to fifty thousand men. More that twelve hundred new buildings were required at the encampment sites: 325 lavatories with hot and cold showers, kitchens, laundries, post exchanges, and base hospitals with one thousand beds. It took until mid-September before facilities were built and furnished. Furthermore, special

Table 3 Pre-World War I Pros Who Coached in the NFL

Player	NFL Team(s) Coached
Arthur "Dutch" Bergman	Washington Redskins 1943
Stanley Cofall	Cleveland Panthers 1920
Paul Des Jardien	Chicago Tigers 1920
William Lone Star Dietz	Boston Redskins 1933–34
Charles "Gus" Dorais	Detroit Lions 1943–47
John Leo "Paddy" Driscoll	Chicago Cardinals 1921–22; Chicago Bears 1956–57
Guilford Falcon	Hammond Pros 1920; Toledo Maroons 1923
Tommy Hughitt	Buffalo All-Americans 1921–24
Barney Lepper	Buffalo All-Americans 1920
Alfred "Greasy" Neale	Philadelphia Eagles 1942–50
Alfred Nesser	Akron Pros 1926
Ted Nesser	Columbus Panhandles 1919–22
Carl Storck	Dayton Triangles 1922–25
Jim Thorpe	Canton Bulldogs 1919–20; Oorang Indians 1922–23
Reuben Ursella	Rock Island Independents 1919–21,1925; Akron Pros 1926

schools for the artillery, aviation, chemical warfare, engineering, and tank corps, together with large embarkation camps in New York City and Newport News, Virginia, had to be built. In the meantime, officers had to be appointed and trained.[18] As a result, the brunt of the draft did not occur until after the 1917 football season had started.

There were five new camps in the region of the country where professional football flourished: Camp Custer in Michigan, Camp Sherman in Ohio, Camp Taylor in Kentucky, Camp Grant in Illinois, and Camp Dodge in Iowa. Each camp needed officers, and professional football players who had attended college were an ideal source for army officers. They were better educated than most American men, and they had the physical fitness and stamina required to train other men of their age.

There was widespread acceptance of the idea that there is "no game like football for rough and tumble training."[19] Walter Camp observed that "football is like the game of war,"[20] and still others reported that "football players feel like soldiers going to the front as the big games approach."[21] General Pershing cabled a message from France back to the general command, recommending athletic training in the camps where men were being taught to shoot, throw grenades, dig trenches, and use the bayonet. He went on to recommend boxing and football as the best fighting exercises.[22] Soldiers from all around the country sent out a call for footballs and other athletic goods.[23]

Colleges also got into the war effort. The University of Michigan, for instance, named its tackling dummy "Kaiser Bill." It was seen as a way of preparing the boys for the front.[24]

By October 1917, the war effort had already begun to thin the ranks of professional football talent. More than 20 percent of the professional football players who played in 1915–16 were given officers appointments in the U.S. Army by the end of October 1917 (see Table 4). In some cases, these players were allowed weekend passes to permit them to play Sunday football. In other cases, they played football for the camp teams that emerged in the fall of 1917 and played games both for the entertainment of army recruits and to raise money for the Red Cross and army camp social needs. In several cases, professional football players on army teams played exhibition games against their old teams.[25]

Some of the camp teams were very good. Camp Sherman's first team had more college all-stars than the Canton Bulldogs and was coached by Nelson Talbott, who had coached the Dayton Triangles in 1916. According to the *Toledo Blade*, September 24, 1917:

Besides Captain Talbot[t] who was an All-American halfback at Yale, and who will lead the team, there is Goebel, Yale guard; Conant, Case lineman; "Bud" Denaple, former Reserve captain, and All-Ohio back; "Brute" Pontius, Michigan tackle and assistant to coach Yost; Kagy, Reserve half, who is well known to Toledo; Whinnery and Smoots of Mt. Union; Marting, famous Yale center and All-American man; Constant Southworth, one of the brothers who put Kenyon on the football map; Dickerson, former Cincinnati University captain; Malcolm Scovill, Yale half; Needham of Dartmouth; Roudebush of Denison; Roger, Ohio University; Layman, University of Virginia; Townsend of Princeton; Gilbreath, University of Tennessee; Edmonds, Michigan and All-Western; Dale Jones and Kurts, of Ohio University, the former being this year's captain.

The prosperity that accompanied all the new work created by the war effort, together with the uprooting of so many young men, resulted in increased interest in football, although there were also victims. Ripon College, for example, was forced to drop football because so many of its players had been called to war.[26] The *Toledo Blade* observed on October 25, 1917:

Despite the war and the hardships it worked in football, the pigskin is being pushed by more eleven's than in any season past. The sport has more followers and public interest is growing stronger.

Conditions brought on by the war have encouraged hundreds of students who would not have taken up football to come out for practice.

Players who left college to help Uncle Sam are playing the game in every can-

Table 4   A Partial List of Pro Football Players in Officer's Training in the Fall of 1917

Camp	College	Pro team
CAMP CUSTER		
N. Jerry Da Prato	Mich. Ag. College	Detroit Heralds
Nig Lennahan	Univ. of Detroit	Detroit Heralds
William Blake Miller	Mich. Ag. College	Detroit Heralds
Dick Shields	Mich. Wesleyan College	Detroit Heralds
Tom Bogle	Univ. of Mich.	Detroit Heralds
		Detroit Maroons
Frank Gardner	Carlisle Institute	Detroit Heralds
		Detroit Maroons
Tom Moriarity	Georgetown Univ.	Detroit Maroons
Ed Kerwin	Georgetown Univ.	Detroit Maroons
Harry Costello	Georgetown Univ.	Canton Bulldogs
William Davis Ward	Georgetown Univ.	Canton Bulldogs
CAMP SHERIDAN		
Ernest Allmendinger	Univ. of Mich.	Ann Arbor Independents
Clarence Erb	Allegheny College	Massillon Tigers
Ray Eichenlaub	Univ. of Notre Dame	Toledo Maroons
William Goebel	Yale Univ.	Cincinnati Celts
George Roudebush	Denison Univ.	Cincinnati Celts
Fred Heyman	Washington and Jefferson College	Massillon Tigers
Edmund L. Kagy	W. Reserve Univ.	Akron Indians
		Massillon Tigers
Ray Falcon	Indiana Poly Tech Institute	Evanston North Ends
Thomas H. King	Univ. of Notre Dame	Cleveland Indians
Melvin L. McCreary	Ohio University	Youngstown Pats
Horace Palmer	Ohio University	Youngstown Pats
Tilly Schuessler	Univ. of Cincinnati	Cincinnati Celts
OTHER LOCATIONS		
Earl Abell	Colgate Univ.	Canton Bulldogs
John Arthur	Rutgers Univ.	Massillon Tigers
H. C. Banjan	Univ. of Notre Dame	Pine Village A.C.
Baird	Carlisle Institute	Fort Wayne Friars
Albert "Bert" Baston	Univ. of Minnesota	Massillon Tigers
Alfred Bergman	Univ. of Notre Dame	Wabash A.A.
Charles "Gus" Dorais	Univ. of Notre Dame	Massillon Tigers
		Fort Wayne Friars
Mal Elward	Univ. of Notre Dame	Fort Wayne Friars
Al Feeney	Univ. of Notre Dame	Fort Wayne Friars
William Garlow	Carlisle Institute	Canton Bulldogs
Charles Helvie	Indiana Univ.	Fort Wayne Friars
		Pine Village A.C.

Camp	College	Pro team
David Walter Hopkins	Univ. of Pennsylvania	Cincinnati Celts
George W. Jones	Holy Cross Univ.	Davenport A.C.
Keith "Deacon" Jones	Univ. of Notre Dame	Fort Wayne Friars
Kent "Skeet" Lambert	Wabash College	Fort Wayne Friars
		Canton Bulldogs
		Detroit Heralds
		Massillon Tigers
William D. Love	Princeton Univ.	Youngstown Pats
Leo McCausland	Univ. of Detroit	Akron Burkharts
McCormick	North Dakota Univ.	Davenport A. C.
F. Bart Macomber	Univ. of Illinois	Youngstown Pats
Cyril Moran	Univ. of Detroit	Detroit Maroons
Frank Mt. Pleasant	Carlisle Institute	Altoona Indians
		N.Y. All Stars
Joe Pliska	Univ. of Notre Dame	Fort Wayne Friars
		Pine Village A.C.
Rudolph W. Propst	Syracuse Univ.	Detroit Heralds
Labe Safro	none	Minn. Marines
Stilwell Saunooke	Carlisle Institute	Altoona Indians
		Pitcairn Quakers
		Youngstown Pats
Chris Schlachter	Syracuse Univ.	Massillon Tigers
Eugene Schobinger	Univ. of Illinois	Evanston N. Ends
J. Lee Snoots	none	Columbus Panhandles
Axel Turnquist	Univ. of Minnesota	Minn. All-Stars
M. J. Truesby	Oberlin Prep School	Canton Bulldogs
William Sykes Tucker	Univ. of Pennsylvania	Detroit Heralds
W. V. Van Aken	Purdue Univ.	Hammond Clabbys
Ivan A. Zaring	Indiana Univ.	Fort Wayne Friars

tonment camp in the country. Some camps have as high as four football teams in action.

Husky young rookies who never played football before are playing it this fall in the Army camps and on college gridirons. In other years these young men did not go in for the pigskin game because they did not have the opportunity. Under military regulations, hundreds turned out for football. The soldier is red blooded and full of life. He loves sport and needs it. Football is a red blooded game.

By the time the season ends, football will have hundreds of followers who never knew its thrills before.

In November 1917, the war also brought a war tax on tickets to football games, boxing exhibitions, and other forms of entertainment. The war tax law was worded in such a way that owners and promoters could not pay it out of their own pockets. The law specifically required a 10 percent surtax. Consequently, the war also brought higher ticket prices.[27]

Finally, the war was reflected in professional football in many unexpected ways. For example, bands began playing the national anthem before the start of the game, a tradition that has been followed ever since 1917. In Dayton, the Triangles enlisted the help of Wright Field army aviators to demonstrate support for the war effort at the opening game of their 1917 season. Planes from the 42nd Aviation Squadron of the U.S. Army flew over the field and dropped a football from one of the planes to launch the game.[28] At other professional football games, the Red Cross passed around a bucket to solicit donations for that agency's war activities, and the Toledo Maroons donated some football equipment so that army boys could play football.[29]

Some of the pro football players became war heroes. Harry Costello, for example, was awarded the British Military Cross for Bravery at Archangel, Russia,[30] and William Sykes Tucker was awarded the Croix de Guerre for gallantry while in France.[31] Others, such as Kent Lambert, Melvin L. McCreary, Rudolph W. Propst, and Lester Thomas Miller, made the military their career as a result of commissions gained in officer's training camps during World War I.[32]

Over the past eighty years, the value of football, and particularly professional football, as a staging ground for life has been seriously undermined. The job market and the training requirements for professional football have changed so dramatically since 1920 that perhaps the only thing that pro football prepares one for today is more football. Year-round conditioning, daily practices, and long seasons have reduced the ancillary benefits of professional football, but salaries paid to modern athletes more than compensate for other lost benefits. The lessons of the earlier period about leadership, teamwork, and camaraderie are still taught by parents and high school coaches, even though it is likely that they no longer reflect the values needed to succeed, now that the country has moved into a postindustrial society.[33]

Even in the first two decades of the twentieth century, some outstanding football players were not good scholars. A number of pioneers in professional football dropped out of college before getting a degree, and some even played college football without leaving any record that they had ever enrolled in that college. For example, Joe "Dolly" Gray from Akron played football for the University of Chicago in 1914, is pictured in game photos, and had flattering words about his performances printed on the sports pages of several of the country's best news-

THE WAR AND THE GAME   -   -   -   By Fontaine Fox

(Copyright, 1917, by The Wheeler Syndicate, Inc.)

The Big Colleges aren't the only ones whose football squads have been reduced by the war.

World War I fostered the growth of pro football with higher wages of the factory workers who supported the game, but America's entrance into the war interrupted the formalization of a national professional football league. (*Pittsburgh Gazette Times*, 3 November 1917.)

papers, but there is no record that he was ever enrolled at the University of Chicago.[34] Likewise, Cornell-Hamburg lineman Cochran played at least two games for De Paul University in Chicago in 1913, but the University has no record that he ever enrolled there.[35] At least one in four independent football players who show college affiliation, among the teams studied, was a college dropout. Some, such as Fred M. Walker,[36]

Paul Des Jardien, and Gideon Charles Smith, later completed their college education, but many had little or no interest in more formal education.

During the second decade of the twentieth century, professional sports and coaching careers were powerful influences promoting occupational and geographic mobility. At a time when most Americans rarely traveled more than a hundred miles from their birthplace and occupational mobility was still difficult to achieve, the desire to succeed drove the sponsors of sports teams to cast a wide net in search of athletes and coaches who could help them win. By 1910, this search frequently extended beyond city and state to region, but it was not until 1915 that player mobility in independent football circles encompassed the entire country. The twenty most successful professional football teams featured players who had grown up in places like Texas, South Carolina, New York, Massachusetts, California, Oregon, Washington, and Kansas, as well as the Midwest, where most of the teams were located.

Increased opportunities for secondary schooling for American teenagers, together with the growing emphasis on physical fitness for city kids, were creating coaching opportunities that professional football players were happy to take. Pro sports, especially for college-educated athletes, offered widespread recognition, travel, extra income during an apprenticeship period, and an introduction to a new set of people in communities that were heretofore unfamiliar to them. These advantages gave pro sports an allure they had not had in earlier times. It is clear from the profiles of those who played professional football during this formative period that the athletes nearly always gained more than they lost by turning professional.

30. Sunday Heroes

Football is a sport of controlled violence in which athletic skill, teamwork, and fast thinking are necessary. This is particularly true of single platoon football, played by the professionals until 1949, where the players had to understand the whole game and, like basketball, were responsible for both offensive and defensive play. The players on the field were on their own, calling their own plays and controlling their own destinies. This gave distinctive personalities to the teams that reflected the strengths and weaknesses of the players.

Unlike baseball, football is fast paced and does not require long periods of concentration or subtle understandings to be appreciated. In baseball, attention is frequently focused on the duel between pitcher and hitter. That contest often hinges on the choice of pitches that only a keen observer and student of the game can detect. By contrast, football is more clearly a team activity in which all eleven players must do their part on every play. While it is possible for a baseball star to shine without team support, no football player can be a star without the help of his teammates.

Football is a game of manly skills and brute strength: there is no place for a gentleman on the football field. Family status or ethnic origins have little impact on winning football games. In short, football is well designed to appeal to blue-collar workers. One might even say that it is a workingman's game, pure and simple.

Like other sports, football had its heroes and its stars. Looking back from a perspective of nearly one hundred years, it is natural to wonder if early professional football players were as good as those who followed. College coaches like Glenn "Pop" Warner, Albert Exendine, Amos Stagg, and Fielding Yost, who were contemporary with the emergence of the professional sport, made disparaging comments about professional football during that period, but were they fair observers?

Glenn S. "Pop" Warner was a maverick among college coaches of his time. He openly paid and lavishly housed his "athletic boys," scheduled long money-making tours, personally pocketed part of the game receipts, and sometimes bet heavily on his own and other games.[1] Nevertheless, Warner was a good judge of football talent, and his former players and those of Notre Dame were the most numerous on professional football rosters during the period. In early November 1917, Coach Warner, at that time head coach at the University of Pittsburgh, decided that his star fullback, George McLaren, needed to improve his punting before the Washington and Jefferson game. So he hired Jim Thorpe to improve McLaren's punting. The *Pittsburgh Gazette-Times* reported that "Thorpe spent most of all afternoon kicking the ball himself and showing McLaren . . . how a major leaguer in the art of punting should perform."[2]

As a result of this coaching experience, noted the *Canton Repository,* Pop Warner "sat on the bench along the north side of the field" during the Canton-Massillon game of November 25, 1917, and "hobnobbed with the players before the game and between halves." Warner claimed that he could see the difference between professional and college football, but he still had a kind word for the Bulldogs. According to Warner, "they play a great defensive game, almost unbeatable, but do not show the team work that is a characteristic of the successful college teams. . . . Give that Canton team a few weeks of practice together under a good coach and they would be hard to beat."[3]

Warner went on to say,

my team of last year would have whipped the Canton team. I am sure, and my team this fall would best Canton. We would best them through superior teamwork. Jim Thorpe has been telling me right along he has the best team in the world: he may have, but I cannot agree with him. Pitt would beat the best professional team in the land if today's play is a sample of what we would have to beat.[4]

Albert Exendine, who had played for Warner a decade earlier and was now head coach at Georgetown, was also at the game and agreed with Pop Warner.[5]

These comments did not sit well in Canton, and the Bulldog management offered to test out Warner's statements on the football field.[6] Jim Thorpe offered to play Warner's Pitt team for charity and wired his challenge to the University of Pittsburgh, declaring that the 1916–17 Canton Bulldogs were the greatest football team ever assembled.[7] Pop Warner, of course, refused the challenge.

Without question, Warner's observation that pro teams in 1917 lacked offensive teamwork was accurate. After all, they changed personnel frequently and rarely had the opportunity to practice together. However, given comparable training and practice times, there is no doubt that the pro players of 1915–17 were every bit as talented as pro players that followed, and some, like Jim Thorpe, would have been great stars in any era. Indeed, the best fifty players of the pre-NFL era could have played for any single platoon professional team before or after the formation of the NFL. More than a hundred players who played professionally during this period went on to play for thirty-seven different National Football League teams between 1920 and 1932. Twenty-four were still playing as starters for NFL teams in 1925.

The idea for naming an all-professional team had some of its first adherents in 1917 when the *Toledo Bee* and the *Cleveland Plain Dealer* named All-Pro teams (see Appendix C).

A list of the best fifty-five professional players of the 1915–17 period might include those shown in Table 5. Those with an asterisk are members of the College Football Hall of Fame. Those with a # were College All-Americans.

Table 5   Fifty-five Best Players, 1915–17

ENDS
John Devereaux, *Dayton Triangles; Detroit Heralds*
Bob Marshall, *Minneapolis Marines* *#
Bob "Nasty" Nash, *Massillon Tigers* #
Alfred E. "Greasy" Neale, *Canton Bulldogs* *
Jesse Reno, *Wabash Athletic Association*
Knute Rockne, *Massillon Tigers; Fort Wayne Friars* *#
Richard "Red" Shields, *Detroit Heralds*
Ernie Soucy, *Canton Bulldogs* #
Carl "Dutch" Thiele, *Cincinnati Celts; Massillon Tigers; Detroit Heralds*
Ray E. Whipple, *Detroit Heralds*
Samuel S. Willaman, *Akron Indians; Cleveland Indians; Canton Bulldogs*

TACKLES AND GUARDS
Frank A. Blocker, *Hammond Clabbys*
Howard "Cub" Buck, *Canton Bulldogs; Pine Village* #
Bob "Butts" Butler, *Canton Bulldogs; Cleveland Indians*#
Edgar C. "Big Ed" Davis, *Pine Village; Canton Bulldogs; Fort Wayne Friars*
Howard "Cap" Edwards, *Canton Bulldogs; Fort Wayne Friars*
Keith "Deacon" Jones, *Massillon Tigers; Fort Wayne Friars*
Clarence "Steamer" Horning, *Detroit Heralds* #
Emmett Keefe, *Pine Village; Hammond Clabbys; Cincinnati Celts*
John Kellison, *Canton Bulldogs*
Alfred Nesser, *Columbus Panhandles; Massillon Tigers; Akron Pros*
Frank Nesser, *Columbus Panhandles; Massillon Tigers; Akron Pros; Detroit Heralds*
John "Doc" Redmond, *Wabash A. A.; Pine Village*
Ed "Unk" Russell, *Canton Bulldogs*
Clarence "Doc" Spears, *Canton Bulldogs* #

Table 5　Fifty-five Best Players, 1915–17 *(continued)*

Norman J. "Dutch" Speck, *Canton Bulldogs*
Claude Thornhill, *McKeesport Olympics; Massillon Tigers*
Aloysius A. "Buzz" Wesbecher, *Massillon Tigers*

CENTERS

Paul "Shorty" Des Jardien, *Cleveland Indians* *#
Robert D. "Bob" Peck, *Youngstown Patricians; Massillon Tigers* *#
David Reese, *Cincinnati Celts; Youngstown Patricians*
Frank Rydzewski, *Fort Wayne Friars*
Ralph "Fats" Waldsmith, *Canton Bulldogs*

QUARTERBACKS

Charles "Gus" Dorais, *Massillon Tigers; Fort Wayne Friars* *#
Milton Ghee, *Canton Bulldogs* #
Reuben Johnson, *Evanston North Ends; Cornell-Hamburgs*
Kent "Skeet" Lambert, *Ft. Wayne Friars; Canton Bulldogs; Detroit Heralds; Massillon Tigers*
Alphonse H. Mahrt, *Dayton Triangles*

HALFBACKS

John Barrett, *Evanston North Ends; Toledo Maroons; Youngstown Patricians; Hammond Clabbys*
Alfred "Dutch" Bergman, *Wabash A. A.*
Stanley Cofall, *Youngstown Pats; Massillon Tigers*
Harry Costello, *Canton Bulldogs* #
John Leo "Paddy" Driscoll, *Hammond Clabbys* *#
Joel P. Mattern, *Massillon Tigers*
George Roudebush, *Cincinnati Celts; Canton Bulldogs*
Norbert Sacksteder, *Dayton Gym-Cadets; Dayton Triangles; Massillon Tigers; Detroit Heralds*
Jim Thorpe, *Canton Bulldogs; Pine Village* *#
Gus Welch, *Canton Bulldogs* #

FULLBACKS

Pete Calac, *Canton Bulldogs; Detroit Braves*
Frank Dunn, *Canton Bulldogs; Youngstown Patricians*
Ray Eichenlaub, *Toledo Maroons; Wabash A.A.* *#
Guilford Falcon, *Evanston North Ends; Wabash A.A.*
George "Carp" Julian, *Canton Bulldogs*
Ted Nesser, *Columbus Panhandles*
Lorin Solon, *Cleveland Indians; Duluth* #

The incomparable star of the era, of course, was James Francis Thorpe. Thorpe was the yard stick against which every athlete of his time measured himself. Even today, the children of the pioneers of professional football will say with evident pride, "he played against Jim

Thorpe." While a student at Carlisle Institute, Thorpe's unofficial best in the 100-yard dash equaled the world's record, a feat that, when translated to today's track conditions, would still make him a world-class sprinter. Thorpe had speed, strength, and stamina. In 1916 and 1917, he carried the ball 105 times in nine games and averaged 5.2 yards per carry. He punted thirty-three times and averaged more than forty yards per punt. He also threw passes, returned punts, and played fearless defense. He played injured, and he played with virtually no training or practice. Few modern athletes could hope for such statistics, as these earlier players had to compete exposed to the elements in shorter games on muddy and snowy fields that were poorly maintained. It was no accident that polls conducted by the Associated Press among 393 sportswriters and broadcasters in 1950 declared Jim Thorpe "the greatest football player" and the "greatest male athlete" of the first half of the twentieth century.[8]

Lest one think that Thorpe was the only star, it must be remembered that players like Reuben Johnson, Kent Lambert, Knute Rockne, Charles Dorais, Stanley Cofall, Paddy Driscoll, and, indeed, all of the players on the list of fifty-five, were genuine stars by any standards. They were skilled athletes whose accomplishments should not be underestimated. In total, thirty-five Walter Camp All-Americans played professional football between 1915 and 1918, eighteen of them first team All-American selections (see Appendix D). An additional sixteen professional players during this three-year period were named to All-American teams by other sportswriters while in college. These numbers leave little doubt that, by 1915, many of the best college players went on to play pro football. Clearly, professional football was becoming well established prior to the creation of the National Football League.[9]

31. Promotion and Financing of Iron-Man Football: 1915–17

Today, the revenue to support professional football comes primarily from television and radio broadcast rights, rent on expensive sky boxes, the sale of licensed sportswear, concessions and programs at the stadium during games, parking fees, and ticket sales. In 1915, the revenue for professional football was limited almost exclusively to ticket sales and grandstand seating. That year, on average, a ticket to a professional football game cost fifty cents for standing room or end zone seats, and approximately 40 percent of the crowd paid an additional twenty-five cents for grandstand seating. By 1917, the average ticket was up to seventy-five cents for general admission, and, for special games, the charge was up to $1 or $1.50 to cover the large guarantees that the best teams charged.

The average crowd for the top twenty teams in 1915 was about twenty-four hundred fans. This translated into a weekly revenue of $600 for home teams and $525 for visiting teams. In order to attract a team that demanded a $1,000 guarantee, it was necessary to draw at least thirty-three hundred paying fans or have merchant subsidies to make up the shortfall. Sometimes, as was the case with the Detroit Heralds-Evanston North Ends game in 1915, the visiting team might lower its guarantee but demand a side bet that allowed them to increase their revenue if they won. Gate receipts were typically split fifty-fifty with the visiting team. Grandstand revenues were usually split sixty-forty in favor of the home team. A weak visiting team might settle for a forty-sixty split on combined revenues.

Low admission charges hampered some teams. The Rock Island Independents, for example, charged twenty-five cents admission to games in 1915.[1] As a consequence, they were only able to pay referees and linesmen $10 per game, and while a small number of players got $25, the rest were paid $5 or $10.[2] Massillon and Canton charged seventy-five cents admission during the regular season and $1 when they played each other. They also charged an additional twenty-five cents for reserved grandstand seats. Some teams, like Youngstown in 1915, passed the hat and hoped for twenty-five cents per person, often averaging only $750 income even with crowds of five thousand.

In 1915, twenty professional football match ups drew three thousand or more paying fans. Seventeen teams were involved in these match-ups. The best estimated average fan attendance occurred in Massillon (3,700), Canton (3,570), Fort Wayne (2,635), Youngstown (5,625), and Detroit (3,057 for the Heralds). Wabash, Toledo, Pine Village, Minneapolis, and Rock Island were capable of drawing large crowds of four thousand to eight thousand people for key games. The visiting teams most likely to draw large crowds were Columbus, Evanston, Canton, and Massillon. Other teams were financially handicapped by the lack of fan support at home. Evanston and Columbus were forced to play almost their entire schedule on the road. Dayton and Cincinnati were kept from the top ranks of independent football by their inability to schedule top flight teams that required large guarantees. By contrast, in 1915 Ivy League and Western Conference college teams often drew twenty thousand to thirty thousand fans to their games, frequently at higher ticket prices than charged by the professionals. It would take years before professional football could achieve crowds that large.

In October 1916, the top twenty independent football teams in the United States were attracting crowds that were double those of the previous year. In 1915, the average attendance was twelve hundred per game, and only ten games during the month drew more than three thousand fans. In October, one year later, sixteen games drew three thousand or more fans, and seven of these games drew more than five thousand fans.

The increase in attendance was not evenly distributed. In 1916, teams like Cleveland, Detroit, Canton, and Massillon averaged more than twice as many fans as the other top twenty teams. In 1915, the range in attendance was relatively narrow, when Youngstown is excluded, because it did not charge admission. In that year, Massillon averaged thirty-seven hundred fans per game, while teams like Dayton and Cincinnati averaged about one thousand fans. Thus, the difference between the team with the best hometown attendance and the fifteenth ranked team was seventeen hundred fans per game. By 1916, the range had widened. Cleveland and Detroit drew more than four thousand fans per game, while Dayton and Cincinnati still hovered around one thousand fans per game.

The largest crowds for a professional football game before World War I were in Detroit, Cleveland, and Canton. The 1916 games between the Cleveland Indians and the Canton Bulldogs, and between Canton and Massillon, drew between eight and ten thousand fans. In 1917, the Detroit Heralds drew fifteen thousand fans to their games against Camp Custer and eight thousand for the Canton Bulldogs. On average, three thousand paying fans at a game was considered a good-sized crowd. Depending on the weather and the reputation of the visiting team, some games drew as few as six hundred or as many as eight thousand or ten thousand fans. Clearly, professional football was still the illegitimate stepchild of college football, which regularly drew crowds of twenty thousand or more for important games and frequently had annual incomes of more than $30,000 for midsized colleges. For example, eighty thousand fans paid an average of $2 per ticket to see the Yale-Harvard game;[3] fifteen thousand fans paid an average of $2 per ticket to see the University of Chicago-Minnesota game in 1914;[4] and seven thousand fans paid $3 each to see the University of Chicago-Minnesota game in Minneapolis in 1915, while an additional four thousand fans paid $1.50 to $2 for tickets to that game.[5] In 1916, the University of Wisconsin's season receipts for home games were $31,705, having grossed $8,000 in their game with the University of Chicago, $5,000 against the University of Minnesota, and $2,000 against the University of Illinois.[6]

The size of professional football crowds was not a function of city size, as Table 6 demonstrates. Large cities like Chicago and Cincinnati showed minimal support for pro football, while small towns like Massillon, Wabash, Rock Island, and Pine Village were staunch supporters of their independent football teams. It is also notable that blue-collar, steel manufacturing cities like Gary, Indiana (50,000 residents), or Lorain, Ohio (35,000 residents), failed to field strong independent football teams, while smaller cities like Massillon and Moline, with similar manufacturing bases, did. Moreover, Canton and Fort Wayne were the same size communities, but Canton regularly outdrew Fort Wayne by fourteen hundred fans per game. The average attendance figures provided in Table 6 are for home games.

Preoccupation with attendance was natural when it was the only source of revenue for most pro football teams. In 1916, the average weekly revenue for the top twenty teams was $1,200 for the home team. The following year it was $1,400. One of the patterns regarding attendance that began to emerge by 1916–17 was the difficulty of small markets to maintain a pro football team. In 1915, Wabash ranked eighth in attendance, but, by 1917, they ranked tenth. More importantly, their revenue in 1915 was only 51 percent of the best teams, and 25 percent in 1917. As costs escalated and the number of paying fans necessary to break even grew, small-market teams were placed in jeopardy. In 1916, the Wabash Athletic Association was nearly insolvent,[7] the Evanston North Ends found it necessary to close operations, and Pine Village actively sought opportunities to play home games in Indianapolis and Lafayette. In 1917, this trend continued. Wabash, Toledo, and Pine Village became less competitive as their home market became smaller in comparison to their competitors, and teams with larger markets got stronger. It would take nearly two decades before some National Football League franchise owners learned the obvious lesson that their ability to survive depended on the size of their market.

Bigger crowds meant a need for more seating and, therefore, more expense. In Fort Wayne, the Friars' management built additional bleachers to accommodate fans.[8] Peggy Parratt's Indians played their games in the summer home of Cleveland's American League baseball team,[9] while, in Detroit, the Heralds moved from Packard Park to Navin Field, the home of the Detroit Tigers, and the Cincinnati Celts played their home games at Redlands Field, the summer home of the Cincinnati Reds.[10] Massillon constructed "seats 14 tiers high and stretching the entire length of the field" on both west and east sides of the Driving Park gridiron.[11] In Davenport, Iowa, the Davenport Athletic Club played at Three-I Park, a minor league baseball field. The Hammond Clabbys scheduled their game with Sheridan, Indiana, in Lafayette to accommodate a larger crowd.[12] Pine Village enlarged its home seating capacity for their game with Decatur by renting "seats from a circus company" to completely encircle the football field with bleachers.[13] In November 1916, Claire Rhodes, the Pine Village manager, leased a football field in Indianapolis for the balance of the season to accommodate larger crowds.[14]

The trend toward larger and better accommodations continued the next year when the Toledo Maroons moved from Armory Park to Swayne Field. The *Toledo Blade* reported, on October 6, 1917, "There is far more space for a playing field than was the case at Armory Park, where play was hampered by the lack of clearance at the ends and sides of the gridiron." Not everyone, however, was happy with the move, as the *Toledo Blade* noted: "There has always been close relationships between Maroon players and spectators, made possible by the size of Ar-

Table 6 The Top 25 Professional Football Teams by City Size, 1915–1917

Team	City Size	Average Attendance	NFL
Chicago Cornell-Hamburgs	2,200,000	2,000	yes
Detroit Heralds	950,000	4,100	yes
Cleveland Indians	750,500	4,100	yes
Cincinnati Celts	382,160	1,000	yes
Minneapolis Marines	375,350	2,600	yes
Toledo Maroons	237,200	2,800	yes
Columbus Panhandles	234,000	700	yes
Akron Pros	189,000	3,500	yes
Dayton Triangles	148,000	1,200	yes
Youngstown Patricians*	125,000	4,000	no
Canton Bulldogs	85,000	4,000	yes
Fort Wayne Friars	85,000	2,600	yes
Altoona Indians	57,200	1,200	no
Racine Regulars	56,500	1,000	yes
Davenport Athletic Association	52,500	3,200	no
McKeesport Olympics	44,300	1,300	no
Decatur Athletic Club	38,000	1,500	yes
Hammond Clabbys	35,500	1,500	yes
Evanston North Ends	35,200	1,200	no
Rock Island Independents	34,000	3,200	yes
Green Bay	29,000	5,000	yes
Moline Red Men	28,200	3,000	no
Massillon Tigers	25,000	4,000	no
Lafayette-Pine Village AC	20,200	2,200	no
Wabash Athletic Association	8,000	2,600	no
Pitcairn Quakers**	5,000	2,500	no

*some free admissions, low price tickets in 1915, but in 1916 averaged 3,122 paid admissions and 4,157 in 1917.
**a suburb of Pittsburgh
  SOURCE: *Collier's World Atlas and Gazetteer,* (New York: Collier & Sons Corporation, 1920). The average game attendance was estimated from newspaper reports.

mory Park, in the past. Considerable comment was indulged in Sunday because the playing field was so far away from the crowd."[15]

As the top ten independent teams incurred greater expenses to accommodate fans and hire key players, they found it necessary to demand higher guarantees when they played out of town. In 1915, $500 guarantees were considered the upper limit for visiting teams. In 1916, the Detroit Heralds, the Massillon Tigers, the Canton Bulldogs, and the Fort Wayne Friars demanded $750 and $1,000 guarantees. The Friars paid $700 a week in salaries to get all-star talent,[16] so it is little wonder that they demanded an $800 guarantee to play away from home. Davenport secured a guarantee of $700 to play in Hammond.[17] Sometimes games were canceled because the guarantee was not secured. On November 17, 1916, for example, the *Canton Repository* reported that "the trip to Detroit on Thanksgiving, with the strong Heralds as opponents of the Bulldogs, has been canceled by Cusack because he could not get a satisfactory guarantee."[18]

In some cases, admission rates were increased to meet higher guarantee requirements. On October 21, 1916, the *Toledo Blade* reported:

Management atop the Maroons has increased the admission to 75 cents for this game, owing to the big guarantee demanded by the Tigers. Gratop [the Toledo Maroons business manager] hesitated before asking the increased price, but finally decided that fans wanted the best to be had and would rather pay an additional quarter to see the Tigers than watch some weak team play at the regular price.

Similarly, Hammond increased its admission price to $1 to make good on its $700 guarantee to Davenport,[19] and Canton increased its admission rate of fifty cents general admission to $1 starting with the Columbus Panhandle game when Jim Thorpe was back on the job and the team was at full strength.[20] Reserved seats added twenty-five cents to Canton prices.[21]

In Fort Wayne, Dayton, Wabash, and Pine Village, they tried to hold the line at fifty cents for general admission to games, but failure to raise prices undermined the financial stability of these teams and contributed to their relative decline in 1917.

Teams did two other things to cope with rising costs. The Hammond Clabbys took only sixteen players with them when they played Sheridan in Lafayette, Indiana, on October 22, 1916. They used all of them during the game and discovered "they could use a couple of extra men very nicely when they meet 'stronger teams'."[22] Some teams also tried crowd-pleasing promotions to increase fan interest and attendance. The Cincinnati Celts, for example, announced that, henceforth, their players would wear numbers on the back of their jerseys to make it easier for fans to watch the game and to identify who did what.[23] They were following the lead of Detroit. On October 22, the Fort Wayne Friars tried using letters as a means of identifying their players, but they apparently dropped the idea after a single game.[24] In 1917, the Toledo Maroons started wearing numbers.[25]

Three types of promotions were popular in professional football circles in 1916: parades, free admission for children under fifteen, and excursions out of town. Many teams started the season with a parade. In

Fort Wayne, for example, "an automobile parade, concert by the Electro-Technic band and the Jefferson Drum Corps, and all sorts of excitement" were the features of the 1916 football season opener.[26] Massillon also held a parade on opening day. In Wabash, the Athletic Association held a "homecoming" parade before an important mid-season game, and Hammond combined out-of-town excursions with parades held in Fort Wayne and Lafayette.[27] The *Hammond Times* supported the latter practice:

> The greatest sporting excursion ever made out of Hammond or into Fort Wayne for the most important professional football game in the west [took place]. . . . A vestibule train of seven coaches with every seat taken left Hammond at eight o'clock Sunday morning and with hardly a stop reached Fort Wayne exactly at eleven—a distance of 180 miles in three hours. . . . At the depot in Fort Wayne a line of march was formed. While the band played "Hail, Hail, the Gang's All Here," the Clabby army went up the main street before the astounded natives. Fort Wayne didn't suppose that any city thought as much of a professional football team as Hammond does.[28]

The parade two weeks later in Lafayette was even more grand. "Shortly after 1 o'clock . . . the Citizen's band of Lafayette serenaded the Hammond team and delegation at the Fowler [Hotel] and then repeated the stunt at the Lahr [Hotel] for the benefit of the Sheridan team. The band then headed a procession to the [ball] park."[29] "Several photographers and a 'moving picture operator' was taking scenes. Max Klein entertained the crowd with several solos." All of the men in the Hammond delegation wore top hats furnished by the Hammond Commercial Club. Other teams organized excursions, but none were better than those organized by the Hammond Clabbys.[30]

On October 22, 1916, the Fort Wayne Friars held their first kids' day at League Park. All youngsters under fifteen were invited to see the game free. All they had to do was go to a local merchant to get a free ticket.[31] The promotion was so popular that it was repeated in 1917.

Promotion did not solve a team's financial problems even when it increased attendance, because the cost of fielding a quality football team continued to rise faster than income. Competition for good players drove up both wages and the guarantees demanded by rivals. In a number of instances, teams entered into bidding wars for key players. Consequently, it became difficult to hold a strong team together, because other teams would try to steal the best players. Peggy Parratt was intimately involved both in having players stolen from him and in raiding other teams. In 1915, his entire first team was lured away with offers of higher wages by Massillon and Canton. The following year, he used the same tactics when he plucked players from Canton, Massillon, and Youngstown.

In addition to bidding for players, teams would sometimes break their contract to play with an opponent when a more attractive offer presented itself. For example, on Thanksgiving Day 1917, in Lafayette, Indiana, there was one unhappy man. Joseph F. Carr and twenty players from the Columbus Panhandle team had traveled all night for what they believed would be a game at League Park with Pine Village. Joe Carr had a signed contract, and the date had been booked in September. In the meantime, however, Claire Rhodes, manager of Pine Village, had also agreed to play in Wabash that same day. So, when Carr showed up there was just an empty stadium, and there was nothing left for him to do except sue Claire Rhodes for expenses and damages or to absorb the costs and to go home mad.[32]

Player contracts, schedules, guarantees, and the number and location of games to be played were subject to the type of abuse that jeopardized team solvency and public support. It was becoming clear to all who were familiar with unregulated pro football during this period that these conditions could not go on indefinitely without endangering the future of the sport. Ruinous wages to key players and the lack of regular schedules and leagues were the bane of pro football in 1916. Many business managers were quick to understand these problems. The 1915–16 professional football seasons demonstrated to most team owners and managers that a league with rules was needed if the sport was to survive.

According to Arthur Daley, sports columnist for the *New York Times*, the pro game was "a haphazard hit or miss affair. Teams would assemble on a Sunday, run through signals in a hotel lobby in the morning, and play together in the afternoon. Teammates one week might be rivals the next. The sport was run virtually on a day to day basis."[33] But there was more stability than many realized. The often repeated story that the Columbus Panhandles found themselves facing Knute Rockne with six different teams in one season is simply not true. A small handful of players such as George Vedderneck, Joe Bergie, Red Fleming, Tom Gormley, George "Bull" Lowe, and Jim "Butchy" Barron played for three teams in one season, and a somewhat larger group played for two teams in a season, but sportswriters have exaggerated the number of players who frequently switched teams during this era. Even so, there was enough pirating to be a problem to managers with big-name players.

The 1916 independent football season marked the beginning of efforts to create a national football league. While these efforts would not bear fruit until September 17, 1920, when the American Professional Football Association was formally organized at a meeting held in the Hupmobile agency of Ralph Hay, the Canton Bulldogs' business manager, the necessary groundwork for that meeting began in 1916. It is not surprising that, by mid-October 1916, there were attempts underway to call a halt to the "football wars" and to discuss regular schedules and an end to player "tampering."

On Tuesday, October 17, the business managers of the pro teams in Canton, Cleveland, Massillon, and Youngstown met in Cleveland to consider how "the big four" could "smoke the pipe of peace" and end the "war in Ohio professional football circles."[34] These four teams agreed to scheduling dates among themselves calling for a fifty-fifty split of all proceeds for those games. They also agreed to "ban all tampering with players on those four teams." That is to say, if one of the teams signed a player, the others were not to offer that player a job for the balance of the season, unless given approval by the team for whom he was playing. The northeast Ohio peace agreement lasted until mid-November, when it was broken by Peggy Parratt who hired two players away from Youngstown.

On October 24, 1916, discussion of a possible "Big Nine" professional football conference surfaced in Indiana.[35] The proposal called for a league composed of Decatur, Columbus, Sheridan, Wabash, Cincinnati, Pine Village, Fort Wayne, Evanston, and Hammond. An argument was made, by the Hammond contingent, that:

in the United States . . . there are hundreds of cities supporting minor league baseball because of the advertising value. In baseball with a daily schedule there are teams that do not draw an average of five hundred people a day and the deficit is made up by the commercial clubs of the cities and credited to value received in advertising. Professional football is a far greater advertising medium. It comes at a time when the sporting columns have been vacated by baseball and space is easily obtained. The Indianapolis papers willingly give Hammond half to three-quarters of a column for football but utterly ignore Hammond baseball games. The size of football crowds in Hammond is three to four times that at a baseball contest. [Moreover,] a season of ten games is a complete football schedule and as five of these games will be played away from home under guarantees, the financial responsibility resting on local backers of a professional team will not be heavy. . . . [Finally, it was argued that] a world of advertising would result from such a conference . . . because of the scores of ex-college stars whose names lend the teams prestige.[36]

In early December, 1916, the Wabash Athletic Association, Fort Wayne Friars, Hammond Clabbys, and Pine Village Athletic Club met to discuss a league that would, according to the *Wabash Plain Dealer,* "delineate salaries for players, establish a regular schedule of games, and regulate admission prices so that professional football could be profitable to its financial backers." Fort Wayne only wanted to play home games because they had better facilities and made more money than their Indiana competitors, so they walked out of the meeting. Tentative arrangements were made, but a conclusion was not reached until September 1917.[37]

Concurrently, Art Gratop, manager of the Toledo Maroons, expressed the issues accurately on December 5, 1916, when he announced his campaign to organize a strong league comprised of the Toledo Maroons, Cleveland Indians, Massillon Tigers, Canton Bulldogs, Detroit Heralds, Cincinnati Celts, Fort Wayne Friars, and the Pine Village Athletic Club. Gratop observed that "ironclad rulings are needed to govern play and protect the various clubs in the circuit." Gratop was "anxious to regulate the lineups, that is prevent too much loading and would make it against the rules to sign college stars for the last game or so, like the Massillon and Canton teams have been doing for years. An organization of this sort would also protect clubs against unreliable players of the Dorais type. . . ."[38]

Dorais was playing for both Massillon and Fort Wayne and would make up stories about injuries to allow him to play on the other team for an important game. A limited arrangement of this type became reality in an agreement between Hammond, Wabash, and Pine Village.[39]

In the meantime, however, professional football remained a marginal business. There were twice as many $500-a-week teams as $1,000-a-week teams among the top twenty independents. Except for the four northeast Ohio teams, Detroit, and perhaps Fort Wayne, all of the other teams were still "wannabees." Columbus could not draw a large enough crowd to support a home game against any of the top twenty teams. Dayton, Toledo, and Cincinnati could not regularly guarantee more than $500 to a visiting team, and Wabash, Pine Village, and Hammond each faced serious limitations when it came to guarantees of over $750. Moreover, Wabash had no showers for visiting teams, and Pine Village was such a small town that it depended on the railroads to help promote a regional following and held its home games in Lafayette or Indianapolis.

Hammond's gate receipts on home games averaged less than $500[40] until they raised their tickets to $1 per person and threatened to play the balance of their games on the road if fan support did not improve.[41] Even then Hammond could only manage to pay its players $10 per game, while other teams averaged $35 a game.[42] This was hardly the foundation for a strong franchise in a regional football league. In trying to stay competitive, some traditional football strongholds began to experience economic pressure. Nineteen-sixteen was the last year that Wabash, Pine Village, Evanston, Columbus, Toledo, and Cincinnati were football powerhouses. By 1917, all of these teams were in decline. Davenport, Cleveland, and Youngstown would shine brightly for a short time, only to disappear from the ranks of professional football. Cleveland, of course, reemerged as a pro football center, but only after several false starts.

From the outset, professional football has been plagued with two nagging problems. The first is its dependence on local community identity and support. Team owners often delude themselves, and endanger the future of the sport, by convincing themselves that they are in a private business, independent of the need for community largess, and that they need answer only to themselves and their stockholders. This is a mistake. Professional football, like many professional sports, depends on stadiums, transportation networks, local traffic control and law enforcement, and an absence of local competition, as well as community pride, participation, and support, to survive. When communities are blackmailed into building new stadiums which require significant tax support or one-sided leases, or when a franchise is moved from one city to another without regard for the public interest, professional football risks alienating the community support it so vitally needs to survive and, incidentally, took so long to build.

The second problem is the disparity inherent when communities of vastly different sizes compete. Unless the big-market teams financially assist the small-market teams, the contest will inevitably be uneven and unfair, and the professional sport will become less competitive and less interesting. This first became evident in 1917, when Wabash and Dayton were unable to remain competitive with Detroit, because Detroit simply hired the best players away from Dayton and its larger market allowed it to hire more college all-stars than Wabash could afford. Nevertheless, small-market teams have made important contributions to professional football. Canton, Massillon, and Akron demonstrated that professional football teams were viable, and small market teams were the first to give African-American athletes an opportunity to play professional football. Yet for nearly a century professional sports leagues have consistently ignored or inadequately addressed the problem of disparate market size among their franchises. Myopic greed appears to be at the root of both the arrogance toward host communities and the reluctance of the owners of large-market franchises to share revenue with those of smaller franchises.

One of the remaining mysteries regarding the early development of professional football is why communities like Akron, Canton, and Massillon had such an important role in the early history of the sport. Perhaps the answer lies in the ingenuity, intensity, or special sense of purpose of such individuals as George "Peggy" Parratt, Jack Cusack, and James Francis Thorpe. Or maybe the area's openness to ethnic diversity give it an advantage. Or perhaps the region's special love of football, shared by so many factory workers in northeast Ohio, was responsible. Surely, all of these ingredients were present. Without question, Parratt, Cusack, and Thorpe were among the most important individuals involved in raising the curtain on professional football, and all were promoting the sport in northeast Ohio. It also is true that Akron and Canton were open to ethnic diversity. In both communities, African-American and Native American players were given fair contracts, ample playing time, and the acceptance normally withheld from them in other parts of the country in those years. And, certainly, the per capita ratio of population to attendance at professional football games in Akron, Canton, Massillon, and Youngstown was among the highest in the nation. Only Wabash and Green Bay were more supportive of independent football than Massillon, and, between 1915 and 1918, only Davenport, Moline, and Rock Island rivaled Akron, Canton, and Youngstown in their support of independent football. Yet, when all is said and done, no one can prove what made northeast Ohio so important to the dawn of professional football.

It is clear, however, that professional football could not have started in New York City, Boston, Philadelphia, or Chicago. There was simply not enough fan support in large cities for such a venture in 1915. Even in Chicago, where ward politicians sponsored independent football, they could not garner crowds of four or five thousand paying fans to support Sunday football. Instead, it was the midsize factory towns of the upper Midwest that created this new enterprise.

In 1915, the Massillon Tigers tried to schedule the opening game of their season with Shelby but were told "our city is now engrossed in a baseball series with neighboring towns and has not had time to think about football."[43] Shelby's response reflected the priorities of the period. Although spawned in big cities, baseball was rooted in rural America and was the principle American sport. Football was an afterthought to be addressed only at the conclusion of the baseball season. It would take nearly forty years to change this alignment. Only in the last half of the twentieth century was the relative importance of the two sports reversed. Throughout the first fifty years of the twentieth century, professional football was a fragile enterprise. Between 1920 and 1950, forty-two different cities were granted NFL franchises, but only nine cities held a franchise in 1950. Gradually, most of the small-market teams were forced out of the business by market forces, making teams like the Columbus Panhandles, the Dayton Triangles, and the Fort Wayne Friars no more than faded or forgotten memories. Today football, not baseball, is the dominant sport in American culture, but it is a different game played in different places than the game played in Canton in 1915.[44] The hardy entrepreneurs who pioneered in professional football risked significant amounts of their limited capital on a dream. Most of them lost money, and few are remembered even by their families, much less the sporting public. City pride and a love of the sport, not a search for wealth or a religious sense of mission, created professional football. Let us hope that these values are not lost as the sport prospers.

Reference Material

Appendices:

APPENDIX A. Rosters and Schedules

APPENDIX B. Professional Players Who Doubled as Coaches

APPENDIX C. All-Professional Teams, 1917

APPENDIX D. Walter Camp All-Americans in Pro Football, 1915–17

Notes

Index

Appendix A

Prior to World War I, professional football teams did not establish team rosters or schedules either prior to or during the football season. Players were sometimes hired week to week, with the caliber of player added often improving as the season progressed. Team schedules were usually open to change. Winning teams arranged to play other winning teams, and less successful teams scheduled regional rivals in hopes of claiming some sort of championship.

The rosters and schedules that follow were pieced together from newspaper accounts. In many instances, it was necessary to examine several different newspapers and a variety of other sources to get a complete record, and in a few cases—the Chicago Cornell-Hamburgs, for example—it was impossible to establish a complete record for 1915 or 1916. Establishing the first names and playing histories of pioneering professional football players was particularly difficult, since that information was sparingly provided in most newspaper accounts. High school and college yearbooks, student directories, city directories, obituaries, census records, newspaper reports, and, on rare occasions, family records were used to research correct spellings of names, accurate first names, and prior playing histories. There were frequently several spellings of a player's name, and whenever possible we chose the name listed in the high school or college year book.

For perhaps thirty-five percent of the players listed, it has not been possible to determine the first name, the correct spelling of the last name, or the playing history, despite exploring records in more than seventy-five libraries. Nevertheless, these rosters and schedules represent a significant contribution to the early history of professional football and demonstrate that many of the finest college football players went on to play professional football before the creation of the National Football League.

Some abbreviations are used: HS stands for high school; (f) is used to indicate that college football experience was limited to the freshman team; * indicates an assumed name; AC stands for athletic club, while AA stands for athletic association. Mc is a traditional abbreviation for Mac and is treated as Mac in the alphabetization of football players in the rosters.

Akron Indians/Shelby Blues, 1915

ROSTER

Manager-Coach: George "Peggy" Parratt

Colors: *Home Field:*

Players	Position	Prior Team
Austin	QB	
Howard Lester Beck	LE,RE	Wash. and Jeff. College
Crane	QB	Hiram College
Crawford	LG	Shelby Blues
Flanders	RG	Univ. of Pennsylvania
Gettis	LH	
Ed Hanley	FB	Univ. of Pittsburgh
Orville Beck Littick	QB	Ohio Wesleyan Univ.
Lowrey	LT	Oberlin College
Miller	LH	Shelby Blues
Papp	C	
George "Peggy" Parratt	QB	Case Institute
Peck	RT	
Phaler	RT	Shelby Blues
Jonathan Fred Potts	RH	Ohio Wesleyan Univ.
Randall	RH	
Arthur "Bugs" Raymond	RT	Ohio State Univ.
Roe	C	Western Reserve Univ.
Schreiner	LH,RH	Elyria Athletics
Schuffler	RH	
Shreffin	C	
"Smoke" Smalley	LE,RE	Mt. Union College; Canton Bulldogs
John M. Smith	FB	Bethany College
Watson	RE	
Carl Weiler	LG	Case Institute
Stanfield Wells	LE	Univ. of Michigan
Samuel S. Willaman	LH,E	Ohio State Univ.
Wilson*	RT	
Zackman	RG	Case Institute
Zieman	LT	

SCHEDULE

Attend.	Date	Opponent	Score
	10/10	canceled at Detroit Maroons	
	10/31	@ Detroit Maroons*	0–21
A2600	11/07	@ TOLEDO MAROONS	0–10
	11/14	@ Dayton Gym-Cadets	0–39
	11/25	@ Marion Questions	7–18
	11/28	Bates Pirates	0–0

* Akron played as Shelby Blues

Won 0   **Lost 4**   **Tied 1**

Akron Burkhardts, 1916

ROSTER

Manager: Stephen "Suey" Welch   *Coach:* Ralph "Fats" Waldsmith
Colors: *Home Field:*

Players	Position	Prior Team
Carl Carderelli	C	Akron Central HS
Chick Conway	RT	
Derby*	RE,RG,LG	Univ. of Pittsburgh
Frank Goettge	FB	Barberton HS
Joe "Dolly" Gray	RH	Univ. of Chicago
Ginn Guinther	RH,LH	
Hinneman	FB	
Tom Holleran	RG, QB	Akron South HS
Cliff "Chief" James	LH	
Bill Jenkins	RE,LH	
Fritz Kerner	LT	Bucknell Univ.
John Larsen	RH,RT	Princeton Univ.
Little	QB,FB	
Lundermuth	LH	West Virginia Univ.
Leo McCausland	RT	Univ. of Detroit
T. McMurray	RE	
Ted Murray	FB	
Niger	LG,RT	
Quinter	LH	
Frederick Stanley Sefton	RE	Colgate
Mike Spering	RG	
Chick Ulrich	LG,LT	
Charles "Shang" Welch	RG	
Howard Welch	LE	Case Univ.
Woozley	RE	

SCHEDULE

Attend.	Date	Opponent	Score
	10/01	@ Cleveland Indians	0–3
	10/08	Massillon Blues	0–0
	10/15	@ Lorain Pros	12–0
	10/22	Youngstown Struthers	47–0
	10/29	@ Cleveland Indians	0–13
	11/05	Imperial Electrics	6–0
	11/12	Barberton Pros	0–10
	11/19	Elyria Andwars	3–0
	11/26	@ Detroit Heralds	7–13
	11/30	Barberton Pros	6–0
	12/03	Old Akron Indians	27–0
	12/10	Barberton Pros	7–0

The team was sponsored by the Akron brewers, Gus and Bill Burkhardt.

Won 7   **Lost 4**   **Tied 1**

Akron Pros, 1917

ROSTER

Managers: Stephen "Suey" Welch and Vernon "Mac" McGinnis
Colors: Blue and Gold   *Home Field:* Grossvater Park

Players	Position	Prior Team
Ralph Rube Bechtol	LH,FB	Coach at Akron South HS; Wooster College
Roy "Tommy" Burrell	LH,RB,QB	sandlot; Cleveland Indians
Carl Carderelli	C	Akron Central HS
Cartwright	FB,RH	
Chick Conway	C	
Park "Tumble" Crisp	LT,RT	Municipal Univ. of Akron; Canton Bulldogs
Dunlop	LG	
Featherstone	QB	
Flaherty	RT	
Malcolm "Red" Fleming	R,HB	Wash. and Jeff. College
"Red" Forrest	RE	Wooster Panthers
Gardner	RH	Virginia Univ.
Joe "Dolly" Gray	RT,LH	Univ. of Chicago
Tom Holleran	QB	Akron South HS
"Fat" Howard	T	
Curly Jenkins	G	
Jones	G	
Layman	C	
I.R. Martin (Johnson*)	HB	Univ. of Missouri
"Bullet" Mitchell	LH,FB	Purdue Univ.; Akron Imperial Electrics
Alfred Nesser	RG,LG	Columbus Panhandles
Frank Nesser	RT,LT,FB	Columbus Panhandles
Carl "Bull" Olsson	LG	Akron Indians, Clev. Indians
Clinton C. Prather	LE,RE,QB	Indiana Univ.
Purdue*	RT	
Frederick S. Sefton (Ralph Colgate*)	LE,RE,LH	Colgate Univ.; Canton Bulldogs
Vern Thomas	LG	
Chick Ulrich	T,G	
Howard Welch	LE	Western Reserve Univ.
Woozley	LE	

SCHEDULE

Attend.	Date	Opponent	Score
	10/07	Salem (OH) Semi-Pro	34–0
	10/14	Columbus Panhandle	3–0
	10/21	Cleveland Tomahawks	40–0
3500	10/28	@ Massillon Tigers	0–14
	11/04	Buffalo All-Stars (Irish-Am. AC)	12–7
6000	11/11	Canton Bulldogs	0–14
	11/18	Massillon Tigers	3–0
	11/25	Snow-game w/Youngstown canceled	
	11/29	Toledo Maroons	27–7

Won 6   **Lost 2**

Altoona Indians, 1915

ROSTER

Manager: Mort Henderson   Coach: Gus Wheelock
Colors: Home Field: Cricket Park

Players	Position	Prior Team
Ameigh	C	
Alex Arcasa	RH	Carlisle Institute
Joe Bender	RH	Carlisle Institute
Joe Bergie	C	Carlisle Institute
Bind	RE	
J. "Auggie" Blair	LT	Univ. of Pittsburgh
H. Brennan	RG	Carlisle Institute
Brown	RE	
Clifford	LT	
Lee Collins	RT	
Craymer	LE	Philadelphia sandlot
Virgil L. Crawford	LG	Susquehanna Univ.
Fitzgerald	FB,RG	
Malcolm "Red" Fleming	HB	Wash. and Jeff. College
Furrier	RT	Carlisle Institute
Gibbons	LE	
Fritz Henderson	LG	Carlisle Institute
Hoffman	RH,LG	Carlisle Institute
Johnston	LG,FB	
Ted Pratt	RE	Carlisle Institute
Stilwell Saunooke	RE,RH,C	Carlisle Institute
Schenk	LE	
Shipp	LG,RG	Carlisle Institute
Carl "King Carl" Snavely	FB	Lebanon Valley College
Stillwell	RT	
William Elwood "Red" Swoope	QB	Susquehanna Univ.; Altoona HS
George Vedderneck	LE,RE	Carlisle Institute
Hugh Wheelock	RT,RG	Carlisle Institute; Lebanon Valley College
Joel Wheelock	QB,LT,FB	Carlisle Institute; Lebanon Valley College Academy
Winnshick	C	Carlisle Institute
Woodring	RG,RE	Carlisle Institute

SCHEDULE

Attend.	Date	Opponent	Score
	10/09	@ Yeagertown	0–6
	10/16	Yeagertown	25–0
	10/23	@ Duquesne Cornells	25–7
	10/30	Pitcairn Quakers	3–0
2400	11/07	@ Canton Bulldogs	0–38
	11/13	Latrobe	13–3
	11/20	Swiss Vale	0–7
3000	11/25	Pitcairn Quakers	10–0

Won 5   **Lost 3**

Altoona Indians, 1916

ROSTER

(Sponsored by the Pennsylvania Railroad)

| Manager: | | *Coach:* Joe Bergie |
| Colors: | | *Home Field:* Cricket Park |

Players	Position	Prior Team
Alex Arcasa	RH	Carlisle Institute
Joe Bender	FB	Carlisle Institute
Joe Bergie	C	Carlisle Institute
Bettwy	RG,RT	Carlisle Institute
J. "Auggie" Blair	RT	Univ. of Pittsburgh
Carr	RH	
Carroll	RH	Holiday YMCA
Crissman	LT	Univ. of Pennsylvania
William Lone Star Dietz	QB	Carlisle Institute
John Joseph Donnelly	LE	Altoona HS
Fitzgerald	RT	Susquehanna Univ.
Foley	LH	McKeesport Olympics
Furrier	RT	Carlisle Institute
Gibson	LH	Carlisle Institute
Hoffman	FB,LH	Carlisle Institute
H.W. Leeiver	LE	
Lindsay	QB	
Pickens	QB	Conway Hall
Pohle	LH,QB	
Ted Pratt (C)	RE,LE	Carlisle Institute
Stilwell Saunooke	RG,FB	Carlisle Institute
Shipp	LG,LT	Carlisle Institute
E.A. Snyder	C	Bucknell College
Speache	LE	
William Elwood "Red" Swoope	QB	Susquehanna Univ., Altoona HS
Ollie Vogel	RT,RE	Penn State Univ.
Hugh Wheelock	LT,RE,RG,C	Carlisle Institute; Lebanon Valley College
Joel Wheelock	RE	Carlisle Institute; Lebanon Valley College Academy
Winnshick	LE,C	Carlisle Institute
Woodring	C	Carlisle Institute
Yarnell	LG	Penn State Univ.

SCHEDULE

Attend.	Date	Opponent	Score
1000	10/1	@ Canton Bulldogs	0–23
	10/8	@ Cleveland Indians	7–29
	10/14	Burnham YMCA	30–0
3800	10/15	@ Massillon Tigers	0–54
	10/21	Lewistown	25–6
1700	10/29	@ Dayton Triangles	0–33
	11/4	Lebanon College	7–0

Won 3   **Lost 4**

Altoona Indians, 1917

ROSTER

Manager:		*Coach:*
Colors:		*Home Field:* Cricket Park

Players	Position	Prior Team
Joe Bender	RH	Carlisle Institute
Bettwy	LT	Carlisle Institute
Black	LG	
Crisstock	LE	
Gibbons	RE	
Lindsay	QB	
Pearson	FB	
Ted Pratt	LH	Carlisle Institute
Quinn	RT	
Shipp	LG, LE	Carlisle Institute
Stuart	RH	
Winnshick	C	Carlisle Institute
Yarnell	RG	Penn State Univ.

Buffalo All-Stars, 1916

ROSTER

Manager: Eugene J. Dooley	*Coach:*
Colors:	*Home Field:* Ryan Park

Players	Position	Prior Team
Armstrong	RG	
Bailey	LG	
Hymie Bleich	RH	Lancaster Malleables
Louis Bleich	RE	Jewish Young Men's Assoc.
Carney	LE	
Eugene J. Dooley	QB	
Floyd	C	
Gregory	RH,RE,LE	
Henneman	LH,RG	
Jacobs	RT	
Douglas Jeffery	LH	Univ. of North Carolina
Johnson	LE	Penn State Univ.
Lynch	RE	
Morganstein	RT,LG	
Frank Mt. Pleasant	QB	Carlisle Institute; Altoona Indians
Provancha	LT	
Newton Scatecherd	LT	Lancaster Malleables
Ted Scatecherd +	LT,RT,RG	Cornell Univ.
Russ Sherman	FB	
Smith	QB	
Wesley Talchief	RG,LG	Carlisle Institute

+ A Henry Edward Schradieck was in the Cornell University class of 1916. There is no record of a Ted Scatecherd.

SCHEDULE

Attend.	Date	Opponent	Score
	10/1	Tonawanda Frontiers	70–0
	10/8	@ Toledo [Ohio] Maroons	0–15
	10/15	@ Canton Bulldogs	0–77
	10/22	Jewish Young Men's Assoc.	won
	10/29	Tonawanda All-Stars	6–0
	11/5	Lancaster Malleables	0–0
	11/12	Buffalo High School All-Stars	20–0
	11/26	Tonawanda All-Stars	6–0

Won 5	**Lost 2**	**Tied 1**

Buffalo All-Stars, 1917

ROSTER

Manager-Coach: Eugene J. Dooley and Abbott

| *Colors:* | | *Home field:* Ryan Park |

Players	*Position*	*Prior Team*
Abbott	RH	Allegheny College
Hymie Bleich	LE,RH	Lancaster Malleables
Colby	RT	
Cummer	C	
Daily	LG	
Dennison	LG	
Donavan	LH	
Eugene J. Dooley	QB	
Floyd	LG,RG	
Bob Gill	LE,RE	Buffalo International League
Gordon	RE	
Gregory	LT,RE	
Hess	C	
Highson	LH	
Douglas Jeffery	LH	Univ. of North Carolina
Johnson	LE,RE	Penn State Univ.
Barney Lepper	RH,RT	(a)
Lynch	RE	
McDermott	LT	
McNerny	LT,RG	
Murphy	RT	
Provanche	LT,LG,LE	
Russ Sherman	FB	
Wesley Talchief	RG,LG	Carlisle Institute
Templeton	QB	Colgate Univ.
Thoma	LT	
Thompson	LT,RE,LE	

(a) While it was reported that he attended Univ. of Rochester, there is no record of his enrollment there.

SCHEDULE

Date	*Opponent*	*Score*
10/7	Niagaras	30–0
10/14	@ Massillon Tigers	6–14
10/21	@ Detroit Heralds	0–67
10/28	Tonawanda All-Stars	0–0
11/4	@ Akron Pros	7–12
11/11	Jamestown	34–12
11/25	Tonawanda All-Stars	16–0
12/1	Fort Dix	lost

Won 3   Lost 4   Tied 1

Canton Bulldogs, 1915

ROSTER

Manager: Jack Cusack   *Coach:* Harry Hazlett
Colors: Red and White   *Home Field:* League Park

Players	Position	Prior Team
Earl C. Abell	LT	Colgate Univ.
Howard Ashley Axtel	LE	Kenyon College; Akron Indians
Robert P. "Butts" Butler	RT	Univ. of Wisconsin
Henry "Hank" Dagenhart	LG	Canton sandlot
William Dagenhart	FB	Canton sandlot
Edgar C. "Big Ed" Davis	RT	Indiana Univ.; Pine Village; Fort Wayne Friars
Don Drumm	RG,LG	Marietta College; Shelby Blues
Howard "Cap" Edwards	LT,LG	Univ. of Notre Dame; Akron Indians
R. Foss	HB	Pittsburgh sandlot
William "Bill" Gardner	RE,LE	Carlisle; Shelby Blues
Goff	LG	Case Univ.
Don Hamilton	QB	Univ. of Notre Dame
Harold "Eddie" Iddings	LH	Univ. of Chicago
George Edward "Carp" Julian	RH	Mich. Agricultural College
John Kellison	RT	W. Va. Wesleyan College
Kent "Skeet" Lambert	QB	Wabash College; Ft. Wayne Friars
Alfred E. "Greasy" Neale (Fisher*)	LH,RH	W. Va. Wesleyan College
Don Peters	FB	Carlisle Institute; No. Ohio Univ.
Harold T. "Dutch" Powell	LG	Ohio State Univ.; Shelby Blues; Akron Indians
Arthur W. "Bugs" Raymond	G	Ohio State Univ.
Art Schlott	RG	Canton sandlot
C. "Whitey" Schultz	C,RT	Shelby Blues
Frederick Sefton	E	Colgate Univ.
Gideon Charles Smith	LT	Michigan Agricultural College
Norman J. "Dutch" Speck	RG	Canton sandlot
Charles Edward Stewart	E	Colgate Univ.
James F. "Jim" Thorpe	LH	Carlisle; Pine Village AC
M. J. Truesby	LH	Painesville sandlot
Eddie Van Alman	LH	Mt. Union College
John Huber "Hube" Wagner	LH,RE	Univ. of Pittsburgh
Ralph "Fats" Waldsmith	C,RT	Buchtel College; Akron Indians
Harry Whitaker	QB	Indiana Univ.
Vince "Wink" Zettler	RE	Canton sandlot

SCHEDULE

Attend.	Date	Opponent	Score
700	10/10	Wheeling AC	75–0
2500	10/17	Columbus Panhandles	7–0
2900	10/24	@ Detroit Heralds	3–9
2000	10/31	No. Cincinnati Colts	41–12
2400	11/07	Altoona Indians	38–0
6000	11/14	@ Massillon Tigers	0–16
	11/21	@ Shelby Blues (canceled)	
8500	11/28	Massillon Tigers	6–0

Won 5   **Lost 2**

Canton Bulldogs, 1916

ROSTER

| Manager: Jack Cusack | | Coach: James F. Thorpe |
| Colors: Red and White | | Home Field: League Park |

Players	Position	Prior Team
James Martin "Butchy" Barron	G	Georgetown Univ.
Bell*	T	Colgate Univ.
Howard "Cub" Buck (Moriarity*)	LT	Univ. of Wisconsin
Pete Calac	FB	Carlisle Institute; W.Va. Wesleyan
Harry Costello (Conley*)	HB	Georgetown Univ.
Park "Tumble" Crisp	LT	Buchtel College
Frank Dunn (Swinehart*)	QB,RH	Dickinson College
Howard "Cap" Edwards	RT	Univ. of Notre Dame
William "Bill" Gardner	RG,LT	Carlisle Institute
William Garlow	C	Carlisle Institute
Milton P. Ghee	QB	Dartmouth College
Thomas F. Gormley	T	Georgetown Univ.
George Edward "Carp" Julian	FB	Michigan Ag. College
John Kellison (Ketcham*)	RT	W. Va. Wesleyan College
Richard C. King	HB	Harvard Univ.
George "Bull" Lowe	HB	Lafayette; Fordham College
George Roudebush	HB	Denison Univ.; Cincinnati Celts
Ed "Unk" Russell	RT	Univ. of Pennsylvania
Art Schlott	G,C	None
Frederick Sefton (Fisher*)	LE,HB	Colgate Univ.
Ernie Soucy (Drake*)	LE	Harvard Univ.
Clarence W. "Doc" Spears	RG	Dartmouth College
Norman J. "Dutch" Speck	LG,RG	Canton sandlot
Charles Edward Stewart (Fisher*)	RE	Colgate Univ.
James F. "Jim" Thorpe	LH	Carlisle Institute
M. J. Truesby	E	Painesville sandlot
Ralph "Fats" Waldsmith	C	Buchtel College
William Davis Ward (Moriarity*)	LT	Georgetown Univ.
Gus Welch	HB	Carlisle Institute
Harry Whitaker	QB	Indiana Univ.
M. E. "Red" Wilkinson	RH	Syracuse Univ.

SCHEDULE

Attend.	Date	Opponent	Score
	10/01	Altoona Indians	23–0
	10/08	Pitcairn Quakers	7–0
4,000	10/15	Buffalo All-Stars	77–0
	10/22	New York All-Stars	67–0
	10/29	Columbus Panhandles	12–0
7,000	11/05	Cleveland Indians	27–0
10,000	11/12	@ Cleveland Indians	14–7
	11/19	@ Youngstown Patricians	6–0
10,000	11/26	@ Massillon Tigers	0–0
10,000	12/02	Massillon Tigers	24–0

Won 9   **Tied 1**

Canton Bulldogs, 1917

ROSTER

Manager: Jack Cusack   *Coach:* James F. Thorpe
Color: Red and White   *Home Field:* League Park

Players	Position	Prior Team
James M."Butchy" Barron	RG	Georgetown Univ.
Beck*	HB	
Howard "Cub" Buck (Black*)	LT	Univ. of Wisconsin
Carpenter*	G, E	Penn State (All-American)
Pete Calac (Anderson*, Andrews*)	RH,FB	Carlisle Institute; W. Va. Wesleyan
Ollie Dreisbach	RT,RG	Municipal Univ. of Akron
Frank Dunn	RH	Dickinson College
Howard "Cap" Edwards	LT	Univ. of Notre Dame
William Garlow	C	Carlisle Institute
Milton Ghee	QB	Dartmouth College
John R. Gilroy	QB	Georgetown Univ.
Jackson	LH	Colgate Univ.
John Kellison (Ketcham*, Harris*)	RT	W. Va. Wesleyan College
John McNamara (Martin*, Moore*)	LH	Georgetown Univ.
I. R. Martin (Brown*)	HB	Univ. of Missouri
Neil Matthews	LT	Univ. of Pennsylvania
Alfred E. "Greasy" Neale (Foster*, Fisher*)	RE,FB,QB	W. Va. Wesleyan College
Ed "Unk" Russell	LG	Univ. of Pennsylvania
John Schwab	RH	Wash. and Jeff. College
Frederick Sefton (Fisher*)	LE	Colgate Univ.
Clarence "Doc" Spears (Patton*)	LG,RG	Dartmouth College
Norman J. "Dutch" Speck	LG	Canton sandlot
Spencer	LT	North Dakota Univ.
Charles E. Stewart	RE,LE	Colgate Univ.
James F. "Jim" Thorpe	LH,RB,QB	Carlisle Institute
Ralph "Fats" Waldsmith	C	Buchtel College
William Davis Ward (Bush*)	LG	Georgetown Univ.
Gus Welch (Wells*)	LH	Carlisle; Dickinson College
Harry Whitaker	QB	Indiana Univ.
Samuel S. Willaman (Williams*)	LE,LH	Ohio State Univ.

SCHEDULE

Attend.	Date	Opponent	Score
	10/07	Pitcairn Quakers	12–7
	10/14	Altoona Indians	80–0
	10/21	Columbus Panhandles	54–0
	10/28	47th Infantry of Syracuse	41–0
8000	11/04	@ Youngstown Patricians	3–0
6000	11/11	@ Akron Pros	14–0
5000	11/18	@ Youngstown Patricians	13–0
	11/25	Massillon Tigers	14–3
8000	11/29	@ Detroit Heralds	7–0
	12/03	Massillon Tigers	0–6

Won 9   **Lost 1**

Cincinnati Celts, 1915

ROSTER

Manager-Coach: Frank Marty

Color: Kelly Green   *Home Field:* Redlands Field

Players	Position	Prior Team
Abbott	C	
Bachman	RT	Ohio State Univ.
Leonard K. "Teddy" Baehr	FB	Univ. of Cincinnati
Albert Henry "Whitey" Bessmeyer	LE	Univ. of Cincinnati
Otto Bessmeyer	RE	
Costello	LG	
Davis	RE,QB	Univ. of Cincinnati
"Cliff" Foscaula	RE	
Earl Dudley "Whitey" Foss	QB	Ohio State Univ.
Thomas Gaither	FB,RH	
Gaylor	RT	Kenyon College
William A. Goebel	RG	Yale Univ.; Shelby Blues; Akron Indians
Herbert John Goosman	RH	Univ. of Cincinnati
Ellis B. Gregg, Jr.	LT	Univ. of Cincinnati
"Augie" Janzen	QB	
Howard Justice	FB	Univ. of Cincinnati
Chet "Shine" Knab	RE	
Frank Lane	RG,LG	sandlot
Lang	LG	
Love	RG	
Magley	C	Notre Dame HS
Meister	LT,RG	
Meyer	RH	
Keene "Peggy" Palmer	LH	
Pavles	RH	
David Reese	C,FB	Denison Univ.
Scheehan	LG	
"Tilly" Schuessler	LH	Univ. of Cincinnati
Tan Snyder	RH	Marietta College
Paul Roy Stewart	LE	Virginia Military Acad.
Weheringer	RH	
Welsh	RT	

SCHEDULE

Attend.	Date	Opponent	Score
3000	10/17	@ Detroit Heralds	6–12
	10/24	@ Dayton Gym-Cadets	0–0
	10/31	Christ Church Reds	
	11/07	West Carrollton	24–0
	11/14	@ Toledo Maroons	0–0
	11/21	Muncie (IN) Congervilles	48–0

Won 2   **Lost 1**   **Tied 2**

Cincinnati Celts, 1916

ROSTER

Manager-Coach: Frank Marty

Colors: Kelly Green   *Home Field:* Redlands Field

Players	Position	Prior Team
Albert Henry "Whitey" Bessmeyer	LE	Univ. of Cincinnati
Otto Bessmeyer	RT,LT	
Blackburn	FB,RG,RE	
Thomas Gaither	FB	
Ellis B. Gregg Jr.	LT	Univ. of Cincinnati
Hackhermes	QB	
Hanson	RG	
Emmett G. Keefe	LG	Univ. of Notre Dame
King	Sub.	
Chet "Shine" Knab	RE,RT	
Frank Lane	RG	
Leyman	RH	
Magley	C	
Meister	LG	
Keene T. Palmer	RH,LH	Univ. of Cincinnati
Pat Reece	LE,RE	Univ. of Cincinnati
David Reese	C,RE	Denison Univ.
George Roudebush	LH	Denison Univ.
Rowlette	QB	
"Tilly" Schuessler	QB,LH	Univ. of Cincinnati
Smith	FB,RT,C	
Tan Snyder	LG,RG	Marietta College
Tony	RG	
William Sykes Tucker	LG,RH,LH	Univ. of Pennsylvania
Weheringer	RH	
Wernecke	LE	

SCHEDULE

Date	Opponent	Score
10/08	@ Detroit Heralds	0–17
10/15	Lebanon, Ohio	61–0
10/22	@ Fort Wayne Friars	6–6
10/29	@ Pine Village AC	9–6
11/05	Lebanon, Ohio	67–7
11/12	Cleveland Indians (2nd team)	25–0
11/19	@ Dayton Triangles	0–6
11/26	Dayton Triangles	10–7
11/30	@ Pine Village AC	3–23
12/03	@ Hammond Clabbys	0–3

Won 5   **Lost 4**   **Tied 1**

Cincinnati Celts, 1917

ROSTER

Manager: Michel   *Coach:* Frank Marty
Colors: Red   *Home Field:* Redlands Field

Players	Position	Prior Team
Otto Bessmeyer	RT	
"Babe" Brock Brooks	LH	
Buehren	LH,RE	
Costello	LG	
Sam Foertmeyer	LT	
Freye	QB	
Thomas Gaither	FB	
Gilbert	RE	Indiana Univ.
Harlam	RB	
Henenson	FB	
David Walter Hopkins	LE	Univ. of Pennsylvania
Hull	RB	
Chet "Shine" Knab	LH,RH	Coaching at Cincinnati HS
Knute	RH	
Ed Krueck	RE,QB	Indiana Normal at Muncie
Frank Lane	RG	
Meister	LG	
Pat O'Brian	RG,LG	
Keene "Peggy" Palmer	LH	
David Reese	C,AB	Denison Univ.
Schockman	RH	
Frank G. "Swede" Sorenson	FB	Ohio State Univ.
Carl "Dutch" Thiele	LE	Denison Univ.
Thompson	LH	
Tully	LH	
Weheringer	RH	
Williams	LE	

SCHEDULE

Attend.	Date	Opponent	Score
	10/14	@ Detroit Heralds	0–14
2200	10/21	@ Fort Wayne Friars	6–21
	10/28	Pine Village @ Lafayette	0–0
	11/04	Pitcairn Quakers	7–6
	11/11	@ Dayton Triangles	0–0
	11/17	Camp Sherman	Exhibition game
	11/25	Dayton Triangles	7–7
	12/01	@ Dayton Triangles	0–13

Won 1   **Lost 3**   **Tied 3**

Cleveland Indians, 1916

ROSTER

Manager/Coach: George "Peggy" Parratt

Colors: Home Field: League Park

Players	Position	Prior Team
James Martin "Butchy" Barron (Roberts*)	RG	Georgetown Univ.
Howard Lester Beck	RE	Wash. and Jeff. College
Bergman	QB	
Brooks	LT	
Roy "Tommy" Burrell	LE	Canton sandlot
Robert "Butts" Butler	RT	Univ. of Wisconsin; Canton Bulldogs
Cass	RE	Western Reserve. Univ.; Massillon Tigers
Boyd Cherry	LE	Ohio State Univ.
E. M. Cole	RG	Univ. of Michigan; Massillon Tigers
Charles Criss	E	Municipal Univ. of Akron
Homer Davidson	QB	Massillon Tigers; Cleveland Central HS
Derby	LE,LH	University of Virginia
Paul R. "Shorty" Des Jardien	C	Univ. of Chicago
Fay*	T	
Flynn	E	
Frey	RG	
Getz	G	Youngstown Patricians
Goldberg	G	Wash. and Jeff. College
Thomas F. Gormley (Gordon*)	RT,LT	Georgetown Univ.
Campbell J. "Honus" Graff	RH,FB	Ohio State Univ.
Ed Hanley	LH,FB	Univ. of Pittsburgh; Massillon Tigers
David Walter "Hoppy" Hopkins	LE	Univ. of Penn; Cincinnati Celts
James*	QB	
Thomas H. King	LT	Univ. of Notre Dame
Lobert*	RE	Villanova Univ.
George "Bull" Lowe (Hunter*)	HB	Lafayette; Fordham Univ.
I. R. Martin	LE,C	Univ. of Missouri
E. N. Mayer	HB	Univ. of Virginia
William Neill	LG	Univ. of Penn; Whitman College
Carl "Bull" Olsson	LG	Akron Indians; Massillon Tigers
George "Peggy" Parratt	QB	Case Institute
Patton	LG	
Louis Edward Pickerel	QB	Ohio State Univ.
Milton "Muff" Portmann	RG	Western Reserve Univ.; Akron Indians
Harold "Dutch" Powell	LG	Ohio State Univ.
Arthur "Dub" Schieber	FB	Ohio State Univ.; Canton Bulldogs
C. "Whitey" Schultz	LG,C	Shelby Blues; Canton Bulldogs
Murray N. Shelton	RE	Cornell Univ.
Gilbert Sinclair	LG	Univ. of Minnesota
Smith	RH	
Lorin Solon (C)	FB	Univ. of Minnesota; Duluth Independents
John "Hube" Wagner	RE	Univ. of Pittsburgh; Canton Bulldogs
Fred M. Walker	LE	Univ. of Chicago
Carl Weiler	LG	Case Institute
Stanfield Wells	E	Univ. of Michigan
Dwight A. Wertz	LH	Western Reserve Univ.
Samuel S. Willaman (Williams)	LH	Ohio State Univ.
Guy L. "Chalky" Williamson	QB	Univ. of Pittsburgh
F. A. Yocum	RH	Oberlin College
Zeeman	LE	

Second Team Members, (Cincinnati Game)

E. Lane	QB	
Marshall	LH	

Cleveland Indians, 1916 *(Continued)*

Players	Position	Prior Team
Miller	LH	
Keene T. Palmer	RH	Univ. of Cincinnati
Spencer	LT	South Dakota State Univ.
Winters	RH	
Witherspoon	C	

SCHEDULE

Attend.	Date	Opponent	Score
	9/24	Elyria	6–3
2,000	10/01	Akron Burkhardts	3–0
4,000	10/08	Altoona Indians	39–7
	10/15	Pittsburgh Pitcairns	14–6
6,000	10/22	Columbus Panhandles	6–9
	10/29	Akron Burkhardts	13–0
	10/29	@ Mendel Pirates of Columbus	13–0
7,000	11/05	@ Canton Bulldogs	0–27
	11/12	@ Cincinnati Celts	0–25
10,000	11/12	Canton Bulldogs	7–14
5,000	11/19	Massillon Tigers	0–0
	11/26	Columbus Panhandles	7–0
8,000	11/30	@ Detroit Heralds	20–6
	12/03	@ Toledo Maroons	3–0

Won 8   **Lost 3**   **Tied 1**

Columbus Panhandles, 1915

ROSTER

Manager: Joe Carr

Colors: Gold and Maroon   *Home Field:* Indianola Park

Players	Position	Prior Team
Hiram Brigham	C	Ohio State Univ. (f)
Dornick	RG	
Charles Dunn	RG,LG,LT	
Hale	LT	
Hannah	LE,RE	
Jason	RT	
Andy Kertzinger	C	
Oscar Kuehner	LT,RG	
Roscoe Kuehner	RE	
Littleton	G	
Alfred Nesser	LG,RG	Massillon Tigers
Frank Nesser	RG,RT,FB	Akron Indians
Fred Nesser	LE	
John Nesser	QB,RH	
Phil Nesser	RT	
Ted Nesser	LH,RT,FB	Massillon Tigers
Louis Edward Pickerel	QB,RH	Ohio State Univ.
Emmett Ruhl	RH	Davis and Elkins
John Schneider	C,LG	
Slain	RE	
Slowly	RG	
J. Lee Snoots	LH	
Snyder	LG	
Pete Vogel	LG	

SCHEDULE

Attend.	Date	Opponent	Score
	09/21	Solderbloom Smokers	40–0
	10/03	Columbus All-Stars	49–0
	10/10	@ Marion (OH) Questions	21–0
2500	10/17	@ Canton Bulldogs	0–7
3700	10/24	@ Toledo Maroons	0–20
3000	10/31	@ Massillon Tigers	16–0
3000	11/07	@ Dayton Gym-Cadets	24–7
	11/14	@ Detroit Mack Park Maroons	7–0
5000	11/21	@ Youngstown Patricians	0–0
	11/24	Columbus Muldoons	19–0
3000	11/25	@ Fort Wayne Friars	0–3
	11/28	Columbus Barracks	26–0
	12/5	Ohio All-Stars	13–0

Won 9   **Lost 3**   **Tied 1**

Columbus Panhandles, 1916

ROSTER

Manager: Joe Carr   *Trainer:* Cororan

Colors: Gold and Maroon   *Home Field:* Indianola Park

Players	Position	Prior Team
Hiram Brigham	C	Ohio State Univ. (f)
Clues	HB	
Cochran	QB	
Compton	LG	
A.R. Godfrey	G	Ohio State Univ.
Henry	LG	
E. Kuchner	LE	
Oscar Kuehner	LT	
Roscoe Kuehner	LE	
Alfred Nesser	RG	
Frank Nesser (C)	RH	
Fred Nesser	LE	
John Nesser	QB	
Phil Nesser	RT	
Raymond Nesser	G,T	
Ted Nesser	FB	
Louis Edward Pickerel	QB	Ohio State Univ.
Emmett Ruhl	RE,LH	Davis and Elkins
Homer Ruhl	LE	
Silbaugh	T	
J. Lee Snoots	LH	

SCHEDULE

Attend.	Date	Opponent	Score
	10/08	@ Marion Questions	54–0
7000	10/15	@ Detroit Heralds	13–7
6000	10/22	@ Cleveland Indians	9–7
	10/29	@ Canton Bulldogs	0–12
3000	11/05	@ Toledo Maroons	7–23
3600	11/12	@ Massillon Tigers	0–10
	11/19	@ Detroit Heralds	15–0
	11/26	@ Cleveland Indians	0–7
	11/30	@ Fort Wayne Friars	0–3
950	12/03	@ Youngstown Patricians	13–0
	12/10	Columbus All-Stars	6–0

Won 6   **Lost 5**

Columbus Panhandles, 1917

ROSTER

Manager: Joe Carr

Colors: Gold and Maroon   *Home Field:* Indianola Park

Players	Position	Prior Team
Hiram Brigham	C	Ohio State Univ.
Cellhouse	RG	
Jerry Corcoran	RH	
John Davis	RE	
Charlie Dunn	C	
Gale	QB	
Hal Gaulke	QB,RH	
Jones	RT	
Kline	LH	
Oscar Kuehner	LT	
Roscoe Kuehner	RE,LE	
Mason	FB	
Mercer	RT,LT	
Joe Muhlbarger	RH	Alderson–Broaddus
Frank Nesser	RT,FB	
Fred Nesser	LE, RG	
John Nesser	E,T	
Phil Nesser	RG	
Ted Nesser	FB	
Homer Rich	LH	
Selwig	LE	

SCHEDULE

Attend.	Date	Opponent	Score
	09/30	@ Newark (OH)	14–6
	10/07	@ Lancaster (OH)	38–6
	10/14	@ Akron Pros	0–3
	10/21	@ Canton Bulldogs	0–54
	10/28	@ Youngstown Patricians	0–30
	11/04	@ Massillon Tigers	0–28
	11/11	@ Toledo Maroons	13–0
	11/18	@ Fort Wayne Friars	0–13
	11/25	@ Detroit Heralds	0–23

Won 3   **Lost 6**

Cornell-Hamburgs (Chicago), 1916

ROSTER

Manager: Bill Finn   *Coach:* Joe McDonough
Colors: *Home Field:* Schorling's Park and Comiskey Park

Players	Position	Prior Team
Arnstein	RE,RT	
Moses Bashaw	RT	Evanston North Ends
Brennan	LT	Holy Cross College
Burson	FB	
Cockran	LE,LT	DePaul Univ.
Devenray	RG	Univ. of Chicago
Kearney (Carney)	LG	
Kruse	C	
LaRos(s)	FB,LE	
McDermott	FB	
Mensch	RH	
Nelkum	C	
Nelson	RE	
Nicholson	LH,RH	
Al Pressler	QB	
William Pressler	RH,LH	
Ryan	QB	
Schneider	LE	

SCHEDULE

Attend.	Date	Opponent	Score
	11/12	Racine Battery C	13–3
	11/19	Beloit	20–7
10,000	11/30	@ Evanston North Ends	7–6

Win-Loss Record Unavailable

Cornell-Hamburgs (Chicago) 1917

ROSTER

| Manager: Bill Finn | Coach: Joe McDonough |
| Assistant Coach: Walter Steffen | Home Field: Comiskey Park |

Players	Position	Prior Team
Anderson	FB	
Brennan	RT,LT	Holy Cross College
Cochran	C,LE,RE	DePaul Univ.
Devenray	RT	Univ. of Chicago
Dock	RG,RT	
Doyle	RT,LE	
B. Geis	LH	
Gels	RH	
Fred Montague Gillies	RT	Cornell Univ.
Harter	RG,LG,C	
Reuben Johnson	QB	Evanston North Ends
Kearney	LG	
Kelly	T	
Kohfeldt	C	
Kolb	FB	
LaRos	RE,LE	
McDonald	C	
McGinty	RG,LG	
Marder	C	
"Baggs" Miller	FB	Lane Tech HS
G. Monahan	RG,LG	Univ. of Chicago
Nicholson	RH	
Pearson	RH	
Al Pressler	LH,QB	
William Pressler	LE,RH	
Tom Shaughnessy	G	Univ. of Notre Dame
Walsh	RT	
Zepp	RE	Wendell Phillips HS

SCHEDULE

Attend.	Date	Opponent	Score
800	09/30	@ East Chicago Gophers	12–20
	10/07	Maywood (IL)	34–0
2000	10/14	@ Racine Battery C	27–0
	10/21	Rockford Badgers	40–0
	10/28	Milwaukee Maples	27–0
	11/04	Racine Battery C	21–0
3000	11/11	@ Hammond Clabbys	3–13
	11/18	@ Davenport AC	6–19
	11/25	Joliet @ Comiskey Park	10–6
1500	11/29	@ Hammond Clabbys	0–15

Won 6   **Lost 4**

Davenport Athletic Club, 1916

ROSTER

Manager: Dr. C. V. McCormack   *Coach:* Victor L. Littig/Carl Anderson
Colors: Brown and Green   *Home field:* Three I Park

Players	Position	Prior Team
"Nig" Clark	G	
Coe	LT	
Raymond "Slim" Crowley	FB,RG,LG	St. Ambrose College
Mark Donavan	QB,FB	
Fred W. Earp	RG	Moline Red Men; Knox College
Erhest	RT	
Flest	LH	
Richard M. Fort	HB,FB	Davenport HS
Freeberg	LE	Moline Red Men; Moline E. Ends
Hauser	RG,C	Moline Red Men
Dilk Holm	QB	sandlot; Moline Red Men; Rock Island Independents
Dick Holmes	LG	
George Jones	QB	St. Ambrose College Coach; Holy Cross College
Thomas Kennedy	RG	Davenport HS; St. Ambrose College
Frank T. Killian	QB	Davenport HS
Archie Raymond Kirk	RT	Univ. of Iowa
Koppas	LG	Univ. of Iowa (not verified)
Ray "Waddle" Kuehl	RH	Moline Red Men; Rock Island HS
Magerkurth	LE,LG	Moline Red Men
"Honey" Meersman	QB	Moline Red Men
Albert Herman Miller	LG	Univ. of Nebraska
Ray Mitten	LT	Davenport HS
Murphy	RE	
Poe	LH	Indiana State College
Edgar Rumberg	LH,QB	Monmouth HS
Runburg	LE, RG	Davenport HS
Charles Schuler	LE,QB	Cornell Univ.
Ward Shaw	C	
Harold Stowe	FB	Moline HS; Moline Red Men
Duffy "Bum" Stuehmer	C,QB,FB,LG	
Herbert Ross Tomson	RH,QB	Davenport HS
Art Wellendorf	Sub.	
E. Carl Wellendorf	RE	
"Red" Wolters	HB,LT	Moline Red Men
"Nig" Wright	RT	Moline Red Men

SCHEDULE

Attend.	Date	Opponent	Score
848	10/1	Oelwein	27–0
1500	10/8	@ Moline Red Men	7–6
3000	10/15	Evanston North Ends	3–0
1200	10/22	Peru Badgers	51–0
3100	10/29	@ Rock Island Independents	6–0
3350	11/5	Moline Red Men	16–9
2970	11/12	Rock Island Independents	0–0
1500	11/19	@ Hammond Clabbys	14–12
	11/26	Spring Valley Moose	7–9
3000	12/3	Minneapolis Marines	7–19

Won 7   **Lost 2**   **Tied 1**

Davenport Athletic Club, 1917

ROSTER

Manager: *Coach:* Malcolm Galvin
Colors: Brown and Green   *Home Field:* Three I Park

Players	Position	Prior Team
Allison	LT,RE	
Mark Donavan	QB	
Doyle	LE	
Fred W. Earp	RG,RT	Knox College; Moline Red Men
Ellison	RE	
Richard M. Fort	FB	Davenport HS
Malcolm Galvin	FB	Univ. of Wisc.; Hammond Clabbys
Hauser	C	
Hufford	C	
George Jones	LH,FB	Holy Cross College
Klinch	LT	
William W. Koch	RT	Davenport HS; Univ. of Wisconsin
Kuchi	RH	
Ray "Waddle" Kuehl	RH	Rock Island HS; Moline Red Men
Lagomarcino	RG	
Cliff "Swede" Lundberg	FB	Moline HS
McCarthy	RE	
McCormack	RE	Camp Dodge; Univ. North Dakota
Magerkurth	LG	Moline Red Men
Bob Marshall	LE	Minneapolis Marines; Univ. of Minnesota
Frank Mayer	LH	Univ. of Minnesota
"Honey" Meersman	FB	Moline Red Men
W. Miller	RT	St. Ambrose College
Ray Mitten	LT	Davenport HS
Parker	LE	
Rogers	LT	
Edgar Rumberg	LT	Monmouth HS
Leslie Shallberg	RG	Moline HS
Herbert Ross Tomson	RH,QB	Davenport HS
Versaluis	RE	Moline Red Men
Weisman	FB	
E. Carl Wellendorf	LE	
Williams	LH	
"Red" Wolters	RT,C,RG	Moline Red Men
Albert "Allie" Woodyatt	QB	Moline HS; Moline Red Men; Spring Valley

SCHEDULE

Attend.	Date	Opponent	Score
1700	09/23	Oelwein	50–0
	09/30	Moline Red Men	31–0
5000	10/07	Rock Island Independents	0–3
	10/14	Hammond Clabbys	3–9
	10/21	Minneapolis Marines	0–40
6000	10/28	Camp Dodge	9–6
1700	11/04	@ Peoria Socials	27–6
4748	11/11	@ Rock Island Independents	12–10
2000	11/18	Cornell-Hamburgs	19–6
	11/25	Bilbow Athletics (St. Paul)	30–2
4000	12/02	Rock Island Independents	7–23

Won 7   **Lost 4**

Dayton Gym-Cadets, 1915

ROSTER

Manager: Gessler   *Coach:*

Colors: Red and Orange   *Home Field:* Westwood Field

Players	Position	Prior Team
Herb Allen	LH	
Burns	RG	
Louis A. Clark	LG	St. Mary's College
Craig	RH	
"Pie" Decker	FB,RH	
Larry Dellinger	LG	St. Mary's College
Gebhart	RH	
Bob Gregor	LT	St. Mary's College
Herbig	RG,LG	
George "Hobby" Kinderdine	C	Miamisburg HS
Harry "Shine" Kinderdine	LE	Miamisburg HS
Alphonse H. Mahrt	QB	St. Mary's College
Louis Partlow	RH	West Carrollton Paper Mill
Gus Redmond	RE	
Rodgers	LT	
Hugh Sacksteder	HB	St. Mary's College
Norbert "Saxie" Sacksteder	LH	St. Mary's College
Bill Sherry	QB	
Carl Storck	LH	YMCA College, Chicago
Walters	RT,FB	
Weaver	LE	
Wenger	C	
Wents	RT	
William Zile	RE	St. Mary's College
George "Babe" Zimmerman	FB	St. Mary's College

SCHEDULE

Attend.	Date	Opponent	Score
	10/10	Valley AC, Cincinnati	50–0
	10/17	@ North Cincinnati	33–7
	10/24	Cincinnati Celts	0–0
3000	10/31	@ Toledo Maroons	20–7
	11/07	Columbus Panhandles	7–24
	11/14	Akron Indians	39–0
	11/21	Dayton Miamis	48–0
	11/25	West Carrollton Paper Mill	20–0
	11/28	Dayton Wolverines	20–0

Won 7   **Lost 1**   **Tied 1**

Dayton Triangles, 1916

ROSTER

Manager: Gessler   *Coach:* Nelson Talbott
Asst. Coach: Carl "Dutch" Thiele   *Home Field:* Highland Park/Westwood Park

Players	Position	Prior Team
Richard "Dick" Abrell	RH	Purdue Univ.
Louis A. Clark	RG	St. Mary's College
Craig	RE	
Crooks	LG	
Crosa	RG	
Harry Cutler	RT	
"Pie" Decker	FB	
Larry Dellinger	LT	St. Mary's College
Ernie Dugan	RE	Gym-Cadets
Lee Fenner	LE	sandlot
Haas	LE	
Ray Lingrel	LH	sandlot
McCorkle	FB,HB	Wash. and Lee Univ.
Mack	RH	
Alphonse H. Mahrt	QB	St. Marys College
Arthur "Red" Murray	LG	
Reeves "Turk" Palmer	FB,RE	Univ. of Cincinnati
Louis Partlow	LH	West Carrolton paper mill
Louis Reese	C,T	sandlot
Norbert "Saxie" Sacksteder	RH	St. Mary's College
"Irish Demon" Sloan	HB	
Earl Stoecklein	LT,RG	
Sweningen	C	
Glen Tidd	RG	sandlot
Williams	RE	
William Zile	LE	St. Mary's College
George "Babe" Zimmerman	FB	St. Mary's College

SCHEDULE

Attend.	Date	Opponent	Score
	10/01	Cincinnati Northerns	72–0
	10/08	Wellston	67–0
	10/15	Elyria Athletics	25–0
7000	10/22	@ Detroit Heralds	14–7
1500	10/29	Altoona Indians	33–0
2000	11/05	Pitcairn Quakers	7–3
	11/12	@ Toledo Maroons	12–0
2500	11/19	Cincinnati Celts	6–0
	11/26	@ Cincinnati	7–10
2000	11/30	Pitcairn Quakers	20–9

Won 9   **Lost 1**

Dayton Triangles 1917

ROSTER

Manager: Michael W. Redelle/Carl Storck   *Coach:*

Colors: *Home Field:* Triangle Park

Players	Position	Prior Team
Richard T. "Dick" Abrell	FB	Purdue Univ.
Jimmy Beckley	LT,RT	sandlot
Bill Clark	G	sandlot
Collins	LE	
Harry Cutler	RT	sandlot
"Pie" Decker	RE	sandlot
Larry Dellinger	LG	St. Mary's College
John Devereaux	RE	St. Mary's College
Ernie Dugan	LH	
Lee Fenner	LE	
George "Hobby" Kinderdine	C	Miamisburg HS
Harry B. "Shine" Kinderdine	RE	Miamisburg HS
Alphonse H. Mahrt	QB	St. Mary's College
Moore	RE	
Louis Partlow	LH	West Carrollton paper mill
David Reese	C	Denison Univ.
Louis Reese	LG	sandlot
Earl Stoecklein	RG	sandlot
Carl "Scummy" Storck	FB	YMCA College, Chicago
Weaver	RH	
George "Babe" Zimmerman	RH,RE	St. Mary's College

SCHEDULE

Attend.	Date	Opponent	Score
	10/06	42nd Aero Squad	54–6
	10/15	Elyria	44–0
3000	10/21	Toledo Maroons	15–0
	10/28	Cleveland Tomahawks	*(canceled wet ground)*
	11/04	McKeesport Olympics	29–0
	11/10	Camp Sherman, U.S. Army	*(half game exhibition)*
	11/11	Cincinnati Celts	0–0
	11/18	@ Toledo Maroons	26–0
	11/25	@ Cincinnati Celts	7–7
	12/01	Cincinnati Celts	13–0

Won 6   **Lost 0**   **Tied 2**

Detroit Heralds 1915

ROSTER

Manager-Coach: William H. Marshall   Asst. Coach: Jose Malcomson
Colors: Red and White   Home Field: Packard Park

Name	Position	Prior Teams
Neno J. "Jerry" Da Prato	FB	Mich. Ag. College
Earl Dunn	FB	Syracuse Univ. (not verified)
Norman "Tango" Glockson	RE	
Gerald Kelly	RH	Detroit College; St. Louis Univ.
H. Kennedy	G	
Percy Latham	QB	
McKenzie	LG	
Joseph Malcomson	RE	Detroit Univ. HS
William Blake Miller	LE	Mich. Ag. College
Mitchell	LG	
Mullens	G	Univ. of Detroit
Lawrence Nadeau	RE	
Bill "Chief" Newashe	LG,RG	Carlisle Institute
Webster H. Pierce	RG	Univ. of Mich.; Michigan Normal College; Adrian College; Mack Park Maroons
Ed Schlee	RH	Mich. Wesleyan Univ; Det. Univ. HS
Harry Schlee	RT	Univ. of Detroit; Det. Univ. HS
Gerald "Guy" Shields	LT	Michigan Wesleyan College
Richard "Red" Shields (c)	LE	
Archie "Dutch" Stewart	C	
G. Herbert "Hubby" Weekes	QB	Univ. of Detroit; Eastern HS
Percy "Shorty" Wilson	LH	St. Louis Univ.

SCHEDULE

Attend.	Date	Opponent	Score
1500	10/03	Cleveland Erin Braun	34–0
	10/10	(Cincinnati canceled)	
3000	10/17	Cincinnati Celts	12–6
2900	10/24	Canton Bulldogs	9–3
2000	10/31	Evanston North Ends	0–6
2000	11/07	Lancaster Malleables	0–0
2000	11/14	Buffalo All-Stars	69–0
8000	11/21	Mack Park Maroons	9–7

Won 5   **Lost 1**   **Tied 1**

Detroit Heralds, 1916

ROSTER

Manager-Coach: William H. Marshall

Colors: Red and White   *Home Field:* Navin Field

Players	Position	Prior Team
Benone	RG	
Bob V. "Rube" Boville (Ruben*)	RE	Wash. and Jeff. College; Detroit Central HS
Lewis S. Castle	LH	Syracuse Univ.
Collins	LT	
Arthur "Red" Cornwell	C	Univ.of Mich.; Detroit Maroons
Earl Dunn	RH,FB	Syracuse Univ. (not verified)
Andrew Clifford "Ox" Edgerton	LT	Alma College
Frank "Birdie" Gardner	LE	Carlisle Institute; Canton Bulldogs
Norman "Tango" Glockson	RE,RG	
Pete Hauser	RG	Carlisle Institute; Detroit Braves
Ty Krentler	FB,LH,QB	Kalamazoo Normal; Detroit Maroons
Kent C. "Skeet" Lambert	QB	Wabash College; Fort Wayne Friars; Massillon Tigers
La Pado	LE	Fort Wayne Friars
Percy Latham	QB	
"Nig" Lennahan	LH	Univ. of Detroit
Bernard "Bertie" Maher	FB	Detroit College; Detroit Maroons
D. Miller	LE	
Mitchell	LG	
Danny Mullane	RE	Detroit Maroons; Univ. of Detroit
Lawrence Nedeau	RE	
Bill "Chief" Newashe	LG	Carlisle Institute
Louis Partlow	LH	Dayton Triangles
Webster H. Pierce	LG,RG	Univ. of Mich.(f); Michigan Normal College; Adrian College
Robinson	RG	
Norbert "Saxie" Sacksteder	RH	Dayton Cadets; St. Mary's College
Harry Schlee	RT	Univ.of Detroit; Detroit Univ. HS
Bill Schultz	RT,HB,E	
Gerald "Guy" Shields	LT	Michigan Wesleyan College
Richard "Red" Shields	LE	
Archie "Dutch" Stewart	C	
Herbert Straight	LG	Mich. Ag. College
William Sykes Tucker	RH	Univ. of Pennsylvania
Percy "Shorty" Wilson	LH,RH	St. Louis Univ.

SCHEDULE

Attend.	Date	Opponent	Score
	10/1	Detroit Ex-Carlisles (Braves)	12–0
	10/08	Cincinnati Celts	17–0
7,000	10/15	Columbus Panhandles	7–13
	10/22	Dayton Triangles	7–14
	10/29	Massillon Tigers	0–6
	11/05	Evanston North Ends	21–9
	11/12	(Pittsburgh) Pitcairn Quakers	15–0
	11/19	Columbus Panhandles	0–15
	11/26	Akron Burkhardts	13–7
8,000	11/30	Cleveland Indians	6–20

Won 5   **Lost 5**

Detroit Heralds, 1917

ROSTER

Manager: John A. Roesink   *Coach:* William H. Marshall
Colors: Red and White   *Home Field:* Navin Field

Players	Position	Prior Team
Booth	RH	
Elmer E. Carroll	LT	Wash. and Jeff. College
Burleigh Cruikshank	G	Wash. and Jeff. College
John Devereaux	RE	St. Mary's College; Dayton Triangles
Earl Dunn	FB	Syracuse Univ.
Andrew C. "Ox" Edgerton	RG	Alma College
Green	HB	
Henning *	LG	Colgate Univ.
Clarence "Steamer" Horning	RT	Colgate Univ.
Ernest "Tommy" Hughitt	QB	Youngstown Pats; Univ. of Mich.
"Nig" Lennahan	RH	Univ. of Detroit
Bernard "Bertie" Maher	RH	Detroit College; Det. Maroons
Danny Mullane	LE	Univ. of Detroit; Det. Maroons
Frank Nesser	LT	Columbus Panhandles; Akron Pros
Rudolph W. Propst	T,FB	Syracuse Univ.
Ross	RG	
Norbert Sacksteder	LH	St. Mary's College; Dayton Gym-Cadets; Massillon Tigers
Gerald "Guy" Shields	LT	Michigan Wesleyan College
Harry Schlee	LT,LG	Det. Univ. HS; Univ. of Detroit
"Nany" Shanks	RT	
Archie "Dutch" Stewart	C	
Herbert Straight	RT,G	Mich. Ag. College
Carl "Dutch" Thiele	LE	Denison Univ.; Cincinnati Celts
Usher	LG	
G. Herbert "Hubby" Weekes	QB	Univ. of Detroit; Eastern HS
Ray E. Whipple	RE	Univ. of Notre Dame
Harry Whitaker	LH,QB	Indiana Univ.
Percy "Short" Wilson	FB	St. Louis Univ.
Windbile	LT,LE	Carlisle Institute

*R. B. Henning played end for Mich. Ag. College in 1914–15.

SCHEDULE

Attend.	Date	Opponent	Score
4000	10/07	Hammond Clabbys	19–0
	10/14	Cincinnati Celts	14–0
	10/21	Buffalo All-Stars	67–0
	10/28	Toledo Maroon	20–0
	11/04	Wabash AA	34–0
15000	11/11	Camp Custer	0–13
3000	11/18	Racine Battery C	19–0
	11/25	Columbus Panhandles	23–0
8000	11/29	Canton Bulldogs	0–7
	12/01	@ Toledo Maroons	23–0

Won 8   **Lost 2**

Detroit Mack Park Maroons, 1915

ROSTER

Manager: John A. Roesink   *Coach:* Bernard "Bertie" Maher
Colors: Maroon and White   *Home Field:* Mack Park

Name	Position	Prior Teams
Thomas Bogle	RT	Univ. of Mich.
Michael H. Boyle	RG,RT	Dartmouth (f); Univ. of Mich.
Arthur "Red" Cornwell	C	Univ. of Mich.
"Red" Cullen	LE	Syracuse Univ.
F. R. Davis	LT,RT	Mich. Ag. College
Dawson	RG	
Deckard	FB	Univ. of Detroit
Dunn	FB	Univ. of Mich. (f)
Eli	RT	Detroit Heralds
Leon C. Exelby	RE	Mich. Ag. College
Goodnow	LH	
Hadden	FB	Univ. of Mich.
"Tacks" Harding	LE	Univ. of Detroit
Hebb	QB	
Ed Kerwin	LG	Georgetown Univ.
Ty Krentler	QB,LH	Kalamazoo Normal School
Faunt V. "Dutch" Lenardson	LG,RT	Univ. of Wyoming; Mich. Ag. College
John Lyons	RE	Univ. of Mich., Ann Arbor Indep.
Thomas McCall	RG	Harvard Univ.
Frank McHale	LT,RG	Univ. of Mich.; Ann Arbor Indep.
Bernard "Bertie" Maher (C)	RH	Detroit College; Detroit Heralds
Jimmy Monat	LH,FB	Detroit Athletic Club
Cyril Moran	C	Univ. of Detroit
Tom Moriarity	LT	Georgetown Univ.
Jimmy Mount	FB	Detroit Univ. HS
Danny Mullane	RG	Univ. of Detroit
Murray	LE,RG,HB	Mich. Ag. College
Parcell	QB	Univ. of Detroit
Robbins	LG	
Smith	LG	
Texas*	LG	
Gus Toumey	FB	Univ. of Detroit; Detroit Univ. HS
Percy "Shorty" Wilson	LH	St. Louis Univ.

SCHEDULE

Attend.	Date	Opponent	Score
	10/03	Toledo Independents	7–0
	10/10	Buffalo Oakdales	12–0
	10/17	Cleveland Blepp Knits	13–0
3000	10/24	Massillon Tigers	7–9
	10/31	Shelby Blues	21–0
	11/07	Ann Arbor Independents	0–0
	11/14	Columbus Panhandles	0–7
8000	11/21	@ Detroit Heralds	7–9
	11/25	@ Toledo Maroons	6–6

Won 4   **Lost 3**   **Tied 2**

Evanston North Ends, 1915

ROSTER

Manager: C. L. Pattison
Colors: Purple and Gold

Coach: Ralph Butow
Home Field: De Paul College Field;
Federal Field; Northwestern University Field

Players	Position	Prior Team
Bates	RH	
Murray J. Battaglia	C	
Bennett	LH,RE	
John Bosdett	LE	Evanston Tech HS
Eppling	RT	
Guilford "Hawk" Falcon	RH,FB	Evanston HS
Favorant	LH	
Fitzgerald	LE,RG	Northwestern Academy
John Hanna	RE	
Hoskins	LH	
James	LT,RG	
Reuben "Rube" Johnson	FB,QB	Evanston HS
Jones	RE	
Henry Norbert Kilby	RH	Evanston HS
Frederick "Blad" Meyers	RG,C	Northwestern Academy
"Baggs" Miller	FB	Lane Tech HS
Max Palm	LT	
Art Pascolini	LE	Univ. of Michigan (f)
Robert Specht	QB,RH	Chicago Mounted Police; Lane Tech HS
Tarrant	RH	
Roy Whitlock	LG,RT	Northwestern Academy

SCHEDULE

Attend.	Date	Opponent	Score
2500	10/03	Illinois All-Stars	34–0
300	10/17	Cabery (IL)	1–0
6000	10/24	@ Wabash AA	0–7
	10/31	@ Detroit Heralds	6–0
3000	11/07	@ Fort Wayne Friars	16–0
	11/14	@ Moline Red Men	26–13
1500	11/21	@ Rockford (IL) AC	24–14
3000	11/25	Moline Red Men	25–0

Won 7   **Lost 1**

Evanston North Ends, 1916

ROSTER

Manager: C. L. Pattison   *Coach:* Moore *[Washington Park, attended Loyola]*
Colors: Purple and Gold   *Home Field:* DePaul College Field; Northwestern Field

Players	Position	Prior Team
John Barrett	LH	Washington and Lee Univ.; Keewatin Academy; Oak Park HS
Moses Bashaw	LE	
Murray J. Battaglia	C	
John Bosdett	LE	Evanston Tech HS
Penn Carolan	FB,RH	Dartmouth Univ.
Eissler	LH	
Eppling	RT	
Guilford "Hawk" Falcon	LE	Evanston HS
Ray C. "Dick" Falcon	C	Evanston Tech HS; Culver Military Academy
Fitzgerald	RE	Northwestern Academy
Geiger	RG,T	Univ. of Illinois
Gilbert	QB	
Graham	RT	
John Hanna	RE	
Reuben "Rube" Johnson	QB	Evanston HS
Kelly	RE	
Henry Norbert Kilby	LHB,QB	Evanston Tech HS
Roger Kilby	RE	Evanston Tech HS
Lindal	LT,G	Northwestern Academy
Frederick "Blad" Meyers	RG	Northwestern Academy
"Baggs" Miller	RH,FB	Lane Tech HS
Olson	RT,C	
Max Palm	LT,RT	Evanston Tech HS
Art Pascolini	LE	Univ. of Michigan (f)
William Riche	RG	DePaul Univ.
St. Germain	LG	Carlisle Institute
Eugene Schobinger	RE,FB,LE	Univ. of Illinois; Illinois All-Stars
Tom Shaughnessy	C	Univ. of Notre Dame; Chicago Blues
Robert Specht	RH,LH	Lane Tech HS; Chicago Mounted Police
Roy Whitlock	LG	Northwestern Academy

SCHEDULE

Attend.	Date	Opponent	Score
	10/01	Milwaukee Maples	28–0
3000	10/08	@ Racine Regulars	12–0
3000	10/15	@ Davenport AC	0–3
5000	10/22	@ Wabash	21–18
	10/29	South Bend	51–3
	11/05	@ Detroit Heralds	9–21
	11/12	@ Fort Wayne Friars	0–14
	11/19	@ Rockford AC	41–0
10,000	11/30	Cornell-Hamburgs	6–7
		(game called for darkness with 3 minutes left)	

Won 5   **Lost 4**

Fort Wayne Friars, 1915

ROSTER

Manager: Leo Beltman
Colors: Black and Gold

Coach: Samuel Byroades
Home Field: League Park

Name	Position	Prior Team
Baird	LE,RE	Carlisle Institute
Baker	LG	
Daniel R. Ball	C	
Alvin "Heine" Berger	FB,RH	Univ. of Notre Dame
Bryan	LG	Friars
Christian C. Chambers	FB,E	Friars
Frank "Coonie" Checkaye	QB	Muncie Congervilles
Edgar C. "Big Ed" Davis	LG	Indiana Univ.; Pine Village AC
"Denny" Dennison	LG,LT	Friars
Howard "Cap" Edwards	RT	Univ. of Notre Dame; Akron Indians; Canton Bulldogs
Al Feeney	C	Univ. of Notre Dame; Marion AC
Louis Island	RE,QB	Haskell; Carlisle Institute; Jackson (MI) All-Stars
Jonard	C	Friars
Keith "Deacon" Jones	LT	Univ. of Notre Dame; Akron Indians
Walt Kennedy	LH	Friars
Kintz	RT	+
Walter Krull	RG	Friars
Laird	RH	Friars
Kent "Skeet" Lambert	QB	Wabash College
La Pado	LE	Friars
Miller	LT	Friars
Monahan	LE	Friars
Orthieb	RH	
Charles E. Pask	LE	Purdue Univ. (f)
Don Peters	FB	Carlisle Institute; Canton Bulldogs
Joe Pliska	LH	Univ. of Notre Dame; Chicago Blues
Reilly	LE,LT,RE	Chicago Blues
Robbins	LG,LT	Friars
Rogers	LG	Friars
"Reb" Russell	LT,RT,RH	Friars
D.C. Smith	RT	Purdue Univ. (f)
Its Strieder	RH,FB,QB	Indiana Univ.
Wilkins	RG	Friars
Ivan Armon Zaring	LT	Indiana Univ.

+ Newspapers report he attended the Univ. of Nebraska, but he did not.

SCHEDULE

Attend.	Date	Opponent	Score
	10/03	South Bend M.A.C.s	58–0
	10/10	Newcastle Maxwell-Briscoes	79–0
	10/17	Muncie Congervilles	109–0
	10/24	Chicago Blues	43–0
	10/31	Racine Regulars	41–6
3500	11/07	Evanston North Ends	0–16
2500	11/14	Ann Arbor Independents	23–3
4500	11/21	Wabash AA	6–6
3000	11/25	Columbus Panhandles	3–0

Won 7   **Lost 1**   **Tied 1**

Fort Wayne Friars, 1916

ROSTER

Manager: Leo Beltman/Carl J. Suedhoff   *Coach:* Samuel Byroades
Colors: Black and Gold   *Home Field:* League Park

Players	Position	Prior Team
Jack Ambrose	QB	Univ. of Maine; Elyria Pros
Baird	RE	Carlisle Institute
Daniel R. Ball	C	
Alvin "Heine" Berger	LH	Univ. of Notre Dame
Christian C. Chambers	FB,LE	
Frank "Coonie" Checkaye	QB	Muncie Congervilles
Daley	LG	
"Denny" Dennison	RG	
Charles "Gus" Dorais	QB	Univ. of Notre Dame; Massillon Tigers
Howard "Cap" Edwards	RT	Univ. of Notre Dame; Canton Bulldogs
Allen "Mal" Elward	LE	Univ. of Notre Dame
Albert Feeney	C	Univ. of Notre Dame; Marian AC
Freeman "Fitz" Fitzgerald	LT	Univ. of Notre Dame
Fred E. Gerberding	HB,QB	
Hunter	RE	
Earl D. Huntington	RE	Univ. of Chicago
Keith "Deacon" Jones	LT	Univ. of Notre Dame; Akron Indians
Kintz	RT	
Gordon A. Laird	LH	
I.R. Martin (Johnson*)	LH	Univ. of Missouri
Miller	LT	
J. Hugh "Pepper" O'Donnell	C,RG,E	Univ. of Notre Dame
Don Peters	FB	Northern Ohio Univ.
Joe Pliska	LH,RH	Univ. of Notre Dame
Quirk	FB	
Smith	LH	
Joseph D. Trimble	LE	Rose Poly Tech
Wilkins	LG	
Ralph "Bull" Young	FB	Wash. and Jeff. College
Ivan Armon Zaring	RT	Indiana Univ.

SCHEDULE

Attend.	Date	Opponent	Score
	10/01	Dayton Gym-Cadets +	101–0
2600	10/08	Hammond Clabbys	9–0
	10/15	Detroit Braves	27–0
	10/22	Cincinnati Celts	6–6
	10/29	Elyria Athletics	24–13
	11/05	Pine Village AC	7–0
	11/12	Evanston North Ends	14–0
5200	11/19	Wabash AA	13–7
5000	11/26	@ Wabash AA	0–3
	11/30	Columbus Panhandles	3–0

+ Officially the team went out of existence, the Dayton Munitions played this game as Gym-Cadets.

Won 8   **Lost 1**   **Tied 1**

Fort Wayne Friars, 1917

ROSTER

Manager: George Fishering/Ed Leech   *Coach:* Earl D. Huntington
Colors: Black and Gold   *Home Field:* League Park

Players	Position	Prior Team
Jack Ambrose	QB	Univ. of Maine
Daniel R. Ball	C	
Moses Bashaw	RG,LE,RT	Evanston North Ends
Walter E. Berghoff	LE	St. Mary's College
Bradley	LE	West Virginia Wesleyan College
Christian C. Chambers	FB	
"Denny" Dennison	LG	
Charles "Gus" Dorais	QB	Univ. of Notre Dame; Massillon Tigers
Allen "Mal" Elward	LE	Univ. of Notre Dame
Al Feeney	C	Univ. of Notre Dame; Marion AC
Norman "Tango" Glockson	RG	Detroit Heralds; Racine Pros
Charles Helvie	RE	Pine Village AC; Indiana Univ.
Horsefield	E	
Earl D. Huntington	LH,RE	Univ. of Chicago
Jetmore	FB	Fort Wayne sandlot
Keith "Deacon" Jones	LT	Univ. of Notre Dame; Akron Indians
Kintz	RH	
Kraege	RG	Army
Lockwood	RT,RG	All State high school/Indiana
Mann	HB	
I. R. Martin (Johnson*)	LH,LE	Univ. of Missouri
Lee Percy Mehlig	LT	Univ. of Wisconsin; Hammond Clabbys
L. T. Parry	LE	
Joe Pliska	LH	Univ. of Notre Dame; Chicago Blues
Raeder	RG	
Robbins	LG	
Knute Rockne	LE	Univ. of Notre Dame; Massillon Tigers
Frank Rydzewski	C	Univ. of Notre Dame
Tom Shaughnessy	RB	Univ. of Notre Dame; Evan. North Ends
Smith	LH,RH	Univ. of Notre Dame; Marian AC
Robert Specht	RH	Lane Tech HS; Evanston North Ends
Thompson	LT	
Wanzer	RT	
Roy Whitlock	RG	Evanston North Ends; Hammond Clabbys
Ralph "Bull" Young	FB	Wash. and Jeff. College
Ivan Armon Zaring	RE	Indiana Univ.

SCHEDULE

Attend.	Date	Opponent	Score
2000	10/07	Camp Custer (Battle Creek)	0–9
2000	10/14	Carlisle Indians	56–0
2200	10/21	Cincinnati Celts	21–6
2500	10/28	Pitcairn Quakers	9–10
3000	11/04	Toledo Maroons	45–7
	11/11	Racine Battery C	28–0
	11/18	Columbus Panhandles	13–0
	11/25	Wabash AA	7–7
	12/02	@ Hammond Clabbys	0–25

Won 5   **Lost 3**   **Tied 1**

Hammond Clabbys, 1916

ROSTER

Manager: F. M. "Heine" Morrow   *Coach:* Edward L. Green
Colors: Yellow and Black   *Home Field:* Hammond's League Park

Players	Position	Prior Team
Benton	RT	
Blair	RH,LH	
Frank A. Blocker	C	Purdue Univ.
Ted Blocker	QB,FB	Indiana Univ. (f)
Howard Ewert	RT	Indiana Univ.
John R. Finn	QB	Purdue Univ.
Ford	RH	
Malcolm E. Galvin	QB,LH	Univ. of Wisconsin
F. Green	RG,LG	
Herbert	RG,LG	
G. Kohl	LE,QB	
Paul D. "Clinks" Meyers	RH	Univ. of Wisconsin
J. Nolan	LE,RE	
Plum	LT,RT	
Henry V. Ruffner	RT	Purdue Univ.
Schillo	C,FB	
L. Seliger	LG	
Melvin J. Stinchfield	RE	Purdue Univ.
Talbot	LH,LE,RH,FB	Purdue Univ.; South Dakota Univ.
George Volkman	LT	Univ. of Wisconsin
Ralph "Bull" Young	HB	Wash. and Jeff. College; Fort Wayne Friars

SCHEDULE

Attend.	Date	Opponent	Score
	09/24	Peru (IL) Second Team	76–0
	10/01	Rockford (IL) Badgers	27–2
2600	10/08	@Ft Wayne Friars	0–9
	10/15	Aurora (IL) Greyhounds	34–6
3000	10/22	Sheridan @ Lafayette	20–0
630	10/29	Montpelier (OH)	56–0
	11/05	Racine Battery C	14–13
1100	11/12	Ann Arbor Independents	30–0
1500	11/19	Davenport AC	12–14
	11/26	@ Elyria Athletics	lost
	11/30	Detroit Harvards	20–0
	12/3	Cincinnati Celts	3–0
5000	12/10	@ Pine Village AC	0–3

Won 9   **Lost 4**

Hammond Clabbys, 1917

ROSTER

Owner/Manager: Paul Parduhn   *Coach:* Edward L. Green
Colors: Golden yellow   *Home Field:* Parduhn Field

Players	Position	Prior Team
John Barrett	RH	Wash. and Lee; Toledo Maroons
Bauer	LE	
Blair	LH	
Frank A. Blocker	RT,C	Purdue Univ.
Ted Blocker	FB	Indiana Univ. (f)
John Leo "Paddy" Driscoll	HB,QB	Northwestern Univ.
Duke	RE	
Gaffney	LH	Oak Park HS (IL)
F. Green	C,RG	
Bernard "Swede" Halstrom	LH	Univ. of Illinois
Wilber W. Henderson	RE,LE	
Wallie Hess (Herrin*)	QB	Indiana Univ.
Johnson	LE	
Emmett G. Keefe	RG	Univ. of Notre Dame; Pine Village AC
G. Kohl	LE,RH	
Kreese	LH	
A. R. Longenecker	FB,HB	Univ. of California; Purdue Univ.
C. M. McCardy	T	Mich. Ag. College
Lee Percy Mehlig	LT,RT	Univ. of Wisconsin
Paul D. "Clinks" Meyers	RH	Univ. of Wisconsin
J. Nolan	QB,E	
Pike	G	
Plum	RG,LG	
Henry V. Ruffner	RT	Purdue Univ.
Schlatter	RH	
L. Seliger	LT	
Thomas J. Shaughnessy (T. Howard Gangway*)	FB,E	Univ. of Notre Dame; Chicago Blues; Evanston North Ends
Harold "Irish" Sheridan	HB	Pine Village AC; Sheridan Warriors
Shill	LG	
Simmons	FB	
Slater	QB	
Thiery	LE,RT	
Thoemes	RE,RH	
George Volkman	LT	Univ. of Wisconsin
Hugo "Hugs" Volkman	G	
Roy Whitlock	T,LG	Evanston North Ends

SCHEDULE

Attend.	Date	Opponent	Score
4000	10/07	@ Detroit Heralds	0–19
2000	10/14	@ Davenport AC	9–3
2000	10/21	Racine Battery C	0–12
800	10/28	Wabash AA	20–9
1700	11/04	@ Pine Village AC	13–0
3000	11/11	Cornell-Hamburgs	13–3
1500	11/18	@ Wabash AA	7–0
1700	11/25	Pine Village AC	6–21
1500	11/29	Cornell-Hamburgs	15–0
2000	12/01	Fort Wayne Friars	25–0

Won 7   **Lost 3**

Massillon Tigers, 1915

ROSTER

President: John "Jack" Whalen Jr.   *Coach:* Joe Collins
Colors: Orange and Black   *Home Field:* Driving Park

Players	Position	Prior Team
Harold A. Boerner	LT	Massillon sandlot
Thomas Bogle	LG	Univ. of Mich.
Howard J. Bowie	LE	Western Reserve Univ.
Maurice "Windy" Briggs (Burne*)	LH	Ohio State Univ.
Burns	LE,RE	
Cass	RE	Western Reserve Univ.
Boyd V. Cherry (White*)	LE,RE	Ohio State Univ.
E. M. Cole	RG	Univ. of Mich.
Joe Collins	FB	Univ. of Notre Dame; Elyria Pros; Akron Indians
Leo "Jock" Collins	FB	Univ. of Pittsburgh
Custer	LG	Massillon sandlot
Homer Davidson	QB	Massillon; Shelby; Elyria Pros; Akron Indians
J. Franklin "Pud" Day (Southern*, Campbell*)	RT	Muhlenberg College
Charles "Gus" Dorais	QB	Univ. of Notre Dame
Clarence Erb	LG	Allegheny College; Canton Bulldogs
Joe Esch	C	Elyria Pros
Charles "Sam" Finnegan	LH	Univ. of Notre Dame
Malcolm D. "Red" (Maurie*) Fleming	LH,RH	Wash. and Jeff. College; Altoona
Jim Flynn	RT	Western Reserve Univ.
Ed Hanley (Hogan*)	FB	Univ. of Pittsburgh
Louis J. Hayes (Lee*, McGuire*)	C	Muhlenberg College
Holston	LT,RG	
Keith "Deacon" Jones	LT,RT	Univ. of Notre Dame; Akron Indians
Edmund L. Kagy	RH	Western Reserve Univ.; Elyria; Akron
Bill Kelleher	LH	Univ. of Notre Dame
Morris	LH	Ohio State Univ.
Alfred Nesser	RE	Columbus Panhandles
Carl "Bull" Olsson	LG	Akron Indians
Milton "Muff" Portmann	RG	Western Reserve Univ.; Akron Indians
David Reese		
Knute Rockne	LE	Univ. of Notre Dame; Akron Indians
Norbert Sacksteder	LH	St. Mary's College; Dayton Gym-Cadets
Smith	LG	
Dwight Arthur Wertz	LH	Western Reserve Univ.; Elyria; Akron

SCHEDULE

Attend.	Date	Opponent	Score
2000	10/10	Cleveland Blepp Knits	41–3
	10/17	Idle	
3000	10/24	@ Det. Mack Park Maroons	9–7
3000	10/31	Columbus Panhandles	0–16
1500	11/07	@ Wheeling AC	47–0
6000	11/14	Canton Bulldogs	16–0
3000	11/21	@ Toledo Maroons	6–3
8500	11/28	@ Canton Bulldogs	0–6

Won 5   **Lost 2**

Massillon Tigers, 1916

ROSTER

Manager: Edmund L. Kagy   *Coach:* Malcolm D. "Red" Fleming
Colors: Orange and Black   *Home Field:* Driving Park

Players	Position	Prior Team
John Arthur	LT	Rutgers Univ.
Albert "Bert" Baston	LE	Univ. of Minnesota
Bemis	QB	
Joe Bergie	FB	Carlisle Institute
Maurice "Windy" Briggs (Maurie*)	QB	Ohio State Univ.
Custer	LG	sandlot
J. Franklin "Pud" Day	RT	Muhlenberg College
John J. Donahue*	QB	
Charles "Gus" Dorais	QB	Univ. of Notre Dame; Ft. Wayne Friars
Freeman "Fitz" Fitzgerald	RG	Univ. of Notre Dame
Malcolm D. "Red" Fleming	RH	Wash. and Jeff.; Altoona Indians
Forbes*	G	
Russell Bryan Goodwin	QB	Wash. and Jeff. College
Ed Hanley (Hogan*)	RE	Univ. of Pittsburgh
Louis J. Hayes	C	Muhlenberg College
Fred "Fritz" Heyman	RE	Wash. and Jeff. College; Massillon HS
Edmund L. Kagy	QB	Western Reserv; Elyria Pros; Akron
Willmon "Fats" Keiser	FB,RH	Bucknell College
Bill Kelleher	FB	Univ. of Notre Dame
Kent "Skeet" Lambert	QB	Wabash College; Detroit Heralds;
		Canton Bulldogs; Fort Wayne Friars
Little*	RT	
Joel P. Mattern (DeMars)*	LH	Univ. of Minnesota
Mullin	QB	
Robert A. "Nasty" Nash	LT	Rutgers Univ.
Carl "Bat" Rambaud	LG	sandlot; Massillon Blues
Dan "Bullet" Riley	LH	sandlot; Canton Bulldogs
Knute Rockne	LE	Univ. of Notre Dame; Akron Indians
Christopher Schlachter (Schmidt*)	LG,LE	Syracuse Univ.
Gilbert Sinclair	LG	Univ. of Minnesota
Howard Parker Talman (Townsend*)	FB	Rutgers Univ.
Carl L. "Dutch" Thiele	LT,LE	Denison Univ.
Jack Townley	RT	Univ. of Minnesota
Fred M. "Iron Man" Walker	T	Univ. of Chicago; Utica (baseball)
Aloysius A. "Buzz" Wesbecher	RT	Wash. and Jeff. College
Frank S. White	RH	Indiana Normal School

SCHEDULE

Attend.	Date	Opponent	Score
2500	10/08	Elyria Athletics	31–0
3800	10/15	Altoona Indians	54–0
6000	10/22	@ Toledo Maroons	15–7
	10/29	@ Detroit Heralds	6–0
	11/05	@ Youngstown Patricians	3–0
3600	11/12	Columbus Panhandles	10–0
5000	11/19	@ Cleveland Indians	0–0
10000	11/26	Canton Bulldogs	0–0
	11/30	Youngstown Patricians	27–0
10000	12/02	@ Canton Bulldogs	0–24

Won 7   **Lost 1**   **Tied 2**

Massillon Tigers, 1917

ROSTER

President: John Whalen Jr.   *Coach:* Bob Nash/Charles Brickley/
Stanly Cofall/Knute Rockne
Colors: Orange and Black   *Home Field:* M.B.A.C. Field on Clay Street

Players	Position	Prior Team
Bawl	LG	Army Ambulance Corp, Allentown
John Beck Jr.	LH	Massillon HS; Buffalo (baseball)
Earl Blackburn	RH	Massillon HS
Charles Brickley	HB	Harvard Univ.
Brown*	LE	Harvard Univ.
Stanley Cofall	FB,LH	Univ. of Notre Dame, Youngstown Pats
Charles Copley	RT	Muhlenberg College
Craig	QB	Army Ambulance Corp, Allentown
Jim Dettling	RE	Univ. of So. Carolina; Muhlenberg College
Dobie	C	Army Ambulance Corp, Allentown
Emmelay*	LH	Univ. of Pittsburgh
Fisher*	RT	Army Ambulance Corp, Allentown
Freeman Fitzgerald	RG	Notre Dame Univ.; Youngstown Pats
Malcolm "Red" Fleming	RH	Wash. and Jeff. College
French*	RE	Penn State Univ.
Jones*	LE	Washington and Lee Univ.
Kelly*	LH	
DeOrmond "Tuss" McLaughry	FB	Mich. Ag. College; Westminster College
Frank B. McNulty	LH	Univ. of Pittsburgh
I. R. Martin (Jones*, Emmely*)	RH	Univ. of Missouri
C. Meyers	RE	Canal Fulton HS
Eugene E. "Shorty" Miller	QB	Penn State Univ.
Robert A. "Nasty" Nash	LT,LE	Rutgers Univ.
Frank Nesser	RT	Columbus Panhandles
Robert D. Peck	C	Univ. of Pitt; Youngstown Pats
Carl "Bat" Rambaud	LG	Massillon Sandlot
Fred "Fritz" Rehor	LG,RG	Univ. of Michigan
Dan "Bullet" Riley	FB	Hiram College; Canton Bulldogs
Knute Rockne	RE	Univ. of Notre Dame; Fort Wayne Friars
Irving William Rogers	RH	Princeton Univ.
Jack Scott	RH	an eastern college
Stuart Briscoe Scruggs	C	Lehigh Univ.
Dale H. Sies	RG	Univ. of Pittsburgh
Claude E. Thornhill	RT	Univ. of Pittsburgh; McKeesport Olympics
Everett Tuttle	G	Oregon Ag. College
Aloysius A. "Buzz" Wesbecher	C,T	Wash. and Jeff. College

SCHEDULE

Attend.	Date	Opponent	Score
	10/14	Buffalo All-Stars	14–6
	10/21	Pitcairn Quakers	27–0
3500	10/28	Akron Pros	14–0
	11/04	Columbus Panhandles	28–0
5000	11/11	@ Youngstown Patricians	6–14
	11/18	@ Akron Pros	0–3
	11/25	@ Canton Bulldogs	3–14
	12/03	@ Canton Bulldogs	6–0

Won 5   **Lost 3**

Minneapolis Marines, 1916

ROSTER

Manager: John Dunne	*Coach:* Russell J. Tollefson
Colors: Maroon and Gold	*Home Field:* Nicollet Park

Players	Position	Prior Team
Walt Buland	RT	
Fred Chicken	LH	Univ. of Kansas
Costello	LH	
John Dunne	RG	
Art Gaustad	RT,LG	
Harry Gunderson	C	sandlot
Charles Jonason	RE	
Kostick	LG	
Dewey Lyle	LT	Univ. of Minnesota;
		Minneapolis Central H.S.
Bob "Rube" Marshall	LE	Univ. of Minnesota
Nelson	C	East Ends (St. Paul)
Edward Novak	RH	
Mike Palmer	LG	sandlot
"Sheepy" Redeen	RE	sandlot
Labe Safro	RH	
Selvig	RG,RT	
Eber F. Simpson Jr.	RH,FB	Univ. of Wisconsin
Edward Sundby	LB,FB	
Russell J. Tollefson	T	Univ. of Minnesota
Reuben "Rube" Ursella	QB	sandlot

SCHEDULE

Attend.	Date	Opponent	Score
1800	10/15	West Duluth	54–3
800	10/22	Merrimacs (St. Paul)	53–0
2000	10/29	East Ends (Minneapolis)	7–0
1200	11/12	Laurels (St. Paul)	34–0
3000	11/19	Banholzers (St. Paul)	39–0
2000	11/26	East Ends (Minneapolis)	17–0
7500	11/30	Minnesota All-Stars	0–0
3000	12/3	@ Davenport AC	19–7

Won 7   **Lost 0**   **Tied 1**

Minneapolis Marines, 1917

ROSTER

Manager: John Dunne   *Coach:*
Colors: Maroon and Gold   *Home Field:* Nicollet Park

Players	Position	Prior Team
Walt Buland	RT	sandlot
Fred Chicken	R	Univ. of Kansas
Costello	LH	
John Dunne	RG	
Art Gaustad	LG	
Goslad	LG	
Harry Gunderson	C,LT	sandlot
Halleran	LT	
Charles Jonason	RH	
Mallory	LT	
Bob "Rube" Marshall	LE	Univ. of Minn.; Minneapolis Central HS
Nelson	C	East Ends (St. Paul)
Edward Novak	LH	
Mike Palmer	LT	sandlot
"Sheepy" Redeen	RE	sandlot
Labe Safro	RH	
Selvig	RG	
Eber F. Simpson Jr.	FB	Univ. of Wisconsin
Edward Sundby	RH	
Reuben "Rube" Ursella	QB	sandlot

SCHEDULE

Attend.	Date	Opponent	Score
	10/7	West Side Tigers (St. Paul)	won
1200	10/14	Seatons (St. Paul)	31–0
	10/21	@ Davenport AC	40–0
2100	0/28	@ Duluth	55–7
	11/4	@ Rock Island Independents	7–3
	11/11	Banholzers (St. Paul)	38–14
	11/18	@ Rock Island Independents	33–14
3500	11/25	Camp Dodge	28–0

Won 8   **Lost 0**

Pine Village Athletic Club, 1915

ROSTER

Manager: Claire Rhodes   *Coach:* Edgar C. "Big Ed" Davis
Colors: *Home Field:* Akers Park, Pine Village

Players	Position	Prior Team
Oral Brier	RE	
Walter Burns	RH	
George Cain	FB	
John Carr	FB	
Lee Christian	RT	
Lloyd Crane	HB	
Edgar C. "Big Ed" Davis	T	Indiana Univ.
Eli Fenters	QB	
Ray Fenters	LH	
Roy Fenters	QB	
Bill Fisher		
Mart Halsema	LH	
Nance Halsema	RG	
Earl Hammil		
Merie Hammil		
Charles Helvie	RE	Indiana Univ.
James Hooker	LT	
Fred Leacentimer	QB	
P. Mann	G	
McKinley Martindale	C	
Charles Metzker	G	
Paul Odle	HB,E	
Joe Pliska	HB	Univ. of Notre Dame
John Prescott		
Claire Rhodes	C	Univ. of Chicago
Lee Rhodes	HB	
Seymour Rhodes		
"Red" Rockhold	C	
Marion Van Sclepen	FB	
Charles Sims	G	
Fred Slinger	LG	
Herman Slinger	LT	
Wilford "Beekie" Smith	T	DePauw College
Elmer Soller		
Foster Strayer	LE	
Earl Strong	RE	
James F. "Jim" Thorpe	HB	Carlisle Institute
Bill Williams	FB	Indiana Univ.
Matthew Winters	T	Indiana Univ.

SCHEDULE

Attend.	Date	Opponent	Score
	10/03	Lafayette	34–0
	10/10	Sheldon (IL)	56–0
	10/17	Marion Club(Indianapolis)	19–0
	10/24	Idle	
1200	10/31	@ Wabash AA	7–0
	11/07	@ Sheridan	13–0
	11/14	@ Indianapolis Mapletons 49–0	1
	11/21	Westville (IL)	64–0
3000	11/25	@ Purdue Univ. All-Stars 29–0	1

Won 8   **Lost 0**

Pine Village Athletic Club, 1916

ROSTER

Manager: Claire Rhodes   Coach: Edgar C. "Big Ed" Davis
Colors: Home Field: Akers Park, Pine Village

Player	Position	Prior Team
Frank Allen	RT	Indiana Univ.
Joe Bergie	C	Carlisle Institute; Pitcairn
Oral "Skinny" Brier	RE	Pine Village AC
Lee Brutus		
Howard "Cub" Buck	LG	Univ. of Wisconsin
Chester	HB	
Carl Dalbow	LG	
Edgar C. "Big Ed" Davis	RT	Indiana Univ.; Fort Wayne Friars
Mark C. Erehart	LH	Indiana Univ.
Eli Fenters	QB	Pine Village AC
Ray Fenters	LH	Pine Village AC
Bill Fisher		
David Earl "Kinks" Hawthorne	LT,LG	DePauw Univ.
Charles Helvie	RE	Indiana Univ.; Marion AC
Leslie Hole		
James Hooker	LT,LG	Pine Village AC
Emmett G. Keefe	RG	Univ. of Notre Dame
Richard C. King (D. Dalbo*)	FB	Harvard Univ.
Arthur C. Krause	RE	Indiana Univ.
Franklin Bart Macomber	QB	Univ. of Illinois
McQullen	C	
McKinley Martindale	C	
Charles Metzker	G	Pine Village AC
Cliff Milligan	C,RE	Indiana Univ.
Minter	LT	
Paul Odle	E	
Harold S. Ofstie	RE,LE	Univ. of Wisconsin
Claire Rhodes	C	Univ. of Chicago
Henry "Hank" Rowan	HB	DePauw Univ.
John Sailor		
Clair Scott	RH,LE	Indiana Univ.
Paul Preston "Chesty" Sheeks	QB	Univ. of South Dakota
Harold "Irish" Sheridan	QB	Sheridan Warriors
Ernie Soucy	LE	Harvard Univ.
Gordon "Doc" Thomas	HB	DePauw Univ.
Harrison Walker	LG	Indiana Univ.
Bill Williams	FB	Indiana Univ.
Matthew Winters	LT	Indiana Univ.; Marion AC

SCHEDULE

Attend.	Date	Opponent	Score
	09/24	Kirkland	46–0
3,000	10/01	@ Renssinger Valparaiso Apollos	37–0
	10/08	Elwood	won
	10/15	@ Wabash AA	0–0
1100	10/22	Decatur Indians	12–7
2000	10/29	Cincinnati Celts	6–9
	11/05	@ Fort Wayne Friars	0–7
	11/12	Wabash AA	7–0
	11/19	Toledo Maroons	0–0
	11/26	Pitcairn Quakers	13–3
	11/30	Cincinnati Celts	23–3
	12/03	Capital Citys of Indianapolis	43–6
5000	12/10	Hammond Clabbys	3–0

Won 9   **Lost 2**   **Tied 2**

Pine Village Athletic Club, 1917

ROSTER

Manager: Claire Rhodes   *Coach:* Edgar C. "Big Ed" Davis
Colors: *Home Field:*

Players	Position	Prior Team
Francis Bacon	FB,RH	Wabash College
Harry C. Banjan	LE	Univ. of Notre Dame
Arthur Bergman	LH	Univ. of Notre Dame
C. J. Borum	LT	Purdue Univ.
Edgar C. "Big Ed" Davis	RT	Indiana Univ.; Fort Wayne Friars
Eli Fenters	QB	(14 years w/Pine Village)
Roy Fenters	LH,LG	(5 years w/Pine Village)
Graham	RE	
Charles Helvie	RE	Indiana Univ.
Hogle	LT	
James Hooker	LG	
Johnson	RH,LE	
Emmett G. Keefe	RG	Univ. of Notre Dame
Richard C. King	FB	Harvard Univ.; Canton Bulldogs
J. McCarthy	LE,RE	
M. McCarthy	QB	
Miller	C	
Cliff Milligan	LG,C,LT	Indiana Univ.
James Patterson	RG	
Jim Phelan	QB	Univ. of Notre Dame
Roum	LT	
Paul Preston "Chesty" Sheeks	QB	Univ. of South Dakota at Vermillion
Homer Stonebraker	C	Wabash College
W. V. Van Aken	RE	Purdue Univ.

SCHEDULE

Date	Opponent	Score
09/30	Peoria Socials @ Lafayette	6–0
10/07	South Bend Jolly Fellows	14–7
10/14	McKeesport Olympics	0–0
10/21	@ Wabash AA	2–0
10/28	Cincinnati Celts @ Lafayette	0–0
11/04	Hammond Clabbys @ Indianapolis	0–13
11/11	Wabash AA @ Lafayette	0–7
11/18	328th Machine Gun Battalion (Camp Custer)	35–0
11/25	@ Hammond Clabbys	21–6
11/29	Wabash AA @ Indianapolis	20–6

Won 6   **Lost 2**   **Tied 2**

Pitcairn Quakers, 1915

ROSTER

Manager: Crowl   *Coach:* George "Cotton" Vedderneck
Colors: *Home Field:*

Players	Position	Prior Team
C. Adams	LG	
R. Adams	LT,RG,C	
J. "Auggie" Blair	RE	Univ. of Pittsburgh
Bowser	FB	
Collins	LT	
G. Crowell (Crowl)	RH,LH	
Kirk	RE	
Lose	QB,RH	
McDowell	LH	
Mauke	LT	
Meyers	LG	
Mockerk	FB	
Morrison	RG	
Nelson "Rocky" Rupp	FB	Mercersburg Acad.
Schreiner	LT	
Seiglev	QB	
Summers	LH, RH	
Frank Vedderneck	LE	
George "Cotton" Vedderneck	RE	Carlisle Institute
Warner	LE	Cornell Univ.
Zeigler	QB	

SCHEDULE

Date	Opponent	Score
10/09	South Fork	105–0
10/30	@ Altoona Indians	0–3
11/13	Irwin (PA)	20–0
11/14	@ Youngstown Patricians	6–17
11/25	@ Altoona Indians	0–10

Pitcairn Quakers, 1916

ROSTER

Manager: P. H. Muteller   *Coach:* Joe Bergie/George "Cotton" Vedderneck
Colors: *Home Field:*

Player	Position	Prior Team
C. Adams	LG	Penn. State; Pitcairn Quakers
Joe Bergie	FB	Carlisle Institute; Altoona Indians
Buldowsky	LT,LG	sandlot
Carroll	LE	West Virginia Univ.
Frank Dunn	FB	Dickinson College
Grubbs	LT	Fort Wayne Friars
Mauke	RT	Altoona Indians
Meyers	LG	
Bill "Chief" Newashe	T	Carlisle Institute; Detroit Heralds
O'Connell	RH	Pitcairn Quakers
Raymond	T	Slippery Rock Acad.
Robbins	RG	Wabash AA; Detroit Heralds
Nelson "Rocky" Rupp	FB	Mercersburg Acad.
Stilwell Saunooke	RH	Carlisle Institute
Schreiner	C,T	Pitcairn Quakers
Summers	LH	Pitcairn Quakers
Sutter	LH	Kiski Acad.
Frank Vedderneck	LE	
George "Cotton" Vedderneck	RE	Carlisle Institute; Altoona Indians
Vedern	LE	
Warner +	LE	Cornell Univ.
Frank S. White	QB	Indiana Normal School

+ No proof of attendance at Cornell Univ.

SCHEDULE

Attend.	Date	Opponent	Score
	9/23	Irwin Scholastics	13–0
	9/30	Perrysville	28–0
1500	10/08	@ Canton Bulldogs	0–7
3000	10/15	@ Cleveland Indians	6–14
	10/22	Latrobe AC	31–0
	10/29	@ Youngstown Patricians	0–7
2000	11/05	@ Dayton Triangles	3–7
3000	11/12	@ Detroit Heralds	0–15
	11/19	Martins Ferry AA @ Wheeling (WV)	19–7
	11/26	@ Pine Village AC	3–13
2000	11/30	@ Dayton Triangles	9–20
	12/02	Nixton Club	22–0
	12/03	Bradley Eagles	7–0
	12/10	S.J. Grenets	13–2

Won 7   **Lost 7**

Pitcairn Quakers, 1917

ROSTER

Manager: P. H. Muteller   *Coach:*
Colors: *Home Field:*

Players	Position	Prior Team
C. Adams	LG	Penn State Univ.
Joe Bergie	C	Carlisle Institute
Bradley	LH,RH,RE	West Va. Wesleyan Univ.
Buldowsky	LF,RG	
Collins	G,T	
Stephen Rowan Crawford	FB	West Virginia Univ.
Malcolm "Red" Fleming	HB	Wash. and Jeff. College; Massillon Tigers
Grayber	FB	
Grubbs	LG	
McIndoe	LT	Wilkinsburg HS ++
Marick	RT	
Meyers	LG	
Miller	RH,LH	
Minde	RT	
O'Connell	HB	Pitcairn for 6 yrs
Plaxico	LE,RE	
Pogue	HB	
Pratt	LT,FB	Carlisle Institute
Stilwell Saunooke	RE	Carlisle Institute
Schiller	LE	
Schreiner	LT	
Stevens	LT	
Summers	HB	Pitcairn for 3 yrs
Sutter	LH	Kiski Acad.
Warner +	RE,LE	Cornell Univ.
Frank S. White	QB	Indiana Normal of Pennsylvania

+ No proof of attendance at Cornell Univ.
++ Reported in the *Youngstown Telegram*, but could not be verified in Wilkinsburg

SCHEDULE

Attend.	Date	Opponent	Score
	10/07	@ Canton Bulldogs	7–12
4000	10/14	Youngstown Patricians	16–10
	10/20	Wheeling Stogis	20–0
	10/21	Massillon Tigers	0–27
2500	10/28	@ Fort Wayne Friars	10–9
	11/04	Cincinnati Celts	6–7
	11/11	Wheeling (WV) @ Martins Ferry	59–0
	11/18	U.S. Army Camp Lee Bradley Eagles	5–6
6000	11/25	McKeesport Olympics	0–3
5000	12/01	McKeesport Olympics	0–0

Won 3   **Lost 5**   **Tied 1**

Racine Regulars, 1915

ROSTER

Racine Football Association
Manager: Otto Jandl
Colors: Blue and White   *Home Field:* Bi-State League Park and
W. I. League Park

Players	Position	Prior Team
Joe Beam	LT	Kenosha sandlot; Woodstock (IL)
Dietrich	RH	
Downing	RE	
Walter Eck	RT	Lawrence College; Milwaukee Ernests
Bob Foster	RH	Marquette Univ.; Milwaukee Ernests
Edward Hegeman	LE	Racine Seidels
Hoffman	B,T	
Kautz	LG,RG	
Scott "Duke" McEachron	LT,LG,FB	Grinnell College
Maxted	QB	
Miller	LH,RE	
Moss	E	
Mossteck	LE,RE,RG	
Murray	RE	Illinois Normal
Ben Nelson	QB	Kenosha HS
Ratchford	LH	
G. "Babe" Ruetz	RG,LG	
Schmitt	RE,LE	
Art Sehl	C	South Dakota Univ.
Semmes	LG,C	
Smith	RE	
Strauss	QB,RT,FB	
Phillip Thoennes	LT,RT	Carroll College
"Red" Wells	FB	Toledo Maroons

SCHEDULE

Attend.	Date	Opponent	Score
	10/03	Milwaukee Maple Leafs	*canceled*
700	10/10	Milwaukee Arlingtons	33–0
1500	10/17	Illinois All-Stars	0–0
	10/24	Milwaukee Ernests	19–7
	10/31	@ Fort Wayne Friars	6–41
	11/07	Illinois All-Stars	13–0
2000	11/14	@ Cornell-Hamburgs @ Comiskey Pk	0–13
	11/21	@ Great Lakes Naval Training Center	
	11/28	@ Appleton	
	12/05	Elgin AC	27–0

Racine Battery C, 1916

ROSTER

Manager: Otto Jandl   *Coaches:* Ted Dumphy, Tom H. Reese, and
Lawrence Mortensen
Colors: Blue and White   *Home Field:* Bi-State League Park

Players	Position	Prior Team
Balzarin	RE	
Joe Beam	LG	Kenosha sandlot
Boehm	LG	
Cargo	LG	
Cleary	RT,LG	
Cowgill	C	
Richard Dick	RE,LH	
Joe Dory	LH	Kenosha HS
John "Jack" Dory	RE,LT	Kenosha HS
Downing	RE	
Walter Eck	LT,RE	Lawrence College; Milwaukee Ernests
Fleary	LG	
Bob Foster	HB	Marquette Univ.; Milwaukee Ernests
Gorman	LT	
O. Hegeman	RT	Racine Seidels
John Heiller	LH,FB	Univ. of Wisconsin
Wallace "Red" Kelly	FB	Marshall HS (Chicago); South Dakota Univ.; Kenosha semi-pros
Krenger	LG	
McCarron	LG	
Scott "Duke" McEachron	LG,LT	Grinnell College
Maxted	QB	
A. Miller	FB,RG	
Morasky	RH	
Murray	RE,LE	Illinois Normal; Ripon College; Milwaukee; Marinette
F. O'Connors	QB, LE	Lawrence Univ.
M. O'Connors	FB	
Pease	E	Ripon College
Tom Reese		
G. "Babe" Ruetz	RG	
Art Sehl	C	South Dakota Univ.
Phillip Thoennes	RT	Carroll College
Wapsted	QB	

SCHEDULE

Attend.	Date	Opponent	Score
	10/1	St. Charles (IL)	41–0
3000	10/8	Evanston North Ends	0–12
	10/15	@ Maywood (IL)	19–6
600	10/22	Schmidt Colts (Milwaukee)	55–7
	10/29	Beloit	6–12
1000	11/5	@ Hammond Clabbys	13–14
3000	11/12	Cornell-Hamburgs	3–13
	11/19	South Bend	13–0
	11/30	@ Toledo Maroons	0–19

Won 4   **lost 5**

Racine Battery C, 1917

ROSTER

President of Assoc.: Ted Schliesman   *Manager:* Ed Hegeman
Colors: Blue and White   *Home Field:* Wisc. Independent League Park

Players	Position	Prior Team
Balzarin	RE	Milwaukee sandlot
Cleary	G	
Joe Dory	LG	Kenosha HS
John "Jack" Dory	RE	Kenosha HS
Walter Eck	LG,LT	Milwaukee HS; Lawrence Univ.
Bob Foster	RH	Marquette Univ.; Milwaukee Ernests
Norman "Tango" Glockson	LG,RG	Detroit Heralds
Edward Hegeman	QB,E	Racine Horlicks
O. Hegeman	C,RG	Racine Seidels
John Heiller	FB	Univ. of Wisconsin
Wallace "Red" Kelly	G,T	Marshall HS (Chi.); So. Dakota Univ.
Grover C. "Dovey" Lutter	C	
McCarron	LR	
Scott "Duke" McEachron	LG	Grinnell College
Meyers	FB	
A. Miller	T	
Morasky	FB	
Mossbach	E	
Murray	RE	Ripon College
Ben Nelson	QB	Kenosha HS
Fred Newton	QB	River Falls Normal College
F. O'Connors	QB,LE	Ripon College
M. O'Connors	FB	
Pabat	T	
Pease	E	Ripon College
Rabbedaux		
Ratchford	RE,RH	
G. "Babe" Ruetz	RG,RT	
Ryan	G,T	
Joe Schnell	RT,RH	Kenosha HS
Richard Schnell	LH	
Schwimmer	T	Cornell-Hamburgs
Art Sehl	C	South Dakota Univ.
Tennis	LE	
Phillip Thoennes	LT,LE	Carrol College
Weber	FB	

SCHEDULE

Attend.	Date	Opponent	Score
	10/07	(No game)	
2000	10/14	Cornell-Hamburgs	0–27
2000	10/21	@ Hammond Clabbys	12–0
	10/28	@ Rock Island Independents	0–12
	10/4	@ Cornell-Hamburgs	0–21
	10/11	@ Fort Wayne Friars	0–28
3000	10/18	@ Detroit Heralds	0–19

Won 1   **Lost 5**

Rock Island Independents, 1915

ROSTER

Manager: Walter H. Flannigan   *Coach:* Leon Liett
Color: Black and Red   *Home Field:* Three I Park

Players	Position	Prior Team
Dick Benson	C	Peoria Socials
Brandt	LH, C	
Victor F. Bredimus	QB	East Des Moines HS
Chander	LT	DeParew College; Palmer College
Cook	HB	
Teddy Davenport	RH	
Keith Dooley	LE	Rock Island HS
Ehrhom	LT	
Gable	G	
Dilk Holm	LE	Davenport sandlot
Jones	G	
Tom Kennedy	FB	St. Ambrose College
Louis Kolls	G	Chattanooga sandlot
Ray Kuehl	HB	Moline Red Men; Rock Island HS
Ernest McGinnis	QB	
Edward "Nips" Murphy	FB	Clinton HS; Univ. of Notre Dame (f)
Phibrook	G,C	
Loyal Robb	LE	Rock Island HS
Arthur W. Salzmann	RT	Rock Island HS
Roy H. Salzmann	RG,LG	Rock Island HS
Patrick Sexton	LE,RE	
Frank "Fat" Smith	LG	Rock Island HS
Edward Swanson	FB	Moline HS

SCHEDULE

Attend.	Date	Opponent	Score
	10/10	900 Block Team	65–0
4000	10/17	Moline Red Men	0–0
	10/25	Dubuque Hawkeyes	74–0
	10/31	Aurora Greyhounds	10–0
	11/07	Des Moines Missions	7–0
	11/14	North Henderson AC	66–0
6000	11/21	Moline Red Men	0–10

Won 5   **Lost 1**   **Tied 1**

Rock Island Independents, 1916

ROSTER

Manager: Walter H. Flannigan   *Coach:* Teddy Davenport
Colors: Black and Red   *Home Field:* Three I Park

Players	Position	Prior Team
Berg	LG	
Brandt	LH,C,RG	
Victor F. Bredimus	QB	East Des Moines HS
Walter C. Brindley	QB,RH	Des Moines Missions; West Des Moines HS
Cox	E	Des Moines Missions
Teddy Davenport	RH,LH	
Keith Dooley	LE	Rock Island HS
Fellows		Cornell-Hamburgs
Gerg	LG	
Bill Gleason		
Edward Rawson "Ted" Guyer	RE,LT	Cornell Univ. (All-American)
Hardy	LT,RT	
Al Jorgensen	HB	
Louis Kolls	C,G	Chattanooga sandlot;
Jacob "Jake" K. Lazerous	LE	East Des Moines HS
Charles McGinnis	LE	St. Ambrose College
Ernest McGinnis	QB	
Ernest McRoberts	HB	Columbus Junction
Edward "Nips" Murphy	FB,QB	Clinton HS; Univ. of Notre Dame(f)
Peoples	FB,RH	Cornell-Hamburgs
Harry Pratt	RE	
George "Paddy" Quinn	HB	
Loyal Robb	LE	Rock Island HS
Arthur W. Salzmann	RT	Rock Island HS
Roy H. Salzmann	LT	Rock Island HS
Patrick Sexton	RE	Rock Island HS
Frank "Fat" Smith	RG,RT	Rock Island HS
Spaulding	RG	
Edward Swanson	FB	Moline HS
Cliff Whisler	FB	Rock Island HS

SCHEDULE

Attend.	Date	Opponent	Score
	10/8	@ Rockford AC	0–25
	10/15	@ Moline Red Men	0–3
1500	10/22	Aurora Greyhounds	21–0
3100	10/29	Davenport AC	0–6
	11/5	Idle	
2970	11/12	@ Davenport AC	0–0
3000	11/19	Moline Red Men	21–3
3000	11/26	Maywood AC	14–0
2500	12/3	Rockford AC	34–6
4000	12/10	Spring Valley Moose	13–0

Won 5   Lost 3   Tied 1

Rock Island Independents, 1917

ROSTER

Manager: Walter H. Flannigan   *Coach:* Dick Liett
Colors: Black and Red   *Home Field:* Douglas Park

Players	Position	Prior Team
Walter C. Brindley	LH	Des Moines Missions; West Des Moines HS
Walt Buland	RT	Minneapolis Marines
Fred Chicken	RH	Minneapolis Marines
Teddy Davenport	RH	
Lee Dempsey	RE	
Bob "Fat" Fosdick	RG	West Des Moines HS
Ted Freeburg	LE	Davenport AC
Harry Gunderson	C	Minneapolis Marines
Edward Rawson "Ted" Guyer	LE	Cornell Univ.
Harty	LT	
Ed Hoar	RE	Moline HS; Spring Valley Moose
Al Jorgenson	G	
Louis Kolls	C	
Jerry "Jay" Mansfield	FB	Des Moines Missions
Mullin	FB	
Edward "Nips" Murphy	QB	Clinton HS; Univ. of Notre Dame (f)
Nelson	RG	
Edward Novak	LH	Minneapolis Marines
O'Leary	RH	
George "Paddy" Quinn	RH	
Qunderson	C	
Loyal Robb	FB	Rock Island HS
Frank "Fat" Smith	LG	Rock Island HS
Reuben "Rube" Ursella	QB	Minneapolis Marines
Wyland	LG	

SCHEDULE

Attend.	Date	Opponent	Score
	09/23	Sterling	33–0
	09/30	Alton Tigers	33–3
5000	10/07	@ Davenport AC	3–0
2000	10/14	Peoria Socials	49–0
2300	10/21	Moline Red Men	20–0
3000	10/28	Racine Regulars	12–0
6425	11/04	Minneapolis Marines	3–7
4748	11/11	Davenport AC	10–12
	11/18	Minneapolis Marines	14–33
	11/25	Idle	
4000	12/02	@ Davenport AC	23–7

Won 7   **Lost 3**

Toledo Maroons, 1915

ROSTER

Manager: Art Gratop	*Coach:* Tom "Doc" Brown
Colors: Maroon and White	*Home Field:* Armory Park

Players	Position	Prior Team
Jimmy Baxter	RH,QB	Kenyon College
King Bowles	FB	Kenyon College
Tom "Doc" Brown	LT	Vanderbilt Univ.
Ray Eichenlaub	FB	Univ. of Notre Dame
Albert Fawcett	G,T	
Hugh F. Hackett	LE	
Hope	RT	
Leslie M. Jones	LT	
Noble H. "Nob" Jones	LT	Scott HS
Lemiow	LH	
Lola	RE	
Rudolph "Babe" Lutz	RE,FB	
Russ McConnell	FB	
Marrow	E	
William "Billy" Marshall	QB	Toledo Central HS; Adrian College
Louis "Dutch" Mauder	LG	
Charles "Chuck" Nichols	LH	Toledo Central HS; Adrian College
Oatis	LG	
Paul "Dutch" Reule	LH	Adrian College; Mississippi State
Bill Roper	RT	
Errett "Monk" Sala	RE	Toledo Central HS; Adrian College
John Schimmel	RG	
Joseph J. Schuette	LG	
Walter J. Semlow	HB	
Harold M. Seubert	FB	Toledo Central HS; Adrian College
Bob Siebert	T	Adrian College
Harold "Sox" Smith	LG	Scott HS
Tompkinson	LG,LT	a Michigan HS
Louis G. Trout	RT,HB	
Bill "Bee" Weiss	C	
Julia "Jules" Weiss	QB,C	Toledo Glenwoods
West	RH	

SCHEDULE

Attend.	Date	Opponent	Score
2000	10/03	Cleveland Blepp Knits	27–0
2200	10/10	Elyria Athletics	13–6
2400	10/17	Ann Arbor Independents	19–0
3700	10/24	Columbus Panhandles	20–0
3000	10/31	Dayton Gym-Cadets	7–20
2600	11/07	Akron Indians	10–0
	11/14	Cincinnati Celts	0–0
3200	11/21	Massillon Tigers	0–3
	11/25	Detroit Mack Park Maroons	6–6
	11/28	Toledo Glenwoods	56–0
1000	12/05	Cleveland Favorite Knits	34–0

Won 7   **Lost 2**   **Tied 2**

Toledo Maroons, 1916

ROSTER

Manager: Art Gratop   *Coach:* Tom Merrill
Colors: Maroon and White   *Home Field:* Armory Park

Players	Position	Prior Team
John Barrett	LH	Oak Park HS; Evanston North Ends; Wash. and Lee Univ.
Jimmy Baxter	RH	Kenyon College
Tom "Doc" Brown	LT	Vanderbilt Univ.
Penn Carolan	RH	Oak Park HS; Dartmouth College (f); Evanston North Ends
John "Jack" Fluhrer	HB	Scott HS
Hugh F. Hackett	LE	
"Golly" Jarvis	HB	Adrian College
Noble H. "Nob" Jones	G,T	Scott HS
Rudolph "Babe" Lutz	LE	
Arthur McIntyre	RE	Scott HS
McMahon	LH	
Wm "Billy" Marshall	QB	Adrian College
Lou "Dutch" Mauder	LG	
Charles "Chuck" Nichols	LH	Toledo Central HS; Adrian College
Bill Roper	RT	
John Schimmel	RG	
Joseph J. Schuette	RT	
Louis G. Trout	RT	
Bill "Bee" Weiss	LH,LE	
Julia "Jules" Weiss	C	
"Red" Wells	FB	Racine Regulars

SCHEDULE

Attend.	Date	Opponent	Score
2500	10/01	Elyria Andwars	9–0
	10/08	Buffalo All-Stars	15–0
	10/15	Akron Imperial Electrics	20–0
6000	10/22	Massillon Tigers	7–15
	10/29	Cleveland Telling Strollers	59–0
3000	11/05	Columbus Panhandles	23–7
	11/12	Dayton Triangles	0–12
	11/19	Pine Village AC	0–0
	11/26	Lancaster, New York	10–0
	11/30	Racine Regulars	19–0
	12/03	Cleveland Indians	0–3

Won 7   **Lost 3**   **Tied 1**

Toledo Maroons, 1917

ROSTER

Manager: Jimmy Baxter   Coach: Byron Dickson
Colors: Maroon and White   Home Field: Swayne Field

Players	Position	Prior Team
Atwiler	RG	
John Tedford Bachman	RE	
Jimmy Baxter	LH	Mercersburg Acad.
Tom "Doc" Brown	LT	Kenyon College
Brubaker	HB	Vanderbilt Univ.
Byrne	QB	
Clark	C	
Dority (Doherty)	RE	
Jim Flynn	LG	
Freehart	LT	
Green	LH	
Hager	QB	
Hartman	T	
Hutchinson	RG	
Leslie M. Jones	LG	
Noble H. "Nob" Jones	G,C	Scott HS
William Kopitke	LH	
Maxy "Mother" Kruse	HB,G	
W. Kruse	LG	
James "Jimmy" Lalond	LH	
Paul S. "Andy" Mason	RT,LG	Toledo Central HS; Purdue Univ.
Lou "Dutch" Mauder	LT	
"Butch" Miller	QB	
"Red" Nicholson	LE,RH	
Frank "Tubby" Roush	FB	Waite HS
John Schimmel	RG	
Schmul	FB,LH	
Joseph J. Schuette	RE	
Smoot	FB	
Stanton	G	
Taylor	LE	
Turner	LE	
Bill "Bee" Weiss	QB	
Julia "Jules" Weiss	C	

SCHEDULE

Attend.	Date	Opponent	Score
2000	10/07	Carlisle Indians (Detroit)	47–0
	10/14	South Bend All-Stars	49–0
5000	10/21	@ Dayton Triangles	0–15
3000	10/28	@ Detroit Heralds	7–20
3000	11/04	@ Fort Wayne Friars	7–45
2000	11/11	Columbus Panhandles	0–13
	11/18	Dayton Triangles	0–26
	11/25	Toledo Navys	7–0
	11/29	@ Akron Pros	7–27
	12/01	@ Detroit Heralds	0–23

Won 3   **Lost 7**

Wabash Athletic Association, 1915

ROSTER

Manager-Coach: Billy Jones

Colors: Blue and White   *Home Field:* Carroll Street Field

Players	Position	Prior Team
Alfred "Dutch" Bergman	RH,LH	Univ. of Notre Dame
Oscar Bricker	RT,LG	Wabash HS
Harry W. "Bud" Caldwell	C	
Mark "Mickey" Erehart	LH,RH	Indiana Univ.
Frank Gurtner	RE	
Moses Johnson	RG,LG	
Mc Murry	RT,FB	
William "Red" Milliner	RE,FB	Wabash HS
J. N. "Rocky" Myers	LE	
Robert W. Palmer	RG	
Jesse Reno	LE	
Claude Rice	RT	
Harry Routh	LG,LT	Purdue Univ.
Sayveskie (Savensky)	LG,RG	
Earnest Scheerer	LG,LT	
Henry Schneider	C	
Lester Simond	RG	Wabash HS
Howard "Red" Smith	FB	
Everett O. "Newt" Tibbs	RH	
George Yarnelle	QB	Wabash HS; Culver Military Academy
J. Kenneth Yarnelle	LH	Wabash HS; Culver Military Academy

SCHEDULE

Attend.	Date	Opponent	Score
	10/03	Dayton Oakwoods	19–14
	10/10	Illinois All-Stars	41–0
	10/17	Jackson, Michigan	49–0
6000	10/24	Evanston North Ends	7–0
1200	10/31	Pine Village AC	0–7
	11/07	Canadian team	24–3
	11/14	Detroit AC	*(canceled)*
4500	11/21	@ Fort Wayne Friars	6–6
	11/25	Corby Hall at Notre Dame	28–0

Won 6   **Lost 1**   **Tied 1**

Wabash Athletic Association, 1916

ROSTER

Manager-Coach: Billy Jones

Colors: Blue and White   *Home Field:* Carroll Street Field

Players	Position	Prior Team
James D. Adams	LH	
Alfred "Dutch" Bergman	FB	Univ. of Notre Dame
Oscar Bricker	RT	Wabash HS
Edward "Eddie" Duggan	FB	Univ. of Notre Dame
G. Ellenray	RH	
K. Ellenray	LH	
Mark "Mickey" Erehart	LH	Indiana Univ.
John Farr	LG	
Gordon	RH	
Frank Gurtner	RE	
Frank M. McHale	LG	Univ. of Michigan
William "Red" Milliner	RH	Wabash HS
Joseph N. "Rocky" Myers	LE	
Robert W. Palmer	RG	
John "Doc" Redmond	RG,RT	Indiana Univ.
Jesse Reno	LE	
Harry Routh	LT	Purdue Univ.
Earnest Scheerer	LG	
Henry Schneider	C,RG	
Homer T. Showalter	RE	Wabash College
Everett O. "Newt" Tibbs	C	
George Yarnelle	QB	
J. Kenneth Yarnelle	LH	Wabash HS; Culver Military Academy
Young	RT	Wabash HS; Culver Military Academy
Myron Edward "Mike" Yount	G,T	Franklin College (f)

SCHEDULE

Attend.	Date	Opponent	Score
	10/1	Muncie Congervilles	25–0
	10/8	Toledo Glenwoods	*canceled*
5000	10/15	Pine Village AC	0–0
5000	10/22	Evanston North Ends	18–21
	10/29	Decatur	42–10
2500	11/5	Wheeling (WV)	32–0
5000	11/12	Pine Village AC @ Lafayette	0–7
5200	11/19	@ Fort Wayne Friars	7–13
5000	11/26	Fort Wayne Friars	3–0
	11/30	Louisville Goldbergs	46–0

Won 5   **Lost 3**   **Tied 1**

Wabash Athletic Association, 1917

ROSTER

Manager-Coach: Billy Jones

Colors: Blue and White   *Home Field:* Carroll Street Field

Players	Position	Prior Team
James D. Adams	LH	
Frank Allen	RT,RE	Indiana Univ.; Pine Village AC
Andrus	RG	
Alfred "Dutch" Bergman	LH	Univ. of Notre Dame
Frank "Coonie" Checkaye	RH	Muncie Congervilles; Fort Wayne Friars
Dempsey	LH	
Guilford Falcon	FB	Evanston HS; Evanston North Ends
Frank Gurtner	RH	
Jacquard	LG	Washington and Lee Univ.
George Jewett	RH	Wabash HS
La Pado	RH	Detroit Heralds; Fort Wayne Friars
Nick McInerney	RT	
McMurray	LG	
Fredrick "Blad" Meyers	RG	Evanston North Ends
William "Red" Milliner	QB	Wabash HS
Nodner	QB	
Max Palm	LT	Evanston North Ends
John "Doc" Redmond	LG	Indiana Univ.
Jesse Reno	LE	
Earnest Scheerer	C,LG	
Henry Schneider	RG	
Homer T. Showalter	RE,LE	Wabash HS; Wabash College
Snyder	C	
Everett O. "Newt" Tibbs	C	
Myron Edward "Mike" Yount	RE,RT	Franklin College (f)

SCHEDULE

Attend.	Date	Opponent	Score
880	10/07	Anderson Remys	20–6
1200	10/14	Toledo Naval Training	20–0
4000	10/21	Pine Village AC	0–2
800	10/28	@ Hammond Clabbys	0–20
	11/04	@ Detroit Heralds	0–34
	11/11	Pine Village AC @ Lafayette	7–0
1500	11/18	Hammond Clabbys	0–7
	11/25	@ Fort Wayne Friars	7–7
	11/29	Pine Village AC	6–20

Won 3   **Lost 5**   **Tied 1**

Youngstown Patricians, 1915

ROSTER

Manager: Joe Omier   *Coach:* Ray Thomas
Colors: Maroon and Gray   *Home Field:* Wright Field

Players	*Position*	*Prior Team*
Russell G. "Busty" Ashbaugh	RE,RT	Brown Univ.; Rayen HS
John Barrett	LH	Washington and Lee Univ.
Benson	RT	Akron HS
Casey	C,RG	
Frank Cavanaugh	C,RG	
Cooper	RH	
Wilber S. Davidson	RH	
Duval (Devon)	RT	Akron sandlot
Leo Eberhardt	RH	Buchtel College
Philip P. Edwards	QB	Oberlin HS; Oberlin College
Fleming	RT	
Ralph Funkhouser	LH	
Getz	LH	Akron HS
Ed "Turk" Gillespie	HB	
Jarvis	HB	Columbus Panhandles
Johnson	LG,RG	
Jones	LT	
Robert Kling	LE	
William E. "Bill" Lavin	LH	Girard HS
Loos	C	
Lucy	RG	
Lutz	LH	
DeOrmond "Tuss" McLaughry	FB	Mich. Ag. College; Wesminster College
Lester Thomas "Red" Miller	RH	Marietta College
George "Curly" Richards	LG,C,LT	
Rudt	C	
R. M. Smith	LT	Penn State Univ.
Steel	LT	
Fred Stiver	RG	Case Univ.
Ray Thomas	QB	Rayen HS; West Virginia Univ.
Elgie Tobin	RG	Penn State Univ.
George "Cotton" Vedderneck	LE	Carlisle Institute; Pitcairn Quakers
Joe Wilkoff	RT	
Wymard	C	
George "Whitey" Yeckel	LG,RE	Western Reserve Univ.

SCHEDULE

Attend.	*Date*	*Opponent*	*Score*
5000	10/10	Alliance	72–0
8000	10/17	Barberton	52–0
5000	10/24	Akron, B.F. Goodrich Team	21–0
5000	10/31	Salem	20–0
6500	11/07	McKeesport Olympics	27–3
4000	11/14	Pitcairn Quakers	17–6
5000	11/21	Columbus Panhandles	0–0
5000	11/28	Washington, DC, Vigilants	13–7

Won 7   **Tied 1**

Youngstown Patricians, 1916

ROSTER

Manager: Frank B. Ward   *Coach:* Ray Thomas
Colors: Maroon and Gray   *Home Field:* Wright Field

Players	Position	Prior Team
Russell G. "Busty" Ashbaugh	QB,LE	Brown Univ.; Rayen HS
Jim "Butchy" Barron	RG	Georgetown Univ.
Clyde E. Bastian	FB	Univ. of Michigan
Jackson "Auggie" Blair	RG	Rayen HS; Univ. of Pittsburgh
Lewis S. Castle	LH	Syracuse Univ.
Dickle	LT	++
Leo Eberhart	LH	Buchtel College
Fessrewell	RH	
Ralph Funkhouser	HB	Youngstown Sandlot
Getz	FB	Akron Central HS
Ed "Turk" Gillespie	HB	Youngstown Sandlot
Tom Gormley	RT	Georgetown Univ.
Haldy	LG	McKeesport Olympics
Douglas McWilliams Hawkins	LE	Ohio Univ.
Hennis	RT	Virginia Military Institute
Earnest "Tommy" Hughitt	QB	Univ. of Mich.
Jarvis	HB	Columbus Panhandles
Johnson	LG	
Jones	LH	
Robert Kling	RE	
Loos	C	
William DeLoss Love	LG,LT	Princeton Univ.
Melvin Lesley McCreary	C	Ohio Univ.
DeOrmond "Tuss" McLaughry	FB	Mich. Ag. College; Westminster College
Lester Thomas Miller	C,LG,FB	Marietta College
Morgan	RE	
Horace "Hoke" Palmer	RH	Ohio Univ.
Petriez	C	
Randolph	RT	
Maurice "Bugs" Raymond	LG	Ohio State Univ.
Charles H. Roberts	LE,RE	Yale Univ.
Stilwell Saunooke	LH	Carlisle; Pitcairn Quakers
R. M. Smith	LT,RT	Penn State Univ.
Steale	RG	
Fred Stiver	RT,LG	Case Univ.
Ray Thomas	QB	Rayen HS; West Virginia Univ.
Elgie Tobin	LG,RG	Penn State Univ.
George "Cotton" Vedderneck	LE,RE	Carlisle Institute; Pitcairn Quakers
Fred M. "Iron Man" Walker	C	Univ. of Chicago; Massillon Tigers
George "Whitey" Yeckel	RG,HB	Barberton HS; Western Reserve Univ.

++ reported to be from Ohio Univ., but not verified

SCHEDULE

Attend.	Date	Opponent	Score
5000	10/01	Lisbon	21–0
	10/08	Ex-Carlisle Indians	42–0
	10/15	Jamestown, New York Alcos	33–0
3000	10/22	Martins Ferry AA (WV)	7–0
4200	10/29	Pitcairn Quakers	7–0
3049	11/05	Massillon Tigers	0–3
3100	11/12	McKeesport (PA) Olympics	20–3
8000	11/19	Canton Bulldogs	0–6
1200	11/26	Washington, DC, Vigilants	10–9
5000	11/30	@ Massillon Tigers	0–27
950	12/03	Columbus Panhandles	0–13

Won 6   **lost 4**

Youngstown Patricians, 1917

ROSTER

Manager: Joseph E. Mullane   *Coach:* Stanley Cofall
Colors: Maroon and Gray   *Homefield:* Wright Field

Players	Position	Prior Team
John Barrett	FB	Wash. and Lee Univ.; Evanston North Ends
Jim "Butchy" Barron	LG,RG	Georgetown Univ.
Howard Barry	LE	Univ. of Pennsylvania
Berwick	RT,RG	
Stanley Cofall	LH	Univ. of Notre Dame
Park "Tumble" Crisp	C	Municipal Univ. of Akron
Freeman Fitzgerald	C,RG	Univ. of Notre Dame
Ralph Funkhouser	LH	Youngstown sandlot
Ed "Turk" Gillespie	HB	Youngstown sandlot
Goode	RG,LG	
Tom Gormley	LT	Georgetown Univ.
Ed Hanley	FB,LH	Univ. of Pittsburgh
Ernest "Tommy" Hughitt	QB	Univ. of Michigan
Jennings	QB	
Jordan	RE	
Bill Kelleher	RE	Univ. of Notre Dame
Franklin "Bart" Macomber	QB,RH	Pine Village AC; Univ. of Illinois
Martin	LE	
Mason	RE	
Mullaney	LG	
Neil		
Olin	G	
Robert D. "Bob" Peck (Cripp*)	C	Univ. of Pittsburgh
David Reese	E	Denison Univ.
Rowland	G	
Ryan	QB	
Schaeffer		
Stephan	RT	
George "Cotton" Vedderneck	LE	Carlisle Institute
Bill Ward	T,LG,RG	Univ. of Pennsylvania
Watkins	RT	
George "Whitey" Yeckel	RG	Western Reserve Univ.

SCHEDULE

Attend.	Date	Opponent	Score
3500	10/7	Wheeling (WV)	36–0
2100	10/14	Pitcairn Quakers	10–16
3500	10/21	Dayton Shamrock-Wolverines	44–0 [7]
2000	10/28	Columbus Panhandles	30–0
8000	11/4	Canton Bulldogs	0–3
5000	11/11	Massillon Tigers	14–6
5000	11/18	Canton Bulldogs	0–13
	11/25	Game w/Akron	*canceled because of snow*

Won 4   **Lost 3**

Appendix B

Professional Players Who Doubled as Coaches

Name	Pro Team	Where They Coached
Ernest J. Allmendinger	Ann Arbor Independents, 1915	Univ. of Michigan
Jack Ambrose	Elyria Pros, 1916	Elyria HS (OH)
	Fort Wayne Friars, 1916	
Russell G. "Busty" Ashbaugh	Youngstown Patricians, 1915–16	South HS, Youngstown
Ralph "Rube" Bechtol	Akron Pros, 1917	South HS, Akron
Maurice "Windy" Briggs	Massillon Tigers, 1915–16	University Hts. HS (OH)
Howard "Cub" Buck	Canton Bulldogs, 1916–17	
	Pine Village, 1916	Univ. of Wisconsin
Robert "Butts" Butler	Canton Bulldogs, 1915	Univ. of Wisconsin
	Cleveland Indians, 1916	
Harry Costello	Canton Bulldogs, 1916	Univ. of Detroit
Edgar C. Davis	Pine Village, 1915–17	
	Canton Bulldogs, 1915	Indiana Univ.
	Fort Wayne Friars, 1915	
William Lone Star Dietz	Altoona, 1916	Wash. State Univ.
Charles "Gus" Dorais	Massillon Tigers,1915–16	Columbia College
	Fort Wayne Friars, 1916–17	(Dubuque Iowa)
Don Drumm	Canton Bulldogs, 1915	Marietta College
Eddie Duggan	Wabash AA, 1916	Franklin College
Philip P. Edwards	Youngstown Patricians, 1915	Rayen HS (Youngstown)
Al Feeney	Fort Wayne Friars, 1915–17	Butler College
Malcolm "Red" Fleming	Altoona Indians, 1915	Wash. and Jeff. College
	Massillon Tigers, 1915–16	Massillon Tigers
	Pitcairn Quakers, 1917	Canal Dover HS (OH)
	Akron Pros, 1917	
Malcolm Galvin	Hammond Clabbys, 1916	Davenport AC,
	Davenport AC, 1917	St. Ambrose College
William Gardner	Canton Bulldogs, 1915	Louisville Manual Training
Milton Ghee	Canton Bulldogs, 1916	Dartmouth College
Russell B. Goodwin	Massillon Tigers, 1916	Wash. and Lee Univ.
Don Hamilton	Canton Bulldogs, 1915	Wittenburg College
Wallie Hess	Hammond Clabbys, 1917	Hammond HS
Earl D. Huntington	Fort Wayne Friars ,1916	U. of Chicago, Friars
George Jones	Davenport AC, 1916–17	St. Ambrose College
Keith "Deacon" Jones	Massillon Tigers, 1915	Univ. of Notre Dame(f)
	Fort Wayne Friars, 1915–17	
Edmund L. Kagy	Massillon Tigers, 1915–16	Massillon Tigers
Bill Kelleher	Massillon Tigers, 1915–16	Kenyon College
John Kellison	Canton Bulldogs, 1915–16	Massillon Tigers
Ed Kerwin	Detroit Maroons, 1915	Univ. of Detroit
Richard C. King	Pine Village AC, 1916	Univ. of Wisconsin
	Canton Bulldogs, 1916	
Orville Littick	Akron Indians, 1915	Ohio Univ.
Thomas McCall	Detroit Maroons, 1915	Univ. of Michigan
Scott "Duke" McEachron	Racine Regulars, 1915–17	Grinnell College
DeOrmond "Tuss" McLaughry	Youngstown Patricians, 1915–16;	
	Massillon Tigers, 1917	Westminster College
I. R. Martin	Massillon Tigers, 1917	Athletic Director, Goodyear Tire Co.

Name	Pro Team	Where They Coached
Joel P. Mattern	Massillon Tigers, 1916	Western Reserve Univ.
Frank Mt. Pleasant	Buffalo All-Stars, 1916	Franklin and Marshall College
Robert "Nasty" Nash	Massillon Tigers, 1916–17	Rutgers Univ.
Alfred Earle "Greasy" Neale	Canton Bulldogs, 1915–17	W. Va. Wesleyan Univ.
George "Peggy" Parratt	Massillon Tigers, 1906	
	Shelby Blues, 1907–12	Shelby Blues
	Akron Indians, 1912–15	Akron Indians
	Cleveland Indians, 1916	Cleveland Indians
Don Peters	Canton Bulldogs, 1915	Ohio Northern Univ.
Louis Pickerel	Cleveland Indians, 1916	Ohio State Univ.
Joe Pliska	Chicago Blues, 1915	Chicago Public HS
	Fort Wayne Friars, 1915–17	
Arthur "Bugs" Raymond	Akron Indians, 1915	Ohio Northern Univ.
	Canton Bulldogs, 1915	
David Reese	Cincinnati Celts, 1915–17	Univ. of Cinncinati
	Youngstown Patricians, 1917	
	Dayton Triangles, 1917	
Knute Rockne	Akron Indians, 1914	Univ. of Notre Dame
	Massillon Tigers, 1915–17	
	Fort Wayne Friars, 1917	
Henry V. Ruffner	Hammond Clabbys, 1916–17	Purdue University
Frederick S. Sefton	Canton Bulldogs, 1915–17	Municipal Univ. of Akron
	Akron Pros, 1917	
Harold M. Seubert	Toledo Maroons, 1915	Scott HS
Paul Sheeks	Pine Village, 1916	Wabash College
Ernie Soucy	Canton Bulldogs, 1916	Univ. of Wisconsin
Claude Thornhill	McKeesport Olympics, 1917	McKeesport Olympics
	Massillon Tigers, 1917	
James F. Thorpe	Pine Village, 1915	Indiana Univ.;
	Canton Bulldogs, 1915–17	Buchtel College; New Philadelpha HS; Canton Bulldogs
Elgie Tobin	Youngtown Patricians, 1915–16	Wash. and Jeff. College
Russell J. Tollefson	Minneapolis Marines, 1916	Minn. Marines; Grinnell College
Harry Whitaker	Canton Bulldogs, 1915–16	Indiana Univ.
	Detroit Heralds, 1917	
Samuel S. Willaman	Akron Indians, 1915	East Tech HS, Cleveland, OH
	Cleveland Indians, 1916	
	Canton Bulldogs, 1917	
Ralph "Bull" Young	Fort Wayne Friars, 1916	DePauw Univ.

Appendix C

All-Professional Teams, 1917

All-Ohio
Cleveland Plain Dealer
(Also reported in the Canton Repository December 10, 1917)

Tommy Burrell, Akron	RE
Charles Copley, Massillon	RT
Clarence Spears, Canton	RG
Bob Peck, Youngstown/Massillon	C
Alfred Nesser, Akron	LG
Claude Thornhill, Massillon	LT
Bob Nash, Massillon	LE
Milton Ghee, Canton	QB
Jim Thorpe, Canton	LH
Stanley Cofall, Youngstown/Massillon	RH
Frank Dunn, Canton	FB

All-Pro
Toledo Bee
(Dec. 11, 1917)

Alfred "Greasy" Neale, Canton
Clarence "Steamer" Horning, Detroit
Frank Blocker, Hammond
Ralph "Fats" Waldsmith, Canton
Frank Nesser, Akron
Clarence Spears, Canton
Ray Whipple, Detroit
Milton Ghee, Canton
Norb Sacksteder, Detroit/Dayton
Pete Calac, Canton
Jim Thorpe, Canton

All-Indiana Pros, 1917
Indianapolis Star

Jesse Reno, Wabash	LE
Henry V. Ruffner, Hammond	LT
John "Doc" Redmond, Wabash	LG
Frank Rydzewski, Ft. Wayne	C
Emmett Keefe, Pine Village	RG
Frank Blocker, Hammond	RT
Wilber Henderson, Hammond	RE
Charles "Gus" Dorais, Ft. Wayne	QB
Paddy Driscoll, Hammond	LH
John Barrett, Hammond	RH
Francis Bacon, Pine Village	FB

Appendix D

Walter Camp All-Americans in Pro Football, 1915–17

Player	Position	College	All-American Yr/Team		Pro Team
Earl Abell	Tackle	Colgate	1915	(1)	Canton
Ernest Allmendinger	Guard	Michigan	1917	(1)	Ann Arbor
Russell Ashbaugh	End	Brown	1911,12	(3)(3)	Youngstown
Bert Baston	End	Minn.	1915,16	(1)(1)	Massillon
Charles Brickley	Half	Harvard	1912,13	(1)(1)	Massillon
Howard Buck	Tackle	Wisc.	1915	(2)	Canton
Bob Butler	Tackle	Wisc.	1912,13	(1)(2)	Canton
Ralph Capron	Quarter	Minn.	1907,11	(3)(3)	Minn. Stars
Harry Costello	Quarter	Custer	1917	(3)	Canton
Burleigh Cruikshank	Center	Wash & Jeff	1914	(3)	Detroit
Paul Des Jardien	Center	Chicago	1913,14	(1)(2)	Cleveland
John Driscoll	Half	Northwestern	1916	(3)	Hammond
Ray Eichenlaub	Full	Notre Dame	1913	(2)	Toledo
Milton Ghee	Quarter	Dartmouth	1914	(1)	Canton
John Gilroy	Half	Georgetown	1916	(3)	Canton
William Goebel	Guard	Yale	1907,8,9	(3)(1)(2)	Cincinnati
Clarence Horning	Tackle	Colgate	1916	(1)	Detroit
Richard King	Half	Harvard	1915	(1)	Pine Village
Bart Macomber	Half	Illinois	1915	(1)	Youngstown
John McGovern	Quarter	Minn.	1910	(3)	Minn. Stars
Bob Marshall	End	Minn.	1906	(2)	Minneapolis
Eugene Miller	Quarter	Penn State	1913	(3)	Massillon
Tom Moriarity	Tackle	Georgetown	1917	(2)	Detroit Maroons
Bob Nash	Tackle	Rutgers	1914	(2)	Massillon
Bob Peck	Center	Pittsburgh	1915,16	(1)(1)	Youngstown
Rudolph Propst	Tackle	Syracuse	1912	(2)	Detroit
Knute Rockne	End	Notre Dame	1913	(3)	Massillon
Christopher Schlachter	Guard	Syracuse	1915	(1)	Massillon
Murray Shelton	End	Cornell	1915	(1)	Cleveland
Lorin Solon	End	Minn.	1913,14	(3)(3)	Cleveland
Clarence Spears	Guard	Dartmouth	1914,15	(3)(1)	Canton
Nelson Talbott	Tackle	Yale	1913	(1)	Dayton
Howard Talman	Half	Rutgers	1913,14	(3)(3)	Massillon
Jim Thorpe	Half	Carlisle	1908,11,12	(3)(1)(1)	Canton
Stanfield Wells	End	Michigan	1910,11	(1)(3)	Akron, Detroit

Notes

Chapter 1

1. "There is a very long history behind the religious and secular control of sports on Sunday," according to Frederick W. Cozens and Florence Scovil Stumpf, *Sports in American Life* (Chicago: University of Chicago Press, 1953), p. 106. As late as 1927, the Pennsylvania Supreme Court upheld a ban on professional sports on Sunday. See *Detroit News,* 6 July 1927, p. 6.

2. Marc S. Maltby, "The Origins and Early Development of Professional Football, 1890–1920" (Ph.D. diss., Ohio University, August, 1987), p. 101.

3. *Collier's Magazine.* 18 October 1924.

4. Bob Carroll, *The Tigers Roar: Professional Football in Ohio: 1903–09* (North Huntington, PA: Professional Football Researchers Association, 1990).

5. *Akron Beacon Journal,* 17 February 1974.

6. Carroll, *The Tigers Roar.*

7. Bob Carroll and Bob Branwart, *Pro Football: From AAA to '03* (North Huntington, PA: Professional Football Researchers Association, 1991).

8. *Biographical Dictionary of American Sports: Football,* ed. David L. Porter (New York: Greenwood Press, 1987), pp. 456–57.

9. Case Institute Archives.

10. *Cleveland Plain Dealer,* 6 July 1959.

11. *Detroit Free Press,* 2–3 November 1907.

12. Jack Cusack, *Pioneer in Pro Football* (Fort Worth, TX: privately printed, 1963).

13. The University of Akron Alumni Office; *Akron Beacon Journal,* 8 December 1913.

14. Case Western Reserve University Archives; *Cleveland Leader,* 14 October 1912, 21 November 1912, 12, 19, 26 October 1914, 2, 9, 16, 24 November 1914; *Gyroscope,* 1923; *Cleveland Plain Dealer,* 17 November 1960.

15. Western Reserve University Alumni Records; *The Rubiayat Yearbook,* 1911; and *Cleveland Leader* October–November 1912, 1913, 1914.

16. Phil Dietrich, *Down Payments: Professional Football 1896–1930 As Viewed from the Summit, Professional Football in Akron.* (North Huntington, PA: Professional Football Researchers Association, 1995).

17. University of Notre Dame Archives; *Cleveland Leader,* 2 November 1914; *Akron Beacon Journal,* 16, 24 November 1914.

18. University of Notre Dame Archives.

19. Glen Schoor, *100 Years of Notre Dame Football* (New York: Morrow, 1987); *Akron Beacon Journal,* November 1914; Porter, *Biographical Dictionary,* pp. 504–07; University of Detroit-Mercy Archives; *Holcad,* 8 December 1913.

20. *Detroit Free Press,* 8 October 1915.

21. *Massillon Independent,* 19 October 1915.

22. Baldwin-Wallace College Archives.

Chapter 2

1. *Arbutus,* Indiana University Yearbook, (Bloomington, IN: 1916).

2. *Washington Post,* 20 November 1916.

3. *Minneapolis Tribune,* 20, 30 November 1916.

4. Murray Sperber, *Shake Down The Thunder: The Creation of Notre Dame Football* (New York: Henry Holt and Company, 1993), pp. 34, 90, 114 ff.

5. *Davenport Daily Times,* 2 October 1916.

6. *Canton Daily News,* 19 November 1915.

7. Michael Oriard, *Reading Football: How the Popular Press Created an American Spectacle* (Chapel Hill, NC: The University of North Carolina Press,1993), pp. 142–93.

8. *Minneapolis Journal,* 30 November 1916, p. 7.

9. *Pittsburgh Gazette-Times,* 25 November 1917.

10. Harry Messick, *The Silent Syndicate* (New York: The Macmillan Company, 1967).

11. David Harris, *The League: The Rise and Decline of the NFL* (New York: Bantam Books, 1986).

12. Amos Alonzo Stagg, *Touchdown!* (New York: Longman's, Green & Company, 1927).

13. *Spalding Official Football Guide, 1915* (Chicago, IL: American Sports Publishing Company, 1915); and John R. Richards, *Inside Dope on Football Coaching* (Chicago: Thos. E. Wilson & Co., 1917).

14. *Ibid.*   15. *Ibid.*   16. *Ibid.*

17. *Fort Wayne Journal-Gazette,* 19 November 1915.

Chapter 3

1 *Toledo Blade,* 19 October 1916.

2. *Minneapolis Journal,* 8, 9, 10 November 1915.

3. *Minneapolis Journal,* 10 November 1915.

4. *Minneapolis Journal,* 17 November 1915.

5. *Minneapolis Journal,* 19 November 1915.

6. *Massillon Independent,* 11 October 1916 and *Minneapolis Tribune,* 20 October 1916.

7. *Toledo Blade,* 20 October 1916.

8. *Pittsburgh Gazette-Times,* 22 October 1916.

9. *Dayton Daily News,* 22 November 1972.

10. "A Ralph By Any Other Name," *The Coffin Corner* 18, no. 6 (1997): 21.

11. Casper Whitney, "Amateur Sport," *Harper's Weekly* (4 November 1893): 1067.

12. Walter Camp, "What Are Athletics Good For?" *Outing* 63 (December 1913): 263.

13. The *Boston Herald,* 1895, quoted in Oriard, *Reading Football,* 159.

14. Papers of Van Hise, University of Wisconsin Dean of the College of Letters and Science, 9 January 1906.

15. *Biennial Report,* University of Wisconsin Regents, 1905–06, p. 18.

16. Merle Curtis, *The University of Wisconsin: A History 1848–1925* (Madison, WI: University of Wisconsin, 1949).

17. *Cleveland Plain Dealer,* 21 January 1922.

18. Sperber, *Shake Down The Thunder; Cleveland Plain Dealer,* 21 January 1922.

19. *Toledo Blade,* 1 November 1916.

20. *Cleveland Plain Dealer,* 10 December 1916.

Chapter 4

1. *Wabash Plain Dealer,* 1 October 1916.

2. *Fort Wayne Journal-Gazette,* 27 October 1916.

3. *Fort Wayne Journal-Gazette,* 31 October 1916; *Wabash Plain Dealer,* 1 November 1916.

4. *Hammond Times,* 6 November 1916.

5. *Wabash Plain Dealer,* 21 November 1916.

6. *Hammond Times,* 30 October 1916.

7. *Davenport Daily Times,* 4, 20 November 1916; *Hammond Times,* 15 November 1916.

8. For an example of a cancellation, see *Dayton Daily News,* 17, 19, 28 October 1916.

9. *Massillon Independent,* 25 October 1916.

Chapter 5

1. *Fort Wayne City Directory, 1915* (Fort Wayne, IN: R. L. Polk & Co., 1915).

2. *Collier's World Atlas* (New York: P. F. Collier & Sons Corp., 1920).

3. Jack Newcombe, *The Best of the Athletic Boys: The White Man's Impact on Jim Thorpe* (New York: Doubleday, 1975), p. 112.

4. *Fort Wayne Journal-Gazette,* 10 November 1913, 12, 25 October 1914.

5. In 1910, Ward Lambert was declared ineligible to play college sports because he was caught playing professional baseball the previous summer. Ward became assistant coach to Jesse Harper, and later went on to coach at Purdue, where he was the first person to introduce the fast break to basketball. He became president of the National Basketball Association in 1946. *Montgomery: Our County Magazine* 4, no. 11 (November 1979).

6. On January 1, 1918, Kent Lambert married his childhood sweetheart Janet Maud Snyder. In March 1918, he went to France with the U.S. Expeditionary Force. After World War I, he stayed in the army. He was transferred to Governor's Island, New York, in 1938, and retired as a colonel in 1950. James Insley Osborne, *Wabash College: The First Hundred Years, 1832–1932* (Crawfordsville, IN, 1932); *Montgomery: Our County Magazine* 4, no. 11 (November 1979); *Athenian,* Crawfordsville High School Yearbook (Crawfordsville, IN: 1909).

7. *Fort Wayne Journal-Gazette,* 23 September 1915.

8. *Fort Wayne Journal-Gazette,* 30 September 1915, 1 October 1915.

9. Emil Klosinski, "Knute Rockne's Pro Football Roots," *The Coffin Corner* 17, no. 1 (spring 1995): 10–16.

10. Sperber, *Shake Down The Thunder.*

11. *Fort Wayne Journal-Gazette,* 4 October 1915.

12. *Fort Wayne Journal-Gazette,* 5 October 1915.

13. *Fort Wayne Journal-Gazette,* 9 October 1915. Christian C. Chambers was a blacksmith with railroad related companies. See *Fort Wayne City Directory* (Fort Wayne, IN: R. L. Polk & Co., 1915–22).

14. *Fort Wayne Journal-Gazette,* 11 October 1915.

15. *Fort Wayne Journal-Gazette,* 18 October 1915.

16. *Fort Wayne Journal-Gazette,* 1 November 1915.

17. *Fort Wayne Journal-Gazette,* 7 November 1915.

18. *Ibid.*

19. *Fort Wayne Journal-Gazette,* 8 November 1915.

20. *Arbutus,* Indiana University Yearbook (Bloomington, IN: 1915).

21. *Fort Wayne Journal-Gazette,* 12 November 1915.

22. *Ibid.*

23. *Fort Wayne Journal-Gazette,* 13 November 1915.

24. *Fort Wayne Journal-Gazette,* 15 November 1915.

25. Purdue University Archives; *Fort Wayne City Directory, 1915* (Fort Wayne, IN: R. L. Polk & Co., 1915).

26. *Fort Wayne Journal-Gazette,* 15, 22 November 1915; *Debris,* Purdue University Yearbook, (Lafayette, IN: 1907).

27. *Fort Wayne Journal-Gazette,* 18 November 1915.

28. *Fort Wayne Journal-Gazette,* 19 November 1915.

29. *Fort Wayne Journal-Gazette,* 22 November 1915.

30. *Fort Wayne Journal-Gazette,* 18 November 1915.

31. *Fort Wayne Journal-Gazette,* 19 November 1915.

32. *Fort Wayne Journal-Gazette,* 22 November 1915; Indiana University Archives.

33. *Fort Wayne Journal-Gazette,* 26 November 1915.

34. *Fort Wayne Journal-Gazette,* 22 November 1915.

35. *Ibid.*   36. *Ibid.*

37. *Fort Wayne Journal-Gazette,* 26 November 1915.

38. *Ibid.*   39. *Ibid.*

40. *Fort Wayne Journal-Gazette,* 28 November 1915.

41. *Ibid.*   42. *Ibid.*

Chapter 6

1. *Columbus Dispatch,* 7 June 1941; Ted Nesser's certificate of death, State of Ohio, Department of Health; and U.S. Bureau of Census, vol. 49, edition 38, sheets 3, 10, and 21, lines 39, 40, and 42, 1900.

2. *Columbus City Directory,* 1901.

3. *Columbus Dispatch,* 7 June 1941.

4. *Columbus Senior Times,* April 1994.

5. *Columbus Dispatch,* 21 May 1939. Born in Columbus on October 22, 1880, Joe went to work

as a machinist for the Panhandle Division of the Pennsylvania Railroad after graduating from high school. When he was twenty, working as a clerk at the Pennsy hub in Columbus, he organized the Panhandle White Sox semiprofessional baseball team. Shortly afterwards, he went to work as assistant sports editor for the *Ohio State Journal* newspaper in Columbus, a job that he kept until 1906.

6. Carroll, *The Tigers Roar.*

7. A "Joe Carr remembers" clipping from a 1938 interview reprinted in the *Pottsville Republican*, 24 October 1987.

8. *Akron Beacon Journal*, 12 March 1967.

9. *Columbus Dispatch*, 6 June 1941.

10. Carroll, *The Tigers Roar.*

11. *Ohio State Journal*, 2 April 1911.

12. *Columbus Senior Times*, April 1994.

13. *Ibid.*

14. *The Makio*, Ohio State University Yearbook, (Columbus, OH: 1915).

15. *Canton Repository*, 18 October 1915.

16. *Toledo Blade*, 6, 10 October 1917.

17. *Detroit Free Press*, 14 November 1915.

18. *Massillon Independent*, 30 October 1915.

19. *Ibid.*

20. *Toledo Blade*, 1 November 1915.

21. *Massillon Independent*, 1 November 1915.

22. *Dayton Daily News*, 8 November 1915.

23. *Detroit Times*, 13 November 1915.

24. *Youngstown Vindicator*, 21 November 1915.

25. *Youngstown Vindicator*, 22 November 1915.

26. *Ibid.*   27. *Ibid.*

28. *Fort Wayne Journal-Gazette*, 26 November 1915.

29. *Ibid.*

30. *Toledo Blade*, 3 December 1915.

31. *Detroit Free Press*, 16 October 1916.

32. *Detroit News*, 16 October 1915.

33. Yale University Archives, Camp Papers, file 505.

34. *Detroit Free Press*, 16 October 1916.

35. *Cleveland Plain Dealer*, 23 October 1916.

36. *Canton Repository*, 30 October 1916.

37. *Toledo Blade*, 4 November 1916.

38. Guy Lewis, "Theodore Roosevelt's Role: The 1905 Football Controversy," *Research Quarterly for Health, Physical Education and Recreation* (October 1969).

39. *Toledo Blade*, 6 November 1916.

40. *Massillon Independent*, 8 November 1916.

41. *Massillon Independent*, 13 November 1916.

42. *Fort Wayne Journal-Gazette*, 2 December 1916.

43. *Detroit News Tribune*, 20 November 1916; *Detroit Free Press*, 19, 20 November 1916.

44. *Detroit News Tribune*, 20 November 1916.

45. *Toledo Blade*, 20 November 1916.

46. *Fort Wayne Journal-Gazette*, 20 December 1916.

47. *Fort Wayne Journal-Gazette*, 2 December 1916.

48. *Detroit Free Press*, 27 May 1917, p. 21.

49. *Toledo Blade*, 24 November 1917.

50. The Columbus Panhandles were one of the original members of the American Professional Football Association and the National Football League. In 1925, their name was changed to the Columbus Tigers. The franchise suspended operations in 1928. See Joe Horrigan, "National Football League Franchise Transactions," *The Coffin Corner* 18, no. 3 (summer 1996): 3–13.

Chapter 7

1. Carroll and Branwart, *Pro Football.*

2. Newcombe, *Best of the Athletic Boys.*

3. *Ibid.* In 1912, Frank Mt. Pleasant was head football coach at Indiana Normal in Indiana, Pennsylvania, where his star quarterback was Frank S. White, who played for the Pitcairn Quakers in 1916–17. See *Instano, 1912*, Indiana Normal School Yearbook (Indiana, PA: 1913).

4. *Canton Repository*, 4 November 1915.

5. Lebanon Valley College Archives, Pennsylvania; Porter, *Biographical Dictionary*, 558–59. Joel Wheelock, the youngest of the brothers from West Depew, Wisconsin, weighed about 180 pounds and had played on the same team as Thorpe in 1911. Joel was enrolled at Lebanon Valley College Academy in 1913 and played on the football, basketball, and track teams at that school for the next three years.

6. *Altoona Mirror*, 11 October 1915.

7. *Altoona Mirror*, 18 October 1915.

8. *Altoona Mirror*, 25 October 1915.

9. Lebanon Valley College Archives, Pennsylvania; Paul Soderberg, Helen Washington, and Jaques Cattell Press, comps. and eds. *The Big Book of Halls of Fame in the United States and Canada* (New York: R. R. Bowker, 1977), pp. 236, 825. King Carl, the son of a Methodist minister, was born on July 30, 1892, in Omaha, Nebraska, and lived in a dozen places around the United States before attending State College High School in Pennsylvania as preparation for college. During the summer, he worked in the Danville rolling mill and, in 1915, was the baseball and football captain for the Lebanon College varsity squads. He would go on to be inducted into the College Football Hall of Fame as an outstanding coach for Bucknell, North Carolina, and Cornell Universities.

10. *Altoona Mirror*, 1 November 1915.

11. *Altoona Mirror*, 29 October 1915.

12. *Altoona Mirror*, 1 November 1915.

13. *Canton Repository*, 5 November 1915. Malcolm "Red" Fleming grew up in Bellwood, just nine miles north of Altoona. After graduation, he went on to play a fifth year of football at Muhlenburg College near Allentown, where they were willing to overlook normal eligibility requirements.

14. *Canton Repository*, 8 November 1915.

15. Carroll and Branwart, *Pro Football.*

16. *Altoona Mirror*, 15 November 1915.

17. *Altoona Mirror*, 22 November 1915.

18. *Massillon Independent*, 22 November 1915.

19. *Toledo Blade*, 26 November 1915.

20. *Altoona Mirror*, 26 November 1915.

21. *Lathorn*, Susquehanna University Yearbook, (Selingrove, PA: 1913), p. 124; (1914), pp. 127, 128, 130, 132, 137; (1915), pp. 54, 123, 129, 133. At five feet ten inches and one-hundred sixty-five

pounds, Red Swoope was a great athlete. After starring in several sports at Altoona High School, he went to Susquehanna University in Selingrove, where he was captain of the varsity football and basketball teams and won four letters in baseball. He was also considered by many to be a candidate for All-American honors in football.

22. *Altoona Mirror,* 23 November 1915.

23. Newcombe, *Best of Athletic Boys,* 152–53. William Lone Star Dietz was born on the Rosebud Reservation in Pine Ridge, South Dakota. His father was a German civil engineer and his mother, Julia One-Star, was a full-blooded Oglala Sioux. Lone Star was a talented artist and a competent coach. He was already a veteran of semiprofessional baseball and football when he was recruited from Friends University in Kansas to play for Carlisle Institute in 1911. In 1913, he was assistant coach to Pop Warner at Carlisle Institute (*Detroit Free Press,* 2 October 1913). In 1914, Lone Star coached at Washington State University and took his team to the first Rose Bowl game that year. He later played pro football with the Columbus Panhandles and, in 1920, for the Hammond Pros. In 1933–34, he went on to become head coach of the Boston Redskins, where his team was second in the eastern division of the NFL [*Canton Repository,* 2 October 1916; Roger Treat, *The Official Encyclopedia of Football,* 10th ed. (Cranbury, NJ: A. S. Barnes and Co., 1972), pp. 61–64]. Joe Bergie was a Chippewa from the Devil's Lake Band in Dakota and, like Dietz and Hugh Wheelock, was one of the linemen who helped Jim Thorpe gain All-American status in 1911.

24. *Canton Repository,* 2 October 1915.

25. *Cleveland Plain Dealer,* 9 October 1916.

26. *Altoona Mirror,* 16 October 1916.

27. *Massillon Independent,* 26 October 1916.

28. *Altoona Mirror,* 23 October 1916.

29. *Dayton Journal,* 30 October 1916.

30. *Altoona Mirror,* 6 November 1916.

Chapter 8

1. *Evanston Index,* 27 January 1912, p. 8.

2. Lutheran Church records, Albert City, Iowa; *Evanston City Directory,* 1907. Reuben Ludvig Emmanuel Johnson was born in Chicago on June 15, 1891, the third child of Johanna Alfred and Hilma Josphine Johnson. In 1892, the family moved to Albert City, Iowa. Sometime after the turn of the century, Reuben's brother Richard moved to Evanston, Illinois, and became a house painter. By the fall of 1906, Reuben had also moved to Evanston and was living with his brother. An excellent all-around athlete, "Rube" Johnson won numerous golf, baseball, and track awards from the Evanston YMCA.

3. *Evanston Review,* 2 July 1954.

4. Lee Corkill, "Falcon Marks 41 Years in Underwater Business," *The Evanston Review,* 2 July 1959, p. 22.

5. *Evanston Review,* 2 July 1959; *The Chicago Tribune,* July 1982. Guilford W. "Hawk" Falcon was born December 16, 1892, in Evanston, Illinois. His father and grandfather were marine salvage contractors and underwater construction experts who specialized in laying underwater pipe.

6. *Evanston Index,* 6 November 1909, 15 October 1910, 25 November 1911.

7. *Evanston Index,* 27 November 1909, 10 April 1958, 28 August 1975. Henry Norbert Kilby was born in Wilmette, Illinois, in 1893. His family moved to Evanston shortly after his birth, and he lived there almost his entire life. In 1913, he was hired as a cable splicer helper for Illinois Bell in Evanston and was promoted to cable splicer four years later.

8. *Evanston Index,* 27 January 1912, 25 October 1913, 22 December 1955. In 1914, Murray went to work for the Bowman Dairy Company, staying with them for forty-one years.

9. *Detroit News Tribune,* 4 November 1916. Patrick J. O'Dea was born in Melbourne, Australia, and played rugby football before coming to America to play football at the University of Wisconsin, where he was named All-American in 1898. O'Dea was considered the best kicker in football at the beginning of the twentieth century, having kicked field goals from 62, 60, and 57 yards later. After graduating from Wisconsin, O'Dea coached at Notre Dame in 1900 and 1901. In 1917, he changed his name and dropped out of sight. He died in 1962. See Porter, *Halls of Fame,* 819–20.

10. *University of Illinois Directory* (Urbana, IL: University of Illinois Press, 1916); *Evanston News-Index,* 4 October 1915.

11. *Racine Journal-News,* 15 October 1916.

12. *Evanston News-Index,* 4 October 1915.

13. *Evanston News-Index,* 18 October 1915.

14. *Evanston News-Index,* 25 October 1915.

15. *Wabash Plain Dealer,* 25 October 1915.

16. *Ibid.*

17. *Detroit Times,* 27 October 1915.

18. *Detroit Free Press,* 1 November 1915.

19. *Detroit Free Press, Detroit Times,* 1 November 1915.

20. *Detroit Free Press,* 1 November 1915.

21. *Fort Wayne Journal-Gazette,* 5 November 1915.

22. *Fort Wayne Journal-Gazette,* 8 November 1915.

23. *Ibid.*

24. *Rock Island Argus,* 15 November 1915.

25. *Evanston Index,* 15 November 1915.

26. *Rock Island Argus,* 20 November 1915.

27. *Evanston News-Index,* 22 November 1915; *Rockford Morning Star,* 23 November 1915, p. 9.

28. *Rock Island Argus,* 26 November 1915.

29. *Clinton Herald,* 5 October 1914.

30. *Evanston News-Index,* 3 October 1916.

31. *Ibid.*

32. *Racine Times-Call,* 7 October 1916.

33. *Racine Times-Call,* 9 October 1916.

34. *Evanston News-Index,* 9 October 1916.

35. *Davenport Daily Times,* 16 October 1916.

36. *Wabash Plain Dealer,* 16 October 1916.

37. *Evanston News-Index* and *Wabash Plain Dealer,* 23 October 1916.

38. *Evanston News-Index,* 1 November 1916.

39. *Detroit News,* 4, 6 November 1916.

40. *Detroit Free Press,* 6 November 1916.

41. The *Evanston Index,* 6 November 1916, reported that Eissler had caught the pass instead of Schobinger.

42. *Detroit News*, 6 November 1916.

43. *Evanston Index*, 16 November 1916.

44. *Detroit Free Press*, 16 November 1916.

45. *Detroit News*, 16 November 1916.

46. *Fort Wayne Journal-Gazette*, 10 November 1916.

47. *Fort Wayne Journal-Gazette*, 12 November 1916.

48. *Fort Wayne Journal-Gazette*, 10 November 1916.

49. *Fort Wayne Journal-Gazette*, 13 November 1916.

50. *Rockford Morning Star*, 21 November 1916, p. 7.

51. *Fort Wayne Journal-Gazette*, 28 November 1916; *Davenport Daily Times*, 1 December 1916.

Chapter 9

1. Carroll, *The Tigers Roar.* "Mother" Kruse became a Toledo policeman; see *Akron Beacon Journal*, 19 October 1912.

2. Toledo Central High School was excluded by Armory Park management from practicing or playing their games at Armory Park in 1908, so it is likely that the Toledo Athletic Association was refused access to the field and had no place to play their games. See *The Almanac*, Toledo Central High School Yearbook, (Toledo, OH: 1908). It also seems likely that, at the baseball team's insistence, Armory Park management wanted to give the field an opportunity to grow grass before the next baseball season.

3. Carroll, *The Tigers Roar; Akron Beacon Journal*, 19 October 1912.

4. *The Almanac*, Toledo Central High School Yearbook, (Toledo, OH: 1909, 1910, 1911). Harry Seubert, in the Class of 1912 (but may have graduated early), was captain of the 1910 Toledo Central High School football team, while Charles Nichols was in the Class of 1910.

5. *Adrian College World*, October 1911.

6. The Michigan Intercollegiate Athletic Association, formed on March 24, 1884, is America's oldest collegiate conference.

7. *Adrian College World*, December 1911.

8. *The Almanac*, Toledo Central High School Yearbook, (Toledo, OH: 1910); Adrian College Archives.

9. Louis G. Trout was a plumber. See *Toledo, Ohio City Directory, 1917–18*.

10. *Toledo Blade*, 2 October 1915.

11. *Massillon Independent*, 8 October 1915.

12. Walter J. Semlow was a salesman for the Willys-Overland Automobile Company. See *Toledo, Ohio City Directory, 1917–18*.

13. *Toledo Blade*, 4 October 1915.

14. *Toledo News Bee*, 5 October 1915.

15. *Toledo Blade*, 16 October 1915.

16. *Toledo Blade*, 13 November 1915.

17. *Fort Wayne Journal-Gazette*, 28 October 1916.

18. *Toledo Blade*, 11 October 1915.

19. *Toledo News Bee*, 18 October 1915.

20. *Fort Wayne Journal-Gazette*, 13 November 1915; *Toledo Blade*, 15 October 1915.

21. *Toledo Blade*, 11 October 1915.

22. *Toledo Blade*, 21 October 1915.

23. *Toledo Blade*, 23 October 1915; Bernie McCarty, *All-America: The Complete Roster of Football Heroes, 1889–1945* (IL: self-published, 1991).

24. *Toledo Blade*, 21 October 1915.

25. *Toledo Blade* and *Toledo News-Bee*, 25 October 1915.

26. *Toledo Blade*, 25 October 1915.

27. *Toledo Blade*, 29 October 1915.

28. *Toledo News-Bee*, 1 November 1915.

29. *Toledo Blade*, 2 November 1915.

30. *Toledo Blade*, 1 November 1915.

31. *Toledo News-Bee* and *Toledo Blade*, 1 November 1915.

32. *Toledo News-Bee*, 1 November 1915.

33. *Toledo Blade*, 2 November 1915.

34. *Toledo Blade*, 4 November 1915.

35. *Massillon Independent*, 8, 9 October 1915.

36. *Toledo News-Bee*, 8 November 1915. Orrville Beck "Bo" Littick from Zanesville, Ohio, was one of Ohio Wesleyan's all-time great athletes, participating in football, basketball, and baseball as part of the class of 1912. He was All-Ohio in football in 1912 and later coached at Ohio University, Centre College, Beloit College, and Ohio Wesleyan University before becoming vice-president and general manager of the Zanesville Publishing Company and general manager of the Southeastern Ohio Broadcasting System in 1929. He replaced his father as president of these companies in 1941. He died September 2, 1953. See *Ohio Wesleyan Magazine* 31, no. 2 (October 1953). Jonathan Fred "Pottsy" Potts from Tippecanoe City, Ohio, was captain of the 1909 Ohio Wesleyan football team. After graduating from Ohio Wesleyan, he received his law degree from Western Reserve University in 1912 and began practicing law in Cleveland. In 1929, he moved from Cleveland Heights to Hollywood, California. He retired to Palm Beach, Florida in 1951. See *Le Bijou 1909*, Ohio Wesleyan University Yearbook, (Columbus, OH: The Champlin Press, 1909), and alumni records, Ohio Wesleyan University.

37. *Toledo News-Bee* and *Toledo Blade*, 8 November 1915.

38. *Toledo News-Bee*, 10 November 1915.

39. *Toledo News-Bee*, 15 November 1915.

40. *Ibid.*

41. *Ibid.*

42. *Toledo Blade*, 13 November 1915.

43. *Massillon Independent*, 22 November 1915.

44. *Toledo News-Bee*, 18 November 1915; *Toledo Blade*, 20 November 1915.

45. *Toledo News-Bee*, 20 November 1915.

46. *Toledo Blade*, 22 November 1915.

47. *Massillon Independent*, 22 November 1915.

48. *Toledo Blade*, 22 November 1915.

49. *Massillon Independent*, 22 November 1915.

50. *Toledo Blade*, 25 November 1915.

51. *Toledo Blade*, 26 November 1915.

52. *The Almanac*, Toledo Central High School Yearbook, (Toledo, OH: 1913), pp. 142, 152. John Fluhrer, Harold Smith, Noble Jones, and Arthur McIntyre were among Clarence Fraim's teammates at Central High School.

53. *Toledo Blade*, 26 November 1915.

54. *Toledo Blade*, 29 November 1915.

55. *Toledo Blade,* 6 December 1915.

56. Shortstop Charles E. Nichols Jr. was captain of the Toledo Central High School baseball team in 1909. See *The Almanac,* Toledo Central High School Yearbook (Toledo, OH: 1909), p. 183. According to the *Toledo, Ohio City Directory, 1917–18,* he worked as a salesman.

57. *Toledo Blade,* 14 October 1916.

58. Arthur McIntyre was in the Toledo Central High School Class of 1912 (See *The Almanac 1909,* p. 107), but was forced to drop out of school on several occasions to help support his family. *The Almanac 1914* reported on page 145, "Art McIntyre is a flashy, dashing end, whose flying tackles were immense. He will be missed as he dropped out of high school [in 1912 after the football season]." In the fall of 1913, he played for Toledo's new Scott High School, and finally graduated from Scott High in the spring of 1914. See *The Scottonian,* Scott High School Yearbook, (Toledo, OH: 1914), p. 146. Arthur R. McIntyre later became an engineer. See *Toledo City Directory, 1917–18.*

59. *The Scottonian,* Scott High School Yearbook, (Toledo, OH: 1915), p. 109.

60. *Toledo Blade,* 2 October 1916.

61. *Detroit Free Press,* 15 November 1915.

62. *Toledo Blade,* 9 October 1916.

63. *Toledo Blade,* 11 October 1916.

64. *Toledo Blade,* 14 October 1916.

65. *Toledo Blade,* 16 October 1916.

66. *Ibid.*

67. *Massillon Independent* and *Toledo Blade,* 23 October 1916.

68. *Toledo Blade,* 23 October 1916.

69. *Ibid.*

70. *Toledo Blade,* 28 October 1916.

71. *Toledo Blade,* 30 October 1916.

72. *Toledo Blade,* 31 October 1916.

73. *Massillon Independent,* 8 November 1916.

74. *Toledo Blade,* 6 November 1916.

75. *Ibid.*   76. *Ibid.*

77. *Toledo Blade,* 13 November 1916.

78. *Toledo Blade,* 18 November 1916. John "Jack" Fluhrer was an all-around athlete, who lettered in football, basketball, and track. He played quarterback for Toledo Central High School from 1910 through the 1912 football season and was captain of the famous Mastodon eleven in 1912. He was known for his uncanny ability to perceive the enemy's plays and forestall their offensive efforts. He played his senior year at Scott High School and planned to attend the University of Pennsylvania in 1914, according to his high school yearbook. See *The Scottonian* (1914), pp. 30, 142.

79. *Toledo Blade,* 17 November 1916.

80. *Detroit Free Press,* 15 November 1915.

81. *Toledo News-Bee,* 27 November 1916.

82. *Racine Journal-News* and *Toledo Blade,* 1 December 1916.

83. *Toledo Blade,* 3 October, December 1916.

84. *Toledo Blade,* 2, 4 December 1916.

85. *Toledo Blade,* 4 December 1916.

86. *Toledo Blade,* 27 September 1917.

87. Joseph J. Schuette was a jeweler with Basch and Company. See *Toledo, Ohio City Directory, 1917–18.*

88. Frank Roush was also captain of his high school basketball team in 1916. See *The Purple and Gold: The Yearbook of Morrison R. Waite High School,* (Toledo, OH: 1915), p. 145; (1916), pp. 82, 165, 179.

89. *The Almanac* (1912), pp. 30, 110, 121; Purdue University Archives; *Toledo, Ohio City Directory, 1917–18.*

90. *Toledo Blade,* 27 September 1917.

91. *Youngstown Telegram,* 23 October 1916.

92. *Toledo Blade,* 5 October 1917.

93. *Toledo Blade,* 10 October 1917.

94. *Toledo Blade,* 8 October 1917.

95. *Toledo News-Bee,* 15 October 1917.

96. *Dayton Daily News,* 22 October 1917.

97. *Toledo Blade,* 22 October 1917.

98. *Detroit Free Press,* 29 October 1917.

99. *Ibid.*

100. *Fort Wayne Journal-Gazette,* 5 November 1917.

101. *Ibid.*

102. *Toledo News-Bee,* 5 November 1915.

103. *Fort Wayne Journal-Gazette,* 12 November 1917.

104. Horrigan, "Franchise Transactions," 3–13.

105. Treat, *Official Encyclopedia of Football,* 34, 38.

Chapter 10

1. Unpublished letter, NFL Football Hall of Fame Archives.

2. *Youngstown Vindicator,* 24 October 1915.

3. *Ibid.*   4. *Ibid.*

5. *Rayen Record,* October 1910.

6. *Rayen Record,* October 1909; Brown University Archives; *Youngstown Vindicator,* 21 October 1917. Ashbaugh graduated from Rayen High School and in 1913 from Brown University, and coached at South High School in Youngstown. He later served as corporal in World War I and become the high school's athletic director. See Brown University Archives. His wife was Thelma E. Ashbaugh and in later years lived at 69 Delason Avenue. Russell died before 1955. See *Youngstown Official City Directory,* 1955 (Akron: The Burch Directory Company, 1955). Elgie Tobin, who lived on Powers Way just off Poland Avenue in Youngstown, was an assistant coach at Washington and Jefferson College in 1915–16 and coached at West Virginia University in 1917.

7. Edwards played football, basketball, and baseball at Oberlin HS before playing these same sports at Oberlin College and Rollins College. After college, he coached at Lewiston High School in Idaho, Columbia College in Florida, and Oberlin Academy. *Rayen Record* (October 1914): p. 16.

8. *Youngstown Vindicator,* 24 October 1915.

9. *Youngstown Vindicator,* 11 October 1915.

10. *Youngstown Vindicator,* 8 October 1915.

11. *Youngstown Vindicator,* 18 October 1915.

12. *Youngstown Vindicator,* 25 October 1915.

13. *Youngstown Vindicator* and *Youngstown Telegram,* 1 November 1915, p. 19.

14. *Youngstown Telegram,* 8 November 1915, p. 19.

15. *Youngstown Vindicator* and *Youngstown Telegram,* 8 November 1915.

16. *Youngstown Vindicator*, 21 November 1915.

17. *Youngstown Telegram* and *Youngstown Vindicator*, 15 November 1915.

18. *Youngstown Telegram*, 22 November 1915.

19. *Youngstown Telegram* and *Youngstown Vindicator*, 22 November 1915.

20. *Youngstown Telegram*, 22 November 1915.

21. NFL Football Hall of Fame Archives.

22. *Washington Star*, 25 October 1915.

23. *Washington Star*, 7 November 1915.

24. *Youngstown Vindicator*, 29 November 1915.

25. *Youngstown Telegram*, 2 October 1916.

26. *Youngstown Telegram*, 23 October 1916; *The 1916 Michiganensian*, University of Michigan Yearbook, (Ann Arbor, MI: 1916), pp. 73, 80, 285, 314.

27. *Youngstown Telegram*, 9, 16, 23, 30 October 1916.

28. *Cleveland Plain Dealer*, 22 October 1916.

29. Horace Dutton "Hoke" Palmer was an all around athlete, having been captain of his college team at Ohio University, a record holder in the shot put, and starting guard on the university's basketball team. *Atheana*, Ohio University Yearbook, (Athens, OH: 1914), pp. 203, 220; (1916), p. 224. See Dougles McWilliams. Hawkins played for Ohio University two years without ever moving beyond the freshman class. He married an Ohio University graduate, who became an elementary school teacher and lived in Tulsa, Oklahoma in 1937. See *Alumni Directory*, Ohio University, 1937. Lester Thomas Miller later became a general in the U.S. Army. See Marietta College Archives.

30. *Massillon Independent*, 30 October 1916.

31. *Massillon Independent*, 4 November 1916.

32. *Youngstown Telegram*, 6 November 1916.

33. *Ibid.*

34. *Massillon Independent*, 6 November 1916.

35. *Youngstown Telegram*, 6 November 1916.

36. *Youngstown Telegram*, 13 November 1916.

37. *Michiganensian*, University of Michigan Yearbook, (Ann Arbor, MI: 1911–15).

38. *Youngstown Telegram*, 16 November 1916.

39. Howard Franklin, "Short Happy Afternoon of Bart Macomber," *Sports Illustrated* 8 no. 16 (October 1958): E3–E4.

40. *Youngstown Vindicator*, 20 November 1916.

41. *Canton Repository*, 20 November 1916.

42. *Youngstown Telegram*, 20 November 1916.

43. *Canton Repository*, 20 November 1916.

44. *Massillon Independent*, 24 November 1916.

45. *Washington Post*, 27 November 1916. The Youngstown newspapers used Cranston's assumed name, Martin, but attributed the Washington touchdown to right halfback, Russell.

46. *Youngstown Telegram* and *Washington Post*, 27 November 1916.

47. *Youngstown Telegram*, 1 December 1916.

48. *Youngstown Telegram*, 4 December 1916.

49. *Cleveland Plain Dealer*, 22 September 1961; *Cleveland Leader*, 11 November 1912; *Toledo Blade*, 24 November 1916; University of Notre Dame Archives; Emil Klosinski, "Knute Rockne's Pro Football Roots," *The Coffin Corner* 17, no. 1 (spring 1995): 10–16.

50. *Youngstown Telegram*, 8 October 1917 and *Youngstown Directory, 1917* (Akron: The Burch Directory Co., 1917), p. 1005. The four carryover players were Yeckel, Gillespie, Vedderneck, and Funkhouser. Russell Ashbaugh was prohibited from playing by public school authorities who felt that a high school football coach should not be allowed to play football on Sunday.

51. *Massillon Independent*, 9 October 1917.

52. *Youngstown Vindicator*, 13 October 1917.

53. *Youngstown Telegram*, 15 October 1917.

54. *Pittsburgh Press*, 15 October 1917.

55. *Youngstown Telegram*, 15 October 1917.

56. *Dayton Daily News*, 18 October 1917.

57. *Youngstown Telegram*, 22 October 1917.

58. *Youngstown Vindicator*, 22 October 1917.

59. *Ibid.*

60. *Toledo Blade*, 23 October 1917.

61. Letter from Milton Silver to University of Illinois Alumni Office, 1972.

62. *Toledo Blade* and *Youngstown Telegram*, 29 October 1917.

63. *Youngstown Vindicator*, 10 October 1917.

64. *Dayton Journal*, 22 October 1916; *Toledo Blade*, 8 November 1916; *Cleveland Plain Dealer*, October, 1917; Porter, *Biographical Dictionary*, p. 463–64.

65. *Akron Beacon Journal*, 1911–14; *Canton Daily News*, 5 November 1917; The University of Akron Alumni Office, 1994.

66. *Canton Repository*, 5 November 1917.

67. *Youngstown Telegram* and *Pittsburgh Gazette-Times*, 5 November 1917.

68. *Youngstown Vindicator*, 27 October 1917; *Massillon Independent*, 1 November 1917.

69. *Massillon Independent*, 1 November 1917.

70. *Massillon Independent*, 2 November 1917.

71. *Fort Wayne Journal-Gazette*, 10–12 November 1917.

72. *Massillon Independent*, 9 November 1917.

73. *Youngstown Telegram* and *Massillon Independent*, 12 November 1917.

74. *Youngstown Telegram*, 19 November 1917.

75. *Pittsburgh Gazette-Times*, 20 November 1917.

76. *Canton Repository*, 19 November 1917.

77. *Ibid.*

78. Gerald Holland, "Greasy Neale: Nothing to Prove, Nothing to Ask," *Sports Illustrated* 21, no. 8 (24 August 1964): 33. Greasy Neale's memory mistakenly places Frank M. Pleasant (rather than Gus Welch) in the huddle, which was not yet in use, but the rest of the story sounds consistent with contemporary reports. It is noteworthy that Neale hit .357 in the 1919 World Series, took Washington and Jefferson College to the Rose Bowl, and coached the Philadelphia Eagles to two NFL Championships.

79. *Akron Beacon Journal*, 24 November 1917.

80. *Ibid.*

81. *Akron Beacon Journal*, 26 November 1917.

82. *Youngstown Telegram*, 26 November 1917.

83. *Massillon Independent*, 28 November 1917.

84. Youngstown was granted an NFL franchise on June 24, 1922, but did not field a team that fall. Horrigan, "Franchise Transactions," 5.

Chapter 11

1. *St. Mary's College Exponent*, 11, no. 10 (December 1913): pp. 392–97.

2. *St. Mary's College Exponent*, 11, no. 10 (December 1913): pp. 395–97.

3. *St. Mary's College Exponent*, 11 (1913) and 12 (1914).

4. *Dayton Sunday News*, 11 November 1917; Dayton University Archives; *St. Mary's College Exponent*, October-December 1913.

5. A profile of Al Mahrt based on an interview of him by John Dye appeared in *the Dayton Daily News*, 10 January 1965, which makes a case that Al was one of the best passers in the NFL prior to 1950. After retiring from football, Al Mahrt became executive vice-president of the Mead Corporation and a wealthy man. He married Marcie Niehaus, who in 1921 was voted the prettiest girl in Dayton. He died in 1970.

6. *St. Mary's College Exponent*, 9, no. 9 (November 1911): p. 424.

7. *St. Mary's College Exponent*, 10, no. 9 (November 1912): p. 433.

8. *St. Mary's College Bulletin*, series 24, no. 2 (1913): 38–41; *Dayton Daily News*, 10 January 1965.

9. Quoted in *St. Mary's College Exponent*, 11, no. 10 (December 1913): 396.

10. *Dayton Daily News*, 8 October 1915.

11. *Dayton Daily News*, 10 October 1915.

12. *Dayton Daily News*, 11 October 1915.

13. *Dayton Daily News*, 18 October 1915.

14. *Dayton Daily News*, 25 October 1915.

15. *Dayton Daily News*, 1 November 1915.

16. *Dayton Daily News*, 8 November 1915.

17. *Dayton Daily News*, 1 November 1915.

18. *Dayton Daily News*, 8 November 1915.

19. *Ibid.*

20. *Dayton News*, 13 November 1915.

21. *Dayton News*, 15 November 1915.

22. *Dayton Daily News*, 22 November 1915; *Massillon Independent*, 22, 29 November 1915.

23. *Dayton Daily News*, 8 October 1915.

24. *Dayton Daily News*, 29 November 1915.

25. Steve Presar, "Present at the Creation: Dayton's Triangles and the NFL," *Miami Valley History* 11 (1989): 19–29.

26. *Dayton Daily News*, 13–14 March 1950.

27. *Dayton Journal*, 2 October 1916.

28. *Dayton Daily News*, 10 January 1965.

29. *Fort Wayne Journal-Gazette*, 1 October 1916.

30. *Dayton Journal*, 2 October 1916.

31. *Dayton Daily News*, 5 October 1916; *Dayton Journal*, 9 October 1916.

32. *Dayton Daily News*, 12 October 1916.

33. *Dayton Daily News*, 16 October 1916.

34. *Dayton Daily News*, 19 October 1916.

35. *Detroit Free Press*, 23 October 1916.

36. *Dayton Daily News*, 23 October 1916.

37. *Ibid.*

38. *Ibid.*

39. *Detroit Free Press*, 23 October 1916.

40. *Ibid.*

41. *Dayton Daily News*, 25 October 1916.

42. *Ibid.*

43. *Dayton Daily News*, 30 October 1916.

44. *Instano*, Indiana Normal School yearbook, (Indiana, PA: 1915).

45. *Dayton Daily News*, 6 November 1916.

46. *Dayton Journal*, 13 November 1916.

47. *Dayton Daily News*, 20 November 1916.

48. *Dayton Journal*, 27 November 1916.

49. *Dayton Daily News*, 29 November 1916.

50. *Dayton Daily News*, 13,14 March 1950.

51. *Dayton Journal*, 1 December 1916.

52. *Dayton Daily News*, 7 October 1917.

53. *Miamisburg News*, 20 February 1947, p. 1.

54. George's youngest brother, Walter, who graduated with the Miamisburg High School class of 1917, also played in the backfields for the Dayton Triangles in the early 1920s. *Mirus*, Miamisburg High School Yearbook, (Miamisburg, OH: 1919) p. 52. Miamisburg Board of Education Records, *Bulldogs on Sunday, 1923* (North Huntington, PA: The Professional Football Researchers Association, 1998) pp. 30–31.

55. *Debris*, Purdue University yearbook, (West Lafayette, IN: 1916). Richard T. "Abe" Abrell was a remarkable man. He was the starting quarterback for Purdue University in 1914, but, in the summer of 1915, he badly mangled his right arm in a milling machine and was unable to play football in 1915. However, in 1916, he was a Purdue "Boilermaker" starter, although no longer a quarterback.

56. *Dayton Daily News*, 8 October 1917.

57. *Toledo Blade*, 22 October 1917.

58. *Dayton Daily News*, 28 October 1917.

59. *Dayton Journal*, 5 November 1917.

60. *Dayton Journal*, 11 November 1917.

61. *Dayton Journal* and *Dayton Daily News*, 12 November 1917.

62. *Dayton Daily News*, 19 November 1917.

63. *Dayton Daily News*, 26 November 1917.

64. Horrigan, "Franchise Transactions," 10.

Chapter 12

1. *Detroit News*, 22 October 1916; University of Detroit-Mercy Archives.

2. University of Detroit-Mercy Archives.

3. *Detroit Free Press*, 8 April 1909. Marshall played left halfback for the Detroit College football team in 1907. See *Detroit Free Press*, 1 November 1907.

4. *Detroit Free Press*, 6 November 1910.

5. *Detroit Free Press*, 5 November 1911 and 20 October 1912. According to *Detroit Free Press*, 12 October 1913, 1910 was the first year Bertie Maher played in the Herald's backfield.

6. *Detroit News*, 22 May 1910; *Detroit Free Press*, 23 May 1910.

7. Richard Bak, *Joe Louis: The Great Black Hope* (Dallas, TX: Taylor Publishing Company, 1996), p.17.

8. *Detroit News*, 22 October 1916.

9. *Detroit Free Press*, 20 October 1913.

10. *Detroit Free Press*, 22 October 1914.

11. *Dayton Daily News*, 22 November 1972.

12. *Detroit News*, 20 June 1935, p. 38; R. L. Polk and Co., *Detroit City Directory, 1902*, p. 1444.

13. Certificate of marriage, Aaron J. Roesink, State of Michigan, 10 August 1903, and R. L. Polk and Co., *Grand Rapids City Directory, 1904*.

14. *Detroit News*, 20 July 1954, p. 25.

15. For facts about John A. Roesink's life, see *Civic Searchlight*, September 1937; *Detroit Free Press*, 20 June 1947 and 27 November 1950; *Detroit News* 20 June 1935, p. 38 and 20 July 1954, p. 25; and

R. L. Polk and Co., *Detroit City Directory, 1902*, p. 1444; 1903, p. 1807; 1904–5, p. 2034; 1908; 1909, p. 1804; 1911, p. 2020; 1912, p. 2152; 1915, p. 2028; 1921–22, p. 1714; 1926–27, p. 1776; and 1941, p. 1517. In 1903, John married Anna Pauline Harrigan, and in 1919 he opened his own men's clothing store at 7 Campus Martius in Detroit. By 1921, he owned three stores, advertised on the wall at Navin Field, and became a close friend of Ty Cobb. He continued to operate Mack Park and to promote semiprofessional sports. In 1920, the Negro National League was formed, and the Detroit franchise rented the 4,000-seat Mack Park for its league games and exhibitions. In 1925, Roesink acquired the Detroit Stars franchise, which he held until 1931. Mack Park was partially destroyed by a fire on July 7, 1929. See E. A. Batchelor, "Afro-American Rooters Are Best Part of The Shows at Mack Park," *Detroit Saturday Night*, 26 August 1922, 2ff; Richard Bak, "Black Diamonds," *Michigan Magazine, Detroit Free Press*, 5 April 1987, pp. 28–32; and Richard Bak, *Turkey Stearnes and the Detroit Stars* (Detroit: Wayne State University Press, 1994).

16. *Detroit Free Press*, 26 October 1913, p. 19.

17. *Detroit Free Press*, 6 November 1910; 12 October 1913.

18. *Detroit Free Press*, 5, 17 October 1915.

19. *Detroit Free Press*, 14 October 1914.

20. The University of Michigan players included Frank McHale, Arthur Cornwell, Tom Bogle, and Dunn (a freshman with the University of Michigan in 1913). See *Michiganensian*, University of Michigan yearbook (Ann Arbor, MI: 1914). Dunn was unable to stay academically eligible, according to the *Detroit Free Press*, 17 October 1915.

21. *Detroit Free Press*, 26, 27 September 1915, 2 October 1915.

22. *Detroit Free Press* and *Detroit News*, 4 October 1915.

23. Ken Hoffman with Larry Bielot, *Spartan Football: 100 Seasons of Gridiron Glory* (Champaign, IL: Sagamore Publishing Co., 1996), p. 22.

24. *Sport International*, ed. Charles Harvey (New York: A. S. Barnes and Company, Inc., 1960), p. 52.

25. *Detroit Free Press*, 10 October 1915.

26. *Detroit News Tribune*, 10 October 1915.

27. *Detroit Free Press* and *Buffalo Courier*, 11 October 1915.

28. *Detroit Free Press*, 12 October 1915.

29. *Detroit Free Press*, 18 October 1915.

30. *Detroit News Tribune*, 17 October 1915.

31. *Detroit Free Press*, 18 October 1915.

32. *Detroit Free Press*, 25 October 1915.

33. *Ibid.*   34. *Ibid.*

35. *Detroit Times*, 25 October 1915.

36. *Detroit Times*, 16 November 1914.

37. *Detroit Times*, 27 October 1915, p. 6.

38. *Detroit Free Press* and *Detroit Times*, 1 November 1915.

39. *Detroit Free Press* and *Detroit Times*, 1 November 1915.

40. *Detroit Times*, November 9, 1915.

41. *Michigan All-Time Athletic Record Books* (Ann Arbor: Olympia Sports Press, 1979).

42. *Detroit Times*, 8 November 1915.

43. *Detroit Free Press*, 8 November 1915.

44. *Detroit Free Press*, 14 November 1915.

45. *Detroit Times*, 15 November 1915.

46. *Detroit Free Press*, 15 November 1915.

47. *Wolverine*, Michigan Agricultural College Yearbook (East Lansing, MI: 1912).

48. Hoffman and Bielot, *Spartan Football*, 28.

49. *Fort Wayne Journal-Gazette*, 17 November 1915.

50. *Lansing State Journal* and *Detroit News*, 10 January 1987. After that, Blake Miller became the golf pro at the Lansing Country Club and died as a result of a fire in 1987 at the age of 97.

51. *Detroit Free Press*, 15 November 1915.

52. *Detroit Free Press*, 21 November 1915.

53. *Detroit Free Press, Detroit News*, and *Detroit Times*, 22 November 1915.

54. *Toledo Blade*, 26 November 1915.

55. *Detroit News Tribune*, 3 December 1917.

56. *Detroit Free Press*, 1, 2 October 1916.

57. *Detroit Free Press*, 2 October 1916.

58. *Montgomery: Our County Magazine* 4, no. 11 (November 1979).

59. *Detroit News Tribune*, 1 October 1916.

60. *Detroit News Tribune*, 6 October 1916.

61. *Detroit News Tribune*, 9 October 1916.

62. *Detroit News Tribune*, 9 October 1916.

63. *Detroit Free Press*, 16 October 1916.

64. *Detroit News Tribune*, 16 October 1916.

65. *Detroit Free Press*, 23 October 1916.

66. *Ibid.*

67. *Detroit News Tribune*, 31 October 1916.

68. *Philadelphia Evening Bulletin* and *Philadelphia Evening Ledger*, 1 May 1918 and 16 January 1920.

69. *Detroit Free Press*, 31 October 1916.

70. *Detroit Free Press*, 6 November 1916, 4 November 1910.

71. *Detroit News Tribune*, 6 November 1916.

72. *Ibid.*   73. *Ibid.*

74. *Detroit Free Press*, 22 November 1920.

75. *Detroit News Tribune*, 6 November 1916.

76. Syracuse University Archives. Castle later became a basketball player for the Detroit Athletic Club and a trader on the floor of the Detroit Stock Exchange

77. *Detroit News Tribune*, 13 November 1916.

78. *Detroit Free Press*, 13 November 1916.

79. *Detroit News Tribune*, 20 November 1916; *Detroit Free Press*, 19 November 1916.

80. *Detroit Free Press*, 27 November 1916.

81. *Detroit Free Press*, 31 November 1916; *Toledo Blade*, 1 December 1916.

82. *Detroit Free Press*, 22 September 1917.

83. *Detroit Free Press*, 7 October 1917.

84. *Youngstown Vindicator*, 13 October 1917.

85. *Detroit Free Press*, 8 October 1917.

86. *Detroit Free Press*, 15 October 1917.

87. *Youngstown Vindicator*, 13 October 1917.

88. *Detroit Free Press*, 22 October 1917; *Buffalo Enquirer*, 22 October 1917, p. 11.

89. Indiana University Archives.

90. *Detroit Free Press*, 29 October 1917.

91. *Detroit Free Press*, 29 October 1917; *Detroit News Tribune*, 4 November 1917.

92. *Detroit Free Press*, 5 November 1917.

93. *Ibid.*

94. *Detroit News,* 12 November 1917.

95. *Detroit Free Press,* 18 November 1917.

96. *Detroit News,* 12 November 1917.

97. *Detroit News,* 18 November 1917.

98. *Detroit Free Press,* 19 November 1917.

99. *Detroit News,* 19 November 1917.

100. *Detroit Free Press,* 19 November 1917.

101. *Detroit News,* 25 November 1917.

102. *Detroit Free Press,* 25 November 1917.

103. *Detroit Times,* 4 May 1924, part 3, p. 6. Horning would later be an assistant coach at the University of Detroit before becoming athletic director at Highland Park High School, in suburban Detroit.

104. *Detroit News,* 26 November 1917.

105. *Detroit News,* 26 November 1917.

106. Syracuse University Archives. Propst had been Assistant Coach at Syracuse in 1914 and 1915, and, starting in 1918, became a career army officer.

107. *Detroit News,* 30 November 1917.

108. *Ibid.*   109. *Ibid.*

110. After graduating from Princeton Theological Seminary, Cruikshank became a Presbyterian minister in Pittsburgh. See *Detroit Free Press,* 17 December 1920.

111. *Detroit News,* 3 December 1917.

112. *Detroit Free Press,* 8, 22 November 1920.

113. *Detroit Free Press,* 11, 18 September 1921. Walter "Tillie" Voss was born in Detroit on March 28, 1897, and lived most of his life in the city.

114. *Detroit News,* 20 June 1935, p. 38.

115. *Detroit Free Press,* 14 November 1921, p.18.

116. *Detroit Free Press,* 14 November 1921.

117. *Detroit Free Press,* 12 November 1921.

118. *Detroit Free Press,* 6 December 1920, 25 November 1921.

119. *Detroit Free Press,* 30 November 1921.

120. *Detroit Free Press,* 6 December 1921.

121. Technically, Detroit was granted a new franchise on August 1, 1925.

122. On August 16, 1927, the Detroit Panthers suspended operations for one year with league permission. See Horrigan, "Franchise Transactions," 8.

123. *Detroit News,* 15 November 1975, p. 1D. Voss played end/tackle in 86 NFL games and caught 57 passes for 1,123 yards. See Joe Marren, "Buffalo's 2-Sports Guys," *The Coffin Corner* 19, no. 4 (1997): 16. He died in Stuart, Florida, December 14, 1975 at the age of seventy-eight.

124. Richard Bak, *Turkey Stearnes and the Detroit Stars* (Detroit: Wayne State University Press, 1994), pp. 189–91.

125. Cemetery records, Olivet Cemetery and *Detroit Free Press,* 21 July 1954. See Burton Historical Collection, Detroit Public Library, and Detroit News Agency Library for the absence of pictures of Mack Park. There are pictures of the ruins after the July 1929 fire at Mack Park. The *Detroit News* and the *Detroit Times* did carry his obituary on 20 July 1954, p. 25.

Chapter 13

1. *Massillon Independent,* 9 October 1917; *Dayton Daily News,* October–November 1915, 22 November 1972, 2 March 1988; *Dayton Journal Herald,* 30 June 1978; *Columbus Dispatch,* 23 March 1949; Denison University Alumni Affairs Office. David E. Reese was born in Youngstown Hill, a coal mining community near Massillon, Ohio, in 1893. His father was killed in a railroad accident two months before he was born. His mother, determined that David would not follow his father's footsteps into the mines, worked hard to allow him to attend Washington High School in Massillon, where he excelled in sports, particularly football. He enrolled at Denison University in Granville, Ohio, in the fall of 1911, and earned sixteen letters in varsity athletics, four each in football, basketball, baseball, and tennis. In 1914, he was co-captain of the Denison University football team and helped lead the football and basketball teams to Ohio Conference championships that school year. George Roudebush and Carl Thiele were teammates on both teams. After graduating from Denison in the spring of 1915, Reese attended the Ohio College of Dental Surgery at the University of Cincinnati and, at this time, began playing professional football. That fall, he played center and fullback with the Cincinnati Celts and the North Cincinnati Athletic Club, for $25 a game.

2. *Detroit News,* 10 October 1915.

3. *Detroit Free Press,* 18 October 1915.

4. *Dayton Daily News,* 25 October 1915.

5. Virginia Military Institute Archives.

6. *Toledo Blade,* 15 November 1915.

7. *Fort Wayne Journal-Gazette,* 14 November 1915.

8. *Cincinnati Enquirer,* 22 November 1915.

9. *Detroit News Tribune,* 9 October 1916.

10. *Detroit News Tribune,* 1, 6 October 1916.

11. *Detroit Free Press,* 9 October 1916.

12. *Detroit News Tribune,* 9 October 1916.

13. *Ibid.*

14. *Fort Wayne Journal-Gazette,* 29 October 1916.

15. *Fort Wayne Journal-Gazette,* 23 October 1916.

16. Denison University Alumni Affairs Office; *The Miami Student,* 19 November 1914, no. 9; *Columbus Dispatch,* 9 June 1985; *Cleveland Plain Dealer,* 1 March 1992, 10 September 1969; *Cleveland Press,* 2 March 1992; *C. A. C. Journal,* October 1969, pp. 50 ff. George Milton "Roudy" Roudebush was born on his father's farm near Newtonville, Ohio, on January 25, 1894. His family had moved to America from Germany in 1660 and, by 1800, held twenty-four hundred acres in central Ohio. His father also was a member of the board of directors of banks in two small Ohio towns. George played all sports in high school. He enrolled at Denison University in Granville, Ohio, in the fall of 1911, and became one of their all-time great athletes. He earned letters in football, basketball, baseball, and tennis. In 1912, he played quarterback for Denison and began throwing the forward pass with proficiency, first in the game against Otterbein and later in other games as well. In subsequent years, he played halfback and helped Denison win two Ohio Conference championships, one for his 1914 football team and one for his 1915 basketball team. He also played semi-professional baseball while in college, for $25 per

game, but, unlike Jim Thorpe, he did not get caught.

17. *Fort Wayne Journal-Gazette,* 23 October 1916.

18. *Cincinnati Enquirer,* 23 October 1916.

19. *Wabash Plain Dealer,* 16 October 1916; *Lafayette Journal,* 30 October 1916.

20. *Lafayette Journal,* 30 October 1916.

21. *Cincinnati Enquirer,* 30 October 1916.

22. *Cincinnati Enquirer,* 1 November 1916.

23. *Cincinnati Enquirer,* 13 November 1916.

24. *Dayton Journal-Herald,* 30 November 1916.

25. *Cincinnati Enquirer* and *Dayton Daily News,* 20 November 1916.

26. *Cincinnati Enquirer,* 27 November 1916.

27. *Lafayette Journal-Courier,* 20 September 1960; October–November 1915–1917 passim. Eli Fenters was born near Pine Village, Indiana, in 1888. He was introduced to football by C. G. Beckett, a teacher in the Pine Village School. Eli never attended college. Instead, after graduating from high school, he took up farming and played Sunday football for the Pine Village Athletic Club as quarterback for more than fourteen years. His brothers Ray and Roy played left halfback and back-up quarterback. In 1915, a number of out-of-town college stars were added to the lineup. By 1916, the entire Pine Village team was made up of top hired players. Years later, Eli declared, "We became professional in 1915." Eli Fenters played until the team went out of business shortly after World War I. In 1923, at the age of thirty-five, he played semiprofessional football for a Kokomo, Indiana team, continuing with them until 1926. He also played professional basketball during these years. In 1926, he gave up farming and became a carpenter. Later, he worked as a millwright and then in a grain elevator until he retired in 1954.

28. *Cincinnati Enquirer,* 1 December 1916.

29. *Cincinnati Enquirer,* 4 December 1916.

30. *Dayton Journal-Herald,* 3 November 1917.

31. Si Burick's column, *Dayton Daily News,* 22 November 1972; Denison University Alumni Affairs Office.

32. *The Makio,* Ohio State University Yearbook (Columbus, OH: 1915, 1916); *Dayton Daily News,* October–November 1917; *The Ohio State University Monthly,* January 1929. Sorenson was born in Norwood Heights, Ohio, in 1896. After playing with the Celts, he remained in the Cincinnati area, where he owned a car dealership

33. *Philadelphia Inquirer,* 26 September 1966; The University Archives and Record Center, University of Pennsylvania. Hopkins had grown up in Cincinnati and graduated from the University of Pennsylvania, in 1916, where he played varsity football for three years while earning a mechanical engineering degree. Hopkins would later become a navy pilot in World War I, earn a Master's Degree in aeronautical engineering at MIT, and retire as vice president of R. S. Products of Philadelphia in 1959.

34. *Detroit Free Press,* 15 October 1917.

35. *Fort Wayne Journal-Gazette,* 17, 21 October 1917.

36. *Fort Wayne Journal-Gazette,* 17 October 1917.

37. *Lafayette Journal,* 29 October 1917.

38. *Pittsburgh Gazette-Times,* 5 November 1917.

39. *Dayton Daily News,* 12 November 1917.

40. *Dayton Daily News,* 25 November 1917.

41. *Dayton Journal-Herald,* 26 November 1917.

42. *Dayton Daily News* and *Dayton Journal,* 26 November 1917.

43. *Dayton Journal-Herald,* 2 December 1917.

44. Horrigan, "Franchise Transactions," 4, 11.

Chapter 14

1. Carroll, *The Tigers Roar.*

2. *Ibid.* Blondy Wallace was a second-team Walter Camp All-American while at the University of Pennsylvania and, in 1905, was coaching linemen at his alma mater. At six feet two inches and 240 pounds, Blondy was a giant by the standards of the day.

3. Cusack, *Pioneer in Pro Football.*

4. *Ibid.*

5. *Akron Beacon Journal,* 16 November 1914.

6. *Massillon Independent,* 5 October 1915.

7. *The Makio,* Ohio State University Yearbook (Columbus, OH: 1910).

8. *The Makio,* Ohio State University Yearbook (Columbus, OH: 1909–12).

9. *Canton Repository,* 19, 20 November 1952.

10. *Canton Repository,* 11 October 1915.

11. *Ibid.*

12. *Massillon Independent,* 18 October 1915.

13. *Detroit News Tribune,* 25 October 1916.

14. *Canton Repository,* 25 October 1915.

15. *Canton Repository,* 22, 19 November 1915; Porter, *Biographical Dictionary,* 420–21; E. Lee North, *Battling the Indians, Panthers, and Nittany Lions* (Washington, PA: Washington and Jefferson College, 1976); and Cusack, *Pioneer in Pro Football.*

16. Kellison died May 7, 1971. *Canton Repository,* October–November, 1915–17 passim; Cusack, *Pioneer in Pro Football;* Treat, *Official Encyclopedia of Football.*

17. Indiana University Archives; Erick Bergvall, ed., and Edward Adams Roy, trans., *The Fifth Olympiad. The Official Report of the Olympic Games of Stockholm 1912,* (Stockholm: Wahlstrom & Wildstrand, 1913), pp. 409–10.

18. Cusack, *Pioneer in Pro Football,* 12.

19. *Massillon Independent,* 4 September 1903.

20. Carroll, *The Tigers Roar.*

21. *Ibid.*

22. Dick Johnson, *Columbus Discovers Football* (Columbus, OH: All American Archives, 1972), p. 5.

23. Carroll, *The Tigers Roar.*

24. *Ibid.*

25. Bob Carroll, *The Ohio League: 1910–1919* (North Huntington, PA: Professional Football Researchers Association, 1997), p. 35.

26. Massillon High School Yearbook, 1913. Becker was a recent graduate from Massillon High School, where he had been a football and basketball player, admired as a "good looker" who "handles himself well" and was "not one of the backward kind" when it came to girls.

27. Oral history records, Massillon Public Library.

28. *Massillon Independent,* 2 October 1915.

29. Cusack, *Pioneer in Pro Football.*

30. *Massillon City Directory,* 1915.

31. *Cleveland Leader,* 26 November 1914. Newly married to Tillie Navorek of Cleveland on the eve of the Ohio Championship game, Collins was pleased to have the job as player-coach of the new Massillon team.

32. Unpublished records, Massillon Public Library.

33. *Detroit Free Press,* 8 October 1915.

34. *Massillon Independent,* 5 October 1915; *Canton Repository,* 7 October 1915.

35. *Detroit Free Press,* 8 October 1915.

36. *Massillon Independent,* 19 October 1915.

37. Western Reserve University Archives; University of Michigan Archives; University of Notre Dame Archives; *Massillon Independent,* 14 December 1979, 11, 24 October 1915, 5 November 1915. Boerner became a captain in the U.S. Army during World War I and in 1924 became a captain in the Massillon Fire Department. Boerner helped to erect the first electric sign in Massillon and was a member of St. Mary's Catholic Church. This single game with the Massillon Tigers was one of the highlights of his life.

38. *Massillon Independent,* 5, 9 October 1915.

39. *Massillon Independent,* 8 October 1915.

40. *Massillon Independent,* 4 October 1915.

41. *Massillon Independent,* 9 October 1915.

42. *Massillon Independent,* 11, 12 October 1915.

43. *Massillon Independent,* 3 October 1915.

44. *Massillon Independent,* 20 October 1915.

45. *Massillon Independent,* 23 October 1915.

46. *Detroit Free Press,* 25 October 1915.

47. Cleveland Board of Education Archives.

48. *Detroit Free Press,* 25 October 1915.

49. *Massillon Independent,* 16 October 1915.

50. *Massillon Independent,* 27 October 1915.

51. *Massillon Independent,* 28 October 1915.

52. *Massillon Independent,* 1 November 1915.

53. Massillon fans left Canton Sunday morning over the Wheeling and Lake Erie Railroad at 10:35 and returned to Harmon, Ohio, at 5:40 where they made connections with a Massillon street car and arrived back in Massillon at 7:25 P.M. *Massillon Independent,* 5 November 1915.

54. *Massillon Independent,* 8 November 1915.

55. *Canton Repository,* 12 November 1915.

56. *Bloomington Herald-Telephone,* 24 November 1979.

57. *Canton Repository,* 14 November 1915.

58. *Canton Repository,* 15 November 1915.

59. *Ibid.*

60. *Canton Repository,* 15, 16 November 1915.

61. Alumni Records, Colgate University. Earl Abell later coached and directed athletics at the Virginia Military Academy before managing the Beaver Canning Company in Beaver Dam, Wisconsin. In the 1920s, he coached at the University of Virginia, Mississippi College, and Colgate before becoming an executive with the American Can Company.

62. *Collier,* 7 December 1915.

63. *Racine Daily Times,* 5 October 1915; *Racine Journal-News,* 12 October 1915; *Canton Daily News,* 24 November 1914.

64. *The Holcad,* Michigan Agricultural College newspaper, 1913–15.

65. *South Bend Tribune,* 22 November 1915.

66. *Massillon Independent,* 26 November 1915.

Chapter 15

1. Grantland Rice, *Collier's,* 9 December 1939.

2. Myron Cope, *The Game That Was: The Early Days of Professional Football* (New York: World Publishing Company, 1970), p. 39.

3. Walter Camp, *Collier's,* 18 December 1915.

4. *University of Wisconsin Alumni Directory,* 1921.

5. John T. Brady, *The Heisman* (New York: Athenaeum Books, 1984).

6. *Canton Repository,* 19 November 1952. Dutch Speck and Jim hunted together and ran together while on the road. Speck began playing for pay in 1904 and played professionally until 1926 when he retired from the game he loved to become deputy Sheriff, then an iron worker, and finally a union official.

7. *Alumni Catalogue, List of Graduates, 1857–1930,* Michigan State College Bulletin (Lansing, MI: Hallenbeck Printing Co., 1931), p. 70. Later he became assistant director of physical education at Hampton Institute in Virginia.

8. *Canton Daily News,* 29 November 1915.

9. *Canton Repository,* 30 November 1915.

10. *Canton Repository,* 29 November 1915.

11. *Canton Daily News, Canton Repository, Massillon Independent,* 29 November 1915 were the sources for what follows.

12. *Canton Repository,* 30 November 1915.

13. Cusack, *Pioneer in Pro Football.*

Chapter 16

1. *Decatur Review,* 20 October 1916.

2. *The Makio,* Ohio State University Yearbook (Columbus, OH: 1912–15). Boyd V. "Bill" Cherry was born in 1894 and grew up in Columbus, Ohio. His parents later moved to the Hyde Park neighborhood of Chicago. Enrolling at Ohio State University in 1911, Boyd stood six feet one inch tall and weighed 165 pounds while playing end in college, and was All-Ohio from 1912 to 1914. In October 1915, he played four games for the Massillon Tigers, before graduating in the spring of 1915.

3. *The Makio,* 1913–15; *The Ohio State University Monthly,* April 1937, September 1939, January 1942, May 1942, May 1944, October 1987. Campbell John "Honus" Graff was born in Hamilton, Ohio, in 1892. He enrolled at Ohio State in engineering in 1912. At six feet tall and 185 pounds, he played football all four years and was captain in 1914. He also lettered in basketball, baseball, and track. When he graduated in 1916, his honors thesis was on hydroelectric power development and traction. In 1917, he married Stella Rogers and had three children. His two sons were later on the Ohio State University football team, and one was its captain. Honus became an industrial engineer, a manufacturer's representative, and a contractor of building specialties in Columbus, Ohio. In 1937, he was a member of the board of overseers for Ohio State University. He was also head of an Oil-O-Matic burner sales agency and sold overhead doors, kitchen cabinets, and medicine cabinets. In 1942 and 1944, he was placed on the Athletic Board of Ohio State. In 1987, he became

a member of the Ohio State University Sports Hall of Fame.

4. *The Makio*, (1910, 1911). Arthur L. Schieber, considered one of the most versatile players on the squad, grew up in Bucyrus, Ohio, and played end and halfback for Ohio State University in 1910–11, where he graduated with a degree in electrical engineering.

5. *Cleveland Plain Dealer*, 25 September 1916.

6. *Washington Post*, 20 November 1916.

7. *Toledo Blade*, 28 September 1916.

8. Howard L. Beck grew up in Shelby, Ohio, and attended Washington and Jefferson College from 1911 to 1914. Washington and Jefferson College Archives.

9. *Cleveland Leader*, 9 October 1916.

10. *Cleveland Plain Dealer*, 16 October 1916.

11. *Ibid.*

12. *Cleveland Plain Dealer*, 23 October 1916.

13. *Ibid.*

14. *Cleveland Plain Dealer*, 29, 30 October 1916.

15. Oberlin College Archives.

16. *The Makio* (1913, 1914, 1915); *Columbus Dispatch*, October–December 1915; *Cleveland Plain Dealer*, 29 October 1916.

17. *The Makio* (1912, 1914, 1915); *Ohio State University Monthly*, February 1926, October 1926, February 1929, November 1929, December 1933, February 1934, October, 1935.

18. *Cleveland Plain Dealer*, 29 October 1916.

19. *Cleveland Plain Dealer*, 30 October 1916.

20. *Canton Repository*, 1 October 1916.

21. *Canton Repository*, 2 October 1916.

22. Georgetown University Archives.

23. *Canton Repository*, 1 October 1916.

24. *Massillon Independent*, 14 October 1916.

25. *Pittsburgh Press*, 1 October 1916.

26. *Georgetown College Journal*, 14 (1912–13): 139.

27. *Canton Repository*, 2 October 1916.

28. *Canton Repository*, 9 October 1916.

29. *Canton Repository*, 16 October 1916.

30. *Canton Repository*, 23 October 1916.

31. Carl Rambaud worked in the building trades as a molder. In later years he married Irene, and he and his brothers owned Rambaud Wallpaper and Paint in Massillon. See *Massillon City Directory*, 1915, 1920, 1923.

32. *Massillon Independent*, 9 October 1916.

33. *Detroit Free Press*, 15 October 1922.

34. *The New York Times*, 7 May 1942; *Massillon Independent*, October–November 1916, October–December 1917; *Fort Wayne Journal Gazette*, November 1916; University of Notre Dame Archives.

35. *Massillon Independent*, 11 October 1916; *Toledo Blade*, 20 October 1916.

36. *Massillon Independent*, 16 October 1916.

37. *Massillon Independent*, 23 October 1916.

38. *Massillon Independent*, 14, 28 October 1916.

39. *Detroit Free Press*, 30 October 1916.

40. *Detroit Free Press*, 29, 30 October 1916.

41. *Massillon Independent*, 30 October 1916.

42. *Canton Repository*, 30 October 1916.

43. *Massillon Independent*, 4 November 1916.

44. *Youngstown Vindicator*, 6 November 1916.

45. *Massillon Independent*, 6 November 1916.

46. *Massillon Independent*, 10 November 1916.

47. *Massillon Independent*, 13 November 1916.

48. *Ibid.*

49. *L'Agenda*, Bucknell University Yearbook, (Lewisburg, PA: 1914, 1915).

50. *L'Agenda*. (1915), 50.

51. *Massillon Independent*, 13 November 1916.

52. *Canton Repository*, 5 November 1916.

53. *Canton Repository*, 5 November 1916.

54. Cusack, *Pioneer in Pro Football*.

55. *Cleveland Plain Dealer*, 6 November 1916.

56. *Canton Repository*, 6 November 1916.

57. *Cleveland Plain Dealer*, 5 November 1916.

58. *Ibid.*

59. *Massillon Independent*, 22 November 1916.

60. See *Cleveland Plain Dealer*, 19 November 1916, for this uncovering of assumed names.

61. *Canton Repository*, 13 November 1916.

62. *Cleveland Plain Dealer*, 13 November 1916.

63. Cusack, *Pioneer in Pro Football*, p. 5.

64. *Cleveland Plain Dealer*, 12 November 1916.

65. *Cleveland Plain Dealer*, 13 November 1916.

66. It was later reported that the player who scored the touchdown the extra point was actually Butchy Barron, not Lowe.

67. *Cleveland Plain Dealer*, 12, 19 November 1916.

68. *Canton Repository*, 13 November 1916.

69. *Aurora Daily Beacon-News*, 12 November 1916, p. 9.

70. For example, see *Chicago Evening Post*, 17 October 1917.

71. Jane R. Smith, "Triumph and Tragedy," *American History* 32, no. 2 (May–June 1997): 34 ff.

72. Frank G. Menke, *The Encyclopedia of Sports* (New York: A. S. Barnes and Company, 1953 and 1975), p. 403.

73. *Dayton Daily News*, 29 October 1916; Newcombe, *Best of the Athletic Boys*; Cusack, *Pioneer in Pro Football*.

74. *Youngstown Vindicator*, 28 October 1915.

75. *Canton Repository*, 20 November 1916.

76. *Massillon Independent*, 22 November 1916; *Canton Repository*, 20, 26 November 1916.

77. *Canton Repository*, 26 November 1916; *Detroit Free Press*, 16 November 1921; *Alumni Catalogue List of Graduates, 1857–1930*, Michigan State College Bulletin (Lansing, MI: Hallenbeck Printing Co., 1931), p. 65; Hoffman and Bielot, *Spartan Football*, 26–27. Later, Julian developed tuberculosis and was confined to a sanitarium in Rochester, Michigan, for several years, before recovering, working for the State of Michigan Department of Agriculture, and going on to become president of the Downtown Coaches Association and the Michigan State University Alumni Association in 1938–40.

78. Newcombe, *Best of the Athletic Boys*.

79. *Canton Repository* and *Massillon Independent*, 27 November 1916.

80. *Canton Repository*, 27 November 1916.

81. *Massillon Independent*, 27 November 1916.

82. *Ibid.*

83. Washington and Jefferson College, Public Information Office; North, *Battling the Indians*, 11.

84. The players present were W. (Fats) Keiser,

Pud Day, J. P. Mattern, A. A. Wesbecher, Fritz Heyman, Skeet Lambert, Lou Hayes, Carl L. Thiele, Robert A. Nash, H. Parker Talman, C. Meyer, Ed Kagy, Red Fleming, and John J. Donahue.

85. *Massillon Independent*, 1 December 1916.

86. *Massillon Independent*, 24 November 1916.

87. *Cleveland Plain Dealer*, 2 December 1916.

88. *Youngstown Telegram*, 2 December 1916.

89. *Cleveland Plain Dealer*, 1 December 1916; also see chapter on assumed names.

90. Cusack, *Pioneer in Pro Football*, p. 23.

91. *Canton Repository*, 3 December 1916.

92. *Cleveland Plain Dealer*, 4 December 1916.

93. *Cincinnati Enquirer*, 13 November 1916.

94. *Massillon Independent*, 23 October 1916.

95. *Massillon Independent*, 15 November 1916.

96. *Cleveland Plain Dealer*, 20 November 1916.

97. *Cleveland Plain Dealer*, 20 November 1916. Washington and Lee University Archives report that no Mayer played football for that school.

98. *Massillon Independent*, 20 November 1916.

99. *Canton Repository*, 20 November 1916.

100. *Cleveland Plain Dealer*, 26 November 1916.

101. *Toledo Blade*, 30 November 1916.

102. *Cleveland Plain Dealer*, 22 November 1916.

103. *Cleveland Plain Dealer*, 2 December 1916; *Canton Repository*, 17 November 1916.

104. *Detroit Free Press*, 31 November 1916.

105. *Toledo Blade*, 1 December 1916.

106. *Toledo Blade*, 1 December 1916.

107. *Toledo Blade*, 1 December 1916; *Cleveland Plain Dealer*, 19 November 1916.

108. *Detroit Free Press*, 1 December 1916.

109. *Cleveland Plain Dealer*, 1 December 1916.

110. *Toledo Blade*, 4 December 1916.

111. *Toledo Blade* and *Cleveland Plain Dealer*, 4 December 1916.

112. *Minneapolis Journal*, 28, 29 November 1916.

113. *Minneapolis Tribune*, 29 October 1916; *Minneapolis Journal*, 21 November 1915, 3 December 1916.

114. *Cincinnati Enquirer*, 13 November 1916.

115. The principle financial backers of the 1916 Cleveland football team were Sam Bernard, vice-president of the Cleveland Baseball Club, and a sportsman, Slayman. See *Massillon Independent*, 20 October 1916.

Chapter 17

1. Princeton University Archives; University of Detroit-Mercy Archives; *Akron Beacon Journal*, October–November 1916. John Larsen was born in Chicago on August 17, 1889. He attended McHenry High School, Evanston Academy, and Notre Dame before graduating from Princeton in 1916. *Nassau Herald*, 1916, p. 157–58.

2. *Minneapolis Journal*, 5 November 1914.

3. *Akron Beacon Journal*, October–November 1909, October–November 1914, 12 March 1967; *Massillon Independent*, 11 October 1915, 10 November 1916; *Detroit Free Press*, 15 November 1916; *Columbus Dispatch*, 25 October 1915, 15 November 1915; Ralph Hickock, *Who Was Who in American Sports* (New York: Hawthorn Books, 1971). During the 1930s, Alfred went to work for the Middleton

Plumbing Company in Akron and remained with them until he retired. He married an Akron girl, Nellie, and had one son and two daughters, seven grandchildren and five great-grandchildren at the time of his death on March 11, 1967.

4. *Buch-tel*, Buchtel College Yearbook, (Akron, OH: 1913–16); *The Holcad*, Michigan Agriculture College newspaper, 3 November 1913; *Canton Repository*, October–November 1916.

5. *Akron Beacon Journal*, 2 October 1917.

6. *Canton Repository*, 15 October 1917.

7. *Canton Repository*, 17 October 1917.

8. *Cleveland Plain Dealer*, 21 October 1917.

9. *Massillon Independent*, 24 October 1917.

10. *Massillon Independent* and *Akron Beacon Journal*, 27 October 1917.

11. *Wolverine*, Michigan Agricultural College Yearbook, (East Lansing, MI: 1912).

12. Westminster College Archives.

13. *Fort Wayne Journal-Gazette*, 10, 16 October 1916, 10 November 1917; *Akron Beacon Journal*, 27 October 1917, Dietrich, *Down Payments*.

14. *Massillon Independent*, 27 October 1917.

15. *Akron Beacon Journal*, 2 October 1917; *Massillon Independent*, 29 October 1917.

16. Indiana University Archives; *Akron Beacon Journal*, 27, 29 October 1917.

17. *Massillon Independent*, 23 October 1917.

18. *Massillon Independent*, 24 October 1917.

19. *Massillon Independent*, 26 October 1917.

20. *Akron Beacon Journal*, 29 October 1917.

21. *Massillon Independent*, 29 October 1917.

22. *Ibid.*

23. *Akron Beacon Journal*, 29 October 1917.

24. *Akron Beacon Journal*, 30 October 1917.

25. *Akron Beacon Journal*, 3 November 1917.

26. *Akron Beacon Journal*, 2 November 1917; *Buffalo Courier*, 5 November 1917.

27. *Akron Beacon Journal*, 3 November 1917.

28. Dietrich, *Down Payments*.

29. *Buffalo Courier*, 5 November 1917.

30. *Massillon Independent*, 6 November 1917; *Buffalo Enquirer*, 5 November 1917, p. 12; *Buffalo Courier*, 5 November 1917.

31. *Canton Repository*, 9 November 1917.

32. *Akron Beacon Journal* and *Massillon Independent*, 12 November 1917.

33. *Akron Beacon Journal*, 9 November 1917.

34. *Canton Repository*, 9 November 1917; *Akron Beacon Journal*, 12 November 1917.

35. *Canton Repository* and *Akron Beacon Journal*, 12 November 1917.

36. *Ibid.*

37. *Akron Beacon Journal*, 12 November 1917.

38. *Ibid.*

39. *Massillon Independent*, 15 November 1917.

40. *Akron Beacon Journal*, 19 November 1917.

41. *Massillon Independent*, 19 November 1917.

42. See *Joliet Evening Herald-News*, 27 November 1917, p. 10, for commentary on how "sand-lot star outpoints Charley Brickley."

43. *Akron Beacon-Journal*, 19 November 1917; Washington and Jefferson College Archives; *The Reporter*, 19 December 1933. Red joined the U.S. Marines, undertook parachute training, and coached the Marine Corps football team at Quan-

tico in 1918. After the war, he coached at Virginia Military Institute for a year. Ultimately, he returned to Belleville, Pennsylvania, where he died at the age of forty-four, eight days after taking a job with the State Highway Department.

44. *Akron Beacon-Journal*, 26 November 1917.

45. As usual, tickets for the game were available at the Howe, Hamilton, Gothic and Long, and Taylor cigar stores in downtown Akron. *Akron Beacon-Journal*, 26 November 1917.

46. James M. Flynn was born in Hoboken, New Jersey, on December 24, 1882. His family moved to Denver, Colorado, and then to Pueblo where he became a fireman and took up professional boxing when he was 18 years old. See *Detroit Free Press*, 5 November 1911, p. 19.

47. *Massillon Independent*, 30 November 1917.

48. Horrigan, "Franchise Transactions," 3–8.

Chapter 18

1. *Canton Repository*, 8 October 1917.

2. Ollie Dreisbach was second-team All-Ohio for the Municipal University of Akron in 1916. See *Cincinnati Enquirer*, December 3, 1916.

3. *Canton Repository*, 15 October 1917.

4. *Ibid.*

5. *Massillon Independent*, October–December 1916–17 passim; Treat, *Official Encyclopedia of Football*, 26, 29, 32, 35.

6. Lehigh University Special Collections.

7. *Massillon Independent*, 13 October 1917.

8. *Massillon Independent*, 15 October 1917.

9. *Massillon Independent*, 19 October 1917.

10. *Massillon Independent*, 20 October 1917.

11. *Massillon Independent*, 22 October 1917.

12. *Pittsburgh Press*, 9 October 1916; *Pittsburgh Gazette Times*, 15 October 1917; *Massillon Independent*, 29 October 1917, 1, 5, 17, 19 November 1917, 1 December 1917; *Cleveland Plain Dealer*, October 1920,1921; Hickok, *Who Was Who*.

13. *Canton Repository*, 22 October 1917.

14. *Youngstown Vindicator*, 27 October 1917.

15. Newcombe,*Best of the Athletic Boys*, 195.

16. *Pittsburgh Press*, 14 October 1917; *Pittsburgh Gazette-Times*, 7 November 1917; Cusack, *Pioneer in Pro Football*.

17. *Canton Repository*, 19 November 1952.

18. *Canton Repository*, 5 November 1917.

19. *Ibid.*

20. *Pittsburgh Gazette-Times*, 5 November 1917.

21. *Massillon Independent*, 1 November 1917.

22. *Massillon Independent*, 6 November 1917.

23. *Youngstown Vindicator*, 27 October 1917.

24. *Ibid.*

25. *Massillon Independent* and *Youngstown Telegram*, 12 November 1917.

26. *Youngstown Vindicator*, 29 October 1917. Brickley had recently married Kathryn Taylor at the Church of the Blessed Sacraments on Long Island, surrounded by brothers who were already in the armed services.

27. *Canton Repository*, 19 November 1917.

28. *Massillon Independent*, 19 November 1917.

29. *Massillon Independent*, 24 November 1917.

30. *Massillon Independent*, 21 November 1917.

31. *Massillon Independent*, 24 November 1917.

32. *Canton Repository*, 26 November 1917.

33. *Canton Repository*, 27 November 1917.

34. *Ibid.*

35. *Canton Repository*, 26 November 1917.

36. *Canton Repository*, 27 November 1917.

37. *Toledo Blade*, 29 November 1917.

38. *Massillon Independent*, 30 November 1917.

39. *Massillon Independent*, 26 November 1917.

40. *Detroit News*, 26 November 1917.

41. *Detroit Free Press*, 25 November 1917.

42. *Detroit Free Press*, 1 December 1917.

43. *Canton Repository*, 30 November 1917.

44. *Cleveland Plain Dealer*, 22 September 1961, October 1917; *Massillon Independent*, 3 December 1917; *Cleveland Leader*, 11 November 1912; University of Notre Dame Archives; *Canton Repository*, 4 December 1917; *Toledo Blade*, 24 November 1916. Stanley Cofall returned to Cleveland in 1929 to work for Standard Oil of Ohio. He formed the Stanco Oil Company in 1931. It later purchased the National Solvent Corporation, which he held until his death. In 1944, he was named to the Cleveland Boxing Commission and served in that capacity for several years. In 1947, he was named to the State Liquor Commission by the governor; later in the year, he resigned that post to devote more time to his business. He died September 21, 1961, at the age of seventy-six, of a heart attack.

45. Irving Rogers, son of the secretary and general adjuster of the Standard Fire Insurance Company, was born in Trenton, New Jersey, on February 7, 1896. After attending the State Model School in Trenton, he entered Princeton in the fall of 1913 and dropped out of school at the end of the academic year. An older and younger brother both graduated from Princeton. Irving worked as a law clerk and stenographer for John A. Roebling's in Trenton until 1930 when he moved to San Diego, where he worked in the U.S. Naval Hospital, then entered the insurance business. He owned and played a Stradivarius violin and played piano for his church, the Open Bible Assembly. He died November 16, 1967. Princeton University Archives.

46. *Massillon Independent*, 1 December 1917.

47. *Massillon Independent*, 3 December 1917.

48. *Canton Repository*, 4 December 1917.

49. *Massillon Independent*, 3 December 1917.

50. *Massillon Independent*, 3 December 1917.

51. Cusack, *Pioneer in Pro Football*, p. 27.

52. Treat, *Official Encyclopedia of Football*, 23.

53. *Ibid.*, 26.

54. Cusack, *Pioneer in Pro Football*, 28.

55. Horrigan, "Franchise Transactions," 6.

56. *Ibid.*, 7.

57. *Detroit Times*, 17 May 1929, p. 27. Tragically, Ben Jones died on May 17, 1929, at the age of thirty-one, from the ill effects of the anesthesia administered at the Cleveland Clinic for a tonsil operation.

58. Treat, *Official Encyclopedia of Football*, 41–42.

59. Horrigan, "Franchise Transactions," 8.

Chapter 19

1. *Davenport Daily Times,* 13 October 1916; *Davenport Democrat and Leader,* 6 November 1916.

2. *Moline Dispatch,* 20 November 1911.

3. *Davenport Daily Times,* 11 September 1916.

4. *Scott County Heritage* (Davenport, IA: privately published, 1991). The Littig family was one of the area's pioneer families, having moved to the Tri-cities area in 1838. At the age of nineteen, Littig's grandfather had fought under Napoleon Bonaparte before emigrating to New Orleans, in 1836, and subsequently moving to Stephenson, Illinois (now Rock Island) in 1838. In 1847, his grandfather built the first brewery in Rock Island and, in 1866, built the Eagle Brewery in Davenport.

Littig's father owned a 360-acre farm in what became Davenport and, at one point, held 560 acres of land in Scott County. Victor Louis Littig was one of seventeen children fathered by John Littig. He attended college in the east before becoming a sportswriter and teacher.

5. *Davenport Daily Times,* 12 October 1916.

6. *Davenport Daily Times,* 13 October 1916

7. *Davenport Daily Times,* 12 October 1916.

8. *Davenport Daily Times,* 18 September 1916.

9. Davenport High School Yearbooks, 1912–16.

10. Saint Ambrose College Archives.

11. Edgar Rumberg grew up in Monmouth, Illinois, where his family belonged to the Swedish Lutheran Church. He did not graduate from high school and moved to Davenport, Iowa, to work in about 1913. Correspondence with the Warren Country Illinois Genealogical Society, Monmouth, Illinois, and *Monmouth Review Atlas,* 29 June 1931.

12. Albert Herman Miller played for the University of Nebraska in 1910. University of Nebraska Archives and Special Collection. In 1916 he was a bookkeeper at the Sieg Iron Company in Davenport, Iowa. *Polk's Directory of Davenport* (Davenport, IA: R. L. Polk & Co., 1916), p. 576.

13. *Monmouth City Directory,* 1911–12, *Polk's Directory of Davenport,* 1916; Knox College Archives. Fred became a department store clerk in his hometown and later at Neustadt's Department Store in Davenport. Later, he helped guide his brother into a career in profootball, and, after his football career, he married Myrtle J. They moved to Chicago, where he died on June 9, 1958. (Earp family genealogy, Warren Co. Public Library, Monmouth, IL.) Fred Earp's younger brother Francis Lewis Earp was also a football player and played for the Rock Island Independents and the Green Bay Packers after playing for four years at Monmouth College. He later was inducted into the Green Bay Packers Hall of Fame. John B. Torinus, *The Packard Legend: An Inside Look* (Neshkoro, WI: Laranmark Press, 1982); *Monmouth College Oracle,* 25 September 1917; *Monmouth College Ravelings,* Monmouth College Yearbook, (Monmouth, IL: 1917–22).

14. *Davenport Daily Times,* 2 October 1916.

15. *Davenport Democrat and Leader,* 9 October 1916.

16. *Davenport Daily Times,* 5, 7 October 1916.

17. *Rock Island Argus,* 14 October 1915.

18. *Ibid.*

19. *Davenport Democrat and Leader,* 9 October 1916.

20. *Davenport Daily News,* 13 October 1916.

21. *Davenport Daily Times,* 16 October 1916.

22. *Davenport Democrat and Leader,* 16 October 1916.

23. *Ibid.*

24. Holy Cross University Archives; St. Ambrose University Archives.

25. *Davenport Daily Times,* 17 October 1916.

26. *Davenport Daily Times,* 18 October 1916.

27. *Davenport Daily Times,* 20 October 1916.

28. *Davenport Daily Times,* 23 October 1916.

29. *Davenport Democrat and Leader,* 23 October 1916.

30. *Davenport Democrat and Leader,* 26 October 1916.

31. *Davenport Democrat and Leader,* 29 October 1916.

32. *Rock Island Argus,* 30 October 1916.

33. *Davenport Democrat and Leader,* 30 October 1916.

34. *Davenport Democrat and Leader,* 30 October 1916; 6 November 1916.

35. *Davenport Democrat and Leader,* 30 October 1916.

36. *Davenport Democrat and Leader,* 1 November 1916.

37. *Davenport Daily Times,* 4 November 1916.

38. Cornell University Archives.

39. *Davenport Democrat and Leader,* 5 November 1916.

40. *Davenport Democrat and Leader,* 6 November 1916.

41. *Ibid.*

42. *Davenport Democrat and Leader,* 10 November 1916.

43. *Davenport Democrat and Leader,* 13 November 1916.

44. *Davenport Daily Times,* 30 November 1916.

45. *Ibid.*

46. *Davenport Daily Times* and *Hammond Times,* 20 November 1916.

47. *Davenport Daily Times,* 20 November 1916.

48. *Ibid.*　　　49. *Ibid.*

50. *Davenport Daily Times,* 21 November 1916.

51. *Ibid.*

52. *Davenport Democrat and Leader,* 11 December 1916.

53. *Davenport Democrat and Leader,* 4 December 1916.

54. *Badger,* University of Wisconsin Yearbook, (Madison, WI: 1916).

55. *Davenport Democrat and Leader,* 4 December 1916.

56. *Ibid.*

57. *Davenport Daily Times,* 25 November 1916.

58. *Davenport Daily Times,* 29 November 1916.

Chapter 20

1. *Moline Dispatch,* 19 November 1911; *Rock Island Argus,* 29 April 1920. Art Salzmann and his brother Roy, who was also a good football player, were the sons of Louis H. Salzmann, a prominent German Lutheran, who had resided in Rock Island

for more than fifty years. Roy was destined to die in 1918.

2. *Rock Island Argus,* 29 September 1921.

3. *Rock Island Argus,* 28 September 1915.

4. Victor Bredimus lived at 1140 Douglas Avenue in Des Moines and attended Highland Park Methodist Church in 1919. His 20-month-old son died on April 29, 1919. See *Des Moines Register,* 30 April 1919, p. 10.

5. *Rock Island Argus,* 25 November 1915.

6. *Rock Island Argus,* 5 October 1915.

7. *Rock Island Argus,* 13 October 1915.

8. *Rock Island Argus,* 15 November 1915.

9. *Rock Island Argus,* 16 November 1915.

10. *Rock Island Argus,* 26 November 1915.

11. *Rock Island Argus,* 25 November 1915.

12. *Rock Island Argus,* 20 November 1915 and 2 October 1916.

13. *Rock Island Argus,* 2 October 1916.

14. *Rockford Morning Star,* 8 October 1916.

15. *Rock Island Argus,* 2 October 1916; St. Ambrose College Archives.

16. *Davenport Democrat and Leader,* 20 October 1916.

17. *Rock Island Argus,* 9, 16 October 1916.

18. *Rock Island Argus,* 8 October 1916.

19. Jacob K. Lazerous was the son of a Isaac Lazerous, junk dealer. He and his sister were members of a very small contingent of Jewish students at East Des Moines High School, where "Jake" was left end on the football team and a member of the basketball team in 1913–15. *The Quill,* Des Moines East High School Yearbook, May 1915, p. 29. Jake served in the U. S. Navy during World War I and was a policeman in Des Moines in 1926. See R. L. Polk, *Des Moines City Directory* (1919), p. 741, (1926), p. 822, (1932), p. 552.

20. *Rock Island Argus,* 12 October 1916; Cornell University Archives.

21. *The Clinton Herald,* 4 October 1914; 26, 27 November 1914.

22. Osborne said that he had never seen the so-called Minnesota shifts nor had them described to him. "He just woke up one night with it in his mind, figured it out and used it with great success." In 1916, Osborne was head coach at Northwestern College in Naperville, Illinois. See *Davenport Democrat,* 29 September 1916; *Rockford Morning Star,* 1, 12, 16 October 1916.

23. *Rock Island Argus,* 16 October 1916.

24. *Rock Island Argus,* 20 October 1916.

25. *Ibid.*

26. *Rock Island Argus,* 23 October 1916.

27. *Rock Island Argus,* 18 November 1916.

28. *Rock Island Argus* and *Davenport Democrat and Leader,* 30 October 1916.

29. *Rock Island Argus,* 13 November 1916.

30. *Rock Island Argus,* 18 November 1916.

31. Walter C. Brindley was president of his senior class at West Des Moines High School in 1914. He was also captain of the West High football team and on the relay team that set the state record for the mile relay in 1912 and again in 1913. He was later a clerk in the post office, an employee of the Ford Motor Company, and an employee of the Phillips Petroleum Co. See *Tatler,* West Des Moines

High School Yearbook, 1912, 1913, 1914; R. L. Polk, *Des Moines City Directory* (1919), p. 201, (1926), p. 203, (1932), p. 187.

32. *Rock Island Argus,* 20 November 1916.

33. *Rock Island Argus,* 24 September 1917.

34. *Hammond Times,* 22 September 1917.

35. *Ambrosian,* St. Ambrose College Yearbook, (Davenport, IA: 1918, 1919); Holy Cross University Archives. George W. Jones became commander of Battery E and was sent to France where he was gassed during the Meuse Argonne offensive. Jones survived the gassing and returned to Worcester, where he coached the football and track teams at the Worcester Academy. In addition to coaching, he became commander of his American Legion post, ran an unsuccessful race—as a Republican—for county sheriff in 1932, and died on November 7, 1951.

36. *Davenport Democrat and Leader,* 8 October 1917.

37. *Hammond Times,* 15 October 1917.

38. *Des Moines Evening Tribune,* 28 October 1917.

39. *Rock Island Argus,* 5 November 1917.

40. *Davenport Democrat and Leader,* 10 November 1917; *Alumni Directory: Davenport /Central High School: North High; West High* (Norfolk, VA: Bernard C. Harris Publishing Co., 1994); Class Rolls Davenport High School 1913 Commencement; *Badger,* University of Wisconsin Yearbook (Madison, WI: 1917). Note: George W. Koch also played tackle for Davenport H.S. in 1914 and graduated in the class of 1915, and it is possible that he and not his brother played for the Davenport AC

41. *Rock Island Argus,* 12 November 1917.

42. *Davenport Democrat and Leader,* 12 November 1917.

43. *Rock Island Argus,* 19 November 1917.

44. *Hammond Times,* 3 December 1917.

45. *Davenport Democrat and Leader,* 3 December 1917.

46. Horrigan, "Franchise Transactions," 3–8.

Chapter 21

1. An interview with John Dunne in 1916 reported that the Minneapolis Marines were organized in 1905. See *Davenport Democrat and Leader,* 4 December 1916.

2. Newcombe, *Best of the Athletic Boys,* 91.

3. *Minneapolis Journal,* 21 October 1917.

4. Menke, *The Encyclopedia of Sports,* 365; *Michigan All-Time Athletic Record Book*; and McCarty, *All-American.*

5. *Minneapolis Journal,* 22 October 1911, 5 November 1911.

6. Hammer lived at 818 Twenty-Second Avenue South in Minneapolis. Hammer, employed by the *Minneapolis Journal,* was a representative of the Minneapolis Typographical Union and was active in the Union Printers Bowling League. *Minneapolis Journal,* 21 October 1917.

7. *The Cyclone,* Grinnell College Yearbook (Grinnell, IA: 1919), p. 78; *Minneapolis Journal,* 9, 15, 19, 23 November 1914. Oscar M. Solem was born in Minneapolis on December 13, 1891, and graduated from the University of Minnesota in 1915,

after playing end on their football team. After WWII, he coached at Luther College, Drake University, the University of Iowa, Springfield College, and Syracuse University, and was inducted into the College Football Hall of Fame for his coaching contributions. His coaching proteges included Bud Wilkinson, Clarence "Biggie" Munn, and Duffy Daugherty. Solem died October 26, 1970. See *The Big Book of Halls of Fame in the United States and Canada.* Compiled and edited by Paul Soderberg, Helen Washington, Jaques Cattell Press. (New York: R. R. Bowker Co., 1977): p. 825.

8. *Minneapolis Journal,* 12 November 1914.

9. *Minneapolis Journal,* 27 November 1914.

10. *Minneapolis Journal,* 18 November 1915.

11. *Minneapolis Journal,* 15 November 1915.

12. *Minneapolis Journal,* 26 November 1915.

13. *Badger,* University of Wisconsin Yearbook (Madison, WI: 1915, 1917).

14. *Des Moines Evening Tribune,* 5 November 1917.

15. *Minneapolis Tribune,* 16 October 1916.

16. *Minneapolis Tribune,* 23, 29 October 1916; 13, 20, and 27 November 1916.

17. *Minneapolis Tribune,* 23 October 1916.

18. *Minneapolis Tribune,* 29 October 1916.

19. *Minneapolis Tribune,* 30 October 1916.

20. *Minneapolis Tribune,* 13 November 1916.

21. *Minneapolis Tribune,* 20 November 1916.

22. *Minneapolis Tribune,* 24 November 1916.

23. *Minneapolis Journal* and *Minneapolis Tribune,* 27 November 1916.

24. *Minneapolis Tribune* and *Minneapolis Journal,* 24, 26, 29, 30 November 1916.

25. *Minneapolis Journal* and *Minneapolis Tribune,* 1 December 1916.

26. *Minneapolis Journal,* 1 December 1916.

27. *Davenport Democrat* and *Minneapolis Journal,* 4 December 1916.

28. *The Cyclone '19,* Grinnell College Yearbook, (Grinnell, IA: 1920), p. 78.

29. *Des Moines Evening Tribune,* 5 November 1917.

30. *St. Paul Pioneer Press,* 5 October 1917.

31. *Minneapolis Tribune,* 13 October 1917.

32. *Minneapolis Tribune,* 13, 15, 19, 29 October 1917, 5, 8, 12, 25, 26 November 1917; *Minneapolis Journal,* 15, 17, 22, 25, 27, 29 October 1917, 5, 11, 12, 19, 20, 26 November 1917.

33. "Sammies" was a slang term frequently used in 1917 to refer to soldiers, because they worked for "Uncle Sam."

34. *Minneapolis Tribune,* 25, 26 November 1917; *Minneapolis Journal,* 26 November 1917.

35. *Detroit Free Press,* 24 October 1921.

36. *Minneapolis Journal,* 21 October 1917.

37. *Minneapolis Journal,* 3 December 1917.

38. Treat, *Official Encyclopedia of Football,* 25.

39. Horrigan, "Franchise Transactions," 5–8.

40. Treat, *Official Encyclopedia of Football,* 34, 37, 40.

Chapter 22

1. *Racine Journal-News,* 15 October 1915.

2. *The Cyclone '19,* Grinnell College Yearbook (Grinnell, IA: 1920) p. 91; Grinnell College Ar-

chives, Grinnell, Iowa. McEachron went on to become a banker, ultimately becoming vice-president of the Federal Reserve Bank of San Francisco and executive secretary of the Oregon Bankers Association.

3. *Racine Journal-News,* 11 October 1915; 5 November 1915, p. 18.

4. *Toledo Blade,* 30 November 1916; *Racine Journal-News,* 17 November 1917.

5. *Racine Daily Times,* 9 October 1915.

6. *Racine Daily Times,* 4, 6 October 1915.

7. *Racine Daily Times,* 9 October 1915.

8. *Racine Daily Times,* 2 October 1915.

9. *Racine Journal-News,* 11 October 1915.

10. *Racine Daily News,* 9 October 1915.

11. *Racine Journal-News,* 11 October 1915.

12. *Racine Journal-News,* 15 October 1915.

13. *Racine Journal-News,* 14 October 1915; *University of Illinois Directory,* alumni section, 1916; *Michigan All-Time Athletic Record Book.*

14. *Racine Journal-News,* 18 October 1915.

15. *Ibid.*

16. *Racine Journal-News,* 23 October 1915.

17. *Racine Journal-News,* 22 October 1915.

18. *Racine Journal News,* 25 October 1915.

19. *Fort Wayne Journal-Gazette,* 1 November 1915.

20. *Racine Journal-News,* 6 November 1915.

21. *Racine Journal-News,* 8 November 1915.

22. *Racine Journal-News,* 12 November 1915; *Hammond Times,* 12 November 1915.

23. *Racine Journal-News,* 15 November 1915.

24. *Racine Journal-News,* 6 December 1915.

25. *Racine Journal-News,* 2 October 1916.

26. *Toledo Blade,* 30 November 1916.

27. *Racine Times-Call,* 9 October 1916.

28. *Ibid.*

29. *Racine Journal-News,* 9 October 1916.

30. *Racine Times-Call,* 14 October 1916.

31. *Racine Times-Call,* 23 October 1916.

32. *Hammond Times,* 13 November 1916.

33. *Racine Times-Call,* 13 November 1916.

34. *Racine Times-Call,* 15 November 1916.

35. *Racine Times-Call,* 20 November 1916.

36. *Toledo Blade,* 1 December 1916.

37. *Racine Times-Call,* 22 September 1917.

38. *Racine Times-Call,* 19 September 1917.

39. *Racine Times-Call,* 9 October 1917.

40. *Racine Times-Call,* 5 October 1917.

41. *Racine Journal-News,* 15 October 1917.

42. The Hegeman brothers appear to be related to H. J. Hegeman of Hegeman's Grocery. See *Racine Journal-News,* 27 October 1915.

43. *Racine Times-Call,* 13 October 1917.

44. *Racine Times-Call* and *Racine Journal-News,* 15 October 1917.

45. *Racine Times-Call,* 18 October 1917.

46. *Racine Times-Call,* 22 October 1917.

47. *Racine Times-Call,* 22 October 1917.

48. *Hammond Times,* 22 October 1917.

49. *Racine Journal-News* and *Racine Times-Call,* 22 October 1917.

50. *Rock Island Argus,* 29 October 1917.

51. *Chicago Tribune,* 5 November 1917.

52. *Fort Wayne Gazette-Journal,* 12 November 1917.

53. Grover C. "Dovey" Lutter became a deputy sheriff in 1918, got married to Helen J. by 1921, and was a loader at H & M Body Corp. in 1925. See *Polk's Racine Directory*, (Racine, WI: R. L. Polk & Co., 1918, 1921, and 1925).

54. *Racine Journal-News*, 12 November 1917.

55. *Racine Journal-News*, 19 November 1917.

56. *Green Bay Press-Gazette*, 12 November 1917.

57. Torinus, *The Packard Legend*.

58. Horrigan, "Franchise Transactions," 5–7. Racine forfeited their NFL franchise February 6, 1926.

Chapter 23

1. Of the twenty-one men who played for the Wabash Athletic Association in 1915, only three played college football, five played high school football, and thirteen were limited to sandlot football, primarily with the Wabash Athletic Association. See U.S. Census Records for Wabash and high school year books for Wabash High School in Wabash Public Library.

2. Mickey Erehart later became a physician and his brother, Archie Dean Erehart, was on the 1915 Indiana University football team. Indiana University Archives.

3. Unpublished material from the Wabash County Historical Museum.

4. *Ibid.*   5. *Ibid.*

6. *Wabash Plain Dealer*, 5 October 1917.

7. William "Red" Milliner was born in May 5, 1882, in New Castle, Indiana, but spent most of his life in Wabash. He attended Wabash High School, where he played football in 1898. He served in World War I, married Loretta Hegel on July 24, 1920, and served as fire chief of Wabash from 1922 to 1930. He was a member of the Christian Church. He died of a heart attack on August 3, 1956. *Sejjin, 1898–89*, Wabash High School Yearbook (Wabash, IN: 1899). *Wabash Plain Dealer*, 4 August 1956.

8. *Wabash Plain Dealer*, 7 June 1978; Wabash College Archives; *Fort Wayne Journal-Gazette*, 22 November 1915.

9. Unpublished materials, Wabash County Historical Museum.

10. Rhodes also operated a detective service that recovered stolen horses and livestock. *Fountain-Warren Democrat*, 4 November 1915.

11. *Wabash Plain Dealer*, 2 October 1915.

12. University of Illinois Archives. According to the 1915 University of Illinois yearbook, *The Illio*, Schobinger was "unquestionably one of the greatest college all-around athletes in the country." He was a member of the 1912 U. S. Olympic track team and could run dashes and hurdles or throw the weights. He was the leading pole vaulter in the Western Conference, was on the varsity water polo team, and was an All-Conference fullback.

13. *Wabash Plain Dealer*, 11 October 1915.

14. *Ibid.*

15. *Wabash Plain Dealer*, 18 October 1915.

16. George Yarnelle played football for Wabash High School in 1906 and later attended Culver Military Academy for a short period of time. After serving in the armed services during World War I, he and his brother, Kenneth, joined their father in operating their family owned lumber yard. He died July 11, 1959. *The Sycamore, 1906*, Wabash High School Yearbook, (Wabash, IN: 1906); *Wabash Plain Dealer*, 12 July 1959. Oscar Bricker graduated from Wabash High School in 1906 and worked for the Wabash Gas Works. *The Sycamore, 1906*, p. 93. Earnest Scheerer, born in August 1891, was the oldest of three brothers, who later owned and operated Scheerer Brothers Grocery. U.S. Bureau of Census, Wabash Census, 1900; Indiana Associated Telephone Corporation, *Telephone Directory, Wabash, Indiana, August 1932*. Harold W. "Bud" Caldwell was born in Wabash September 18, 1887. He married Edith Lucille Webb in St. Joseph, Michigan, on January 14, 1912. He belonged to the South Side EUB Church, the Moose and Eagles lodges, and worked for the Railway Express for 38 years. He died January 28, 1962. *Wabash Plain Dealer*, 29 January 1962.

17. *Wabash Plain Dealer* and *Evanston News-Index*, 25 October 1915.

18. *Fountain Warren-Democrat*, 7 October 1915.

19. *Wabash Plain Dealer*, 1 November 1915.

20. *Wabash Plain Dealer*, 8 November 1915.

21. *Wabash Plain Dealer*, 11 November 1915.

22. *Fort Wayne Journal-Gazette*, 18 November 1915.

23. *Fort Wayne Journal-Gazette*, 19 November 1915.

24. *Fort Wayne Journal-Gazette*, 22 November 1915.

25. *Ibid.*

26. *Wabash Plain Dealer*, 22 November 1915.

27. *Fort Wayne Journal-Gazette*, 22 November 1915.

28. *Ibid.*

29. *Fort Wayne Journal-Gazette* and *Wabash Plain Dealer*, 22 November 1915.

30. *Indianapolis Times*, 22 November 1915.

31. *Wabash Plain Dealer*, 22 November 1915.

32. Homer was captain of the Wabash High School basketball team in 1909 and 1910. According to his high school yearbook, "An athlete—the best in the school, and at his studies he is no fool." See *The Sycamore, 1910; Wabash Plain Dealer*, 7 June 1978. Homer married Hazel Marie Morrow on January 14, 1915, in the home of her father John Morrow, a staunch Republican. Homer T. Showalter began his political career, in 1915, when he organized the Wabash County Young Men's Republican Club. The group soon had more than thirteen hundred members. When Homer T. graduated from Wabash College in the spring of 1916, he returned to his hometown where he entered the monument business with his brother Jim. Later he became an insurance broker. Homer was a well-liked person, many said "a Crackerjack of a person." In the late 1920s, he ran for mayor of Wabash on the slogan, "Homer T.: a Go-Getter! I'm for you. Are you for me? Cast your vote for Homer T." He served as the Mayor of Wabash for ten years. He taught Sunday school from 1921 to 1945, was an officer in the local Kiwanis Club for

thirty-three years, was an active Mason, and was an active Wabash College alumnus and booster. He also organized the Polar Bear Club of Wabash.

33. Paul Purman, "Harper Hailed as Wonder-Man, Wizard of Western College Football Directors," *Joliet Evening Herald-News,* 19 November 1917, p. 6.

34. *South Bend Tribune,* 18 October 1950; University of Notre Dame Archives.

35. Upon graduation in spring 1915, Alfred Bergman played professional baseball. In 1916, he played second base for the Cleveland Americans in the major leagues. He was given an unconditional release by the Cleveland Indians Baseball Team on October 2, 1916, ending his major league baseball career. While serving in the army, he was gassed and then contracted tuberculosis. He spent thirty years in a TB hospital in Fort Wayne, Indiana, unable to leave because of his illness and frequently unable to have visitors. His brother, Arthur "Dutch" Bergman, played football at Notre Dame and played a game or two with the Pine Village Athletic Association. Arthur Bergman ultimately became coach of the Washington Redskins and took them to a National Football League championship. Alfred Bergman conquered TB in 1950 and died on June 21, 1961. University of Notre Dame Archives; *Fort Wayne Journal-Gazette,* 9 October 1917; *Toledo Blade,* 2 October 1916.

36. Fifteen years later, more than one-third of the men who played for the Wabash Athletic Association between 1915 and 1918 still lived and worked in Wabash. See Indiana Associated Telephone Corporation, *Telephone Directory, Wabash, Indiana, August 1932.*

37. *Wabash Plain Dealer,* 1 October 1916.

38. *Wabash Plain Dealer,* 12 October 1916.

39. Henry Schneider, son of Rudolph and Madeline Schneider from Switzerland, was born in Wabash in September 1884 and did not attend Wabash High School. U. S. Bureau of Census, Wabash, 1900; Wabash High School yearbooks.

40. *Wabash Plain Dealer,* 16 October 1916.

41. *Ibid.*

42. *Decatur Review,* 16 October 1916.

43. *Decatur Review,* 15 October 1916.

44. *Decatur Review,* 23 October 1916.

45. *Evanston News-Index,* 23 October 1916; *Wabash Plain Dealer,* 18 October 1916.

46. Frank Gurtner grew up in Wabash and later operated the South Side Grocery Store in Wabash. See Indiana Associated Telephone Corporation, *Telephone Directory, Wabash, Indiana, August 1932.*

47. *Wabash Plain Dealer,* 23 October 1916.

48. *Ibid.*

49. University of Illinois, Archives. A graduate of Sullivan High School in Decatur, Pogue returned home after college to become secretary of the Association on Commerce. Later, he was a lieutenant in the U. S. Army Airforce in World War I, owned a lumber company, a building company, and a development company, became president of the University of Illinois Board of Trustees, and was active in the Democratic Party.

50. *Decatur Review,* 20 October 1916.

51. *Wabash Plain Dealer,* 30 October 1916.

52. *Decatur Herald,* 30 October 1916.

53. *Wabash Plain Dealer,* 6 November 1916.

54. *Ibid.*

55. *Wabash Plain Dealer,* 13 November 1916.

56. *Wabash Plain Dealer,* 5 October 1917.

57. *Wabash Plain Dealer,* 8 October 1917.

58. *Wabash Plain Dealer,* 13 October 1917.

59. Soderberg, Washington, and Press, *Halls of Fame,* 706.

60. *Crawfordsville Journal Review,* 9 December 1977; *Fort Wayne Journal-Gazette,* November 1919 and December–March 1922, 1924; *Detroit News,* 29 January 1923; Herb Schwomeyer, *Hoosier Hysteria* (Greenfield, IN: privately published, 1970); and *Wabash Plain Dealer,* 22 October 1917.

61. *Indianapolis News,* 19 November 1915; University of South Dakota, Special Collections, I. D. Weeks Library. Homer Stonebraker, Pine Village's starting center, was born November 1, 1895. Stonebraker, at six feet four inches tall, led his high school basketball team from Wingate, Indiana, to the state high school basketball championship in 1913 and 1914. Stonebraker was on the All-State team both years. In 1915, 1916, and 1917, he was an All-American basketball player for Wabash College. Stonebraker was still a football and basketball star with Wabash College in the fall of 1917 and was playing illegally. In 1919, he was hired as the coach and starting center for the Fort Wayne Knights of Columbus professional basketball team. Later, he played professional basketball for the Detroit Jerry McCartys, the Fort Wayne Hoosiers, and the Chicago Bruins. He played in the original National Basketball Association, and many considered him the best center to play basketball prior to 1930. When Homer Stonebraker retired from pro basketball in 1928, Abe Saperstein, founder of the Harlem Globetrotters, called him the greatest all-around center he had ever seen. In 1962, Stonebraker was inducted into the Indiana Basketball Hall of Fame. He was sheriff of Cass County for two terms and an executive in the Allison Division of General Motors for thirty-one years. He died of heart ailments on December 8, 1977.

62. *Wabash Plain Dealer,* 22 October 1917.

63. *Ibid.*

64. After the game, Myron Yount entered the army and later served in France. Following the war, he worked for I.J. Case and then International Harvester before entering business for himself in 1940. In 1950, he became a veteran affairs official for the State of Indiana. Franklin College Alumni Office, 1952.

65. *Hammond Times,* 29 October 1917.

66. *Wabash Plain Dealer,* 29 October 1917.

67. *Wabash Plain Dealer,* 12 November 1917.

68. *Wabash Plain Dealer,* 19 November 1917.

69. *Ibid.*

70. *Fort Wayne Journal-Gazette,* 24 November 1917.

71. *Ibid.*

72. *Fort Wayne Journal-Gazette,* 26 November 1917.

73. *Ibid.*

74. *Wabash Plain Dealer,* 30 November 1917.

75. *Hammond Times,* 25, 26 September 1917.

Chapter 24

1. Oriand, *Reading Football*, 232.

2. *Ft. Wayne Journal-Gazette*, 24 November 1916; Menke, *Encyclopedia of Sports*, 368.

3. Soderberg, Washington, and Press, *Halls of Fame*, 821.

4. See *Rockford Morning Star*, 27 September 1914, 23 November 1916. Also see Porter, *Biographical Dictionary*, 476–78.

5. *Chicago Tribune*, 28 October 1916.

6. *Detroit News*, 4 November 1917; Porter,*Biographical Dictionary*, 497.

7. In October 1917, Fred "Duke" Slater, a native of Clinton, Iowa, was accused of stealing a watch while at the University of Iowa gym and was pressured to leave school to avoid legal charges. He stayed in college and went on to become a judge in Cook County, Illinois. For details, see *St. Paul Pioneer Press*, 16 October 1917. For more on his accomplishments, see *Biographical Dictionary of American Sports: Football*. (1987): pp. 550–51.

8. It is interesting to note that all of the African-American professional football players in this era attended predominately white, integrated high schools.

9. *Daily Globe*, 16 September 1904. Also see Edna and Art Rust, *Illustrated History of the Black Athlete* (Garden City, NY: Doubleday and Company, 1985), pp. 227–35.

10. E. Rust and A. Rust, *Black Athlete*, 236.

11. *Minneapolis Journal*, 21 October 1917; *Racine Journal News*, 7 November 1917.

12. *Akron Beacon Journal*, February 17, 1974; E. Rust and A. Rust, *Black Athlete*, 229.

13. *Minneapolis Journal*, 29 October 1916.

14. *New Castle Independent Daily Times*, 13 October 1916.

15. *Racine Journal-News*, 5 October 1915.

16. *Cincinnati Enquirer*, 17 October 1916.

17. *Toledo Blade*, 10 October 1917.

18. *The Almanac*, Toledo Central High School Yearbook (Toledo, OH: 1913), pp. 73, 138, 142, 152. Clarence Fraim, whose nickname was "Smoke," played halfback or fullback on offense, and tackle on defense. He was an outstanding ground gainer and a sure tackler. He graduated from high school in 1913.

19. *Toledo Blade*, 7 October 1916.

20. *Toledo Blade*, 4 October 1916.

21. Roberts, *Black Sports*, November 1975; E. Rust and A. Rust, *Black Athlete*, 227–28.

22. *Wabash Plain Dealer*, 9 October 1916.

23. *The Sycamore, 1910*, Wabash High School Yearbook, Wabash High School Class of 1911 (Wabash, IN: 1910).

24. *Toledo Blade*, 14 October 1916.

25. *Chicago Tribune*, 28 October 1916.

26. E. Rust and A. Rust, *Black Athlete*, 236–40.

27. *Ibid.*

Chapter 25

1. *Fort Wayne Journal-Gazette*, 17 September 1916.

2. Wilfred P. Schoenberg, *Gonzaga University: Seventy-Five years, 1887–1962* (Spokane, WA: Gonzaga University Press, 1971).

3. University of Detroit-Mercy Archives.

4. Schoor, *Notre Dame Football;* Porter, *Biographical Dictionary*, p. 148 ; University of Detroit-Mercy Archives; *Massillon Independent*, November 1915, October–November 1916; *Fort Wayne Gazette-Journal*, November 1916, October–November, 1917. On May 20, 1917, Dorais married Vila Fettgather of Dubuque, and they later had five children. After 1948, he served on the Detroit City Council and operated an automobile agency in Wabash, Indiana. He died in his home in Birmingham, Michigan, on January 4, 1954.

5. *Akron Beacon Journal*, 24 November 1914; *Cleveland Plain Dealer*, 22 September 1961; *Fort Wayne Journal-Gazette*, October–November 1916, 10 October 1917, October 1919.

6. *Fort Wayne Journal-Gazette*, 24 September 1916.

7. *Fort Wayne Journal-Gazette*, 27, 28 September 1916.

8. *Fort Wayne Journal-Gazette*, 2 October 1916.

9. *Fort Wayne Journal-Gazette*, 9 October 1916.

10. *Hammond Times and Fort Wayne Journal-Gazette*, 9 October 1916.

11. *Fort Wayne Journal-Gazette*, 16 October 1916.

12. *Ibid.*   13. *Ibid.*

14. *Fort Wayne Journal-Gazette*, 20 October 1916.

15. *Fort Wayne Journal-Gazette*, 22 October 1916.

16. Sperber, *Shake Down The Thunder*, 52, 368–70, 447–51; *Fort Wayne Journal-Gazette*, 16, 22, 23, 29, 30 October 1916.

17. *Fort Wayne Journal-Gazette*, 23 October 1916.

18. *Fort Wayne Journal-Gazette*, 29 October 1916.

19. *Lafayette Journal*, October–November 1915–17, 1919 passim; Indiana University Archives; Treat, *Official Encyclopedia of Football*, pp. 28, 30, 33. In 1919, he became a practicing physician in Muncie, Indiana.

20. Ivy Chamnese and Burton D. Meyer, *History of Indiana University, 1903–1937*, vol. 2 (Bloomington, IN: Indiana University, 1952).

21. *Fort Wayne Journal-Gazette*, 6 November 1916.

22. *Mirage*, DePauw University Yearbook, DePauw University (Greencastle, IN: 1912).

23. DePauw University Archives and Special Collections; *Akron Beacon Journal*, 6 December 1960. Hawthorne went on to become a physician and surgeon. He moved to Akron, Ohio, in 1921, where he set up a general medical practice and lived the rest of his life. He was married and had four children. He died of a heart attack on December 5, 1960.

24. *Fort Wayne Journal-Gazette*, 4 November 1916.

25. *Fort Wayne Journal-Gazette*, 6 November 1916.

26. *Ibid.*   27. *Ibid.*

28. *Fort Wayne Journal-Gazette*, 10 November 1916.

29. University of Notre Dame Archives. In World War II, Elward was a lieutenant commander in the U. S. Navy. His son, who was also in the navy, was killed in action in 1943.

30. *Fort Wayne Journal-Gazette*, 12 November 1916.

31. *Toledo Blade*, 13 November 1916.

32. *Fort Wayne Journal-Gazette*, 13 November 1916.

33. *Fort Wayne Journal-Gazette*, 16 November 1916.

34. *Fort Wayne Journal-Gazette*, 19 November 1916.

35. *Wabash Plain Dealer*, 21 November 1916.

36. *Ibid.*

37. *Wabash Plain Dealer*, 27 November 1916.

38. *Fort Wayne Journal-Gazette*, 4, 27 November 1916.

39. *Fort Wayne Journal-Gazette*, 30 November 1916.

40. *Ibid.*   41. *Ibid.*

Chapter 26

1. Earl Huntington was born in Genesco, Kansas, and received a B.S. degree from the University of Chicago in 1915, where he played football from 1912 through 1914. University of Chicago Archives.

2. Mather Kahn, *Michigan State: The First 100 Years* (East Lansing, MI: Michigan State University Press, 1955), p. 327.

3. *Fort Wayne Journal-Gazette*, 8 October 1917.

4. *Fort Wayne Journal-Gazette*, 10, 14 October 1917.

5. Gustav A. Berghoff was one of Fort Wayne's industrial leaders. Born in Dortmund, Germany, Gustav arrived in Fort Wayne in February 1883 at the age of twenty and started making washing powder. Four years later, he and his three brothers started making beer. One brother moved to Chicago where he started a brewery and opened a restaurant that is still a landmark in the Chicago loop. In 1892, Gustav took over the Summit City Soap Works, which he reincorporated as the Rub-No-More Company, which made soap, glycerin, stearic acid, oleic acid, pitch, and red oil. Gustav married Julia Jauch of Dayton, Ohio. They had four sons. Gustav's brother, Harry, served as mayor of Fort Wayne. Bert J. Griswold, *Builders of Greater Fort Wayne* (Fort Wayne: Bert J. Griswold, 1926), pp. 36, 656. Walter Berghoff grew up in Fort Wayne and, in 1912, went away to St. Mary's High School in Dayton, Ohio, his mother's hometown, where he played football. In 1916, he attended the college program at St. Mary's where he majored in chemistry and played on the varsity football and tennis teams. In spring 1917, he returned home to work in his father's businesses, and that fall he played end for the Fort Wayne Friars. Dayton University Archives; *Fort Wayne Journal-Gazette*, 1 October 1916, October–November, 1917; St. Mary's College Sixty-Fifth Annual Commencement, 15 June 1915; *Hammond Times*, 3 December 1917. Walter E. Berghoff served in the army in World War I. After prohibition went into effect, Walter E. Berghoff became assistant superintendent of the Rub-No-More Plant. *Polk's Fort Wayne City Directory, 1922*, p.172. Later, he became president of the Hoff-Brau Brewing Corporation. He died February 23, 1948, at the age of 50. *Fort Wayne Journal-Gazette*, 24 February 1948.

6. *Fort Wayne Journal-Gazette*, 15 October 1917.

7. *Indianapolis News*, 19 November 1915.

8. Washington and Jefferson College Archives.

9. *Massillon Independent*, 19 October 1917, 5 November 1917; *Toledo Blade*, 22 October 1916; *Detroit Free Press*, 29 November 1917.

10. *Fort Wayne Journal-Gazette*, 21 October 1917.

11. *Fort Wayne Journal-Gazette*, 22 October 1917.

12. *Fort Wayne Journal-Gazette*, 25, 26 October 1917.

13. *Fort Wayne Journal-Gazette*, 29 October 1917.

14. *Ibid.*

15. *Fort Wayne Journal-Gazette*, 30 October 1917.

16. *Fort Wayne Journal-Gazette*, 29 October 1917.

17. *Fort Wayne Journal-Gazette*, 30 October 1917.

18. *Fort Wayne Journal-Gazette*, 1, 2 November 1917.

19. *Fort Wayne Journal-Gazette*, 5 November 1917.

20. *Fort Wayne Journal-Gazette*, 10 November 1917.

21. *Fort Wayne Journal-Gazette*, 12 November 1917.

22. *Wabash Plain Dealer*, 12 November 1917.

23. *Fort Wayne Journal-Gazette*, November 1917; *Hammond Times*, November–December 1917; Treat, *Official Encyclopedia of Football*, 29, 30, 33, 37, 39, 45.

24. *Fort Wayne Journal-Gazette*, 26 November 1917.

25. *Fort Wayne Journal-Gazette*, 27 November 1917.

26. *Ibid.*

27. *Fort Wayne Journal-Gazette*, 26 November 1917.

28. *Massillon Independent, Fort Wayne Journal-Gazette* and *Hammond Times*, 1, 3 December 1917.

29. University of Notre Dame Archives; *Fort Wayne Journal-Gazette*, 8 December 1917. After football, Keefe worked as an engineer in the research and development department of the Pullman Company on Chicago's south side. He was married to Nellie Mulborn and had a son, a daughter, and five grandchildren at the time of his death.

30. *Hammond Times*, 3 December 1917.

31. *Detroit Free Press*, 28 August 1921, 11 September 1921.

32. This lack of interest is reflected in the high school yearbooks for Fort Wayne High Schools during the first two decades of the twentieth century.

Chapter 27

1. *Hammond Times*, 15, 25, 27 October 1915.

2. *Hammond Times*, 25 October 1915.

3. *Indianapolis News*, 13 October 1915.

4. *Lafayette Journal*, 4 December 1916.

5. *Hammond Times*, 2 October 1916.

6. *Ibid.*

7. *Debris*, Purdue University Yearbook, (West Lafayette, IN: 1909).

8. *Debris*, 1912.

9. *Debris*, 1915.

10. *Ibid.*

11. *Hammond Times* and *Fort Wayne Journal-Gazette*, 9 October 1916.

12. *Hammond Times*, 9 October 1916.

13. *Fort Wayne Journal-Gazette,* 5 October 1916.

14. *Hammond Times,* 9 October 1916.

15. *Hammond Times* and *Fort Wayne Journal-Gazette,* 9 October 1916.

16. *Fort Wayne Journal-Gazette,* 9 October 1916.

17. *Hammond Times,* 9 October 1916. Ralph Young grew up just fifteen miles south of Hammond in Crown Point, Indiana.

18. *Hammond Times,* 16 October 1916.

19. *Ibid.*   20. *Ibid.*

21. *Hammond Times,* 23 October 1916.

22. *Lake County Times,* 23 October 1916.

23. *Lafayette Journal,* 23 October 1916.

24. *Hammond Times,* 23 October 1916.

25. *Hammond Times,* 25 October 1916.

26. *Hammond Times,* 30 October 1916.

27. *Ibid.*

28. *Hammond Times,* 31 October 1916.

29. *Ibid.*

30. *Hammond Times,* 6 November 1916.

31. *Ibid.*

32. *Lafayette Journal,* 5 December 1916; *Davenport Daily Times,* 18 November 1916.

33. *Davenport Daily Times,* 20 November 1916.

34. *Ibid.*

35. *Cleveland Leader,* 27 November 1916.

36. *Akron Beacon Journal,* 6 December 1960. Hawthorne later went to medical school at the Indiana University, then moved to Akron, Ohio, where he practiced general medicine.

37. DePauw University Archives, 1994. In the winter of 1915–16, Rowan dropped out of college to work for the Canadian Copper Company, and, in fall 1916, he returned to Indiana, where he took a job with the U.S. Steel Corporation in Gary. Concurrently, he played several games for Pine Village. He was later a sales manager for a New York fertilizer firm.

38. *Decatur Review,* 13 October 1916.

39. *Hammond Times,* 16 October 1916; *Lafayette Journal,* 5 December 1916.

40. *Lafayette Journal,* 15 December 1916.

Chapter 28

1. *Hammond Times,* 25, 26 September 1917.

2. *Ibid.*

3. *Hammond Times,* 26 September 1917.

4. *Hammond Times,* 22 September 1917.

5. *Hammond Times,* 2 October 1917.

6. The Chicago Athletic Association's semi-pro football team of 1896, sponsored by Republican politician "Big Bill" Thompson, proved that sports and politics mixed quite nicely (*Boston Globe,* 27 November 1896), so the Democrats in the back-of-the-[stock]yards area formed the Hamburg Athletic Association. Both athletic clubs were designed primarily for political purposes, and their sponsors were more interested in winning Chicago elections than winning football games beyond the city limits. Indeed, the Chicago Athletic Association helped Big Bill become Chicago's mayor from 1915 to 1923, and again from 1927 to 1931.

7. Len O'Connor, *Clout: Mayor Daley and His City* (Chicago: Henry Regnery Co., 1975); Eugene Kennedy, *Himself! The Life and Times of Mayor Richard J. Daley* (New York: The Viking Press, 1978).

8. *Hammond Times,* 2 October 1917.

9. *Hammond Times,* 22 September 1917, 6 October 1917.

10. *Detroit Free Press,* 8 October 1917.

11. *Ibid.*

12. *Chicago Tribune,* 30 June 1968; Porter, *Biographical Dictionary,* 152.

13. Bernard Christian Halstrom attended the University of Illinois in 1914 and 1915 as an architectural engineering student. His family lived in the Hyde Park area of Chicago at 5487 Ellis Avenue. See *University of Illinois Directory* (Urbana-Champaign: University of Illinois Press, 1916).

14. *Hammond Times,* 13 October 1917.

15. *Hammond Times,* 15 October 1917.

16. *Hammond Times,* 22 October 1917; *Racine Call,* 22 October 1917.

17. *Hammond Times,* 22 October 1917.

18. *Ibid.*

19. *Rockford Morning Star,* 23 October 1917.

20. *Wabash Plain Dealer,* 30 October 1917.

21. *Hammond Times,* 27 October 1917.

22. *Hammond Times,* 29 October 1917.

23. *Ibid.*

24. *Hammond Times* and *Wabash Plain Dealer,* 29, 30 October 1917.

25. *Hammond Times,* 30 October 1917.

26. *Chicago Evening Post,* 5 November 1917, p. 10.

27. *Hammond Times,* 22 November 1917.

28. *Chicago Evening Post,* 12 November 1917, p. 6.

29. *Hammond Times,* 19 November 1917.

30. *Ibid.*

31. *Hammond Times,* 22 November 1917.

32. *Hammond Times,* 26 November 1917.

33. *Ibid.*

34. *Joliet Evening Herald-News,* 27 November 1917, p. 10.

35. *Joliet Evening Herald-News,* 26 November 1917, p. 10.

36. *Chicago Evening Post,* 27 November 1917, p. 11; *Joliet Evening Herald-News,* 26 November 1917, p. 10.

37. *Hammond Times,* 28 November 1917.

38. *Hammond Times,* 30 November 1917.

39. *Ibid.*   40. *Ibid.*

41. University of Notre Dame Archives.

42. *Hammond Times,* 3 December 1917.

43. *Ibid.*

44. *Hammond Times,* 11 December 1917.

45. *Hammond Times,* 7, 8 December 1917.

46. *Hammond Times,* 7 December 1917.

47. *Hammond Times,* 13 December 1917.

48. *Canton Daily News,* 30 November 1917.

49. *Hammond Times,* 11 December 1917.

50. *Pittsburgh Gazette-Times,* 26 November 1917.

51. *Canton Repository,* 27 November 1917.

52. Jimmy Clabby started fighting professionally in 1906 at the age of 16.

53. *Detroit Free Press,* 7 October 1931.

54. Bob Carroll, "Doc Young and the Hammond Pros," *The Coffin Corner* 17, no. 1 (spring 1995): 20–22.

Chapter 29

1. *Social Problems in Athletics: Essays in the Sociology of Sports*, ed. Daniel M. Landers. (Urbana, IL: University of Illinois Press, 1976), pp.186–94.

2. James S. Pressley and Roger L. Whitley, "Let's Hear It for the 'Dumb Jock': What Athletics Contribute to the Academic Program," *NASSP Bulletin* 89, no. 580 (May 1996): 74–83.

3. Bureau of the Census, *Historical Statistics of the United States, Colonial Times to 1970*, 1 (Washington, D.C.: U.S. Department of Commerce, U.S. Government Printing Office, 1975), pp. H. 412–32. African-American children were less likely than white children to attend school at the beginning of the twentieth century. Only thirty-one percent attended grade school. Ibid., pp. H. 520–30.

4. *Evanston Index*, 22 December 1955.

5. Bureau of the Census, *Historical Statistics*, pp. H. 751–65. In 1910, approximately five percent of the college-age population attended college.

6. Twenty-four NFL players became physicians between 1921 and 1970, but the number declined as the football season lengthened and the physical demands became greater. See *The Coffin Corner* 16, no. 1 (late winter 1994), 23–24.

7. *Miamisburg News*, 20 February 1947, p. 1. Harry Kinderdine served as a deputy sheriff for fourteen years before being elected sheriff of Montgomery County, Ohio in 1944. Kinderdine was a veteran of WWI, serving eleven months in France before finding employment in local machine shops and warehouses. He was appointed deputy sheriff in 1930.

8. Bureau of the Census, *Historical Statistics*, pp. H. 751–65. The percentage of seventeen year olds graduating from high school increased from 6.3 percent in 1900 to 14.5 percent in 1917. Ibid., pp. H. 598–601. The average number of days of school attended per pupil, for all children attending school, increased from 99 days per pupil in 1900 to 121 days per pupil in 1920. Ibid., pp. H. 520–30.

9. J. Edmund Welch, "Edward Hitchcock, M.D., Founder of Physical Education in the College Curriculum," in Earle F. Zeigler, *A History of Physical Education & Sport in the United States and Canada* (Champaign, IL: Stripes Publishing Co., 1975), pp. 124 ff.

10. Mabel Lee, *A History of Physical Education and Sports in the USA* (New York: John Wiley & Sons, 1983), pp. 86–88. Princeton University adopted PE in 1876, Oberlin in 1885, the University of Wisconsin in 1890, Indiana University in 1891, the University of Chicago and the University of Illinois in 1893, the University of Michigan in 1894, the University of Minnesota in 1896, Ohio State University in 1897, the University of Iowa in 1899, and the University of Missouri in 1900.

11. Ibid., 83. In 1855, Cincinnati was the first city to adopt PE for elementary and secondary schools. Cleveland was next in 1870, followed by Milwaukee in 1876, Chicago in 1886, Davenport in 1887, Moline and Detroit in 1890, Indianapolis and Dayton in 1892, and St. Paul in 1894.

12. Ibid., 165–66, 258.

13. See Richard G. Wettan, "Social Stratification in the New York City's Athletic Clubs, 1865–1915," *Journal of Sports History* 3 (spring 1976): 45–56, and Lee, *A History of Physical Education*, 82.

14. Allison Danzig and Peter Brandwein, *Sport's Golden Age* (New York: Harper & Brothers, 1948).

15. Like so many of the coaches on this list, Ralph Young made a significant contribution to the next generation of athletes. Before becoming Athletic Director at Michigan State University, as their track coach he helped to mold Fred Alderman into an Olympic gold medal winner in the 1928 games held in Amsterdam. See *Detroit News*, 19 June 1927, 6 August 1928.

16. *The Michigan Alumnus*, 22 (January 1916): 194.

17. Mark Sullivan, *Our Times: The United States 1900–1925*, Vol. 5, *Over Here 1914–1918* (New York: Charles Scribner's Sons, 1933), p. 286.

18. *Ibid.*, pp. 302–13.

19. *Minneapolis Journal*, 21 October 1917.

20. *Milwaukee Journal*, 29 October 1917.

21. *Minneapolis Tribune*, 2 November 1916.

22. *Minneapolis Journal*, 21 October 1917.

23. *Minneapolis Journal*, 21 October 1917; *Minneapolis Tribune*, 2 November 1917.

24. *Green Bay Press-Gazette*, 20 October 1917.

25. *Fort Wayne Journal-Gazette*, 13 October 1917; *Detroit Free Press*, 10,12 November 1917; *Davenport Democrat and Leader*, 29 October 1917; *Dayton Daily News*, 11 November 1917.

26. *Detroit Free Press*, 30 September 1917.

27. *Toledo Blade*, 29 October 1917.

28. *Dayton Daily News*, 7, 8 October 1917.

29. *Toledo Blade*, 24 September 1917.

30. *Varsity News*, University of Detroit, 2, no. 5 (November 1918): 6.

31. *Philadelphia Evening Bulletin*, 1 May 1918.

32. *Montgomery: Our County Magazine* 4, no. 11 (November 1979); *Alumni Directory*, Ohio University, 1937; Syracuse University Archives; Marietta College Archives.

33. Landers, *Social Problems in Athletics*, 184–96.

34. Letter from University of Chicago Library Archives, 28 July 1997. For an example of picture and coverage see *Minneapolis Journal*, 5 November 1914. It seems likely that Joe Gray was a freshman, got injured, and dropped out of school. An article in the *Minneapolis Journal*, 18 November 1914, said, "Gray won't suit up Saturday for the University of Chicago, he has played his last game for the team because of an injured ankle."

35. For record of his play for De Paul see *De Paul Minerval*, November 1913, pp. 84–85. For absence of enrollment records see De Paul University Archives.

36. Fred M. Walker coached the Michigan Agricultural College baseball and basketball teams in 1923 and 1924. See *Detroit Times*, 8 May 1924, p. 24.

Chapter 30

1. Sperber, *Shake Down The Thunder*, 35.

2. *Pittsburgh Gazette-Times*, 2 November 1917.

3. *Canton Repository*, 27 November 1917.

4. *Pittsburgh Gazette-Times*, 27 November 1917.

5. *Pittsburgh Gazette-Times*, 26 November 1917.

6. *Massillon Independent,* 28 November 1917.

7. *Canton Repository,* 27 November 1917.

8. *Current Biography,* ed. Anna Rothe (New York: The H. W. Wilson Co., 1951), pp. 569–72.

Chapter 31

1. *Rock Island Argus,* 20 November 1915.

2. *Rock Island Argus,* 16 November 1915, 20 October 1916.

3. *Minneapolis Journal,* 26 November 1916.

4. *Minneapolis Journal,* 22 November 1914.

5. *Minneapolis Journal,* 5 November 1915.

6. *Minneapolis Tribune,* 29 November 1916. The University of Wisconsin increased its stadium seating capacity in 1917. See *The Des Moines Evening Tribune,* 31 October 1917.

7. *Wabash Plain Dealer,* 23 October 1916.

8. *Fort Wayne Journal-Gazette,* 17 September 1916.

9. *Toledo Blade,* 5 October 1916.

10. *Detroit News,* 1 October 1916.

11. *Massillon Independent,* 22 November 1916.

12. *Lafayette Journal,* 24 October 1916.

13. *Lafayette Journal,* 21 October 1916.

14. *Hammond Times,* 6 November 1916.

15. *Toledo Blade,* 10 October 1917.

16. *Hammond Times,* 9 October 1916.

17. *Hammond Times,* 3 November 1916.

18. *Canton Repository,* 17 November 1916.

19. *Lafayette Journal,* 5 December 1916; *Davenport Daily Times,* 18 November 1916.

20. *Canton Repository,* 1, 29 October 1916.

21. *Ibid.*

22. *Hammond Times,* 23 October 1916.

23. *Fort Wayne Journal-Gazette,* 20 October 1916.

24. *Ibid.*

25. *Toledo Blade,* 10 October 1917.

26. *Fort Wayne Journal-Gazette,* 1 October 1916.

27. *Hammond Times,* 9, 23 October 1916; also see *Fort Wayne Journal-Gazette,* 9 October 1916; *Lafayette Journal,* 23 October 1916.

28. *Hammond Times,* 8 October 1916.

29. *Hammond Times,* 24 October 1916.

30. *Lafayette Journal,* 23 October 1916.

31. *Fort Wayne Journal-Gazette,* 22 October 1916.

32. *Hammond Times,* 30 November 1917. For a biography of Joe Carr, see Porter, *Biographical Dictionary,* 97.

33. Danzig and Brandwein, *Sport's Golden Age.*

34. *Massillon Independent,* 18, 20, 26 October 1916.

35. *Hammond Times,* 25 October 1916.

36. *Ibid.*

37. *Wabash Plain Dealer,* 2 December 1916.

38. *Toledo Blade,* 6 December 1916.

39. *Hammond Times,* 25, 26 September 1917.

40. *Hammond Times,* 16 October 1916.

41. *Hammond Times,* 31 October 1916.

42. *Lafayette Journal,* 15 December 1916.

43. *Massillon Independent,* 4 October 1915.

44. *The Sporting News,* the one-hundred-and-twelve-year-old St. Louis-based, weekly sports publication that did not even recognize pro football until 1942, spent eight months in 1996 interviewing sports fanatics and discovered that the National Football League is far and away the most popular sports organization.

Index

Abell, Earl, 30, 189, 191, 194, 196–97, 367, 372, 476
Abrell, Richard T. "Able," 129–30, 472
Adams, 100, 265, 268, 275
Adrian College, 53, 82–83, 89
African-American football players, 198, 275–76, 318–23, 378–79, 392–93
Akron Burkhardts, 24, 151, 204, 206–207, 232, 373
Akron Imperial Electrics, 36, 90, 151, 233
Akron Indians, 6–14, 17, 22, 24, 27, 86, 137, 141, 173–74, 177, 181–82, 188–89, 192–93, 202, 239, 279, 319, 326, 373, 379
Akron, OH, 5–14, 16, 22, 112, 115–16, 180, 222
Akron, University of (Buchtel College, Municipal University of Akron), 90, 220, 232, 236
Akron Pros, 24, 63, 116, 160, 174, 232–39, 323, 379–80, 386, 392–93
Allegheny Athletic Association, 64
Allegheny College, 9, 236, 372
Allen, Frank, 313, 315, 342, 352
Allentown Army Ambulance Corps, 248
Alliance, OH, 99, 206, 233
Allmendinger, Ernest J., 44, 372
Alma College, 150, 164
Altoona Indians, 16, 24, 64–68, 125, 177, 204, 210, 212, 240–41, 318, 373 386
Altoona, PA, 3, 22, 38, 64
Ambrose, Jack, 83, 90, 97, 330, 336, 339, 341, 345
American Professional Football Association, 23, 97, 128, 131, 160, 171, 239, 252, 273, 294, 364, 390
Ann Arbor Independents, 5, 44, 84, 134, 141, 320, 351, 372
anti-professional attitudes, 20, 29–32
Armory Park (Toledo), 52, 82–83, 87, 90–91, 93–94, 144, 212, 385
Ashbaugh, Russell Gillman "Busty," 31, 55–56, 98–100, 102–103, 105–106, 213, 221, 470–71
assumed names, 29–32
attendance, 383–86
Aurora Greyhounds, 23, 70, 268–69, 318, 348–49
Axtell, Howard, 139, 182

Bacon, Francis, 314
Baird, 286, 327, 347, 372
Baker, Charles A. "Doc," 6, 319

Ball, Daniel R., 40–46, 286, 327, 332, 347
Banjan, Harry C., 299, 313, 372
Barberton Pros, 99, 151, 187, 232
Barrett, Charlie, 210
Barrett, John "Johnny," 59, 77–78, 91–94, 107, 110–11, 127, 245, 258–59, 288, 290, 308, 310, 332, 361–62, 380
Barron, Jim "Butchy," 93, 102, 113, 217–18, 230, 245, 252, 389
Bashaw, Moses, 362
Bastian, Clyde E., 102
Baston, Bert, 30, 225, 280, 372
Battaglia, Murray J., 70, 76, 366
Battery "C" (First Wisconsin Artillery), see Racine Regulars
Battle Creek, MI, 152, 338–39
Baxter, Jimmy, 53, 59, 83–84, 86, 89–92, 94
Beam, 286, 289
Bechtol, Rube, 235
Beck, Howard Lester, 19, 86, 166, 204–205
Becker, Fred J., 181–82, 185, 225, 228, 475
Beltman, Leo, 37
Bender, Joe, 65
Berger, Alvin "Heine," 39, 41, 45, 62, 165, 286, 302, 327, 333, 336, 347
Berghoff, Walter E., 97, 339–41, 345, 362, 367, 486
Bergie, Joe, 66, 147, 204, 212, 242, 340
Bergman, Alfred H. "Dutch," 74, 154, 295, 299–306, 309–17, 334–35, 372, 380, 484
Bergman, Arthur, 370
Bessmeyer, Albert Henry "Whitey," 87, 162–63, 165–66, 328
Bessmeyer, Otto, 87, 162–63, 170–71
Bethany College, 210
Bilbow Athletics (St. Paul), 272
Blackburn, Earl, 241–42, 245
Blair, Jackson "Auggie," 67, 102
Bleich, Hynie, 318
Bleich, Louis, 318
Blocker, Frank Adolphus, 152, 271, 314–15, 345–48, 353–54, 356–57, 359, 362, 380
Blocker, George, 316, 346
Blocker, Ted, 152, 291, 315, 346–50
Bloomberg, W.S. "Red," 225
Bloomington, IN, 178, 187
blue laws, 3, 184
blue-collar workers, 16–19, 377, 384
Blueitt, 319
Boerner, Harold A., 182, 367, 476

Bogle, Thomas, 55, 137–39, 143, 152, 183, 372
Bosdett, John, 289, 308
Boville, Bob "Rube," 31, 79, 148
Bowie, Howard J., 182
Bowles, King, 83, 89
Boyle, Michael H., 55, 268
Brandt, 269
Bredimus, Victor, 266, 270, 481
Brennan, H., 65, 359
Bricker, Oscar, 300–301, 305–306
Brickley, Charles E., 238–39, 246, 248–49, 251, 342
Brier, Oral "Skinny," 309
Brier, W. J., 32
Briggs, Maurice "Windy," 31, 147, 186, 190–92, 199, 200–201, 212, 367
Brigham, Hiram, 53, 57, 62
Brindley, Walter C., 270–72, 479, 481, 487
Broadway Athletic Club (Cleveland), 7
Brooklyn Lakewoods, 23, 90
Brooks, 206–207
Brown (Tufts), 319, 322
Brown, Tom "Doc," 85, 87, 91, 93
Brown University, 55, 98, 212, 221, 238, 244–45, 319
Buchtel College, 10, 98–99, 112, 191–92, 215, 232–33, 248, see also Akron, University of
Bucknell University, 67, 125, 215
Buck, Howard "Cub," 31, 93, 105, 113, 167, 207–208, 221, 223, 237, 245, 252, 278, 294, 330, 379
Buffalo All-Stars, 23–24, 36, 90, 93, 143, 153, 160, 211, 236, 240–43, 318
Buffalo Oakdales, 90, 137–38, 183
Buland, Walter, 273, 275, 277, 281
Buldowsky, 340
Burkhardt, Bill, 232
Burkhardt, Gus, 232
Burrell, Roy "Tommy," 166, 202, 206, 215, 232–33, 235, 237
Butler, Bill, 49
Butler, Edward "Sol," 323
Butler, Robert Parker "Butts," 151, 188–89, 191–92, 194–95, 202, 207, 215, 379
Byroades, Samuel, 39–40, 42, 336

Cabery, IL, 73–74
Calac, Pete, 112, 114, 145, 156, 158, 174, 208, 225–26, 240–41, 243–44, 248, 250, 252–53, 380
Caldwell, Harold W. "Bud," 300
Camp Custer, 142, 152, 154–55, 293, 338
Camp Dodge, 271, 273, 280–81
Camp Gettysburg, 250
Camp MacArthur, 326
Camp Sherman, 128, 168, 171
Camp, Walter, 20, 31, 58, 110, 112, 122, 156–58, 169, 188–89, 191, 202, 213, 220, 223, 249–50, 310, 318–19, 355, 370, 381, 464

Cantillon, Mike, 280
Canton Athletic Club, 172
Canton Bulldogs, 5, 7, 12, 14, 17, 19, 22, 24, 37, 39, 45–46, 48, 52–53, 58–59, 61, 66–67, 76, 86, 101–102, 105, 107, 112–15, 120–21, 125, 131, 137, 139–40, 145, 152–53, 156, 158–59, 166, 172–82, 185–90, 201–29, 233, 237–38, 240–53, 294, 312, 318, 324, 331, 335, 338–39, 344, 365, 372–73, 378–88, 390–93
Canton, OH, 3, 9, 12, 14, 16, 19–23, 29, 48, 65
Canton Professionals, 9, 172, 175, 180
Capron, George and Ralph, 277, 280
Carderelli, Carl "Squash," 232–37
Carlisle Institute, 8, 36, 38, 46, 55, 64, 77, 90, 94, 101, 103, 110, 124, 145, 174, 177, 191–92, 204, 214–15, 219–20, 222, 242–43, 248, 275, 372–73
Carlson, Archie, 280
Carolan, Penn, 77–79, 91, 93, 256–59, 288, 290, 308, 332
Carpenter, Walker, 159–60
Carr, Joseph F.19, 47, 49–50, 55, 67, 84, 128, 245, 389
Carroll, Elmer E., 156
Carroll Street Field (Wabash), 74, 78, 300, 306, 313
Case School of Applied Science (Pennsylvania State), 7–8, 30, 86, 90, 98
Castle, Lewis S., 149–51
Chamberlin, Guy, 252–53
Chambers, Christian C., 40–41, 302, 322–23, 338
Checkaye, Frank "Connie," 41–42, 44, 46, 80, 154, 163, 165, 302, 304, 313–15, 327, 332–33, 336, 342
Cherry, Boyd, 87, 166, 182, 186, 190, 192, 195, 200, 202, 206, 476
Chicago Athletic Club, 355
Chicago Bears, 39, 160, 343, 357
Chicago Blues, 41, 45
Chicago Cardinals, 31, 203, 343, 357
Chicago Cornell-Hamburgs, 24, 72, 80–81, 265, 272, 285, 287–92, 348, 355–62, 375, 380, 386
Chicago, IL, 11, 16, 21, 386
Chicago Ripmores, 69, 72, 285
Chicago Tigers, 203, 329, 343–44
Chicago, University of, 20, 32, 39, 72, 151, 202, 215, 232, 275, 298, 303, 329, 339, 374–75, 384
Chicken, Fred, 273, 277–79, 281–82
child labor, 367
Childs, Clarence C., 17, 178
chop blocking, 24
Churchill, 260
cigar stores, 23, 45, 234, 239, 266–67, 479
Cincinnati Celts, 19, 20, 24, 86–87, 109, 117, 120, 127, 130–31, 137–38, 145–46, 148, 152, 156, 162–71, 177, 227, 279, 328, 330, 339–40, 351, 353–54, 372–73, 379–80, 383, 386–87, 390–92

Cincinnati, North, *see* North Cincinnati Colts
Cincinnati, OH, 5, 20, 187
Cincinnati Reds, 31, 171, 179
Cincinnati, University of, 109, 162, 165
Clabby, Jimmy, 152, 262, 346, 363–64
Clark, Harry, 192
Clay, William, 129
Cleveland Blepp Knits, 36, 83, 137–38, 182–83
Cleveland Erin Brauns, 83, 137
Cleveland Favorite Knits, 89
Cleveland Indians, 62, 67, 93, 102, 106–107, 151, 166, 188, 202–207, 212–19, 227–31, 232–33, 243, 324, 365, 373, 379–80, 383, 386, 390–92
Cleveland, OH, 17, 21, 58, 61, 253
Cleveland Panthers, 161, 212, 233, 243, 343
Cleveland Telling-Strollers, 91
Cleveland Tomahawk, 83, 129, 134, 234
coaching as a profession, 368, 461–62
Cochran, 375
Cofall, Stanley B., 40, 107, 110, 114, 116, 245–51, 370, 380, 479
Cohen, Abe and David, 318, 348
Cole, E. M., 87, 93, 139, 166, 182, 191, 202, 206
Colgate University, 30, 158, 189, 191–92, 215, 240, 252, 373
college attendance and graduation, 365
Collins, Joe, 11–12, 129, 139, 181, 185, 476
Columbus Muldoons, 47, 56
Columbus, OH, 5, 22, 38, 49, 52, 57, 84, 115, 174, 363
Columbus Panhandles, 16, 19–20, 24, 37, 46–47, 49–63, 67, 84, 90–91, 100–102, 106–107, 110, 121–22, 127, 141, 143, 146, 150–51, 155–56, 162, 166, 175, 183–84, 189, 205–206, 213–15, 229, 232–34, 242–43, 245, 250, 330–31, 337, 354, 373, 379–80, 383–86, 389–91, 394
Comiskey Park, 287, 361
Conners, Ed, 187, 191, 200
Conway, Chick, 232, 237
Copley, Charles, 234, 241, 251
Cornell University, 30, 151, 191, 210, 260, 268, 277, 361
Cornell-Hamburgs, *see* Chicago Cornell-Hamburgs
Cornwell, Arthur "Red," 55, 57, 61, 88, 139, 143, 145, 164
Cortland Hotel, 200, 226, 252
Cosgrove, 191, 200
Costello, 277, 281
Costello, Harry, 67, 105, 152–55, 159, 171, 208, 210–11, 215–17, 221, 240, 338–39, 372, 374, 380
Crawford, Stephen Rowan, 240, 340
Crisp, Park "Tumble," 207–208, 233, 235, 238–39

Crowley, Raymond "Slim," 255, 260
Cruikshank, Burliegh Edmond, 159, 367, 474
cultural diversity, 393
Cusack, Jack, 9, 37, 172–74, 177–78, 185, 188–89, 191, 197, 201, 207–208, 210–11, 217, 222, 226–27, 229, 252, 387, 393
Cutler, Harry, 124, 167, 170

Da Prato, Nero J. "Jerry," 30, 141, 143–44, 152, 154, 160–61, 338, 372
Dagenhart, Henry "Hank," 52, 173–74, 177
Dagenhart, William "Bill," 139, 173–74
Daley, Richard J., 355–56
Dartmouth College, 77, 86, 105, 207, 221–23, 248, 258
Davenport Athletic Club, 24, 35–37, 78, 168, 254–66, 269–74, 276, 280–81, 294, 335, 350–57, 361, 383, 393
Davenport, IA, 1, 16, 21, 78
Davenport, Ted, 261, 266–67, 269
Davidson, Homer, 8, 139, 182–83, 202, 205–206, 215
Davidson, Wilber S., 99–100
Davis, Edgar C. "Big Ed," 44, 93, 167, 189, 191–92, 299, 301, 306, 309, 311, 313, 330–32, 352, 362, 367, 379
Davis, F. R., 55, 162–63
Day, J. Franklin, 44, 55, 87, 103, 147, 186, 191, 211, 214, 228
Dayton Gym-Cadets, 16, 24, 46, 54, 85–89, 101, 117–24, 147, 162–63, 177, 182, 192, 297, 324, 380
Dayton Munitions, 123, 324, 327, 347
Dayton Oakwoods, 117, 299
Dayton, OH, 5, 14, 16, 19, 23, 168
Dayton Shamrock Wolverines, 109
Dayton Triangles, 24, 96, 109, 120, 124–31, 151, 159–60, 167–69, 170–71, 324, 331, 379–80, 383, 386, 392, 394
Dayton, University of (St. Mary's College), 54, 85, 92, 117, 199, 313
Dayton Wolverines, 122, 168
Decatur (Illinois) Indians, 23, 202, 308, 310
Decatur Stanleys, 357
Decker, "Pie," 85, 117, 128
Dellinger, Larry, 54, 117, 124
Denison College, 109, 127, 152, 162, 165, 168, 211, 213, 356, 373
Dennison, "Denny," 340
De Paul University, 73, 77–78, 375
DePauw University, 297–98, 329, 339, 352
Des Jardien, Paul "Shorty," 93, 151, 202–204, 207, 215, 228, 230, 370, 380
Des Moines, 23, 260, 268
Detroit Athletic Club 139, 149
Detroit Braves, 36, 94, 327, 339, 380
Detroit Harvards, 320–21, 351
Detroit Heralds, 16, 19, 24, 37, 39, 42, 57–58, 61, 63, 70, 74, 76, 79–80, 88, 90, 93, 96, 120, 123–27, 130–62, 166, 168–

69, 175, 177, 212–13, 225, 229–30, 232,
  250, 266, 283, 288, 292–93, 312–13,
  315, 318, 324, 327, 339, 355–56, 372–
  73, 379–80, 383–87
Detroit Mack Park Maroons, 14, 24, 46, 55,
  57, 88, 101, 133, 135–44, 152, 160–64,
  182–83, 211, 306, 372–73
Detroit, MI, 5–6, 9, 16, 19, 21, 132, 149,
  159, 302
Detroit Tigers, 120, 160–61, 356
Detroit, University of, (Detroit College),
  124, 132, 134–37, 148, 160–61, 232,
  325–26
Dettling, Jim, 234, 242
Devereaux, John, 96, 117, 119–20,
  129–30, 379
Dickinson College, 210, 225, 248
Dietz, William "Lone Star," 66, 370, 468
Donahue, Jack J., 181
Donovan, Mark, 260, 272
Dooley, Eugene "Gene," 153, 237
Dooley, Keith, 268
Dorais, Charles "Gus," 12, 44, 80, 87–88,
  97, 103, 132, 165, 170, 186–99, 203,
  210, 213, 222–23, 227–28, 293, 316,
  324–27, 332–48, 362, 369–70, 372, 380,
  391, 485
Dory, Joe, 77, 288, 291, 350
Dory, John "Jack," 289, 291
Dougherty, Bud, 277, 280
Dowling, John "Jack," 225
Downing, 387–88
Doyle, Tommy, 355
Dries, Frank, 277–78
Dreisbach, Ollie, 237, 240–41, 248, 479
Driscoll, John Leo "Paddy," 30, 271,
  291–92, 314–15, 344–45, 355–63, 370,
  380
Driving Park, 54, 60, 182, 184, 187, 214,
  222
Duggan, Edward, 303, 305–306, 311
Duluth Independents, 3, 23, 227, 380
Dunn, Earl, 293
Dunn, Frank, 380
Dunne, John, 264, 277–78, 282

Earp, Francis Lewis "Jugs," 294
Earp, Fred W., 255–64, 267, 480
Earp, Wyatt, 78, 255
East Chicago Gophers, 356
Eberwein, 44, 141
Eck, Walter, 41, 77, 155, 283, 286, 288, 291
Edgerton, Andrew "Ox," 150, 152, 164
Edwards, Howard "Cap," 11, 27, 45–48,
  52, 65, 80, 139, 165, 182, 189, 191–93,
  208, 210, 225, 237, 240, 302, 326–27,
  332–36, 338, 347, 379
Edwards, Philip P., 98–100, 470
Eichenlaub, Ray, 53, 83–89, 121, 144, 163,
  372, 380
Eisenhower, Dwight D., 250
Eissler, 79–80
Elgin, IL, 70, 288, 320

Elward, Allen "Mal," 80, 165, 293, 332–34,
  342, 372, 485
Elyria Athletics, 202, 211, 232, 328, 330,
  351, 353
Elyria, OH, 5, 23, 36, 83, 90, 97
Elyria Pros, 10, 123, 151, 173, 182, 193
encampments, 369–70, see also Camps
entrepreneurs 18–20
Erb, Clarence, 9, 182, 372
Erehart, Mark G. "Mickey," 295–96,
  300–301
Esch, Joe, 182
Evanston, IL, 5, 38, 47, 69–70, 359, 386
Evanston North Ends, 16, 24, 42, 62,
  69–81, 91, 97, 140, 148, 154, 186, 245,
  297, 300–301, 305, 308, 310, 313–4,
  332, 348–49, 256–58, 262, 265–67, 272,
  287–88, 290, 355, 358, 361, 365, 372–
  73, 380, 382, 386, 390
Evansville Crimson Giants, 174
Exelby, Leon C., 136–37
Exendine, Albert, 377–78

factory worker prosperity, 17–18
Falcon, Guilford, 42, 69–70, 76, 81, 97,
  140, 154, 258, 288, 300, 313–17,
  342–44, 370, 380, 486
Falcon, Ray, 258, 372
Feeney, Al, 45–47, 56, 62, 80, 165, 252,
  293, 302, 327, 332–33, 336, 338
Fenner, Lee, 96, 124, 128, 167
Fenters, Eli, 166, 180, 299, 301, 306,
  308–309, 311, 314, 353, 360, 475
Fenters, Ray "Snowy, 299, 301, 306,
  308–309, 311, 330, 353
Fenters, Roy "Squint," 309, 314
financing football, 382–394
Finn, Bill, 361
Finn, Johnny, R. 168, 262, 289, 346,
  349–51, 354
Finnegan, Charles "Sam," 54, 182–84
First Regiment of Chicago, 346
Fisher, J. P., 225
Fitzgerald, Freeman C., 78, 107, 116, 147–
  48, 205, 211–13, 222, 228, 251, 338, 345
Flannigan, Walter H., 259, 266–69,
  272–73, 323
Flemming, Malcolm "Red," 30, 61, 65–66,
  87–88, 91, 100, 103, 106, 147, 186,
  190–200, 210–14, 222–24, 227–28,
  334–39, 241–42, 389, 467, 478
Fluhrer, John "Jack," 470
Flynn, Jim M., 139, 182, 239, 479
Foertmeyer, Sam, 170
Foley, J. J., 173, 181
Follis, Charles W., 319–20
Football: as blue-collar sport, 16–19, 377,
  384; compared with baseball, 377;
  equipment, 26–27; formations, 193–94;
  and immigrants, 365; rules, 24–27, 193;
  and war, 369–75
Ford Motor Company, 94, 145, 243
Forest, "Red," 233

Fort Benjamin Harrison Indianapolis),303
Fort, Richard M., 78, 255, 258, 261–63
Fort Taylor, 326, 339
Fort Wayne Friars, 13, 16, 19, 24, 34–48, 56, 62, 75, 96–97, 123, 130, 145, 163, 165, 168–69, 189, 204–205, 208, 210, 212, 225, 228, 235, 249, 265, 273, 286, 288, 292–93, 297, 302–304, 312–13, 315–18, 324–45, 347–48, 353–55, 360, 362–63, 372–73, 379–80, 386–87, 390–94
Fort Wayne, IN, 5, 19, 21, 23, 35, 38, 56, 70, 80, 81
Fort Wayne Vets, 73, 111, 326, 345
Foster, Robert "Bobby," 41, 77, 155, 283, 286–93
Fraim, Clarence "Smoke," 88–89, 318, 320–22, 485
Franklin College, 303–304, 313
Freeburg, 257, 259–61, 268
Frey, 170, 206–207
Funkhouser, Ralph, 99

Gaither, Tom, 138, 146, 162–64, 171
Galvin, Malcolm E., 30, 271–72, 278, 347–51, 354
Gardner, Bill, 8, 52, 139, 175, 178, 191–92, 208, 237, 239
Gardner, Frank, 45, 152, 154, 196–97, 200, 239
Garlow, Bill, 208, 215, 222, 226, 363, 372
Gaskeen, Harry, 116
Gaustad, Art, 277, 282
George Williams College, 127–28
Georgetown University, 39, 67, 92, 102, 107, 109–10, 135, 207, 210, 214–15, 218, 372
Getz, 55, 100, 103, 105, 206, 214
Ghee, Milton, 105–106, 13–15, 158, 207–208, 221–26, 237, 240–41, 244, 246, 248, 250, 362, 380
Gilbert (Evanston), 78, 310
Gillespie, Ed, 99
Gillies, Fredrick Montague, 361
Gilroy, John, 107
Glockson, Norman "Tango," 61, 124, 139–40, 145, 148, 177, 291–92, 342, 357
Goebel, William, 8, 168, 371–72
Goldberg, 204, 318
Gonzaga College, 325–26
Goodrich, Jack, 181
Goodwin, Russell, 106, 210, 224–25
Goosman, Herbert, 168
Gormley, Thomas F., 93, 102–103, 110, 207–210, 214, 219, 228, 230, 389
Graf, Frank and Stanley, 129
Graff, Campbell "Honus," 93, 151, 166, 202, 229–30, 476
Graham, Harold "Peg," 262, 268
Grand Rapids, MI, 134, 233
Gratop, Arthur, 82–84, 91, 93
Gray, Joe "Dolly," 151, 207, 232–37, 374, 488

Green Bay Packers, 223, 273, 326, 344
Green Bay, WI, 293, 386, 393
Green, Edward L., 346, 348, 354, 359–60
Green, Sebastian "Babe," 49
Gregg, Ellis B., Jr., 163
Grinnell College, 259, 275, 279–80, 283–84, 288, 291
Grossvater Park (Akron), 232–35, 239, 244
Guarantees, 22, 382–87, 381
Gunderson, Harry, 273, 277, 281–82
Gurtner, Frank, 305, 310, 313, 315, 484
Guyer, Edward "Ted" Rawson, 268, 292
Guyon, Joe, 77, 190, 252

Hackett, Hugh, 83–84, 87, 89–92
Hadden, 55, 139
Halas, George, 97, 323
Halstrom, Bernard "Swede," 191–92, 271, 315–16, 357–63, 487
Halter, H. H., 172
Hamburg Club, 355, 487
Hamilton, Don, 52, 139–40, 174–75, 177, 187–88
Hammer, Frank, 275, 278, 481
Hammond All-Stars, 343
Hammond Clabbys Athletic Club, 24, 35, 62, 152, 168–69, 289, 291–92, 312–15, 329, 335, 341, 373, 379–80, 386–87, 390–92
Hammond, IN, 17, 19, 21, 348–50
Hammond Pros, 174, 203
Hampton Institute, 198
Hanley, Ed, 86, 190–91, 194–200, 202, 204–205, 207, 211, 215
Hanna, John, 72, 76, 300, 308
Hansen, Harold, 279
Hansen, Herman, 267
Hanson, Jack, 280
Harding, "Tacks," 138
Harper, Jesse, 12, 303
Harvard University, 44, 55, 84, 93, 168, 211, 215, 222, 238, 246, 311, 360
Haskell Institute, 38, 275
Hauser, 255, 263
Hawkins, Douglas McWilliams, 102
Hawthorne, David Earl "Kinks," 309, 330, 352, 485, 487
Hayes, Louis J., 87, 103, 186, 190–91, 211, 214, 228
Hazlett, Harry, 9
Hegeman, Ed and O., 291
Heiller, John, 289
Heisman, John, 192
Helvie, Charles, 93, 97, 168, 299, 306, 311, 313, 341, 362, 372
Henderson, Mort, 64
Henderson, Wilber, 314, 345, 358–59, 362
Hendricks, Vincent, 225
Henry, Wilber "Fats," 252
Hess, Wallie, 152, 356
Heyman, Fred, 103, 106, 147, 214, 224, 228, 372
Highland Park, MI, 94, 158

Hole, Leslie, 41, 309
Holleran, Tom, 232–33, 235, 237, 239
Holm, Dilk, 256, 263
Holy Cross, College of the, 373, 259–60
Hooker, James, 299, 306, 309
Hopkins, David Walter "Hoppy," 93, 169, 367, 373, 475
Hopkins, Steve, 278–79, 318–19
Horning, Clarence "Steamer," 97, 156, 158–61, 250, 379, 474
Horween [Horowitz], Ralph, 31
Howard, "Fat," 237
"Howling Hundred," 45, 334
Huddle, 26, 193
Hughitt, Ernest F. "Tommy," 105–106, 109–10, 114, 116, 152, 169, 221, 224, 245–46, 356, 370
Huntington, Earl D., 169–70, 335, 338, 340–41
Huntington, IN, 295–96
Hutchins, J. B., 295, 297

Iddings, Harold "Eddie," 139, 177
Illinois All-Stars, 72–73, 285, 287, 300
Illinois, University of, 12, 30, 72–73, 77, 110–11, 167, 193, 202, 271, 300, 310, 314, 352, 357, 373
Indiana Normal College in PA (Indiana University), 125–26, 167, 204, 209, 222, 235, 340–42
Indiana University, 30, 43–44, 93, 96, 152–53, 178, 186, 191, 278, 295, 298, 300, 306, 311, 313, 322, 330–34, 347, 353, 372
Indianapolis, IN, 35, 235, 298, 364, 385
Irish American Athletic Club, 236
Ironton Lions, 179
Island, Louis, 38, 40–42

Jackson, OH, 52, 206
Jackson, MI, All-Stars, 38
James, Cliff "Chief," 232
Jamestown, NY ALCOs, 102
Jandl, Otto, 41, 283–85
Jeffrey, Douglas, 90, 153, 236
Jenzen, 163
Jim Crow laws, 319
Joliet, IL (Wilson Steel Semi-Pros), 354, 361
Jonason, Charles, 277
Jones, Ben, 253
Jones, Billy, 34–35, 297, 299–302, 311–13, 354
Jones, George W., 258–63, 271, 373, 481
Jones, Keith "Deacon," 11, 62, 87, 139, 165, 182, 191–92, 197, 199, 326–27, 332–33, 338–40, 345–47, 362, 373, 379
Jones, Leslie M., 94
Jones, Noble, 94
Jones (Ohio Wesleyan), 9, 191
Jones, Ralph, 39
Johnson, Moses, 300
Johnson, Reuben "Rube" L. E., 42, 67, 72,

74, 77–80, 140–41, 148, 150, 249, 258, 272, 288–91, 300, 308–10, 355, 359, 361, 366–67, 380, 468
Julian, George "Carp," 58, 105, 139, 174–76, 187, 191–96, 207–208, 211, 213, 215–16, 221–22, 240, 380, 477

Kagy, Edmund Leroy, 87, 139, 147, 183, 187, 191, 193–95, 211, 214, 228, 370, 372
Keefe, Emmett G., 92, 167, 306, 309, 314, 330, 344–45, 362, 379, 486
Keewatin Academy, 77
Keiser, Willmon "Fat," 215
Kelleher, Bill, 110, 116, 191, 194, 196, 211, 245
Kellison, John, 30–31, 97, 112, 114, 178, 186, 208, 221–22, 240, 243–44, 252, 379
Kelly, Gerald, 37, 139, 177
Kelly, Wallace "Red," 290, 292
Kennedy, Thomas, 255, 266
Kennedy, Walt, 39–41, 47
Kenyon College, 9, 53, 83, 119, 162
Kerwin, Ed, 152, 154, 372
"Kicking Swede" see Rube Johnson
Kilby, Henry Norbert, 42, 69–70, 76, 79, 140, 258, 468
Kilby, Roger, 12, 58, 81
Killian, Frank T., 255
Kinderdine, George "Hobby," 54, 129–30
Kinderdine, Harry "Shine," 96, 129–30, 367, 488
King, Richard S. C., 31, 93, 168, 170, 208, 311, 314, 317, 330, 360
King, Thomas H., 93, 166, 204, 206, 372
Kirk, Archie Raymond, 264
Klein, Max, 348–49
Knab, Chet "Shine," 87, 146, 162, 165–71, 327
Knox College, 55, 223
Koch, William W. "Polly," 272, 278, 481
Kohl, G., 349, 356, 359–62
Kolls, Louis, 292
Krause, Arthur, C., 167, 309, 311, 330
Krentler, Ty, 88, 139, 141, 145
Krueck, Ed, 170
Krull, Walter, 40, 286
Kruse, Maxy "Mother," 82, 94
Ku Klux Klan, 45, 319
Kuehl, Ray "Waddle," 255–56, 260–63, 266–67, 351
Kuehner, Oscar, 52–53, 143
Kuehner, Roscoe, 52–54

La Pado, 39–41, 47, 286, 317
La Ross, 287, 359, 362
Lafayette, IN, 130, 165, 170, 301, 311, 315, 354
Lalond, Jimmy, 94, 96
Lambeau, E. L. "Curley," 294
Lambert, Kent "Skeet," 39–48, 56–58, 61, 75, 103, 124, 145–48, 164, 189, 191,

193–95, 197, 199, 213–14, 224, 228, 286, 302–303, 324, 373–74, 380, 466
Lambert, Ward "Piggie," 39, 303, 466
Lancaster Malleables, 23, 90, 93, 141, 318–19
Lane, Frank, 87, 162, 164, 170–71
Larsen, John, 4, 78, 207, 232
Latham, Percy, 137–39, 145, 177
Latrobe, PA, 46, 64–66, 172
Laub, Bill, 6, 172
Lavin, Bill, 99
Lawrence College (University), 41, 155, 283, 288
Lazerous, Jacob K. "Jake," 268, 318, 481
Lebanon, OH, 36, 165–66
Lebanon Valley College (PA), 65, 67
Lehigh University, 211, 241, 278
Lenardson, Faunt "Dutch," 55, 88, 137, 139
Lennahan, "Nig," 61, 80, 124, 150–51, 153–54, 164, 372
Lepper, Barney, 236–37, 370
Lisbon, OH, Semi-Pros, 102
Littick, Orrville Beck, 9, 86, 367, 469
Littig, Victor L., 19, 254, 256–58, 480
Lockwood (All-State player), 338–40, 362
Lodwick, John H. "Johnny," 225
Longenecker, A. R., 152, 291–92, 356–60
Longman, "Shorty," 12, 181
Lord, Edwin B., 225
Louisville Goldbergs, 1, 312
Love, William DeLoss, 373
Lowe, George "Bull," 208, 217, 252, 389
Lutter, Grover C. "Dovey," 291, 293, 367, 483
Lyle, Dewey, 275, 277, 281–2
Lyman, "Link," 252–3
Lyons, John, 44

McBride, Arthur "Mickey," 21
McCall, Thomas, 44, 55, 84
McCardy, C. M., 345, 362
McCausland, Leo, 31, 207, 232, 373
McConnell, Russ, 83, 86, 89
McCorkle, 127
McCormick, Dr. C. V., 254
McCormick (SD), 271, 273, 373
McCreary, Melvin Lesley, 106, 108, 374
McDonald, Henry, 319
McDonough, Joel "Big Joe," 355–56, 362, 372
McEachron, Scott "Duke," 41, 283–85, 288–89, 482
McGinnis, Ernest, 266
McGinnis, Vernon "Mac," 115, 232, 235
McGovern, John, 275, 277–78, 280
McHale, Frank, M., 44, 55, 137, 305–306
McIntyre, Arthur, 89–91, 470
Mack, Connie, 4, 172
Mack Park, 134–34, 141, 160–61, see also Detroit Mack Park Maroons
McKeesport Olympics, 24, 36, 99–100, 109, 129, 187, 243, 380, 386

McLaren, George, 378
McLaughry, DeOrmond C. "Tuss," 55, 102, 114, 116, 234, 241, 246–47, 251, 369
McNamara, 240–41, 248
Macomber, Franklin Bartlett "Bart," 30, 105, 107, 109–113, 167–68, 245, 352, 361, 373, 441
Magerkurth, 257, 269
Maher, Bernard "Bertie," 57, 61, 88, 132, 136–45, 150, 153–54, 164, 183, 250, 293
Mahrt, Alphonse H., 54, 85, 92, 96, 117, 119–31, 147, 167, 171, 367, 380, 472
Maine, University of, 83, 330
Malcomson, Joseph, 137
Marietta College, 7, 179, 214
Marion Club of Indianapolis, 301
Marion Owls (OH), 297
Marion Questions, 52, 57
Markoe, John, 277
Marquette University, 41, 77, 141, 155, 212, 283, 288, 357
Marrow, Forest M. "Heine," 347–48
Marshall, Bob, 264, 273, 275–77, 281–82, 318–19, 323, 379
Marshall, William "Billy," 53, 82–85, 87, 89–91, 93–94, 132, 134, 140, 144–45
Marshall, William H., 156, 159–60
Martin, I. R., 93, 228, 233–34, 242, 245, 252, 327, 332, 338, 341–44, 389
Martin, Reverend Father Charles Alfred, 98, 116
Martindale, McKinley, 299, 309
Martins Ferry Athletic Club (Ohio), 102, 109, 184
Marty, Frank, 166
Mason, Paul Sinclair "Andy," 94, 367
Massillon Blues (team), 151, 182, 232
Massillon, OH, 4, 14, 16, 19–20, 22–23, 29, 181
Massillon Tigers, 4–7, 13–14, 19, 22–24, 46, 48, 52–54, 60–61, 65–67, 76, 79, 86–91, 101–107, 113–16, 120–26, 131, 137–39, 145, 157, 152, 160, 166, 172, 177–78, 180–89, 190–202, 205, 210–15, 221–28, 233–36, 240–253, 312, 325, 335, 339, 344, 359, 372–73, 378–79, 382, 390–94
Mattern, Joel P., 31, 61, 91, 103, 147, 205, 211–12, 214, 222, 227–28, 380
Matthews, Neil, 248
Mauder, Louis "Dutch," 83, 86, 89, 94, 96
Maugher, Louis P., 225
Maxted, 286, 288–89
Mayer, E. N., 62, 228–29
Maywood Athletic Club, 37
Maywood, IL, 23, 270, 289
Meersman, "Honey," 264, 267, 272
Mehlig, Lee Percy, 338, 345, 361–62
Meister, 162–63, 171
Mendel Pirates (Columbus, OH), 206
Mercersburg Academy, 94
Merkle, Fred, 82, 144

Merrill, Tom, 90, 94
Metzer, Charles, 299, 309
Meyers, C., 241–42
Meyers, Frederick "Blad," 258, 308, 317
Meyers, Paul Duncan "Clinks," 262, 278, 291, 315, 346, 348–51, 356–57, 360
Michigan Agricultural College (MSU), 30, 55, 88, 94, 136–37, 141–43, 175–77, 189, 191, 197–98, 243, 247, 293, 318, 338, 372
Michigan Intercollegiate Athletic Association, 82
Michigan State University, see Michigan Agricultural College
Michigan, University of, 5, 9, 32, 44, 53, 55, 84, 86, 88, 102–103, 137, 139, 141, 152, 164, 169, 182–83, 191–92, 204, 221, 241, 249, 251, 306, 391
Miller, Albert Herman, 255, 480
Miller, "Baggs," 78–79, 332
Miller, "Butch," (Toledo), 96
Miller, D., 150
Miller, John, 6
Miller, Eugene Elseworth "Shorty," 114, 234–35, 238–39, 241–42, 245, 251
Miller, Lester Thomas, 103, 214
Miller, S. S., 225
Miller, William Blake, 30, 142–43, 152, 154–55, 338, 372, 473
Milligan, Cliff "Tuck," 93, 167, 306, 309, 311, 313, 352
Milliner, William Burgess "Red," 35, 154, 297, 300, 304–306, 309, 312–17, 322, 333, 343–44, 367, 483
"Million Dollar Line," 72, 333
Milwaukee Ernsts, 283, 285–86
Milwaukee Maple Leafs, 77, 282–83
Minneapolis Marines, 24, 37, 212, 264, 271–73, 275–82, 318–19, 379, 383, 386
Minneapolis, MN, 1, 5, 19, 105, 221, 230
Minnesota All-Stars, 264, 275, 277, 280
Minnesota East Ends, 278–79
Minnesota, University of, 20, 30, 93, 205, 211, 214, 222, 225, 227, 260, 264, 275, 277–80, 318, 373, 384
Mitchell, Bullet (Akron), 90, 232–33, 236–37
Mitten, Ray, 255, 257
Moline Red Men, 24, 76, 254–63, 266–71, 287–88, 348
Monnett, Marvin, 350, 354
Monon Railroad, 38, 299, 349
Montpelier, OH, 350
Moran, Cyril, 136, 373
Morgan Park, IL, 72–73, 285
Moriarity, Tom, 135, 144, 154–55, 210–11, 372
Morin, Ed, 94
Morningside College, 281
Morrell, 277
Morrison, 319, 322
Mossteck, 285
Mount, Jimmy, 138–39

Mt. Pleasant, Frank, 38, 64, 90, 363, 373, 467
Mount Union College, 6, 180
Muhlenberg College, 186, 191, 214, 241–42, 251
Mullane, Danny, 57, 96, 139, 150, 153, 155, 161, 250
Mullane, Joseph E., 109
Muncie Congerville Athletic Club, 41, 162–63, 304–305
Muncie Flyers, 171, 296
Muncie, IN, 23, 38, 41, 70, 331
Murphy, Edward "Nips," 256, 259, 266, 268, 270, 292
Murray, Arthur "Red," 55, 124
Murray, Floyd, 348
Mussel Brewing Co., 40, 107
Muteller, P. H., 35

Nash, Robert A. "Nasty," 103, 213–14, 222, 227–28, 234, 236, 241–42, 245, 251, 379
National Football League, 16, 23, 29, 49, 97, 128, 131, 161, 171, 179, 233, 239, 252–53, 273, 281–82, 294, 303, 323, 337, 357, 364, 368
Navin Field (Detroit), 58, 96, 124, 145, 152–55, 158, 160–63, 178–79, 187, 190–95, 199, 212, 229, 237–38, 250, 283, 293, 356, 370, 385
Navin, Frank, 134
Neale, Alfred E. "Greasy," 30–31, 65, 112, 114–15, 158, 161, 178–79, 186–87, 190–91, 222, 198, 199, 237–38, 243, 246, 248, 250, 369–70, 379, 471
Nebraska, University of, 255
Nedeau, 43, 145
Neid, Frank, 239, 323
Neill, William, 30, 215
Nelson, "Bones," 287
Nesser brothers, 6, 18–20, 46–47, 49–63, 84, 100, 106, 121, 141, 143, 149, 177, 183, 205, 214, 232, 234, 245, 282
Nesser, Alfred L., 49–50, 53–54, 58, 60–63, 160, 232–35, 237, 239, 366, 370, 379, 476
Nesser, Frank, 49–52, 54, 56, 58, 60–63, 92, 115–16, 141, 146, 151, 156, 183–84, 205, 214, 233, 235–39, 249, 379
Nesser, Fred W., 49–50, 53, 56, 58, 60, 84, 92, 121, 141
Nesser, John, 49–50, 52, 58, 60–61
Nesser, Phillip, 49–50, 53, 58–60, 92, 233
Nesser, Raymond, 49–50, 60
Nesser, Theodore, 49, 380
Nesser, Theodore "Ted" Jr., 49–54, 56, 58, 60, 62, 121, 141, 146, 175, 183–84, 205, 214, 233, 370
New York Giants, 144, 178, 226, 233, 241
Newashe, Bill "Chief," 124, 137–40, 162
newspaper coverage, 19–20
Nichols, Charles E. Jr. "Chuck," 59, 82–84, 87–89, 470

Nichols, John, 277
Nicholson, "Red," 94, 96, 358
Nicollet Park, 278, 281
Nolan, J., 346–48, 356, 359
North Carolina, University of, 90
North Cincinnati Colts, 39, 120, 123
Northwestern University, 30, 76, 80, 355, 357
Notre Dame, University of, 11–13, 20, 23, 30, 39–48, 53, 62, 77, 80, 83–84, 93, 96, 107, 110, 119, 139, 144, 152, 163, 165, 167, 181–82, 186, 191–93, 204, 211–12, 222, 232, 241, 250–51, 268, 278, 286, 292–95, 302–303, 306, 308, 311, 313–15, 324–34, 336, 343–44, 347, 356, 358, 362, 378
Novak, Edward, 273, 281
Numbered jerseys, 134, 327–28

Oak Park, IL, 77, 105, 111, 121
Oak Park High School, 77, 91
Oberlin College, 9, 98, 206, 373
Oberlin, Monk, 173
O'Brian, Pat, 170
O'Conners, Frank., 288
O'Dea, Patrick J., 72, 74, 468
Odle, Paul, 299, 309
O'Donnell, J. Hugh "Pepper," 165, 328, 330, 333, 336–38
Oelwein, IA, 256, 271
Ofstie, Harold Sigvold "Hod," 167, 351, 353
Ohio State University, 20, 52, 55, 57, 60, 86, 115, 169, 182, 186, 200, 206 214–15, 248
Ohio University, 8, 102–104, 107–108, 214, 373
Ohio Wesleyan College, 9, 86
Olsson, Carl "Bull," 182–83, 202, 206, 227, 232–33, 235, 237
Omier, Joe, 55, 98
Oneida Tribe, 38
O'Neill, William, 338
Oregon Agricultural College, 246
O'Rourke, "Cameo," 83
O'Rourke, Frank, 35
Osborne, Clint, 259, 268, 481

Packard Park, 134, 136–37, 140, 143
Palm, Max, 76–77, 154, 308, 313–14
Palmer, Horace Dutton "Hoke," 102–104, 214, 471
Palmer, Keene T. "Peggy," 87, 127, 166–68
Palmer, Mike, 275, 277, 282
Panhandle Division, Pennsylvania RR, 49, 51
Parcell, 88, 141, 144
Parduhn Field, 350–51, 358
Parduhn, Paul, 354, 358, 360, 362–64
Parratt, George Waterson "Peggy," 5, 9–14, 67, 85–86, 93, 121, 137, 141, 151, 166, 172–73, 181–82, 202–206, 215–17, 227–29, 231, 385, 388, 390, 393

Partlow, Lou, 122, 124, 127–30, 147, 167, 171
Pascolini, Art, 42, 72, 75–76, 258
Pask, Charles E., 44, 46
Patricians, *see* Youngstown Patricians
Pattison, C. L. "Pat," 69, 76
Peck, Robert D. "Bob," 107, 110, 112, 115–16, 244–45, 345, 363, 380
Penn State University, 8, 20, 55, 102–103, 113, 125, 214
Pennsylvania Railroad, 22, 38, 49, 53, 55, 64, 66, 125, 183, 232, 342
Pennsylvania, University of, 5, 93, 102, 148, 151, 215, 219, 222, 241, 248, 346, 373
Peoria Socials (Illinois team), 271–72
Peru, IL, 346–48
Peters, Don, 46, 52, 139, 174–75, 327
Phelan, Jim, 40
Philadelphia Eagles, 179
physical education, 366–69
physicians in football, 172, 358, 366, 488
Pickerel, Louis Edward "Pick," 52–54, 60, 121, 206
Pickering, Earl, 280
Pierce, Webster, 137
Piero, Ed, 172
Pine Village Athletic Club, 5, 16, 19, 23–24, 34–35, 44, 62, 78, 92–93, 105, 111, 130, 152, 165–70, 186, 189, 207–208, 223, 298–99, 301, 306–18, 330, 335, 341–44, 349–55, 358–62, 365, 372–73, 379–80, 383–86, 390–91
Pitcairn Quakers, 16, 22, 24, 35–37, 65–67, 100, 102–103, 109, 125–26, 128, 130, 150, 170, 204, 211, 234–35, 240, 242–43, 318, 340–41, 386
Pittsburgh, PA, 35–36, 180, 210
Pittsburgh, University of, 67, 80, 83, 107, 109, 112, 178, 191, 204, 215, 220, 242, 251, 378
Plazico, 341
Pliska, Joe, 41, 45–46, 80, 96, 165, 170, 286, 299, 301–302, 316, 327, 332–36, 339–43, 327, 362, 373
Pogue, Harold, 202, 310–11, 484
Pollard, Frederick D. "Fritz," 238, 318–19, 323
Portmann, Milton Claudius "Muff," 11, 87, 182, 191–93, 199, 202, 207, 215
Potts, Jonathan Fred "Pottsy," 86, 367
Powell, Harold Thompson "Dutch," 139, 174, 182, 189, 202, 206, 227, 367
Powers, Paul, 102
prairie football, 358
Prather, Clinton C., 235–36
preparation for life, 369–70, 374–75
Pressler, William "Billie," 287, 290
Princeton University, 232, 373
Professional Football Hall of Fame, 179
progressive movement, impact of, 367
Propst, Rudolph W., 156–59, 367, 373–74
Pulford, George R., 85, 91

punt-out, 26
Purdue University, 39, 44–45, 90, 94, 129, 152, 168, 232, 262, 271, 289, 291, 298, 302, 306, 314, 332, 336, 346–47, 373
Purdue University All-Stars, 189

Racine Football Association, 283, 290
Racine Legion, 294
Racine Regulars, 16, 24, 90, 93, 155, 272, 283–94, 341–42, 332, 350, 353, 355, 357, 359, 386
Racine, WI, Battery C, 5, 16, 77
Rambaud, Carl "Bat," 211, 234, 241, 477
Ratchford, 291
Raymond, Arthur "Bugs," 86, 189
Redeen, "Sheepy," 275, 277, 282
Redelle, Michael W. "Mike," 122–23, 128
Redlands Field (Cincinnati), 166, 171
Redmond, John Thomas "Doc," 305–308, 313–16, 334, 336, 379, 343
Reece, Pat, 167
Reese, David E., 31, 109, 162, 165, 167, 170–71, 327, 380, 474
Reese, Lou, 124
Rehor, Fred "Fritz," 234, 241, 249, 251–52
religious opposition to Sunday football, 22–23
Reilly, 45–47, 56
Reno, Jesse, 45, 74, 154, 300–302, 305–306, 310–15, 336–37, 344–45, 379
Reule, Paul "Dutch," 53, 82–84, 87–89, 121, 141
Reutz, G. "Babe," 291
revenue, 382–87, 391–92
Rhodes, Claire, 34–35, 92, 298–99, 301, 306, 309, 354, 483
Roberts, Charles H., 102–103, 214
Robeson, Paul, 319, 323
Roche, Jack, 267–69
Rochester Jeffersons (NY team), 23, 90, 158
Rockford Athletic Club (IL), 23, 76, 80, 267–68, 270
Rockford Badgers, 347–48, 358
Rock Island, IL, 5, 16, 70
Rock Island Independents, 29, 160, 212, 254, 269, 261, 266–74, 276, 281–82, 288, 292, 303, 312, 318, 323, 344, 348, 354, 365, 383, 386, 393
Rockne, Knute, 11–13, 32, 40, 51, 54, 87–88, 91, 103, 107, 112, 139, 147–48, 181–84, 191–92, 205, 212–13, 222, 224, 227–28, 234, 241, 249–52, 277, 294, 316, 324–28, 334, 343–44, 369, 379, 389
Roesink, John Aaron, 132–34, 136, 144, 156, 159–61, 472–73
Rogers, Irving William, 251, 479
Rooney, Art, 239, 343
Roosevelt, Theodore, 59
Rosenthal, Boleslaus, 277
Roudebush, George, 31, 127, 163, 165–68, 207–208, 211, 327–28, 367, 371–72, 380, 474

Roush, Frank "Tubby," 94–96
Routh, Harry, 44–46, 302, 306, 308, 334–36
Rowan, Henry "Hank," 352, 367, 487
Ruffner, Henry V., 289, 347, 359, 362
Ruhl, Emmett, 52–53, 58, 60, 92, 146, 205
Ruhl, Homer, (Ruh), 61, 151
Rumberg, Edgar, 255, 480
Rush, Jimmy, 277–78
Russell, Ed "Unk," 208, 210, 215, 222, 237–38, 248–49, 379
Russell, Reb, 286
Rutgers University, 214, 222, 241, 251, 319
Rydzewski, Frank N., 30, 315–16, 343–44, 362–63, 380

Sacksteder, Hugh J., 117, 119–20
Sacksteder, Norbert, 54, 85, 87–88, 92, 96, 117, 119, 121–27, 147, 151–60, 167, 169, 192, 196–99, 250, 252–53, 293, 356, 380
Safro, Labe, 278–79, 281, 373
Saint Ambrose College, 255, 258–61, 271
Saint Louis, 29, 41, 148
Saint Mary's College (University of Dayton), 54, 85, 117, 192, 199, 313
Saint Paul Banholzers (team), 275, 278–79, 318–19
Saint Paul Bilbow Athletics (team), 272
Saint Thomas College, 277, 280
Sala, Errett "Monk," 82–89
Salem, OH, Semi-Pros, 43–44, 99, 206, 233
Salzmann, Arthur W., 361, 366–68, 480
Salzmann, Roy H., 267–68, 480
Saunooke, Stilwell, 66, 102–103, 214, 363, 373
Sayveskie, 300
Schachter, Christopher, 30, 107, 212, 214, 222, 228, 373
Scheerer, Earnest, 300, 313
Schieber, Arthur L. "Dub," 202, 207, 215, 477
Schimmel, John, 83, 87, 91, 94, 96
Schlee, Ed, 143
Schlee, Harry, 124, 137, 139–40, 153, 164, 177
Schliesman, Ted, 291
Schlott, Art, 174, 208
Schmidt Colts (team), 284, 289
Schneider, Henry, 305–306, 313, 484
Schneider, John, 47, 50, 52
Schnell, Joe, 292
Schnell, Richard, 291
Schobinger, Eugene "Gene," 72–73, 77–79, 148, 258, 285, 287–88, 290, 300, 332, 345, 373, 483
school attendance, influence on professional football, 366, 376
Schuette, Joseph J., 94, 96, 318, 367
Schuler, Charles, 260
Schultz, Adolph "Germany," 5, 44
Schultz, Bill, 148, 150, 164
Schultz, Guy "Germany," 5, 6

Schultz, "Whitey," 93, 139, 166, 174, 202, 206, 215, 227
Schussler, "Tilly," 87, 145–46, 162–67, 327–28, 372
Schuster, William A. "Bill," 181, 185, 225
Schwab, John, 237, 240
Scott, Clair, 167–68, 186, 311, 330, 332
Scruggs, Stuart Briscoe, 241, 242
Seattle, Washington Athletic Club, 137
Sefton, Frederick, 30, 189, 208, 210, 223, 232, 236–37, 240–41, 244, 248
Seliger, Herbert L., 347, 356, 359, 362
Semlow, Walter J., 83, 89
Seubert, Harold M. "Harry," 82, 89, 469
Shanks, "Nany," 96, 153–54,159
Shaughnessy, Thomas J. "Tom," 41, 258, 308, 314, 338–39, 358, 362–63
Sheeks, Paul Preston "Chesty," 170, 314
Shelburne, John, 323
Shelby Blues, 5, 6, 22, 141, 173–74, 182, 319–20
Shelby, OH, 5–11, 14, 49
Shelton, Murry N., 151
Sheridan, Harold "Irish," 152, 306, 308–309, 330, 356–57, 360
Sheridan Warriors, 349, 353, 390
Shields, Gerald "Guy," 137, 139, 153, 160, 177, 293, 361, 392
Shields, Richard "Red," 61, 79, 124, 137–40, 143–59, 162–64, 177, 250, 379
shift formations, 254–56, 259, 268
Showalter, Homer T., 46, 154, 297, 302–303, 305–309, 313–16, 334, 344, 367, 483
Sibila, Paul V., 225
side backs, 194
Siebert, Bob, 89
Simmons, 359–60
Simpson, Eber F., Jr., 264, 278, 282
Sinclair, Gilbert, 30, 225, 230, 280
Slater, Fred "Duke," 268, 319, 323, 485
small market teams, 392–93
Smith, Andrew "Dope," 44
Smith, Dan, 277
Smith, Frank "Fat," 266–67, 292
Smith, Gideon Charles, 30, 189, 192, 197–201, 318, 376
Smith, R. M., 102–103, 214
Snavely, Carl G. "King Carl," 65, 369, 467
Snoots, J. Lee, 52, 54, 48, 63, 143, 205, 373
Snyder, E. A., 67
Snyder, Tan, 87
social mobility, 366, 376
Solem, Oscar M. "Ossie," 275, 481–82
Solon, Lorin, 30, 62, 93, 151, 227–30, 277–78, 380
Sommer, Frank, 94
Sorenson, Frank G. "Swede," 169–70, 340
Soucy, Ernie, 93, 105, 379
South Bend, IN, 11, 23, 38–40, 79, 96, 153, 189, 290–91
South Bend Silver Edgers, 39–40, 297

Spears, Clarence "Doc," 31, 208, 222, 226, 248, 252, 367, 379
Specht, Robert, 42, 75–76, 78–81, 96, 140, 197, 258, 293, 300, 308, 310, 316, 333, 339, 341–44, 362
Speck, Norman "Dutch," 18, 173–74, 177, 192, 208, 211, 215, 237, 240–41, 244, 252–53, 282, 366–67, 380, 476
Spring Valley Moose (team), 23, 263, 270
Stagg, Amos Alonzo, 32, 298, 303, 377
steel shoulder support, 46
Stewart, Archie "Dutch," 61, 124, 137, 140, 145, 151, 153–54, 156, 164, 177, 208, 210, 215, 222
Stewart, Charles Edward, 30, 189, 237, 240–44
Stinchfield, Melvin Joshua "Red," 347–48
Stivers, Fred, 98, 102–103, 213
Stonebraker, Homer, 31, 303, 314, 484
Storch, Carl "Skummy," 127–29, 370
Straight, Herbert, 151–54, 159, 293, 356
Stuehmer, Duffy "Bum," 255–56, 260, 262
Suedhoff, Carl J., 34, 347
Swope, William Elwood "Red," 66, 467–68
Syracuse University, 107, 116, 124, 156–57, 192, 214, 222, 244, 373

Talbott, Nelson S., 122–23, 128, 147, 371
Talchief, Wesley, 236
Talman, Howard Parker, 31, 222, 227
Taylor, 94, 96
Taylorville, IL, 23, 35
Thiele, Carl "Dutch," 103, 123, 145, 152–53, 156, 168–70, 211, 213, 228, 250, 340, 356, 379
Thoennes (Thoennis), Phillip, 41, 77, 283, 288
Thomas, Gordon "Doc," 168, 367
Thomas, Ray, 55–56, 98–100, 102–103, 105, 116, 214, 221
Thompson, 155, 170
Thornhill, Claudia (Claude) Earl "Tiny," 107, 109, 113, 234, 242–45, 251, 369, 380
Thorpe, James Francis "Jim," 17–18, 30, 58, 65–66, 74, 87, 97, 105, 110, 112, 115, 145, 156–59, 174, 178, 185–200, 208, 215–17, 219–22, 225–27, 237–38, 240, 243–44, 246, 248–52, 282, 331, 334, 338, 359, 370, 378–81, 393
Tibbs, Everett "Newt," 44, 305, 313–14
Tobin, Elgie, 55–56, 99, 102, 160, 470
Toledo Glenwoods, 88–89, 137, 318, 320–22, 305
Toledo Maroons, 16, 19, 24, 29, 46, 52–53, 63, 81–97, 105, 121, 125, 127, 130, 153–54, 158–59, 162–63, 177–78, 182–84, 212, 229–30, 239, 241, 283, 290, 318, 320, 335, 339, 345, 361, 374, 380, 383, 386, 391–92
Toledo, OH, 5, 14, 19, 82–83, 283
Tollefson, Russell J., 264, 278–80
Tompkinson, 83, 89

Tomson, Herbert Ross, 255, 259
Toumey, Gus, 141, 143
Townley, Jack, 20, 30, 222, 225
Triangle Park, 170–71
Trout, Louis G., 83, 85–87
Truesby, M. J., 52, 174–77, 208, 373
tuberculosis, *see* George Julian and Alfred
    Bergman
Tucker, William Sykes, 148, 374
Turnquist, Axel, 278, 280–81, 373

Ulrich, Chick, 232
Union (Colored) Giants, 267
United States Navy Great Lakes Training
    School, 284, 344, 357, 363
United States Olympic team, 64, 72–73,
    178, 220
Ursella, Ruben, 264, 273, 275, 277–82, 370
Usher, 153–54

Van Aken, W.V., 170, 373
Van Alman, Eddie, 52, 173, 175
Van Alman, Norm, 173
Vedderneck (Vetterneck), George "Cotton,"
    55–56, 65–66, 100–101, 103, 110, 116,
    389
Villanova University, 217
Virginia, University of, 216, 228
Vogel, Joel, 67
Vogt, Frank A., 225
Volkman, George, 152, 292, 346–48,
    356–57, 359, 362
Voss, Walter C. "Tilly," 160–61

Wabash Athletic Association, 24, 34–37,
    51, 62, 71–74, 78, 81, 154, 186, 288,
    295–317, 320–22, 328, 334, 336,
    342–44, 354–55, 358–61, 365, 372–73,
    380, 383–86, 390–93
Wabash College, 39, 124, 191, 214, 286,
    302–303, 314
Wabash, IN, 5, 16, 19, 35, 47, 70, 78, 118,
    319
Wagner, John Huber "Hube," 93, 178, 191,
    193–96, 202, 214, 228, 243
Waldsmith, Ralph "Fats," 10, 65, 111–12,
    115, 139, 174, 191–93, 208, 215, 225,
    237, 240, 244–45, 252, 380
Walker, Fredrick M. "Iron Man," 230, 375,
    488
Wallace, Charles E. "Blondy," 172, 180,
    475
Walter Camp All-Americans, *see* Camp,
    Walter
Ward, Frank, 280
Ward, William Davis, 208, 210–11, 215,
    248, 338
war, preparation for, 369–375
war tax law, 373
Warner, Glen S. "Pop," 32, 64, 112, 145,
    208, 219–20, 243, 377–78
Washington and Jefferson College (PA),
    65, 79, 86, 106, 156, 159, 161, 179,
        191–92, 204–205, 210, 214, 222, 224,
        241, 315, 329, 339–40, 347, 378
Washington and Lee University, 77, 110,
    224, 228
Washington Vigilants, 24, 101, 103, 106,
    224
Weeks, G. Herbert "Hubby," 143, 153,
    293
Weheringer, 163–66
Weiler, Carl, 30, 86
Weiss, Billy "Bee," 83, 90, 94
Weiss, Julia "Jules," 83, 85–87, 90–91, 96
Welch, Gus, 208, 226, 246, 248, 380
Welch, Howard, 232–39
Welch, Stephen "Suey," 115, 232, 235
Wellendorf, Albert "Art," 255
Wellendorf, E. Carl, 255–56
Wells, "Red," 89–90, 93–94, 283, 286
Wells, Stanfield, 9, 86, 204, 207
Wenig, Wellston Poe, 281
Wertz, Dwight, 8–11, 139, 182, 202, 206,
    215, 227, 367
Wesbecher, Aloysius A. "Buzz," 31, 210,
    222, 234, 245, 379
West Virginia University, 55, 93, 98, 214
West Virginia Wesleyan College, 114,
    178–79, 191, 222, 244
Western Reserve University (OH), 8–11,
    86, 139, 180, 182, 191, 206, 214–15,
    372
Westminster College, 55, 234, 241, 247,
    251
Westwood Field (Dayton), 120, 127, 166
Whalen, Jr., John "Jack," 181, 185, 225
Wheeling, WV, 36, 174, 184, 224, 311
Wheelock, Hugh, 65
Wheelock, Joel, 65, 167, 467
Whipple, Ray, 96, 152–61, 250, 293, 356,
    379
Whitaker (Whitacer), Harry, 30, 96,
    153–59, 189, 206–10, 217, 221–22,
    250
White, Frank S., 204, 242
Whitlock, Roy258, 308, 314, 358–59
Whitney, Casper, 20, 31
Wilkinson, M. E. "Red," 105–106, 208,
    215, 221–22
Willaman, Samuel S. "Willie," 31, 86, 115,
    206, 221, 246, 248, 379
Williams, Bill, 167, 170–71, 299, 306–307,
    309, 330
Williamson, Guy "Chalky," 204–207,
    228–29
Wilson, Percy, 61, 124, 137–39, 143, 147,
    150–51, 162–64, 177
Wilson, Woodrow, 319, 369
Winters, Matthew, 44, 93, 167, 299, 306,
    309, 316, 330
Wisconsin, University of, 30, 32, 93, 99,
    105, 151–52, 167, 188–89, 191, 194,
    215, 221–23, 271–72, 278, 300, 346–47,
    352, 361, 384
Wolters, "Red," 255–58, 263–64, 267

Woodyatt, Albert "Allie," 263, 268–69, 271
Wright, "Nig," 257, 269
Wright, Walter, 82

Yale University, 8, 40, 76, 102, 123, 147,
    214, 244, 277, 280, 332, 373
Yarnelle, George, 35, 74, 300–310, 316,
    334, 336, 483
Yarnelle, J. Kenneth, 304–12, 316, 334–36,
    483
Yeckel, George, 214
Yocum, F. A., 206
Yost, Fielding, 32, 377
Young, Dr. Alva Andrew, 323, 358, 364
Young, Ralph "Bull" 293, 327–32, 339–42,
    347–50, 354, 362–64, 369, 487–88

Youngstown, OH, 6, 16, 21, 23, 98–99, 234
Youngstown Patricians, 16, 24, 55, 62, 81,
    98–116, 125, 149, 152–53, 187, 207,
    212–14, 217–18, 221, 224, 239, 242–47,
    250–51, 361, 373, 380, 383, 386,
    390–93
Youngstown Struthers, 151
Yount, Myron "Mike," 203, 313–14, 484

Zaring, Ivan Armon, 42–44, 47, 373
Zeeman, 206–207
Zettler, Vince, 174–75
Zile, William, 117
Zimmerman, George "Babe," 54, 85, 92,
    96, 117, 120, 123–24, 128–31, 171
Zuppke, Bob, 105, 110, 221

About the Author

Keith McClellan lives in Oak Park, Michigan, where he edits *Employee Assistance Quarterly*. He has a BA from the University of Northern Iowa and did graduate work at the University of Chicago, receiving several fellowships for his studies. He has published sixty articles in a variety of journals, including *Indiana Social Studies Quarterly* and *The Journal of Drug Education*. Since 1993, he has been a member of the Professional Football Research Association.

About the Book

The Sunday Game was designed and typeset on a MacIntosh in Quark-XPress by Kachergis Book Design of Pittsboro, North Carolina. The typeface, Meridien, was designed by Adrian Frutiger in 1957 for the French foundry Deberny & Peignot.

This book was printed on sixty-pound Glatfelter Natural Smooth and bound by Braun-Brumfield, Inc. of Ann Arbor, Michigan.